George MacDonald
Christian Writings

Cover Photograph: peasap

ISBN: 978-1-78139-366-6

© 2013 Benediction Classics, Oxford.

Contents

UNSPOKEN SERMONS FIRST SERIES

UNSPOKEN SERMONS SERIES TWO

UNSPOKEN SERMONS SERIES THREE

A BOOK OF STRIFE IN THE FORM OF

THE DIARY OF AN OLD SOUL

THE HOPE OF THE GOSPEL

BIBLICAL INDEX

UNSPOKEN SERMONS FIRST SERIES

Comfort ye, comfort ye my people

These Ears of Corn. gathered and rubbed in my hands upon broken Sabbaths, I offer first to my Wife, and then to my other Friends.

THE CHILD IN THE MIDST.

And he came to Capernaum: and, being in the house, he asked them, What was it that ye disputed among yourselves by the way? But they held their peace: for by the way they had disputed among themselves who should be the greatest. And he sat down, and called the twelve, and saith unto them, If any man desire to be first, the same shall be last of all, and servant of all. And he took a child, and set him in the midst of them: and when he had taken him in his arms, he said unto them, Whosoever shall receive one of such children in my name, receiveth me; and whosoever shall receive me, receiveth not me, but him that sent me.——MARK ix. 33-37.

Of this passage in the life of our Lord, the account given by St Mark is the more complete. But it may be enriched and its lesson rendered yet more evident from the record of St Matthew.

"Verily I say unto you, Except ye be converted, and become as little children, ye shall not enter into the kingdom of heaven. Whosoever shall humble himself as this little child, the same is greatest in the kingdom of heaven. And whoso shall receive one such little child in my name receiveth me. But whoso shall offend one of these little ones that believe in me, it were better for him that a millstone were hanged about his neck, and that he were drowned in the depth of the sea."

These passages record a lesson our Lord gave his disciples against ambition, against emulation. It is not for the sake of setting forth this lesson that I write about these words of our Lord, but for the sake of a truth, a revelation about God, in which his great argument reaches its height.

He took a little child—possibly a child of Peter; for St Mark says that the incident fell at Capernaum, and "in the house,"—a child there-fore with some of the characteristics of Peter, whose very faults were those of a childish nature. We might expect the child of such a father to possess the childlike countenance and bearing essential to the con-veyance of the lesson which I now desire to set forth as contained in the passage.

For it must be confessed that there are children who are not child-like. One of the saddest and not least common sights in the world is the face of a child whose mind is so brimful of worldly wisdom that the human childishness has vanished from it, as well as the divine childlikeness. For the *childlike* is the divine, and the very word "mar-shals me the way that I was going." But I must delay my ascent to the final argument in order to remove a possible difficulty, which, in turn-ing us towards one of the grandest truths, turns us away from the truth which the Lord had in view here.

The difficulty is this: Is it like the *Son of man* to pick out the beau-tiful child, and leave the common child unnoticed? What thank would he have in that? Do not even the publicans as much as that? And do not our hearts revolt against the thought of it? Shall the mother's heart cleave closest to the deformed of her little ones? and shall "Christ as we believe him" choose according to the sight of the eye? Would he turn away from the child born in sin and taught iniquity, on whose pinched face hunger and courage and love of praise have combined to stamp the cunning of avaricious age, and take to his arms the child of honest parents, such as Peter and his wife, who could not help looking more good than the other? That were not he who came to seek and to save that which was lost. Let the man who loves his brother say which, in his highest moments of love to God, which, when he is nearest to that ideal humanity whereby *a man* shall be a hiding-place from the wind, he would clasp to his bosom of refuge. Would it not be the evil-faced child, because he needed it most? Yes; in God's name, yes. For is not that the divine way? Who that has read of the lost sheep, or the found prodigal, even if he had no spirit bearing witness with his spirit, will dare to say that it is not the divine way? Often, no doubt, it will *appear* otherwise, for the childlike child is easier to save than the oth-er, and may *come* first. But the rejoicing in heaven is greatest over the sheep that has wandered the farthest—perhaps was born on the wild hill-side, and not in the fold at all. For such a prodigal, the elder broth-er in heaven prays thus—"Lord, think about my poor brother more than about me, for I know thee, and am at rest in thee. I am with thee always."

Why, then, do I think it necessary to say that this child was proba-bly Peter's child, and certainly a child that looked childlike because it was childlike? No amount of evil can *be* the child. No amount of evil, not to say in the face, but in the habits, or even in the heart of the child, can make it cease to be a child, can annihilate the divine idea of childhood which moved in the heart of God when he made that child after his own image. It is the essential of which God speaks, the real by which he judges, the undying of which he is the God.

Heartily I grant this. And if the object of our Lord in taking the child in his arms had been to teach love to our neighbour, love to hu-manity, the ugliest child he could have found, would, perhaps, have served his purpose best. The man who receives any, and more plainly he who receives the repulsive child, because he is the offspring of God, because he is his own brother born, must receive the Father in thus receiving the child. Whosoever gives a cup of cold water to a lit-tle one, refreshes the heart of the Father. To do as God does, is to receive God; to do a service to one of his children is to receive the Fa-ther. Hence, any human being, especially if wretched and woe-begone and outcast, would do as well as a child for the purpose of setting forth this love of God to the human being. Therefore something more is probably intended here. The lesson will be found to lie not in the *hu-manity*, but in the *childhood* of the child.

Again, if the disciples could have seen that the essential childhood was meant, and not a blurred and half-obliterated childhood, the most selfish child might have done as well, but could have done no better than the one we have supposed in whom the true childhood is more evident. But when the child was employed as a manifestation, utter-ance, and sign of the truth that lay in his childhood, in order that the eyes as well as the ears should be channels to the heart, it was essen-tial— not that the child should be beautiful but—that the child should be childlike; that those qualities which wake in our hearts, at sight, the love peculiarly belonging to childhood, which is, indeed, but the per-ception of the childhood, should at least glimmer out upon the face of the *chosen type*. Would such an unchildlike child as we see sometimes, now in a great house, clothed in purple and lace, now in a squalid close, clothed in dirt and rags, have been fit for our Lord's purpose, when he had to say that his listeners must become like this child?

5

when the lesson he had to present to them was that of the divine nature of the child, that of childlikeness? Would there not have been a contrast between the child and our Lord's words, ludicrous except for its horror, especially seeing he set forth the individuality of the child by saying, "this little child," "one of such children," and "these little ones that believe in me?" Even the feelings of pity and of love that would arise in a good heart upon further contemplation of such a child, would have turned it quite away from the lesson our Lord intended to give.

That this lesson did lie, not in the humanity, but in the childhood of the child, let me now show more fully. The disciples had been disputing who should be the greatest, and the Lord wanted to show them that such a dispute had nothing whatever to do with the way things went in his kingdom. Therefore, as a specimen of his subjects, he took a child and set him before them. It was not, it could not be, in virtue of his humanity, it was in virtue of his childhood that this child was thus presented as representing a subject of the kingdom. It was not to show the scope but the nature of the kingdom. He told them they could not enter into the kingdom save by becoming little children—by humbling themselves. For the idea of ruling was excluded where childlikeness was the one essential quality. It was to be no more who should rule, but who should serve; no more who should look down upon his fellows from the conquered heights of authority—even of sacred authority, but who should look up honouring humanity, and ministering unto it, so that humanity itself might at length be persuaded of its own honour as a temple of the living God. It was to impress this lesson upon them that he showed them the child. Therefore, I repeat, the lesson lay in the *childhood* of the child.

But I now approach my especial object; for this lesson led to the enunciation of a yet higher truth, upon which it was founded, and from which indeed it sprung. Nothing is required of man that is not first in God. It is because God is perfect that we are required to be perfect. And it is for the revelation of God to all the human souls, that they may be saved by knowing him, and so becoming like him, that this child is thus chosen and set before them in the gospel. He who, in giving the cup of water or the embrace, comes into contact with the essential childhood of the child—that is, embraces the *childish* humanity of it, (not he who embraces it out of love to humanity, or even love to God as the Father of it)—is partaker of the meaning, that is, the blessing, of this passage. It is the recognition of the childhood as divine that will show the disciple how vain the strife after relative place or honour in the great kingdom.

6

THE CHILD IN THE MIDST.

For it is *In my name*. This means *as representing me*; and, there-fore, *as being like me*. Our Lord could not commission any one to be received in his name who could not more or less represent him; for there would be untruth and unreason. Moreover, he had just been tell-ing the disciples that they must become like this child; and now, when he tells them to receive *such* a little child in his name, it must surely imply something in common between them all—something in which the child and Jesus meet—something in which the child and the disci-ples meet. What else can that be than the spiritual childhood? *In my name* does not mean *because I will it*. An arbitrary utterance of the will of our Lord would certainly find ten thousand to obey it, even to suffering, for one that will be able to receive such a vital truth of his character as is contained in the words; but it is not obedience alone that our Lord will have, but obedience to the *truth*, that is, to the Light of the World, truth beheld and known. *In my name*, if we take all we can find in it, the full meaning which alone will harmonize and make the passage a whole, involves a revelation from resemblance, from fitness to represent and so reveal. He who receives a child, then, in the name of Jesus, does so, perceiving wherein Jesus and the child are one, what is common to them. He must not only see the *ideal* child in the child he receives—that reality of loveliness which constitutes true childhood, but must perceive that the child is like Jesus, or rather, that the Lord is like the child, and may be embraced, yea, is embraced, by every heart childlike enough to embrace a child for the sake of his childness. I do not therefore say that none but those who are thus con-scious in the act partake of the blessing. But a special sense, a lofty knowledge of blessedness, belongs to the act of embracing a child as the visible likeness of the Lord himself. For the blessedness is the per-ceiving of the truth—the blessing is the truth itself—the God-known truth, that the Lord has the heart of a child. The man who perceives this knows in himself that he is blessed—blessed because that is true.

But the argument as to the meaning of our Lord's words, *in my name*, is incomplete, until we follow our Lord's enunciation to its sec-ond and higher stage: "He that receiveth me, receiveth him that sent me." It will be allowed that the connection between the first and sec-ond link of the chain will probably be the same as the connection between the second and third. I do not say it is necessarily so; for I aim at no logical certainty. I aim at showing, rather than at proving, to my reader, by means of my sequences, the idea to which I am approach-ing. For if, once he beholds it, he cannot receive it, if it does not shew itself to him to be true, there would not only be little use in convincing him by logic, but I allow that he can easily suggest other possible connections in the chain, though, I assert, none so symmetrical. What, then, is the connection between the second and third? How is it that he who receives the Son receives the Father? Because the Son is as the Father; and he whose heart can perceive the essential in Christ, has the essence of the Father—that is, sees and holds to it by that recognition, and is one therewith by recognition and worship. What, then, next, is the connection between the first and second? I think the same. "He that sees the essential in this child, the pure childhood, sees that which is the essence of me," grace and truth—in a word, childlikeness. It follows not that the former is perfect as the latter, but it is the same in kind, and therefore, manifest in the child, reveals that which is in Jesus.

Then to receive a child in the name of Jesus is to receive Jesus; to receive Jesus is to receive God; therefore to receive the child is to receive God himself.

That such is the feeling of the words, and that such was the feeling in the heart of our Lord when he spoke them, I may show from another golden thread that may be traced through the shining web of his golden words.

What is the kingdom of Christ? A rule of love, of truth—a rule of service. The king is the chief servant in it. "The kings of the earth have dominion: it shall not be so among you." "The Son of Man came to minister." "My Father worketh hitherto, and I work." The great Workman is the great King, labouring for his own. So he that would be greatest among them, and come nearest to the King himself, must be the servant of all. It is *like king like subject* in the kingdom of heaven. No rule of force, as of one kind over another kind. It is the rule of *kind*, of *nature*, of deepest nature—of *God*. If, then, to enter into this kingdom, we must become children, the spirit of children must be its pervading spirit throughout, from lowly subject to lowliest king. The lesson added by St Luke to the presentation of the child is: "For he that is least among you all, the same shall be great." And St Matthew says: "Whosoever shall humble himself as this little child, the same is greatest in the kingdom of heaven." Hence the sign that passes between king and subject. The subject kneels in homage to the kings of the earth: the heavenly king takes his subject in his arms. This is the sign of the kingdom between them. This is the all-pervading relation of the kingdom.

To give one glance backward, then:

8

To receive the child because God receives it, or for its humanity, is one thing; to receive it because it is like God, or for its childhood, is another. The former will do little to destroy ambition. Alone it might argue only a wider scope to it, because it admits all men to the arena of the strife. But the latter strikes at the very root of emulation. As soon as even service is done for the honour and not for the service-sake, the doer is that moment outside the kingdom. But when we receive the child in the name of Christ, the very childhood that we receive to our arms is humanity. We love its humanity in its childhood, for childhood is the deepest heart of humanity—its divine heart; and so in the name of the child we receive all humanity. Therefore, although the lesson is not about humanity, but about childhood, it returns upon our race, and we receive our race with wider arms and deeper heart. There is, then, no other lesson lost by receiving this; no heartlessness shown in insisting that the child was a lovable—a childlike child.

If there is in heaven a picture of that wonderful teaching, doubtless we shall see represented in it a dim childhood shining from the faces of all that group of disciples of which the centre is the Son of God with a child in his arms. The childhood, dim in the faces of the men, must be shining trustfully clear in the face of the child. But in the face of the Lord himself, the childhood will be triumphant—all his wisdom, all his truth upholding that radiant serenity of faith in his father. Verily, O Lord, this childhood is life. Verily, O Lord, when thy tenderness shall have made the world great, then, children like thee, will all men smile in the face of the great God.

But to advance now to the highest point of this teaching of our Lord: "He that receiveth me receiveth him that sent me." To receive a child in the name of God is to receive God himself. How to receive him? As alone he can be received,—by knowing him as he is. To know him is to have him in us. And that we may know him, let us now receive this revelation of him, in the words of our Lord himself. Here is the argument of highest import founded upon the teaching of our master in the utterance before us.

God is represented in Jesus, for that God is like Jesus: Jesus is represented in the child, for that Jesus is like the child. Therefore God is represented in the child, for that he is like the child. God is child-like. In the true vision of this fact lies the receiving of God in the child.

Having reached this point, I have nothing more to do with the argument; for if the Lord meant this—that is, if this be a truth, he that is able to receive it will receive it: he that hath ears to hear it will hear it.

For our Lord's arguments are for the presentation of the truth, and the truth carries its own conviction to him who is able to receive it.

But the word of one who has seen this truth may help the dawn of a like perception in those who keep their faces turned towards the east and its aurora; for men may have eyes, and, seeing dimly, want to see more. Therefore let us brood a little over the idea itself, and see whether it will not come forth so as to commend itself to that spirit, which, one with the human spirit where it dwells, searches the deep things of God. For, although the true heart may at first be shocked at the truth, as Peter was shocked when he said, "That be far from thee, Lord," yet will it, after a season, receive it and rejoice in it.

Let me then ask, do you believe in the Incarnation? And if you do, let me ask further, Was Jesus ever less divine than God? I answer for you, Never. He was lower, but never less divine. Was he not a child then? You answer, "Yes, but not like other children." I ask, "Did he not look like other children?" If he looked like them and was not like them, the whole was a deception, a masquerade at best. I say he was a child, whatever more he might be. God is man, and infinitely more. Our Lord became flesh, but did not *become* man. He took on him the form of man: he was man already. And he was, is, and ever shall be divinely childlike. He could never have been a child if he would ever have ceased to be a child, for in him the transient found nothing. Childhood belongs to the divine nature. Obedience, then, is as divine as Will, Service as divine as Rule. How? Because they are one in their nature; they are both a doing of the truth. The love in them is the same. The Fatherhood and the Sonship are one, save that the Fatherhood looks down lovingly, and the Sonship looks up lovingly. Love is all. And God is all in all. He is ever seeking to get down to us—to be the divine man to us. And we are ever saying, "That be far from thee, Lord!" We are careful, in our unbelief, over the divine dignity, of which he is too grand to think. Better pleasing to God, it needs little daring to say, is the audacity of Job, who, rushing into his presence, and flinging the door of his presence-chamber to the wall, like a troubled, it may be angry, but yet faithful child, calls aloud in the ear of him whose perfect Fatherhood he has yet to learn: "Am I a sea or a whale, that thou settest a watch over me?"

Let us dare, then, to climb the height of divine truth to which this utterance of our Lord would lead us.

Does it not lead us up hither: that the devotion of God to his creatures is perfect? that he does not think about himself but about them?

that he wants nothing for himself, but finds his blessedness in the out-going of blessedness.

Ah! it is a terrible—shall it be a lonely glory this? We will draw

near with our human response, our abandonment of self in the faith of

Jesus. He gives himself to us—shall not we give ourselves to him? Shall we not give ourselves to each other whom he loves?

For when is the child the ideal child in our eyes and to our hearts? Is it not when with gentle hand he takes his father by the beard, and turns that father's face up to his brothers and sisters to kiss? when even the lovely selfishness of love-seeking has vanished, and the heart is absorbed in loving?

In this, then, is God like the child: that he is simply and altogether our friend, our father—our more than friend, father, and mother—our infinite love-perfect God. Grand and strong beyond all that human im-agination can conceive of poet-thinking and kingly action, he is delicate beyond all that human tenderness can conceive of husband or wife, homely beyond all that human heart can conceive of father or mother. He has not two thoughts about us. With him all is simplicity of purpose and meaning and effort and end—namely, that we should be as he is, think the same thoughts, mean the same things, possess the same blessedness. It is so plain that any one may see it, every one ought to see it, every one shall see it. It must be so. He is utterly true and good to us, nor shall anything withstand his will.

How terribly, then, have the theologians misrepresented God in the measures of the low and showy, not the lofty and simple humanities! Nearly all of them represent him as a great King on a grand throne, thinking how grand he is, and making it the business of his being and the end of his universe to keep up his glory, wielding the bolts of a Jupiter against them that take his name in vain. They would not allow this, but follow out what they say, and it comes much to this. Brothers, have you found our king? There he is, kissing little children and saying they are like God. There he is at table with the head of a fisherman lying on his bosom, and somewhat heavy at heart that even he, the be-loved disciple, cannot yet understand him well. The simplest peasant who loves his children and his sheep were—no, not a truer, for the other is false, but—a true type of our God beside that monstrosity of a monarch.

The God who is ever uttering himself in the changeful profusions of nature; who takes millions of years to form a soul that shall under-stand him and be blessed; who never needs to be, and never is, in haste; who welcomes the simplest thought of truth or beauty as the return for seed he has sown upon the old fallows of eternity, who rejoices in the response of a faltering moment to the age-long cry of his wisdom in the streets; the God of music, of painting, of building, the Lord of Hosts, the God of mountains and oceans; whose laws go forth from one unseen point of wisdom, and thither return without an atom of loss; the God of history working in time unto christianity; this God is the God of little children, and he alone can be perfectly, abandonedly simple and devoted. The deepest, purest love of a woman has its well-spring in him. Our longing desires can no more exhaust the fulness of the treasures of the Godhead, than our imagination can touch their measure. Of him not a thought, not a joy, not a hope of one of his creatures can pass unseen; and while one of them remains unsatisfied, he is not Lord over all.

Therefore, with angels and with archangels, with the spirits of the just made perfect, with the little children of the kingdom, yea, with the Lord himself, and for all them that know him not, we praise and magnify and laud his name in itself, saying *Our Father*. We do not draw back for that we are unworthy, nor even for that we are hard-hearted and care not for the good. For it is his childlikeness that makes him our God and Father. The perfection of his relation to us swallows up all our imperfections, all our defects, all our evils; for our childhood is born of his fatherhood. That man is perfect in faith who can come to God in the utter dearth of his feelings and his desires, without a glow or an aspiration, with the weight of low thoughts, failures, neglects, and wandering forgetfulness, and say to him, "Thou art my refuge, because thou art my home."

Such a faith will not lead to presumption. The man who can pray such a prayer will know better than another, that God is not mocked; that he is not a man that he should repent; that tears and entreaties will not work on him to the breach of one of his laws; that for God to give a man because he asked for it that which was not in harmony with his laws of truth and right, would be to damn him—to cast him into the outer darkness. And he knows that out of that prison the childlike, imperturbable God will let no man come till he has paid the uttermost farthing.

And if he should forget this, the God to whom he belongs does not forget it, does not forget him. Life is no series of chances with a few providences sprinkled between to keep up a justly failing belief, but one providence of God; and the man shall not live long before life itself shall remind him, it may be in agony of soul, of that which he has forgotten. When he prays for comfort, the answer may come in dismay and terror and the turning aside of the Father's countenance; for love itself will, for love's sake, turn the countenance away from that which is not lovely; and he will have to read, written upon the dark wall of his imprisoned conscience, the words, awful and glorious, *Our God is a consuming fire.*

THE CONSUMING FIRE.

Our God is a consuming fire.— HEBREWS xii. 29.

Nothing is inexorable but love. Love which will yield to prayer is imperfect and poor. Nor is it then the love that yields, but its alloy. For if at the voice of entreaty love conquers displeasure, it is love asserting itself, not love yielding its claims. It is not love that grants a boon unwillingly; still less is it love that answers a prayer to the wrong and hurt of him who prays. Love is one, and love is changeless.

For love loves unto purity. Love has ever in view the absolute loveliness of that which it beholds. Where loveliness is incomplete, and love cannot love its fill of loving, it spends itself to make more lovely, that it may love more; it strives for perfection, even that itself may be perfected—not in itself, but in the object. As it was love that first created humanity, so even human love, in proportion to its divinity, will go on creating the beautiful for its own outpouring. There is nothing eternal but that which loves and can be loved, and love is ever climbing towards the consummation when such shall be the universe, imperishable, divine.

Therefore all that is not beautiful in the beloved, all that comes between and is not of love's kind, must be destroyed.

And our God is a consuming fire.

If this be hard to understand, it is as the simple, absolute truth is hard to understand. It may be centuries of ages before a man comes to see a truth—ages of strife, of effort, of aspiration. But when once he does see it, it is so plain that he wonders he could have lived without seeing it. That he did not understand it sooner was simply and only that he did not see it. To see a truth, to know what it is, to understand it, and to love it, are all one. There is many a motion towards it, many a misery for want of it, many a cry of the conscience against the neglect of it, many a dim longing for it as an unknown need before at length the eyes come awake, and the darkness of the dreamful night yields to the light of the sun of truth. But once beheld it is for ever. To see one divine fact is to stand face to face with essential eternal life.

For this vision of truth God has been working for ages of ages. For this simple condition, this apex of life, upon which a man wonders like a child that he cannot make other men see as he sees, the whole labour of God's science, history, poetry—from the time when the earth gathered itself into a lonely drop of fire from the red rim of the driving sun-wheel to the time when Alexander John Scott worshipped him from its face—was evolving truth upon truth in lovely vision, in torturing law, never lying, never repenting; and for this will the patience of God labour while there is yet a human soul whose eyes have not been opened, whose child-heart has not yet been born in him. For this one condition of humanity, this simple beholding, has all the outthinking of God flowed in forms innumerable and changeful from the foundation of the world; and for this, too, has the divine destruction been going forth; that his life might be our life, that in us, too, might dwell that same consuming fire which is essential love.

Let us look at the utterance of the apostle which is crowned with this lovely terror: "Our God is a consuming fire."

"Wherefore, we receiving a kingdom which cannot be moved, let us have grace, whereby we may serve God acceptably with reverence and godly fear, for our God is a consuming fire."—We have received a kingdom that cannot be moved—whose nature is immovable: let us have grace to serve the Consuming Fire, our God, with divine fear; not with the fear that cringes and craves, but with the bowing down of all thoughts, all delights, all loves before him who is the life of them all, and will have them all pure. The kingdom he has given us cannot be moved, because it has nothing weak in it: it is of the eternal world, the world of being, of truth. We, therefore, must worship him with a fear pure as the kingdom is unshakeable. He will shake heaven and earth, that only the unshakeable may remain, (*verse* 27): he is a consuming fire, that only that which cannot be consumed may stand forth eternal. It is the nature of God, so terribly pure that it destroys all that is not pure as fire, which demands like purity in our worship. He will have purity. It is not that the fire will burn us if we do not worship thus; but that the fire will burn us until we worship thus; yea, will go on burning within us after all that is foreign to it has yielded to its force, no longer with pain and consuming, but as the highest consciousness of life, the presence of God. When evil, which alone is consumable, shall have passed away in his fire from the dwellers in the immovable kingdom, the nature of man shall look the nature of God in the face, and his fear shall then be pure; for an eternal, that is a holy fear, must spring from a knowledge of the nature, not from a sense of the power. But that which cannot be consumed must be one within itself, a simple existence; therefore in such a soul the fear towards God will be one with the homeliest love. Yea, the fear of God will cause a man to flee, not from him, but from himself; not from him, but to him, the Father of himself, in terror lest he should do Him wrong or his neighbour wrong. And the first words which follow for the setting forth of that grace whereby we may serve God acceptably are these—"Let brotherly love continue." To love our brother is to worship the Consuming Fire.

The symbol of *the consuming fire* would seem to have been suggested to the writer by the fire that burned on the mountain of the old law. That fire was part of the revelation of God there made to the Israelites. Nor was it the first instance of such a revelation. The symbol of God's presence, before which Moses had to put off his shoes, and to which it was not safe for him to draw near, was a fire that *did not consume the bush in which it burned.* Both revelations were of terror. But the same symbol employed by a writer of the New Testament should mean more, not than it meant before, but than it was before employed to express; for it could not have been employed to express more than it was possible for them to perceive. What else than terror could a nation of slaves, into whose very souls the rust of their chains had eaten, in whose memory lingered the smoke of the flesh-pots of Egypt, who, rather than not eat of the food they liked best, would have gone back to the house of their bondage—what else could such a nation see in that fire than terror and destruction? How should they think of purification by fire? They had yet no such condition of mind as could generate such a thought. And if they had had the thought, the notion of the suffering involved would soon have overwhelmed the notion of purification. Nor would such a nation have listened to any teaching that was not supported by terror. Fear was that for which they were fit. They had no worship for any being of whom they had not to be afraid.

Was then this show upon Mount Sinai a device to move obedience, such as bad nurses employ with children? a hint of vague and false horror? Was it not a true revelation of God?

If it was not a true revelation, it was none at all, and the story is either false, or the whole display was a political trick of Moses. Those who can read the mind of Moses will not easily believe the latter, and those who understand the scope of the pretended revelation, will see

16

no reason for supposing the former. That which would be politic, were it a deception, is not therefore excluded from the possibility of another source. Some people believe so little in a cosmos or ordered world, that the very argument of fitness is a reason for unbelief.

At all events, if God showed them these things, God showed them what was true. It was a revelation of himself. He will not put on a mask. He puts on a face. He will not speak out of flaming fire if that flaming fire is alien to him, if there is nothing in him for that flaming fire to reveal. Be his children ever so brutish, he will not terrify them with a lie.

It was a revelation, but a partial one; a true symbol, not a final vision.

No revelation can be other than partial. If for true revelation a man must be told all the truth, then farewell to revelation; yea, farewell to the sonship. For what revelation, other than a partial, can the highest spiritual condition receive of the infinite God? But it is not therefore untrue because it is partial. Relatively to a lower condition of the receiver, a more partial revelation might be truer than that would be which constituted a fuller revelation to one in a higher condition; for the former might reveal much to him, the latter might reveal nothing. Only, whatever it might reveal, if its nature were such as to preclude development and growth, thus chaining the man to its incompleteness, it would be but a false revelation fighting against all the divine laws of human existence. The true revelation rouses the desire to know more by the truth of its incompleteness.

Here was a nation at its lowest: could it receive anything but a partial revelation, a revelation of fear? How should the Hebrews be other than terrified at that which was opposed to all they knew of themselves, beings judging it good to honour a golden calf? Such as they were, they did well to be afraid. They were in a better condition, acknowledging if only a terror *above* them, flaming on that unknown mountain height, than stooping to worship the idol below them. Fear is nobler than sensuality. Fear is better than no God, better than a god made with hands. In that fear lay deep hidden the sense of the infinite. The worship of fear is true, although very low; and though not acceptable to God in itself, for only the worship of spirit and of truth is acceptable to him, yet even in his sight it is precious. For he regards men not as they are merely, but as they shall be; not as they shall be merely, but as they are now growing, or capable of growing, towards that image after which he made them that they might grow to it. Therefore a thousand stages, each in itself all but valueless, are of inestimable worth as the necessary and connected gradations of an infinite progress. A condition which of declension would indicate a devil, may of growth indicate a saint. So far then the revelation, not being final any more than complete, and calling forth the best of which they were now capable, so making future and higher revelation possible, may have been a true one.

But we shall find that this very revelation of fire is itself, in a higher sense, true to the mind of the rejoicing saint as to the mind of the trembling sinner. For the former sees farther into the meaning of the fire, and knows better what it will do to him. It is a symbol which needed not to be superseded, only unfolded. While men take part *with* their sins, while they feel as if, separated from their sins, they would be no longer themselves, how can they understand that the lightning word is a Saviour—that word which pierces to the dividing between the man and the evil, which will slay the sin and give life to the sinner? Can it be any comfort to them to be told that God loves them so that he will burn them clean. Can the cleansing of the fire appear to them anything beyond what it must always, more or less, be—a process of torture? They do not want to be clean, and they cannot bear to be tortured. Can they then do other, or can we desire that they should do other, than fear God, even with the fear of the wicked, until they learn to love him with the love of the holy. To them Mount Sinai is crowned with the signs of vengeance. And is not God ready to do unto them even as they fear, though with another feeling and a different end from any which they are capable of supposing? He is against sin: in so far as, and while, they and sin are one, he is against them—against their desires, their aims, their fears, and their hopes; and thus he is altogether and always *for them*. That thunder and lightning and tempest, that blackness torn with the sound of a trumpet, that visible horror billowed with the voice of words, was all but a faint image to the senses of the slaves of what God thinks and feels against vileness and selfishness, of the unrest of unassuageable repulsion with which he regards such conditions; that so the stupid people, fearing somewhat to do as they would, might leave a little room for that grace to grow in them, which would at length make them see that evil, and not fire, is the fearful thing; yea, so transform them that they would gladly rush up into the trumpet-blast of Sinai to escape the flutes around the golden calf. Could they have understood this, they would have needed no Mount Sinai. It was a true, and of necessity a partial revelation— partial in order to be true.

THE CONSUMING FIRE.

Even Moses, the man of God, was not ready to receive the revelation in store; not ready, although from love to his people he prayed that God would even blot him out of his book of life. If this means that he offered to give himself as a sacrifice *instead* of them, it would show reason enough why he could not be glorified with the vision of the Redeemer. For so he would think to appease God, not seeing that God was as tender as himself, not seeing that God is the Reconciler, the Redeemer, not seeing that the sacrifice of the heart is the atonement for which alone he cares. He would be blotted out, that their names might be kept in. Certainly when God told him that he that had sinned should suffer for it, Moses could not see that this was the kindest thing that God could do. But I doubt if that was what Moses meant. It seems rather the utterance of a divine despair:—he would not survive the children of his people. He did not care for a love that would save him alone, and send to the dust those thousands of calf-worshipping brothers and sisters. But in either case, how much could Moses have understood, if he had seen the face instead of the back of that form that passed the clift of the rock amidst the thunderous vapours of Sinai? Had that form turned and that face looked upon him, the face of him who was more man than any man; the face through which the divine emotion would, in the ages to come, manifest itself to the eyes of men, bowed, it might well be, at such a moment, in anticipation of the crown with which the children of the people for whom Moses pleaded with his life, would one day crown him; the face of him who was bearing and was yet to bear their griefs and carry their sorrows, who is now bearing our griefs and carrying our sorrows; the face of the Son of God, who, instead of accepting the sacrifice of one of his creatures to satisfy his justice or support his dignity, gave himself utterly unto them, and therein to the Father by doing his lovely will; who suffered unto the death, not that men might not suffer, but that their suffering might be like his, and lead them up to his perfection; if that face, I say, had turned and looked upon Moses, would Moses have lived? Would he not have died, not of splendour, not of sorrow, (terror was not there,) but of the actual sight of the incomprehensible? If infinite mystery had not slain him, would he not have gone about dazed, doing nothing, having no more any business that he could do in the world, seeing God was to him altogether unknown? For thus a full revelation would not only be no revelation, but the destruction of all revelation.

"May it not then hurt to say that God is Love, all love, and nothing other than love? It is not enough to answer that such is the truth, even

19

granted that it is. Upon your own showing, too much revelation may hurt by dazzling and blinding."

There is a great difference between a mystery of God that no man understands, and a mystery of God laid hold of, let it be but by one single man. The latter is already a revelation; and, passing through that man's mind, will be so presented, it may be so *feebly* presented, that it will not hurt his fellows. Let God conceal as he will: (although I believe he is ever destroying concealment, ever giving all that he can, all that men can receive at his hands, that he does not want to conceal anything, but to reveal everything,) the light which any man has received is not to be put under a bushel; it is for him and his fellows. In sowing the seed he will not withhold his hand because there are thorns and stony places and waysides. He will think that in some cases even a bird of the air may carry the matter, that the good seed may be too much for the thorns, that that which withers away upon the stony place may yet leave there, by its own decay, a deeper soil for the next seed to root itself in. Besides, they only can receive the doctrine who have ears to hear. If the selfish man could believe it, he would misinterpret it; but he cannot believe it. It is not possible that he should. But the loving soul, oppressed by wrong teaching, or partial truth claiming to be the whole, will hear, understand, rejoice.

For, when we say that God is Love, do we teach men that their fear of him is groundless? No. As much as they fear will come upon them, possibly far more. But there is something beyond their fear,—a divine fate which they cannot withstand, because it works along with the human individuality which the divine individuality has created in them. The wrath will consume what they *call* themselves; so that the selves God made shall appear, coming out with tenfold consciousness of being, and bringing with them all that made the blessedness of the life the men tried to lead without God. They will know that now first are they fully themselves. The avaricious, weary, selfish, suspicious old man shall have passed away. The young, ever young self, will remain. That which they *thought* themselves shall have vanished: that which they *felt* themselves, though they misjudged their own feelings, shall remain— remain glorified in repentant hope. For that which cannot be shaken shall remain. That which is immortal in God shall remain in man. The death that is in them shall be consumed.

It is the law of Nature—that is, the law of God—that all that is destructible shall be destroyed. When that which is immortal buries itself in the destructible—when it receives all the messages from without, through the surrounding region of decadence, and none from within, from the eternal doors—it cannot, though immortal still, know its own immortality. The destructible must be burned out of it, or begin to be burned out of it, before it can *partake* of eternal life. When that is all burnt away and gone, then it has eternal life. Or rather, when the fire of eternal life has possessed a man, then the destructible is gone utterly, and he is pure. Many a man's work must be burned, that by that very burning he may be saved—"so as by fire." Away in smoke go the lordships, the Rabbi-hoods of the world, and the man who acquiesces in the burning is saved by the fire; for it has destroyed the destructible, which is the vantage point of the deathly, which would destroy both body and soul in hell. If still he cling to that which can be burned, the burning goes on deeper and deeper into his bosom, till it reaches the roots of the falsehood that enslaves him—possibly by looking like the truth.

The man who loves God, and is not yet pure, courts the burning of God. Nor is it always torture. The fire shows itself sometimes only as light—still it will be fire of purifying. The consuming fire is just the original, the active form of Purity,—that which makes pure, that which is indeed Love, the creative energy of God. Without purity there can be as no creation so no persistence. That which is not pure is corruptible, and corruption cannot inherit incorruption.

The man whose deeds are evil, fears the burning. But the burning will not come the less that he fears it or denies it. Escape is hopeless. For Love is inexorable. Our God is a consuming fire. He shall not come out till he has paid the uttermost farthing.

If the man resists the burning of God, the consuming fire of Love, a terrible doom awaits him, and its day will come. He shall be cast into the outer darkness who hates the fire of God. What sick dismay shall then seize upon him! For let a man think and care ever so little about God, he does not therefore exist without God. God is here with him, upholding, warming, delighting, teaching him—making life a good thing to him. God gives him himself, though he knows it not. But when God withdraws from a man as far as that can be without the man's ceasing to be; when the man feels himself abandoned, hanging in a ceaseless vertigo of existence upon the verge of the gulf of his being, without support, without refuge, without aim, without end—for the soul has no weapons wherewith to destroy herself—with no inbreathing of joy, with nothing to make life good;—then will he listen in agony for the faintest sound of life from the closed door; then, if the moan of suffering humanity ever reaches the ear of the outcast of darkness, he will be ready to rush into the very heart of the Consuming

Fire to know life once more, to change this terror of sick negation, of unspeakable death, for that region of painful hope. Imagination cannot mislead us into too much horror of being without God—that one living death. Is not this

to be worse than worst Of those that lawless and incertain thoughts Imagine howling?

But with this divine difference: that the outer darkness is but the most dreadful form of the consuming fire—the fire without light—the darkness visible, the black flame. God hath withdrawn himself, but not lost his hold. His face is turned away, but his hand is laid upon him still. His heart has ceased to beat into the man's heart, but he keeps him alive by his fire. And that fire will go searching and burning on in him, as in the highest saint who is not yet pure as he is pure.

But at length, O God, wilt thou not cast Death and Hell into the lake of Fire—even into thine own consuming self? Death shall then die everlastingly,

And Hell itself will pass away,

And leave her dolorous mansions to the peering day.

Then indeed wilt thou be all in all. For then our poor brothers and sisters, every one—O God, we trust in thee, the Consuming Fire—shall have been burnt clean and brought home. For if their moans, myriads of ages away, would turn heaven for us into hell—shall a man be more merciful than God? Shall, of all his glories, his mercy alone not be infinite? Shall a brother love a brother more than The Father loves a son?—more than The Brother Christ loves his brother? Would he not die yet again to save one brother more?

As for us, now will we come to thee, our Consuming Fire. And thou wilt not burn us more than we can bear. But thou wilt burn us. And although thou seem to slay us, yet will we trust in thee even for that which thou hast not spoken, if by any means at length we may attain unto the blessedness of those *who have not seen and yet have believed.*

THE HIGHER FAITH.

Jesus saith unto him, Thomas, because thou hast seen me, thou hast believed: blessed are they that have not seen, and yet have believed.—JOHN xx. 29.

The aspiring child is often checked by the dull disciple who has learned his lessons so imperfectly that he has never got beyond his school-books. Full of fragmentary rules, he has perceived the principle of none of them. The child draws near to him with some outburst of unusual feeling, some scintillation of a lively hope, some wide-reaching imagination that draws into the circle of religious theory the world of nature, and the yet wider world of humanity, for to the child the doings of the Father fill the spaces; he has not yet learned to divide between God and nature, between Providence and grace, between love and benevolence;—the child comes, I say, with his heart full, and the answer he receives from the dull disciple is—"God has said nothing about that in his word, therefore we have no right to believe anything about it. It is better not to speculate on such matters. However desirable it may seem to us, we have nothing to do with it. It is not revealed." For such a man is incapable of suspecting, that what has remained hidden from him may have been revealed to the babe. With the authority, therefore, of years and ignorance, he forbids the child, for he believes in no revelation but the Bible, and in the word of that alone. For him all revelation has ceased with and been buried in the Bible, to be with difficulty exhumed, and, with much questioning of the decayed form, re-united into a rigid skeleton of metaphysical and legal contrivance for letting the love of God have its way unchecked by the other perfections of his being.

But to the man who would live throughout the whole divine form of his being, not confining himself to one broken corner of his kingdom, and leaving the rest to the demons that haunt such deserts, a thousand questions will arise to which the Bible does not even allude. Has he indeed nothing to do with such? Do they lie beyond the sphere of his responsibility? "Leave them," says the dull disciple. "I cannot," returns the man. "Not only does that degree of peace of mind without which action is impossible, depend upon the answers to these questions, but my conduct itself must correspond to these answers." "Leave them at least till God chooses to explain, if he ever will." "No. Questions imply answers. He has put the questions in my heart; he holds the answers in his. I will seek them from him. I will wait, but not till I have knocked. I will be patient, but not till I have asked. I will seek until I find. He has something for me. My prayer shall go up unto the God of my life."

Sad, indeed, would the whole matter be, if the Bible had told us *everything* God meant us to believe. But herein is the Bible itself greatly wronged. It nowhere lays claim to be regarded as *the* Word, *the* Way, *the* Truth. The Bible leads us to Jesus, the inexhaustible, the ever unfolding Revelation of God. It is Christ "in whom are hid all the treasures of wisdom and knowledge," not the Bible, save as leading to him. And why are we told that these treasures are *hid* in him who is the *Revelation* of God? Is it that we should despair of finding them and cease to seek them? Are they not hid in him that they may be revealed to us in due time—that is, when we are in need of them? Is not their hiding in him the mediatorial step towards their unfolding in us? Is he not the Truth?—the Truth to men? Is he not the High Priest of his brethren, to answer all the troubled questionings that arise in their dim humanity? For it is his heart which

Contains of good, wise, just, the perfect shape.

Didymus answers, "No doubt, what we know not now, we shall know hereafter." Certainly there may be things which the mere passing into another stage of existence will illuminate; but the questions that come here, must be inquired into here, and if not answered here, then there too until they be answered. There is more hid in Christ than we shall ever learn, here or there either; but they that begin first to inquire will soonest be gladdened with revelation; and with them he will be best pleased, for the slowness of his disciples troubled him of old. To say that we must wait for the other world, to know the mind of him who came to this world to give himself to us, seems to me the foolishness of a worldly and lazy spirit. The Son of God *is* the Teacher of men, giving to them of his Spirit—that Spirit which manifests the deep things of God, being to a man the mind of Christ. The great heresy of the Church of the present day is unbelief in this Spirit. The mass of the Church does not believe that the Spirit has a revelation for every man individually—a revelation as different from the revelation of the Bible, as the food in the moment of passing into living brain and nerve differs from the bread and meat. If we were once filled with the mind of Christ, we should know that the Bible had done its work, was fulfilled, and had for us passed away, that thereby the Word of our God might abide for ever. The one use of the Bible is to make us look at Jesus, that through him we might know his Father and our Father, his God and our God. Till we thus know Him, let us hold the Bible dear as the moon of our darkness, by which we travel towards the east; not dear as the sun whence her light cometh, and towards which we haste, that, walking in the sun himself, we may no more need the mirror that reflected his absent brightness.

But this doctrine of the Spirit is not my end now, although, were it not true, all our religion would be vain, that of St Paul and that of Socrates. What I want to say and show, if I may, is, that a man will please God better by believing some things that are not told him, than by confining his faith to those things that are expressly said—said to arouse in us the truth-seeing faculty, the spiritual desire, the prayer for the good things which God will give to them that ask him.

"But is not this dangerous doctrine? Will not a man be taught thus to believe the things he likes best, even to pray for that which he likes best? And will he not grow arrogant in his confidence?"

If it be true that the Spirit strives with our spirit; if it be true that God teaches men, we may safely leave those dreaded results to him. If the man is of the Lord's company, he is safer with him than with those who would secure their safety by hanging on the outskirts and daring nothing. If he is not taught of God in that which he hopes for, God will let him know it. He will receive, something else than he prays for. If he can pray to God for anything not good, the answer will come in the flames of that consuming fire. These will soon bring him to some of his spiritual senses. But it will be far better for him to be thus sharply tutored, than to go on a snail's pace in the journey of the spiritual life. And for arrogance, I have seen nothing breed it faster or in more offensive forms than the worship of the letter.

And to whom shall a man, whom the blessed God has made, look for what he likes best, but to that blessed God? If we have been indeed enabled to see that God is our Father, as the Lord taught us, let us advance from that truth to understand that he is far more than father—that his nearness to us is beyond the embodiment of the highest idea of father; that the fatherhood of God is but a step towards the Godhood for them that can receive it. What a man likes best *may* be God's will, may be the voice of the Spirit striving *with* his spirit, not against it; and if, as I have said, it be not so—if the thing he asks is not according to his will—there is that consuming fire. The danger lies, not in asking from God what is not good, nor even in hoping to receive it from him, but in not asking him, in not having him of our council. Nor will the fact that we dare not inquire his will, preserve us from the necessity of acting in some such matter as we call unrevealed, and where shall we find ourselves then? Nor, once more, for such a disposition of mind is it likely that the book itself will contain much of a revelation.

The whole matter may safely be left to God.

But I doubt if a man *can* ask anything from God that is bad. Surely one who has begun to pray to him is child enough to know the bad from the good when it has come so near him, and dares not pray for *that*. If you refer me to David praying such fearful prayers against his enemies, I answer, you must read them by your knowledge of the man himself and his history. Remember that this is he who, with the burning heart of an eastern, yet, when his greatest enemy was given into his hands, instead of taking the vengeance of an eastern, contented himself with cutting off the skirt of his garment. It was justice and right that he craved in his soul, although his prayers took a wild form of words. God heard him, and gave him what contented him. In a good man at least, "revenge is," as Lord Bacon says, "a kind of wild justice," and is easily satisfied. The hearts desire upon such a one's enemies is best met and granted when the hate is changed into love and compassion.

But it is about hopes rather than prayers that I wish to write.

What should I think of my child, if I found that he limited his faith in me and hope from me to the few promises he had heard me utter! The faith that limits itself to the promises of God, seems to me to partake of the paltry character of such a faith in my child—good enough for a Pagan, but for a Christian a miserable and wretched faith. Those who rest in such a faith would feel yet more comfortable if they had God's bond instead of his word, which they regard not as the outcome of his character, but as a pledge of his honour. They try to believe in the truth of his word, but the truth of his Being, they understand not. In his oath they persuade themselves that they put confidence: in *himself* they do not believe, for they know him not. Therefore it is little wonder that they distrust those swellings of the heart which are his drawings of the man towards him, as sun and moon heave the ocean mass heavenward. Brother, sister, if such is your faith, you will not, must not stop there. You must come out of this bondage of the law to which you give the name of grace, for there is little that is gracious in it. You will yet know the dignity of your high calling, and the love of God that passeth knowledge. He is not afraid of your presumptuous approach to him. It is you who are afraid to come near him. He is not watching over his dignity. It is you who fear to be sent away as the disciples would have sent away the little children. It is you who think so much about your souls and are so afraid of losing your life, that you dare not draw near to the Life of life, lest it should consume you.

Our God, we will trust thee. Shall we not find thee equal to our faith? One day, we shall laugh ourselves to scorn that we looked for so little from thee; for thy giving will not be limited by our hoping.

O thou of little faith! "in everything,"—I am quoting your own Bible; nay, more, I am quoting a divine soul that knew his master Christ, and in his strength opposed apostles, not to say christians, to their faces, because they could not believe more than a little in God; could believe only for themselves and not for their fellows; could believe for the few of the chosen nation, for whom they had God's ancient *word*, but could not believe for the multitude of the nations, for the millions of hearts that God had made to search after him and find him;—"In everything," says St Paul, "In everything, by prayer and supplication, with thanksgiving, let your requests be made known unto God." For this *everything*, nothing is too small. That it should trouble us is enough. There is some principle involved in it worth the notice even of God himself, for did he not make us so that the thing does trouble us? And surely for this *everything*, nothing can be too great. When the Son of man cometh and findeth too much faith on the earth—may God in his mercy slay us. Meantime, we will hope and trust.

Do you count it a great faith to believe what God has said? It seems to me, I repeat, a little faith, and, if alone, worthy of reproach. To believe what he has not said is faith indeed, and blessed. For that comes of believing in HIM. Can you not believe in God himself? Or, confess,—do you not find it so hard to believe what he has said, that even that is almost more than you can do? If I ask you why, will not the true answer be—"Because we are not quite sure that he did say it"? If you believed in God you would find it easy to believe the word. You would not even need to inquire whether he had *said* it: you would know that he meant it.

Let us then dare something. Let us not always be unbelieving children. Let us keep in mind that the Lord, not forbidding those who insist on seeing before they will believe, blesses those who have not seen and yet have believed—those who trust in him more than that— who believe without the sight of the eyes, without the hearing of the ears. They are blessed to whom a wonder is not a fable, to whom a mystery is not a mockery, to whom a glory is not an unreality—who are content to ask, "Is it like Him?" It is a dull-hearted, unchildlike people that will be always putting God in mind of his promises. Those promises are good to reveal what God is; if they think them good as binding God, let them have it so for the hardness of their hearts. They prefer the Word to the Spirit: it is theirs.

Even such will leave us—some of them will, if not all—to the "uncovenanted mercies of God." We desire no less; we hope for no better. Those are the mercies beyond our height, beyond our depth, beyond our reach. We know in whom we have believed, and we look for that which it hath not entered into the heart of man to conceive. Shall God's thoughts be surpassed by man's thoughts? God's giving by man's asking? God's creation by man's imagination? No. Let us climb to the height of our Alpine desires; let us leave them behind us and ascend the spear-pointed Himmalays of our aspirations; still shall we find the depth of God's sapphire above us; still shall we find the heavens higher than the earth, and his thoughts and his ways higher than our thoughts and our ways.

Ah Lord! be thou in all our being; as not in the Sundays of our time alone, so not in the chambers of our hearts alone. We dare not think that thou canst not, carest not; that some things are not for thy beholding, some questions not to be asked of thee. For are we not all thine— utterly thine? That which a man speaks not to his fellow, we speak to thee. Our very passions we hold up to thee, and say, "Behold, Lord! Think about us; for thus thou hast made us." We would not escape from our history by fleeing into the wilderness, by hiding our heads in the sands of forgetfulness, or the repentance that comes of pain, or the lethargy of hopelessness. We take it, as our very life, in our hand, and flee with it unto thee. Triumphant is the answer which thou boldest for every doubt. It may be we could not understand it yet, even if thou didst speak it "with most miraculous organ." But thou shalt at least find faith in the earth, O Lord, if thou comest to look for it now—the faith of ignorant but hoping children, who know that they do not know, and believe that thou knowest.

And for our brothers and sisters, who cleave to what they call thy word, thinking to please thee so, they are in thy holy safe hands, who hast taught us that *whosoever shall speak a word against the Son of man, it shall be forgiven him*; though unto him that blasphemes against the Holy Ghost, it shall not be forgiven_.

IT SHALL NOT BE FORGIVEN.

_And whosoever shall speak a word against the Son of man, it shall be forgiven him: but unto him that blasphemeth against the Holy Ghost, it shall not be forgiven.—LUKE xi. 18.

Whatever belonging to the region of thought and feeling is uttered in words, is of necessity uttered imperfectly. For thought and feeling are infinite, and human speech, although far-reaching in scope, and marvellous in delicacy, can embody them after all but approximately and suggestively. Spirit and Truth are like the Lady Una and the Red Cross Knight; Speech like the dwarf that lags behind with the lady's "bag of needments."

Our Lord had no design of constructing a system of truth in intellectual forms. The truth of the moment in its relation to him, The Truth, was what he spoke. He spoke out of a region of realities which he knew could only be suggested—not represented—in the forms of intellect and speech. With vivid flashes of life and truth his words invade our darkness, rousing us with sharp stings of light to will our awaking, to arise from the dead and cry for the light which he can give, not in the lightning of words only, but in indwelling presence and power.

How, then, must the truth fare with those who, having neither glow nor insight, will build intellectual systems upon the words of our Lord, or of his disciples? A little child would better understand Plato than they St Paul. The meaning in those great hearts who knew our Lord is too great to enter theirs. The sense they find in the words must be a sense small enough to pass through their narrow doors. And if mere words, without the interpreting sympathy, may mean, as they may, almost anything the receiver will or can attribute to them, how shall the man, bent at best on the salvation of his own soul, understand, for instance, the meaning of that apostle who was ready to encounter banishment itself from the presence of Christ, that the beloved brethren of his nation might enter in? To men who are not simple, simple words are the most inexplicable of riddles.

If we are bound to search after what our Lord means—and he speaks that we may understand—we are at least equally bound to refuse any interpretation which seems to us unlike him, unworthy of him. He himself says, "Why do ye not of your own selves judge what is right?" In thus refusing, it may happen that, from ignorance or misunderstanding, we refuse the verbal form of its true interpretation, but we cannot thus refuse the spirit and the truth of it, for those we could not have seen without being in the condition to recognize them as the mind of Christ. Some misapprehension, I say, some obliquity, or some slavish adherence to old prejudices, may thus cause us to refuse the true interpretation, but we are none the less bound to refuse and wait for more light. To accept that as the will of our Lord which to us is inconsistent with what we have learned to worship in him already, is to introduce discord into that harmony whose end is to unite our hearts, and make them whole.

"Is it for us," says the objector who, by some sleight of will, believes in the word apart from the meaning for which it stands, "to judge of the character of our Lord?" I answer, "This very thing he requires of us." He requires of us that we should do him no injustice. He would come and dwell with us, if we would but open our chambers to receive him. How shall we receive him if, avoiding judgment, we hold this or that daub of authority or tradition hanging upon our walls to be the real likeness of our Lord? Is it not possible at least that, judging unrighteous judgment by such while we flatter ourselves that we are refusing to judge, we may close our doors against the Master himself as an impostor, not finding him like the picture that hangs in our oratory. And if we do not judge—humbly and lovingly—who is to judge for us? Better to refuse even the truth for a time, than, by accepting into our intellectual creed that which our heart cannot receive, not seeing its real form, to introduce hesitation into our prayers, a jar into our praises, and a misery into our love. If it be the truth, we shall one day see it another thing than it appears now, and love it because we see it lovely; for all truth is lovely. "Not to the unregenerate mind." But at least, I answer, to the mind which can love that Man, Christ Jesus; and that part of us which loves him let us follow, and in its judgements let us trust; hoping, beyond all things else, for its growth and enlightenment by the Lord, who is that Spirit. Better, I say again, to refuse the right *form*, than, by accepting it in misapprehension of what it really is, to refuse the spirit, the truth that dwells therein. Which of these, I pray, is liker to the sin against the Holy Ghost? To mistake the meaning of the Son of man may well fill a man with sadness. But to care so little for him as to receive as his what the noblest part of our nature rejects as low and poor, or selfish and wrong, that surely is more like the sin against the Holy Ghost that can never be forgiven; for it is a sin against the truth itself, not the embodiment of it in him.

Words for their full meaning depend upon their source, the person who speaks them. An utterance may even seem commonplace, till you are told that thus spoke one whom you know to be always thinking, always feeling, always acting. Recognizing the mind whence the words proceed, you know the scale by which they are to be understood. So the words of God cannot mean just the same as the words of man. "Can we not, then, understand them?" Yes, we can understand them—we can understand them *more* than the words of men. Whatever a good word means, as used by a good man, it means just infinitely more as used by God. And the feeling or thought expressed by that word takes higher and higher forms in us as we become capable of understanding him,—that is, as we become like him.

I am far less anxious to show what the sin against the Holy Ghost means, than to show what the nonforgiveness means; though I think we may arrive at some understanding of both. I cannot admit for a moment that there is anything in the Bible too mysterious to be looked into; for the Bible is a *revelation*, an unveiling. True, into many things uttered there I can see only a little way. But that little way is the way of life; for the depth of their mystery is God. And even setting aside the duty of the matter, and seeking for justification as if the duty were doubtful, it is reason enough for inquiring into such passages as this before me, that they are often torture to human minds, chiefly those of holy women and children. I knew a child who believed she had committed the sin against the Holy Ghost, because she had, in her toilette, made an improper use of a pin. Dare not to rebuke me for adducing the diseased fancy of a child in a weighty matter of theology. "Despise not one of these little ones." Would the theologians were as near the truth in such matters as the children. *Diseased fancy!* The child knew, *and was conscious that she knew,* that she was doing wrong because she had been forbidden. *There was rational ground for her fear.* How would Jesus have received the confession of the darling? *He* would not have told her she was silly, and "never to mind." Child as she was, might he not have said to her, "I do not condemn thee: go and sin no more"?

To reach the first position necessary for the final attainment of our end, I will inquire what the divine forgiveness means. And in order to arrive at this naturally, I will begin by asking what the human forgiveness means; for, if there be any meaning in the Incarnation, it is through the Human that we must climb up to the Divine.

31

I do not know that it is of much use to go back to the Greek or the English word for any primary idea of the act—the one meaning *a sending away*, the other, *a giving away*. It will be enough if we look at the feelings associated with the exercise of what is called *forgiveness*.

A man will say: "*I* forgive, but I cannot forget. Let the fellow never come in my sight again." To what does such a forgiveness reach? To the remission or sending away of the penalties which the wronged believes he can claim from the wrong-doer.

But there is no sending away of the wrong itself from between them.

Again, a man will say: "He has done a very mean action, but he has the worst of it himself in that he is capable of doing so. I despise him too much to desire revenge. I will take no notice of it. I forgive him. I don't care."

Here, again, there is no sending away of the wrong from between them— no *remission* of the sin.

A third will say: "I suppose I must forgive him; for if I do not forgive him, God will not forgive me."

This man is a *little* nearer the truth, inasmuch as a ground of sympathy, though only that of common sin, is recognized as between the offender and himself.

One more will say: "He has wronged me grievously. It is a dreadful thing to me, and more dreadful still to him, that he should have done it. He has hurt me, but he has nearly killed himself. He shall have no more injury from it that I can save him. I cannot feel the same towards him yet; but I will try to make him acknowledge the wrong he has done me, and so put it away from him. Then, perhaps, I shall be able to feel towards him as I used to feel. For this end I will show him all the kindness I can, not forcing it upon him, but seizing every fit opportunity; not, I hope, from a wish to make myself great through bounty to him, but because I love him so much that I want to love him more in reconciling him to his true self. I would destroy this evil deed that has come between us. I send it away. And I would have him destroy it from between us too, by abjuring it utterly."

Which comes nearest to the divine idea of forgiveness? nearest, though with the gulf between, wherewith the heavens are higher than the earth?

For the Divine creates the Human, has the creative power in excess of the Human. It is the Divine forgiveness that, originating itself, creates our forgiveness, and therefore can do so much more. It can take up all our wrongs, small and great, with their righteous attendance of griefs and sorrows, and carry them away from between our God and us.

Christ is God's Forgiveness.

Before we approach a little nearer to this great sight, let us consider the human forgiveness in a more definite embodiment—as between a father and a son. For although God is so much more to us, and comes so much nearer to us than a father can be or come, yet the fatherhood is the last height of the human stair whence our understandings can see him afar off, and where our hearts can first know that he is nigh, even in them.

There are various kinds and degrees of wrongdoing, which need varying kinds and degrees of forgiveness. An outburst of anger in a child, for instance, scarcely wants forgiveness. The wrong in it may be so small, that the parent has only to influence the child for self-restraint, and the rousing of the will against the wrong. The father will not feel that such a fault has built up any wall between him and his child. But suppose that he discovered in him a habit of sly cruelty towards his younger brothers, or the animals of the house, how differently would he feel! Could his forgiveness be the same as in the former case? Would not the different evil require a different *form* of forgiveness? I mean, would not the forgiveness have to take the form of that kind of punishment fittest for restraining, in the hope of finally rooting out, the wickedness? Could there be true love in any other kind of forgiveness than this? A passing-by of the offence might spring from a poor human kindness, but never from divine love. It would not be *remission*. Forgiveness can never be indifference. Forgiveness is love towards the unlovely.

Let us look a little closer at the way a father might feel, and express his feelings. One child, the moment the fault was committed, the father would clasp to his bosom, knowing that very love in its own natural manifestation would destroy the fault in him, and that, the next moment, he would be weeping. The father's hatred of the sin would burst forth in his pitiful tenderness towards the child who was so wretched as to have done the sin, and so destroy it. The fault of such a child would then cause no interruption of the interchange of sweet affections. The child is forgiven at once. But the treatment of another upon the same principle would be altogether different. If he had been guilty of baseness, meanness, selfishness, deceit, self-gratulation in the evil brought upon others, the father might *say* to himself: "I cannot forgive him. This is beyond forgiveness." He might *say* so, and keep saying so, while all the time he was striving to let forgiveness find its way that it might lift him from the gulf into which he had fallen. His love might grow yet greater because of the wandering and loss of his son. For love is divine, and then most divine when it loves according to *needs* and not according to *merits*. But the forgiveness would be but in the process of making, as it were, or of drawing nigh to the sinner. Not till his opening heart received the divine flood of destroying affection, and his own affection burst forth to meet it and sweep the evil away, could it be said to be finished, to have arrived, could the son be said to *be* forgiven.

God is forgiving us every day—sending from between him and us our sins and their fogs and darkness. Witness the shining of his sun and the falling of his rain, the filling of their hearts with food and gladness, that he loves them that love him not. When some sin that we have committed has clouded all our horizon, and hidden him from our eyes, he, forgiving us, ere we are, and that we may be, forgiven, sweeps away a path for this his forgiveness to reach our hearts, that it may by causing our repentance destroy the wrong, and make us able even to forgive ourselves. For some are too proud to forgive themselves, till the forgiveness of God has had its way with them, has drowned their pride in the tears of repentance, and made their heart come again like the heart of a little child.

But, looking upon forgiveness, then, as the perfecting of a work ever going on, as the contact of God's heart and ours, in spite and in destruction of the intervening wrong, we may say that God's love is ever in front of his forgiveness. God's love is the prime mover, ever seeking to perfect his forgiveness, which latter needs the human condition for its consummation. The love is perfect, working out the forgiveness. God loves where he cannot yet forgive—where forgiveness in the full sense is as yet simply impossible, because no contact of hearts is possible, because that which lies between has not even begun to yield to the besom of his holy destruction.

Some things, then, between the Father and his children, as between a father and his child, may comparatively, and in a sense, be made light of—I do not mean made light of in themselves: away they must go— inasmuch as, evils or sins though they be, they yet leave room for the dwelling of God's Spirit in the heart, forgiving and cleansing away the evil. When a man's evil is thus fading out of him, and he is growing better and better, that is the forgiveness coming into him more and more. Perfect in God's will, it is having its perfect work in the mind of the man. When the man hath, with his whole nature, cast away his sin, there is no room for forgiveness any more, for God dwells in him, and he in God. With the voice of Nathan, "Thou art the man," the forgiveness of God laid hold of David, the heart of the king was humbled to the dust; and when he thus awoke from the moral lethargy that had fallen upon him, he found that he was still with God. "When I awake," he said, "I am still with thee."

But there are two sins, not of individual deed, but of spiritual condition, which *cannot be forgiven*; that is, as it seems to me, which cannot be excused, passed by, made little of by the tenderness even of God, inasmuch as they will allow no forgiveness to come into the soul, they will permit no good influence to go on working alongside of them; they shut God out altogether. Therefore the man guilty of these can never receive into himself the holy renewing saving influences of God's forgiveness. God is outside of him in every sense, save that which springs from his creating relation to him, by which, thanks be to God, he yet keeps a hold of him, although against the will of the man who will not be forgiven. The one of these sins is against man; the other against God.

The former is unforgivingness to our neighbour; the shutting of him out from our mercies, from our love—so from the universe, as far as we are a portion of it—the murdering therefore of our neighbour. It may be an infinitely less evil to murder a man than to refuse to forgive him. The former may be the act of a moment of passion: the latter is the heart's choice. It is *spiritual* murder, the worst, to hate, to brood over the feeling that excludes, that, in our microcosm, kills the image, the idea of the hated. We listen to the voice of our own hurt pride or hurt affection (only the latter without the suggestion of the former, thinketh no evil) to the injury of the evil-doer. In as far as we can, we quench the relations of life between us; we close up the passages of possible return. This is to shut out God, the Life, the One. For how are we to receive the forgiving presence while we shut out our brother from our portion of the universal forgiveness, the final restoration, thus refusing to let God be All in all? If God appeared to us, how could he say, "I forgive you," while we remained unforgiving to our neighbour? Suppose it possible that he should say so, his forgiveness would be no good to us while we were uncured of our unforgivingness. It would not touch us. It would not come near us. Nay, it would hurt us, for we should think ourselves safe and well, while the horror of disease was eating the heart out of us. Tenfold the forgiveness lies in the words, "If ye forgive not men their trespasses, neither will your heavenly Father forgive your trespasses." Those words are kindness indeed. God holds the unforgiving man with his hand, but turns his face away from him. If, in his desire to see the face of his Father, he turns his own towards his brother, then the face of God turns round and seeks his, for then the man may look upon God and not die. With our forgiveness to our neighbour, in flows the Consciousness of God's forgiveness to us; or even with the effort, we become capable of believing that God can forgive us. No man who will not forgive his neighbour, can believe that God is willing, yea, wanting to forgive him, can believe that the dove of God's peace is hovering over a chaotic heart, fain to alight, but finding no rest for the sole of its foot. For God to say to such a man, "I cannot forgive you," is love as well as necessity. If God said, "I forgive you," to a man who hated his brother, and if (as is impossible) that voice of forgiveness should reach the man, what would it mean to him? How would the man interpret it? Would it not mean to him, "You may go on hating. I do not mind it. You have had great provocation, and are justified in your hate"? No doubt God takes what wrong there is, and what provocation there is, into the account; but the more provocation, the more excuse that can be urged for the hate, the more reason, if possible, that the hater should be delivered from the hell of his hate, that God's child should be made the loving child that he meant him to be. The man would think, not that God loved the sinner, but that he forgave the sin, which God never does. Every sin meets with its due fate—inexorable expulsion from the paradise of God's Humanity. He loves the sinner so much that he cannot forgive him in any other way than by banishing from his bosom the demon that possesses him, by lifting him out of that mire of his iniquity.

No one, however, supposes for a moment that a man who has once refused to forgive his brother, shall therefore be condemned to endless unforgiveness and unforgivingness. What is meant is, that while a man continues in such a mood, God cannot be with him as his friend; not that he will not be his friend, but the friendship being all on one side— that of God—must take forms such as the man will not be able to recognize as friendship. Forgiveness, as I have said, is not love merely, but love *conveyed as love* to the erring, so establishing peace towards God, and forgiveness towards our neighbour.

To return then to our immediate text: Is the refusal of forgiveness contained in it a condemnation to irrecoverable impenitence? Strange righteousness would be the decree, that because a man has done wrong— let us say has done wrong so often and so much that he *is* wrong—he shall for ever remain wrong! Do not tell me the condemnation is only negative—a leaving of the man to the consequences of his own will, or at most a withdrawing from him of the Spirit which he has despised. God will not take shelter behind such a jugglery of logic or metaphysics. He is neither schoolman nor theologian, but our Father in heaven. He knows that that in him would be the same unforgiving-ness for which he refuses to forgive man. The only tenable ground for supporting such a doctrine is, that God *cannot* do more; that Satan has overcome; and that Jesus, amongst his own brothers and sisters in the image of God, has been less strong than the adversary, the destroyer. What then shall I say of such a doctrine of devils as that, even if a man did repent, God would not or could not forgive him?

Let us look at "*the* unpardonable sin," as this mystery is commonly called, and see what we can find to understand about it.

All sin is unpardonable. There is no compromise to be made with it. We shall not come out except clean, except having paid the utter-most farthing. But the special unpardonableness of those sins, the one of which I have spoken and that which we are now considering, lies in their shutting out God from his *genial*, his especially spiritual, influ-ences upon the man. Possibly in the case of the former sin, I may have said this too strongly; possibly the love of God may have some part even in the man who will not forgive his brother, although, if he con-tinues unforgiving, that part must decrease and die away; possibly resentment against our brother, might yet for a time leave room for some divine influences by its side, although either the one or the other must speedily yield; but the man who denies truth, who consciously resists duty, who says there is no truth, or that the truth he sees is not true, who says that which is good is of Satan, or that which is bad is of God, supposing him to know that it is good or is bad, denies the Spirit, shuts out the Spirit, and therefore cannot be forgiven. For without the Spirit no forgiveness can enter the man to cast out the satan. Without the Spirit to witness with his spirit, no man could know himself for-given, even if God appeared to him and said so. The full forgiveness is, as I have said, when a man feels that God is forgiving him; and this cannot be while he opposes himself to the very essence of God's will.

As far as we can see, the men of whom this was spoken were men who resisted the truth with some amount of perception that it was the truth; men neither led astray by passion, nor altogether blinded by their abounding prejudice; men who were not excited to condemn one form of truth by the love which they bore to another form of it; but men so set, from selfishness and love of influence, against one whom they saw to be a good man, that they denied the goodness of what they knew to be good, in order to put down the man whom they knew to be good, because He had spoken against them, and was ruining their influence and authority with the people by declaring them to be no better than they knew themselves to be. Is not this to be Satan? to be in hell? to be corruption? to be that which is damned? Was not this their *condition* unpardonable? How, through all this mass of falsehood, could the pardon of God reach the essential humanity within it? Crying as it was for God's forgiveness, these men had almost separated their humanity from themselves, had taken their part with the powers of darkness. Forgiveness while they were such was an impossibility. No. Out of that they must come, else there was no word of God for them. But the very word that told them of the unpardonable state in which they were, was just the one form the voice of mercy could take in calling on them to repent. They must hear and be afraid. I dare not, cannot think that they refused the truth, knowing all that it was; but I think they refused the truth, knowing that it was true—not carried away, as I have said, by wild passion, but by cold self-love, and envy, and avarice, and ambition; not merely doing wrong knowingly, but setting their whole natures knowingly against the light. Of this nature must the sin against the Holy Ghost surely be. "This is the condemnation," (not the sins that men have committed, but the condition of mind in which they choose to remain,) "that light is come into the world, and men loved darkness rather than light, because their deeds were evil." In this sin against the Holy Ghost, I see no single act alone, although it must find expression in many acts, but a wilful condition of mind,

As far removed from God and light of heaven,
As from the centre thrice to the utmost pole.

For this there could be no such excuse made as that even a little light might work beside it; for there light could find no entrance and no room; light was just what such a mind was set against, almost because it was what it was. The condition was utterly bad.

But can a man really fall into such a condition of spiritual depravity?

That is my chief difficulty. But I think it may be. And wiser people than I, have thought so. I have difficulty in believing it, I say; yet I think it must be so. But I do not believe that it is a fixed, a final condition. I do not see why it should be such any more than that of the man who does not forgive his neighbour. If you say it is a worse offence, I say, Is it too bad for the forgiveness of God?

But is God able to do anything more with the man? Or how is the man ever to get out of this condition? If the Spirit of God is shut out from his heart, how is he to become better?

The Spirit of God is the Spirit whose influence is known by its witnessing with our spirit. But may there not be other powers and means of the Spirit preparatory to this its highest office with man? God who has made us can never be far from any man who draws the breath of life—nay, must be in him; not necessarily in his heart, as we say, but still in him. May not then one day some terrible convulsion from the centre of his being, some fearful earthquake from the hidden gulfs of his nature, shake such a man so that through all the deafness of his death, the voice of the Spirit may be faintly heard, the still small voice that comes after the tempest and the earthquake? May there not be a fire that even such can feel? Who shall set bounds to the consuming of the fire of our God, and the purifying that dwells therein?

The only argument that I can think of, which would with me have weight against this conclusion, is, that the revulsion of feeling in any one who had thus sinned against the truth, when once brought to acknowledge his sin, would be so terrible that life would never more be endurable, and the kindest thing God could do would be to put such a man out of being, because it had been a better thing for him never to have been born. But he who could make such a man repent, could make him so sorrowful and lowly, and so glad that he had repented, that he would wish to live ever that he might ever repent and ever worship the glory he now beheld. When a man gives up self, his past sins will no longer oppress him. It is enough for the good of life that God lives, that the All-perfect exists, and that we can behold him.

"Father, forgive them, for they know not what they do," said the Divine, making excuse for his murderers, not after it was all over, but at the very moment when he was dying by their hands. Then Jesus had forgiven them already. His prayer the Father must have heard, for he and the Son are one. When the Father succeeded in answering his prayer, then his forgiveness in the hearts of the murderers broke out in sorrow, repentance, and faith. Here was a sin dreadful enough surely— but easy for our Lord to forgive. All that excuse for the misled populace! Lord Christ be thanked for that! That was like thee! But must we believe that Judas, who repented even to agony, who repented so that his high-prized life, self, soul, became worthless in his eyes and met with no mercy at his own hand,—must we believe that he could find no mercy in such a God? I think, when Judas fled from his hanged and fallen body, he fled to the tender help of Jesus, and found it—I say not how. He was in a more hopeful condition now than during any moment of his past life, for he had never repented before. But I believe that Jesus loved Judas even when he was kissing him with the traitor's kiss; and I believe that he was his Saviour still. And if any man remind me of his words, "It had been good for that man if he had not been born," I had not forgotten them, though I know that I now offer nothing beyond a conjectural explanation of them when I say: Judas had got none of the good of the world into which he had been born. He had not inherited the earth. He had lived an evil life, out of harmony with the world and its God. Its love had been lost upon him. He had been brought to the very Son of God, and had lived with him as his own familiar friend; and he had not loved him more, but less than himself. Therefore it had been all useless. "It had been good for that man if he had not been born;" for it was all to try over again, in some other way—inferior perhaps, in some other world, in a lower school. He had to be sent down the scale of creation which is ever ascending towards its Maker. But I will not, cannot believe, O my Lord, that thou wouldst not forgive thy enemy, even when he repented, and did thee right. Nor will I believe that thy holy death was powerless to save thy foe—that it could not reach to Judas. Have we not heard of those, thine own, taught of thee, who could easily forgive their betrayers in thy name? And if thou forgivest, will not thy forgiveness find its way at last in redemption and purification?

Look for a moment at the clause preceding my text: "He that denieth me before men shall be denied before the angels of God." What does it mean? Does it mean—"Ah! you are mine, but not of my sort. You denied me. Away to the outer darkness"? Not so. "It shall be forgiven to him that speaketh against the Son of man;" for He may be but the truth revealed *without* him. Only he must have shame before the universe of the loving God, and may need the fire that burneth and consumeth not.

But for him that speaketh against the Spirit of Truth, against the Son of God revealed *within* him, he is beyond the teaching of that Spirit now. For how shall he be forgiven? The forgiveness would touch him no more than a wall of stone. Let him know what it is to be without the God he hath denied. Away with him to the Outer Darkness! Perhaps *that* will make him repent.

My friends, I offer this as only a contribution towards the understanding of our Lord's words. But if we ask him, he will lead us into all truth. And let us not be afraid to think, for he will not take it ill.

But what I have said must be at least a part of the truth.

No amount of discovery in his words can tell us more than *we* have discovered, more than we have seen and known to be true. For all the help the best of his disciples can give us is only to discover, to see for ourselves. And beyond all our discoveries in his words and being, there lie depths within depths of truth that we cannot understand, and yet shall be ever going on to understand. Yea, even now sometimes we seem to have dim glimpses into regions from which we receive no word to bring away.

The fact that some things have become to us so much more simple than they were, and that great truths have come out of what once looked common, is ground enough for hope that such will go on to be our experience through the ages to come. Our advance from our former ignorance can measure but a small portion of the distance that lies, and must ever lie, between our childishness and his manhood, between our love and his love, between our dimness and his mighty vision. To him ere long may we all come, all children, still children, more children than ever, to receive from his hand the *white stone, and in the stone a new name written, which no man knoweth saving he that receiveth it.*

THE NEW NAME.

To him that overcometh, I will give a white stone, and in the stone a new name written, which no man knoweth saving he that receiveth it.— REV. ii. 17.

Whether the Book of the Revelation be written by the same man who wrote the Gospel according to St John or not, there is, at least, one element common to the two—the mysticism.

I use the word *mysticism* as representing a certain mode of embodying truth, common, in various degrees, to almost all, if not all, the writers of the New Testament. The attempt to define it thoroughly would require an essay. I will hazard but one suggestion towards it: A mystical mind is one which, having perceived that the highest expression of which the truth admits, lies in the symbolism of nature and the human customs that result from human necessities, prosecutes thought about truth so embodied by dealing with the symbols themselves after logical forms. This is the highest mode of conveying the deepest truth; and the Lord himself often employed it, as, for instance, in the whole passage ending with the words, "If therefore the light that is in thee be darkness, how great is the darkness!"

The mysticism in the Gospel of St John is of the simplest, and, therefore, noblest nature. No dweller in this planet can imagine a method of embodying truth that shall be purer, loftier, truer to the truth embodied. There may be higher modes in other worlds, or there may not—I cannot tell; but of all our modes these forms are best illustrations of the highest. Apparently the mysticism of St John's own nature enabled him to remember and report with sufficient accuracy the words of our Lord, always, it seems to me, of a recognizably different kind from those of any of the writers of the New Testament—chiefly, perhaps, in the simplicity of their poetical mysticism.

But the mysticism in the Book of the Revelation is more complicated, more gorgeous, less poetic, and occasionally, I think, perhaps arbitrary, or approaching the arbitrary; *reminding* one, in a word, of the mysticism of Swedenborg. Putting aside both historical and literary criticism, in neither of which with regard to the authorship of these two books have I a right even to an opinion, I would venture to suggest that possibly their difference in tone is just what one might expect when the historian of a mystical teacher and the recorder of his mystical sayings, proceeds to embody his own thoughts, feelings, and inspirations; that is, when the revelation flows no longer from the lips of the Master, but through the disciple's own heart, soul, and brain. For surely not the most idolatrous of our Bible-worshipping brothers and sisters will venture to assert that the Spirit of God could speak as freely by the lips of the wind-swayed, reed-like, rebukable Peter, or of the Thomas who could believe his own eyes, but neither the word of his brethren, nor the nature of his Master, as by the lips of Him who was blind and deaf to everything but the will of him that sent him.

Truth is truth, whether from the lips of Jesus or Balaam. But, in its deepest sense, *the truth* is a condition of heart, soul, mind, and strength towards God and towards our fellow—not an utterance, not even a *right* form of words; and therefore such truth coming forth in words is, in a sense, the person that speaks. And many of the utterances of truth in the Revelation, commonly called of St John, are not merely lofty in form, but carry with them the conviction that the writer was no mere "trumpet of a prophecy," but spoke that he did know, and testified that he had seen.

In this passage about the gift of the white stone, I think we find the essence of religion.

What the notion in the mind of the writer with regard to the white stone was, is, I think, of comparatively little moment. I take the stone to belong more to the arbitrary and fanciful than to the true mystical imagery, although for the bringing out of the mystical thought in which it is concerned, it is of high and honourable dignity. For fancy itself will subserve the true imagination of the mystic, and so be glorified. I doubt if the writer himself associated any essential meaning with it. Certainly I will not allow that he had such a poor notion in it as that of a voting pebble—white, because the man who receives it is accepted or chosen. The word is used likewise for a precious stone set as a jewel. And the writer thought of it mystically, a mode far more likely to involve a reference to nature than to a political custom. What his mystic meaning may be, must be taken differently by different minds. *I* think he sees in its whiteness purity, and in its substance indestructibility. But I care chiefly to regard the stone as the vehicle of the name,—as the form whereby the name is represented as passing from God to the man, and what is involved in this communication is what I wish to show. If my reader will not acknowledge my representation as St John's meaning, I yet hope so to set it forth that he shall see the representation to be true in itself, and then I shall willingly leave the interpretation to its fate.

I say, in brief, the giving of the white stone with the new name is the communication of what God thinks about the man to the man. It is the divine judgment, the solemn holy doom of the righteous man, the "Come, thou blessed," spoken to the individual.

In order to see this, we must first understand what is the idea of a name,—that is, what is the perfect notion of a name. For, seeing the mystical energy of a holy mind here speaks of God as giving something, we must understand that the essential thing, and not any of its accidents or imitations, is intended.

A name of the ordinary kind in this world, has nothing essential in it. It is but a label by which one man and a scrap of his external history may be known from another man and a scrap of his history. The only names which have significance are those which the popular judgment or prejudice or humour bestows, either for ridicule or honour, upon a few out of the many. Each of these is founded upon some external characteristic of the man, upon some predominant peculiarity of temper, some excellence or the reverse of character, or something which he does or has done well or ill enough, or at least, singularly enough, to render him, in the eyes of the people, worthy of such distinction from other men. As far as they go, these are real names, for, in some poor measure, they express individuality.

The true name is one which expresses the character, the nature, the being, the *meaning* of the person who bears it. It is the man's own symbol,—his soul's picture, in a word,—the sign which belongs to him and to no one else. Who can give a man this, his own name? God alone. For no one but God sees what the man is, or even, seeing what he is, could express in a name-word the sum and harmony of what he sees. To whom is this name given? To him that overcometh. When is it given? When he has overcome. Does God then not know what a man is going to become? As surely as he sees the oak which he put there lying in the heart of the acorn. Why then does he wait till the man has become by overcoming ere he settles what his name shall be? He does not wait; he knows his name from the first. But as—although repentance comes because God pardons—yet the man becomes aware of the pardon only in the repentance; so it is only when the man has become his name that God gives him the stone with the name upon it, for then first can he understand what his name signifies. It is the blossom, the perfection, the completion, that determines the name; and God foresees that from the first, because he made it so; but the tree of the soul, before its blossom comes, cannot understand what blossom it is to bear, and could not know what the word meant, which, in representing its own unarrived completeness, named itself. Such a name cannot be given until the man *is* the name.

God's name for a man must then be the expression in a mystical word—a word of that language which all who have overcome understand—of his own idea of the man, that being whom he had in his thought when he began to make the child, and whom he kept in his thought through the long process of creation that went to realize the idea. To tell the name is to seal the success—to say, "In thee also I am well pleased."

But we are still in the region of symbol. For supposing that such a form were actually observed between God and him that overcometh, it would be no less a symbol—only an acted one. We must therefore look deeper still for the fulness of its meaning. Up to this point little has been said to justify our expectations of discovery in the text. Let us, I say, look deeper. We shall not look long before we find that the mystic symbol has for its centre of significance the fact of the personal individual relation of every man to his God. That every man has affairs, and those his first affairs, with God, stands to the reason of every man who associates any meaning or feeling with the words, Maker, Father, God. Were we but children of a day, with the understanding that some one had given us that one holiday, there would be something to be thought, to be felt, to be done, because we knew it. For then our nature would be according to our fate, and we could worship and die. But it would be only the praise of the dead, not the praise of the living, for death would be the deepest, the lasting, the overcoming. We should have come out of nothingness, not out of God. He could only be our Maker, not our Father, our Origin. But now we know that God cannot be the God of the dead—must be the God of the living; inasmuch as to know that we died, would freeze the heart of worship, and we could not say Our God, or feel him worthy of such worth-ship as we could render. To him who offers unto this God of the living his own self of sacrifice, to him that overcometh, him who has brought his individual life back to its source, who knows that he is *one* of God's children, *this* one of the Father's making, he giveth the white stone. To him who climbs on the stair of all his God-born efforts and God-given victories up to the height of his being—that of looking face to face upon his ideal self in the bosom of the Father—God's *him*, realized in him through the Father's love in the Elder Brother's devotion—to him God gives the new name written.

But I leave this, because that which follows embraces and intensifies this individuality of relation in a fuller development of the truth. For the name is one "which no man knoweth saving he that receiveth it." Not only then has each man his individual relation to God, but each man has his peculiar relation to God. He is to God a peculiar being, made after his own fashion, and that of no one else; for when he is perfected he shall receive the new name which no one else can understand. Hence he can worship God as no man else can worship him,— can understand God as no man else can understand him. This or that man may understand God more, may understand God better than he, but no other man can understand God as he understands him. God give me grace to be humble before thee, my brother, that I drag not my simulacrum of thee before the judgment-seat of the unjust judge, but look up to thyself for what revelation of God thou and no one else canst give. As the fir-tree lifts up itself with a far different need from the need of the palm-tree, so does each man stand before God, and lift up a different humanity to the common Father. And for each God has a different response. With every man he has a secret—the secret of the new name. In every man there is a loneliness, an inner chamber of peculiar life into which God only can enter. I say not it is *the innermost chamber*—but a chamber into which no brother, nay, no sister can come.

From this it follows that there is a chamber also—(O God, humble and accept my speech)—a chamber in God himself, into which none can enter but the one, the individual, the peculiar man,—out of which chamber that man has to bring revelation and strength for his brethren. This is that for which he was made—to reveal the secret things of the Father.

By his creation, then, each man is isolated with God; each, in respect of his peculiar making, can say, "*my* God;" each can come to him alone, and speak with him face to face, as a man speaketh with his friend. There is no *massing* of men with God. When he speaks of gathered men, it is as a spiritual *body*, not a *mass*. For in a body every smallest portion is individual, and therefore capable of forming a part of the body.

See, now, what a significance the symbolism of our text assumes. Each of us is a distinct flower or tree in the spiritual garden of God,—precious, each for his own sake, in the eyes of him who is even now making us,—each of us watered and shone upon and filled with life, for the sake of his flower, his completed being, which will blossom out of him at last to the glory and pleasure of the great gardener. For each has within him a secret of the Divinity; each is growing towards the revelation of that secret to himself, and so to the full reception, according to his measure, of the divine. Every moment that he is true to his true self, some new shine of the white stone breaks on his inward eye, some fresh channel is opened upward for the coming glory of the flower, the conscious offering of his whole being in beauty to the Maker. Each man, then, is in God's sight worth. Life and action, thought and intent, are sacred. And what an end lies before us! To have a consciousness of our own ideal being flashed into us from the thought of God! Surely for this may well give way all our paltry self-consciousnesses, our self-admirations and self-worships! Surely to know what he thinks about us will pale out of our souls all our thoughts about ourselves! and we may well hold them loosely now, and be ready to let them go. Towards this result St Paul had already drawn near, when he who had begun the race with a bitter cry for deliverance from the body of his death, was able to say that he judged his own self no longer.

"But is there not the worst of all dangers involved in such teaching— the danger of spiritual pride?" If there be, are we to refuse the spirit for fear of the pride? Or is there any other deliverance from pride except the spirit? Pride springs from supposed success in the high aim: with attainment itself comes humility. But here there is no room for ambition. Ambition is the desire to be above one's neighbour; and here there is no possibility of comparison with one's neighbour: no one knows what the white stone contains except the man who receives it. Here is room for endless aspiration towards the unseen ideal; none for ambition. Ambition would only be higher than others; aspiration would be high. Relative worth is not only unknown—to the children of the kingdom it is unknowable. Each esteems the other better than himself. How shall the rose, the glowing heart of the summer heats, rejoice against the snowdrop risen with hanging head from the white bosom of the snow? Both are God's thoughts; both are dear to him; both are needful to the completeness of his earth and the revelation of himself.

"God has cared to make me for himself," says the victor with the white stone, "and has called me that which I like best; for my own name must be what I would have it, seeing it is myself. What matter whether I be called a grass of the field, or an eagle of the air? a stone to build into his temple, or a Boanerges to wield his thunder? I am his; his idea, his making; perfect in my kind, yea, perfect in his sight; full of him, revealing him, alone with him. Let him call me what he will. The name shall be precious as my life. I seek no more."

Gone then will be all anxiety as to what his neighbour may think about him. It is enough that God thinks about him. To be something to God—is not that praise enough? To be a thing that God cares for and would have complete for himself, because it is worth caring for—is not that life enough?

Neither will he thus be isolated from his fellows. For that we say of one, we say of all. It is as *one* that the man has claims amongst his fellows. Each will feel the sacredness and awe of his neighbour's dark and silent speech with his God. Each will regard the other as a prophet, and look to him for what the Lord hath spoken. Each, as a high priest returning from his Holy of Holies, will bring from his communion some glad tidings, some gospel of truth, which, when spoken, his neighbours shall receive and understand. Each will behold in the other a marvel of revelation, a present son or daughter of the Most High, come forth from him to reveal him afresh. In God each will draw nigh to each.

Yes, there will be danger—danger as everywhere; but he giveth more grace. And if the man who has striven up the heights should yet fall from them into the deeps, is there not that fire of God, the consuming fire, which burneth and destroyeth not?

To no one who has not already had some speech with God, or who has not at least felt some aspiration towards the fount of his being, can all this appear other than foolishness. So be it.

But, Lord, help them and us, and make our being grow into thy likeness. If through ages of strife and ages of growth, yet let us at last see thy face, and receive the white stone from thy hand. That thus we may grow, give us day by day our daily bread. Fill us with the words that proceed out of thy mouth. Help us to lay up *treasures in heaven, where neither moth nor rust doth corrupt.*

THE HEART WITH THE TREASURE.

Lay not up for yourselves treasures upon earth, where moth and rust doth corrupt, and where thieves break through and steal. But lay up for yourselves treasures in heaven, where neither moth nor rust doth corrupt, and where thieves do not break through nor steal. For where your treasure is, there will your heart be also.— MATT. vi. 19-21.

To understand the words of our Lord is the business of life. For it is the main road to the understanding of The Word himself. And to receive him is to receive the Father, and so to have Life in ourselves. And Life, the higher, the deeper, the simpler, the original, is the business of life.

The Word is that by which we live, namely, Jesus himself; and his words represent, in part, in shadow, in suggestion, himself. Any utterance worthy of being called *a truth*, is human food: how much more *The Word*, presenting no abstract laws of our being, but the vital relation of soul and body, heart and will, strength and rejoicing, beauty and light, to Him who first gave birth to them all! The Son came forth to *be*, before our eyes and in our hearts, that which he had made us for, that we might behold *the truth* in him, and cry out for the living God, who, in the highest sense of all is The Truth, not as understood, but as understanding, living, and being, doing and creating the truth. "I am the truth," said our Lord; and by those who are in some measure like him in being the truth, the Word can be understood. Let us try to understand him.

Sometimes, no doubt, the Saviour would have spoken after a different *fashion* of speech, if he had come to Englishmen, instead of to Jews. But the lessons he gave would have been the same; for even when questioned about a matter for its passing import, his reply contained the enunciation of the great human principle which lay in it, and *that* lies changeless in every variation of changeful circumstance. With the light of added ages of Christian experience, it ought to be easier for us to understand his words than it was for those who heard him.

What, I ask now, is here the power of his word *For: For where your treasure is, there will your heart be also*? The meaning of the reason thus added is not obvious upon its surface. It has to be sought for because of its depth at once and its simplicity. But it is so complete, so imaginatively comprehensive, so immediately operative on the conscience through its poetic suggestiveness, that when it is once understood, there is nothing more to be said, but everything to be done.

"Why not lay up for ourselves treasures upon earth?"

"Because there the moth and rust and the thief come."

"And so we should lose those treasures!"

"Yes; by the moth and the rust and the thief."

"Does the Lord then mean that the *reason* for not laying up such treasures is their transitory and corruptible nature?"

"No. He adds a *For*: 'For where your treasure is, there will your heart be also.'"

"Of course the heart will be where the treasure is; but what has that to do with the argument?"

This: that what is with the treasure must fare as the treasure; that the heart which haunts the treasure-house where the moth and rust corrupt, will be exposed to the same ravages as the treasure, will itself be rusted and moth-eaten.

Many a man, many a woman, fair and flourishing to see, is going about with a rusty moth-eaten heart within that form of strength or beauty.

"But this is only a figure."

True. But is the reality intended, less or more than the figure? Does not *the rust and the moth* mean more than disease? And does not *the heart* mean more than the heart? Does it not mean a deeper heart, the heart of your own self, not of your body? of the *self* that suffers, not pain, but misery? of the self whose end is not comfort, or enjoyment, but blessedness, yea, ecstasy? a heart which is the inmost chamber wherein springs the divine fountain of your being? a heart which God

50

regards, though you may never have known its existence, not even when its writhings under the gnawing of the moth and the slow fire of the rust have communicated a dull pain to that outer heart which sends the blood to its appointed course through your body? If God sees that heart corroded with the rust of cares, riddled into caverns and films by the worms of ambition and greed, then your heart is as God sees it, for God sees things as they are. And one day you will be compelled to see, nay, to *feel* your heart as God sees it; and to know that the cankered thing which you have within you, a prey to the vilest of diseases, is indeed the centre of your being, your very heart.

Nor does the lesson apply to those only who worship Mammon, who give their lives, their best energies to the accumulation of wealth: it applies to those equally who in any way worship the transitory; who seek the praise of men more than the praise of God; who would make a show in the world by wealth, by taste, by intellect, by power, by art, by genius of any kind, and so would gather golden opinions to be treasured in a storehouse of earth.

Nor to such only, but surely to those as well whose pleasures are of a more evidently transitory nature still, such as the pleasures of the senses in every direction—whether lawfully or unlawfully indulged, if the joy of being is centred in them—do these words bear terrible warning. For the hurt lies not in this—that these pleasures are false like the deceptions of magic, for such they are not: pleasures they are; nor yet in this—that they pass away, and leave a fierce disappointment behind: that is only so much the better; but the hurt lies in this—that the immortal, the infinite, created in the image of the everlasting God, is housed with the fading and the corrupting, and clings to them as its good—clings to them till it is infected and interpenetrated with their proper diseases, which assume in it a form more terrible in proportion to the superiority of its kind, that which is mere decay in the one becoming moral vileness in the other, that which fits the one for the dunghill casting the other into the outer darkness; creeps, that it may share with them, into a burrow in the earth, where its budded wings wither and damp and drop away from its shoulders, instead of haunting the open plains and the high-uplifted table-lands, spreading abroad its young pinions to the sun and the air, and strengthening them in further and further flights, till at last they should become strong to bear the God-born into the presence of its Father in Heaven. Therein lies the hurt.

He whose heart is sound because it haunts the treasure-house of heaven may *be tempted of the devil*, but will be first *led up of the Spirit into the wilderness.*

THE TEMPTATION IN THE WILDERNESS.

Then was Jesus led up of the Spirit into the wilderness, to be tempted of the devil. And when he had fasted forty days and forty nights, he was afterward an hungered. And when the tempter came to him, he said, if thou be the Son of God, command that these stones be made bread. But he answered and said, It is written, Man shall not live by bread alone, but by every word that proceedeth out of the mouth of God. Then the devil taketh him up into the holy city, and setteth him on a pinnacle of the temple, and saith unto him, If thou be the Son of God, cast thyself down; for it is written, He shall give his angels charge concerning thee, and in their hands they shall bear thee up, lest at any time thou dash thy foot against a stone. Jesus said unto him, It is written again, thou shall not tempt the Lord thy God. Again, the devil taketh him up into an exceeding high mountain, and showeth him all the kingdoms of the world, and the glory of them: and saith unto him, All these things will I give thee, if thou wilt fall down and worship me. Then saith Jesus unto him, Get thee hence, Satan; for it is written, Thou shalt

worship the Lord thy God, and him only shalt thou serve. Then the devil leaveth him; and, behold, angels came and ministered unto him.—MATT. iv. 1-11.

This narrative must have one of two origins. Either it is an invention, such as many tales told of our Lord in the earlier periods of Christianity; or it came from our Lord himself, for, according to the story, except the wild beasts, of earthly presence there was none at his Temptation.

As to the former of the two origins: The story bears upon it no sign of human invention. The man who could see such things as are here embodied, dared not invent such an embodiment for them. To one in doubt about the matter it will be helpful, I think, to compare this story with the best of those for which one or other of the apocryphal gospels is our only authority—say the grand account of the Descent into Hell in the Gospel according to Nicodemus.

If it have not this origin, there is but the other that it can have—

Our Lord himself. To this I will return presently.

And now, let us approach the subject from another side.

With this in view, I ask you to think how much God must know of which we know nothing. Think what an abyss of truth was our Lord, out of whose divine darkness, through that revealing countenance, that uplifting voice, those hands whose tenderness has made us great, broke all holy radiations of human significance. Think of his understanding, imagination, heart, in which lay the treasures of wisdom and knowledge. Must he not have known, felt, imagined, rejoiced in things that would not be told in human words, could not be understood by human hearts? Was he not always bringing forth out of the light inaccessible? Was not his very human form a veil hung over the face of the truth that, even in part by dimming the effulgence of the glory, it might reveal? What could be conveyed must be thus conveyed: an infinite More must lie behind. And even of those things that might be partially revealed to men, could he talk to his Father and talk to his disciples in altogether the same forms, in altogether the same words? Would what he said to God on the mountain-tops, in the dim twilight or the gray dawn, never be such that his disciples could have understood it no more than the people, when the voice of God spoke to him from heaven, could distinguish that voice from the inarticulate thunderings of the element?

THE TEMPTATION IN THE WILDERNESS.

There is no attempt made to convey to us even the substance of the battle of those forty days. Such a conflict of spirit as for forty days absorbed all the human necessities of *The Man* in the cares of the Godhead could not be rendered into forms intelligible to us, or rather, could not be in itself intelligible to us, and therefore could not take any form of which we could lay hold. It is not till the end of those forty days that the divine event begins to dawn out from the sacred depths of the eternal thought, becomes human enough to be made to appear, admits of utterance, becomes capable of being spoken in human forms to the ears of men, though yet only in a dark saying, which he that hath ears to hear may hear, and he that hath a heart to understand may understand. For the mystery is not left behind, nor can the speech be yet clear unto men.

At the same moment when the approaching event comes within human ken, may from afar be dimly descried by the God-upheld intelligence, the same humanity seizes on the Master, and he is an hungered. The first sign that he has come back to us, that the strife is approaching its human result, is his hunger. On what a sea of endless life do we float, are our poor necessities sustained—not the poorest of them dissociated from the divine! Emerging from the storms of the ocean of divine thought and feeling into the shallower waters that lave the human shore, bearing with him the treasures won in the strife, our Lord is straightway an hungered; and from this moment the temptation is human, and can be in some measure understood by us.

But could it even then have been conveyed to the human mind in merely intellectual forms? Or, granting that it might, could it be so conveyed to those who were only beginning to have the vaguest, most error-mingled and confused notions about our Lord and what he came to do? No. The inward experiences of our Lord, such as could be conveyed to them at all, could be conveyed to them only in a parable. For far plainer things than these, our Lord chose this form. The form of the parable is the first in which truth will admit of being embodied. Nor is this all: it is likewise the fullest; and to the parable will the teacher of the truth ever return. Is he who asserts that the passage contains a simple narrative of actual events, prepared to believe, as the story, so interpreted, indubitably gives us to understand, that a visible demon came to our Lord and, himself the prince of worldly wisdom, thought, by quoting Scripture after the manner of the priests, to persuade a good man to tempt God; thought, by the promise of power, to prevail upon him to cast aside every claim he had upon the human race, in falling down and worshipping one whom he knew to be the adversary of

Truth, of Humanity, of God? How could Satan be so foolish? or, if Satan might be so foolish, wherein could such temptation so presented have tempted our Lord? and wherein would a victory over such be a victory for the race?

Told as a parable, it is as full of meaning as it would be bare if received as a narrative.

Our Lord spake then this parable unto them, and so conveyed more of the truth with regard to his temptation in the wilderness, than could have been conveyed by any other form in which the truth he wanted to give them might have been embodied. Still I do not think it follows that we have it exactly as he told it to his disciples. A man will hear but what he can hear, will see but what he can see, and, telling the story again, can tell but what he laid hold of, what he seemed to himself to understand. His effort to reproduce the impression made upon his mind will, as well as the impression itself, be liable to numberless altering, modifying, even, in a measure, discomposing influences. But it does not, therefore, follow that the reproduction is false. The mighty hosts of life-bearing worlds, requiring for the freedom of their courses, and the glory of their changes, such awful abysses of space, dwindle in the human eye to seeds of light sown upon a blue plain. How faint in the ears of man is the voice of their sphere-born thunder of adoration! Yet are they lovely indeed, uttering speech and teaching knowledge. So this story may not be just as the Lord told it, and yet may contain in its mirror as much of the truth as we are able to receive, and as will afford us sufficient scope for a life's discovery. The modifying influences of the human channels may be essential to God's revealing mode. It is only by seeing them first from afar that we learn the laws of the heavens.

And now arises the question upon the right answer to which depends the whole elucidation of the story: *How could the Son of God be tempted?*

If any one say that he was not moved by those temptations, he must be told that then they were no temptations to him, and he was not tempted; nor was his victory of more significance than that of the man who, tempted to bear false witness against his neighbour, abstains from robbing him of his goods. For human need, struggle, and hope, it bears no meaning; and we must reject the whole as a fantastic folly of crude invention; a mere stage-show; a lie for the poor sake of the fancied truth; a doing of evil that good might come; and, with how many fragments soever of truth its mud may be filled, not in any way to be received as a divine message.

56

But asserting that these were real temptations if the story is to be received at all, am I not involving myself in a greater difficulty still? For how could the Son of God be tempted with evil—with that which must to him appear in its true colours of discord, its true shapes of deformity? Or how could he then be the Son of his Father who cannot be tempted with evil?

In the answer to this lies the centre, the essential germ of the whole interpretation: He was not tempted with Evil but with Good; with inferior forms of good, that is, pressing in upon him, while the higher forms of good held themselves aloof, biding their time, that is, God's time. I do not believe that the Son of God could be tempted with evil, but I do believe that he could be tempted with good—to yield to which temptation would have been evil in him—ruin to the universe. But does not all evil come from good?

Yes; but it has come *from* it. It is no longer good. A good corrupted is no longer a good. Such could not tempt our Lord. Revenge may originate in a sense of justice, but it is revenge not justice; an evil thing, for it would be fearfully unjust. Evil is evil whatever it may have come from. The Lord could not have felt tempted to take vengeance upon his enemies, but he might have felt tempted to destroy the wicked from the face of the earth—to destroy them from the face of the earth, I say, not to destroy them for ever. To that I do not think he could have felt tempted.

But we shall find illustration enough of what I mean in the matter itself. Let us look at the individual temptations represented in the parable.

The informing idea which led to St Matthew's arrangement seems to me superior to that showing itself in St Luke's. In the two accounts, the closes, while each is profoundly significant, are remarkably different.

Now let us follow St Matthew's record.

And we shall see how the devil tempted him *to* evil, but not *with* evil.

First, He was hungry, and the devil said, *Make bread of this stone.*

The Lord had been fasting for forty days—a fast impossible except during intense mental absorption. Let no one think to glorify this fast by calling it miraculous. Wonderful such fasts are on record on the part of holy men; and inasmuch as the Lord was more of a man than his brethren, insomuch might he be farther withdrawn in the depths of his spiritual humanity from the outer region of his physical nature. So much the slower would be the goings on of that nature; and fasting in his case might thus be extended beyond the utmost limits of similar fasts in others. This, I believe, was all—and this all infinite in its relations. This is the grandest, simplest, and most significant, and, therefore, the divinest way of regarding his fast. Hence, at the end of the forty days, it was not hunger alone that made food tempting to him, but that exhaustion of the whole system, wasting itself all the time it was forgotten, which, reacting on the mind when the mind was already worn out with its own tension, must have deadened it so, that (speaking after the experience of his brethren, which alone will explain his,) it could for the time see or feel nothing of the spiritual, and could only *believe in* the unfelt, the unseen. What a temptation was here! There is no sin in wishing to eat; no sin in procuring food honestly that one may eat. But it rises even into an awful duty, when a man knows that to eat will restore the lost vision of the eternal; will, operating on the brain, and thence on the mind, render the man capable of hope as well as of faith, of gladness as well as of confidence, of praise as well as of patience. Why then should he not eat? Why should he not put forth the power that was in him that he might eat? Because such power was his, not to take care of himself, but to work the work of him that sent him. Such power was his not even to honour his Father save as his Father chose to be honoured, who is far more honoured in the ordinary way of common wonders, than in the extraordinary way of miracles. Because it was God's business to take care of him, his to do what the Father told him to do. To make that stone bread would be to take the care out of the Father's hands, and turn the divinest thing in the universe into the merest commonplace of self-preservation.

And in nothing was he to be beyond his brethren, save in faith. No refuge for him, any more than for them, save in the love and care of the Father. Other refuge, let it be miraculous power or what you will, would be but hell to him. God is refuge. God is life. "Was he not to eat when it came in his way? And did not the bread come in his way, when his power met that which could be changed into it?"

Regard that word *changed*. The whole matter lies in that. Changed from what? From what God had made it. Changed into what? Into what he did not make it. Why changed? Because the Son was hungry, and the Father would not feed him with food convenient for him! The Father did not give him a stone when he asked for bread. It was Satan that brought the stone and told him to provide for himself. The Father said, That is a stone. The Son would not say, That is a loaf. No one creative *fiat* shall contradict another. The Father and the Son are of one mind. The Lord could hunger, could starve, but would not change into another thing what his Father had made one thing[1].

If we regard the answer he gave the devil, we shall see the root of the matter at once: "Man shall not live by bread alone, but by every word that proceedeth out of the mouth of God." Yea even by the word which made that stone that stone. Everything is all right. It is life indeed for him to leave that a stone, which the Father had made a stone. It would be death to him to alter one word that He had spoken.

"Man shall not live by bread alone." There are other ways of living besides that which comes by bread. A man will live by the word of God, by what God says to him, by what God means between Him and him, by the truths of being which the Father alone can reveal to his child, by the communion of love between them. Without the bread he will die, as men say; but he will not find that he dies. He will only find that the tent which hid the stars from him is gone, and that he can see the heavens; or rather, the earthly house will melt away from around him, and he will find that he has a palace-home about him, another and loftier word of God clothing upon him. So the man lives by the word of God even in refusing the bread which God does not give him, for, instead of dying because he does not eat, he rises into a higher life even of the same kind.

For I have been speaking of the consciousness of existence, and not of that higher spiritual life on which all other life depends. That of course can for no one moment exist save from the heart of God. When a man tries to live by bread and not by the word that comes out of that

---

[1] There was no such change in the feeding of the multitudes. The fish and the bread were fish and bread before. I think this is significant as regards the true nature of a miracle, and its relation to the ordinary ways of God. There was in these miracles, and I think in all, only a hastening of appearances; the doing of that in a day, which may ordinarily take a thousand years, for with God time is not what it is with us. He makes it. And the hastening of a process does not interfere in the least with cause and effect in the process, nor does it render the process one whit more miraculous. In deed, the wonder of the growing corn is to me greater than the wonder of feeding the thousands. It is easier to understand the creative power going forth at once—immediately— than through the countless, the lovely, the seemingly forsaken wonders of the corn-field. To the merely scientific man all this is pure nonsense, or at best belongs to the region of the fancy. The time will come, I think, when he will see that there is more in it, namely, a higher reason, a loftier science, how incorrectly soever herein indicated.

heart of God, he may think he lives, but he begins to die or is dead. Our Lord says, "I can do without the life that comes of bread: without the life that comes of the word of my Father, I die indeed." Therefore he does not think twice about the matter. That God's will be done is all his care. That done, all will be right, and all right with him, whether he thinks about himself or not. For the Father does not forget the child who is so busy trusting in him, that he cares not even to pray for himself.

In the higher aspect of this first temptation, arising from the fact that a man cannot feel the things he believes except under certain conditions of physical well-being dependent upon food, the answer is the same: A man does not live by his feelings any more than by bread, but by the Truth, that is, the Word, the Will, the uttered Being of God.

I am even ashamed to yield here to the necessity of writing what is but as milk for babes, when I would gladly utter, if I might, only that which would be as bread for men and women. What I must say is this: that, by *the Word of God*, I do not understand *The Bible*. The Bible is *a* Word of God, the chief of his written words, because it tells us of The Word, the Christ; but everything God has done and given man to know is a word of his, a will of his; and inasmuch as it is a will of his, it is a necessity to man, without which he cannot live: the reception of it is man's life. For inasmuch as God's utterances are a whole, every smallest is essential: he speaks no foolishness—there are with him no vain repetitions. But by *the word* of the God and not Maker only, who is God just because he *speaks* to men, I must understand, in the deepest sense, every revelation of Himself in the heart and consciousness of man, so that the man knows that God is there, nay, rather, that he is here. Even Christ himself is not The Word of God in the deepest sense *to a man*, until he is this Revelation of God to the man,—until the Spirit that is the meaning in the Word has come to him,—until the speech is not a sound as of thunder, but the voice of words; for a word is more than an utterance— it is a sound to be understood. No word, I say, is fully a Word *of* God until it is a Word *to* man, until the man therein recognizes God. This is that for which the word is spoken. The words of God are as the sands and the stars,—they cannot be numbered; but the end of all and each is this—to reveal God. Nor, moreover, can the man know that any one of them is the word of God, save as it comes thus to him, is a revelation of God in him. It is *to* him that it may be *in* him; but till it is *in* him he cannot *know* that it was *to* him. God must be God *in* man before man can know that he is God, or

THE TEMPTATION IN THE WILDERNESS.

that he has received aright, and for that for which it was spoken, any one of his words[1].

If, by any will of God—that is, any truth in him—we live, we live by it tenfold when that will has become a word to us. When we receive it, his will becomes our will, and so we live by God. But the word of God once understood, a man must live by the faith of what God is, and not by his own feelings even in regard to God. It is the Truth itself, that which God is, known by what goeth out of his mouth, that man lives by. And when he can no longer *feel* the truth, he shall not therefore die. He lives because God is true; and he is able to know that he lives because he knows, having once understood the word, that God is truth. He believes in the God of former vision, lives by that word therefore, when all is dark and there is no vision.

We now come to the second attempt of the Enemy. "Then if God is to be so trusted, try him. Fain would I see the result. Shew thyself his darling. Here is the word itself for it: He shall give his angels charge concerning thee; not a stone shall hurt thee. Take him at his word. Throw thyself down, and strike the conviction into me that thou art the Son of God. For thou knowest thou dost not look like what thou sayest thou art."

Again, with a written word, in return, the Lord meets him. And he does not quote the scripture for logical purposes—to confute Satan intellectually, but as giving even Satan the reason of his conduct. Satan quotes Scripture as a verbal authority; our Lord meets him with a Scripture by the truth in which he regulates his conduct.

If we examine it, we shall find that this answer contains the same principle as the former, namely this, that to the Son of God the will of God is Life. It was a temptation to shew the powers of the world that he was the Son of God; that to him the elements were subject; that he was above the laws of Nature, because he was the Eternal Son; and thus stop the raging of the heathen, and the vain imaginations of the people. It would be but to shew them the truth. But he was the *Son* of God: what was his *Father's* will? Such was not the divine way of convincing the world of sin, of righteousness, of judgment. If the Father told him to cast himself down, that moment the pinnacle pointed naked to the sky. If the devil threw him down, let God send his angels; or, if

---

[1] No doubt the humble spirit will receive the testimony of every one whom he reveres, and look in the direction indicated for a word from the Father; but till he thus receives it in his heart, he cannot know what the word spoken of is.

better, allow him to be dashed to pieces in the valley below. But never will he forestall the divine will. The Father shall order what comes next. The Son will obey. In the path of his work he will turn aside for no stone. There let the angels bear him in their hands if need be. But he will not choose the path because there is a stone in it. He will not choose at all. He will go where the Spirit leads him.

I think this will throw some light upon the words of our Lord, "If ye have faith and doubt not, if ye shall say unto this mountain, Be thou removed, and be thou cast into the sea; it shall be done." Good people, amongst them John Bunyan, have been tempted to tempt the Lord their God upon the strength of this saying, just as Satan sought to tempt our Lord on the strength of the passage he quoted from the Psalms. Happily for such, the assurance to which they would give the name of faith generally fails them in time. Faith is that which, knowing the Lord's will, goes and does it; or, not knowing it, stands and waits, content in ignorance as in knowledge, because God wills; neither pressing into the hidden future, nor careless of the knowledge which opens the path of action. It is its noblest exercise to act with uncertainty of the result, when the duty itself is certain, or even when a course seems with strong probability to be duty[1]. But to put God to the question in any other way than by saying, What wilt thou have me to do? is an attempt to compel God to declare himself, or to hasten his work. This probably was the sin of Judas. It is presumption of a kind similar to the making of a stone into bread. It is, as it were, either a forcing of God to act where he has created no need for action, or the making of a case wherein he shall seem to have forfeited his word if he does not act. The man is therein dissociating himself from God so far that, instead of acting by the divine will from within, he acts in God's face, as it were, to see what he will do. Man's first business is, "What does God want me to do?" not "What will God do if I do so and so?" To tempt a parent after the flesh in such a manner would be impertinence: to tempt God so is the same vice in its highest form—a natural result of that condition of mind which is worse than all the so-called cardinal sins, namely, spiritual pride, which attributes the tenderness and love of God not to man's being and man's need, but to some distinguishing excellence in the individual himself, which causes the Father to love

---

[1] In the latter case a man may be mistaken, and his work will be burned, but by that very fire he will be saved. Nothing saves a man more than the burning of his work, except the doing of work that can stand the fire.

him better than his fellows, and so pass by his faults with a smile. Not thus did the Son of God regard his relation to his Father. The faith which will remove mountains is that confidence in God which comes from seeking nothing but his will. A man who was thus faithful would die of hunger sooner than say to the stone, *Be bread*; would meet the scoffs of the unbelieving without reply and with apparent defeat, sooner than say to the mountain, *Be thou cast into the sea*, even if he knew that it would be torn from its foundations at the word, except he knew first that God would have it so.

And thus I am naturally brought to consider more fully how this should be a real temptation to the Son of Man. It would be good to confound his adversaries; to force conviction upon them that he was the God-supported messenger he declared himself. Why should he have Adversaries a moment longer to interfere between him and the willing hearts which would believe if they could? The answer to all this was plain to our Lord, and is plain to us now: It was not the way of the Father's will. It would not fall in with that gradual development of life and history by which the Father works, and which must be the way to breed free, God-loving wills. It would be violent, theatrical, therefore poor in nature and in result,—not God-like in any way. Everything in God's doing comes harmoniously with and from all the rest. Son of Man, his history shall be a man's history, shall be The Man's history. Shall that begin with an exception? Yet it might well be a temptation to Him who longed to do all he could for men. He was the Son of God: why should not the sons of God know it?

But as this temptation in the wilderness was an epitome and type of the temptations to come, against which for forty days he had been making himself strong, revolving truth beyond our reach, in whose light every commonest duty was awful and divine, a vision fit almost to oppress a God in his humiliation, so we shall understand the whole better if we look at his life in relation to it. As he refused to make stones bread, so throughout that life he never wrought a miracle to help himself; as he refused to cast himself from the temple to convince Satan or glory visibly in his Sonship, so he steadily refused to give the sign which the human Satans demanded, notwithstanding the offer of conviction which they held forth to bribe him to the grant. How easy it seems to have confounded them, and strengthened his followers! But such conviction would stand in the way of a better conviction in his disciples, and would do his adversaries only harm. For neither could not in any true sense be convinced by such a show: it could but prove his power. It might prove so far the presence of a God; but would it prove that God? Would it bring him nearer to them, who could not see him in the face of his Son? To say *Thou art God*, without knowing what the *Thou* means—of what use is it? God is a name only, except we know *God*. Our Lord did not care to be so acknowledged.

On the same principle, the very miracles which from their character did partially reveal his character to those who already had faith in him, he would not do where unbelief predominated. He often avoided cities and crowds, and declined mighty works because of unbelief. Except for the loving help they gave the distressed, revealing him to their hearts as the Redeemer from evil, I doubt if he would have wrought a single miracle. I do not think he cared much about them. Certainly, as regarded the onlookers, he did not expect much to result from those mighty deeds. A mere marvel is practically soon forgotten, and long before it is forgotten, many minds have begun to doubt the senses, their own even, which communicated it. Inward sight alone can convince of truth; signs and wonders never. No number of signs can do more than convey a probability that he who shews them knows that of which he speaks. They cannot convey the truth. But the vision of the truth itself, in the knowledge of itself, a something altogether beyond the region of signs and wonders, is the power of God, is salvation. This vision was in the Lord's face and form to the pure in heart who were able to see God; but not in his signs and wonders to those who sought after such. Yet it is easy to see how the temptation might for a moment work upon a mind that longed to enter upon its labours with the credentials of its truth. How the true heart longs to be received by its brethren—to be known in its truth! But no. The truth must show itself in God's time, in and by the labour. The kingdom must come in God's holy human way. Not by a stroke of grandeur, but by years of love, yea, by centuries of seeming bafflement, by aeons of labour, must he grow into the hearts of the sons and daughters of his Father in heaven. The Lord himself *will* be bound by the changeless laws which are the harmony of the Fathers being and utterance. He will *be*, not seem. He will be, and thereby, not therefore, seem. Yet, once more, even on him, the idea of asserting the truth in holy power such as he could have put forth, must have dawned in grandeur. The thought was good: to have yielded to it would have been the loss of the world; nay, far worse—ill inconceivable to the human mind—the God of obedience had fallen from his throne, and—all is blackness.

But let us not forget that the whole is a faint parable—faint I mean in relation to the grandeur of the reality, as the ring and the shoes are poor types (yet how dear!) of the absolute love of the Father to his prodigal children.

We shall now look at the third temptation. The first was to help himself in his need; the second, perhaps, to assert the Father; the third to deliver his brethren.

To deliver them, that is, after the fashion of men—from the outside still. Indeed, the whole Temptation may be regarded as the contest of the seen and the unseen, of the outer and inner, of the likely and the true, of the show and the reality. And as in the others, the evil in this last lay in that it was a temptation to save his brethren, instead of doing the Will of his Father.

Could it be other than a temptation to think that he might, if he would, lay a righteous grasp upon the reins of government, leap into the chariot of power, and ride forth conquering and to conquer? Glad visions arose before him of the prisoner breaking jubilant from the cell of injustice; of the widow lifting up the bowed head before the devouring Pharisee; of weeping children bursting into shouts at the sound of the wheels of the chariot before which oppression and wrong shrunk and withered, behind which sprung the fir-tree instead of the thorn, and the myrtle instead of the brier. What glowing visions of holy vengeance, what rosy dreams of human blessedness—and all from his hand—would crowd such a brain as his!—not like the castles-in-the-air of the aspiring youth, for he builds at random, because he knows that he cannot realize; but consistent and harmonious as well as grand, because he knew them within his reach. Could he not mould the people at his will? Could he not, transfigured in his snowy garments, call aloud in the streets of Jerusalem, "Behold your King?" And the fierce warriors of his nation would start at the sound; the ploughshare would be beaten into the sword, and the pruning-hook into the spear; and the nation, rushing to his call, learn war yet again indeed,—a grand, holy war—a crusade—no; we should not have had *that* word; but a war against the tyrants of the race—the best, as they called themselves— who trod upon their brethren, and would not suffer them even to look to the heavens.—Ah! but when were his garments white as snow? When, through them, glorifying them as it passed, did the light stream from his glorified body? Not when he looked to such a conquest; but when, on a mount like this, he "spake of the decease that he should *accomplish* at Jerusalem"! Why should this be "the sad end of the war"? "Thou shalt worship the Lord thy God, and him only shalt thou serve." Not even thine own visions of love and truth, O Saviour of the world, shall be thy guides to thy goal, but the will of thy Father in heaven.

But how would he, thus conquering, be a servant of Satan? Wherein would this be a falling-down and a worshipping of him (that is, an acknowledging of the worth of him) who was the lord of misrule and its pain?

I will not inquire whether such an enterprise could be accomplished without the worship of Satan,—whether men could be managed for such an end without more or less of the trickery practised by every ambitious leader, every self-serving conqueror—without double-dealing, tact, flattery, finesse. I will not inquire into this, because, on the most distant supposition of our Lord being the leader of his country's armies, these things drop out of sight as impossibilities. If these were necessary, such a career for him refuses to be for a moment imagined. But I will ask whether to know better and do not so well, is not a serving of Satan;—whether to lead men on in the name of God as towards the best when the end is not the best, is not a serving of Satan;—whether to flatter their pride by making them conquerors of the enemies of their nation instead of their own evils, is not a serving of Satan;—in a word, whether, to desert the mission of God, who knew that men could not be set free in that way, and sent him to be a man, a true man, the one man, among them, that his life might become their life, and that so they might be as free in prison or on the cross, as upon a hill-side or on a throne,—whether, so deserting the truth, to give men over to the lie of believing other than spirit and truth to be the worship of the Father, other than love the fulfilling of the law, other than the offering of their best selves the service of God, other than obedient harmony with the primal love and truth and law, freedom,— whether, to desert God thus, and give men over thus, would not have been to fall down and worship the devil. Not all the sovereignty of God, as the theologians call it, delegated to the Son, and administered by the wisdom of the Spirit that was given to him without measure, could have wrought the kingdom of heaven in one corner of our earth. Nothing but the obedience of the Son, the obedience unto the death, the absolute *doing* of the will of God because it was the truth, could redeem the prisoner, the widow, the orphan. But it would redeem them by redeeming the conquest-ridden conqueror too, the stripe-giving jailer, the unjust judge, the devouring Pharisee himself with the insatiable moth-eaten heart. The earth should be free because Love was stronger than Death. Therefore should fierceness and wrong and hypocrisy and God-service play out their weary play. He would not pluck the spreading

66

branches of the tree; he would lay the axe to its root. It would take time; but the tree would be dead at last—dead, and cast into the lake of fire. It would take time; but his Father had time enough and to spare. It would take courage and strength and self-denial and endurance; but his Father could give him all. It would cost pain of body and mind, yea, agony and torture; but those he was ready to take on himself. It would cost him the vision of many sad and, to all but him, hopeless sights; he must see tears without wiping them, hear sighs without changing them into laughter, see the dead lie, and let them lie; see Rachel weeping for her children and refusing to be comforted; he must look on his brothers and sisters crying as children over their broken toys, and must not mend them; he must go on to the grave, and they not know that thus he was setting all things right for them. His work must be one with and completing God's Creation and God's History. The disappointment and sorrow and fear he could, he would bear. The will of God should be done. Man should be free,—not merely man as he thinks of himself, but man as God thinks of him. The divine idea shall be set free in the divine bosom; the man on earth shall see his angel face to face. He shall grow into the likeness of the divine thought, free not in his own fancy, but in absolute divine fact of being, as in God's idea. The great and beautiful and perfect will of God *must* be done.

"Get thee hence, Satan: for it is written, Thou shalt worship the Lord thy God, and him only shalt thou serve."

It was when Peter would have withstood him as he set his face steadfastly to meet this death at Jerusalem, that he gave him the same kind of answer that he now gave to Satan, calling him Satan too.

"Then the devil leaveth him, and behold angels came and ministered unto him."

So saith St Matthew. They brought him the food he had waited for, walking in the strength of the word. He would have died if it had not come now.

"And when the devil had ended all the temptation, he departed from him for a season."

So saith St Luke.

Then Satan ventured once more. When?

Was it then, when at the last moment, in the agony of the last faint, the Lord cried out, "Why hast thou forsaken me?" when, having done the great work, having laid it aside clean and pure as the linen cloth that was ready now to infold him, another cloud than that on the mount overshadowed his soul, and out of it came a voiceless persuasion that, after all was done, God did not care for his work or for him?

Even in those words the adversary was foiled—and for ever. For when he seemed to be forsaken, his cry was still, "*My God! my God!*"

THE ELOI.

**_"My God, my God, why hast thou forsaken me?"_—
ST MATTHEW xxvii. 46.**

I do not know that I should dare to approach this, of all utterances into which human breath has ever been moulded, most awful in import, did I not feel that, containing both germ and blossom of the final devotion, it contains therefore the deepest practical lesson the human heart has to learn. The Lord, the Revealer, hides nothing that can be revealed, and will not warn away the foot that treads in naked humility even upon the ground of that terrible conflict between him and Evil, when the smoke of the battle that was fought not only with garments rolled in blood but with burning and fuel of fire, rose up between him and his Father, and for the one terrible moment ere he broke the bonds of life, and walked weary and triumphant into his arms, hid God from the eyes of his Son. He will give us even to meditate the one thought that slew him at last, when he could bear no more, and fled to the Father to know that he loved him, and was well-pleased with him. For Satan had come at length yet again, to urge him with his last temptation; to tell him that although he had done his part, God had forgotten his; that although he had lived by the word of his mouth, that mouth had no word more to speak to him; that although he had refused to tempt him, God had left him to be tempted more than he could bear; that although he had worshipped none other, for that worship God did not care. The Lord hides not his sacred sufferings, for truth is light, and would be light in the minds of men. The Holy Child, the Son of the Father, has nothing to conceal, but all the Godhead to reveal. Let us then put off our shoes, and draw near, and bow the head, and kiss those feet that bear for ever the scars of our victory. In those feet we clasp the safety of our suffering, our sinning brotherhood.

It is with the holiest fear that we should approach the terrible fact of the sufferings of our Lord. Let no one think that those were less because he was more. The more delicate the nature, the more alive to all that is lovely and true, lawful and right, the more does it feel the antagonism of pain, the inroad of death upon life; the more dreadful is that breach of the harmony of things whose sound is torture. He felt more than man could feel, because he had a larger feeling. He was even therefore worn out sooner than another man would have been. These sufferings were awful indeed when they began to invade the region about the will; when the struggle to keep consciously trusting in God began to sink in darkness; when the Will of The Man put forth its last determined effort in that cry after the vanishing vision of the Father: *My God, my God, why hast thou forsaken me?* Never had it been so with him before. Never before had he been unable to see God beside him. Yet never was God nearer him than now. For never was Jesus more divine. He could not see, could not feel him near; and yet it is "*My* God" that he cries.

Thus the Will of Jesus, in the very moment when his faith seems about to yield, is finally triumphant. It has no *feeling* now to support it, no beatific vision to absorb it. It stands naked in his soul and tortured, as he stood naked and scourged before Pilate. Pure and simple and surrounded by fire, it declares for God. The sacrifice ascends in the cry, *My God*. The cry comes not out of happiness, out of peace, out of hope. Not even out of suffering comes that cry. It was a cry *in* desolation, but it came out of Faith. It is the last voice of Truth, speaking when it can but cry. The divine horror of that moment is unfathomable by human soul. It was blackness of darkness. And yet he would believe. Yet he would hold fast. God was his God yet. *My God*— and in the cry came forth the Victory, and all was over soon. Of the peace that followed that cry, the peace of a perfect soul, large as the universe, pure as light, ardent as life, victorious for God and his brethren, he himself alone can ever know the breadth and length, and depth and height.

Without this last trial of all, the temptations of our Master had not been so full as the human cup could hold; there would have been one region through which we had to pass wherein we might call aloud upon our Captain-Brother, and there would be no voice or hearing: he had avoided the fatal spot! The temptations of the desert came to the young, strong man with his road before him and the presence of his God around him; nay, gathered their very force from the exuberance of his conscious faith. "Dare and do, for God is with thee," said the devil.

"I know it, and therefore I will wait," returned the king of his brothers. And now, after three years of divine action, when his course is run, when the old age of finished work is come, when the whole frame is tortured until the regnant brain falls whirling down the blue gulf of fainting, and the giving up of the ghost is at hand, when the friends have forsaken him and fled, comes the voice of the enemy again at his ear: "Despair and die, for God is not with thee. All is in vain. Death, not Life, is thy refuge. Make haste to Hades, where thy torture will be over. Thou hast deceived thyself. He never was with thee. He was the God of Abraham. Abraham is dead. Whom makest thou thyself?" "My God, my God, why hast thou forsaken me?" the Master cries. For God was his God still, although he had forsaken him—forsaken *his vision* that his faith might glow out triumphant; forsaken *himself?* no; come nearer to him than ever; come nearer, even as—but with a yet deeper, more awful pregnancy of import—even as the Lord himself withdrew from the bodily eyes of his friends, that he might dwell in their profoundest being.

I do not think it was our Lord's deepest trial when in the garden he prayed that the cup might pass from him, and prayed yet again that the will of the Father might be done. For that will was then present with him. He was living and acting in that will. But now the foreseen horror has come. He is drinking the dread cup, and the Will has vanished from his eyes. Were that Will visible in his suffering, his will could bow with tearful gladness under the shelter of its grandeur. But now his will is left alone to drink the cup of The Will in torture. In the sickness of this agony, the Will of Jesus arises perfect at last; and of itself, unsupported now, declares—a naked consciousness of misery hung in the waste darkness of the universe—declares for God, in defiance of pain, of death, of apathy, of self, of negation, of the blackness within and around it; calls aloud upon the vanished God.

This is the Faith of the Son of God. God withdrew, as it were, that the perfect Will of the Son might arise and go forth to find the Will of the Father.

Is it possible that even then he thought of the lost sheep who could not believe that God was their Father; and for them, too, in all their loss and blindness and unlove, cried, saying the word they might say, knowing for them that *God* means *Father* and more, and knowing now, as he had never known till now, what a fearful thing it is to be without God and without hope? I dare not answer the question I put.

But wherein or what can this Alpine apex of faith have to do with the creatures who call themselves Christians, creeping about in the valleys, hardly knowing that there are mountains above them, save that they take offence at and stumble over the pebbles washed across their path by the glacier streams? I will tell you. We are and remain such creeping Christians, because we look at ourselves and not at Christ; because we gaze at the marks of our own soiled feet, and the trail of our own defiled garments, instead of up at the snows of purity, whither the soul of Christ clomb. Each, putting his foot in the footprint of the Master, and so defacing it, turns to examine how far his neighbour's footprint corresponds with that which he still calls the Master's, although it is but his own. Or, having committed a petty fault, I mean a fault such as only a petty creature could commit, we mourn over the defilement to ourselves, and the shame of it before our friends, children, or servants, instead of hastening to make the due confession and amends to our fellow, and then, forgetting our paltry self with its well-earned disgrace, lift up our eyes to the glory which alone will quicken the true man in us, and kill the peddling creature we so wrongly call our *self*. The true self is that which can look Jesus in the face, and say *My Lord*.

When the inward sun is shining, and the wind of thought, blowing where it lists amid the flowers and leaves of fancy and imagination, rouses glad forms and feelings, it is easy to look upwards, and say *My God*. It is easy when the frosts of external failure have braced the mental nerves to healthy endurance and fresh effort after labour, it is easy then to turn to God and trust in him, in whom all honest exertion gives an ability as well as a right to trust. It is easy in pain, so long as it does not pass certain undefinable bounds, to hope in God for deliverance, or pray for strength to endure. But what is to be done when all feeling is gone? when a man does not know whether he believes or not, whether he loves or not? when art, poetry, religion are nothing to him, so swallowed up is he in pain, or mental depression, or disappointment, or temptation, or he knows not what? It seems to him then that God does not care for him, and certainly he does not care for God. If he is still humble, he thinks that he is so bad that God cannot care for him. And he then believes for the time that God loves us only because and when and while we love him; instead of believing that God loves us always because he is our God, and that we live only by his love. Or he does not believe in a God at all, which is better.

So long as we have nothing to say to God, nothing to do with him, save in the sunshine of the mind when we feel him near us, we are poor creatures, willed upon, not willing; reeds, flowering reeds, it may be, and pleasant to behold, but only reeds blown about of the wind; not bad, but poor creatures.

And how in such a condition do we generally act? Do we not sit mourning over the loss of our feelings? or worse, make frantic efforts to rouse them? or, ten times worse, relapse into a state of temporary atheism, and yield to the pressing temptation? or, being heartless, consent to remain careless, conscious of evil thoughts and low feelings alone, but too lazy, too content to rouse ourselves against them? We know we must get rid of them some day, but meantime—never mind; we do not *feel* them bad, we do not feel anything else good; we are asleep and we know it, and we cannot be troubled to wake. No impulse comes to arouse us, and so we remain as we are.

God does not, by the instant gift of his Spirit, make us always feel right, desire good, love purity, aspire after him and his will. Therefore either he will not, or he cannot. If he will not, it must be because it would not be well to do so. If he cannot, then he would not if he could; else a better condition than God's is conceivable to the mind of God— a condition in which he could save the creatures whom he has made, better than he can save them. The truth is this: He wants to make us in his own image, *choosing the good, refusing* the evil. How should he effect this if he were *always* moving us from within, as he does at divine intervals, towards the beauty of holiness? God gives us room *to be*; does not oppress us with his will; "stands away from us," that we may act from ourselves, that we may exercise the pure will for good. Do not, therefore, imagine me to mean that we can do anything of ourselves without God. If we choose the right at last, it is all God's doing, and only the more his that it is ours, only in a far more marvellous way his than if he had kept us filled with all holy impulses precluding the need of choice. For up to this very point, for this very point, he has been educating us, leading us, pushing us, driving us, enticing us, that we may choose him and his will, and so be tenfold more his children, of his own best making, in the freedom of the will found our own first in its loving sacrifice to him, for which in his grand fatherhood he has been thus working from the foundations of the earth, than we could be in the most ecstatic worship flowing from the divinest impulse, without this *willing* sacrifice. For God made our individuality as well as, and a greater marvel than, our dependence; made our *apartness* from himself, that freedom should bind us divinely dearer to himself, with a new and inscrutable marvel of love; for the Godhead is still at the root, is the making root of our individuality, and the freer the man, the stronger the bond that binds him to him who made his freedom. He

made our wills, and is striving to make them free; for only in the per-
fection of our individuality and the freedom of our wills call we be
altogether his children. This is full of mystery, but can we not see
enough in it to make us very glad and very peaceful?

Not in any other act than one which, in spite of impulse or of
weakness, declares for the Truth, for God, does the will spring into
absolute freedom, into true life.

See, then, what lies within our reach every time that we are thus
lapt in the folds of night. The highest condition of the human will is in
sight, is attainable. I say not the highest condition of the Human Be-
ing; that surely lies in the Beatific Vision, in the sight of God. But the
highest condition of the Human Will, as distinct, not as separated from
God, is when, not seeing God, not seeming to itself to grasp him at all,
it yet holds him fast. It cannot continue in this condition, for, not find-
ing, not seeing God, the man would die; but the will thus asserting
itself, the man has passed from death into life, and the vision is nigh at
hand. Then first, thus free, in thus asserting its freedom, is the individ-
ual will one with the Will of God; the child is finally restored to the
father; the childhood and the fatherhood meet in one; the brotherhood
of the race arises from the dust; and the prayer of our Lord is an-
swered, "I in them and thou in me, that they may be made perfect in
one." Let us then arise in God-born strength every time that we feel the
darkness closing, or Become aware that it has closed around us, and
say, "I am of the Light and not of the Darkness."

Troubled soul, thou art not bound to feel, but thou art bound to
arise. God loves thee whether thou feelest or not. Thou canst not love
when thou wilt, but thou art bound to fight the hatred in thee to the
last. Try not to feel good when thou art not good, but cry to Him who
is good. He changes not because thou changest. Nay, he has an espe-
cial tenderness of love towards thee for that thou art in the dark and
hast no light, and his heart is glad when thou dost arise and say, "I will
go to my Father." For he sees thee through all the gloom through
which thou canst not see him. Will thou his will. Say to him: "My
God, I am very dull and low and hard; but thou art wise and high and
tender, and thou art my God. I am thy child. Forsake me not." Then
fold the arms of thy faith, and wait in quietness until light goes up in
thy darkness. Fold the arms of thy Faith I say, but not of thy Action:
bethink thee of something that thou oughtest to do, and go and do it, if
it be but the sweeping of a room, or the preparing of a meal, or a visit
to a friend. Heed not thy feelings: Do thy work.

As God lives by his own will, and we live in him, so has he given to us power to will in ourselves. How much better should we not fare if, finding that we are standing with our heads bowed away from the good, finding that we have no feeble inclination to seek the source of our life, we should yet *will* upwards toward God, rousing that essence of life in us, which he has given us from his own heart, to call again upon him who is our Life, who can fill the emptiest heart, rouse the deadest conscience, quicken the dullest feeling, and strengthen the feeblest will!

Then, if ever the time should come, as perhaps it must come to each of us, when all consciousness of well-being shall have vanished, when the earth shall be but a sterile promontory, and the heavens a dull and pestilent congregation of vapours, when man nor woman shall delight us more, nay, when God himself shall be but a name, and Jesus an old story, then, even then, when a Death far worse than "that phantom of grisly bone" is griping at our hearts, and having slain love, hope, faith, forces existence upon us only in agony, then, even then, we shall be able to cry out with our Lord, "My God, my God, why hast thou forsaken me?" Nor shall we die then, I think, without being able to take up his last words as well, and say, "*Father, into thy hands I commend my spirit.*"

THE HANDS OF THE FATHER.

"Father, into thy hand I commend my spirit."— St Luke xxiii. 46.

Neither St Matthew nor St Mark tells us of any words uttered by our Lord after the *Eloi*. They both, along with St Luke, tell us of a cry with a loud voice, and the giving up of the ghost; between which cry and the giving up, St Luke records the words, "Father, into thy hands I commend my spirit." St Luke says nothing of the Eloi prayer of desolation. St John records neither the *Eloi*, nor the *Father into thy hands*, nor the loud cry. He tells us only that after Jesus had received the vinegar, he said, "*It is finished*," and bowed his head, and gave up the ghost.

Will the Lord ever tell us why he cried so? Was it the cry of relief at the touch of death? Was it the cry of victory? Was it the cry of gladness that he had endured to the end? Or did the Father look out upon him in answer to his *My God*, and the blessedness of it make him cry aloud because he could not smile? Was such his condition now that the greatest gladness of the universe could express itself only in a loud cry? Or was it but the last wrench of pain ere the final repose began? It may have been all in one. But never surely in all books, in all words of thinking men, can there be so much expressed as lay unarticulated in that cry of the Son of God. Now had he made his Father Lord no longer in the might of making and loving alone, but Lord in right of devotion and deed of love. Now should inward sonship and the spirit of glad sacrifice be born in the hearts of men; for the divine obedience was perfected by suffering. He had been amongst his brethren what he would have his brethren be. He had done for them what he would have them do for God and for each other. God was henceforth inside and beneath them, as well as around and above them, suffering with them and for them, giving them all he had, his very life-being, his essence of existence, what best he loved, what best he was. He had been among them, their God-brother. And the mighty story ends with a cry.

Then the cry meant, *It is finished*; the cry meant, *Father, into thy hands I commend my spirit*. Every highest human act is just a giving back to God of that which he first gave to us. "Thou God hast given me: here again is thy gift. I send my spirit home." Every act of worship is a holding up to God of what God hath made us. "Here, Lord, look what I have got: feel with me in what thou hast made me, in this thy own bounty, my being. I am thy child, and know not how to thank thee save by uplifting the heave-offering of the overflowing of thy life, and calling aloud, 'It is thine: it is mine. I am thine, and therefore I am mine.'" The vast operations of the spiritual as of the physical world, are simply a turning again to the source.

The last act of our Lord in thus commending his spirit at the close of his life, was only a summing up of what he had been doing all his life. He had been offering this sacrifice, the sacrifice of himself, all the years, and in thus sacrificing he had lived the divine life. Every morning when he went out ere it was day, every evening when he lingered on the night-lapt mountain after his friends were gone, he was offering himself to his Father in the communion of loving words, of high thoughts, of speechless feelings; and, between, he turned to do the same thing in deed, namely, in loving word, in helping thought, in healing action towards his fellows; for the way to worship God while the daylight lasts is to work; the service of God, the only "divine service," is the helping of our fellows.

I do not seek to point out this commending of our spirits to the Father as a duty: that is to turn the highest privilege we possess into a burden grievous to be borne. But I want to shew that it is the simplest blessedest thing in the human world.

For the Human Being may say thus with himself: "Am I going to sleep—to lose consciousness—to be helpless for a time—thoughtless—dead? Or, more awful consideration, in the dreams that may come may I not be weak of will and scant of conscience?—Father, into thy hands I commend my spirit. I give myself back to thee. Take me, soothe me, refresh me, 'make me over again.' Am I going out into the business and turmoil of the day, where so many temptations may come to do less honourably, less faithfully, less kindly, less diligently than the Ideal Man would have me do?—Father, into thy hands. Am I going to do a good deed? Then, of all times,—Father, into thy hands; lest the enemy should have me now. Am I going to do a hard duty, from which I would gladly be turned aside,—to refuse a friend's request, to urge a neighbour's conscience?—Father, into thy hands I commend my spirit. Am I in pain? Is illness coming upon me to shut out the glad visions of a healthy brain, and bring me such as are troubled and untrue?—Take my spirit, Lord, and see, as thou art wont, that it has no more to bear than it can bear. Am I going to die? Thou knowest, if only from the cry of thy Son, how terrible that is; and if it comes not to me in so terrible a shape as that in which it came to him, think how poor to bear I am beside him. I do not know what the struggle means; for, of the thousands who pass through it every day, not one enlightens his neighbour left behind; but shall I not long with agony for one breath of thy air, and not receive it? shall I not be torn asunder with dying?—I will question no more: Father, into thy hands I commend my spirit. For it is thy business, not mine. Thou wilt know every shade of my suffering; thou wilt care for me with thy perfect fatherhood; for that makes my sonship, and inwraps and infolds it. As a child I could bear great pain when my father was leaning over me, or had his arm about me: how much nearer my soul cannot thy hands come!—yea, with a comfort, father of me, that I have never yet even imagined; for how shall my imagination overtake thy swift heart? I care not for the pain, so long as my spirit is strong, and into thy hands I commend that spirit. If thy love, which is better than life, receive it, then surely thy tenderness will make it great."

Thus may the Human Being say with himself.

Think, brothers, think, sisters, we walk in the air of an eternal fatherhood. Every uplifting of the heart is a looking up to The Father. Graciousness and truth are around, above, beneath us, yea, *in* us. When we are least worthy, then, most tempted, hardest, unkindest, let us yet commend our spirits into his hands. Whither else dare we send them? How the earthly father would love a child who would creep into his room with angry, troubled face, and sit down at his feet, saying when asked what he wanted: "I feel so naughty, papa, and I want to get good"! Would he say to his child: "How dare you! Go away, and be good, and then come to me?" And shall we dare to think God would send us away if we came thus, and would not be pleased that we came, even if we were angry as Jonah? Would we not let all the tenderness of our nature flow forth upon such a child? And shall we dare to think that if we being evil know how to give good gifts to our children, God will not give us his own spirit when we come to ask him? Will not some heavenly dew descend cool upon the hot anger? some genial rain-drop on the dry selfishness? some glance of sunlight on the cloudy hopelessness? Bread, at least, will be given, and not a stone; water, at least, will be sure, and not vinegar mingled with gall.

Nor is there anything we can ask for ourselves that we may not ask for another. We may commend any brother, any sister, to the common fatherhood. And there will be moments when, filled with that spirit which is the Lord, nothing will ease our hearts of their love but the commending of all men, all our brothers, all our sisters, to the one Father. Nor shall we ever know that repose in the Father's hands, that rest of the Holy Sepulchre, which the Lord knew when the agony of death was over, when the storm of the world died away behind his retiring spirit, and he entered the regions where there is only life, and therefore all that is not music is silence, (for all noise comes of the conflict of Life and Death)—we shall never be able, I say, to rest in the bosom of the Father, till the fatherhood is fully revealed to us in the love of the brothers. For he cannot be our father save as he is their father; and if we do not see him and feel him as their father, we cannot know him as ours. Never shall we know him aright until we rejoice and exult for our race that he is *the* Father. He that loveth not his brother whom he hath seen, how can he love God whom he hath not seen? To rest, I say, at last, even in those hands into which the Lord commended his spirit, we must have learned already to love our neighbour as ourselves.

LOVE THY NEIGHBOUR

Thou shalt love thy neighbor as thyself.— ST
MATTHEW xxii. 39.

The original here quoted by our Lord is to be found in the words of
God to Moses, (*Leviticus* xix. 18:) *"Thou shalt not avenge, nor bear
any grudge against the children of thy people, but thou shalt love thy
neighbour as thyself: I am the Lord"* Our Lord never thought of being
original. The older the saying the better, if it utters the truth he wants
to utter. In him it becomes fact: The *Word* was made *flesh*. And so, in
the wondrous meeting of extremes, the words he spoke were no more
words, but spirit and life.

The same words are twice quoted by St Paul, and once by St James,
always in a similar mode: Love they represent as the fulfilling of the
law.

Is the converse true then? Is the fulfilling of the law love? The
apostle Paul says: "Love worketh no ill to his neighbour, therefore
love is the fulfilling of the law." Does it follow that *working no ill* is
love? Love will fulfil the law: will the law fulfil love? No, verily. If a
man keeps the law, I know he is a lover of his neighbour. But he is not
a lover because he keeps the law: he keeps the law because he is a lov-
er. No heart will be content with the law for love. The law cannot fulfil
love.

"But, at least, the law will be able to fulfil itself, though it reaches
not to love."

I do not believe it. I am certain that it is impossible to keep the law
towards one's neighbour except one loves him. The law itself is infi-
nite, reaching to such delicacies of action, that the man who tries most
will be the man most aware of defeat. We are not made for law, but for
love. Love is law, because it is infinitely more than law. It is of an al-

together higher region than law—is, in fact, the creator of law. Had it not been for love, not one of the *shall-nots* of the law would have been uttered. True, once uttered, they shew themselves in the form of justice, yea, even in the inferior and worldly forms of prudence and self-preservation; but it was love that spoke them first. Were there no love in us, what sense of justice could we have? Would not each be filled with the sense of his own wants, and be for ever tearing to himself? I do not say it is *conscious* love that breeds justice, but I do say that without love in our nature justice would never be born. For I do not call that justice which consists only in a sense of *our own* rights. True, there are poor and withered forms of love which are immeasurably below justice now; but even now they are of speechless worth, for they will grow into that which will supersede, because it will necessitate, justice.

Of what use then is the law? To lead us to Christ, the Truth,—to waken in our minds a sense of what our deepest nature, the presence, namely, of God *in* us, requires of us,—to let us know, in part by failure, that the purest effort of will of which we are capable cannot lift us up even to the abstaining from wrong to our neighbour. What man, for instance, who loves not his neighbour and yet wishes to keep the law, will dare be confident that never by word, look, tone, gesture, silence, will he bear false witness against that neighbour? What man can judge his neighbour aright save him whose love makes him refuse to judge him? Therefore are we told to love, and not judge. It is the sole justice of which we are capable, and that perfected will comprise all justice. Nay more, to refuse our neighbour love, is to do him the greatest wrong. But of this afterwards. In order to fulfil the commonest law, I repeat, we must rise into a loftier region altogether, a region that is above law, because it is spirit and life and makes the law: in order to keep the law towards our neighbour, we must love our neighbour. We are not made for law, but for grace—or for faith, to use another word so much misused. We are made on too large a scale altogether to have any pure relation to mere justice, if indeed we can say there is such a thing. It is but an abstract idea which, in reality, will not be abstracted. The law comes to make us long for the needful grace,—that is, for the divine condition, in which love is all, for God is Love.

Though the fulfilling of the law is the practical form love will take, and the neglect of it is the conviction of lovelessness; though it is the mode in which a man's *will* must begin at once to be love to his neighbour, yet, that our Lord meant by the love of our neighbour; not the fulfilling of the law towards him, but that condition of being which results in the fulfilling of the law and more, is sufficiently clear from his story of the good Samaritan. "Who is my neighbour?" said the lawyer. And the Lord taught him that every one to whom he could be or for whom he could do anything was his neighbour, therefore, that each of the race, as he comes within the touch of one tentacle of our nature, is our neighbour. Which of the inhibitions of the law is illustrated in the tale? Not one. The love that is more than law, and renders its breach impossible, lives in the endless story, coming out in active kindness, that is, the recognition of kin, of *kind*, of nighness, of *neighbourhood*; yea, in tenderness and loving-kindness— the Samaritan-heart akin to the Jew-heart, the Samaritan hands neighbours to the Jewish wounds.

Thou shalt love thy neighbour as thyself.

So direct and complete is this parable of our Lord, that one becomes almost ashamed of further talk about it. Suppose a man of the company had put the same question to our Lord that we have been considering, had said, "But I may keep the law and yet not love my neighbour," would he not have returned: "Keep thou the law thus, not in the letter, but in the spirit, that is, in the truth of action, and thou wilt soon find, O Jew, that thou lovest thy Samaritan"? And yet, when thoughts and questions arise in our minds, he desires that we should follow them. He will not check us with a word of heavenly wisdom scornfully uttered. He knows that not even his words will apply to every question of the willing soul; and we know that his spirit will reply. When we want to know more, that more will be there for us. Not every man, for instance, finds his neighbour in need of help, and he would gladly hasten the slow results of opportunity by true thinking. Thus would we be ready for further teaching from that Spirit who is the Lord.

"But how," says a man, who is willing to recognize the universal neighbourhead, but finds himself unable to fulfil the bare law towards the woman even whom he loves best,—"How am I then to rise into that higher region, that empyrean of love?" And, beginning straightway to try to love his neighbour, he finds that the empyrean of which he spoke is no more to be reached in itself than the law was to be reached in itself. As he cannot keep the law without first rising into the love of his neighbour, so he cannot love his neighbour without first rising higher still. The whole system of the universe works upon this law—the driving of things upward towards the centre. The man who will love his neighbour can do so by no immediately operative exercise of the will. It is the man fulfilled of God from whom he came and by whom he is, who alone can as himself love his neighbour who came from God too and is by God too. The mystery of individuality and consequent relation is deep as the beginnings of humanity, and the questions thence arising can be solved only by him who has, practically, at least, solved the holy necessities resulting from his origin. In God alone can man meet man. In him alone the converging lines of existence touch and cross not. When the mind of Christ, the life of the Head, courses through that atom which the man is of the slowly revivifying body, when he is alive too, then the love of the brothers is there as conscious life. From Christ through the neighbours comes the life that makes him a part of the body.

It *is* possible to love our neighbour as ourselves. Our Lord *never* spoke hyperbolically, although, indeed, that is the supposition on which many unconsciously interpret his words, in order to be able to persuade themselves that they believe them. We may see that it is possible before we attain to it; for our perceptions of truth are always in advance of our condition. True, no man can see it perfectly until he is it; but we must see it, that we may be it. A man who knows that he does not yet love his neighbour as himself may believe in such a condition, may even see that there is no other goal of human perfection, nothing else to which the universe is speeding, propelled by the Father's will. Let him labour on, and not faint at the thought that God's day is a thousand years: his millennium is likewise one day—yea, this day, for we have him, The Love, in us, working even now the far end.

But while it is true that only when a man loves God with all his heart, will he love his neighbour as himself, yet there are mingled processes in the attainment of this final result. Let us try to aid such operation of truth by looking farther. Let us suppose that the man who believes our Lord both meant what he said, and knew the truth of the matter, proceeds to endeavour obedience in this of loving his neighbour as himself. He begins to think about his neighbours generally, and he tries to feel love towards them. He finds at once that they begin to classify themselves. With some he feels no difficulty, for he loves them already, not indeed because they *are*, but because they have, by friendly qualities, by showing themselves lovable, that is loving, already, moved his feelings as the wind moves the waters, that is without any self-generated action on his part. And he feels that this is nothing much to the point; though, of course, he would be farther from the desired end if he had none such to love, and farther still if he loved none such. He recalls the words of our Lord, "If ye love them which love you, what reward have ye?" and his mind fixes upon—let us say—one of a second class, and he tries to love him. The man is no enemy—we have not come to that class of neighbours yet—but he is dull, uninteresting—in a negative way, he thinks, unlovable. What is he to do with him? With all his effort, he finds the goal as far off as ever.

Naturally, in his failure, the question arises, "Is it my duty to love him who is unlovable?"

Certainly not, if he is unlovable. But that is a begging of the question.

Thereupon the man falls back on the primary foundation of things, and asks—

"How, then, is the man to be loved by me? Why should I love my neighbour as myself?"

We must not answer "Because the Lord says so." It is because the Lord says so that the man is inquiring after some help to obey. No man can love his neighbour merely because the Lord says so. The Lord says so because it is right and necessary and natural, and the man wants to feel it thus right and necessary and natural. Although the Lord would be pleased with any man for doing a thing because he said it, he would show his pleasure by making the man more and more dissatisfied until he knew why the Lord had said it. He would make him see that he could not in the deepest sense—in the way the Lord loves—obey any command until he saw the reasonableness of it. Observe I do not say the man ought to put off obeying the command until he see its reasonableness: that is another thing quite, and does not lie in the scope of my present supposition. It is a beautiful thing to obey the rightful source of a command: it is a more beautiful thing to worship the radiant source of our light, and it is for the sake of obedient vision that our Lord commands us. For then our heart meets his: we see God.

Let me represent in the form of a conversation what might pass in the man's mind on the opposing sides of the question.—"Why should I love my neighbour?"

"He is the same as I, and therefore I ought to love him."

"Why? I am I. He is he."

"He has the same thoughts, feelings, hopes, sorrows, joys, as I."

"Yes; but why should I love him for that? He must mind his, I can only do with mine."

"He has the same consciousness as I have. As things look to me, so things look to him."

"Yes; but I cannot get into his consciousness, nor he into mine. I feel myself, I do not feel him. My life flows through my veins, not through his. The world shines into my consciousness, and I am not conscious of his consciousness. I wish I could love him, but I do not see why. I am an individual; he is an individual. My self must be closer to me than he can be. Two bodies keep me apart from his self. I am isolated with myself."

Now, here lies the mistake at last. While the thinker supposes a duality in himself which does not exist, he falsely judges the individuality a separation. On the contrary, it is the sole possibility and very bond of love. *Otherness* is the essential ground of affection. But in spiritual things, such a unity is pre-supposed in the very contemplation of them by the spirit of man, that wherever anything does not exist that ought to be there, the space it ought to occupy, even if but a blank, assumes the appearance of a separating gulf. The negative looks a positive. Where a man does not love, the not-loving must seem rational. For no one loves because he sees why, but because he loves. No human reason can he given for the highest necessity of divinely created existence. For reasons are always from above downwards. A man must just feel this necessity, and then questioning is over. It justifies itself. But he who has not felt has it not to argue about. He has but its phantom, which he created himself in a vain effort to understand, and which he supposes to be it. Love cannot be argued about in its absence, for there is no reflex, no symbol of it near enough to the fact of it, to admit of just treatment by the algebra of the reason or imagination. Indeed, the very talking about it raises a mist between the mind and the vision of it. But let a man once love, and all those difficulties which appeared opposed to love, will just be so many arguments for loving.

Let a man once find another who has fallen among thieves; let him be a neighbour to him, pouring oil and wine into his wounds, and binding them up, and setting him on his own beast, and paying for him at the inn; let him do all this merely from a sense of duty; let him even, in the pride of his fancied, and the ignorance of his true calling, bate no jot of his Jewish superiority; let him condescend to the very baseness of his own lowest nature; yet such will be the virtue of obeying an eternal truth even to his poor measure, of putting in actuality what he has not even seen in theory, of doing the truth even without believing it, that even if the truth does not after the deed give the faintest glimmer as truth in the man, he will yet be ages nearer the truth than before, for he will go on his way loving that Samaritan neighbour a little more than his Jewish dignity will justify. Nor will he question the reasonableness of so doing, although he may not care to spend any logic upon its support. How much more if he be a man who would love his neighbour if he could, will the higher condition unsought have been found in the action! For man is a whole; and so soon as he *unites himself* by obedient action, the truth that is in him makes itself known to him, shining from the new whole. For his action is his response to his maker's design, his individual part in the creation of himself, his yielding to the All in all, to the tides of whose harmonious cosmo-plastic life all his being thenceforward lies open for interpenetration and assimilation. When will once begins to aspire, it will soon find that action must precede feeling, that the man may know the foundation itself of feeling.

With those who recognize no authority as the ground of tentative action, a doubt, a suspicion of truth ought to be ground enough for putting it to the test.

The whole system of divine education as regards the relation of man and man, has for its end that a man should love his neighbour as himself. It is not a lesson that he can learn by itself, or a duty the obligation of which can be shown by argument, any more than the difference between right and wrong can be defined in other terms than their own. "But that difference," it may be objected, "manifests itself of itself to every mind: it is self-evident; whereas the loving of one's neighbour is *not* seen to be a primary truth; so far from it, that far the greater number of those who hope for an eternity of blessedness through him who taught it, do not really believe it to be a truth; believe, on the contrary, that the paramount obligation is to take care of one's self at much risk of forgetting one's neighbour."

But the human race generally has got as far as the recognition of right and wrong; and therefore most men are born capable of making the distinction. The race has not yet lived long enough for its latest offspring to be born with the perception of the truth of love to the neighbour. It is to be seen by the present individual only after a long reception of and submission to the education of life. And once seen, it is believed.

The whole constitution of human society exists for the express end, I say, of teaching the two truths by which man lives, Love to God and Love to Man. I will say nothing more of the mysteries of the parental relation, because they belong to the teaching of the former truth, than that we come into the world as we do, to look up to the love over us, and see in it a symbol, poor and weak, yet the best we can have or receive of the divine love[1]. And thousands more would find it easy to love God if they had not such miserable types of him in the self-seeking, impulse-driven, purposeless, faithless beings who are all they have for father and mother, and to whom their children are no dearer than her litter is to the unthinking dam. What I want to speak of now, with regard to the second great commandment, is the relation of brotherhood and sisterhood. Why does my brother come of the same father and mother? Why do I behold the helplessness and confidence of his infancy? Why is the infant laid on the knee of the child? Why do we grow up with the same nurture? Why do we behold the wonder of the sunset and the mystery of the growing moon together? Why do we share one bed, join in the same games, and attempt the same exploits? Why do we quarrel, vow revenge and silence and endless enmity, and, unable to resist the brotherhood within us, wind arm in arm and forget all within the hour? Is it not that Love may grow lord of all between him and me? Is it not that I may feel towards him what there are no words or forms of words to express— a love namely, in which the divine self rushes forth in utter self-forgetfulness to live in the contemplation of the brother—a love that is stronger than death,—glad and proud and satisfied? But if love stop there, what will be the result? Ruin to itself; loss of the brotherhood. He who loves not his brother for deeper reasons than those of a common parentage will cease to love him at all. The love that enlarges not its borders, that is not ever spreading and including, and deepening, will contract, shrivel, decay, die. I have had the sons of my mother that I may learn the universal brotherhood. For there is a bond between me and the most wretched liar that ever died for the murder he would not even confess, closer infinitely than that which springs only from having one father and mother. That we are the sons and the daughters of God born from his heart, the outcoming offspring of his love, is a bond closer than all other bonds in one. No man ever loved his own child aright who did not love him for his humanity, for his divinity, to the utter forgetting of his origin from himself. The son of my mother is indeed my brother by this greater and closer bond as well; but if I recognize that bond be-

---

[1] It might be expressed after a deeper and truer fashion by saying that, God making human affairs after his own thoughts, they are therefore such as to be the best teachers of love to him and love to our neighbour. This is an immeasurably nobler and truer manner of regarding them than as a scheme or plan invented by the divine intellect.

tween him and me at all, I recognize it for my race. True, and thank God! the greater excludes not the less; it makes all the weaker bonds stronger and truer, nor forbids that where all are brothers, some should be those of our bosom. Still my brother according to the flesh is my first neighbour, that we may be very nigh to each other, whether we will or no, while our hearts are tender, and so may learn *brotherhood*. For our love to each other is but the throbbing of the heart of the great brotherhood, and could come only from the eternal Father, not from our parents. Then my second neighbour appears, and who is he? Whom I come in contact with soever. He with whom I have any transactions, any human dealings whatever. Not the man only with whom I dine; not the friend only with whom I share my thoughts; not the man only whom my compassion would lift from some slough; but the man who makes my clothes; the man who prints my book; the man who drives me in his cab; the man who begs from me in the street, to whom, it may be, for brotherhood's sake, I must not give; yea, even the man who condescends to me. With all and each there is a chance of doing the part of a neighbour, if in no other way yet by speaking truly, acting justly, and thinking kindly. Even these deeds will help to that love which is born of righteousness. All true action clears the springs of right feeling, and lets their waters rise and flow. A man must not choose his neighbour; he must take the neighbour that God sends him. In him, whoever he be, lies, hidden or revealed, a beautiful brother. The neighbour is just the man who is next to you at the moment, the man with whom any business has brought you in contact.

Thus will love spread and spread in wider and stronger pulses till the whole human race will be to the man sacredly lovely. Drink-debased, vice-defeatured, pride-puffed, wealth-bollen, vanity-smeared, they will yet be brothers, yet be sisters, yet be God-born neighbours. Any rough-hewn semblance of humanity will at length be enough to move the man to reverence and affection. It is harder for some to learn thus than for others. There are whose first impulse is ever to repel and not to receive. But learn they may, and learn they must. Even these may grow in this grace until a countenance unknown will awake in them a yearning of affection rising to pain, because there is for it no expression, and they can only give the man to God and be still.

And now will come in all the arguments out of which the man tried in vain before to build a stair up to the sunny heights of love. "Ah brother! thou hast a soul like mine," he will say. "Out of thine eyes thou lookest, and sights and sounds and odours visit thy soul as mine, with wonder and tender comforting. Thou too lovest the faces of thy neighbours. Thou art oppressed with thy sorrows, uplifted with thy joys. Perhaps thou knowest not so well as I, that a region of gladness surrounds all thy grief, of light all thy darkness, of peace all thy tumult. Oh, my brother! I will love thee. I cannot come very near thee: I will love thee the more. It may be thou dost not love thy neighbour; it may be thou thinkest only how to get from him, how to gain by him. How lonely then must thou be! how shut up in thy poverty-stricken room, with the bare walls of thy selfishness, and the hard couch of thy unsatisfaction! I will love thee the more. Thou shalt not be alone with thyself. Thou art not me; thou art another life—a second self; therefore I can, may, and will love thee."

When once to a man the human face is the human face divine, and the hand of his neighbour is the hand of a brother, then will he understand what St Paul meant when he said, "I could wish that myself were accursed from Christ for my brethren." But he will no longer understand those who, so far from feeling the love of their neighbour an essential of their being, expect to be set free from its law in the world to come. There, at least, for the glory of God, they may limit its expansive tendencies to the narrow circle of their heaven. On its battlements of safety, they will regard hell from afar, and say to each other, "Hark! Listen to their moans. But do not weep, for they are our neighbours no more." St Paul would be wretched before the throne of God, if he thought there was one man beyond the pale of his mercy, and that as much for God's glory as for the man's sake. And what shall we say of the man Christ Jesus? Who, that loves his brother, would not, upheld by the love of Christ, and with a dim hope that in the far-off time there might be some help for him, arise from the company of the blessed, and walk down into the dismal regions of despair, to sit with the last, the only unredeemed, the Judas of his race, and be himself more blessed in the pains of hell, than in the glories of heaven? Who, in the midst of the golden harps and the white wings, knowing that one of his kind, one miserable brother in the old-world-time when men were taught to love their neighbour as themselves, was howling unheeded far below in the vaults of the creation, who, I say, would not feel that he must arise, that he had no choice, that, awful as it was, he must gird his loins, and go down into the smoke and the darkness and the fire, travelling the weary and fearful road into the far country to find his brother?—who, I mean, that had the mind of Christ, that had the love of the Father?

But it is a wild question. God is, and shall be, All in all. Father of our brothers and sisters! thou wilt not be less glorious than we, taught of Christ, are able to think thee. When thou goest into the wilderness to seek, thou wilt not come home until thou hast found. It is because we hope not for them in thee, not knowing thee, not knowing thy love, that we are so hard and so heartless to the brothers and sisters whom thou hast given us.

One word more: This love of our neighbour is the only door out of the dungeon of self, where we mope and mow, striking sparks, and rubbing phosphorescences out of the walls, and blowing our own breath in our own nostrils, instead of issuing to the fair sunlight of God, the sweet winds of the universe. The man thinks his consciousness is himself; whereas his life consisteth in the inbreathing of God, and the consciousness of the universe of truth. To have himself, to know himself, to enjoy himself, he calls life; whereas, if he would forget himself, tenfold would be his life in God and his neighbours. The region of man's life is a spiritual region. God, his friends, his neighbours, his brothers all, is the wide world in which alone his spirit can find room. Himself is his dungeon. If he feels it not now, he will yet feel it one day—feel it as a living soul would feel being prisoned in a dead body, wrapped in sevenfold cerements, and buried in a stone-ribbed vault within the last ripple of the sound of the chanting people in the church above. His life is not in knowing that he lives, but in loving all forms of life. He is made for the All, for God, who is the All, is his life. And the essential joy of his life lies abroad in the liberty of the All. His delights, like those of the Ideal Wisdom, are with the sons of men. His health is in the body of which the Son of Man is the head. The whole region of life is open to him—nay, he must live in it or perish.

Nor thus shall a man lose the consciousness of well-being. Far deeper and more complete, God and his neighbour will flash it back upon him— pure as life. No more will he agonize "with sick assay" to generate it in the light of his own decadence. For he shall know the glory of his own being in the light of God and of his brother.

But he may have begun to love his neighbour, with the hope of ere long loving him as himself, and notwithstanding start back affrighted at yet another word of our Lord, seeming to be another law yet harder than the first, although in truth it is not another, for without obedience to it the former cannot be attained unto. He has not yet learned to love his neighbour as himself whose heart sinks within him at the word, *I say unto you, Love your enemies.*

LOVE THINE ENEMY.

Ye have heard that it hath been said, Thou shalt love thy neighbour, and hate thine enemy; but I say unto you, Love your enemies, bless them that curse you, do good to them that hate you, and pray for them which despitefully use you, and persecute you; that ye may be the children of your Father which is in heaven; for he maketh his sun to rise on the evil and on the good, and sendeth rain on the just and on the unjust. For if ye love them which love you, what reward have ye? do not even the publicans the same? And if ye salute your brethren only, what do ye more than others? do not even the publicans so? Be ye therefore perfect, even as your Father which is in heaven is perfect.— St Matthew v. 43-48.

Is not this at length *too* much to expect? Will a man ever love his enemies? He may come to do good to them that hate him; but when will he pray for them that despitefully use him and persecute him? When? When he is the child of his Father in heaven. Then shall he love his neighbour as himself, even if that neighbour be his enemy. In the passage in Leviticus (xix. 18,) already referred to as quoted by our Lord and his apostles, we find the neighbour and the enemy are one. "Thou shalt not avenge, nor bear any grudge against the children of thy people, but thou shalt love thy neighbour as thyself: I am the Lord."

Look at the glorious way in which Jesus interprets the scripture that went before him. "*I am the Lord*,"—"That ye may be perfect, as your Father in heaven is perfect."

Is it then reasonable to love our enemies? God does; therefore it must be the highest reason. But is it reasonable to expect that man should become capable of doing so? Yes; on one ground: that the divine energy is at work in man, to render at length man's doing divine as his nature is. For this our Lord prayed when he said: "That they all may be one, as thou, Father, art in me, and I in thee, that they also may be one in us." Nothing could be less likely to human judgment: our Lord knows that one day it will come.

Why should we love our enemies? The deepest reason for this we cannot put in words, for it lies in the absolute reality of their being, where our enemies are of one nature with us, even of the divine nature. Into this we cannot see, save as into a dark abyss. But we can adumbrate something of the form of this deepest reason, if we let the thoughts of our heart move upon the face of the dim profound.

"Are our enemies men like ourselves?" let me begin by asking. "Yes." "Upon what ground? The ground of their enmity? The ground of the wrong they do us?" "No." "In virtue of cruelty, heartlessness, injustice, disrespect, misrepresentation?" "Certainly not. *Humanum est errare* is a truism; but it possesses, like most truisms, a latent germ of worthy truth. The very word *errare* is a sign that there is a way so truly the human that, for a man to leave it, is to *wander*. If it be human to wander, yet the wandering is not humanity. The very words *humane* and *humanity* denote some shadow of that loving-kindness which, when perfected after the divine fashion, shall include even our enemies. We do not call the offering of human sacrifices, the torturing of captives, cannibalism—humanity. Not because they do such deeds are they men. Their humanity must be deeper than those. It is in virtue of the divine essence which is in them, that pure essential humanity, that we call our enemies men and women. It is this humanity that we are to love—a something, I say, deeper altogether than and independent of the region of hate. It is the humanity that originates the claim of neighbourhead; the neighbourhood only determines the occasion of its exercise." "Is this humanity in every one of our enemies?" "Else there were nothing to love." "Is it there in very deed?—Then we *must* love it, come between us and it what may."

But how can we love a man or a woman who is cruel and unjust to us?— who sears with contempt, or cuts off with wrong every tendril we would put forth to embrace?—who is mean, unlovely, carping, uncertain, self-righteous, self-seeking, and self-admiring?—who can even sneer, the most inhuman of human faults, far worse in its essence than mere murder?

These things cannot be loved. The best man hates them most; the worst man cannot love them. But are these the man? Does a woman bear that form in virtue of these? Lies there not within the man and the woman a divine element of brotherhood, of sisterhood, a something lovely and lovable,—slowly fading, it may be,—dying away under the fierce heat of vile passions, or the yet more fearful cold of sepulchral selfishness—but there? Shall that divine something, which, once awakened to be its own holy self in the man, will loathe these unlovely things tenfold more than we loathe them now—shall this divine thing have no recognition from us? It is the very presence of this fading humanity that makes it possible for us to hate. If it were an animal only, and not a man or a woman that did us hurt, we should not hate: we should only kill. We hate the man just because we are prevented from loving him. We push over the verge of the creation—*we damn*—just because we cannot embrace. For to embrace is the necessity of our deepest being. That foiled, we hate. Instead of admonishing ourselves that there is our enchained brother, that there lies our enchanted, disfigured, scarce recognizable sister, captive of the devil, to break, how much sooner, from their bonds, that we love them!—we recoil into the hate which would fix them there; and the dearly lovable reality of them we sacrifice to the outer falsehood of Satan's incantations, thus leaving them to perish. Nay, we murder them to get rid of them, we *hate* them. Yet within the most obnoxious to our hate, lies that which, could it but show itself as it is, and as it will show itself one day, would compel from our hearts a devotion of love. It is not the unfriendly, the unlovely, that we are told to love, but the brother, the sister, who is unkind, who is unlovely. Shall we leave our brother to his desolate fate? Shall we not rather say, "With my love at least shalt thou be compassed about, for thou hast not thy own lovingness to infold thee; love shall come as near thee as it may; and when thine comes forth to meet mine, we shall be one in the indwelling God"?

Let no one say I have been speaking in a figure merely. That I have been so speaking I know. But many things which we see most vividly and certainly are more truly expressed by using a right figure, than by attempting to give them a clear outline of logical expression. My figure means a truth.

If any one say, "Do not make such vague distinctions. There is the person. Can you deny that that person is unlovely? How then can you love him?" I answer, "That person, with the evil thing cast out of him, will be yet more the *person*, for he will be his real self. The thing that now makes you dislike him is separable from him, is therefore not he, makes himself so much less himself, for it is working death in him. Now he is in danger of ceasing to be a person at all. When he is clothed and in his right mind, he will be a person indeed. You *could* not then go on hating him. Begin to love him now, and help him into the loveliness which is his. Do not hate him although you can. The personalty, I say, though clouded, besmeared, defiled with the wrong, lies deeper than the wrong, and indeed, so far as the wrong has reached it, is by the wrong injured, yea, so far, it may be, destroyed."

But those who will not acknowledge the claim of love, may yet acknowledge the claim of justice. There are who would shrink with horror from the idea of doing injustice to those, from the idea of loving whom they would shrink with equal horror. But if it is impossible, as I believe, without love to be just, much more cannot justice co-exist with hate. The pure eye for the true vision of another's claims can only go with the loving heart. The man who hates can hardly be delicate in doing justice, say to his neighbour's love, to his neighbour's predilections and peculiarities. It is hard enough to be just to our friends; and how shall our enemies fare with us? For justice demands that we shall think rightly of our neighbour as certainly as that we shall neither steal his goods nor bear false witness against him. Man is not made for justice from his fellow, but for love, which is greater than justice, and by including supersedes justice. *Mere* justice is an impossibility, a fiction of analysis. It does not exist between man and man, save relatively to human *law*. Justice to be justice must be much more than justice. Love is the law of our condition, without which we can no more render justice than a man can keep a straight line walking in the dark. The eye is not single, and the body is not full of light. No man who is even indifferent to his brother can recognize the claims which his humanity has upon him. Nay, the very indifference itself is an injustice.

I have taken for granted that the fault lies with the enemy so considered, for upon the primary rocks would I build my foundation. But the question must be put to each man by himself, "Is my neighbour indeed my enemy, or am I my neighbour's enemy, and so take him to be mine?—awful thought! Or, if he be mine, am not I his? Am I not refusing to acknowledge the child of the kingdom within his bosom, so killing the child of the kingdom within my own?" Let us claim for ourselves no more indulgence than we give to him. Such honesty will end in severity at home and clemency abroad. For we are accountable for the ill in ourselves, and have to kill it; for the good in our neighbour, and have to cherish it. He only, in the name and power of God, can kill the bad in him; we can cherish the good in him by being good to it across all the evil fog that comes between our love and his good.

Nor ought it to be forgotten that this fog is often the result of misapprehension and mistake, giving rise to all kinds of indignations, resentments, and regrets. Scarce anything about us is just as it seems, but at the core there is truth enough to dispel all falsehood and reveal life as unspeakably divine. O brother, sister, across this weary fog, dim-lighted by the faint torches of our truth-seeking, I call to the divine in thee, which is mine, not to rebuke thee, not to rouse thee, not to say "Why hatest thou me?" but to say "I love thee; in God's name I love thee." And I will wait until the true self looks out of thine eyes, and knows the true self in me.

But in the working of the Divine Love upon the race, my enemy is doomed to cease to be my enemy, and to become my friend. One flash of truth towards me would destroy my enmity at once; one hearty confession of wrong, and our enmity passes away; from each comes forth the brother who was inside the enemy all the time. For this The Truth is at work. In the faith of this, let us love the enemy now, accepting God's work in reversion, as it were; let us believe as seeing his yet invisible triumph, clasping and holding fast our brother, in defiance of the changeful wiles of the wicked enchantment which would persuade our eyes and hearts that he is not our brother, but some horrible thing, hateful and hating.

But again I must ask, What if *we* are in the wrong and do the wrong, and hate because we have injured? What then? Why, then, let us cry to God as from the throat of hell; struggle, as under the weight of a spiritual incubus; cry, as knowing the vile disease that cleaveth fast unto us; cry, as possessed of an evil spirit; cry, as one buried alive, from the sepulchre of our evil consciousness, that He would take pity upon us the chief of sinners, the most wretched and vile of men, and send some help to lift us from the fearful pit and the miry clay. Nothing will help but the Spirit proceeding from the Father and the Son, the spirit of the Father and the Brother casting out and revealing. It will be with tearing and foaming, with a terrible cry and a lying as one dead, that such a demon will go out. But what a vision will then arise in the depths of the purified soul!

"Be ye therefore perfect, even as your father which is in heaven is perfect." "Love your enemies, and ye shall be the children of the highest." It is the divine glory to forgive.

Yet a time will come when the Unchangeable will cease to forgive; when it will no more belong to his perfection to love his enemies; when he will look calmly, and have his children look calmly too, upon the ascending smoke of the everlasting torments of our strong brothers, our beautiful sisters! Nay, alas! the brothers are weak now; the sisters are ugly now!

O brother, believe it not. "O Christ!" the redeemed would cry, "where art thou, our strong Jesus? Come, our grand brother. See the suffering brothers down below! See the tormented sisters! Come, Lord of Life! Monarch of Suffering! Redeem them. For us, we will go down into the burning, and see whether we cannot at least carry through the howling flames a drop of water to cool their tongues."

Believe it not, my brother, lest it quench forgiveness in thee, and thou be not forgiven, but go down with those thy brothers to the torment; whence, if God were not better than that phantom *thou* callest God, thou shouldst *never* come out; but whence assuredly thou shalt come out when thou hast paid the uttermost farthing; when thou hast learned of God in hell what thou didst refuse to learn of him upon the gentle-toned earth; what the sunshine and the rain could not teach thee, nor the sweet compunctions of the seasons, nor the stately visitings of the morn and the eventide, nor the human face divine, nor the word that was nigh thee in thy heart and in thy mouth—the story of Him who was mighty to save, because he was perfect in love.

O Father, thou art All-in-all, perfect beyond the longing of thy children, and we are all and altogether thine. Thou wilt make us pure and loving and free. We shall stand fearless in thy presence, because perfect in thy love. Then shall thy children be of good cheer, infinite in the love of each other, and eternal in thy love. Lord Jesus, let the heart of a child be given to us, that so we may arise from the grave of our dead selves and die no more, but see face to face *the God of the Living*.

THE GOD OF THE LIVING.

He is not a God of the dead, but of the living: for all live unto him.— ST LUKE xx. 38.

It is a recurring cause of perplexity in our Lord's teaching, that he is too simple for us; that while we are questioning with ourselves about the design of Solomon's earring upon some gold-plated door of the temple, he is speaking about the foundations of Mount Zion, yea, of the earth itself, upon which it stands. If the reader of the Gospel supposes that our Lord was here using a verbal argument with the Sadducees, namely, "I *am* the God of Abraham, Isaac, and Jacob; therefore they *are*," he will be astonished that no Sadducee was found with courage enough to reply: "All that God meant was to introduce himself to Moses as the same God who had aided and protected his fathers while they were alive, saying, I am he that was the God of thy fathers. They found me faithful. Thou, therefore, listen to me, and thou too shalt find me faithful unto the death."

But no such reply suggested itself even to the Sadducees of that day, for their eastern nature could see argument beyond logic. Shall God call himself the God of the dead, of those who were alive once, but whom he either could not or would not keep alive? Is that the Godhood, and its relation to those who worship it? The changeless God of an ever-born and ever-perishing torrent of life; of which each atom cries with burning heart, *My God*! and straightway passes into the Godless cold! "Trust in me, for I took care of your fathers once upon a time, though they are gone now. Worship and obey me, for I will be good to you for threescore years and ten, or thereabouts; and after that, when you are not, and the world goes on all the same without you, I will call myself your God still." God changes not. Once God he is always God. If he has once said to a man, "I am thy God, and that

man has died the death of the Sadducee's creed," then we have a right
to say that God is the God of the dead.

"And wherefore should he not be so far the God of the dead, if dur-
ing the time allotted to them here, he was the faithful God of the
living?" What Godlike relation can the ever-living, life-giving,
changeless God hold to creatures who partake not of his life, who have
death at the very core of their being, are not worth their Maker's keep-
ing alive? To let his creatures die would be to change, to abjure his
Godhood, to cease to be that which he had made himself. If they are
not worth keeping alive, then his creating is a poor thing, and he is not
so great, nor so divine as even the poor thoughts of those his dying
creatures have been able to imagine him. But our Lord says, "All live
unto him." With Him death is not. Thy life sees our life, O Lord. All of
whom *all* can be said, are present to thee. Thou thinkest about us, eter-
nally more than we think about thee. The little life that burns within
the body of this death, glows unquenchable in thy true-seeing eyes. If
thou didst forget us for a moment then indeed death would be. But un-
to thee we live. The beloved pass from our sight, but they pass not
from thine. This that we call death, is but a form in the eyes of men. It
looks something final, an awful cessation, an utter change. It seems
not probable that there is anything beyond. But if God could see us
before we were, and make us after his ideal, that we shall have passed
from the eyes of our friends can be no argument that he beholds us no
longer. "All live unto Him." Let the change be ever so great, ever so
imposing; let the unseen life be ever so vague to our conception, it is
not against reason to hope that God could see Abraham, after his Isaac
had ceased to see him; saw Isaac after Jacob ceased to see him; saw
Jacob after some of the Sadducees had begun to doubt whether there
ever had been a Jacob at all. He remembers them; that is, he carries
them in his mind: he of whom God thinks, lives. He takes to himself
the name of *Their God*. The Living One cannot name himself after the
dead; when the very Godhead lies in the giving of life. Therefore they
must be alive. If he speaks of them, remembers his own loving
thoughts of them, would he not have kept them alive if he could; and if
he could not, how could he create them? Can it be an easier thing to
call into life than to keep alive?

"But if they live to God, they are aware of God. And if they are
aware of God, they are conscious of their own being: Whence then the
necessity of a resurrection?"

For their relation to others of God's children in mutual revelation;
and for fresh revelation of God to all.—But let us inquire what is

meant by the resurrection of the body. "With what body do they come?"

Surely we are not required to believe that the same body is raised again. That is against science, common sense, Scripture. St Paul represents the matter quite otherwise. One feels ashamed of arguing such a puerile point. Who could wish his material body which has indeed died over and over again since he was born, never remaining for one hour composed of the same matter, its endless activity depending upon its endless change, to be fixed as his changeless possession, such as it may then be, at the moment of death, and secured to him in worthless identity for the ages to come? A man's material body will be to his consciousness at death no more than the old garment he throws aside at night, intending to put on a new and a better in the morning. To desire to keep the old body seems to me to argue a degree of sensual materialism excusable only in those pagans who in their Elysian fields could hope to possess only such a thin, fleeting, dreamy, and altogether funebrial existence, that they might well long for the thicker, more tangible bodily being in which they had experienced the pleasures of a tumultuous life on the upper world. As well might a Christian desire that the hair which has been shorn from him through all his past life should be restored to his risen and glorified head.

Yet not the less is the doctrine of the Resurrection gladdening as the sound of the silver trumpet of its visions, needful as the very breath of life to our longing souls. Let us know what it means, and we shall see that it is thus precious.

Let us first ask what is the use of this body of ours. It is the means of Revelation to us, the *camera* in which God's eternal shows are set forth. It is by the body that we come into contact with Nature, with our fellow-men, with all their revelations of God to us. It is through the body that we receive all the lessons of passion, of suffering, of love, of beauty, of science. It is through the body that we are both trained outwards from ourselves, and driven inwards into our deepest selves to find God. There is glory and might in this vital evanescence, this slow glacier-like flow of clothing and revealing matter, this ever uptossed rainbow of tangible humanity. It is no less of God's making than the spirit that is clothed therein.

We cannot yet have learned all that we are meant to learn through the body. How much of the teaching even of this world can the most diligent and most favoured man have exhausted before he is called to leave it! Is all that remains to be lost? Who that has loved this earth can but believe that the spiritual body of which St Paul speaks will be a yet higher channel of such revelation? The meek who have found that their Lord spake true, and have indeed inherited the earth, who have seen that all matter is radiant of spiritual meaning, who would not cast a sigh after the loss of mere animal pleasure, would, I think, be the least willing to be without a body, to be unclothed without being again clothed upon. Who, after centuries of glory in heaven, would not rejoice to behold once more that patient-headed child of winter and spring, the meek snowdrop? In whom, amidst the golden choirs, would not the vision of an old sunset wake such a song as the ancient dwellers of the earth would with gently flattened palm hush their throbbing harps to hear?

All this revelation, however, would render only *a* body necessary, not this body. The fulness of the word *Resurrection* would be ill met if this were all. We need not only a body to convey revelation to us, but a body to reveal us to others. The thoughts, feelings, imaginations which arise in us, must have their garments of revelation whereby shall be made manifest the unseen world within us to our brothers and sisters around us; else is each left in human loneliness. Now, if this be one of the uses my body served on earth before, the new body must be like the old. Nay, it must be the same body, glorified as we are glorified, with all that was distinctive of each from his fellows more visible than ever before. The accidental, the nonessential, the unrevealing, the incomplete will have vanished. That which made the body what it was in the eyes of those who loved us will be tenfold there. Will not this be the resurrection of the body? of the same body though not of the same dead matter? Every eye shall see the beloved, every heart will cry, "My own again!—more mine because more himself than ever I beheld him!" For do we not say on earth, "He is not himself to-day," or "She looks her own self;" "She is more like herself than I have seen her for long"? And is not this when the heart is glad and the face is radiant? For we carry a better likeness of our friends in our hearts than their countenances, save at precious seasons, manifest to us.

Who will dare to call anything less than this a resurrection? Oh, how the letter killeth! There are who can believe that the dirt of their bodies will rise the same as it went down to the friendly grave, who yet doubt if they will know their friends when they rise again. And they call *that* believing in the resurrection!

What! shall a man love his neighbour as himself, and must he be content not to know him in heaven? Better be content to lose our consciousness, and know ourselves no longer. What! shall God be the God of the families of the earth, and shall the love that he has thus created towards father and mother, brother and sister, wife and child, go moaning and longing to all eternity; or worse, far worse, die out of our bosoms? Shall God be God, and shall this be the end?

Ah, my friends! what will resurrection or life be to me, how shall I continue to love God as I have learned to love him through you, if I find he cares so little for this human heart of mine, as to take from me the gracious visitings of your faces and forms? True, I might have a gaze at Jesus, now and then; but he would not be so good as I had thought him. And how should I see him if I could not see you? God will not take you, has not taken you from me to bury you out of my sight in the abyss of his own unfathomable being, where I cannot follow and find you, myself lost in the same awful gulf. No, our God is an unveiling, a revealing God. He will raise you from the dead, that I may behold you; that that which vanished from the earth may again stand forth, looking out of the same eyes of eternal love and truth, holding out the same mighty hand of brotherhood, the same delicate and gentle, yet strong hand of sisterhood, to me, this me that knew you and loved you in the days gone by. I shall not care that the matter of the forms I loved a thousand years ago has returned to mingle with the sacred goings on of God's science, upon that far-off world wheeling its nursery of growing loves and wisdoms through space; I shall not care that the muscle which now sends the ichor through your veins is not formed of the very particles which once sent the blood to the pondering brain, the flashing eye, or the nervous right arm; I shall not care, I say, so long as it is yourselves that are before me, beloved; so long as through these forms I know that I look on my own, on my loving souls of the ancient time; so long as my spirits have got garments of revealing after their own old lovely fashion, garments to reveal themselves to me. The new shall then be dear as the old, and for the same reason, that it reveals the old love. And in the changes which, thank God, must take place when the mortal puts on immortality, shall we not feel that the nobler our friends are, the more they are themselves; that the more the idea of each is carried out in the perfection of beauty, the more like they are to what we thought them in our most exalted moods, to that which we saw in them in the rarest moments of profoundest communion, to that which we beheld through the veil of all their imperfections when we loved them the truest?

Lord, evermore give us this Resurrection, like thine own in the body of thy Transfiguration. Let us see and hear, and know, and be seen, and heard, and known, as thou seest, hearest, and knowest. Give us glorified bodies through which to reveal the glorified thoughts which shall then inhabit us, when not only shalt thou reveal God, but each of us shall reveal thee.

And for this, Lord Jesus, come thou, the child, the obedient God, that we may be one with thee, and with every man and woman whom thou hast made, in the Father.

END OF FIRST SERIES

UNSPOKEN SERMONS SERIES TWO

THESE ALSO AFTER EIGHTEEN YEARS TO MY WIFE

CORAGGIO, BORDIGHERA
January 1885

THE WAY.

'If thou wouldest be perfect.'—ST. MATTHEW xix 21.

For reasons many and profound, amongst the least because of the fragmentary nature of the records, he who would read them without the candle of the Lord—that is, the light of truth in his inward parts—must not merely fall into a thousand errors—a thing for such a one of less moment—but must fail utterly of perceiving and understanding the life therein struggling to reveal itself—the life, that is, of the Son of Man, the thought, the feeling, the intent of the Lord himself, that by which he lived, that which is himself, that which he poured out for us. Yet the one thing he has to do with is this life of Jesus, his inner nature and being, manifested through his outer life, according to the power of sight in the spiritual eye that looks thereupon.

In contemplating the incident revealing that life of which I would now endeavour to unfold the truth, my readers who do not *study* the Greek Testament must use the revised version. Had I not known and rejoiced in it long before the revision appeared, I should have owed the revisers endless gratitude, if for nothing more than the genuine reading of St. Matthew's report of the story of the youth who came to our Lord. Whoever does not welcome the change must fail to see its preciousness.

Reading then from the revised version, we find in St. Matthew the commencement of the conversation between Jesus and the young man very different from that given in the Gospels of St. Mark and St. Luke. There is not for that the smallest necessity for rejecting either account; they blend perfectly, and it is to me a joy unspeakable to have both. Put together they give a completed conversation. Here it is as I read it;

let my fellow students look to the differing, far from opposing, reports, and see how naturally they combine.

'Good Master,' said the kneeling youth, and is interrupted by the Master:—

'Why callest thou me good?' he returns. 'None is good save one, even

God.'

Daring no reply to this, the youth leaves it, and betakes himself to his object in addressing the Lord.

'What good thing shall I do,' he says, 'that I may have eternal life?'

But again the Lord takes hold of the word *good*:—

'Why askest thou me concerning that which is good?' he rejoins. 'One there is who is good.—But if thou wouldest enter into life, keep the commandments.'

'Which?'

'Thou shalt not kill, Thou shalt not commit adultery, Thou shalt not steal, Thou shalt not bear false witness, Honour thy father and thy mother; and, Thou shalt love thy neighbour as thyself.'

'All these things have I observed: what lack I yet?'

'If thou wouldest be perfect, go, sell that thou hast, and give to the poor, and thou shalt have treasure in heaven; and come, follow me.'

Let us regard the story.

As Jesus went out of a house (see St. Mark x. 10 and 17), the young man came running to him, and kneeling down in the way, addressed him as 'Good Master.'

The words with which the Lord interrupts his address reveal the whole attitude of the Lord's being. At that moment, at every and each moment, just as much as when in the garden of Gethsemane, or encountering any of those hours which men call crises of life, his whole thought, his whole delight, was in the thought, in the will, in the being of his Father. The joy of the Lord's life, that which made it life to him, was the Father; of him he was always thinking, to him he was always turning. I suppose most men have some thought of pleasure or satisfaction or strength to which they turn when action pauses, life becomes for a moment still, and the wheel sleeps on its own swiftness: with Jesus it needed no pause of action, no rush of renewed consciousness, to send him home; his thought was ever and always his Father. To its home in the heart of the Father his heart ever turned. That was his treasure-house, the jewel of his mind, the mystery of his gladness, claiming all degrees and shades of delight, from peace and calmest content to ecstasy. His life was hid in God. No vain show could enter at his eyes; every truth and grandeur of life passed before him as it was; neither ambition nor disappointment could distort them to his eternal childlike gaze; he beheld and loved them from the bosom of the Father. It was not for himself he came to the world—not to establish his own power over the doings, his own influence over the hearts of men: he came that they might know the Father who was his joy, his life. The sons of men were his Father's children like himself: that the Father should have them all in his bosom was the one thought of his heart: that should be his doing for his Father, cost him what it might! He came to do his will, and on the earth was the same he had been from the beginning, the eternal first. He was not interested in himself, but in his Father and his Father's children. He did not care to hear himself called good. It was not of consequence to him. He was there to let men see the goodness of the Father in whom he gloried. For that he entered the weary dream of the world, in which the glory was so dulled and clouded. 'You call *me* good! You should know my Father!'

For the Lord's greatness consisted in his Father being greater than he: who calls into being is greater than who is called. The Father was always the Father, the Son always the Son; yet the Son is not of himself, but by the Father; he does not live by his own power, like the Father. If there were no Father, there would be no Son. All that is the Lord's is the Father's, and all that is the Father's he has given to the Son. The Lord's goodness is of the Father's goodness; because the Father is good the Son is good. When the word *good* enters the ears of the Son, his heart lifts it at once to his Father, the Father of all. His words contain no denial of goodness in himself: in his grand self- regard he was not the original of his goodness, neither did he care for his own goodness, except to be good: it was to him a matter of course. But for his Father's goodness, he would spend life, suffering, labour, death, to make that known! His other children must learn to give him his due, and love him as did the primal Son! The Father was all in all to the Son, and the Son no more thought of his own goodness than an honest man thinks of his honesty. When the good man sees goodness, he thinks of his own evil: Jesus had no evil to think of, but neither does he think of his goodness; he delights in his Father's. 'Why callest thou me good? None is good save one, even God.'

Checked thus, the youth turns to the question which, working in his heart, had brought him running, and made him kneel: what good thing shall he do that he may have eternal life? It is unnecessary to inquire precisely what he meant by *eternal life*. Whatever shape the thing took to him, that shape represented a something he needed and had not got—a something which, it was clear to him, could be gained only in some path of good. But he thought to gain a thing by a doing, when the very thing desired was *a being*: he would have that as a possession which must possess him.

The Lord cared neither for isolated truth nor for orphaned deed. It was truth in the inward parts, it was the good heart, the mother of good deeds, he cherished. It was the live, active, knowing, breathing good he came to further. He cared for no speculation in morals or religion. It was good men he cared about, not notions of good things, or even good actions, save as the outcome of life, save as the bodies in which the primary live actions of love and will in the soul took shape and came forth. Could he by one word have set at rest all the questionings of philosophy as to the supreme good and the absolute truth, I venture to say that word he would not have uttered. But he would die to make men good and true. His whole heart would respond to the cry of sad publican or despairing pharisee, 'How am I to be good?'

When the Lord says, 'Why askest thou me concerning that which is good?' we must not put emphasis on the *me*, as if the Lord refused the question, as he had declined the epithet: he was the proper person to ask, only the question was not the right one: the good thing was a small matter; the good Being was all in all[1]. 'Why ask me about the good thing? There is one living good, in whom the good thing, and all good, is alive and ever operant. Ask me not about the good thing, but the good person, the good being—the origin of all good'—who, because he is, can make good. He is the one live good, ready with his life to communicate living good, the power of being, and so doing good, for he makes good itself to exist. It is not with this good thing and that good thing we have to do, but with that power whence comes our power even to speak the word *good*. We have to do with him to whom no one can look without the need of being good waking up in his heart; to think about him is to begin to be good. To do a good thing is to do a good thing; to know God is to be good. It is not to make us do all things right he cares, but to make us hunger and thirst after a righteousness possessing which we shall never need to think of what is or is not good, but shall refuse the evil and choose the good by a motion of

---

[1] As it stands, it is difficult to read the passage without putting emphasis on the *me*, which spoils the sense. I think it would better be, 'Why dost thou ask me concerning &c.?'

the will which is at once necessity and choice. You see again he refers him immediately as before to his Father.

But I am anxious my reader should not mistake. Observe, the question in the young man's mind is not about the doing or not doing of something he knows to be right; had such been the case, the Lord would have permitted no question at all; the one thing he insists upon is the *doing* of the thing we know we ought to do. In the instance present, the youth looking out for some unknown good thing to do, he sends him back to the doing of what he knows, and that in answer to his question concerning the way to eternal life.

A man must have something to do in the matter, and may well ask such a question of any teacher! The Lord does not for a moment turn away from it, and only declines the form of it to help the youth to what he really needs. He has, in truth, already more than hinted where the answer lies, namely, in God himself, but that the youth is not yet capable of receiving; he must begin with him farther back: 'If thou wouldest enter into life, keep the commandments;'—for verily, if the commandments have nothing to do with entering into life, why were they ever given to men? This is his task—he must keep the commandments.

Then the road to eternal life is the keeping of the commandments! Had the Lord *not* said so, what man of common moral sense would ever dare say otherwise? What else can be the way into life but the doing of what the Lord of life tells the creatures he has made, and whom he would have live for ever, that they must do? It is the beginning of the way. If a man had kept all those commandments, yet would he not therefore have in him the life eternal; nevertheless, without keeping of the commandments there is no entering into life; the keeping of them is the path to the gate of life; it is not life, but it is the way—so much of the way to it. Nay, the keeping of the commandments, consciously or unconsciously, has closest and essential relation to eternal life.

The Lord says nothing about the first table of the law: why does he not tell this youth as he did the lawyer, that to love God is everything?

He had given him a glimpse of the essence of his own life, had pointed the youth to the heart of all—for him to think of afterwards: he was not ready for it yet. He wanted eternal life: to love God with all our heart, and soul, and strength, and mind, is to know God, and to know him *is* eternal life; that is the end of the whole saving matter; it is no human beginning, it is the grand end and eternal beginning of all things; but the youth was not capable of it. To begin with that would be as sensible as to say to one asking how to reach the top of some mountain, 'Just set your foot on that shining snow-clad peak, high there in the blue, and you will at once be where you wish to go.' 'Love God with all your heart, and eternal life is yours:'—it would have been to mock him. Why, he could not yet see or believe that that was eternal life! He was not yet capable of looking upon life even from afar! How many *Christians* are? How many know that they are not? How many care that they are not? The Lord answers his question directly, tells him what to do—a thing he can do—to enter into life: he must keep the commandments!—and when he asks, 'Which?' specifies only those that have to do with his neighbour, ending with the highest and most difficult of them.

'But no man can perfectly keep a single commandment of the second table any more than of the first.'

Surely not—else why should they have been given? But is there no meaning in the word *keep*, or *observe*, except it be qualified by *perfectly*? Is there no keeping but a perfect keeping?

'None that God cares for.'

There I think you utterly wrong. That no keeping but a perfect one will *satisfy* God, I hold with all my heart and strength; but that there is none else he cares for, is one of the lies of the enemy. What father is not pleased with the first tottering attempt of his little one to walk? What father would be satisfied with anything but the manly step of the full-grown son?

When the Lord has definitely mentioned the commandments he means, the youth returns at once that he *has* observed those from his youth up: are we to take his word for it? The Lord at least takes his word for it: he looked on him and loved him. Was the Lord deceived in him? Did he tell an untruth? or did the Master believe he had kept the commandments perfectly? There must be a keeping of the commandments, which, although anything but perfect, is yet acceptable to the heart of him from whom nothing is hid. In that way the youth had kept the commandments. He had for years been putting forth something of his life-energy to keep them. Nor, however he had failed of perfection, had he missed the end for which they were given him to keep. For the immediate end of the commandments never was that men should succeed in obeying them, but that, finding they could not do that which yet must be done, finding the more they tried the more was required of them, they should be driven to the source of life and law—of their life and his law—to seek from him such reinforcement of life as should make the fulfilment of the law as possible, yea, as natural, as necessary. This result had been wrought in the youth. His observance had given him no satisfaction; he was not at rest; but he desired eternal life—of which there was no word in the law: the keeping of the law had served to develop a hunger which no law or its keeping could fill. Must not the imperfection of his keeping of the commandments, even in the lower sense in which he read them, have helped to reveal how far they were beyond any keeping of his, how their implicit demands rose into the infinitude of God's perfection?

Having kept the commandments, the youth needed and was ready for a further lesson: the Lord would not leave him where he was; he had come to seek and to save. He saw him in sore need of perfection—the thing the commonplace Christian thinks he can best do without—the thing the elect hungers after with an eternal hunger. Perfection, the perfection of the Father, is eternal life. 'If thou wouldest be perfect,' said the Lord. What an honour for the youth to be by him supposed desirous of perfection! And what an enormous demand does he, upon the supposition, make of him! To gain the perfection he desired, the one thing lacking was, that he should sell all that he had, give it to the poor, and follow the Lord! Could this be all that lay between him and entering into life? God only knows what the victory of such an obedience might at once have wrought in him! Much, much more would be necessary before perfection was reached, but certainly the next step, to sell and follow, would have been the step into life: had he taken it, in the very act would have been born in him that whose essence and vitality is eternal life, needing but process to develop it into the glorious consciousness of oneness with The Life.

There was nothing like this in the law: was it not hard?—Hard to let earth go, and take heaven instead? for eternal life, to let dead things drop? to turn his hack on Mammon, and follow Jesus? lose his rich friends, and he of the Master's household? Let him say it was hard who does not know the Lord, who has never thirsted after righteousness, never longed for the life eternal!

The youth had got on so far, was so pleasing in the eyes of the Master, that he would show him the highest favour he could; he would take him to be with him—to walk with him, and rest with him, and go from him only to do for him what he did for his Father in heaven—to plead with men, he a mediator between God and men. He would set him free at once, a child of the kingdom, an heir of the life eternal.

I do not suppose that the youth was one whom ordinary people would call a lover of money; I do not believe he was covetous, or desired even the large increase of his possessions; I imagine he was just like most good men of property: he valued his possessions—looked on them as a good. I suspect that in the case of another, he would have regarded such possession almost as a merit, a desert; would value a man more who had *means*, value a man less who had none—like most of my readers. They have not a notion how entirely they will one day have to alter their judgment, or have it altered for them, in this respect: well for them if they alter it for themselves!

From this false way of thinking, and all the folly and unreality that accompany it, the Lord would deliver the young man. As the thing was, he was a slave; for a man is in bondage to what ever he cannot part with that is less than himself. He could have taken his possessions from him by an exercise of his own will, but there would have been little good in that; he wished to do it by the exercise of the young man's will: that would be a victory indeed for both! So would he enter into freedom and life, delivered from the bondage of mammon by the lovely will of the Lord in him, one with his own. By the putting forth of the divine energy in him, he would escape the corruption that is in the world through lust—that is, the desire or pleasure of *having*.

The young man would not.

Was the Lord then premature in his demand on the youth? Was he not ready for it? Was it meant for a test, and not as an actual word of deliverance? Did he show the child a next step on the stair too high for him to set his foot upon? I do not believe it. He gave him the very next lesson in the divine education for which he was ready. It was possible for him to respond, to give birth, by obedience, to the redeemed and redeeming will, and so be free. It was time the demand should be made upon him. Do you say, 'But he would not respond, he would not obey!'? Then it was time, I answer, that he should refuse, that he should know what manner of spirit he was of, and meet the confusions of soul, the sad searchings of heart that must follow. A time comes to every man when he must obey, or make such refusal—*and know it*.

Shall I then be supposed to mean that the refusal of the young man was of necessity final? that he was therefore lost? that because he declined to enter into life the door of life was closed against him? Verily, I have not so learned Christ. And that the lesson was not lost, I see in this, that he went away sorrowful. Was such sorrow, in the mind of an earnest youth, likely to grow less or to grow more? Was all he had gone through in the way of obedience to be of no good to him? Could the nature of one who had kept the commandments be so slight that, after having sought and talked with Jesus, held communion with him who is the Life, he would care less about eternal life than before?

Many, alas! have looked upon his face, yet have never seen him, and have turned back; some have kept company with him for years, and denied him; but their weakness is not the measure of the patience or the resources of God. Perhaps this youth was never one of the Lord's so long as he was on the earth, but perhaps when he saw that the Master himself cared nothing for the wealth he had told him to cast away, that, instead of ascending the throne of his fathers, he let the people do with him what they would, and left the world the poor man he had lived in it, by its meanest door, perhaps then he became one of those who sold all they had, and came and laid the money at the apostles' feet. In the meantime he had that in his soul which made it heavy: by the gravity of his riches the world held him, and would not let him rise. He counted his weight his strength, and it was his weakness. Moneyless in God's upper air he would have had power indeed. Money is the power of this world—power for defeat and failure to him who holds it—a weakness to be overcome ere a man can be strong; yet many decent people fancy it a power of the world to come! It is indeed a little power, as food and drink, as bodily strength, as the winds and the waves are powers; but it is no mighty thing for the redemption of men; yea, to the redemption of those who have it, it is the saddest obstruction. To make this youth capable of eternal life, clearly—and the more clearly that he went away sorrowful—the first thing was to make a poor man of him! He would doubtless have gladly devoted his wealth to the service of the Master, yea, and gone with him, *as a rich man*, to spend it for him. But part with it to free him for his service— that he could not—*yet*!

And how now would he go on with his keeping of the commandments? Would he not begin to see more plainly his shortcomings, the larger scope of their requirements? Might he not feel the keeping of them more imperative than ever, yet impossible without something he had not? The commandments can never be kept while there is a strife to keep them: the man is overwhelmed in the weight of their broken pieces. It needs a clean heart to have pure hands, all the power of a live soul to keep the law—a power of life, not of struggle; the strength of love, not the effort of duty.

One day the truth of his conduct must dawn upon him with absolute clearness. Bitter must be the discovery. He had refused the life eternal! had turned his back upon The Life! In deepest humility and shame, yet with the profound consolation of repentance, he would return to the Master and bemoan his unteachableness. There are who, like St. Paul, can say, 'I did wrong, but I did it in ignorance; my heart was not right,

and I did not know it:' the remorse of such must be very different from
that of one who, brought to the point of being capable of embracing
the truth, turned from it and refused to be set free. To him the time will
come, God only knows its hour, when he will see the nature of his
deed, *with the knowledge that he was dimly seeing it so even when he
did it*: the alternative had been put before him. And all those months,
or days, or hours, or moments, he might have been following the Mas-
ter, hearing the words he spoke, through the windows of his eyes
looking into the very gulfs of Godhead!

The sum of the matter in regard to the youth is this:—He had begun
early to climb the eternal stair. He had kept the commandments, and
by every keeping had climbed. But because he was *well to do*—a
phrase of unconscious irony—he felt well to be—quite, but for that
lack of eternal life! His possessions gave him a standing in the
world—a position of consequence—of value in his eyes. He knew
himself looked up to; he liked to be looked up to; he looked up to him-
self because of his *means*, forgetting that *means* are but tools, and poor
tools too. To part with his wealth would be to sink to the level of his
inferiors! Why should he not keep it? why not use it in the service of
the Master? What wisdom could there be in throwing away such a
grand advantage? He could devote it, but he could not cast it from
him! He could devote it, but he could not devote himself! He could not
make himself naked as a little child and let his Father take him! To
him it was not the word of wisdom the 'Good Master' spoke. How
could precious money be a hindrance to entering into life! How could
a rich man believe he would be of more value without his money? that
the casting of it away would make him one of God's Anakim? that the
battle of God could be better fought without its impediment? that his
work refused as an obstruction the aid of wealth? But the Master had
repudiated money that he might do the will of his Father; and the dis-
ciple must be as his master. Had he done as the Master told him, he
would soon have come to understand. Obedience is the opener of eyes.

There is this danger to every good youth in keeping the command-
ments, that he will probably think of himself more highly than he
ought to think. He may be correct enough as to the facts, and in his
deductions, and consequent self-regard, be anything but fair. He may
think himself a fine fellow, when he is but an ordinarily reasonable
youth, trying to do but the first thing necessary to the name or honour
of a man. Doubtless such a youth is exceptional among youths; but the
number of fools not yet acknowledging the first condition of manhood
nowise alters the fact that he who has begun to recognize duty, and

acknowledge the facts of his being, is but a tottering child on the path of life. He is on the path; he is as wise as at the time he can be; the Father's arms are stretched out to receive him; but he is not therefore a wonderful being; not therefore a model of wisdom; not at all the admirable creature his largely remaining folly would, in his worst moments, that is when he feels best, persuade him to think himself; he is just one of God's poor creatures. What share this besetting sin of the *good young man* may have had in the miserable failure of this one, we need not inquire; but it may well be that he thought the Master under-valued his work as well as his wealth, and was less than fair to him.

To return to the summing up of the matter:—

The youth, climbing the stair of eternal life, had come to a landing-place where not a step more was visible. On the cloud-swathed platform he stands looking in vain for further ascent. What he thought with himself he wanted, I cannot tell: his idea of eternal life I do not know; I can hardly think it was but the poor idea of living for ever, all that commonplace minds grasp at for eternal life—its mere concomitant shadow, in itself not worth thinking about, not for a moment to be disputed, and taken for granted by all devout Jews: when a man has eternal life, that is, when he is one with God, what should he do but live for ever? without oneness with God, the continuance of existence would be to me the all but unsurpassable curse—the unsurpassable itself being, a God other than the God I see in Jesus; but whatever his idea, it must have held in it, though perhaps only in solution, all such notions as he had concerning God and man and a common righteousness. While thus he stands, then, alone and helpless, behold the form of the Son of Man! It is God himself come to meet the climbing youth, to take him by the hand, and lead him up his own stair, the only stair by which ascent can be made. He shows him the first step of it through the mist. His feet are heavy; they have golden shoes. To go up that stair he must throw aside his shoes. He must walk bare- footed into life eternal. Rather than so, rather than stride free- limbed up the everlasting stair to the bosom of the Father, he will keep his precious shoes! It is better to drag them about on the earth, than part with them for a world where they are useless!

But how miserable his precious things, his golden vessels, his embroidered garments, his stately house, must have seemed when he went back to them from the face of the Lord! Surely it cannot have been long before in shame and misery he cast all from him, even as Judas cast from him the thirty pieces of silver, in the agony of every one who wakes to the fact that he has preferred money to the Master!

For, although never can man be saved without being freed from his possessions, it is yet only *hard*, not impossible, *for a rich man to enter into the kingdom of God.*

THE HARDNESS OF THE WAY.

"Children, how hard is it!"— St. Mark x. 24.

I suspect there is scarcely a young man rich and thoughtful who is not ready to feel our Lord's treatment of this young man hard. He is apt to ask, "Why should it be difficult for a rich man to enter into the kingdom of heaven?" He is ready to look upon the natural fact as an arbitrary decree, arising, shall I say? from some prejudice in the divine mind, or at least from some objection to the joys of well-being, as re-garded from the creatures' side. Why should the rich fare differently from other people in respect of the world to come? They do not per-ceive that the law is they *shall* fare like other people, whereas they want to fare as rich people. A condition of things in which it would be easy for a rich man to enter into the kingdom of heaven is to me in-conceivable. There is no kingdom of this world into which a rich man may not easily enter—in which, if he be but rich enough, he may not be the first: a kingdom into which it would be easy for a rich man to enter could be no kingdom of heaven. The rich man does not by any necessity of things belong to the kingdom of Satan, but into that king-dom he is especially welcome, whereas into the kingdom of heaven he will be just as welcome as another man.

I suspect also that many a rich man turns from the record of this in-cident with the resentful feeling that there lies in it a claim upon his whole having; while there are many, and those by no means only of the rich, who cannot believe the Lord really meant to take the poor fellow's money from him. To the man born to riches they seem not merely a natural, but an essential condition of well-being; and the man who has *made* his money, feels it his by the labour of his soul, the travail of the day, and the care of the night. Each feels a right to have and to hold the things he possesses; and if there is a necessity for his entering into the kingdom of heaven, it is hard indeed that right and necessity should confront each other, and constitute all but a bare impossibility! Why should he not 'make the best of both worlds'? He would compromise, if he might; he would serve Mammon a little, and God much. He would not have such a 'best of both worlds' as comes of putting the lower in utter subservience to the higher—of casting away the treasure of this world and taking the treasure of heaven instead. He would gain as little as may be of heaven—but something, with the loss of as little as possible of the world. That which he desires of heaven is not its best; that which he would not yield of the world is its most worthless.

I can well imagine an honest youth, educated in Christian forms, thus reasoning with himself:—'Is the story of general relation? Is this demand made upon me? If I make up my mind to be a Christian, shall I be required to part with all I possess? It must have been comparatively easy in those times to give up the kind of things they had! If I had been he, I am sure I should have done it—at the demand of the Saviour in person. Things are very different now! Wealth did not then imply the same social relations as now! I should be giving up so much more! Neither do I love money as he was in danger of doing: in all times the Jews have been Mammon-worshippers! I try to do good with my money! Besides, am I not a Christian already? Why should the same thing be required of me as of a young Jew? If every one who, like me, has a conscience about money, and cares to use it well, had to give up all, the power would at once be in the hands of the irreligious; they would have no opposition, and the world would go to the devil! We read often in the Bible of rich men, but never of any other who was desired to part with all that he had! When Ananias was struck dead, it was not because he did not give up all his money, but because he pretended to have done so. St. Peter expressly says, 'While it remained was it not thine own? and after it was sold, was it not in thine own power?' How would the Lord have been buried but for the rich Joseph? Besides, the Lord said, "If thou wouldst be perfect, go, sell that thou hast." I cannot be perfect; it is hopeless; and he does not expect it.'—It would be more honest if he said, 'I do not want to be perfect; I am content to be saved.' Such as he do not care for being perfect as their Father in heaven is perfect, but for being what they call *saved*. They little think that without perfection there is no salvation—that perfection is salvation: they are one.—'And again,' he adds, in conclusion triumphant, 'the text says, "How hard is it for them that trust in riches to enter into the kingdom of God!" I do not trust in my riches. I know that they can do nothing to save me!'

I will suppose myself in immediate communication with such a youth. I should care little to set forth anything called truth, except in siege for surrender to the law of liberty. If I cannot persuade, I would be silent. Nor would I labour to instruct the keenest intellect; I would rather learn for myself. To persuade the heart, the will, the action, is alone worth the full energy of a man. His strength is first for his own, then for his neighbour's manhood. He must first pluck out the beam out of his own eye, then the mote out of his brother's—if indeed the mote in his brother's be more than the projection of the beam in his own. To make a man happy as a lark, *might be* to do him grievous wrong: to make a man wake, rise, look up, turn, is worth the life and death of the Son of the Eternal.

I say then to the youth:—

'Have you kept—have you been keeping the commandments?'

'I will not dare to say that,' I suppose him to answer. 'I ought to know better than that youth how much is implied in the keeping of the commandments!'

'But,' I ask insisting, 'does your answer imply that, counting the Lord a hard master, you have taken the less pains to do as he would have you? or that, bending your energies to the absolute perfection he requires, you have the more perceived the impossibility of fulfilling the law? Can you have failed to note that it is the youth who has been for years observing the commandments on whom the further, and to you startling, command is laid, to part with all that he has? Surely not! Are you then one on whom, because of correspondent condition, the same command could be laid? Have you, in any sense like that in which the youth answered the question, kept the commandments? Have you, unsatisfied with the result of what keeping you have given them, and filled with desire to be perfect, gone kneeling to the Master to learn more of the way to eternal life? or are you so well satisfied with what you are, that you have never sought eternal life, never hungered and thirsted after the righteousness of God, the perfection of your being? If this latter be your condition, then be comforted; the Master does not require of you to sell what you have and give to the poor. *You* follow him! *You* go with him to preach good tidings!—you who care not for righteousness! You are not one whose company is desirable to the Master. Be comforted, I say: he does not want you; he will not ask you to open your purse for him; you may give or withhold; it is nothing to him. What! is he to be obliged to one outside his kingdom—to the untrue, the ignoble, for money? Bring him a true heart, an obedient hand: he has given his life-blood for that; but your money—he neither needs it nor cares for it.'

'Pray, do not deal harshly with me. I confess I have not been what I ought, but I want to repent, and would fain enter into life. Do not think, because I am not prepared, without the certainty that it is required of me, to cast from me all I have that I have no regard for higher things.'

'Once more, then, *go and keep the commandments*. It is not come to your money yet. The commandments are enough for you. You are not yet a child in the kingdom. You do not care for the arms of your father; you value only the shelter of his roof. As to your money, let the commandments direct you how to use it. It is in you but pitiable presumption to wonder whether it is required of you to sell all that you have. When in keeping the commandments you have found the great reward of loving righteousness—the further reward of discovering that, with all the energy you can put forth, you are but an unprofitable servant; when you have come to know that the law can be kept only by such as need no law; when you have come to feel that you would rather pass out of being than live on such a poor, miserable, selfish life as alone you can call yours; when you are aware of a something beyond all that your mind can think, yet not beyond what your heart can desire—a something that is not yours, seems as if it never could be yours, which yet your life is worthless without; when you have come therefore to the Master with the cry, "What shall I do that I may inherit eternal life?" it may be he will then say to you, "Sell all that you have and give to the poor, and come follow me." If he do, then will you be of men most honourable if you obey—of men most pitiable if you refuse. Till then you would be no comfort to him, no pleasure to his friends. For the young man to have sold all and followed him would have been to accept God's patent of peerage: to you it is not offered. Were one of the disobedient, in the hope of the honour, to part with every straw he possessed, he would but be sent back to keep the commandments in the new and easier circumstances of his poverty.

'Does this comfort you? Then alas for you! A thousand times alas! Your relief is to know that the Lord has no need of you—does not require you to part with your money, does not offer you himself instead! You do not indeed sell him for thirty pieces of silver, but you are glad not to buy him with all that you have! Wherein do you differ from the youth of the story? In this, that he was invited to do more, to do everything, to partake of the divine nature; you have not had it in your power to refuse; you are not fit to be invited. Such as you can never enter the kingdom. You would not even know you were in heaven if you were in it; you would not see it around you if you sat on the very footstool of the throne.'

'But I do not trust in my riches; I trust in the merits of my Lord and Saviour. I trust in his finished work, I trust in the sacrifice he has offered.'

'Yes; yes!—you will trust in anything but the Man himself who tells you it is hard to be saved! Not all the merits of God and his Christ can give you eternal life; only God and his Christ can; and they cannot, would not if they could, without your keeping the commandments. The knowledge of the living God *is* eternal life. What have you to do with his merits? You have to know his being, himself. And as to trusting in your riches—who ever imagined he could have eternal life by his riches? No man with half a conscience, half a head, and no heart at all, could suppose that any man trusting in his riches to get him in, could enter the kingdom. That would be too absurd. The money- confident Jew might hope that, as his riches were a sign of the favour of God, that favour would not fail him at the last; or their possession might so enlarge his self-satisfaction that he could not entertain the idea of being lost; but *trust in his riches*!—no. It is the last refuge of the riches-lover, the riches-worshipper, the man to whom their possession is essential for his peace, to say he does not trust in them to take him into life. Doubtless the man who thinks of nothing so much, trusts in them in a very fearful sense; but hundreds who do so will yet say, "I do not trust in my riches; I trust in—" this or that stock-phrase.'

'You forget yourself; you are criticizing the Lord's own words: he said, "How hard is it *for them that trust in riches* to enter into the kingdom of heaven!"'

'I do not forget myself; to this I have been leading you:—our Lord, I believe, never said those words. The reading of both the Sinaitic and the Vatican manuscript, the oldest two we have, that preferred, I am glad to see, by both Westcott and Tischendorf, though not by Tregelles or the Revisers, is, "Children, how hard is it to enter into the kingdom of God!" These words I take to be those of the Lord. Some copyist, with the mind at least of a rich man, dissatisfied with the Lord's way of regarding money, and like yourself anxious to compromize, must forsooth affix his marginal gloss—to the effect that it is not the possessing of riches, but the trusting in them, that makes it difficult to enter into the kingdom! *Difficult*? Why, it is eternally impossible for the man who trusts in his riches to enter into the kingdom! it is for the man who has riches it is difficult. Is the Lord supposed to teach that for a man who trusts in his riches it is *possible* to enter the kingdom? that, though impossible with men, this is possible with God? God take the Mammon-worshipper into his glory! No! the Lord never said it. The annotation of Mr. Facingbothways crept into the text, and stands in the English version. Our Lord was not in the habit of explaining away his hard words. He let them stand in all the glory of the burning fire wherewith they would purge us. Where their simplicity finds corresponding simplicity, they are understood. The twofold heart must mistake. It is hard for a rich man, just because he is a rich man, to enter into the kingdom of heaven.'

Some, no doubt, comfort themselves with the thought that, if it be so hard, the fact will be taken into account: it is but another shape of the fancy that the rich man must be differently treated from his fellows; that as he has had his good things here, so he must have them there too. Certain as life they will have absolute justice, that is, fairness, but what will that avail, if they enter not into the kingdom? It is life they must have; there is no enduring of existence without *life*. They think *they can do without eternal life, if only they may live for ever*! Those who know what eternal life means count it the one terror to have to live on without it.

Take then the Lord's words thus: 'Children, how hard is it to enter into the kingdom of God!' It is quite like his way of putting things. Calling them first to reflect on the original difficulty for every man of entering into the kingdom of God, he reasserts in yet stronger phrase the difficulty of the rich man: 'It is easier for a camel to go through a needle's eye, than for a rich man to enter into the kingdom of God.' It always was, always will be, hard to enter into the kingdom of heaven. It is hard even to believe that one must be born from above—must pass into a new and unknown consciousness. The law-faithful Jew, the ceremonial Christian, shrinks from the self-annihilation, the Life of grace and truth, the upper air of heavenly delight, the all-embracing love that fills the law full and sets it aside. They cannot accept a condition of being as in itself eternal life. And hard to believe in, this life, this kingdom of God, this simplicity of absolute existence, is hard to enter. How hard? As hard as the Master of salvation could find words to express the hardness: 'If any man cometh unto me, and hateth not .... his own life also, he cannot be my disciple.' And the rich man must find it harder than another to hate his own life. There is so much associated with it to swell out the self of his consciousness, that the difficulty of casting it from him as the mere ugly shadow of the self God made, is vastly increased.

None can know how difficult it is to enter into the kingdom of heaven, but those who have tried—tried hard, and have not ceased to try. I care not to be told that one may pass at once into all possible sweetness of assurance; it is not assurance I desire, but the thing itself; not the certainty of eternal life, but eternal life. I care not what other preachers may say, while I know that in St. Paul the spirit and the flesh were in frequent strife. They only, I repeat, know how hard it is to enter into life, who are in conflict every day, are growing to have this conflict every hour—nay, begin to see that no moment is life, without the presence that maketh strong. Let any tell me of peace and content, yea, joy unspeakable as the instant result of the new birth; I deny no such statement, refuse no such testimony; all I care to say is, that, if by salvation they mean less than absolute oneness with God, I count it no salvation, neither would be content with it if it included every joy in the heaven of their best imagining. If they are not righteous even as he is righteous, they are not saved, whatever be their gladness or their content; they are but on the way to be saved. If they do not love their neighbour—not as themselves: that is a phrase ill to understand, and not of Christ, but—as Christ loves him, I cannot count them entered into life, though life may have begun to enter into them. Those whose idea of life is simply an eternal one, best know how hard it is to enter into life. The Lord said, 'Children how hard is it to enter into the kingdom!' the disciples little knew what was required of them!

Demands unknown before are continually being made upon the Christian: it is the ever fresh rousing and calling, asking and sending of the Spirit that worketh in the children of obedience. When he thinks he has attained, then is he in danger; when he finds the mountain he has so long been climbing show suddenly a distant peak, radiant in eternal whiteness, and all but lost in heavenly places, a peak whose glory- crowned apex it seems as if no human foot could ever reach— then is there hope for him; proof there is then that he has been climbing, for he beholds the yet unclimbed; he sees what he could not see before; if he knows little of what he is, he knows something of what he is not. He learns ever afresh that he is not in the world as Jesus was in the world; but the very wind that breathes courage as he climbs is the hope that one day he shall be like him, seeing him as he is.

Possessions are *Things*, and *Things* in general, save as affording matter of conquest and means of spiritual annexation, are very ready to prove inimical to the better life. The man who for consciousness of well-being depends upon anything but life, the life essential, is a slave; he hangs on what is less than himself. He is not perfect who, deprived of every *thing*, would not sit down calmly content, aware of a well-being untouched; for none the less would he be possessor of all things, the child of the Eternal. *Things* are given us, this body first of things, that through them we may be trained both to independence and true possession of them. We must possess them; they must not possess us. Their use is to mediate—as shapes and manifestations in lower kind of the things that are unseen, that is, in themselves unseeable, the things that belong, not to the world of speech, but the world of silence, not to the world of showing, but the world of being, the world that cannot be shaken, and must remain. These things unseen take form in the things of time and space—not that they may exist, for they exist in and from eternal Godhead, but that their being may be known to those in training for the eternal; these things unseen the sons and daughters of God must possess. But instead of reaching out after them, they grasp at their forms, reward the things seen as the things to be possessed, fall in love with the bodies instead of the souls of them. There are good people who can hardly believe that, if the young man had consented to give up his wealth, the Lord would not then have told him to keep it; they too seem to think the treasure in heaven insufficient as a substitute. They cannot believe he would have been better off without his wealth. 'Is not wealth power?' they ask. It is indeed power, and so is a wolf hid in the robe; it is power, but as of a brute machine, of which the owner ill knows the handles and cranks, valves and governor. The multitude of those who read the tale are of the same mind as the youth himself—in his worst moment, as he turned and went—with one vast difference, that they are not sorrowful.

Things can never be really possessed by the man who cannot do without them—who would not be absolutely, divinely content in the consciousness that the cause of his being is within it—and *with him*. I would not be misunderstood: no man can have the consciousness of God with him and not be content; I mean that no man who has not the Father so as to be eternally content in him alone, can possess a sunset or a field of grass or a mine of gold or the love of a fellow-creature according to its nature—as God would have him possess it—in the eternal way of inheriting, having, and holding. He who has God, has all things, after the fashion in which he who made them has them. To man, woman, and child, I say—if you are not content, it is because God is not with you as you need him, not with you as he would be with you, as you *must* have him; for you need him as your body never needed food or air, need him as your soul never hungered after joy, or peace, or pleasure.

It is imperative on us to get rid of the tyranny of *things*. See how imperative: let the young man cling with every fibre to his wealth, what God can do he will do; his child shall not be left in the hell of possession! Comes the angel of death!—and where are the things that haunted the poor soul with such manifold hindrance and obstruction! The world, and all that is in the world, drops and slips, from his feet, from his hands, carrying with it his body, his eyes, his ears, every pouch, every coffer, that could delude him with the fancy of possession.

'Is the man so freed from the dominion of things? does Death so serve him—so ransom him? Why then hasten the hour? Shall not the youth abide the stroke of Time's clock—await the Inevitable on its path to free him?'

Not so!—for then first, I presume, does the man of things become aware of their tyranny. When a man begins to abstain, then first he recognizes the strength of his passion; it may be, when a man has not a thing left, he will begin to know what a necessity he had made of things; and if then he begin to contend with them, to cast out of his soul what Death has torn from his hands, then first will he know the full passion of possession, the slavery of prizing the worthless part of the precious.

'Wherein then lies the service of Death? He takes the sting, but leaves the poison!'

In this: it is not the fetters that gall, but the fetters that soothe, which eat into the soul. When the fetters of gold are gone, on which the man delighted to gaze, though they held him fast to his dungeon-wall, buried from air and sunshine, then first will he feel them in the soreness of their lack, in the weary indifference with which he looks on earth and sea, on space and stars. When the truth begins to dawn upon him that those fetters were a horror and a disgrace, then will the good of saving death appear, and the man begin to understand that having never was, never could be well-being; that it is not by possessing we live, but by life we possess. In this way is the loss of the things he thought he had, a motioning, hardly *towards*, yet in favour of deliverance. It may seem to the man the first of his slavery when it is in truth the beginning of his freedom. Never soul was set free without being made to feel its slavery; nothing but itself can enslave a soul, nothing without itself free it.

When the drunkard, free of his body, but retaining his desire unable to indulge it, has time at length to think, in the lack of the means of destroying thought, surely there dawns for him then at last a fearful hope!—not until, by the power of God and his own obedient effort, he is raised into such a condition that, be the temptation what it might, he would not yield for an immortality of unrequited drunkenness—all its delights and not one of its penalties—is he saved.

Thus death may give a new opportunity—with some hope for the multitude counting themselves Christians, who are possessed by *things* as by a legion of devils; who stand well in their church; whose lives are regarded as stainless; who are kind, friendly, give largely, believe in the redemption of Jesus, talk of the world and the church; yet whose care all the time is to heap up, to make much into more, to add house to house and field to field, burying themselves deeper and deeper in the ash-heap of *Things*.

But it is not the rich man only who is under the dominion of things; they too are slaves who, having no money, are unhappy from the lack of it. The man who is ever digging his grave is little better than he who already lies mouldering in it. The money the one has, the money the other would have, is in each the cause of an eternal stupidity. To the one as to the other comes the word, '*How is it that ye do not understand?*'

THE CAUSE OF SPIRITUAL STUPIDITY.

'How is it that ye do not understand?'— ST. MARK viii. 21.

After feeding the four thousand with seven loaves and a few small fishes, on the east side of the Sea of Galilee, Jesus, having crossed the lake, was met on the other side by certain Pharisees, whose attitude towards him was such that he betook himself again to the boat, and recrossed the lake. On the way the disciples bethought them that they had in the boat but a single loaf: probably while the Lord was occupied with the Pharisees, one of them had gone and bought it, little thinking they were about to start again so soon. Jesus, still occupied with the antagonism of the leaders of the people, and desirous of destroying their influence on his disciples, began to warn them against them. In so doing he made use of a figure they had heard him use before—that of leaven as representing a hidden but potent and pervading energy: the kingdom of heaven, he had told them, was like leaven hid in meal, gradually leavening the whole of it. He now tells them to beware of the leaven of the Pharisees. The disciples, whose minds were occupied with their lack of provisions, the moment they heard the word leaven, thought of bread, concluded it must be because of its absence that he spoke of leaven, and imagined perhaps a warning against some danger of defilement from Pharisaical cookery: 'It is because we have taken no bread!' A leaven like that of the Pharisees was even then at work in their hearts; for the sign the Pharisees sought in the mockery of unbelief, they had had a few hours before, and had already, in respect of all that made it of value, forgotten.

It is to the man who is trying to live, to the man who is obedient to the word of the Master, that the word of the Master unfolds itself. When we understand the outside of things, we think we have them: the

Lord puts his things in subdefined, suggestive shapes, yielding no satisfactory meaning to the mere intellect, but unfolding themselves to the conscience and heart, to the man himself, in the process of life-effort. According as the new creation, that of reality, advances in him, the man becomes able to understand the words, the symbols, the parables of the Lord. For life, that is, action, is alone the human condition into which the light of the Living can penetrate; life alone can assimilate life, can change food into growth. See how the disciples here fooled themselves!

See how the Lord calls them to their senses. He does not tell them in so many words where they are wrong; he attacks instead the cause in themselves which led to their mistake—a matter always of infinitely more consequence than any mistake itself: the one is a live mistake, an untruth in the soul, the other a mere dead blunder born of it. The word-connection therefore between their blunder and our Lord's exhortation, is not to be found; the logic of what the Lord said, is not on the surface. Often he speaks not to the words but to the thought; here he speaks not even to the thought, but to the whole mode of thinking, to the thought-matrix, the inward condition of the men.

He addresses himself to rouse in them a sense of their lack of confidence in God, which was the cause of their blunder as to his meaning. He reminds them of the two miracles with the loaves, and the quantity of fragments left beyond the need. From one of these miracles they had just come; it was not a day behind them; yet here they were doubting already! He makes them go over the particulars of the miracles—hardly to refresh their memories-they were tenacious enough of the marvel, but to make their hearts dwell on them; for they had already forgotten or had failed to see their central revelation—the eternal fact of God's love and care and compassion. They knew the number of the men each time, the number of the loaves each time, the number of the baskets of fragments they had each time taken up, but they forgot the Love that had so broken the bread that its remnants twenty times outweighed its loaves.

Having thus questioned them like children, and listened as to the answers of children, he turns the light of their thoughts upon themselves, and, with an argument to the man which overleaps all the links of its own absolute logic, demands, 'How is it that ye do not understand?' Then they did understand, and knew that he did not speak to them of the leaven of bread, but of the teaching of the Pharisees and of the Sadducees. He who trusts can understand; he whose mind is set at ease can discover a reason.

How otherwise than by rebuking and quelling their anxiety, could those words have made them see what then they saw? What connection was there between 'How many baskets took ye up?' and 'How is it that ye do not understand?' What had the miracles to do with their discovering that when he spoke of leaven, it was not of the leaven of bread? If not of the leaven of bread, how did the reference to those miracles of bread make them recognize the fact?

The lesson he would have had them learn from the miracle, the natural lesson, the only lesson worthy of the miracle, was, that God cared for his children, and could, did, and would provide for their necessities. This lesson they had not learned. No doubt the power of the miracle was some proof of his mission, but the love of it proved it better, for it made it worth proving: it was a throb of the Father's heart. The ground of the Master's upbraiding is not that they did not understand him, but that they did not trust God; that, after all they had seen, they yet troubled themselves about bread. Because we easily imagine ourselves in want, we imagine God ready to forsake us. The miracles of Jesus were the ordinary works of his Father, wrought small and swift that we might take them in. The lesson of them was that help is always within God's reach when his children want it—their design, to show what God is—not that Jesus was God, but that his Father was God—that is, was what he was, for no other kind of God could be, or be worth believing in, no other notion of God be worth having. The mission undertaken by the Son, was not to show himself as having all power in heaven and earth, but to reveal his Father, to show him to men such as he is, that men may know him, and knowing, trust him. It were a small boon indeed that God should forgive men, and not give himself. It would be but to give them back themselves; and less than God just as he is will not comfort men for the essential sorrow of their existence. Only God the gift can turn that sorrow into essential joy: Jesus came to give them God, who is eternal life.

Those miracles of feeding gave the same lesson to their eyes, their hands, their mouths, that his words gave to their ears when he said, 'seek not ye what ye shall eat, or what ye shall drink, neither be ye of doubtful mind; for your Father knoweth that ye have need of these things;' 'Seek ye first the kingdom of God, and his righteousness, and all these things shall be added unto you.' So little had they learned it yet, that they remembered the loaves but forgot the Father—as men in their theology forget the very [Greek: *Theou logos*]. Thus forgetting, they were troubled about provision for the day, and the moment leaven was mentioned, thought of bread. *What else could he mean? The con-*

nection was plain! The Lord reminds them of the miracle, which had they believed after its true value, they would not have been so occupied as to miss what he meant. It had set forth to them the truth of God's heart towards them; revealed the loving care without which he would not be God. Had they learned this lesson, they would not have needed the reminder; for their hearts would not have been so filled with discomfort as to cause them mistake his word. Had they but said with themselves that, though they had but one loaf, they had him who makes all the loaves, they would never have made the foolish blunder they did.

The answer then to the Lord's reproach, 'How is it that ye do not understand?' is plainly this: their minds were so full of care about the day's bread, that they could not think with simplicity about anything else; the mere mention of leaven threw them floundering afresh in the bog of their unbelief. When the Lord reminded them of what their eyes had seen, so of what he was and what God was, and of the foolishness of their care—the moment their fear was taught to look up, that moment they began to see what the former words of the Lord must have meant: their minds grew clear enough to receive and reflect in a measure their intent.

The care of the disciples was care for the day, not for the morrow; the word *morrow* must stand for any and every point of the future. The next hour, the next moment, is as much beyond our grasp and as much in God's care, as that a hundred years away. Care for the next minute is just as foolish as care for the morrow, or for a day in the next thousand years—in neither can we do anything, in both God is doing everything. Those claims only of the morrow which have to be prepared to-day are of the duty of to-day; the moment which coincides with work to be done, is the moment to be minded; the next is nowhere till God has made it.

Their lack of bread seems to have come from no neglect, but from the immediacy of the Lord's re-embarkation; at the same time had there been a want of foresight, that was not the kind of thing the Lord cared to reprove; it was not this and that fault he had come to set right, but the primary evil of life without God, the root of all evils, from hatred to discourtesy. Certain minor virtues also, prudence amongst the rest, would thus at length be almost, if not altogether, superseded. If a man forget a thing, God will see to that: man is not lord of his memory or his intellect. But man is lord of his will, his action; and is then verily to blame when, remembering a duty, he does not do it, but puts it off, and so forgets it. If a man lay himself out to do the immediate duty of the moment, wonderfully little forethought, I suspect, will be found needful. That forethought only is right which has to determine duty, and pass into action. To the foundation of yesterday's work well done, the work of the morrow will be sure to fit. Work done is of more consequence for the future than the foresight of an archangel.

With the disciples as with the rich youth, it was *Things* that prevented the Lord from being understood. Because of possession the young man had not a suspicion of the grandeur of the call with which Jesus honoured him. He thought he was hardly dealt with to be offered a patent of Heaven's nobility—he was so very rich! *Things* filled his heart; things blocked up his windows; things barricaded his door, so that the very God could not enter. His soul was not empty, swept, and garnished, but crowded with meanest idols, among which his spirit crept about upon its knees, wasting on them the gazes that belonged to his fellows and his Master. The disciples were a little further on than he; they had left all and followed the Lord; but neither had they yet got rid of *Things*. The paltry solitariness of a loaf was enough to hide the Lord from them, to make them unable to understand him. Why, having forgotten, could they not trust? Surely if he had told them that for his sake they must go all day without food, they would not have minded! But they lost sight of God, and were as if either he did not see, or did not care for them.

In the former case it was the possession of wealth, in the latter the not having more than a loaf, that rendered incapable of receiving the word of the Lord: the evil principle was precisely the same. If it be *Things* that slay you, what matter whether things you have, or things you have not? The youth, not trusting in God, the source of his riches, cannot brook the word of his Son, offering him better riches, more direct from the heart of the Father. The disciples, forgetting who is lord of the harvests of the earth, cannot understand his word, because filled with the fear of a day's hunger. He did not trust in God as having given; they did not trust in God as ready to give. We are like them when, in *any* trouble, we do not trust him. It is hard on God, when his children will not let him give; when they carry themselves so that he must withhold his hand, lest he harm them. To take no care that they acknowledge whence their help comes, would be to leave them worshippers of idols, trusters in that which is not.

Distrust is atheism, and the barrier to all growth. Lord, we do not understand thee, because we do not trust thy Father—whole-hearted to us, as never yet was mother to her first-born! Full of care, as if he had none, we think this and that escapes his notice, for this and that he does not think! While we who are evil would die to give our children bread to eat, we are not certain the only Good will give us anything of what we desire! The things of thy world so crowd our hearts, that there is no room in them for the things of thy heart, which would raise ours above all fear, and make us merry children in our Father's house! Surely many a whisper of the watching Spirit we let slip through brooding over a need not yet come to us! To-morrow makes to-day's whole head sick, its whole heart faint. When we should be still, sleeping or dreaming, we are fretting about an hour that lies a half sun's-journey away! Not so doest thou, Lord! thou doest the work of thy Father! Wert thou such as we, then should we have good cause to be troubled! But thou knowest it is difficult, *things* pressing upon every sense, to believe that the informing power of them is in the unseen; that out of it they come; that, where we can descry no hand directing, a will, nearer than any hand, is moving them from within, causing them to fulfil his word! Help us to obey, to resist, to trust.

The care that is filling your mind at this moment, or but waiting till you lay the book aside to leap upon you—that need which is no need, is a demon sucking at the spring of your life.

'No; mine is a reasonable care—an unavoidable care, indeed!'

'Is it something you have to do this very moment?'

'No.'

'Then you are allowing it to usurp the place of something that is required of you this moment!'

'There is nothing required of me at this moment.'

'Nay, but there is—the greatest thing that can be required of man.'

'Pray, what is it?'

'Trust in the living God. His will is your life.'

'He may not will I should have what I need!'

'Then you only think you need it. Is it a good thing?'

'Yes, it is a good thing.'

'Then why doubt you shall have it?'

'Because God may choose to have me go without it.'

'Why should he?'

'I cannot tell.'

'Must it not be in order to give you something instead?'

'I want nothing instead.'

'I thought I was talking to a Christian!'

'I can consent to be called nothing else.'

'Do you not, then, know that, when God denies anything a child of his values, it is to give him something *he* values?'

'But if I do not want it?'

'You are none the less miserable just because you do not have it. Instead of his great possessions the young man was to have the company of Jesus, and treasure in heaven. When God refused to deliver a certain man from a sore evil, concerning which he three times besought him, unaccustomed to be denied, he gave him instead his own graciousness, consoled him in person for his pain.'

'Ah, but that was St. Paul!'

'True; what of that?'

'He was one by himself!'

'God deals with all his children after his own father-nature. No scripture is of private interpretation even for a St. Paul. It sets forth God's way with man. If thou art not willing that God should have his way with thee, then, in the name of God, be miserable—till thy misery drive thee to the arms of the Father.'

'I do trust him in spiritual matters.'

'Everything is an affair of the spirit. If God has a way, then that is the only way. Every little thing in which you would have your own way, has a mission for your redemption; and he will treat you as a naughty child until you take your Father's way for yours.'

There will be this difference, however, between the rich that loves his riches and the poor that hates his poverty—that, when they die, the heart of the one will be still crowded with things and their pleasures, while the heart of the other will be relieved of their lack; the one has had his good things, the other his evil things. But the rich man who held his *things* lightly, nor let them nestle in his heart; who was a channel and no cistern; who was ever and always forsaking his money—starts, in the new world, side by side with the man who accepted, not hated, his poverty. Each will say, 'I am free!'

For the only air of the soul, in which it can breathe and live, is the present God and the spirits of the just: that is our heaven, our home, our all-right place. Cleansed of greed, jealousy, vanity, pride, possession, all the thousand forms of the evil self, we shall be God's children on the hills and in the fields of that heaven, not one desiring to be before another, any more than to cast that other out; for ambition and hatred will then be seen to be one and the same spirit.—'What thou hast, I have; what thou desirest, I will; I give to myself ten times in giving once to thee. My want that thou mightst have, would be rich possession.' But let me be practical; for thou art ready to be miserable over trifles, and dost not believe God good enough to care for thy care:

I would reason with thee to help thee rid of thy troubles, for they hide from thee the thoughts of thy God.

The things readiest to be done, those which lie not at the door but on the very table of a man's mind, are not merely in general the most neglected, but even by the thoughtful man, the oftenest let alone, the oftenest postponed. The Lord of life demanding high virtue of us, can it be that he does not care for the first principles of justice? May a man become strong in righteousness without learning to speak the truth to his neighbour? Shall a man climb the last flight of the stair who has never set foot on the lowest step? Truth is one, and he who does the truth in the small thing is of the truth; he who will do it only in a great thing, who postpones the small thing near him to the great thing farther from him, is not of the truth. Let me suggest some possible parallels between ourselves and the disciples maundering over their one loaf—with the Bread of Life at their side in the boat. We too dull our understandings with trifles, fill the heavenly spaces with phantoms, waste the heavenly time with hurry. To those who possess their souls in patience come the heavenly visions. When I trouble myself over a trifle, even a trifle confessed—the loss of some little article, say—spurring my memory, and hunting the house, not from immediate need, but from dislike of loss; when a book has been borrowed of me and not returned, and I have forgotten the borrower, and fret over the missing volume, while there are thousands on my shelves from which the moments thus lost might gather treasure holding relation with neither moth, nor rust, nor thief; am I not like the disciples? Am I not a fool whenever loss troubles me more than recovery would gladden? God would have me wise, and smile at the trifle. Is it not time I lost a few things when I care for them so unreasonably? This losing of things is of the mercy of God; it comes to teach us to let them go. Or have I forgotten a thought that came to me, which seemed of the truth, and a revealment to my heart? I wanted to keep it, to have it, to use it by and by, and it is gone! I keep trying and trying to call it back, feeling a poor man till that thought be recovered—to be far more lost, perhaps, in a note-book, into which I shall never look again to find it! I forget that it is live things God cares about—live truths, not things set down in a book, or in a memory, or embalmed in the joy of knowledge, but things lifting up the heart, things active in an active will. True, my lost thought might have so worked; but had I faith in God, the maker of thought and memory, I should know that, if the thought was a truth, and so alone worth anything, it must come again; for it is in God—so, like the dead, not beyond my reach: kept for me, I shall have it again.

'These are foolish illustrations—not worth writing!'

If such things are not, then the mention of them is foolish. If they are, then he is foolish who would treat them as if they were not. I choose them for their smallness, and appeal especially to all who keep house concerning the size of trouble that suffices to hide word and face of God.

With every haunting trouble then, great or small, the loss of thousands or the lack of a shilling, go to God, and appeal to him, the God of your life, to deliver you, his child, from that which is unlike him, therefore does not belong to you, but is antagonistic to your nature. If your trouble is such that you cannot appeal to him, the more need you should appeal to him! Where one cannot go to God, there is something specially wrong. If you let thought for the morrow, or the next year, or the next month, distress you; if you let the chatter of what is called the public, peering purblind into the sanctuary of motive, annoy you; if you seek or greatly heed the judgment of men, capable or incapable, you set open your windows to the mosquitoes of care, to drown with their buzzing the voice of the Eternal!

If you tell me that but for care, the needful work of the world would be ill done—'What work,' I ask, 'can that be, which will be better done by the greedy or anxious than by the free, fearless soul? Can care be a better inspirer of labour than the sending of God? If the work is not his work, then, indeed, care may well help it, for its success is loss. But is he worthy the name of man who, for the fear of starvation, will do better work than for the joy that his labour is not in vain in the Lord? I know as well as you that you are not likely to get rich that way; but neither will you block up the gate of the kingdom of heaven against yourself.

Ambition in every shape has to do with *Things*, with outward advantages for the satisfaction of self-worship; it is that form of pride, foul shadow of Satan, which usurps the place of aspiration. The sole ambition that is of God is the ambition to rise above oneself; all other is of the devil. Yet is it nursed and cherished in many a soul that thinks itself devout, filling it with petty cares and disappointments, that swarm like bats in its air, and shut out the glory of God. The love of the praise of men, the desire of fame, the pride that takes offence, the puffing-up of knowledge, these and every other form of Protean self-worship—we must get rid of them all. We must be free. The man whom another enslaves may be free as God; to him who is a slave in himself, God will not enter in; he will not sup with him, for he cannot be his friend. He will sit by the humblest hearth where the daily food is prepared; he will not eat in a lumber-room, let the lumber be thrones and crowns. *Will not*, did I say? *Cannot*, I say. Men full of things would not once partake with God, were he by them all the day.

Nor will God force any door to enter in. He may send a tempest about the house; the wind of his admonishment may burst doors and windows, yea, shake the house to its foundations; but not then, not so, will he enter. The door must be opened by the willing hand, ere the foot of Love will cross the threshold. He watches to see the door move from within. Every tempest is but an assault in the siege of love. The terror of God is but the other side of his love; it is love outside the house, that would be inside—love that knows the house is no house, only a place, until it enter—no home, but a tent, until the Eternal dwell there. *Things* must be cast out to make room for their souls— the eternal truths which in things find shape and show.

But who is sufficient to cast them out? If a man take courage and encounter the army of bats and demon-snakes that infests the place of the Holy, it is but to find the task too great for him; that the temple of God will not be cleansed by him; that the very dust he raises in sweeping is full of corruptive forces. Let such as would do what they must yet cannot, be what they must yet cannot, remember, with hope and courage, that he who knows all about our being, once *spake a parable to the end that they ought always to pray, and not to faint.*

THE WORD OF JESUS ON PRAYER.

'They ought always to pray.'—ST. LUKE xviii. I.

The impossibility of doing what we would as we would, drives us to look for help. And this brings us to a new point of departure. Everything difficult indicates something more than our theory of life yet embraces, checks some tendency to abandon the strait path, leaving open only the way ahead. But there is a reality of being in which all things are easy and plain—oneness, that is, with the Lord of Life; to pray for this is the first thing; and to the point of this prayer every difficulty hedges and directs us. But if I try to set forth something of the reasonableness of all prayer, I beg my readers to remember that it is for the sake of action and not speculation; if prayer be anything at all, it is a thing to be done: what matter whether you agree with me or not, if you do not pray? I would not spend my labour for that; I desire it to serve for help to pray, not to understand how a man might pray and yet be a reasonable soul.

First, a few words about the parable itself.

It is an instance, by no means solitary, of the Lord's use of a tale about a very common or bad person, to persuade, reasoning *a fortiori*, of the way of the All-righteous. Note the points: 'Did the unrighteous judge, to save himself from annoyance, punish one with whom he was not offended, for the sake of a woman he cared nothing about? and shall not the living Justice avenge his praying friends over whose injuries he has to exercise a long-suffering patience towards their enemies?'—for so I would interpret the phrase, as correctly translated in the Revision, 'and he is long-suffering over them.'—'I say unto you, that he will avenge them speedily. Howbeit when the Son of Man cometh, shall he find faith on the earth?'

Here then is a word of the Lord about prayer: it is a comfort that he recognizes difficulty in the matter—sees that we need encouragement to go on praying, that it looks as if we were not heard, that it is no wonder we should be ready to faint and leave off. He tells a parable in which the suppliant has to go often and often to the man who can help her, gaining her end only at the long last. Actual delay on the part of God, we know from what follows, he does not allow; the more plain is it that he recognizes how the thing must look to those whom he would have go on praying. Here as elsewhere he teaches us that we must not go by the look of things, but by the reality behind the look. A truth, a necessity of God's own willed nature, is enough to set up against a whole army of appearances. It looks as if he did not hear you: never mind; he does; it must be that he does; go on as the woman did; you too will be heard. She is heard at last, and in virtue of her much going; God hears at once, and will avenge speedily. The unrighteous judge cared nothing for the woman; those who cry to God are his own cho- sen— plain in the fact that they cry to him. He has made and appointed them to cry: they do cry: will he not hear them? They exist that they may pray; he has chosen them that they may choose him; he has called them that they may call him—that there may be such communion, such interchange as belongs to their being and the being of their Fa- ther. The gulf of indifference lay between the poor woman and the unjust judge; God and those who seek his help, are closer than two hands clasped hard in love: he will avenge them speedily. It is a bold assertion in the face of what seems great delay—an appearance acknowledged in the very groundwork of the parable. Having made it, why does he seem to check himself with a sigh, adding, Howbeit when the Son of Man cometh, shall he find faith on the earth?' After all he had said, and had yet to say, after all he had done, and was going on to do, when he came again, after time given for the holy leaven to work, would he find men trusting the Father? Would he find them, even then, beyond the tyranny of appearances, believing in spite of them? Would they be children enough towards God to know he was hearing them and working for them, though they could not hear him or see him work?—to believe the ways of God so wide, that even on the breadth of his track was room for their understanding to lose its way—what they saw, so small a part of what he was doing, that it could give them but little clue to his end? that it was because the goal God had in view for them was so high and afar, that they could detect no movement of approach thereto? The sigh, the exclamation, never meant that God might be doing something more than he was doing, but that the Father would have a dreary time to wait ere his children would know, that is, trust in him. The utterance recognizes the part of man, his slowly yielded part in faith, and his blame in troubling God by not trusting in him. If men would but make haste, and stir themselves up to take hold on God! They were so slow of heart to believe! They could but would not help it and do better!

He seems here to refer to his second coming—concerning the time of which, he refused information; concerning the mode of which, he said it would be unexpected; but concerning the duty of which, he insisted it was *to be ready*: we must be faithful, and at our work. Do those who say, lo here or lo there are the signs of his coming, think to be too keen for him, and spy his approach? When he tells them to watch lest he find them neglecting their work, they stare this way and that, and watch lest he should succeed in coming like a thief! So throughout: if, instead of speculation, we gave ourselves to obedience, what a difference would soon be seen in the world! Oh, the multitude of so-called religious questions which the Lord would answer with, 'strive to enter in at the strait gate'! Many eat and drink and talk and teach in his presence; few do the things he says to them! Obedience is the one key of life.

I would meet difficulties, not answer objections; I would remove stumbling-blocks from the path of him who would pray; I would help him to pray. If, seeing we live not by our own will, we live by another will, then is there reason, and then only can there be reason in prayer. To him who refuses that other will, I have nothing to say. The hour may come when he will wish there were some one to pray to; now he is not of those whom I can help.

If there be a God, and I am his creature, there may be, there should be, there must be some communication open between him and me. If any one allow a God, but one scarce good enough to care about his creatures, I will yield him that it were foolish to pray to such a God; but the notion that, with all the good impulses in us, we are the offspring of a cold-hearted devil, is so horrible in its inconsistency, that I would ask that man what hideous and cold-hearted disregard to the truth makes him capable of the supposition! To such a one God's terrors, or, if not his terrors, then God's sorrows yet will speak; the divine something in him will love, and the love be left moaning.

If I find my position, my consciousness, that of one from home, nay, that of one in some sort of prison; if I find that I can neither rule the world in which I live nor my own thoughts or desires; that I cannot quiet my passions, order my likings, determine my ends, will my growth, forget when I would, or recall what I forget; that I cannot love where I would, or hate where I would; that I am no king over myself; that I cannot supply my own needs, do not even always know which of my seeming needs are to be supplied, and which treated as impostors; if, in a word, my own being is everyway too much for me; if I can neither understand it, be satisfied with it, nor better it—may it not well give me pause—the pause that ends in prayer? When my own scale seems too large for my management; when I reflect that I cannot account for my existence, have had no poorest hand in it, neither, should I not like it, can do anything towards causing it to cease; when I think that I can do nothing to make up to those I love, any more than to those I hate, for evils I have done them and sorrows I have caused them; that in my worst moments I disbelieve in my best, in my best loathe my worst; that there is in me no wholeness, no unity; that life is not a good to me, for I scorn myself—when I think all or any such things, can it be strange if I think also that surely there ought to be somewhere a being to account for me, one to account for himself, and make the round of my existence just; one whose very being accounts and is necessary to account for mine; whose presence in my being is imperative, not merely to supplement it, but to make to myself my existence a good? For if not rounded in itself, but dependent on that which it knows not and cannot know, it cannot be to itself a good known as a good—a thing of reason and well-being: it will be a life longing for a *logos* to be the interpretative soul of its *cosmos*—a *logos* it cannot have. To know God present, to have the consciousness of God where he is the essential life, must be absolutely necessary to that life! He that is made in the image of God must know him or be desolate: the child must have the Father! Witness the dissatisfaction, yea desolation of my soul—wretched, alone, unfinished, without him! It cannot act from itself, save in God; acting from what seems itself without God, is no action at all, it is a mere yielding to impulse. All within is disorder and spasm. There is a cry behind me, and a voice before; instincts of betterment tell me I must rise above my present self—perhaps even above all my possible self: I see not how to obey, how to carry them out! I am shut up in a world of consciousness, an unknown *I* in an unknown world: surely this world of my unwilled, unchosen, compelled existence, cannot be shut out from him, cannot be unknown to him, cannot be impenetrable, impermeable, unpresent to him from whom I am! nay, is it not his thinking in which I think? is it not by his consciousness that I am conscious? Whatever passes in me must be as naturally known to him as to me, and more thoroughly, even to infinite degrees. My thought must lie open to him: if he makes me think, how can I elude him in thinking? 'If I should spread my wings toward the dawn, and sojourn at the last of the sea, even there thy hand would lead me, and thy right hand would hold me!' If he has determined the being, how shall any mode of that being be hidden from him? If I speak to him, if I utter words ever so low; if I but think words to him; nay, if I only think to him, surely he, my original, in whose life and will and no otherwise I now think concerning him, hears, and knows, and acknowledges! Then shall I not think to him? Shall I not tell him my troubles—how he, even he, has troubled me by making me?—how unfit I am to be that which I am?—that my being is not to me a good thing yet?—that I need a law that shall account to me for it in righteousness—reveal to me how I am to make it a good— how I am to *be* a good, and not an evil? Shall I not tell him that I need him to comfort me? his breath to move upon the face of the waters of the Chaos he has made? Shall I not cry to him to be in me rest and strength? to quiet this uneasy motion called life, and make me live indeed? to deliver me from my sins, and make me clean and glad? Such a cry is of the child to the Father: if there be a Father, verily he will hear, and let the child know that he hears! Every need of God, lifting up the heart, is a seeking of God, is a begging for himself, is profoundest prayer, and the root and inspirer of all other prayer.

If it be reasonable for me to cry thus, if I cannot but cry, it is reasonable that God should hear, he cannot but hear. A being that could not hear or would not answer prayer, could not be God.

'But, I ask, all this admitted—is what you call a necessary truth an existent fact? You say, "It must be so;" I say, "What if there is no God!" Convince me that prayer is heard, and I shall know. Why should the question admit of doubt? Why should it require to be reasoned about? We know that the wind blows: why should we not know that God answers prayer?'

I reply, What if God does not care to have you know it at second hand? What if there would be no good in that? There is some testimony on record, and perhaps there might be much were it not that, having to do with things so immediately personal, and generally so delicate, answers to prayer would naturally not often be talked about; but no testimony concerning the thing can well be conclusive; for, like a reported miracle, there is always some way to daff it; and besides, the conviction to be got that way is of little value; it avails nothing to know the thing by the best of evidence.

As to the evidence itself, adduction of proof is scarce possible in respect of inward experience, and to this class belongs the better part of the evidence: the testimony may be truthful, yet the testifier utterly self-deceived! How am I to know the thing as he says he knows it? How am I to judge of it? There is king David:—Poetry!—old poetry!—and in the most indefinite language in the world! Doubtless he is little versed in the utterance of the human soul, who does not recognize in many of the psalms a cry as true as ever came from depth of pain or height of deliverance; but it may all have been but now the jarring and now the rhythmical movement of the waves of the psychical aether!—I lay nothing upon testimony for my purpose now, knowing the things that can be said, and also not valuing the bare assent of the intellect. The sole assurance worth a man's having, even if the most incontestable evidence were open to him from a thousand other quarters, is that to be gained only from personal experience—that assurance in himself which he can least readily receive from another, and which is least capable of being transmuted into evidence for another. The evidence of Jesus Christ could not take the place of that. A truth is of enormous import in relation to the life—that is the heart, and conscience, and will; it is of little consequence merely as a fact having relation to the understanding. God may hear all prayers that ever were offered to him, and a man may believe that he does, nor be one whit the better for it, so long as God has no prayers of his to hear, he no answers to receive from God. Nothing in this quarter will ever be gained by investigation. Reader, if you are in any trouble, try whether God will not help you; if you are in no need, why should you ask questions about prayer? True, he knows little of himself who does not know that he is wretched, and miserable, and poor, and blind, and naked; but until he begins at least to suspect a need, how can he pray? And for one who does not want to pray, I would not lift a straw to defeat such a one in the argument whether God hears or does not hear prayer: for me, let him think what he will! it matters nothing in heaven or in earth: whether in hell I do not know.

As to the so-called scientific challenge to prove the efficacy of prayer by the result of simultaneous petition, I am almost ashamed to allude to it. There should be light enough in science itself to show the proposal absurd. A God capable of being so moved in one direction or another, is a God not worth believing in—could not be the God believed in by Jesus Christ—and he said he knew. A God that should fail to hear, receive, attend to one single prayer, the feeblest or worst, I cannot believe in; but a God that would grant every request of every man or every company of men, would be an evil God—that is no God, but a demon. That God should hang in the thought-atmosphere like a windmill, waiting till men enough should combine and send out prayer in sufficient force to turn his outspread arms, is an idea too absurd. God waits to be gracious not to be tempted. A man capable of proposing such a test, could have in his mind no worthy representative idea of a God, and might well disbelieve in any: it is better to disbelieve than believe in a God unworthy.

'But I want to believe in God. I want to know that there is a God that answers prayer, that I may believe in him. There was a time when I believed in him. I prayed to him in great and sore trouble of heart and mind, and he did not hear me. I have not prayed since.'

How do you know that he did not hear you?

'He did not give me what I asked, though the weal of my soul hung on it.'

In your judgment. Perhaps he knew better.

'I am the worse for his refusal. I would have believed in him if he had heard me.'

Till the next desire came which he would not grant, and then you would have turned your God away. A desirable believer you would have made! A worthy brother to him who thought nothing fit to give the Father less than his all! You would accept of him no decision against your desire! That ungranted, there was no God, or not a good one! I think I will not argue with you more. This only I will say: God has not to consider his children only at the moment of their prayer. Should he be willing to give a man the thing he knows he would afterwards wish he had not given him? If a man be not fit to be refused, if he be not ready to be treated with love's severity, what he wishes may perhaps be given him in order that he may wish it had not been given him; but barely to give a man what he wants because he wants it, and without farther purpose of his good, would be to let a poor ignorant child take his fate into his own hands—the cruelty of a devil. Yet is every prayer heard; and the real soul of the prayer may require, for its real answer, that it should not be granted in the form in which it is requested.

'To have a thing in another shape, might be equivalent to not having it at all.'

If you knew God, you would leave that to him. He is not mocked, and he will not mock. But he knows you better than you know yourself, and would keep you from fooling yourself. He will not deal with you as the child of a day, but as the child of eternal ages. You shall be satisfied, if you will but let him have his way with the creature he has made. The question is between your will and the will of God. He is not one of those who give readiest what they prize least. He does not care to give anything but his best, or that which will prepare for it. Not many years may pass before you confess, 'Thou art a God who hears prayer, and gives a better answer.' You may come to see that the desire of your deepest heart would have been frustrated by having what seemed its embodiment then. That God should as a loving father listen, hear, consider, and deal with the request after the perfect tenderness of his heart, is to me enough; it is little that I should go without what I pray for. If it be granted that any answer which did not come of love, and was not for the final satisfaction of him who prayed, would be unworthy of God; that it is the part of love and knowledge to watch over the wayward, ignorant child; then the trouble of seemingly unanswered prayers begins to abate, and a lovely hope and comfort takes its place in the child-like soul. To hear is not necessarily to grant— God forbid! but to hear is necessarily to attend to—sometimes as necessarily to refuse.

'Concerning this thing,' says St. Paul, 'I besought the Lord thrice, that it might depart from me. And he hath said unto me, My grace is sufficient for thee; power is made perfect in weakness.' God had a better thing for Paul than granting his prayer and removing his complaint: he would make him strong; the power of Christ should descend and remain upon him; he would make him stronger than his suffering, make him a sharer in the energy of God. Verily, if we have God, we can do without the answer to any prayer.

'But if God is so good as you represent him, and if he knows all that we need, and better far than we do ourselves, why should it be necessary to ask him for anything?'

I answer, What if he knows prayer to be the thing we need first and most? What if the main object in God's idea of prayer be the supplying of our great, our endless need—the need of himself? What if the good of all our smaller and lower needs lies in this, that they help to drive us to God? Hunger may drive the runaway child home, and he may or may not be fed at once, but he needs his mother more than his dinner. Communion with God is the one need of the soul beyond all other need; prayer is the beginning of that communion, and some need is the motive of that prayer. Our wants are for the sake of our coming into communion with God, our eternal need. If gratitude and love immediately followed the supply of our needs, if God our Saviour was the one thought of our hearts, then it might be unnecessary that we should ask for anything we need. But seeing we take our supplies as a matter of course, feeling as if they came out of nothing, or from the earth, or our own thoughts, instead of out of a heart of love and a will which alone is force, it is needful that we should be made feel some at least of our wants, that we may seek him who alone supplies all of them, and find his every gift a window to his heart of truth. So begins a communion, a talking with God, a coming-to-one with him, which is the sole end of prayer, yea, of existence itself in its infinite phases. We must ask that we may receive; but that we should receive what we ask in respect of our lower needs, is not God's end in making us pray, for he could give us everything without that: to bring his child to his knee, God with-holds that man may ask.

In regard, however, to the high necessities of our nature, it is in or-der that he may be able to give that God requires us to ask—requires by driving us to it—by shutting us up to prayer. For how can he give into the soul of a man what it needs, while that soul cannot receive it? The ripeness for receiving is the asking. The blossom-cup of the soul, to be filled with the heavenly dews, is its prayer. When the soul is hungry for the light, for the truth—when its hunger has waked its higher energies, thoroughly roused the will, and brought the soul into its highest condition, that of action, its only fitness for receiving the things of God, that action is prayer. Then God can give; then he can be as he would towards the man; for the glory of God is to give him-self.—We thank thee, Lord Christ, for by thy pain alone do we rise towards the knowledge of this glory of thy rather and our Father.

And even in regard to lower things—what it may be altogether un-fit to do for a man who does not recognize the source of his life, it may be in the highest sense fit to grant him when he comes to that source to ask for it. Even in the case of some individual desire of one who in the main recognizes the Father, it may be well to give him asking whom, not asking, it would not benefit. For the real good of every gift it is essential, first, that the giver be in the gift—as God always is, for he is love—and next, that the receiver know and receive the giver in the gift. Every gift of God is but a harbinger of his greatest and only suf-ficing gift—that of himself. No gift unrecognized as coming from God is at its own best; therefore many things that God would gladly give us, things even that we need because we are, must wait until we ask for them, that we may know whence they come: when in all gifts we find him, then in him we shall find all things.

Sometimes to one praying will come the feeling rather than ques-tion: 'Were it not better to abstain? If this thing be good, will he not give it me? Would he not be better pleased if I left it altogether to him?' It comes, I think, of a lack of faith and childlikeness—taking form, perhaps, in a fear lest, asking for what was not good, the prayer should be granted. Such a thought has no place with St. Paul; he says, 'Casting all your care upon him, for he careth for you;' 'In everything making your request known unto him.' It may even come of ambition after spiritual distinction. In every request, heart and soul and mind ought to supply the low accompaniment, 'Thy will be done;' but the making of any request brings us near to him, into communion with our Life. Does it not also help us to think of him in all our affairs, and learn in everything to give thanks? Anything large enough for a wish to light upon, is large enough to hang a prayer upon: the thought of him to whom that prayer goes will purify and correct the desire. To say, 'Father, I should like this or that,' would be enough at once, if the wish were bad, to make us know it and turn from it. Such prayer about things must of necessity help to bring the mind into true and simple relation with him; to make us remember his will even when we do not see what that will is. Surely it is better and more trusting to tell him all without fear or anxiety. Was it not thus the Lord carried himself towards his Father when he said, 'If it be possible, let this cup pass from me'? But there was something he cared for more than his own fear— his Father's will: 'Nevertheless, not my will, but thine be done.' There is no apprehension that God might be displeased with him for saying what he would like, and not leaving it all to his Father. Neither did he regard his Father's plans as necessarily so fixed that they could not be altered to his prayer. The true son-faith is that which comes with boldness, fearless of the Father doing anything but what is right fatherly, patient, and full of loving-kindness. We must not think to please him by any asceticism even of the spirit; we must speak straight out to him. The true child will not fear, but lay bare his wishes to the perfect Father. The Father may will otherwise, but his grace will be enough for the child.

There could be no riches but for need. God himself is made rich by man's necessity. By that he is rich to give; through that we are rich by receiving.

As to any notion of prevailing by entreaty over an unwilling God, that is heathenish, and belongs to such as think him a hard master, or one like the unjust judge. What so quenching to prayer as the notion of unwillingness in the ear that hears! And when prayer is dull, what makes it flow like the thought that God is waiting to give, wants to give us everything! 'Let us therefore come boldly to the throne of

146

grace, that we may obtain mercy, and find grace to help in time of need.' We shall be refused our prayer if that be better; but what is good our Father will give us with divine good will. The Lord spoke his parable 'to the end that they ought always to pray, *and not to faint*.'

MAN'S DIFFICULTY CONCERNING PRAYER.

'—*and not to faint*.'— ST. LUKE xviii. 1.

'How should any design of the All-wise be altered in response to prayer of ours!' How are we to believe such a thing?

By reflecting that he is the All-wise, who sees before him, and will not block his path. Such objection springs from poorest idea of God in relation to us. It supposes him to have cares and plans and intentions concerning our part of creation, irrespective of us. What is the whole system of things for, but our education? Does God care for suns and planets and satellites, for divine mathematics and ordered harmonies, more than for his children? I venture to say he cares more for oxen than for those. He lays no plans irrespective of his children; and, his design being that they shall be free, active, live things, he sees that space be kept for them: they need room to struggle out of their chrysalis, to undergo the change that comes with the waking will, and to enter upon the divine sports and labours of children in the house and domain of their Father. Surely he may keep his plans in a measure unfixed, waiting the free desire of the individual soul! Is not the design of the first course of his children's education just to bring them to the point where they shall pray? and shall his system appointed to that end be then found hard and fast, tooth-fitted and inelastic, as if informed of no live causing soul, but an unself-knowing force—so that he cannot answer the prayer because of the system which has its existence for the sake of the prayer? True, in many cases, the prayer, far more than the opportunity of answering it, is God's end; but how will the further end of the prayer be reached, which is oneness between the heart of the child and of the Father? how will the child go on to pray if he knows the Father cannot answer him? *Will not* may be for love, but how with a self-imposed *cannot*? How could he be Father, who creating, would not make provision, would not keep room for the babbled prayers of his children? Is his perfection a mechanical one? Has he himself no room for choice—therefore can give none? There must be a Godlike region of choice as there is a human, however little we may be able to conceive it. It were a glory in such system that its suns themselves wavered and throbbed at the pulse of a new child-life.

What perfection in a dwelling would it be that its furniture and the paths between were fitted as the trays and pigeon-holes of a cabinet? What stupidity of perfection would that be which left no margin about God's work, no room for change of plan upon change of fact—yea, even the mighty change that, behold now at length, his child is praying! See the freedom of God in his sunsets—never a second like one of the foregone!—in his moons and skies—in the ever-changing solid earth!— all moving by no dead law, but in the harmony of the vital law of liberty, God's creative perfection—all ordered from within. A divine perfection that were indeed, where was no liberty! where there could be but one way of a thing! I may move my arm as I please: shall God be unable so to move his? If but for himself, God might well desire no change, but he is God for the sake of his growing creatures; all his making and doing is for them, and change is the necessity of their very existence. They need a mighty law of liberty, into which shall never intrude one atom of chance. Is the one idea of creation the begetting of a free, grand, divine will in us? and shall that will, praying with the will of the Father, find itself cramped, fettered, manacled by foregone laws? Will it not rather be a new-born law itself, working new things? No man is so tied by divine law that he can nowise modify his work: shall God not modify his? Law is but mode of life-action. Is it of his perfection that he should have no scope, no freedom? Is he but the prisoned steam in the engine, pushing, escaping, stopped—his way ordered by valve and piston? or is he an indwelling, willing, ordering power? Law is the slave of Life. Is not a man's soul, as it dwells in his body, a dim-shadowing type of God in and throughout his universe? If you say, he has made things to go, set them going, and left them— then I say, If his machine interfered with his answering the prayer of a single child, he would sweep it from him—not to bring back chaos, but to make room for his child. But order is divine, and cannot be obstructive to its own higher ends; it must subserve them. Order, free order, neither chaos, nor law unpossessed and senseless, is the home of Thought. If you say There can be but one perfect way, I answer, Yet the perfect way to bring a thing so far, to a certain crisis, can ill be the perfect way to carry it on after that crisis: the plan will have to change then. And as this crisis depends on a will, all cannot be in exact, though in live preparation for it. We must remember that God is not occupied with a grand toy of worlds and suns and planets, of attractions and repulsions, of agglomerations and crystallizations, of forces and waves; that these but constitute a portion of his workshops and tools for the bringing out of righteous men and women to fill his house of love withal. Would he have let his Son die for a law of nature, as we call it? These doubtless are the outcome of willed laws of his own being; but they take their relations in matter only for the sake of the birth of sons and daughters, that they may yet again be born from above, and into the higher region whence these things issue; and many a modification of the ideal, rendering it less than complete, must be given to those whose very doom being to grow or perish implies their utter inability to lay hold of the perfect. The best *means* cannot be the ideal Best. The embodiment of uplifting truth for the low, cannot be equal to that for the higher, else it will fail, and prove for its object not good; but, as the low ascend, their revelation will ascend also.

That God cannot interfere to modify his plans, interfere without the change of a single law of his world, is to me absurd. If we can change, God can change, else is he less free than we—his plans, I say, not principles, not ends: God himself forbid!—change them after divine fashion, above our fashions as the heavens are higher than the earth. And as in all his miracles Jesus did only in miniature what his Father does ever in the great—in far wider, more elaborate, and beautiful ways, I will adduce from them an instance of answer to prayer that has in it a point bearing, it seems to me, most importantly on the thing I am now trying to set forth. Poor, indeed, was the making of the wine in the earthen pots of stone, compared with its making in the lovely growth of the vine with its clusters of swelling grapes—the live roots gathering from the earth the water that had to be borne in pitchers and poured into the great vases; but it is precious as the interpreter of the same, even in its being the outcome of our Lord's sympathy with ordinary human rejoicing. There is however an element in its origin that makes it yet more precious to me—the regard of our Lord to a wish of his mother. Alas, how differently is the tale often received! how misunderstood!

His mother had suggested to him that here was an opportunity for appearing in his own greatness, the potent purveyor of wine for the failing feast. It was not in his plan, as we gather from his words; for the Lord never pretended anything, whether to his enemy or his mother; he is The True. He lets her know that he and she have different outlooks, different notions of his work: 'What to me and thee, woman?' he said: 'my hour is not yet come;' but there was that in his look and tone whence she knew that her desire, scarce half-fashioned into request, was granted. What am I thence to conclude, worthy of the Son of God, and the Son of Mary, but that, at the prayer of his mother, he made room in his plans for the thing she desired? It was not his wish then to work a miracle, but if his mother wished it, he would! He did for his mother what for his own part he would rather have let alone. Not always did he do as his mother would have him; but this was a case in which he could do so, for it would interfere nowise with the will of his Father. Was the perfect son, for, being perfect, he must be perfect every way, to be the only son of man who needed do nothing to please his mother—nothing but what fell in with his plan for the hour? Not so could he be the root, the living heart of the great response of the children to the Father of all! not so could the idea of the grand family ever be made a reality! Alas for the son who would not willingly for his mother do something which in itself he would rather not do! If it would have hurt his mother, if it had been in any way turning from the will of his Father in heaven, he would not have done it: that would have been to answer her prayer against her. His yielding makes the story doubly precious to my heart. The Son then could change his intent, and spoil nothing: so, I say, can the Father; for the Son does nothing but what he sees the Father do.

Finding it possible to understand, however, that God may answer prayers to those who pray for themselves, what are we to think concerning prayer for others? One may well say, It would surely be very selfish to pray only for ourselves! but the question is of the use, not of the character of the action: if there be any good in it, let us pray for all for whom we feel we can pray; but is there to be found in regard to prayer for others any such satisfaction as in regard to prayer for ourselves? The ground is changed—if the fitness of answering prayer lies in the praying of him who prays: the attitude necessary to reception does not belong to those *for* whom prayer is made, but to him *by* whom it is made. What fitness then can there be in praying for others? Will God give to another for our asking what he would not give without it? Would he not, if it could be done without the person's self, do it without a second person? If God were a tyrant, one whose heart might be softened by the sight of anxious love; or if he were one who might be informed, enlightened, reasoned with; or one in whom a setting forth of character, need, or claim might awake interest; then would there be plain reason in prayer for another—which yet, however disinterested and loving, must be degrading, as offered to one unworthy of prayer. But if we believe that God is the one unselfish, the one good being in the universe, and that his one design with his children is to make them perfect as he is perfect; if we believe that he not only would once give, but is always giving himself to us for our life; if we believe—which once I heard a bishop decline to acknowledge—that God does his best for *every* man; if also we believe that God knows every man's needs, and will, for love's sake, not spare one pang that may serve to purify the soul of one of his children; if we believe all this, how can we think he will in any sort alter his way with one because another prays for him? The prayer would arise from nothing in the person prayed for; why should it initiate a change in God's dealing with him?

The argument I know not how to answer. I can only, in the face of it, and feeling all the difficulty, say, and say again, 'Yet I believe I may pray for my friend—for my enemy—for anybody! Yet and yet, there is, there must be some genuine, essential good and power in the prayer of one man for another to the maker of both—and that just because their maker is perfect, not less than very God.' I shall not bring authority to bear, for authority can at best but make us believe reason there, it cannot make us see it. The difficulty remains the same even when we hear the Lord himself pray to his Father for those the Father loves because they have received his Son—loves therefore with a special love, as the foremost in faith, the elect of the world—loves not merely because they must die if he did not love them, but loves from the deeps of divine approval. Those who believe in Jesus will be satisfied, in the face of the incomprehensible, that in what he does reason and right must lie; but not therefore do we understand. At the same time, though I cannot explain, I can show some ground upon which, even had he not been taught to do so, but left alone with his heart, a man might yet, I think, pray for another.

If God has made us to love like himself, and like himself long to help; if there are for whom we, like him, would give our lives to lift them from the evil gulf of their ungodliness; if the love in us would, for the very easing of the love he kindled, gift another—like himself who chooses and cherishes even the love that pains him; if, in the midst of a sore need to bless, to give, to help, we are aware of an utter impotence; if the fire burns and cannot out; and if all our hope for ourselves lies in God—what is there for us, what can we think of, what

152

do, but go to God?—what but go to him with this our own difficulty and need? And where is the natural refuge, there must be the help. There can be no need for which he has no supply. The best argument that he has help, is that we have need. If I can be helped through my friend, I think God will take the thing up, and do what I cannot do— help my friend that I may be helped—perhaps help me to help him. You see, in praying for another we pray for ourselves—for the relief of the needs of our love; it is not prayer for another alone, and thus it comes under the former kind. Would God give us love, the root of power, in us, and leave that love, whereby he himself creates, alto- gether helpless in us? May he not at least expedite something for our prayers? Where he could not alter, he could perhaps expedite, in view of some help we might then be able to give. If he desires that we should work with him, that work surely helps him!

There are some things for which the very possibility of supposing them are an argument; but I think I can go a little farther here, and im- agine at least the *where* if not the *how*, the divine conditions in which the help for another in answer to prayer is born, the divine region in which its possibility must dwell.

God is ever seeking to lift us up into the sharing of his divine na- ture; God's kings, such men, namely, as with Jesus have borne witness to the truth, share his glory even on the throne of the Father. See the grandeur of the creative love of the Holy! nothing less will serve it than to have his children, through his and their suffering, share the throne of his glory! If such be the perfection of the Infinite, should that perfection bring him under bonds and difficulties, and not rather set him freer to do the thing he would in the midst of opposing forces? If his glory be in giving himself, and we must share therein, giving our- selves, why should we not begin here and now? If he would have his children fellow-workers with him; if he has desired and willed that not only by the help of his eternal Son, but by the help also of the children who through him have been born from above, other and still other children shall be brought to his knee, to his fireside, to the plenty of his house, why should he not have kept some margin of room wherein their prayers may work for those whom they have to help, who are of the same life as they? I cannot tell how, but may not those prayers in some way increase God's opportunity for working his best and highest will? Dealing with his children, the good ones may add to his power with the not yet good—add to his means of helping them. One way is clear: the prayer will react upon the mind that prays, its light will grow, will shine the brighter, and draw and enlighten the more. But there must be more in the thing. Prayer in its perfect idea being a rising up into the will of the Eternal, may not the help of the Father become one with the prayer of the child, and for the prayer of him he holds in his arms, go forth for him who wills not yet to be lifted to his embrace? To his bosom God himself cannot bring his children at once, and not at all except through his own suffering and theirs. But will not any good parent find some way of granting the prayer of the child who comes to him, saying, 'Papa, this is my brother's birthday: I have nothing to give him, and I do love him so! could you give me something to give him, or give him something for me?'

'Still, could not God have given the gift without the prayer? And why should the good of any one depend on the prayer of another?'

I can only answer with the return question, 'Why should my love be powerless to help another?' But we must not tie God to our measures of time, or think he has forgotten that prayer even which, apparently unanswered, we have forgotten. Death is not an impervious wall; through it, beyond it, go the prayers. It is possible we may have some to help in the next world because we have prayed for them in this: will it not be a boon to them to have an old friend to their service? I but speculate and suggest. What I see and venture to say is this: If in God we live and move and have our being; if the very possibility of loving lies in this, that we exist in and by the live air of love, namely God himself, we must in this very fact be nearer to each other than by any bodily proximity or interchange of help; and if prayer is like a pulse that sets this atmosphere in motion, we must then by prayer come closer to each other than are the parts of our body by their complex nerve- telegraphy. Surely, in the Eternal, hearts are never parted! surely, through the Eternal, a heart that loves and seeks the good of another, must hold that other within reach! Surely the system of things would not be complete in relation to the best thing in it—love itself, if love had no help in prayer. If I love and cannot help, does not my heart move me to ask him to help who loves and can?—him without whom life would be to me nothing, without whom I should neither love nor care to pray!—will he answer, 'Child, do not trouble me; I am already doing all I can'? If such answer came, who that loved would not be content to be nowhere in the matter? But how if the eternal, limitless Love, the unspeakable, self-forgetting God-devotion, which, demanding all, gives all, should say, 'Child, I have been doing all I could; but now you are come, I shall be able to do more! here is a corner for you, my little one: push at this thing to get it out of the way'! How if he should answer, 'Pray on, my child; I am hearing you; it goes through

154

me in help to him. We are of one mind about it; I help and you help. I shall have you all safe home with me by and by! There is no fear, only we must work, and not lose heart. Go, and let your light so shine before men that they may see your good things, and glorify me by knowing that I am light and no darkness'!—what then? Oh that lovely picture by Michelangelo, with the young ones and the little ones come to help God to make Adam!

But it may be that the answer to prayer will come in a shape that seems a refusal. It may come even in an increase of that from which we seek deliverance. I know of one who prayed to love better: a sore division came between—out of which at length rose a dawn of tenderness.

Our vision is so circumscribed, our theories are so small—the garment of them not large enough to wrap us in; our faith so continually fashions itself to the fit of our dwarf intellect, that there is endless room for rebellion against ourselves: we must not let our poor knowledge limit our not so poor intellect, our intellect limit our faith, our faith limit our divine hope; reason must humbly watch over all—reason, the candle of the Lord.

There are some who would argue for prayer, not on the ground of any possible answer to be looked for, but because of the good to be gained in the spiritual attitude of the mind in praying. There are those even who, not believing in any ear to hear, any heart to answer, will yet pray. They say it does them good; they pray to nothing at all, but they get spiritual benefit.

I will not contradict their testimony. So needful is prayer to the soul that the mere attitude of it may encourage a good mood. Verily to pray to that which is not, is in logic a folly; yet the good that, they say, comes of it, may rebuke the worse folly of their unbelief, for it indicates that prayer is natural, and how could it be natural if inconsistent with the very mode of our being? Theirs is a better way than that of those who, believing there is a God, but not believing that he will give any answer to their prayers, yet pray to him; that is more foolish and more immoral than praying to the No-god. Whatever the God be to whom they pray, their prayer is a mockery of him, of themselves, of the truth.

On the other hand, let God give no assent to the individual prayer, let the prayer even be for something nowise good enough to be a gift of God, yet the soul that prays will get good of its prayer, if only in being thereby brought a little nearer to the Father, and making way for coming again. Prayer does react in good upon the praying soul, irrespective of answer. But to pray for the sake of the prayer, and without regard to there being no one to hear, would to me indicate a nature not merely illogical but morally false, did I not suspect a vague undetected apprehension of a Something diffused through the All of existence, and some sort of shadowiest communion therewith.

There are moods of such satisfaction in God that a man may feel as if nothing were left to pray for, as if he had but to wait with patience for what the Lord would work; there are moods of such hungering desire, that petition is crushed into an inarticulate crying; and there is a communion with God that asks for nothing, yet asks for everything. This last is the very essence of prayer, though not petition. It is possible for a man, not indeed to believe in God, but to believe that there is a God, and yet not desire to enter into communion with him; but he that prays and does not faint will come to recognize that to talk with God is more than to have all prayers granted—that it is the end of all prayer, granted or refused. And he who seeks the Father more than anything he can give, is likely to have what he asks, for he is not likely to ask amiss.

Even such as ask amiss may sometimes have their prayers answered. The Father will never give the child a stone that asks for bread; but I am not sure that he will never give the child a stone that asks for a stone. If the Father say, 'My child, that is a stone; it is no bread;' and the child answer, 'I am sure it is bread; I want it;' may it not be well he should try his bread?

But now for another point in the parable, where I think I can give some help—I mean the Lord's apparent recognition of delay in the answering of prayer: in the very structure of the parable he seems to take delay for granted, and says notwithstanding, 'He will avenge them speedily!'

The reconciling conclusion is, that God loses no time, though the answer may not be immediate.

He may delay because it would not be safe to give us at once what we ask: we are not ready for it. To give ere we could truly receive, would be to destroy the very heart and hope of prayer, to cease to be our Father. The delay itself may work to bring us nearer to our help, to increase the desire, perfect the prayer, and ripen the receptive condition.

Again, not from any straitening in God, but either from our own condition and capacity, or those of the friend for whom we pray, time may be necessary to the working out of the answer. God is limited by regard for our best; our best implies education; in this we must ourselves have a large share; this share, being human, involves time. And perhaps, indeed, the better the gift we pray for, the more time is necessary to its arrival. To give us the spiritual gift we desire, God may have to begin far back in our spirit, in regions unknown to us, and do much work that we can be aware of only in the results; for our consciousness is to the extent of our being but as the flame of the volcano to the world-gulf whence it issues: in the gulf of our unknown being God works behind our consciousness. With his holy influence, with his own presence, the one thing for which most earnestly we cry, he may be approaching our consciousness from behind, coming forward through regions of our darkness into our light, long before we begin to be aware that he is answering our request—has answered it, and is visiting his child. To avenge speedily must mean to make no delay beyond what is absolutely necessary, to begin the moment it is possible to begin. Because the Son of Man did not appear for thousands of years after men began to cry out for a Saviour, shall we imagine he did not come the first moment it was well he should come? Can we doubt that to come a moment sooner would have been to delay, not to expedite, his kingdom? For anything that needs a process, to begin to act at once is to be speedy. God does not put off like the unrighteous judge; he does not delay until irritated by the prayers of the needy; he will hear while they are yet speaking; yea, before they call he will answer.

The Lord uses words without anxiety as to the misuse of them by such as do not search after his will in them; and the word *avenge* may be simply retained from the parable without its special meaning therein; yet it suggests a remark or two.

Of course, no prayer for any revenge that would gratify the selfishness of our nature, a thing to be burned out of us by the fire of God, needs think to be heard. Be sure, when the Lord prayed his Father to forgive those who crucified him, he uttered his own wish and his Father's will at once: God will never punish according to the abstract abomination of sin, as if men knew what they were doing. 'Vengeance is mine,' he says: with a right understanding of it, we might as well pray for God's vengeance as for his forgiveness; that vengeance is, to destroy the sin—to make the sinner abjure and hate it; nor is there any satisfaction in a vengeance that seeks or effects less. The man himself must turn against himself, and so be for himself. If nothing else will do, then hell-fire; if less will do, whatever brings repentance and self-repudiation, is God's repayment.

Friends, if any prayers are offered against us; if the vengeance of God be cried out for, because of some wrong you or I have done, God grant us his vengeance! Let us not think that we shall get off!

But perhaps the Lord was here thinking, not of persecution, or any form of human wrong, but of the troubles that most trouble his true disciple; and the suggestion is comforting to those whose foes are within them, for, if so, then he recognizes the evils of self, against which we fight, not as parts of ourselves, but as our foes, on which he will avenge the true self that is at strife with them. And certainly no evil is, or ever could be, of the essential being and nature of the creature God made! The thing that is not good, however associated with our being, is against that being, not of it—is its enemy, on which we need to be avenged. When we fight, he will avenge. Till we fight, evil shall have dominion over us, a dominion to make us miserable; other than miserable can no one be, under the yoke of a nature contrary to his own. Comfort thyself then, who findest thine own heart and soul, or rather the things that move therein, too much for thee: God will avenge his own elect. He is not delaying; he is at work for thee. Only thou must pray, and not faint. Ask, ask; it shall be given you. Seek most the best things; to ask for the best things is to have them; the seed of them is in you, or you could not ask for them.

But from whatever quarter come our troubles, whether from the world outside or the world inside, still let us pray. In his own right way, the only way that could satisfy us, for we are of his kind, will God answer our prayers with help. He will avenge us of our adversaries, and that speedily. Only let us take heed that we be adversaries to no man, but fountains of love and forgiving tenderness to all. And from no adversary, either on the way with us, or haunting the secret chamber of our hearts, let us hope to be delivered till we *have paid the last farthing.*

THE LAST FARTHING.

'Verily I say unto thee, thou shalt by no means come out thence, till thou have paid the last farthing.'— ST. MATTHEW v. 26.

There is a thing wonderful and admirable in the parables, not readily grasped, but specially indicated by the Lord himself—their unintelligibility to the mere intellect. They are addressed to the conscience and not to the intellect, to the will and not to the imagination. They are strong and direct but not definite. They are not meant to explain anything, but to rouse a man to the feeling, 'I am not what I ought to be, I do not the thing I ought to do!' Many maundering interpretations may be given by the wise, with plentiful loss of labour, while the child who uses them for the necessity of walking in the one path will constantly receive light from them. The greatest obscuration of the words of the Lord, as of all true teachers, comes from those who give themselves to interpret rather than do them. Theologians have done more to hide the gospel of Christ than any of its adversaries. It was not for our understandings, but our will, that Christ came. He who does that which he sees, shall understand; he who is set upon understanding rather than doing, shall go on stumbling and mistaking and speaking foolishness. He has not that in him which can understand that kind. The gospel itself, and in it the parables of the Truth, are to be understood only by those who walk by what they find. It is he that runneth that shall read, and no other. It is not intended by the speaker of the parables that any other should know intellectually what, known but intellectually, would be for his injury—what knowing intellectually he would imagine he had grasped, perhaps even appropriated. When the pilgrim of the truth comes on his journey to the region of the parable, he finds its interpretation. It is not a fruit or a jewel to be stored, but a well springing by the wayside.

Let us try to understand what the Lord himself said about his parables. It will be better to take the reading of St. Matthew xiii. 14-15, as it is plainer, and the quotation from Isaiah vi. 9-10) is given in full—after the Septuagint, and much clearer than in our version from the Hebrew:—in its light should be read the corresponding passages in the other Gospels: in St. Mark's it is so compressed as to be capable of quite a different and false meaning: in St. John's reference, the blinding of the heart seems attributed directly to the devil:—the purport is, that those who by insincerity and falsehood close their deeper eyes, shall not be capable of using in the matter the more superficial eyes of their understanding. Whether this follows as a psychical or metaphysical necessity, or be regarded as a special punishment, it is equally the will of God, and comes from him who is the live Truth. They shall not see what is not for such as they. It is the punishment of the true Love, and is continually illustrated and fulfilled: if I know anything of the truth of God, then the objectors to Christianity, so far as I am acquainted with them, do not; their arguments, not in themselves false, have nothing to do with the matter; they see the thing they are talking against, but they do not see the thing they think they are talking against.

This will help to remove the difficulty that the parables are plainly for the teaching of the truth, and yet the Lord speaks of them as for the concealing of it. They are for the understanding of that man only who is practical—who does the thing he knows, who seeks to understand vitally. They reveal to the live conscience, otherwise not to the keenest intellect—though at the same time they may help to rouse the conscience with glimpses of the truth, where the man is on the borders of waking. Ignorance may be at once a punishment and a kindness: all punishment is kindness, and the best of which the man at the time is capable: 'Because you will not do, you shall not see; but it would be worse for you if you did see, not being of the disposition to do.' Such are punished in having the way closed before them; they punish themselves; their own doing results as it cannot but result on them. To say to them certain things so that they could understand them, would but harden them more, because they would not do them; they should have but parables—lanterns of the truth, clear to those who will walk in their light, dark to those who will not. The former are content to have the light cast upon their way; the latter will have it in their eyes, and cannot: if they had, it would but blind them. For them to know more would be their worse condemnation. They are not fit to know more; more shall not be given them yet; it is their punishment that they are in the wrong, and shall keep in the wrong until they come out of it. 'You choose the dark; you shall stay in the dark till the terrors that dwell in the dark affray you, and cause you to cry out.' God puts a seal upon the will of man; that seal is either his great punishment, or his mighty favour: 'Ye love the darkness, abide in the darkness:' 'O woman, great is thy faith: be it done unto thee even as thou wilt!'

What special meaning may be read in the different parts of magistrate, judge, and officer, beyond the general suggestion, perhaps, of the tentative approach of the final, I do not know; but I think I do know what is meant by 'agree on the way,' and 'the uttermost farthing.' The parable is an appeal to the common sense of those that hear it, in regard to every affair of righteousness. Arrange what claim lies against you; compulsion waits behind it. Do at once what you must do one day. As there is no escape from payment, escape at least the prison that will enforce it. Do not drive Justice to extremities. Duty is imperative; it must be done. It is useless to think to escape the eternal law of things; yield of yourself, nor compel God to compel you.

To the honest man, to the man who would fain be honest, the word is of right gracious import. To the untrue, it is a terrible threat; to him who is of the truth, it is sweet as most loving promise. He who is of God's mind in things, rejoices to hear the word of the changeless Truth; the voice of the Right fills the heavens and the earth, and makes his soul glad; it is his salvation. If God were not inexorably just, there would be no stay for the soul of the feeblest lover of right: 'thou art true, O Lord: one day I also shall be true!' 'Thou shalt render the right, cost you what it may,' is a dread sound in the ears of those whose life is a falsehood: what but the last farthing would those who love righteousness more than life pay? It is a joy profound as peace to know that God is determined upon such payment, is determined to have his children clean, clear, pure as very snow; is determined that not only shall they with his help make up for whatever wrong they have done, but at length be incapable, by eternal choice of good, under any temptation, of doing the thing that is not divine, the thing God would not do.

There has been much cherishing of the evil fancy, often without its taking formal shape, that there is some way of getting out of the region of strict justice, some mode of managing to escape doing *all* that is required of us; but there is no such escape. A way to avoid any demand of righteousness would be an infinitely worse way than the road to the everlasting fire, for its end would be eternal death. No, there is

no escape. There is no heaven with a little of hell in it—no plan to re-
tain this or that of the devil in our hearts or our pockets. Out Satan
must go, every hair and feather! Neither shalt thou think to be deliv-
ered from the necessity of *being* good by being made good. God is the
God of the animals in a far lovelier way, I suspect, than many of us
dare to think, but he will not be the God of a man by making a good
beast of him. Thou must be good; neither death nor any admittance
into good company will make thee good; though, doubtless, if thou be
willing and try, these and all other best helps will be given thee. There
is no clothing in a robe of imputed righteousness, that poorest of legal
cobwebs spun by spiritual spiders. To me it seems like an invention of
well-meaning dulness to soothe insanity; and indeed it has proved a
door of escape out of worse imaginations. It is apparently an old 'doc-
trine;' for St. John seems to point at it where he says, 'Little children,
let no man lead you astray; he that doeth righteousness is righteous
even as he is righteous.' Christ is our righteousness, not that we should
escape punishment, still less escape being righteous, but as the live
potent creator of righteousness in us, so that we, with our wills receiv-
ing his spirit, shall like him resist unto blood, striving against sin; shall
know in ourselves, as he knows, what a lovely thing is righteousness,
what a mean, ugly, unnatural thing is unrighteousness. He *is* our right-
eousness, and that righteousness is no fiction, no pretence, no
imputation.

One thing that tends to keep men from seeing righteousness and
unrighteousness as they are, is, that they have been told many things
are righteous and unrighteous, which are neither the one nor the other.
Righteousness is just fairness—from God to man, from man to God
and to man; it is giving every one his due—his large mighty due. He is
righteous, and no one else, who does this. And any system which tends
to persuade men that there is any salvation but that of becoming right-
eous even as Jesus is righteous; that a man can be made good, as a
good dog is good, without his own willed share in the making; that a
man is saved by having his sins hidden under a robe of imputed right-
eousness—that system, so far as this tendency, is of the devil and not
of God. Thank God, not even error shall injure the true of heart; it is
not wickedness. They grow in the truth, and as love casts out fear, so
truth casts out falsehood.

I read, then, in this parable, that a man had better make up his mind
to be righteous, to be fair, to do what he can to pay what he owes, in
any and all the relations of life—all the matters, in a word, wherein
one man may demand of another, or complain that he has not received

fair play. Arrange your matters with those who have anything against you, while you are yet together and things have not gone too far to be arranged; *you will have to do it*, and that under less easy circumstances than now. Putting off is of no use. You must. The thing has to be done; there are means of compelling you.

'In this affair, however, I am in the right.'

'If so, very well—for this affair. But I have reason to doubt whether you are capable of judging righteously in your own cause:—do you hate the man?'

'No, I don't hate him.'

'Do you dislike him?'

'I can't say I *like* him.'

'Do you love him as yourself?'

'Oh, come! come! no one does that!'

'Then no one is to be trusted when he thinks, however firmly, that he is all right, and his neighbour all wrong, in any matter between them.'

'But I don't say I am all right, and he is all wrong; there may be something to urge on his side: what I say is, that I am more in the right than he.'

'This is not fundamentally a question of things: it is a question of condition, of spiritual relation and action, towards your neighbour. If in yourself you were all right towards him, you could do him no wrong. Let it be with the individual dispute as it may, you owe him something that you do not pay him, as certainly as you think he owes you something he will not pay you.'

'He would take immediate advantage of me if I owned that.'

'So much the worse for him. Until you are fair to him, it does not matter to you whether he is unfair to you or not.'

'I beg your pardon—it is just what does matter! I want nothing but my rights. What can matter to me more than my rights?'

'Your duties—your debts. You are all wrong about the thing. It is a very small matter *to you* whether the man give you your rights or not; it is life or death to you whether or not you give him his. Whether he pay you what you count his debt or no, you will be compelled to pay him all you owe him. If you owe him a pound and he you a million, you must pay him the pound whether he pay you the million or not; there is no business-parallel here. If, owing you love, he gives you hate, you, owing him love, have yet to pay it. A love unpaid you, a justice undone you, a praise withheld from you, a judgment passed on you without judgment, will not absolve you of the debt of a love unpaid, a justice not done, a praise withheld, a false judgment passed: these uttermost farthings—not to speak of such debts as the world itself counts grievous wrongs—you must pay him, whether he pay you or not. We have a good while given us to pay, but a crisis will come—come soon after all—comes always sooner than those expect it who are not ready for it—a crisis when the demand unyielded will be followed by prison.

The same holds with every demand of God: by refusing to pay, the man makes an adversary who will compel him—and that for the man's own sake. If you or your life say, 'I will not,' then he will see to it. There is a prison, and the one thing we know about that prison is, that its doors do not open until entire satisfaction is rendered, the last farthing paid.

The main debts whose payment God demands are those which lie at the root of all right, those we owe in mind, and soul, and being. Whatever in us can be or make an adversary, whatever could prevent us from doing the will of God, or from agreeing with our fellow—all must be yielded. Our every relation, both to God and our fellow, must be acknowledged heartily, met as a reality. Smaller debts, if any debt can be small, follow as a matter of course.

If the man acknowledge, and would pay if he could but cannot, the universe will be taxed to help him rather than he should continue unable. If the man accepts the will of God, he is the child of the Father, the whole power and wealth of the Father is for him, and the uttermost farthing will easily be paid. If the man denies the debt, or acknowledging does nothing towards paying it, then—at last—the prison! God in the dark can make a man thirst for the light, who never in the light sought but the dark. The cells of the prison may differ in degree of darkness; but they are all alike in this, that not a door opens but to payment. There is no day but the will of God, and he who is of the night cannot be for ever allowed to roam the day; unfelt, unprized, the light must be taken from him, that he may know what the darkness is. When the darkness is perfect, when he is totally without the light he has spent the light in slaying, then will he know darkness.

I think I have seen from afar something of the final prison of all, the innermost cell of the debtor of the universe; I will endeavour to convey what I think it may be.

It is the vast outside; the ghastly dark beyond the gates of the city of which God is the light—where the evil dogs go ranging, silent as the dark, for there is no sound any more than sight. The time of signs is over. Every sense has its signs, and they were all misused: there is no sense, no sign more—nothing now by means of which to believe. The man wakes from the final struggle of death, in absolute loneliness— such a loneliness as in the most miserable moment of deserted childhood he never knew. Not a hint, not a shadow of anything outside his consciousness reaches him. All is dark, dark and dumb; no motion—not the breath of a wind! never a dream of change! not a scent from far-off field! nothing to suggest being or thing besides the man himself, no sign of God anywhere. God has so far withdrawn from the man, that he is conscious only of that from which he has withdrawn. In the midst of the live world he cared for nothing but himself; now in the dead world he is in God's prison, his own separated self. He would not believe in God because he never saw God; now he doubts if there be such a thing as the face of a man—doubts if he ever really saw one, ever anything more than dreamed of such a thing:—he never came near enough to human being, to know what human being really was— so may well doubt if human beings ever were, if ever he was one of them.

Next after doubt comes reasoning on the doubt: 'The only one must be God! I know no one but myself: I must myself be God—none else!' Poor helpless dumb devil!—his own glorious lord god! Yea, he will imagine himself that same resistless force which, without his will, without his knowledge, is the law by which the sun burns, and the stars keep their courses, the strength that drives all the engines of the world. His fancy will give birth to a thousand fancies, which will run riot like the mice in a house but just deserted: he will call it creation, and *his*. Having no reality to set them beside, nothing to correct them by; the measured order, harmonious relations, and sweet graces of God's world nowhere for him; what he thinks, will be, for lack of what God thinks, the man's realities: what others can he have! Soon, misery will beget on imagination a thousand shapes of woe, which he will not be able to rule, direct, or even distinguish from real presences—a whole world of miserable contradictions and cold-fever-dreams.

But no liveliest human imagination could supply adequate representation of what it would be to be left without a shadow of the presence of God. If God gave it, man could not understand it: he knows neither God nor himself in the way of the understanding. For not he who cares least about God was in this world ever left as God could leave him. I doubt if any man could continue following his wickedness from whom God had withdrawn.

The most frightful idea of what could, to his own consciousness, befall a man, is that he should have to lead an existence with which

God had nothing to do. The thing could not be; for being that is
caused, the causation ceasing, must of necessity cease. It is always in,
and never out of God, that we can live and do. But I suppose the man
so left that he seems to himself utterly alone, yet, alas! with himself—
smallest interchange of thought, feeblest contact of existence, dullest
reflection from other being, impossible: in such evil case I believe the
man would be glad to come in contact with the worst-loathed insect: it
would be a shape of life, something beyond and besides his own huge,
void, formless being! I imagine some such feeling in the prayer of the
devils for leave to go into the swine. His worst enemy, could he but be
aware of him, he would be ready to worship. For the misery would be
not merely the absence of all being other than his own self, but the
fearful, endless, unavoidable presence of that self. Without the correc-
tion, the reflection, the support of other presences, being is not merely
unsafe, it is a horror—for anyone but God, who is his own being. For
him whose idea is God's, and the image of God, his own being is far
too fragmentary and imperfect to be anything like good company. It is
the lovely creatures God has made all around us, in them giving us
himself, that, until we know him, save us from the frenzy of alone-
ness—for that aloneness is Self, Self, Self. The man who minds only
himself must at last go mad if God did not interfere.

Can there be any way out of the misery? Will the soul that could
not believe in God, with all his lovely world around testifying of him,
believe when shut in the prison of its own lonely, weary all-and- noth-
ing? It would for a time try to believe that it was indeed nothing, a
mere glow of the setting sun on a cloud of dust, a paltry dream that
dreamed itself—then, ah, if only the dream might dream that it was no
more! that would be the one thing to hope for. Self-loathing, and that
for no sin, from no repentance, from no vision of better, would begin
and grow and grow; and to what it might not come no soul can tell—of
essential, original misery, uncompromising self disgust! Only, then, if
a being be capable of self-disgust, is there not some room for hope—as
much as a pinch of earth in the cleft of a rock might yield for the
growth of a pine? Nay, there must be hope while there is existence; for
where there is existence there must be God; and God is for ever good,
nor can be other than good. But alas, the distance from the light! Such
a soul is at the farthest verge of life's negation!—no, not the farthest! a
man is nearer heaven when in deepest hell than just ere he begins to
reap the reward of his doings—for he is in a condition to receive the
smallest show of the life that is, as a boon unspeakable. All his years
in the world he received the endless gifts of sun and air, earth and sea

and human face divine, as things that came to him because that was their way, and there was no one to prevent them; now the poorest thinning of the darkness he would hail as men of old the glow of a descending angel; it would be as a messenger from God. Not that he would think of God! it takes long to think of God; but hope, not yet seeming hope, would begin to dawn in his bosom, and the thinner darkness would be as a cave of light, a refuge from the horrid self of which he used to be so proud.

A man may well imagine it impossible ever to think so unpleasantly of himself! But he has only to let things go, and he will make it the real, right, natural way to think of himself. True, all I have been saying is imaginary; but our imagination is made to mirror truth; all the things that appear in it are more or less after the model of things that are; I suspect it is the region whence issues prophecy; and when we are true it will mirror nothing but truth. I deal here with the same light and darkness the Lord dealt with, the same St. Paul and St. John and St. Peter and St. Jude dealt with. Ask yourself whether the faintest dawn of even physical light would not be welcome to such a soul as some refuge from the dark of the justly hated self.

And the light would grow and grow across the awful gulf between the soul and its haven—its repentance—for repentance is the first pressure of the bosom of God; and in the twilight, struggling and faint, the man would feel, faint as the twilight, another thought beside his, another thinking Something nigh his dreary self—perhaps the man he had most wronged, most hated, most despised—and would be glad that some one, whoever, was near him: the man he had most injured, and was most ashamed to meet, would be a refuge from himself—oh, how welcome!

So might I imagine a thousand steps up from the darkness, each a little less dark, a little nearer the light—but, ah, the weary way! He cannot come out until he have paid the uttermost farthing! Repentance once begun, however, may grow more and more rapid! If God once get a willing hold, if with but one finger he touch the man's self, swift as possibility will he draw him from the darkness into the light. For that for which the forlorn, self-ruined wretch was made, was to be a child of God, a partaker of the divine nature, an heir of God and joint heir with Christ. Out of the abyss into which he cast himself, refusing to be the heir of God, he must rise and be raised. To the heart of God, the one and only goal of the human race—the refuge and home of all and each, he must set out and go, or the last glimmer of humanity will die from him. Whoever will live must cease to be a slave and become a child of God. There is no half-way house of rest, where ungodliness may be dallied with, nor prove quite fatal. Be they few or many cast into such prison as I have endeavoured to imagine, there can be no deliverance for human soul, whether in that prison or out of it, but in paying the last farthing, in becoming lowly, penitent, self-refusing—so receiving the sonship, and learning to cry, *Father*!

ABBA, FATHER!

'—the spirit of adoption, whereby we cry, Abba, Father.'-ROMANS viii. 15.

The hardest, gladdest thing in the world is, to cry *Father*! from a full heart. I would help whom I may to call thus upon the Father.

There are things in all forms of the systematic teaching of Christianity to check this outgoing of the heart—with some to render it simply impossible. The more delicate the affections, the less easy to satisfy, the readier are they to be damped and discouraged, yea quite blown aside; even the suspicion of a cold reception is enough to paralyze them. Such a cold wind blowing at the very gate of heaven—thank God, *outside* the gate!—is the so-called doctrine of *Adoption*. When a heart hears—and believes, or half believes—that it is not the child of God by origin, from the first of its being, but may possibly be adopted into his family, its love sinks at once in a cold faint: where is its own father, and who is this that would adopt it? To myself, in the morning of childhood, the evil doctrine was a mist through which the light came struggling, a cloud-phantom of repellent mien—requiring maturer thought and truer knowledge to dissipate it. But it requires neither much knowledge nor much insight to stand up against its hideousness; it needs but love that will not be denied, and courage to question the phantom.

A devout and honest scepticism on God's side, not to be put down by anything called authority, is absolutely necessary to him who would know the liberty wherewith Christ maketh free. Whatever any company of good men thinks or believes, is to be approached with respect; but nothing claimed or taught, be the claimers or the teachers who they may, must come between the soul and the spirit of the father, who is himself the teacher of his children. Nay, to accept authority may be to refuse the very thing the 'authority' would teach; it may remain alto-gether misunderstood just for lack of that natural process of doubt and inquiry, which we were intended to go through by him who would have us understand.

As no scripture is of private interpretation, so is there no feeling in human heart which exists in that heart alone, which is not, in some form or degree, in every heart; and thence I conclude that many must have groaned like myself under the supposed authority of this doctrine. The refusal to look up to God as our Father is the one central wrong in the whole human affair; the inability, the one central misery: whatever serves to clear any difficulty from the way of the recognition of the Father, will more or less undermine every difficulty in life.

'Is God then not my Father,' cries the heart of the child, 'that I need to be adopted by him? Adoption! that can never satisfy me. Who is my father? Am I not his to begin with? Is God not my very own Father? Is he my Father only in a sort or fashion—by a legal contrivance? Truly, much love may lie in adoption, but if I accept it from any one, I allow myself the child of another! The adoption of God would indeed be a blessed thing if another than he had given me being! but if he gave me being, then it means no reception, but a repudiation.—"O Father, am I not your child?"'

'No; but he will adopt you. He will not acknowledge you his child, but he will call you his child, and be a father to you.'

'Alas!' cries the child, 'if he be not my father, he cannot become my father. A father is a father from the beginning. A primary relation can-not be superinduced. The consequence might be small where earthly fatherhood was concerned, but the very origin of my being—alas, if he be only a maker and not a father! Then am I only a machine, and not a child—not a man! It is false to say I was created in his image!

'It avails nothing to answer that we lost our birthright by the fall. I do not care to argue that *I* did not fall when Adam fell; for I have fall-en many a time, and there is a shadow on my soul which I or another may call a curse; I cannot get rid of a something that always intrudes between my heart and the blue of every sky. But it avails nothing, ei-ther for my heart or their argument, to say I have fallen and been cast out: can any repudiation, even that of God, undo the facts of an exist-ent origin? Nor is it merely that he made me: by whose power do I go on living? When he cast me out, as you say, did I then begin to draw my being from myself—or from the devil? In whom do I live and move and have my being? It cannot be that I am not the creature of God.'

'But creation is not fatherhood.'

'Creation in the image of God, is. And if I am not in the image of God, how can the word of God be of any meaning to me? "He called them gods to whom the word of God came," says the Master himself. To be fit to receive his word implies being of his kind. No matter how his image may have been defaced in me: the thing defaced is his image, remains his defaced image—an image yet that can hear his word. What makes me evil and miserable is, that the thing spoiled in me is the image of the Perfect. Nothing can be evil but in virtue of a good hypostasis. No, no! nothing can make it that I am not the child of God. If one say, "Look at the animals: God made them: you do not call them the children of God!" I answer: "But I am to blame; they are not to blame! I cling fast to my blame: it is the seal of my childhood." I have nothing to argue from in the animals, for I do not understand them. Two things only I am sure of: that God is to them "a faithful creator;" and that the sooner I put in force my claim to be a child of God, the better for them; for they too are fallen, though without blame.'

'But you are evil: how can you be a child of the Good?'

'Just as many an evil son is the child of a good parent.'

'But in him you call a good parent, there yet lay evil, and that accounts for the child being evil.'

'I cannot explain. God let me be born through evil channels. But in whatever manner I may have become an unworthy child, I cannot thereby have ceased to be a child of God—his child in the way that a child must ever be the child of the man of whom he comes. Is it not proof— this complaint of my heart at the word *Adoption*? Is it not the spirit of the child, crying out, "Abba, Father"?'

'Yes; but that is the spirit of adoption; the text says so.'

'Away with your adoption! I could not even be adopted if I were not such as the adoption could reach—that is, of the nature of God. Much as he may love him, can a man adopt a dog? I must be of a nature for the word of God to come to—yea, so far, of the divine nature, of the image of God! Heartily do I grant that, had I been left to myself, had God dropped me, held no communication with me, I could never have thus cried, never have cared when they told me I was not a child of God. But he has never repudiated me, and does not now desire to adopt me. Pray, why should it grieve me to be told I am not a child of God, if I be not a child of God? If you say—Because you have learned to love him, I answer—Adoption would satisfy the love of one who was not but would be a child; for me, I cannot do without a father, nor can any adoption give me one.'

171

'But what is the good of all you say, if the child is such that the father cannot take him to his heart?'

'Ah, indeed, I grant you, nothing!—so long as the child does not desire to be taken to the father's heart; but the moment he does, then it is everything to the child's heart that he should be indeed the child of him after whom his soul is thirsting. However bad I may be, I am the child of God, and therein lies my blame. Ah, I would not lose my blame! in my blame lies my hope. It is the pledge of what I am, and what I am not; the pledge of what I am meant to be, what I shall one day be, the child of God in spirit and in truth.'

'Then you dare to say the apostle is wrong in what he so plainly teaches?'

'By no means; what I do say is, that our English presentation of his teaching is in this point very misleading. It is not for me to judge the learned and good men who have revised the translation of the New Testament—with so much gain to every one whose love of truth is greater than his loving prejudice for accustomed form;—I can only say, I wonder what may have been their reasons for retaining this word *adoption*. In the New Testament the word is used only by the apostle Paul. Liddell and Scott give the meaning—"Adoption as a son," which is a mere submission to popular theology: they give no reference except to the New Testament. The relation of the word [Greek: *niothesia*] to the form [Greek: *thetos*], which means "taken," or rather, "*placed* as one's child," is, I presume, the sole ground for the so translating of it: usage plentiful and invariable could not justify that translation here, in the face of what St. Paul elsewhere shows he means by the word. The Greek word *might* be variously meant—though I can find no use of it earlier than St. Paul; the English can mean but one thing, and that is not what St. Paul means. "The spirit of adoption" Luther translates "the spirit of a child;" *adoption* he translates *kindschaft*, or *childship*'

Of two things I am sure—first, that by *niothesia* St. Paul did not intend *adoption*; and second, that if the Revisers had gone through what I have gone through because of the word, if they had felt it come between God and their hearts as I have felt it, they could not have allowed it to remain in their version.

Once more I say, the word used by St Paul does not imply that God adopts children that are not his own, but rather that a second time he fathers his own; that a second time they are born—this time from above; that he will make himself tenfold, yea, infinitely their father: he will have them back into the very bosom whence they issued, issued

172

that they might learn they could live nowhere else; he will have them one with himself. It was for the sake of this that, in his Son, he died for them.

Let us look at the passage where he reveals his use of the word. It is in another of his epistles—that to the Galatians iv. 1-7.

'But I say that so long as the heir is a child, he differeth nothing from a bondservant, though he is lord of all; but is under guardians and stewards until the term appointed of the father. So we also, when we were children, were held in bondage under the rudiments of the world: but when the fulness of the time came, God sent forth his Son, born of a woman, born under the law, that he might redeem them which were under the law, that we might receive the adoption of sons. And because ye are sons, God sent forth the Spirit of his Son into our hearts, crying, Abba, Father. So that thou art no longer a bondservant, but a son; and if a son, then an heir through God.'

How could the Revisers choose this last reading, 'an heir through God,' and keep the word *adoption*? From the passage it is as plain as St. Paul could make it, that, by the word translated *adoption*, he means the raising of a father's own child from the condition of tutelage and subjection to others, a state which, he says, is no better than that of a slave, to the position and rights of a son. None but a child could become a son; the idea is—a spiritual coming of age; *only when the child is a man is he really and fully a son.* The thing holds in the earthly relation. How many children of good parents—good children in the main too—never know those parents, never feel towards them as children might, until, grown up, they have left the house—until, perhaps, they are parents themselves, or are parted from them by death! To be a child is not necessarily to be a son or daughter. The childship is the lower condition of the upward process towards the sonship, the soil out of which the true sonship shall grow, the former without which the latter were impossible. God can no more than an earthly parent be content to have only children: he must have sons and daughters— children of his soul, of his spirit, of his love—not merely in the sense that he loves them, or even that they love him, but in the sense that they love like him, love as he loves. For this he does not adopt them; he dies to give them himself, thereby to raise his own to his heart; he gives them a birth from above; they are born again out of himself and into himself—for he is the one and the all. His children are not his real, true sons and daughters until they think like him, feel with him, judge as he judges, are at home with him, and without fear before him because he and they mean the same thing, love the same things, seek the same

ends. For this are we created; it is the one end of our being, and in-
cludes all other ends whatever. It can come only of unbelief and not
faith, to make men believe that God has cast them off, repudiated
them, said they are not, yea never were, his children—and he all the
time spending himself to make us the children he designed, foreor-
dained—children who would take him for their Father! He is our
father all the time, for he is true; but until we respond with the truth of
children, he cannot let all the father out to us; there is no place for the
dove of his tenderness to alight. He is our father, but we are not his
children. Because we are his children, we must become his sons and
daughters. Nothing will satisfy him, or do for us, but that we be one
with our father! What else could serve! How else should life ever be a
good! Because we are the sons of God, we must become the sons of
God.

There may be among my readers—alas for such!—to whom the
word *Father* brings no cheer, no dawn, in whose heart it rouses no
tremble of even a vanished emotion. It is hardly likely to be their fault.
For though as children we seldom love up to the mark of reason;
though we often offend; and although the conduct of some children is
inexplicable to the parent who loves them; yet, if the parent has been
but ordinarily kind, even the son who has grown up a worthless man,
will now and then feel, in his better moments, some dim reflex of
childship, some faintly pleasant, some slightly sorrowful remembrance
of the father around whose neck his arms had sometimes clung. In my
own childhood and boyhood my father was the refuge from all the ills
of life, even sharp pain itself. Therefore I say to son or daughter who
has no pleasure in the name *Father*, 'You must interpret the word by
all that you have missed in life. Every time a man might have been to
you a refuge from the wind, a covert from the tempest, the shadow of a
great rock in a weary land, that was a time when a father might have
been a father indeed. Happy you are yet, if you have found man or
woman such a refuge; so far have you known a shadow of the perfect,
seen the back of the only man, the perfect Son of the perfect Father.
All that human tenderness can give or desire in the nearness and readi-
ness of love, all and infinitely more must be true of the perfect
Father—of the maker of fatherhood, the Father of all the fathers of the
earth, specially the Father of those who have specially shown a father-
heart.'

This Father would make to himself sons and daughters indeed—
that is, such sons and daughters as shall be his sons and daughters not
merely by having come from his heart, but by having returned thith-

er—children in virtue of being such as whence they came, such as choose to be what he is. He will have them share in his being and nature—strong wherein he cares for strength; tender and gracious as he is tender and gracious; angry where and as he is angry. Even in the small matter of power, he will have them able to do whatever his Son Jesus could on the earth, whose was the life of the perfect man, whose works were those of perfected humanity. Everything must at length be subject to man, as it was to The Man. When God can do what he will with a man, the man may do what he will with the world; he may walk on the sea like his Lord; the deadliest thing will not he able to hurt him:— 'He that believeth on me, the works that I do shall he do also; and greater than these shall he do.'

> God, whose pleasure brought
> Man into being, stands away
> As it were, an handbreath off, to give
> Boom for the newly-made to live.

He has made us, but we have to be. All things were made *through* the Word, but that which was made *in* the Word was life, and that life is the light of men: they who live by this light, that is, live as Jesus lived—by obedience, namely, to the Father, have a share in their own making; the light becomes life in them; they are, in their lower way, alive with the life that was first born in Jesus, and through him has been born in them—by obedience they become one with the godhead: 'As many as received him, to them gave he power to become the sons of God.' He does not *make* them the sons of God, but he gives them power to become the sons of God: in choosing and obeying the truth, man becomes the true son of the Father of lights.

It is enough to read with understanding the passage I have quoted from his epistle to the Galatians, to see that the word *adoption* does not in the least fit St. Paul's idea, or suit the things he says. While we but obey the law God has laid upon us, without knowing the heart of the Father whence comes the law, we are but slaves—not necessarily ignoble slaves, yet slaves; but when we come to think *with* him, when the mind of the son is as the mind of the Father, the action of the son the same as that of the Father, then is the son *of* the Father, then are we the sons of God. And in both passages—this, and that which, from his epistle to the Romans, I have placed at the head of this sermon—we find the same phrase, *Abba, Father*, showing, if proof were needful, that he uses the word [Greek: uiothesia] the same sense in both: nothing can well be plainer, that needs consideration at all, than what that sense is. Let us glance at the other passages in which he uses the same word: as he alone of the writers of the New Testament does use it, so, for aught I know, he may have made it for himsef. One of them is in the same eighth chapter of the epistle to the Romans; this I will keep to the last. Another is in the following chapter, the fourth verse; in it he speaks of the [Greek: viothesia], literally the *son-placing* (that is, the placing of sons in the true place of sons), as belonging to the Jews. On this I have but to remark that 'whose is the [Greek: viothesia]' cannot mean either that they had already received it, or that it belonged to the Jews more than to the Gentiles; it can only mean that, as the elder-brother-nation, they had a foremost claim to it, and would naturally first receive it; that, in their best men, they had always been nearest to it. It must be wrought out first in such as had received the preparation necessary; those were the Jews; of the Jews was the Son, bringing the [Greek: viothesia], the sonship, to all. Therefore theirs was the [Greek: viothesia], just as theirs was the gospel. It was to the Jew first, then to the Gentile—though many a Gentile would have it before many a Jew. Those and only those who out of a true heart cry '*Abba, Father,*' be they of what paltry little so-called church, other than the body of Christ, they may, or of no otherat all, are the sons and daughters of God.

St. Paul uses the word also in his epistle to the Ephesians, the first chapter, the fifth verse. 'Having predestinated us unto the adoption of children by Jesus Christ to himself,' says the authorized version; 'Having foreordained us unto adoption as sons through Jesus Christ unto himself,' says the revised—and I see little to choose between them: neither gives the meaning of St. Paul. If there is anything gained by the addition of the words 'of children' in the one case, and 'as sons' in the other, to translate the word for which 'adoption' alone is made to serve in the other passages, the advantage is only to the minus- side, to that of the wrong interpretation.

Children we were; true sons we could never be, save through The Son. He brothers us. He takes us to the knees of the Father, beholding whose face we grow sons indeed. Never could we have known the heart of the Father, never felt it possible to love him as sons, but for him who cast himself into the gulf that yawned between us. In and through him we were foreordained to the sonship: sonship, even had we never sinned, never could we reach without him. We should have been little children loving the Father indeed, but children far from the sonhood that understands and adores. 'For as many as are led by the spirit of God, these are sons of God;' 'If any man hath not the spirit of Christ, he is none of his;' yea, if we have not each other's spirits, we do not belong to each other. There is no unity but having the same spirit. There is but one spirit, that of truth.

It remains to note yet another passage.

That never in anything he wrote was it St. Paul's intention to contribute towards a system of theology, it were easy to show: one sign of the fact is, that he does not hesitate to use this word he has perhaps himself made, in different, and apparently opposing, though by no means contradictory senses: his meanings always vivify each other. His ideas are so large that they tax his utterance and make him strain the use of words, but there is no danger to the honest heart, which alone he regards, of misunderstanding them, though 'the ignorant and unsteadfast wrest them' yet. At one time he speaks of the sonship as being the possession of the Israelite, at another as his who has learned to cry *Abba, Father*; and here, in the passage I have now last to consider, that from the 18th to the 25th verse of this same eighth chapter of his epistle to the Romans, he speaks of the *niothesia* as yet to come—and as if it had to do, not with our spiritual, but our bodily condition. This use of the word, however, though not the same use as we find anywhere else, is nevertheless entirely consistent with his other uses of it.

The 23rd verse says, 'And not only so, but ourselves also, which have the first fruits of the spirit, even we ourselves groan within ourselves, waiting for adoption, the redemption of our body.'

It is nowise difficult to discern that the ideas in this and the main use are necessarily associated and more than consistent. The putting of a son in his true, his foreordained place, has outward relations as well as inward reality; the outward depends on the inward, arises from it, and reveals it. When the child whose condition under tutors had passed away, took his position as a son, he would naturally change his dress and modes of life: when God's children cease to be slaves doing right from law and duty, and become his sons doing right from the essential love of God and their neighbour, they too must change the garments of their slavery for the robes of liberty, lay aside the body of this death, and appear in bodies like that of Christ, with whom they inherit of the Father. But many children who have learned to cry *Abba, Father*, are yet far from the liberty of the sons of God. Sons they are and no longer children, yet they groan as being still in bondage!— Plainly the apostle has no thought of working out an idea; with burning heart he is writing a letter: he gives, nevertheless, lines plentifully sufficient for us to work out his idea, and this is how it takes clear shape:—

We are the sons of God the moment we lift up our hearts, seeking to be sons—the moment we begin to cry *Father*. But as the world must be redeemed in a few men to begin with, so the soul is redeemed in a few of its thoughts and wants and ways, to begin with: it takes a long time to finish the new creation of this redemption. Shall it have taken millions of years to bring the world up to the point where a few of its inhabitants shall desire God, and shall the creature of this new birth be perfected in a day? The divine process may indeed now go on with tenfold rapidity, for the new factor of man's fellow-working, for the sake of which the whole previous array of means and forces existed, is now developed; but its end is yet far below the horizon of man's vision:—

The apostle speaks at one time of the thing as to come, at another time as done—when it is but commenced: our ways of thought are such. A man's heart may leap for joy the moment when, amidst the sea-waves, a strong hand has laid hold of the hair of his head; he may cry aloud, 'I am saved;'—and he may be safe, but he is not saved; this is far from a salvation to suffice. So are we sons when we begin to cry Father, but we are far from perfected sons. So long as there is in us the least taint of distrust, the least lingering of hate or fear, we have not received the sonship; we have not such life in us as raised the body of Jesus; we have not attained to the resurrection of the dead—by which word, in his epistle to the Philippians (iii. 2), St. Paul means, I think, the same thing as here he means by the sonship which he puts in apposition with the redemption of the body:—

Until our outward condition is that of sons royal, sons divine; so long as the garments of our souls, these mortal bodies, are mean—torn and dragged and stained; so long as we groan under sickness and weakness and weariness, old age, forgetfulness, and all heavy things; so long we have not yet received the sonship in full—we are but getting ready one day to creep from our chrysalids, and spread the great heaven-storming wings of the psyches of God. We groan being burdened; we groan, waiting for the sonship—to wit, the redemption of the body—the uplifting of the body to be a fit house and revelation of the indwelling spirit— nay, like that of Christ, a fit temple and revelation of the deeper indwelling God. For we shall always need bodies to manifest and reveal us to each other—bodies, then, that fit the soul with absolute truth of presentment and revelation. Hence the revealing of the sons of God, spoken of in the 19th verse, is the same thing as the redemption of the body; the body is redeemed when it is made fit for the sons of God; then it is a revelation of them—the thing it was meant for, and always, more or less imperfectly, was. Such it shall be, when truth is strong enough in the sons of God to make it such—for it is the soul that makes the body. When we are the sons of God in heart and soul, then shall we be the sons of God in body too: 'we shall be like him, for we shall see him as he is.'

I care little to speculate on the kind of this body; two things only I will say, as needful to be believed, concerning it: first, that it will be a body to show the same self as before—but, second, a body to show the being truly—without the defects, that is, and imperfections of the former bodily revelation. Even through their corporeal presence shall we then know our own infinitely better, and find in them endlessly more delight, than before. These things we must believe, or distrust the Father of our spirits. Till this redemption of the body arrives, the [Greek: uiothesia] is not wrought out, is only upon the way. Nor can it come but by our working out the salvation he is working in us.

This redemption of the body—its deliverance from all that is amiss, awry, unfinished, weak, worn out, all that prevents the revelation of the sons of God, is called by the apostle, not certainly the *adoption*, but the [Greek: niothesia], the sonship in full manifestation. It is the slave yet left in the sons and daughters of God that has betrayed them into even permitting the word *adoption* to mislead them!

To see how the whole utterance hangs together, read from the 18th verse to the 25th, especially noticing the 19th: 'For the earnest expectation of the creation waiteth for the revealing' (*the outshining*) 'of the sons of God.' When the sons of God show as they are, taking, with the character, the appearance and the place that belong to their sonship; when the sons of God sit with *the* Son of God on the throne of their Father; then shall they be in potency of fact the lords of the lower creation, the bestowers of liberty and peace upon it; then shall the creation, subjected to vanity for their sakes, find its freedom in their freedom, its gladness in their sonship. The animals will glory to serve them, will joy to come to them for help. Let the heartless scoff, the unjust despise! the heart that cries *Abba, Father*, cries to the God of the sparrow and the oxen; nor can hope go too far in hoping what that God will do for the creation that now groaneth and travaileth in pain because our higher birth is delayed. Shall not the judge of all the earth do right? Shall my heart be more compassionate than his?

If to any reader my interpretation be unsatisfactory, I pray him not to spend his strength in disputing my faith, but in making sure his own progress on the way to freedom and sonship. Only to the child of God is true judgment possible. Were it otherwise, what would it avail to

179

prove this one or that right or wrong? Right opinion on questions the most momentous will deliver no man. Cure for any ill in me or about me there is none, but to become the son of God I was born to be. Until such I am, until Christ is born in me, until I am revealed a son of God, pain and trouble will endure—and God grant they may! Call this presumption, and I can only widen my assertion: until you yourself are the son of God you were born to be, you will never find life a good thing. If I presume for myself, I presume for you also. But I do not presume. Thus have both Jesus Christ and his love-slave Paul represented God—as a Father perfect in love, grand in self-forgetfulness, supreme in righteousness, devoted to the lives he has uttered. I will not believe less of the Father than I can conceive of glory after the lines he has given me, after the radiation of his glory in the face of his Son. He is the express image of the Father, by which we, his imperfect images, are to read and understand him: imperfect, we have yet perfection enough to spell towards the perfect.

It comes to this then, after the grand theory of the apostle:—The world exists for our education; it is the nursery of God's children, served by troubled slaves, troubled because the children are themselves slaves—children, but not good children. Beyond its own will or knowledge, the whole creation works for the development of the children of God into the sons of God. When at last the children have arisen and gone to their Father; when they are clothed in the best robe, with a ring on their hands and shoes on their feet, shining out at length in their natural, their predestined sonship; then shall the mountains and the hills break forth before them into singing, and all the trees of the field shall clap their hands. Then shall the wolf dwell with the lamb, and the leopard lie down with the kid and the calf, and the young lion and the fatling together, and a little child shall lead them. Then shall the fables of a golden age, which faith invented, and unbelief threw into the past, unfold their essential reality, and the tale of paradise prove itself a truth by becoming a fact. Then shall every ideal show itself a necessity, aspiration although satisfied put forth yet longer wings, and the hunger after righteousness know itself blessed. Then first shall we know what was in the Shepherd's mind when he said, '*I came that they may have life, and may have it abundantly.*'

LIFE.

'*I came that they may have life, and may have it abundantly.*'— St. John x. 10.

In a word, He came to supply all our lack—from the root outward; for what is it we need but more life? What does the infant need but more life? What does the bosom of his mother give him but life in abundance? What does the old man need, whose limbs are weak and whose pulse is low, but more of the life which seems ebbing from him? Weary with feebleness, he calls upon death, but in reality it is life he wants. It is but the encroaching death in him that desires death. He longs for rest, but death cannot rest; death would be as much an end to rest as to weariness: even weakness cannot rest; it takes strength as well as weariness to rest. How different is the weariness of the strong man after labour unduly prolonged, from the weariness of the sick man who in the morning cries out, 'Would God it were evening!' and in the evening, 'Would God it were morning!' Low-sunk life imagines itself weary of life, but it is death, not life, it is weary of. Never a cry went out after the opposite of life from any soul that knew what life is. Why does the poor, worn, out-worn suicide seek death? Is it not in reality to escape from death?—from the death of homelessness and hunger and cold; the death of failure, disappointment, and distraction; the death of the exhaustion of passion; the death of madness—of a household he cannot rule; the death of crime and fear of discovery? He seeks the darkness because it seems a refuge from the death which possesses him. He is a creature possessed by death; what he calls his life is but a dream full of horrible phantasms.

'More life!' is the unconscious prayer of all creation, groaning and travailing for the redemption of its lord, the son who is not yet a son. Is not the dumb cry to be read in the faces of some of the animals, in the look of some of the flowers, and in many an aspect of what we call Nature? All things are possible with God, but all things are not easy. It is easy for him *to be*, for there he has to do with his own perfect will: it is not easy for him to create—that is, after the grand fashion which alone will satisfy his glorious heart and will, the fashion in which he is now creating us. In the very nature of being—that is, God—it must be hard—and divine history shows how hard—to create that which shall be not himself, yet like himself. The problem is, so far to separate from himself that which must yet on him be ever and always and utterly dependent, that it shall have the existence of an individual, and be able to turn and regard him—choose him, and say, 'I will arise and go to my Father,' and so develop in itself the highest *Divine* of which it is capable—the will for the good against the evil—the will to be one with the life whence it has come, and in which it still is—the will to close the round of its procession in its return, so working the perfection of reunion—to shape in its own life the ring of eternity—to live immediately, consciously, and active-willingly from its source, from its own very life—to restore to the beginning the end that comes of that beginning—to be the thing the maker thought of when he willed, ere he began to work its being.

I imagine the difficulty of doing this thing, of effecting this creation, this separation from himself such that will in the creature shall be possible—I imagine, I say, the difficulty of such creation so great, that for it God must begin inconceivably far back in the infinitesimal regions of beginnings—not to say before anything in the least resembling man, but eternal miles beyond the last farthest-pushed discovery in *protoplasm*—to set in motion that division from himself which in its grand result should be individuality, consciousness, choice, and conscious choice—choice at last pure, being the choice of the right, the true, the divinely harmonious. Hence the final end of the separation is not individuality; that is but a means to it; the final end is oneness—an impossibility without it. For there can be no unity, no delight of love, no harmony, no good in being, where there is but one. Two at least are needed for oneness; and the greater the number of individuals, the greater, the lovelier, the richer, the diviner is the possible unity.

God is life, and the will-source of life. In the outflowing of that life, I know him; and when I am told that he is love, I see that if he were not love he would not, could not create. I know nothing deeper in him than love, nor believe there is in him anything deeper than love— nay, that there can be anything deeper than love. The being of God is love, therefore creation. I imagine that from all eternity he has been creating. As he saw it was not good for man to be alone, so has he never been alone himself;—from all eternity the Father has had the Son, and the never-begun existence of that Son I imagine an easy outgoing of the Father's nature; while to make other beings—beings like us, I imagine the labour of a God, an eternal labour. Speaking after our poor human fashions of thought—the only fashions possible to us—I imagine that God has never been contented to be alone even with the Son of his love, the prime and perfect idea of humanity, but that he has from the first willed and laboured to give existence to other creatures who should be blessed with his blessedness—creatures whom he is now and always has been developing into likeness with that Son—a likeness for long to be distant and small, but a likeness to be for ever growing: perhaps never one of them yet, though unspeakably blessed, has had even an approximate idea of the blessedness in store for him.

Let no soul think that to say God undertook a hard labour in willing that many sons and daughters should be sharers of the divine nature, is to abate his glory! The greater the difficulty, the greater is the glory of him who does the thing he has undertaken—without shadow of compromise, with no half-success, but with a triumph of absolute satisfaction to innumerable radiant souls! He knew what it would cost!—not energy of will alone, or merely that utterance and separation from himself which is but the first of creation, though that may well itself be pain—but sore suffering such as we cannot imagine, and could only be God's, in the bringing out, call it birth or development, of the God-life in the individual soul—a suffering still renewed, a labour thwarted ever by that soul itself, compelling him to take, still at the cost of suffering, the not absolutely best, only the best possible means left him by the resistance of his creature. Man finds it hard to get what he wants, because he does not want the best; God finds it hard to give, because he would give the best, and man will not take it. What Jesus did, was what the Father is always doing; the suffering he endured was that of the Father from the foundation of the world, reaching its climax in the person of his Son. God provides the sacrifice; the sacrifice is himself. He is always, and has ever been, sacrificing himself to and for his creatures. It lies in the very essence of his creation of them. The worst heresy, next to that of dividing religion and righteousness, is to divide the Father from the Son—in thought or feeling or action or intent; to represent the Son as doing that which the Father does not himself do. Jesus did nothing but what the Father did and does. If Jesus suffered for men, it was because his Father suffers for men; only he came close to men through his body and their senses, that he might bring their spirits close to his Father and their Father, so giving them life, and losing what could be lost of his own. He is God our Saviour: it is because God is our Saviour that Jesus is our Saviour. The God and Father of Jesus Christ could never possibly be satisfied with less than giving himself to his own! The unbeliever may easily imagine a better God than the common theology of the country offers him; but not the lovingest heart that ever beat can even reflect the length and breadth and depth and height of that love of God which shows itself in his Son—one, and of one mind, with himself. The whole history is a divine agony to give divine life to creatures. The outcome of that agony, the victory of that creative and again creative energy, will be radiant life, whereof joy unspeakable is the flower. Every child will look in the eyes of the Father, and the eyes of the Father will receive the child with an infinite embrace.

The life the Lord came to give us is a life exceeding that of the highest undivine man, by far more than the life of that man exceeds the life of the animal the least human. More and more of it is for each who will receive it, and to eternity. The Father has given to the Son to have life in himself; that life is our light. We know life only as light; it is the life in us that makes us see. All the growth of the Christian is the more and more life he is receiving. At first his religion may hardly be distinguishable from the mere prudent desire to save his soul; but at last he loses that very soul in the glory of love, and so saves it; self becomes but the cloud on which the white light of God divides into harmonies unspeakable.

'In the midst of life we are in death,' said one; it is more true that in the midst of death we are in life. Life is the only reality; what men call death is but a shadow—a word for that which cannot be—a negation, owing the very idea of itself to that which it would deny. But for life there could be no death. If God were not, there would not even be nothing. Not even nothingness preceded life. Nothingness owes its very idea to existence.

One form of the question between matter and spirit is, which was first, and caused the other—things or thoughts; whether things without thought caused thought, or thought without things caused things. To those who cannot doubt that thought was first, causally preceding the earliest material show, it is easily plain that death can be the cure for nothing, that the cure for everything must be life—that the ills which come with existence, are from its imperfection, not of itself— that what we need is more of it. We who *are*, have nothing to do with death; our relations are alone with life. The thing that can mourn can mourn only from lack; it cannot mourn because of being, but because of not enough being. We are vessels of life, not yet full of the wine of life; where the wine does not reach, there the clay cracks, and aches, and is distressed. Who would therefore pour out the wine that is there, instead of filling to the brim with more wine! All the being must partake of essential being; life must be assisted, upheld, comforted, every part, with life. Life is the law, the food, the necessity of life. Life is everything. Many doubtless mistake the joy of life for life itself; and, longing after the joy, languish with a thirst at once poor and inextinguishable; but even that thirst points to the one spring. These love self, not life, and self is but the shadow of life. When it is taken for life itself, and set as the man's centre, it becomes a live death in the man, a devil he worships as his god; the worm of the death eternal he clasps to his bosom as his one joy!

The soul compact of harmonies has more life, a larger being, than the soul consumed of cares; the sage is a larger life than the clown; the poet is more alive than the man whose life flows out that money may come in; the man who loves his fellow is infinitely more alive than he whose endeavour is to exalt himself above him; the man who strives to be better, than he who longs for the praise of the many; but the man to whom God is all in all, who feels his life-roots hid with Christ in God, who knows himself the inheritor of all wealth and worlds and ages, yea, of power essential and in itself, that man has begun to be alive indeed.

Let us in all the troubles of life remember—that our one lack is life—that what we need is more life—more of the life-making presence in us making us more, and more largely, alive. When most oppressed, when most weary of life, as our unbelief would phrase it, let us bethink ourselves that it is in truth the inroad and presence of death we are weary of. When most inclined to sleep, let us rouse ourselves to live. Of all things let us avoid the false refuge of a weary collapse, a hopeless yielding to things as they are. It is the life in us that is discontented; we need more of what is discontented, not more of the cause of its discontent. Discontent, I repeat, is the life in us that has not enough of itself, is not enough to itself, so calls for more. He has the victory who, in the midst of pain and weakness, cries out, not for death, not for the repose of forgetfulness, but for strength to fight; for more power, more consciousness of being, more God in him; who, when sorest wounded, says with Sir Andrew Barton in the old ballad:—

> Fight on my men, says Sir Andrew Barton,
>   I am hurt, but I am not slain;
> I'll lay me down and bleed awhile,
>   And then I'll rise and fight again;

—and that with no silly notion of playing the hero—what have creatures like us to do with heroism who are not yet barely honest!—but because so to fight is the truth, and the only way.

If, in the extreme of our exhaustion, there should come to us, as to Elijah when he slept in the desert, an angel to rouse us, and show us the waiting bread and water, how would we carry ourselves? Would we, in faint unwillingness to rise and eat, answer, 'Lo I am weary unto death! The battle is gone from me! It is lost, or unworth gaining! The world is too much for me! Its forces will not heed me! They have worn me out! I have wrought no salvation even for my own, and never should work any, were I to live for ever! It is enough; let me now return whence I came; let me be gathered to my fathers and be at rest!'? I should be loth to think that, if the enemy, in recognizable shape, came roaring upon us, we would not, like the red-cross knight, stagger, heavy sword in nerveless arm, to meet him; but, in the feebleness of foiled effort, it wants yet more faith to rise and partake of the food that shall bring back more effort, more travail, more weariness. The true man trusts in a strength which is not his, and which he does not feel, does not even always desire; believes in a power that seems far from him, which is yet at the root of his fatigue itself and his need of rest—rest as far from death as is labour. To trust in the strength of God in our weakness; to say, 'I am weak: so let me be: God is strong;' to seek from him who is our life, as the natural, simple cure of all that is amiss with us, power to do, and be, and live, even when we are weary,—this is the victory that overcometh the world. To believe in God our strength in the face of all seeming denial, to believe in him out of the heart of weakness and unbelief, in spite of numbness and weariness and lethargy; to believe in the wide-awake real, through all the stupefying, enervating, distorting dream; to will to wake, when the very being seems athirst for a godless repose;—these are the broken steps up to the high fields where repose is but a form of strength, strength but a form of joy, joy but a form of love. 'I am weak,' says the true soul, 'but not so weak that I would not be strong; not so sleepy that I would not see the sun rise; not so lame but that I would walk! Thanks be to him who perfects strength in weakness, and gives to his beloved while they sleep!'

LIFE.

If we will but let our God and Father work his will with us, there can be no limit to his enlargement of our existence, to the flood of life with which he will overflow our consciousness. We have no conception of what life might be, of how vast the consciousness of which we could be made capable. Many can recall some moment in which life seemed richer and fuller than ever before; to some, such moments arrive mostly in dreams: shall soul, awake or asleep, infold a bliss greater than its Life, the living God, can seal, perpetuate, enlarge? Can the human twilight of a dream be capable of generating or holding a fuller life than the morning of divine activity? Surely God could at any moment give to a soul, by a word to that soul, by breathing afresh into the secret caves of its being, a sense of life before which the most exultant ecstasy of earthly triumph would pale to ashes! If ever sunlit, sail-crowded sea, under blue heaven flecked with wind-chased white, filled your soul as with a new gift of life, think what sense of existence must be yours, if he whose thought has but fringed its garment with the outburst of such a show, take his abode with you, and while thinking the gladness of a God inside your being, let you know and feel that he is carrying you as a father in his bosom!

I have been speaking as if life and the consciousness of it were one; but the consciousness of life is not life; it is only the outcome of life. The real life is that which is of and by itself—is life because it wills itself—which is, in the active, not the passive sense: this can only be God. But in us there ought to be a life correspondent to the life that is God's; in us also must be the life that wills itself—a life in so far resembling the self-existent life and partaking of its image, that it has a share in its own being. There is an original act possible to the man, which must initiate the reality of his existence. He must live in and by willing to live. A tree lives; I hardly doubt it has some vague consciousness, known by but not to itself, only to the God who made it; I trust that life in its lowest forms is on the way to thought and blessedness, is in the process of that separation, so to speak, from God, in which consists the creation of living souls; but the life of these lower forms is not life in the high sense—in the sense in which the word is used in the Bible: true life knows and rules itself; the eternal life is life come awake. The life of the most exalted of the animals is not such whatever it may become, and however I may refuse to believe their fate and being fixed as we see them. But as little as any man or woman would be inclined to call the existence of the dog, looking strange lack out of his wistful eyes, an existence to be satisfied with—his life an end sufficient in itself, as little could I, looking on the human pleasure, the human refinement, the common human endeavour around me, consent to regard them as worthy the name of life. What in them is true dwells amidst an unchallenged corruption, demanding repentance and labour and prayer for its destruction. The condition of most men and women seems to me a life in death, an abode in unwhited sepulchres, a possession of withering forms by spirits that slumber, and babble in their dreams. That they do not feel it so, is nothing. The sow wallowing in the mire may rightly assert it her way of being clean, but theirs is not the life of the God-born. The day must come when they will hide their faces with such shame as the good man yet feels at the memory of the time when he lived like them. There is nothing for man worthy to be called life, but the life eternal—God's life, that is, after his degree shared by the man made to be eternal also. For he is in the image of God, intended to partake of the life of the most high, to be alive as he is alive. Of this life the outcome and the light is righteousness, love, grace, truth; but the life itself is a thing that will not be defined, even as God will not be defined: it is a power, the formless cause of form. It has no limits whereby to be defined. It shows itself to the soul that is hungering and thirsting after righteousness, but that soul cannot show it to another, save in the shining of its own light. The ignorant soul understands by this life eternal only an endless elongation of consciousness; what God means by it is a being like his own, a being beyond the attack of decay or death, a being so essential that it has no relation whatever to nothingness; a something which is, and can never go to that which is not, for with that it never had to do, but came out of the heart of Life, the heart of God, the fountain of being; an existence partaking of the divine nature, and having nothing in common, any more than the Eternal himself, with what can pass or cease: God owes his being to no one, and his child has no lord but his Father.

This life, this eternal life, consists for man in absolute oneness with God and all divine modes of being, oneness with every phase of right and harmony. It consists in a love as deep as it is universal, as conscious as it is unspeakable; a love that can no more be reasoned about than life itself—a love whose presence is its all-sufficing proof and justification, whose absence is an annihilating defect: he who has it not cannot believe in it: how should death believe in life, though all the birds of God are singing jubilant over the empty tomb! The delight of such a being, the splendour of a consciousness rushing from the wide open doors of the fountain of existence, the ecstasy of the spiritual sense into which the surge of life essential, immortal, increate, flows in silent fulness from the heart of hearts—what may it, what must it not be, in the great day of God and the individual soul!

What then is our practical relation to the life original? What have we to do towards the attaining to the resurrection from the dead? If we did not make, could not have made ourselves, how can we, now we are made, do anything at the unknown roots of our being? What relation of conscious unity can be betwixt the self-existent God, and beings who live at the will of another, beings who could not refuse to be—cannot even cease to be, but must, at the will of that other, go on living, weary of what is not life, able to assert their relation to life only by refusing to be content with what is not life?

The self-existent God is that other by whose will we live; so the links of the unity must already exist, and can but require to be brought together. For the link in our being wherewith to close the circle of immortal oneness with the Father, we must of course search the deepest of man's nature: there only, in all assurance, can it be found. And there we do find it. For the *will* is the deepest, the strongest, the divinest thing in man; so, I presume, is it in God, for such we find it in Jesus Christ. Here, and here only, in the relation of the two wills, God's and his own, can a man come into vital contact—on the eternal idea, in no one-sided unity of completest dependence, but in willed harmony of dual oneness—with the All-in-all. When a man can and does entirely say, 'Not my will, but thine be done'—when he so wills the will of God as to do it, then is he one with God—one, as a true son with a true father. When a man wills that his being be conformed to the being of his origin, which is the life in his life, causing and bearing his life, therefore absolutely and only of its kind, one with it more and deeper than words or figures can say—to the life which is itself, only more of itself, and more than itself, causing itself—when the man thus accepts his own causing life, *and sets himself to live the will of that causing life*, humbly eager after the privileges of his origin,—thus receiving God, he becomes, in the act, a partaker of the divine nature, a true son of the living God, and an heir of all he possesses: by the obedience of a son, he receives into himself the very life of the Father. Obedience is the joining of the links of the eternal round. Obedience is but the other side of the creative will. Will is God's will, obedience is man's will; the two make one. The root-life, knowing well the thousand troubles it would bring upon him, has created, and goes on creating other lives, that, though incapable of self-being, they may, by willed obedience, share in the bliss of his essential self-ordained being. If we do the will of God, eternal life is ours—no mere continuity of existence, for that in itself is worthless as hell, but a being that is one with the essential Life, and so within his reach to fill with the abundant and endless outgoings of his love. Our souls shall be vessels ever growing, and ever as they grow, filled with the more and more life proceeding from the Father and the Son, from God the ordaining, and God the obedient. What the delight of the being, what the abundance of the life he came that we might have, we can never know until we have it. But even now to the holy fancy it may sometimes seem too glorious to support—as if we must die of very life—of more being than we could bear—to awake to a yet higher life, and be filled with a wine which our souls were heretofore too weak to hold! To be for one moment aware of such pure simple love towards but one of my fellows as I trust I shall one day have towards each, must of itself bring a sense of life such as the utmost effort of my imagination can but feebly shadow now—a mighty glory of consciousness!—not to be always present, indeed, for my love, and not my glory in that love, is my life. There would be, even in that one love, in the simple purity of a single affection such as we were created to generate, and intended to cherish, towards all, an expansion of life inexpressible, unutterable. For we are made for love, not for self. Our neighbour is our refuge; *self* is our demon-foe. Every man is the image of God to every man, and in proportion as we love him, we shall know the sacred fact. The precious thing to human soul is, and one day shall be known to be, every human soul. And if it be so between man and man, how will it not be betwixt the man and his maker, between the child and his eternal Father, between the created and the creating Life? Must not the glory of existence be endlessly redoubled in the infinite love of the creature—for all love is infinite— to the infinite God, the great one life, than whom is no other—only shadows, lovely shadows of him!

Reader to whom my words seem those of inflation and foolish excitement, it can be nothing to thee to be told that I seem to myself to speak only the words of truth and soberness; but what if the cause why they seem other to thy mind be—not merely that thou art not whole, but that thy being nowise thirsts after harmony, that thou art not of the truth, that thou hast not yet begun to live? How should the reveller, issuing worn and wasted from the haunts where the violent seize joy by force to find her perish in their arms—how should such reveller, I say, break forth and sing with the sons of the morning, when the ocean of light bursts from the fountain of the east? As little canst thou, with thy mind full of petty cares, or still more petty ambitions, understand the groaning and travailing of the creation. It may indeed be that thou art honestly desirous of saving thy own wretched soul, but as yet thou canst know but little of thy need of him who is *the first and the last and the living one*.

THE FEAR OF GOD.

'And when I saw him, I fell at his feet as one dead. And he laid his right hand upon me, saying, Fear not; I am the first and the last and the Living one.'—Rev. i. 17-18.

It is not alone the first beginnings of religion that are full of fear. So long as love is imperfect, there is room for torment. That lore only which fills the heart—and nothing but love can fill any heart—is able to cast out fear, leaving no room for its presence. What we find in the beginnings of religion, will hold in varying degree, until the religion, that is the love, be perfected.

The thing that is unknown, yet known to be, will always be more or less formidable. When it is known as immeasurably greater than we, and as having claims and making demands upon us, the more vaguely these are apprehended, the more room is there for anxiety; and when the conscience is not clear, this anxiety may well mount to terror. According to the nature of the mind which occupies itself with the idea of the Supreme, whether regarded as maker or ruler, will be the kind and degree of the terror. To this terror need belong no exalted ideas of God; those fear him most who most imagine him like their own evil selves, only beyond them in power, easily able to work his arbitrary will with them. That they hold him but a little higher than themselves, tends nowise to unity with him: who so far apart as those on the same level of hate and distrust? Power without love, dependence where is no righteousness, wake a worship without devotion, a loathliness of servile flattery. Neither, where the notion of God is better, but the conscience is troubled, will his goodness do much to exclude apprehension. The same consciousness of evil and of offence which gave rise to the bloody sacrifice, is still at work in the minds of most who call themselves Christians. Naturally the first emotion of man towards the being he calls God, but of whom he knows so little, is fear.

Where it is possible that fear should exist, it is well it should exist, cause continual uneasiness, and be cast out by nothing less than love. In him who does not know God, and must be anything but satisfied with himself, fear towards God is as reasonable as it is natural, and serves powerfully towards the development of his true humanity. Neither the savage, nor the self-sufficient sage, is rightly human. It matters nothing whether we regard the one or the other as degenerate or as undeveloped—neither I say is human; the humanity is there, but has to be born in each, and for this birth everything natural must do its part; fear is natural, and has a part to perform nothing but itself could perform in the birth of the true humanity. Until love, which is the truth towards God, is able to cast out fear, it is well that fear should hold; it is a bond, however poor, between that which is and that which creates—a bond that must be broken, but a bond that can be broken only by the tightening of an infinitely closer bond. Verily, God must be terrible to those that are far from him; for they fear he will do, yea, he is doing with them what they do not, cannot desire, and can ill endure. Such as many men are, such as all without God would become, they must prefer a devil, because of his supreme selfishness, to a God who will die for his creatures, and insists upon giving himself to them, insists upon their being unselfish and blessed like himself. That which is the power and worth of life they must be, or die; and the vague consciousness of this makes them afraid. They love their poor existence as it is; God loves it as it must be—and they fear him.

The false notions of men of low, undeveloped nature both with regard to what is good and what the Power requires of them, are such that they cannot but fear, and devotion is lost in the sacrifices of ingratiation: God takes them where they are, accepts whatever they honestly offer, and so helps them to outgrow themselves, preparing them to offer the true offering, and to know him whom they ignorantly worship. He will not abolish their fear except with the truth of his own being. Till they apprehend that, and in order that they may come to apprehend it, he receives their sacrifices of blood, the invention of their sore need, only influencing for the time the modes of them. He will destroy the lie that is not all a lie only by the truth which is all true. Although he loves them utterly, he does not tell them there is nothing in him to make them afraid. That would be to drive them from him for ever. While they are such as they are, there is much in him that cannot but affright them; they ought, they do well to fear him. It is, while they remain what they are, the only true relation between them. To remove that fear from their hearts, save by letting them know his love with its purifying fire, a love which for ages, it may be, they cannot know, would be to give them up utterly to the power of evil. Persuade men that fear is a vile thing, that it is an insult to God, that he will none of it—while yet they are in love with their own will, and slaves to every movement of passionate impulse, and what will the consequence be? That they will insult God as a discarded idol, a superstition, a falsehood, as a thing under whose evil influence they have too long groaned, a thing to be cast out and spit upon. After that how much will they learn of him? Nor would it be long ere the old fear would return—with this difference, perhaps, that instead of trembling before a live energy, they would tremble before powers which formerly they regarded as inanimate, and have now endowed with souls after the imagination of their fears. Then would spiritual chaos with all its monsters be come again. God being what he is, a God who loves righteousness; a God who, rather than do an unfair thing, would lay down his Godhead, and assert himself in ceasing to be; a God who, that his creature might not die of ignorance, died as much as a God could die, and that is divinely more than man can die, to give him himself; such a God, I say, may well look fearful from afar to the creature who recognizes in himself no imperative good; who fears only suffering, and has no aspiration—only wretched ambition! But in proportion as such a creature comes nearer, grows towards him in and for whose likeness he was begun; in proportion, that is, as the eternal right begins to disclose itself to him; in proportion as he becomes capable of the idea that his kind belongs to him as he could never belong to himself; approaches the capacity of seeing and understanding that his individuality can be perfected only in the love of his neighbour, and that his being can find its end only in oneness with the source from which it came; in proportion, I do not say as he sees these things, but as he nears the possibility of seeing them, will his terror at the God of his life abate; though far indeed from surmising the bliss that awaits him, he is drawing more nigh to the goal of his nature, the central secret joy of sonship to a God who loves righteousness and hates iniquity, does nothing he would not permit in his creature, demands nothing of his creature he would not do himself.

The fire of God, which is his essential being, his love, his creative power, is a fire unlike its earthly symbol in this, that it is only at a distance it burns—that the farther from him, it burns the worse, and that when we turn and begin to approach him, the burning begins to change to comfort, which comfort will grow to such bliss that the heart at length cries out with a gladness no other gladness can reach, 'Whom have I in heaven but thee? and there is none upon earth that I desire besides thee!' The glory of being, the essence of life and its joy, shining upon the corrupt and deathly, must needs, like the sun, consume the dead, and send corruption down to the dust; that which it burns in the soul is not of the soul, yea, is at utter variance with it; yet so close to the soul is the foul fungous growth sprung from and subsisting upon it, that the burning of it is felt through every spiritual nerve: when the evil parasites are consumed away, that is when the man yields his self and all that self's low world, and returns to his lord and God, then that which, before, he was aware of only as burning, he will feel as love, comfort, strength—an eternal, ever-growing life in him. For now he lives, and life cannot hurt life; it can only hurt death, which needs and ought to be destroyed. God is life essential, eternal, and death cannot live in his sight; for death is corruption, and has no existence in itself, living only in the decay of the things of life. If then any child of the father finds that he is afraid before him, that the thought of God is a discomfort to him, or even a terror, let him make haste—let him not linger to put on any garment, but rush at once in his nakedness, a true child, for shelter from his own evil and God's terror, into the salvation of the Father's arms, the home whence he was sent that he might learn that it was home. What father being evil would it not win to see the child with whom he was vexed running to his embrace? how much more will not the Father of our spirits, who seeks nothing but his children themselves, receive him with open arms!

Self, accepted as the law of self, is the one demon-enemy of life; God is the only Saviour from it, and from all that is not God, for God is life, and all that is not God is death. Life is the destruction of death, of all that kills, of all that is of death's kind.

When John saw the glory of the Son of Man, he fell at his feet as one dead. In what way John saw him, whether in what we vaguely call a vision, or in as human a way as when he leaned back on his bosom and looked up in his face, I do not now care to ask: it would take all glorious shapes of humanity to reveal Jesus, and he knew the right way to show himself to John. It seems to me that such words as were spoken can have come from the mouth of no mere vision, can have been allowed to enter no merely tranced ear, that the mouth of the very Lord himself spoke them, and that none but the living present Jesus could have spoken or may be supposed to speak them; while plainly John received and felt them as a message he had to give again. There are also, strangely as the whole may affect us, various points in his description of the Lord's appearance which commend themselves even to our ignorance by their grandeur and fitness. Why then was John overcome with terror? We recall the fact that something akin to terror overwhelmed the minds of the three disciples who saw his glory on the mount; but since then John had leaned on the bosom of his Lord, had followed him to the judgment seat and had not denied his name, had borne witness to his resurrection and suffered for his sake—and was now 'in the isle that is called Patmos, for the word of God and the testimony of Jesus:' why, I say, was he, why should he be afraid? No glory even of God *should* breed terror; when a child of God is afraid, it is a sign that the word *Father* is not yet freely fashioned by the child's spiritual mouth. The glory can breed terror only in him who is capable of being terrified by it; while he is such it is well the terror should be bred and maintained, until the man seek refuge from it in the only place where it is not—in the bosom of the glory.

There is one point not distinguishable in the Greek: whether is meant, 'one like unto *the* Son of Man,' or, 'one like unto *a* son of Man:' the authorized version has the former, the revised prefers the latter. I incline to the former, and think that John saw him like the man he had known so well, and that it was the too much glory, dimming his vision, that made him unsure, not any perceived unlikeness mingling with the likeness. Nothing blinds so much as light, and their very glory might well render him unable to distinguish plainly the familiar features of *The* Son of Man.

But the appearance of The Son of Man was not intended to breed terror in the son of man to whom he came. Why then was John afraid? why did the servant of the Lord fall at his feet as one dead? Joy to us that he did, for the words that follow—surely no phantasmic outcome of uncertain vision or blinding terror! They bear best sign of their source: however given to his ears, they must be from the heart of our great Brother, the one Man, Christ Jesus, divinely human!

It was still and only the imperfection of the disciple, unfinished in faith, so unfinished in everything a man needs, that was the cause of his terror. This is surely implied in the words the Lord said to him when he fell! The thing that made John afraid, he speaks of as the thing that ought to have taken from him all fear. For the glory that he saw, the head and hair pouring from it such a radiance of light that they were white as white wool—snow-white, as his garments on mount Hermon; in the midst of the radiance his eyes like a flame of fire, and his countenance as the sun shineth in his strength; the darker glow of the feet, yet as of fine brass burning in a furnace—as if they, in memory of the twilight of his humiliation, touching the earth took a humbler glory than his head high in the empyrean of undisturbed perfection; the girdle under his breast, golden between the snow and the brass;—what were they all but the effulgence of his glory who was himself the effulgence of the Father's, the poor expression of the unutterable verity which was itself the reason why John ought not to be afraid?—'He laid his right hand upon me, saying unto me, Fear not; I am the first and the last, and the living one.'

Endless must be our terror, until we come heart to heart with the fire- core of the universe, the first and the last and the living one!

But oh, the joy to be told, by Power himself, the first and the last, the living one—told what we can indeed then see *must* be true, but which we are so slow to believe—that the cure for trembling is the presence of Power; that fear cannot stand before Strength; that the visible God is the destruction of death; that the one and only safety in the universe, is the perfect nearness of the Living One! God is being; death is nowhere! What a thing to be taught by the very mouth of him who knows! He told his servant Paul that strength is made perfect in weakness; here he instructs his servant John that the thing to be afraid of is weakness, not strength. All appearances of strength, such as might rightly move terror, are but false appearances; the true Strong is the *One*, even as the true Good is the *One*. The Living One has the power of life; the Evil One but the power of death—whose very nature is a self-necessity for being destroyed.

But the glory of the mildest show of the Living One is such, that even the dearest of his apostles, the best of the children of men, is cowed at the sight. He has not yet learned that glory itself is a part of his inheritance, yea is of the natural condition of his being; that there is nothing in the man made in the image of God alien from the most glorious of heavenly shows: he has not learned this yet, and falls as dead before it—when lo, the voice of him that was and is and is for evermore, telling him not to be afraid—for the very reason, the one only reason, that he is the first and the last, the living one! For what shall be the joy, the peace, the completion of him that lives, but closest contact with his Life?—a contact close as ere he issued from that Life, only in infinitely higher kind, inasmuch as it is now willed on *both* sides. He who has had a beginning, needs the indwelling power of that beginning to make his being complete—not merely complete to his consciousness, but complete in itself—justified, rounded, ended where it began—with an 'endless ending.' Then is it complete even as God's is complete, for it is one with the self-existent, blossoming in the air of that world wherein it is rooted, wherein it lives and grows. Far indeed from trembling because he on whose bosom he had leaned when the light of his love was all but shut in now stands with the glory of that love streaming forth, John Boanerges ought to have felt the more joyful and safe as the strength of the living one was more manifested. It was never because Jesus was clothed in the weakness of the flesh that he was fit to be trusted, but because he was strong with a strength able to take the weakness of the flesh for the garment wherein it could best work its work: that strength was now shining out with its own light, so lately pent within the revealing veil. Had John been as close in spirit to the Son of Man as he had been in bodily presence, he would have indeed fallen at his feet, but not as one dead—as one too full of joy to stand before the life that was feeding his; he would have fallen, but not to lie there senseless with awe the most holy; he would have fallen to embrace and kiss the feet of him who had now a second time, as with a resurrection from above, arisen before him, in yet heavenlier plenitude of glory.

It is the man of evil, the man of self-seeking design, not he who would fain do right, not he who, even in his worst time, would at once submit to the word of the Master, who is reasonably afraid of power. When God is no longer the ruler of the world, and there is a stronger than he; when there is might inherent in evil, and making-energy in that whose nature is destruction; then will be the time to stand in dread of power. But even then the bad man would have no security against the chance of crossing some scheme of the lawless moment, where disintegration is the sole unity of plan, and being ground up and destroyed for some no-idea of the Power of darkness. And then would be the time for the good—no, not to tremble, but to resolve with the Lord of light to endure all, to let every billow of evil dash and break upon him, nor do the smallest ill, tell the whitest lie for God—knowing that any territory so gained could belong to no kingdom of heaven, could be but a province of the kingdom of darkness. If there were two powers, the one of evil, the other of good, as men have not unnaturally in ignorance imagined, his sense of duty would reveal the being born of the good power, while he born of the evil could have no choice but be evil. But Good only can create; and if Evil were ever so much the stronger, the duty of men would remain the same—to hold by the Living One, and defy Power to its worst—like Prometheus on his rock, defying Jove, and for ever dying—thus for ever foiling the Evil. For

Evil can destroy only itself and its own; it could destroy no enemy— could at worst but cause a succession of deaths, from each of which the defiant soul would rise to loftier defiance, to more victorious endurance— until at length it laughed Evil in the face, and the demongod shrunk withered before it. In those then who believe that good is the one power, and that evil exists only because for a time it subserves, cannot help subserving the good, what place can there be for fear? The strong and the good are one; and if our hope coincides with that of God, if it is rooted in his will, what should we do but rejoice in the effulgent glory of the First and the Last?

The First and the Last is the inclosing defence of the castle of our being; the Master is before and behind; he began, he will see that it be endless. He garrisons the place; he is the living, the live-making one.

The reason then for not fearing before God is, that he is all-glorious, all-perfect. Our being needs the all-glorious, all-perfect God. The children can do with nothing less than the Father; they need the infinite one. Beyond all wherein the poor intellect can descry order; beyond all that the rich imagination can devise; beyond all that hungriest heart could long, fullest heart thank for—beyond all these, as the heavens are higher than the earth, rise the thought, the creation, the love of the God who is in Christ, his God and our God, his Father and our Father.

Ages before the birth of Jesus, while, or at least where yet even Moses and his law were unknown, the suffering heart of humanity saw and was persuaded that nowhere else lay its peace than with the first, the last, the living one:—

O that thou woudest hide me in the grave,... and remember me!... Thou shalt call, and I will answer thee: thou wilt have a desire to the work of thine hands.

THE VOICE OF JOB.

'O that thou wouldest hide me in the grave, that thou wouldest keep me secret, until thy wrath be past, that thou wouldest appoint me a set time, and remember me! If a man die, shall he live again? all the days of my appointed time will I wait, till my change come. Thou shalt call, and I will answer thee: thou wilt have a desire to the work of thine hands.'—Job xiv. 13-15.

The book of Job seems to me the most daring of poems: from a position of the most vantageless realism, it assaults the very citadel of the ideal! Its hero is a man seated among the ashes, covered with loathsome boils from head to foot, scraping himself with a potsherd. Sore in body, sore in mind, sore in heart, sore in spirit, he is the instance- type of humanity in the depths of its misery—all the waves and billows of a world of adverse circumstance rolling free over its head. I would not be supposed to use the word *humanity* either in the abstract, or of the mass concrete; I mean the humanity of the individual endlessly repeated: Job, I say, is *the human being*—a centre to the sickening assaults of pain, the ghastly invasions of fear: these, one time or another, I presume, threaten to overwhelm every man, reveal him to himself as enslaved to the external, and stir him up to find some way out into the infinite, where alone he can rejoice in the liberty that belongs to his nature. Seated in the heart of a leaden despair, Job cries aloud to the Might unseen, scarce known, which yet he regards as the God of his life. But no more that of a slave is his cry, than the defiance of Prometheus hurled at Jupiter from his rock. He is more overwhelmed than the Titan, for he is in infinite perplexity as well as pain; but no more than in that of Prometheus is there a trace of the cowardly in his cry. Before the Judge he asserts his innocence, and will not grovel— knowing indeed that to bear himself so would be to insult the holy. He feels he has not deserved such suffering, and will neither tell nor listen to lies for God.

Prometheus is more stonily patient than Job. Job is nothing of a Stoic, but bemoans himself like a child—a brave child who seems to himself to suffer wrong, and recoils with horror-struck bewilderment from the unreason of the thing. Prometheus has to do with a tyrant whom he despises, before whom therefore he endures with unbewailing unsubmission, upheld by the consciousness that he is fighting the battle of humanity against an all but all-powerful Selfishness: endurance is the only availing weapon against him, and he will endure to the ever-delayed end! Job, on the other hand, is the more troubled because it is He who is at the head and the heart, who is the beginning and the end of things, that has laid his hand upon him with such a heavy torture that he takes his flesh in his teeth for pain. He cannot, will not believe *him* a tyrant; but, while he pleads against his dealing with himself, loves him, and looks to him as the source of life, the power and gladness of being. He dares not think God unjust, but not therefore can he allow that he has done anything to merit the treatment he is receiving at his hands. Hence is he of necessity in profoundest perplexity, for how can the two things be reconciled? The thought has not yet come to him that that which it would be unfair to lay upon him as punishment, may yet be laid upon him as favour—by a love supreme which would give him blessing beyond all possible prayer— blessing he would not dare to ask if he saw the means necessary to its giving, but blessing for which, once known and understood, he would be willing to endure yet again all that he had undergone. Therefore is he so sorely divided in himself. While he must not think of God as having mistaken him, the discrepancy that looks like mistake forces itself upon him through every channel of thought and feeling. He had nowise relaxed his endeavour after a godly life, yet is the hand of the God he had acknowledged in all his ways uplifted against him, as rarely against any transgressor!—nor against him alone, for his sons and daughters have been swept away like a generation of vipers! The possessions, which made him the greatest of all the men of the east, have been taken from him by fire and wind and the hand of the enemy! He is poor as the poorest, diseased as the vilest, bereft of the children which were his pride and his strength! The worst of all with which fear could have

201

dismayed him is come upon him; and worse now than all, death is denied him! His prayer that, as he came naked from the womb, so he may return naked and sore to the bosom of the earth, is not heard; he is left to linger in self-loathing, to encounter at every turn of agonized thought the awful suggestion that God has cast him off! He does not deny that there is evil in him; for—'Dost thou open thine eyes upon such an one,' he pleads, 'and bringest *me* into judgment with *thee*?' but he does deny that he has been a wicked man, a doer of the thing he knew to be evil: he does deny that there is any guile in him. And who, because he knows and laments the guile in himself, will dare deny that there was once a Nathanael in the world? Had Job been Calvinist or Lutheran, the book of Job would have been very different. His perplexity would then have been—how God being just, could require of a man more than he could do, and punish him as if his sin were that of a perfect being who chose to do the evil of which he knew all the enormity. For me, I will call no one Master but Christ—and from him I learn that his quarrel with us is that we will not do what we know, will not come to him that we may have life. How endlessly more powerful with men would be expostulation grounded, not on what they have done, but on what they will not do!

Job's child-like judgment of God had never been vitiated and perverted, to the dishonouring of the great Father, by any taint of such low theories as, alas! we must call the popular: explanations of God's ways by such as did not understand *Him*, they are acceptable to such as do not care to know him, such as are content to stand afar off and stare at the cloud whence issue the thunders and the voices; but a burden threatening to sink them to Tophet, a burden grievous to be borne, to such as would arise and go to the Father. The contradiction between Job's idea of the justice of God and the things which had befallen him, is constantly haunting him; it has a sting in it far worse than all the other misery with which he is tormented; but it is not fixed in the hopelessness of hell by an accepted explanation more frightful than itself. Let the world-sphinx put as many riddles as she will, she can devour no man while he waits an answer from the world-redeemer. Job refused the explanation of his friends because he knew it false; to have accepted such as would by many in the present day be given him, would have been to be devoured at once of the monster. He simply holds on to the skirt of God's garment—besieges his door—keeps putting his question again and again, ever haunting the one source of true answer and reconciliation. No answer will do for him but the answer that God only can give; for who but God can justify God's ways to his creature?

From a soul whose very consciousness is contradiction, we must not look for logic; misery is rarely logical; it is itself a discord; yet is it nothing less than natural that, *feeling* as if God wronged him, Job should yet be ever yearning after a sight of God, straining into his presence, longing to stand face to face with him. He would confront the One. He is convinced, or at least cherishes as his one hope the idea, that, if he could but get God to listen to him, if he might but lay his case clear before him, God would not fail to see how the thing was, and would explain the matter to him—would certainly give him peace; the man in the ashes would know that the foundations of the world yet stand sure; that God has not closed his eyes, or—horror of all horrors— ceased to be just! Therefore would he order his words before him, and hear what God had to say; surely the Just would set the mind of his justice-loving creature at rest!

His friends, good men, religious men, but of the pharisaic type— that is, men who would pay their court to God, instead of coming into his presence as children; men with traditional theories which have served their poor turn, satisfied their feeble intellectual demands, they think others therefore must accept or perish; men anxious to appease God rather than trust in him; men who would rather receive salvation from God, than God their salvation—these his friends would persuade Job to the confession that he was a hypocrite, insisting that such things could not have come upon him but because of wickedness, and as they knew of none open, it must be for some secret vileness. They grow angry with him when he refuses to be persuaded against his knowledge of himself. They insist on his hypocrisy, he on his righteousness. Nor may we forget that herein lies not any overweening on the part of Job, for the poem prepares us for the right understanding of the man by telling us in the prologue, that God said thus to the accuser of men: 'Hast thou considered my servant Job, that there is none like him in the earth, a perfect and an upright man, one that feareth God, and escheweth evil?' God gives Job into Satan's hand with confidence in the result; and at the end of the trial approves of what Job has said concerning himself. But the very appearance of God is enough to make Job turn against himself: his part was to have trusted God altogether, in spite of every appearance, in spite of every reality! He will justify himself no more. He sees that though God has not been punishing him for his sins, yet is he far from what he ought to be, and must become:

'Behold,' he says, 'I am vile; what shall I answer thee? I will lay mine hand upon my mouth.'

But let us look a little closer at Job's way of thinking and speaking about God, and his manner of addressing him—so different from the pharisaic in all ages, in none more than in our own.

Waxing indignant at the idea that his nature required such treatment— 'Am I a sea or a whale,' he cries out, 'that thou settest a watch over me?' *Thou knowest that I am not wicked.* 'Thou settest a print upon the heels of my feet!'—*that the way I have gone may be known by my footprints!* To his friends he cries: 'Will ye speak wickedly for God? and talk deceitfully for him?' *Do you not know that I am the man I say?* 'Will ye accept His person?'—*siding with Him against me?* 'Will ye contend for God?'—*be special pleaders for him, his partisains*? 'Is it good that He should search you out? or as one man mocketh another, do ye so mock Him?'—*saying what you do not think*? 'He will surely reprove you, if ye do secretly accept persons!'—*even the person of God himself!*

Such words are pleasing in the ear of the father of spirits. He is not a God to accept the flattery which declares him above obligation to his creatures; a God to demand of them a righteousness different from his own; a God to deal ungenerously with his poverty-stricken children; a God to make severest demands upon his little ones! Job is confident of receiving justice. There is a strange but most natural conflict of feeling in him. His faith is in truth profound, yet is he always complaining. It is but the form his faith takes in his trouble. Even while he declares the hardness and unfitness of the usage he is receiving, he yet seems assured that, to get things set right, all he needs is admission to the presence of God—an interview with the Most High. To be heard must be to have justice. He uses language which, used by any living man, would horrify the religious of the present day, in proportion to the lack of truth in them, just as it horrified his three friends, the honest pharisees of the time, whose religion was 'doctrine' and rebuke. God speaks not a word of rebuke to Job for the freedom of his speech:—he has always been seeking such as Job to worship him. It is those who know only and respect the outsides of religion, such as never speak or think of God but as the *Almighty* or *Providence*, who will say of the man who would go close up to God, and speak to him out of the deepest in the nature he has made, 'he is irreverent.' To utter the name of God in the drama—highest of human arts, is with such men blasphemy. They pay court to God, not love him; they treat him as one far away, not as the one whose bosom is the only home. They accept God's person.

'Shall not his excellency'—another thing quite than that you admire—
'make you afraid? Shall not his dread'—another thing quite than that to
which you show your pagan respect—'fall upon you?'

In the desolation of this man, the truth of God seems to him, yet
more plainly than hitherto, the one thing that holds together the world
which by the word of his mouth came first into being. If God be not
accessible, nothing but despair and hell are left the man so lately the
greatest in the east. Like a child escaping from the dogs of the street,
he flings the door to the wall, and rushes, nor looks behind him, to
seek the presence of the living one. Bearing with him the burden of his
death, he cries, 'Look what thou hast laid upon me! Shall mortal man,
the helpless creature thou hast made, bear cross like this?' He would
cast his load at the feet of his maker!—God is the God of comfort,
known of man as the refuge, the life-giver, or not known at all. But
alas! he cannot come to him! Nowhere can he see his face! He has hid
himself from him! 'Oh that I knew where I might find him! that I
might come even to his seat! I would order my cause before him, and
fill my mouth with arguments. I would know the words which he
would answer me, and understand what he would say unto me. Will he
plead against me with his great power? No! but he would put strength
in me. There the righteous might dispute with him; so should I be de-
livered for ever from my judge. Behold, I go forward, but he is not
there; and backward, but I cannot perceive him: on the left hand,
where he doth work, but I cannot behold him: he hideth himself on the
right hand, that I cannot see him: but he knoweth the way that I take:
when he hath tried me, I shall come forth as gold.'

He cannot find him! Yet is he in his presence all the time, and his
words enter into the ear of God his Saviour.

The grandeur of the poem is that Job pleads his cause with God
against all the remonstrance of religious authority, recognizing no one
but God, and justified therein. And the grandest of all is this, that he
implies, if he does not actually say, that God *owes* something to his
creature. This is the beginning of the greatest discovery of all—that
God owes *himself* to the creature he has made in his image, for so he
has made him incapable of living without him. This, his creatures'
highest claim upon him, is his divinest gift to them. For the fulfilling
of this their claim he has sent his son, that he may himself, the father
of him and of us, follow into our hearts. Perhaps the worst thing in a
theology constructed out of man's dull *possible*, and not out of the be-
ing and deeds and words of Jesus Christ, is the impression it conveys
throughout that God acknowledges no such obligation. Are not we the

clay, and he the potter? how can the clay claim from the potter? We are the clay, it is true, but *his* clay, but spiritual clay, live clay, with needs and desires—and *rights*; we are clay, but clay worth the Son of God's dying for, that it might learn to consent to be shaped unto honour. We can have no merits—a *merit* is a thing impossible; but God has given us rights. Out of him we have nothing; but, created by him, come forth from him, we have even rights towards him—ah, never, never *against* him! his whole desire and labour is to make us capable of claiming, and induce us to claim of him the things whose rights he bestowed in creating us. No claim had we to be created: that involves an absurdity; but, being made, we have claims on him who made us: our needs are our claims. A man who will not provide for the hunger of his child, is condemned by the whole world.

'Ah, but,' says the partisan of God, 'the Almighty stands in a relation very different from that of an earthly father: there is no parallel.' I grant it: there is no parallel. The man did not create the child, he only yielded to an impulse created in himself: God is infinitely more bound to provide for *his* child than any man is to provide for his. The relation is infinitely, divinely closer. It is God to whom every hunger, every aspiration, every desire, every longing of our nature is to be referred; he made all our needs—made us the creatures of a thousand necessities—and have we no claim on him? Nay, we have claims innumerable, infinite; and his one great claim on us is that we should claim our claims of him.

It is terrible to represent God as unrelated to us in the way of appeal to his righteousness. How should he be righteous without owing us anything? How would there be any right for the judge of all the earth to do if he owed nothing? Verily he owes us nothing that he does not pay like a God; but it is of the devil to imagine imperfection and disgrace in obligation. So far is God from thinking so that in every act of his being he lays himself under obligation to his creatures. Oh, the grandeur of his goodness, and righteousness, and fearless unselfishness! When doubt and dread invade, and the voice of love in the soul is dumb, what can please the father of men better than to hear his child cry to him from whom he came, 'Here I am, O God! Thou hast made me: give me that which thou hast made me needing.' The child's necessity, his weakness, his helplessness, are the strongest of all his claims. If I am a whale, I can claim a sea; if I am a sea, I claim room to roll, and break in waves after my kind; if I am a lion, I seek my meat from God; am I a child, this, beyond all other claims, I claim— that, if any of my needs are denied me, it shall be by the love of a father, who will let me see his face, and allow me to plead my cause before him. And this must be just what God desires! What would he have, but that his children should claim their father? To what end are all his dealings with them, all his sufferings with and for and in them, but that they should claim their birthright? Is not their birthright what he made them for, made in them when he made them? Is it not what he has been putting forth his energy to give them ever since first he began them to be—the divine nature, God himself? The child has, and must have, a claim on the father, a claim which it is the joy of the father's heart to acknowledge. A created need is a created claim. God is the origin of both need and supply, the father of our necessities, the abundant giver of the good things. Right gloriously he meets the claims of his child! The story of Jesus is the heart of his answer, not primarily to the prayers, but to the divine necessities of the children he has sent out into his universe.

Away with the thought that God could have been a perfect, an adorable creator, doing anything less than he has done for his children! that any other kind of being than Jesus Christ could have been worthy of all-glorifying worship! that his nature demanded less of him than he has done! that his nature is not absolute love, absolute self-devotion— could have been without these highest splendours!

In the light of this truth, let us then look at the words at the head of this sermon: '*Oh that thou wouldest hide me in the grave*!' Job appeals to his creator, whom his sufferings compel him to regard as displeased with him, though he knows not why. *We* know he was not displeased but Job had not read the preface to his own story. He prays him to hide him, and forget him for a time, that the desire of the maker to look again upon the creature he had made, to see once more the work of his hands, may awake within him; that silence and absence and loss may speak for the buried one, and make the heart of the parent remember and long after the face of the child; then 'thou shalt call and I will answer thee: thou wilt have a desire to the work of thine hands;' then will he rise in joy, to plead with confidence the cause of his righteousness. For God is nigher to the man than is anything God has made: what can be closer than the making and the made? that which is, and that which is because the other is? that which wills, and that which answers, owing to the will, the heart, the desire of the other, its power to answer? What other relation imaginable could give claims to compare with those arising from such a relation? God must love his creature that looks up to him with hungry eyes—hungry for life, for acknowledgment, for justice, for the possibilities of living that life which the making life has made him alive for the sake of living. The whole existence of a creature is a unit, an entirety of claim upon his creator:— just *therefore*, let him do with me as he will—even to seating me in the ashes, and seeing me scrape myself with a potsherd!— not the less but ever the more will I bring forward my claim! assert it—insist on it— assail with it the ear and the heart of the father. Is it not the sweetest music ear of maker can hear?—except the word of perfect son, 'Lo, I come to do thy will, O God!' We, imperfect sons, shall learn to say the same words too: that we may grow capable and say them, and so enter into our birthright, yea, become partakers of the divine nature in its divinest element, that Son came to us—died for the slaying of our self-ishness, the destruction of our mean hollow pride, the waking of our childhood. We are his father's debtors for our needs, our rights, our claims, and he will have us pay the uttermost farthing. Yes, so true is the Father, he will even compel us, through misery if needful, to put in our claims, for he knows we have eternal need of these things: without the essential rights of his being, who can live?

I protest, therefore, against all such teaching as, originating in and fostered by the faithlessness of the human heart, gives the impression that the exceeding goodness of God towards man is not the natural and necessary outcome of his being. The root of every heresy popular in the church draws its nourishment merely and only from the soil of un-belief. The idea that God would be God all the same, as glorious as he needed to be, had he not taken upon himself the divine toil of bringing home his wandered children, had he done nothing to seek and save the lost, is false as hell. Lying for God could go no farther. As if the idea of God admitted of his being less than he is, less than perfect, less than all-in-all, less than Jesus Christ! less than Love absolute, less than entire unselfishness! As if the God revealed to us in the New Testament were not his own perfect necessity of loving-kindness, but one who has made himself better than, by his own nature, by his own love, by the laws which he willed the laws of his existence, he needed to be! They would have it that, being unbound, he deserves the greater homage! So it might be, if he were not our father. But to think of the living God not as our father, but as one who has condescended greatly, being nowise, in his own willed grandeur of righteous nature, bound to do as he has done, is killing to all but a slavish devotion. It is to think of him as nothing like the God we see in Jesus Christ.

It will be answered that we have fallen, and God is thereby freed from any obligation, if any ever were. It is but another lie. No amount of wrong-doing in a child can ever free a parent from the divine necessity of doing all he can to deliver his child; the bond between them cannot be broken. It is the vulgar, slavish, worldly idea of freedom, that it consists in being bound to nothing. Not such is God's idea of liberty! To speak as a man—the more of vital obligation he lays on himself, the more children he creates, with the more claims upon him, the freer is he as creator and giver of life, which is the essence of his Godhead: to make scope for his essence is to be free. Our Lord teaches us that the truth, known by obedience to him, will make us free: our freedom lies in living the truth of our relations to God and man. For a man to be alone in the universe would be to be a slave to unspeakable longings and lonelinesses. And again to speak after the manner of men: God could not be satisfied with himself without doing all that a God and Father could do for the creatures he had made—that is, without doing just what he has done, what he is doing, what he will do, to deliver his sons and daughters, and bring them home with rejoicing. To answer the cry of the human heart, 'Would that I could see him! would that I might come before him, and look upon him face to face!' he sent his son, the express image of his person. And again, that we might not be limited in our understanding of God by the constant presence to our weak and dullable spiritual sense of any embodiment whatever, he took him away. Having seen him, in his absence we understand him better. That we might know him he came; that we might go to him he went. If we dare, like Job, to plead with him in any of the heart-eating troubles that arise from the impossibility of loving such misrepresentation of him as is held out to us to love by our would-be teachers; if we think and speak out before him that which seems to us to be right, will he not be heartily pleased with his children's love of righteousness—with the truth that will not part him and his righteousness? Verily he will not plead against us with his great power, but will put strength in us, and where we are wrong will instruct us. For the heart that wants to do and think aright, the heart that seeks to worship him as no tyrant, but as the perfectly, absolutely righteous God, is the delight of the Father. To the heart that will not call that righteousness which it feels to be unjust, but clings to the skirt of his garment, and lifts pleading eyes to his countenance—to that heart he will lay open the riches of his being—riches which it has not entered that heart to conceive. 'O Lord, they tell me I have so offended against thy law that, as I am, thou canst not look upon me, but threatenest me with eternal banishment from thy presence. But if thou look not upon me, how can I ever be other than I am? Lord, remember I was born in sin: how then can I see sin as thou seest it? Remember, Lord, that I have never known myself clean: how can I cleanse myself? Thou must needs take me as I am and cleanse me. Is it not impossible that I should behold the final goodness of good, the final evilness of evil? how then can I deserve eternal torment? Had I known good and evil, seeing them as thou seest them, then chosen the evil, and turned away from the good, I know not what I should not deserve; but thou knowest it has ever been something good in the evil that has enticed my selfish heart—nor mine only, but that of all my kind. Thou requirest of us to forgive: surely thou forgivest freely! Bound thou mayest be to destroy evil, but art thou bound to keep the sinner alive that thou mayest punish him, even if it make him no better? Sin cannot be deep as life, for thou art the life; and sorrow and pain go deeper than sin, for they reach to the divine in us: thou canst suffer, though thou wilt not sin. To see men suffer might make us shun evil, but it never could make us hate it. We might see thereby that thou hatest sin, but we never could see that thou lovest the sinner. Chastise us, we pray thee, in loving kindness, and we shall not faint. We have done much that is evil, yea, evil is very deep in us, but we are not all evil, for we love righteousness; and art not thou thyself, in thy Son, the sacrifice for our sins, the atonement of out breach? Thou hast made us subject to vanity, but hast thyself taken thy godlike share of the consequences. Could we ever have come to know good as thou knowest it, save by passing through the sea of sin and the fire of cleansing? They tell me I must say *for Christ's sake*, or thou wilt not pardon: it takes the very heart out of my poor love to hear that thou wilt not pardon me except because Christ has loved me; but I give thee thanks that nowhere in the record of thy gospel, does one of thy servants say any such word. In spite of all our fears and grovelling, our weakness, and our wrongs, thou wilt be to us what thou art—such a perfect Father as no most loving child-heart on earth could invent the thought of! Thou wilt take our sins on thyself, giving us thy life to live withal. Thou bearest our griefs and carriest our sorrows; and surely thou wilt one day enable us to pay every debt we owe to each other! Thou wilt be to us a right generous, abundant father! Then truly our hearts shall be jubilant, because thou art what thou art—infinitely beyond all we could imagine. Thou wilt humble and raise us up. Thou hast given thyself to us that, having thee, we may be eternally alive with thy life. We run within the circle of what men call thy wrath, and find ourselves clasped in the zone of thy love!'

But be it well understood that when I say *rights*, I do not mean *merits*—of any sort. We can deserve from him nothing at all, in the sense of any right proceeding from ourselves. All our rights are such as the bounty of love inconceivable has glorified our being with— bestowed for the one only purpose of giving the satisfaction, the fulfilment of the same—rights so deep, so high, so delicate, that their satisfaction cannot be given until we desire it—yea long for it with our deepest desire. The giver of them came to men, lived with men, and died by the hands of men, that they might possess these rights abundantly: more not God could do to fulfil his part—save indeed what he is doing still every hour, every moment, for every individual. Our rights are rights with God himself at the heart of them. He could recall them if he pleased, but only by recalling us, by making us cease. While we exist, by the being that is ours, they are ours. If he could not fulfil our rights to us—because we would not have them, that is—if he could not make us such as to care for these rights which he has given us out of the very depth of his creative being, I think he would have to uncreate us. But as to deserving, that is absurd: he had to die in the endeavour to make us listen and receive. 'When ye shall have done all the things that are commanded you, say, We are unprofitable servants; we have done that which it was our duty to do.' Duty is a thing prepaid: it can never have desert. There is no claim on God that springs from us: all is from him.

But, lest it should be possible that any unchildlike soul might, in arrogance and ignorance, think to stand upon his rights *against* God, and demand of him this or that after the will of the flesh, I will lay before such a possible one some of the things to which he has a right, yea, perhaps has first of all a right to, from the God of his life, because of the beginning he has given him—because of the divine germ that is in him. He has a claim on God, then, a divine claim, for any pain, want, disappointment, or misery, that would help to show him to himself as the fool he is; he has a claim to be punished to the last scorpion of the whip, to be spared not one pang that may urge him towards repentance; yea, he has a claim to be sent out into the outer darkness, whether what we call hell, or something speechlessly worse, if nothing less will do. He has a claim to be compelled to repent; to be hedged in on every side; to have one after another of the strong, sharp-toothed sheep-dogs of the great shepherd sent after him, to thwart him in any desire, foil him in any plan, frustrate him of any hope, until he come to see at length that nothing will ease his pain, nothing make life a thing worth having, but the presence of the living God within him; that nothing is good but the will of God; nothing noble enough for the desire of the heart of man but oneness with the eternal. For this God must make him yield his very being, that He may enter in and dwell with him.

211

That the man would enforce none of these claims, is nothing; for it is not a man who owes them to him, but the eternal God, who by his own will of right towards the creature he has made, is bound to discharge them. God has to answer to himself for his idea; he has to do with the need of the nature he made, not with the self-born choice of the self- ruined man. His candle yet burns dim in the man's soul; that candle must shine as the sun. For what is the all-pervading dissatisfaction of his wretched being but an unrecognized hunger after the righteousness of his father. The soul God made is thus hungering, though the selfish, usurping self, which is its consciousness, is hungering only after low and selfish things, ever trying, but in vain, to fill its mean, narrow content, with husks too poor for its poverty-stricken desires. For even that most degraded chamber of the soul which is the temple of the deified Self, cannot be filled with less than God; even the usurping Self must be miserable until it cease to look at itself in the mirror of Satan, and open the door of its innermost closet to the God who means to dwell there, and make peace.

He that has looked on the face of God in Jesus Christ, whose heart overflows, if ever so little, with answering love, sees God standing with full hands to give the abundance for which he created his children, and those children hanging back, refusing to take, doubting the God-heart which knows itself absolute in truth and love.

It is not at first easy to see wherein God gives Job any answer; I cannot find that he offers him the least explanation of why he has so afflicted him. He justifies him in his words; he says Job has spoken what is right concerning him, and his friends have not; and he calls up before him, one after another, the works of his hands. The answer, like some of our Lord's answers if not all of them, seems addressed to Job himself, not to his intellect; to the revealing, God-like imagination in the man, and to no logical faculty whatever. It consists in a setting forth of the power of God, as seen in his handywork, and wondered at by the men of the time; and all that is said concerning them has to do with their show of themselves to the eyes of men. In what belongs to the deeper meanings of nature and her mediation between us and God, the appearances of nature are the truths of nature, far deeper than any scientific discoveries in and concerning them. The show of things is that for which God cares *most,* for their show is the face of far deeper things than they; we see in them, in a distant way, as in a glass darkly, the face of the unseen. It is through their show, not through their analysis, that we enter into their deepest truths. What they say to the childlike soul is the truest thing to be gathered of them. To know a

212

primrose is a higher thing than to know all the botany of it—just as to know Christ is an infinitely higher thing than to know all theology, all that is said about his person, or babbled about his work. The body of man does not exist for the sake of its hidden secrets; its hidden secrets exist for the sake of its outside—for the face and the form in which dwells revelation: its outside is the deepest of it. So Nature as well exists primarily for her face, her look, her appeals to the heart and the imagination, her simple service to human need, and not for the secrets to be discovered in her and turned to man's farther use. What in the name of God is our knowledge of the elements of the atmosphere to our knowledge of the elements of Nature? What are its oxygen, its hydrogen, its nitrogen, its carbonic acid, its ozone, and all the possible rest, to the blowing of the wind on our faces? What is the analysis of water to the babble of a running stream? What is any knowledge of things to the heart, beside its child-play with the Eternal! And by an infinite decomposition we should know nothing more of what a thing really is, for, the moment we decompose it, it ceases to be, and all its meaning is vanished. Infinitely more than astronomy even, which destroys nothing, can do for us, is done by the mere aspect and changes of the vault over our heads. Think for a moment what would be our idea of greatness, of God, of infinitude, of aspiration, if, instead of a blue, far withdrawn, light-spangled firmament, we were born and reared under a flat white ceiling! I would not be supposed to depreciate the labours of science, but I say its discoveries are unspeakably less precious than the merest gifts of Nature, those which, from morning to night, we take unthinking from her hands. One day, I trust, we shall be able to enter into their secrets from within them—by natural contact between our heart and theirs. When we are one with God we may well understand in an hour things that no man of science, prosecuting his investigations from the surface with all the aids that keenest human intellect can supply, would reach in the longest lifetime. Whether such power will ever come to any man in this world, or can come only in some state of existence beyond it, matters nothing to me: the question does not interest me; life is one, and things will be then what they are now; for God is one and the same there and here; and I shall be the same there I am here, however larger the life with which it may please the Father of my being to endow me.

The argument implied, not expressed, in the poem, seems to be this— that Job, seeing God so far before him in power, and his works so far beyond his understanding that they filled him with wonder and admiration—the vast might of the creation, the times and the seasons, the marvels of the heavens, the springs of the sea, and the gates of death; the animals, their generations and providing, their beauties and instincts; the strange and awful beasts excelling the rest, behemoth on the land, leviathan in the sea, creatures, perhaps, now vanished from the living world;—that Job, beholding these things, ought to have reasoned that he who could work so grandly beyond his understanding, must certainly use wisdom in things that touched him nearer, though they came no nearer his understanding: 'shall he that contendeth with the Almighty instruct him? he that reproveth God, let him answer it.' 'Wilt thou also disannul my judgment? wilt thou condemn me that thou mayest be righteous?' In this world power is no *proof* of righteousness; but was it likely that he who could create should be unrighteous? Did not all he made move the delight of the beholding man? Did such things foreshadow injustice towards the creature he had made in his image? If Job could not search his understanding in these things, why should he conclude his own case wrapt in the gloom of injustice? Did he understand his own being, history, and destiny? Should not God's ways in these also be beyond his understanding? Might he not trust him to do him justice? In such high affairs as the rights of a live soul, might not matters be involved too high for Job? The maker of Job was so much greater than Job, that his ways with him might well be beyond his comprehension! God's thoughts were higher than his thoughts, as the heavens were higher than the earth!

The true child, the righteous man, will trust absolutely, against all appearances, the God who has created in him the love of righteousness.

God does not, I say, tell Job why he had afflicted him: he rouses his child-heart to trust. All the rest of Job's life on earth, I imagine, his slowly vanishing perplexities would yield him ever fresh meditations concerning God and his ways, new opportunities of trusting him, light upon many things concerning which he had not as yet begun to doubt, added means of growing in all directions into the knowledge of God. His perplexities would thus prove of divinest gift. Everything, in truth, which we cannot understand, is a closed book of larger knowledge and blessedness, whose clasps the blessed perplexity urges us to open. There is, there can be, nothing which is not in itself a righteous intelligibility—whether an intelligibility for us, matters nothing. The awful thing would be, that anything should be in its nature unintelligible: that would be the same as *no God*. That God knows is enough for me; I shall know, if I can know. It would be death to think God did not know; it would be as much as to conclude there was no God to know.

How much more than Job are we bound, who know him in his Son as Love, to trust God in all the troubling questions that force themselves upon us concerning the motions and results of things! With all those about the lower animals, with all those about such souls as seem never to wake from, or seem again to fall into the sleep of death, we will trust him.

In the confusion of Job's thoughts—how could they be other than confused, in the presence of the awful contradiction of two such facts staring each other in the face, that God was just, yet *punishing* a righteous man as if he were wicked?—while he was not yet able to generate, or to receive the thought, that approving love itself might be inflicting or allowing the torture—that such suffering as his was granted only to a righteous man, that he might be made perfect—I can well imagine that at times, as the one moment he doubted God's righteousness, and the next cried aloud, 'Though he slay me, yet will I trust in him,' there must in the chaos have mingled some element of doubt as to the existence of God. Let not such doubt be supposed a yet further stage in unbelief. To deny the existence of God may, paradoxical as the statement will at first seem to some, involve less unbelief than the smallest yielding to doubt of his goodness. I say *yielding*; for a man may be haunted with doubts, and only grow thereby in faith. Doubts are the messengers of the Living One to rouse the honest. They are the first knock at our door of things that are not yet, but have to be, understood; and theirs in general is the inhospitable reception of angels that do not come in their own likeness. Doubt must precede every deeper assurance; for uncertainties are what we first see when we look into a region hitherto unknown, unexplored, unannexed. In all Job's begging and longing to see God, then, may well be supposed to mingle the mighty desire to be assured of God's being. To acknowledge is not to be sure of God. One great point in the poem is—that when Job hears the voice of God, though it utters no word of explanation, it is enough to him to hear it: he knows that God is, and that he hears the cry of his creature. That he is there, knowing all about him, and what had befallen him, is enough; he needs no more to reconcile seeming contradictions, and the worst ills of outer life become endurable. Even if Job could not at first follow his argument of divine probability, God settled everything for him when, by answering him out of the whirlwind, he showed him that he had not forsaken him. It is true that nothing but a far closer divine presence can ever make life a thing fit for a son of man—and that for the simplest of all reasons, that he is made in the image of God, and it is for him absolutely imperative that he should have in him the reality of which his being is the image: while he has it not in him, his being, his conscious self, is but a mask, a spiritual emptiness; but for the present, Job, yielding to God, was calmed and satisfied. Perhaps he came at length to see that, if anything God could do to him would trouble him so as to make him doubt God—if he knew him so imperfectly who could do nothing ill, then it was time that he should be so troubled, that the imperfection of his knowledge of God and his lack of faith in him should be revealed to him—that an earthquake of his being should disclose its hollowness, and at the same time bring to the surface the gold of God that was in him. To know that our faith is weak is the first step towards its strengthening; to be capable of distrusting is death; to know that we are, and cry out, is to begin to live—to begin to be made such that we cannot distrust—such that God may do anything with us and we shall never doubt him. Until doubt is impossible, we are lacking in the true, the childlike knowledge of God; for either God is such that one *may* distrust him, or he is such that to distrust him is the greatest injustice of which a man can be guilty. If then we are able to distrust him, either we know God imperfect, or we do not know him. Perhaps Job learned something like this; anyhow, the result of what he had had to endure was a greater nearness to God. But all that he was required to receive at the moment was the argument from God's loving wisdom in his power, to his loving wisdom in everything else. For power is a real and a good thing, giving an immediate impression that it proceeds from goodness. Nor, however long it may last after goodness is gone, was it ever born of anything but goodness. In a very deep sense, power and goodness are one. In the deepest fact they are one.

Seeing God, Job forgets all he wanted to say, all he thought he would say if he could but see him. The close of the poem is grandly abrupt. He had meant to order his cause before him; he had longed to see him that he might speak and defend himself, imagining God as well as his righteous friends wrongfully accusing him; but his speech is gone from him; he has not a word to say. To justify himself in the presence of Him who is Righteousness, seems to him what it is— foolishness and worthless labour. If God do not see him righteous, he is not righteous, and may hold his peace. If he is righteous, God knows it better than he does himself. Nay, if God do not care to justify him, Job has lost his interest in justifying himself. All the evils and imper- fections of his nature rise up before him in the presence of the one pure, the one who is right, and has no selfishness in him. 'Behold,' he cries, 'I am vile; what shall I answer thee? I will lay mine hand upon my mouth. Once have I spoken; but I will not answer: yea, twice; but I will proceed no further.' Then again, after God has called to witness for him behemoth and leviathan, he replies, 'I know that thou canst do everything, and that no thought can be withholden from thee. Who is he that hideth counsel without knowledge?' This question was the word with which first God made his presence known to him; and in the mouth of Job now repeating the question, it is the humble confession, '*I am that foolish man.*'—'Therefore,' he goes on, 'have I uttered that I understood not; things too wonderful for me, which I knew not.' He had not knowledge enough to have a right to speak. 'Hear, I beseech thee, and I will speak:'—In the time to come, he will yet cry—to be taught, not to justify himself. 'I will demand of thee, and declare thou unto me.'—The more diligently yet will he seek to know the counsel of God. That he cannot understand will no longer distress him; it will only urge him to fresh endeavour after the knowledge of him who in all his doings is perfect. 'I have heard of thee by the hearing of the ear: but now mine eye seeth thee. Wherefore I abhor myself, and repent in dust and ashes.'

Job had his desire: he saw the face of God—and abhorred himself in dust and ashes. He sought justification; he found self-abhorrence. Was this punishment? The farthest from it possible. It was the best thing—to begin with—that the face of God could do for him. Blessedest gift is self-contempt, when the giver of it is the visible glory of the Living One. For there to see is to partake; to be able to behold that glory is to live; to turn from and against self is to begin to be pure of heart. Job was in the right when he said that he did not deserve to be in such wise punished for his sins: neither did he deserve to see the face of God, yet had he that crown of all gifts given him—and it was to see himself vile, and abhor himself. By very means of the sufferings against which he had cried out, the living one came near to him, and he was silent. Oh the divine generosity that will grant us to be abashed and self-condemned before the Holy!—to come so nigh him as to see ourselves dark spots against his brightness! Verily we must be of his kind, else no show of him could make us feel small and ugly and un-clean! Oh the love of the Father, that he should give us to compare ourselves with him, and be buried in humility and shame! To be re-buked before him is to be his. Good man as Job was, he had never yet been right near to God; now God has come near to him, has become very real to him; he knows now in very deed that God is he with whom he has to do. He had laid all these troubles upon him that He might through them draw nigh to him, and enable him to know him.

Two things are clearly contained in, and manifest from this poem:—that not every man deserves for his sins to be punished everlastingly from the presence of the Lord; and that the best of men, when he sees the face of God, will know himself vile. God is just, and will never deal with the sinner as if he were capable of sinning the pure sin; yet if the best man be not delivered from himself, that self will sink him into Tophet.

Any man may, like Job, plead his cause with God—though possibly it may not be to like justification: he gives us liberty to speak, and will hear with absolute fairness. But, blessed be God, the one result for all who so draw nigh to him will be—to see him plainly, surely right, the perfect Saviour, the profoundest refuge even from the wrongs of their own being, yea, nearer to them always than any wrong they could commit; so seeing him, they will abhor themselves, and rejoice in him. And, as the poem indicates, when we turn from ourselves to him, becoming true, that is, being to God and to ourselves what we are, he will turn again our captivity; they that have sown in tears shall reap in joy; they shall doubtless come again with rejoicing, bringing their sheaves with them. Then will the waters that rise from God's fountains, run in God's channels.

For the prosperity that follows upon Job's submission, is the embodiment of a great truth. Although a man must do right if it send him to Hades, yea, even were it to send him for ever to hell itself, yet, while the Lord liveth, we need not fear: *all* good things must grow out of and hang upon the one central good, the one law of life— the Will, the One Good. To submit absolutely to him is the only reason: circumstance as well as all being must then bud and blossom as the rose. And it will!—what matter whether in this world or the next, if one day I know my life as a perfect bliss, having neither limitation nor hindrance nor pain nor sorrow more than it can dominate in peace and perfect assurance?

I care not whether the book of Job be a history or a poem. I think it is both—I do not care how much relatively of each. It was probably, in the childlike days of the world, a well-known story in the east, which some man, whom God had made wise to understand his will and his ways, took up, and told after the fashion of a poet. What its age may be, who can certainly tell!—it must have been before Moses. I would gladly throw out the part of Elihu as an interpolation. One in whom, of all men I have known, I put the greatest trust, said to me once what amounted to this: 'There is as much difference between the language of the rest of the poem and that of Elihu, as between the language of Chaucer and that of Shakspere.'

The poem is for many reasons difficult, and in the original to me inaccessible; but, through all the evident inadequacy of our translation, who can fail to hear two souls, that of the poet and that of Job, crying aloud with an agonized hope that, let the evil shows around them be what they may, truth and righteousness are yet the heart of things. The faith, even the hope of Job seems at times on the point of giving way; he struggles like a drowning man when the billow goes over him, but with the rising of his head his courage revives. Christians we call ourselves!—what would not our faith be, were it as much greater than Job's as the word from the mouth of Jesus is mightier than that he heard out of the whirlwind! Here is a book of faith indeed, ere the law was given by Moses: Grace and Truth have visited us—but where is our faith?

Friends, our cross may be heavy, and the *via dolorosa* rough; but we have claims on God, yea the right to cry to him for help. He has spent, and is spending himself to give us our birthright, which is righteousness. Though we shall not be condemned for our sins, we cannot be saved but by leaving them; though we shall not be condemned for the sins that are past, we shall be condemned if we love the darkness rather than the light, and refuse to come to him that we may have life. God is offering us the one thing we cannot live without—his own self: we must make room for him; we must cleanse our hearts that he may come in; we must do as the Master tells us, who knew all about the Father and the way to him—*we must deny ourselves, and take up our cross daily, and follow him.*

SELF-DENIAL.

'And he said unto all, If any man would come after me, let him deny himself, and take up his cross daily, and follow me. For whosoever would save his life shall lose it; but whosoever shall lose his life for my sake, the same shall save it.'—St. Luke ix. 23-24.

Christ is the way out, and the way in; the way from slavery, conscious or unconscious, into liberty; the way from the unhomeliness of things to the home we desire but do not know; the way from the stormy skirts of the Father's garments to the peace of his bosom. To picture him, we need not only endless figures, but sometimes quite opposing figures: he is not only the door of the sheepfold, but the shepherd of the sheep; he is not only the way, but the leader in the way, the rock that followed, and the captain of our salvation. We must become as little children, and Christ must be born in us; we must learn of him, and the one lesson he has to give is himself: he does first all he wants us to do; he is first all he wants us to be. We must not merely do as he did; we must see things as he saw them, regard them as he regarded them; we must take the will of God as the very life of our being; we must neither try to get our own way, nor trouble ourselves as to what may be thought or said of us. The world must be to us as nothing.

I would not be misunderstood if I may avoid it: when I say *the world*, I do not mean the world God makes and means, yet less the human hearts that live therein; but the world man makes by choosing the perversion of his own nature—a world apart from and opposed to God's world. By *the world* I mean all ways of judging, regarding, and thinking, whether political, economical, ecclesiastical, social, or individual, which are not divine, which are not God's ways of thinking, regarding, or judging; which do not take God into account, do not set his will supreme, as the one only law of life; which do not care for the truth of things, but the customs of society, or the practice of the trade; which heed not what is right, but the usage of the time. From everything that is against the teaching and thinking of Jesus, from the world in the heart of the best man in it, specially from the world in his own heart, the disciple must turn to follow him. The first thing in all progress is to leave something behind; to follow him is to leave one's self behind. 'If any man would come after me, let him deny himself.'

Some seem to take this to mean that the disciple must go against his likings because they are his likings; must be unresponsive to the tendencies and directions and inclinations that are his, because they are such, and his; they seem to think something is gained by abstinence from what is pleasant, or by the doing of what is disagreeable—that to thwart the lower nature is in itself a good. Now I will not dare say what a man may not get good from, if the thing be done in simplicity and honesty. I believe that when a man, for the sake of doing the thing that is right, does in mistake that which is not right, God will take care that he be shown the better way—will perhaps use the very thing which is his mistake to reveal to him the mistake it is. I will allow that the mere effort of will, arbitrary and uninformed of duty, partaking of the character of tyranny and even schism, may add to the man's power over his lower nature; but in that very nature it is God who must rule and not the man, however well he may mean. From a man's rule of himself, in smallest opposition, however devout, to the law of his being, arises the huge danger of nourishing, by the pride of self-conquest, a far worse than even the unchained animal self—the demoniac self. True victory over self is the victory of God in the man, not of the man alone. It is not subjugation that is enough, but subjugation by God. In whatever man does without God, he must fail miserably—or succeed more miserably. No portion of a man can rule another portion, for God, not the man, created it, and the part is greater than the whole. In effecting what God does not mean, a man but falls into fresh ill conditions. In crossing his natural, therefore in themselves right inclinations, a man may develop a self-satisfaction which in its very nature is a root of all sin. Doing the thing God does not require of him, he puts himself in the place of God, becoming not a law but a law-giver to himself, one who commands, not one who obeys. The diseased satisfaction which some minds feel in laying burdens on themselves, is a pampering, little as they may suspect it, of the most dangerous appetite of that self which they think they are mortifying. All the creatures of God are good, received with thanksgiving; then only can any one of them become evil, when it is used in relations in which a higher law forbids it, or when it is refused for the sake of self- discipline, in relations in which no higher law forbids, and God therefore allows it. For a man to be his own schoolmaster, is a right dangerous position; the pupil cannot be expected to make progress—except, indeed, in the wrong direction. To enjoy heartily and thankfully, and do cheerfully without, when God wills we should, is the way to live in regard to things of the lower nature; these must nowise be confounded with the things of *the world*. If any one say this is dangerous doctrine, I answer, 'The law of God is enough for me, and for laws invented by man, I will none of them. They are false, and come all of rebellion. God and not man is our judge.'

Verily it is not to thwart or tease the poor self Jesus tells us. That was not the purpose for which God gave it to us I He tells us we must leave it altogether—yield it, deny it, refuse it, lose it: thus only shall we save it, thus only have a share in our own being. The self is given to us that we may sacrifice it; it is ours that we like Christ may have somewhat to offer—not that we should torment it, but that we should deny it; not that we should cross it, but that we should abandon it utterly: then it can no more be vexed.

'What can this mean?—we are not to thwart, but to abandon? How abandon, without thwarting?'

It means this:—we must refuse, abandon, deny self altogether as a ruling, or determining, or originating element in us. It is to be no longer the regent of our action. We are no more to think, 'What should I like to do?' but 'What would the Living One have me do?' It is not selfish to take that which God has made us to desire; neither are we very good to yield it—we should only be very bad not to do so, when he would take it from us; but to yield it heartily, without a struggle or regret, is not merely to deny the Self a thing it would like, but to deny the Self itself, to refuse and abandon it. The Self is God's making— only it must be the 'slave of Christ,' that the Son may make it also the free son of the same Father; it must receive all from him—not as from nowhere; as well as the deeper soul, it must follow him, not its own desires. It must not be its own law; Christ must be its law. The time will come when it shall be so possessed, so enlarged, so idealized, by the indwelling God, who is its deeper, its deepest self, that there will be no longer any enforced denial of it needful; it has been finally denied and refused and sent into its own obedient place; it has learned to

222

receive with thankfulness, to demand nothing; to turn no more upon its own centre, or any more think to minister to its own good. God's eternal denial of himself, revealed in him who for our sakes in the flesh took up his cross daily, will have been developed in the man; his eternal rejoicing will be in God—and in his fellows, before whom he will cast his glad self to be a carpet for their walk, a footstool for their rest, a stair for their climbing.

To deny oneself then, is to act no more from the standing-ground of self; to allow no private communication, no passing influence between the self and the will; not to let the right hand know what the left hand doeth. No grasping or seeking, no hungering of the individual, shall give motion to the will; no desire to be conscious of worthiness shall order the life; no ambition whatever shall be a motive of action; no wish to surpass another be allowed a moment's respite from death; no longing after the praise of men influence a single throb of the heart. To deny the self is to shrink from no dispraise or condemnation or contempt of the community, or circle, or country, which is against the mind of the Living one; for no love or entreaty of father or mother, wife or child, friend or lover, to turn aside from following him, but forsake them all as any ruling or ordering power in our lives; we must do nothing to please them that would not first be pleasing to him. Bight deeds, and not the judgment thereupon; true words, and not what reception they may have, shall be our care. Not merely shall we not love money, or trust in it, or seek it as the business of life, but, whether we have it or have it not, we must never think of it as a windfall from the tree of event or the cloud of circumstance, but as the gift of God. We must draw our life, by the uplooking, acknowledging will, every moment fresh from the living one, the causing life, not glory in the mere consciousness of health and being. It is God feeds us, warms us, quenches our thirst. The will of God must be to us all in all; to our whole nature the life of the Father must be the joy of the child; we must know our very understanding his—that we live and feed on him every hour in the closest, veriest way: to know these things in the depth of our knowing, is to deny ourselves, and take God instead. To try after them is to begin the denial, to follow him who never sought his own. So must we deny all anxieties and fears. When young we must not mind what the world calls failure; as we grow old, we must not be vexed that we cannot remember, must not regret that we cannot do, must not be miserable because we grow weak or ill: we must not mind anything. We have to do with God who can, not with ourselves where we cannot; we have to do with the Will, with the Eternal Life of the Father of our spirits, and not with the being which we could not make, and which is his care. He is our care; we are his; our care is to will his will; his care, to give us all things. This is to deny ourselves. 'Self, I have not to consult you, but him whose idea is the soul of you, and of which as yet you are all unworthy. I have to do, not with you, but with the source of you, by whom it is that any moment you exist— the Causing of you, not the caused you. You may be my consciousness, but you are not my being. If you were, what a poor, miserable, dingy, weak wretch I should be! but my life is hid with Christ in God, whence it came, and whither it is returning—with you certainly, but as an obedient servant, not a master. Submit, or I will cast you from me, and pray to have another consciousness given me. For God is more to me than my consciousness of myself. He is my life; you are only so much of it as my poor half-made being can grasp—as much of it as I can now know at once. Because I have fooled and spoiled you, treated you as if you were indeed my own self, you have dwindled yourself and have lessened me, till I am ashamed of myself. If I were to mind what you say, I should soon be sick of you; even now I am ever and anon disgusted with your paltry, mean face, which I meet at every turn. No! let me have the company of the Perfect One, not of you! of my elder brother, the Living One! I will not make a friend of the mere shadow of my own being! Good-bye, Self! I deny you, and will do my best every day to leave you behind me.'

And in this regard we must not fail to see, or seeing ever forget, that, when Jesus tells us we must follow him, we must come to him, we must believe in him, he speaks first and always as *the Son* of the Father—and that in the active sense, as the obedient God, not merely as one who claims the sonship for the ground of being and so of further claim. He is the Son of the Father as the Son who obeys the Father, as the Son who came expressly and only to do the will of the Father, as the messenger whose delight it is to do the will of him that sent him. At the moment he says *Follow me*, he is following the Father; his face is set homeward. He would have us follow him because he is bent on the will of the Blessed. It is nothing even thus to think of him, except thus we *believe* in him—that is, so do. To believe in him is to do as he does, to follow him where he goes. We must believe in him *practically*—altogether practically, as he believed in his Father; not as one concerning whom we have to hold something, but as one whom we have to follow out of the body of this death into life eternal. It is not to follow him to take him in any way theoretically, to hold this or that theory about why he died, or wherein lay his atonement: such

224

things can be revealed only to those who follow him in his active be-
ing and the principle of his life—who do as he did, live as he lived.
There is no other following. He is all for the Father; we must be all for
the Father too, else are we not following him. To follow him is to be
learning of him, to think his thoughts, to use his judgments, to see
things as he saw them, to feel things as he felt them, to be hearted,
souled, minded, as he was—that so also we may be of the same mind
with his Father. This it is to deny self and go after him; nothing less,
even if it be working miracles and casting out devils, is to be his disci-
ple. Busy from morning to night doing great things for him on any
other road, we should but earn the reception, 'I never knew you.' When
he says, 'Take my yoke upon you,' he does not mean a yoke which he
would lay upon our shoulders; it is his own yoke he tells us to take,
and to learn of him—it is the yoke he is himself carrying, the yoke his
perfect Father had given him to carry. The will of the Father is the
yoke he would have us take, and bear also with him. It is of this yoke
that he says, *It is easy*, of this burden, *It is light*. He is not saying, 'The
yoke I lay upon you is easy, the burden light;' what he says is, 'The
yoke I carry is easy, the burden on my shoulders is light.' With the
garden of Gethsemane before him, with the hour and the power of
darkness waiting for him, he declares his yoke easy, his burden light.
There is no magnifying of himself. *He first* denies himself, and takes
up his cross—then tells us to do the same. The Father magnifies the
Son, not the Son himself; the Son magnifies the Father.

We must be jealous for God against ourselves, and look well to the
cunning and deceitful Self—ever cunning and deceitful until it is in-
formed of God—until it is thoroughly and utterly denied, and God is to
it also All-in-all—till we have left it quite empty of our will and our
regard, and God has come into it, and made it—not indeed an *adytum*,
but a *pylon* for himself. Until then, its very denials, its very turnings
from things dear to it for the sake of Christ, will tend to foster its self-
regard, and generate in it a yet deeper self- worship. While it is not
denied, only thwarted, we may through satisfaction with conquered
difficulty and supposed victory, minister yet more to its self-
gratulation. The Self, when it finds it cannot have honour because of
its gifts, because of the love lavished upon it, because of its conquests,
and the 'golden opinions bought from all sorts of people,' will please
itself with the thought of its abnegations, of its unselfishness, of its
devotion to God, of its forsakings for his sake. It may not *call* itself,
but it will soon *feel* itself a saint, a superior creature, looking down
upon the foolish world and its ways, walking on high 'above the smoke

and stir of this dim spot;'—all the time dreaming a dream of utter folly, worshipping itself with the more concentration that it has yielded the approbation of the world, and dismissed the regard of others: even they are no longer necessary to its assurance of its own worths and merits! In a thousand ways will Self delude itself, in a thousand ways befool its own slavish being. Christ sought not his own, sought not anything but the will of his Father: we have to grow diamond-clear, true as the white light of the morning. Hopeless task!—were it not that he offers to come himself, and dwell in us.

I have wondered whether the word of the Lord, 'take up his cross,' was a phrase in use at the time: when he used it first he had not yet told them that he would himself be crucified. I can hardly believe this form of execution such a common thing that the figure of bearing the cross had come into ordinary speech. As the Lord's idea was new to men, so I think was the image in which he embodied it. I grant it *might*, being such a hateful thing in the eyes of the Jews, have come to represent the worst misery of a human being; but would they be ready to use as a figure a fact which so sorely manifested their slavery? I hardly think it. Certainly it had not come to represent the thing he was now teaching, that self-abnegation which he had but newly brought to light—nay, hardly to the light yet—only the twilight; and nothing less, it seems to me, can have suggested the terrible symbol!

But we must note that, although the idea of the denial of self is an entire and absolute one, yet the thing has to be done *daily*: we must keep on denying. It is a deeper and harder thing than any sole effort of most herculean will may finally effect. For indeed the will itself is not pure, is not free, until the Self is absolutely denied. It takes long for the water of life that flows from the well within us, to permeate every out-lying portion of our spiritual frame, subduing everything to itself, making it all of the one kind, until at last, reaching the outermost folds of our personality, it casts out disease, our bodies by indwelling right-eousness are redeemed, and the creation delivered from the bondage of corruption into the liberty of the glory of the children of God. Every day till then we have to take up our cross; every hour to see that we are carrying it. A birthright may be lost for a mess of pottage, and what Satan calls a trifle must be a thing of eternal significance.

Is there not many a Christian who, having begun to deny himself, yet spends much strength in the vain and evil endeavour to accommo-date matters between Christ and the dear Self—seeking to save that which so he must certainly lose—in how different a way from that in which the Master would have him lose it! It is one thing to have the loved self devoured of hell in hate and horror and disappointment; another to yield it to conscious possession by the living God himself, who will raise it then first and only to its true individuality, freedom, and life. With its cause within it, then, indeed, it shall be saved!—how then should it but live! Here is the promise to those who will leave all and follow him: '*Whosoever shall lose his life, for my sake, the same shall save it*,'—in St. Matthew, '*find it.*' What speech of men or angels will serve to shadow the dimly glorious hope! To lose ourselves in the salvation of God's heart! to be no longer any care to ourselves, but know God taking divinest care of us, his own! to be and feel just a resting-place for the divine love—a branch of the tree of life for the dove to alight upon and fold its wings! to be an open air of love, a thoroughfare for the thoughts of God and all holy creatures! to know one's self by the reflex action of endless brotherly presence—yearning after nothing from any, but ever pouring out love by the natural motion of the spirit! to revel in the hundredfold of everything good we may have had to leave for his sake—above all, in the unsought love of those who love us as we love them—circling us round, bathing us in bliss—never reached after, ever received, ever welcomed, altogether and divinely precious! to know that God and we mean the same thing, that we are in the secret, the child's secret of existence, that we are pleasing in the eyes and to the heart of the Father! to live nestling at his knee, climbing to his bosom, blessed in the mere and simple being which is one with God, and is the outgoing of his will, justifying the being by the very facts of the being, by its awareness of itself as bliss!—what a self is this to receive again from him for that we left, forsook, refused! We left it paltry, low, mean; he took up the poor cinder of a consciousness, carried it back to the workshop of his spirit, made it a true thing, radiant, clear, fit for eternal companying and indwelling, and restored it to our having and holding for ever!

All high things can be spoken only in figures; these figures, having to do with matters too high for them, cannot *fit* intellectually; they can be interpreted truly, understood aright, only by such as have the spiritual fact in themselves. When we speak of a man and his soul, we imply a self and a self, reacting on each other: we cannot divide ourselves so; the figure suits but imperfectly. It was never the design of the Lord to explain things to our understanding—nor would that in the least have helped our necessity; what we require is a means, a word, whereby to think with ourselves of high things: that is what a true figure, for a figure may be true while far from perfect, will always be to us. But the imperfection of his figures cannot lie in excess. Be sure that, in dealing with any truth, its symbol, however high, must come short of the glorious meaning itself holds. It is the low stupidity of an unspiritual nature that would interpret the Lord's meaning as less than his symbols. The true soul sees, or will come to see, that his words, his figures always represent more than they are able to present; for, as the heavens are higher than the earth, so are the heavenly things higher than the earthly signs of them, let the signs be good as ever sign may be. There is no joy belonging to human nature, as God made it, that shall not be enhanced a hundredfold to the man who gives up himself—though, in so doing, he may seem to be yielding the very essence of life. To yield self is to give up grasping at things in their second causes, as men call them, but which are merely God's means, and to receive them direct from their source—to take them seeing whence they come, and not as if they came from nowhere, because no one appears presenting them. The careless soul receives the Father's gifts as if it were a way things had of dropping into his hand. He thus grants himself a slave, dependent on chance and his own blundering endeavour—yet is he ever complaining, as if some one were accountable for the checks which meet him at every turn. For the good that comes to him, he gives no thanks—who is there to thank? at the disappointments that befall him he grumbles—there must be some one to blame! He does not think to what Power it could be of any consequence, nay, what power would not be worse than squandered, to sustain him after his own fashion, in his paltry, low-aimed existence! How could a God pour out his being to uphold the merest waste of his creatures? No world could ever be built or sustained on such an idea. It is the children who shall inherit the earth; such as will not be children, cannot possess. The hour is coming when all that art, all that science, all that nature, all that animal nature, in ennobling subjugation to the higher even as man is subject to the Father, can afford, shall be the possession, to the endless delight, of the sons and daughters of God: to him to whom he is all in all, God is able to give these things; to another he cannot give them, for he is unable to receive them who is outside the truth of them. Assuredly we are not to love God for the sake of what he can give us; nay, it is impossible to love him save because he is our God, and altogether good and beautiful; but neither may we forget what the Lord does not forget, that, in the end, when the truth is victorious, God will answer his creature in the joy of his heart. For what is joy but the harmony of the spirit! The good Father made his children to be joyful; only, ere they can enter into his joy, they must be like himself, ready to sacrifice joy to truth. No promise of such joy is an appeal to selfishness. Every reward held out by Christ is a pure thing; nor can it enter the soul save as a death to selfishness. The heaven of Christ is a loving of all, a forgetting of self, a dwelling of each in all, and all in each. Even in our nurseries, a joyful child is rarely selfish, generally righteous. It is not selfish to be joyful. What power could prevent him who sees the face of God from being joyful?—that bliss is his which lies behind all other bliss, without which no other bliss could ripen or last. The one bliss of the universe is the presence of God— which is simply God being to the man, and felt by the man as being, that which in his own nature he is—the indwelling power of his life. God must be to his creature what he is in himself, for it is by his essential being alone, that by which he is, that he can create. His presence is the unintermittent call and response of the creative to the created, of the father to the child. Where can be the selfishness in being so made happy? It may be deep selfishness to refuse to be happy. Is there selfishness in the Lord's seeing of the travail of his soul and being satisfied? Selfishness consists in taking the bliss from another; to find one's bliss in the bliss of another is not selfishness. Joy is not selfishness; and the greater the joy thus reaped, the farther is that joy removed from selfishness. The one bliss, next to the love of God, is the love of our neighbour. If any say, 'You love because it makes you blessed,' I deny it: 'We are blessed, I say, because we love.' No one could attain to the bliss of loving his neighbour who was selfish and sought that bliss from love of himself. Love is unselfishness. In the main we love because we cannot help it. There is no merit in it: how should there be in any love?—but neither is it selfish. There are many who confound righteousness with merit, and think there is nothing righteous where there is nothing meritorious. 'If it makes you happy to love,' they say, 'where is your merit? It is only selfishness!' There is no merit, I reply, yet the love that is born in us is our salvation from selfishness. It is of the very essence of righteousness. Because a thing is joyful, it does not follow that I do it for the joy of it; yet when the joy is in others, the joy is pure. That *certain* joys should be joys, is the very denial of selfishness. The man would be a demoniacally selfish man, whom love itself did not make joyful. It is selfish to enjoy in content beholding others lack; even in the highest spiritual bliss, to sit careless of others would be selfishness, and the higher the bliss, the worse the selfishness; but surely that bliss is right altogether of which a great part consists in labour that others may share it. Such, I will not doubt—the labour to bring others in to share with us, will be a great part of our heavenly content and gladness. The making, the redeeming

Father will find plenty of like work for his children to do. Dull are those, little at least can they have of Christian imagination, who think that where all are good, things must be dull. It is because there is so little good yet in them, that they know so little of the power or beauty of merest life divine. Let such make haste to be true. Interest will there be and variety enough, not without pain, in the ministration of help to those yet wearily toiling up the heights of truth—perhaps yet unwilling to part with miserable self, which cherishing they are not yet worth being, or capable of having.

Some of the things a man may have to forsake in following Christ, he has not to forsake because of what they are in themselves. Neither nature, art, science, nor fit society, is of those things a man will lose in forsaking himself: they are God's, and have no part in the world of evil, the false judgments, low wishes, and unrealities generally, that make up the conscious life of the self which has to be denied: such will never be restored to the man. But in forsaking himself to do what God requires of him—his true work in the world, that is, a man may find he has to leave some of God's things—not to repudiate them, but for the time to forsake them, because they draw his mind from the absolute necessities of the true life in himself or in others. He may have to deny himself in leaving them—not as bad things, but as things for which there is not room until those of paramount claim have been so heeded, that these will no longer impede but further them. Then he who knows God, will find that knowledge open the door of his understanding to all things else. He will become able to behold them from within, instead of having to search wearily into them from without. This gave to king David more understanding than had all his teachers. Then will the things he has had to leave, be restored to him a hundred fold. So will it be in the forsaking of friends. To forsake them for Christ, is not to forsake them as evil. It is not to cease to love them, 'for he that loveth not his brother whom he hath seen, how can he love God whom he hath not seen?' it is—not to allow their love to cast even a shadow between us and our Master; to be content to lose their approval, their intercourse, even their affection, where the Master says one thing and they another. It is to learn to love them in a far higher, deeper, tenderer, truer way than before—a way which keeps all that was genuine in the former way, and loses all that was false. We shall love *their* selves, and disregard our own.

I do not forget the word of the Lord about *hating father and mother*: I have a glimpse of the meaning of it, but dare not attempt explaining it now. It is all against the self—not against the father and mother.

There is another kind of forsaking that may fall to the lot of some, and which they may find very difficult: the forsaking of such notions of God and his Christ as they were taught in their youth—which they held, nor could help holding, at such time as they began to believe—of which they have begun to doubt the truth, but to cast which away seems like parting with every assurance of safety.

There are so-called doctrines long accepted of good people, which how any man can love God and hold, except indeed by fast closing of the spiritual eyes, I find it hard to understand. If a man care more for opinion than for life, it is not worth any other man's while to persuade him to renounce the opinions he happens to entertain; he would but put other opinions in the same place of honour—a place which can *belong* to no opinion whatever: it matters nothing what such a man may or may not believe, for he is not a true man. By holding with a school he supposes to be right, he but bolsters himself up with the worst of all unbelief—opinion calling itself faith—unbelief calling itself religion. But for him who is in earnest about the will of God, it is of endless consequence that he should think rightly of God. He cannot come close to him, cannot truly know his will, while his notion of him is in any point that of a false god. The thing shows itself absurd. If such a man seem to himself to be giving up even his former assurance of salvation, in yielding such ideas of God as are unworthy of God, he must none the less, if he will be true, if he would enter into life, take up that cross also. He will come to see that he must follow *no* doctrine, be it true as word of man could state it, but the living Truth, the Master himself.

Good souls many will one day be horrified at the things they now believe of God. If they have not thought about them, but given themselves to obedience, they may not have done them much harm as yet; but they can make little progress in the knowledge of God, while, if but passively, holding evil things true of him. If, on the other hand, they do think about them, and find in them no obstruction, they must indeed be far from anything to be called a true knowledge of God. But there are those who find them a terrible obstruction, and yet imagine, or at least fear them true: such must take courage to forsake the false in *any* shape, to deny their old selves in the most seemingly sacred of prejudices, and follow Jesus, not as he is presented in the tradition of the elders, but as he is presented by himself, his apostles, and the spirit of truth. There are 'traditions of men' after Christ as well as before him, and far worse, as 'making of none effect' higher and better things; and we have to look to it, *how we have learned Christ.*

THE TRUTH IN JESUS.

'But ye did not so learn Christ; if so be that ye heard him, and were taught in him, even as truth is in Jesus: that ye put away, as concerning your former manner of life, the old man, which waxeth corrupt after the lusts of deceit.'[1] —Eph. iv. 20-22.

How have we learned Christ? It ought to be a startling thought, that we may have learned him wrong. That must he far worse than not to have learned him at all: his place is occupied by a false Christ, hard to exorcise! The point is, whether we have learned Christ as he taught himself, or as men have taught him who thought they understood, but did not understand him. Do we think we know him—with notions fleshly, after low, mean human fancies and explanations, or do we indeed know him—after the spirit, in our measure as God knows him? The Christian religion, throughout its history, has been open to more corrupt misrepresentation than ever the Jewish could be, for as it is higher and wider, so must it yield larger scope to corruption:—have we learned Christ in false statements and corrupted lessons about him, or have we learned *himself*? Nay, true or false, is only our brain full of things concerning him, or does he dwell himself in our hearts, a learnt, and ever being learnt lesson, the power of our life?

I have been led to what I am about to say, by a certain utterance of one in the front rank of those who assert that we can know nothing of the 'Infinite and Eternal energy from which all things proceed;' and the utterance is this:—

---

[1] That is, 'which is still going to ruin through the love of the lie.'

'The visiting on Adam's descendants through hundreds of genera-
tions dreadful penalties for a small transgression which they did not
commit; the damning of all men who do not avail themselves of an
alleged mode of obtaining forgiveness, which most men have never
heard of; and the effecting a reconciliation by sacrificing a son who
was perfectly innocent, to satisfy the assumed necessity for a propitia-
tory victim; are modes of action which, ascribed to a human ruler,
would call forth expressions of abhorrence; and the ascription of them
to the Ultimate Cause of things, even not felt to be full of difficulties,
must become impossible.'

I do not quote the passage with the design of opposing either clause
of its statement, for I entirely agree with it: almost it feels an absurdity
to say so. Neither do I propose addressing a word to the writer of it, or
to any who hold with him. The passage bears out what I have often
said—that I never yet heard a word from one of that way of thinking,
which even touched anything I hold. One of my earliest recollections
is of beginning to be at strife with the false system here assailed. Such
paganism I scorn as heartily in the name of Christ, as I scorn it in the
name of righteousness. Rather than believe a single point involving its
spirit, even with the assurance thereby of such salvation as the system
offers, I would join the ranks of those who 'know nothing,' and set my-
self with hopeless heart to what I am now trying with an infinite hope
in the help of the pure originating One— to get rid of my miserable
mean self, comforted only by the chance that death would either leave
me without thought more, or reveal something of the Ultimate Cause
which it would not be an insult to him, or a dishonour to his creature,
to hold concerning him. Even such a chance alone might enable one to
live.

I will not now enquire how it comes that the writer of the passage
quoted seems to put forward these so-called beliefs as representing
Christianity, or even the creed of those who call themselves Christians,
seeing so many, and some of them of higher rank in literature than
himself, believing in Christ with true hearts, believe not one of such
things as he has set down, but hold them in at least as great abhorrence
as he: his answer would probably be, that, even had he been aware of
such being the fact, what he had to deal with was the forming and rul-
ing notions of religious society;—and that such are the things held by
the bulk of both educated and uneducated calling themselves Chris-
tians, however many of them may vainly think by an explanatory
clause here and there to turn away the opprobrium of their falsehood,
while they remain virtually the same—that such are the things so held,

I am, alas! unable to deny. It helps nothing, I repeat, that many, think-ing little on the matter, use *quasi* mitigated forms to express their tenets, and imagine that so they indicate a different class of ideas: it would require but a brief examination to be convinced that they are not merely analogous—they are ultimately identical.

But had I to do with the writer, I should ask how it comes that, re-fusing these dogmas as abominable, and in themselves plainly false, yet knowing that they are attributed to men whose teaching has done more to civilize the world than that of any men besides—how it comes that, seeing such teaching as this could not have done so, he has not taken such pains of enquiry as must surely have satisfied a man of his faculty that such was not their teaching; that it was indeed so different, and so good, that even the forced companionship of such horrible lies as those he has recounted, has been unable to destroy its regenerative power. I suppose he will allow that there was a man named Jesus, who died for the truth he taught: can he believe he died for such alleged truth as that? Would it not be well, I would ask him, to enquire what he did really teach, according to the primary sources of our knowledge of him? If he answered that the question was uninteresting to him, I should have no more to say; nor did I now start to speak of him save with the object of making my position plain to those to whom I would speak—those, namely, who call themselves Christians.

If of them I should ask, 'How comes it that such opinions are held concerning the Holy One, whose ways you take upon you to set forth?' I should be met by most with the answer, 'Those are the things he tells us himself in his word; we have learned them from the Scriptures;' by many with explanations which seem to them so to explain the things that they are no longer to be reprobated; and by others with the remark that better ideas, though largely held, had not yet had time to show themselves as the belief of the thinkers of the nation. Of those whose presentation of Christian doctrine is represented in the quotation above, there are two classes—such as are content it should be so, and such to whom those things are grievous, but who do not see how to get rid of them. To the latter it may be some little comfort to have one who has studied the New Testament for many years and loves it be-yond the power of speech to express, declare to them his conviction that there is not an atom of such teaching in the whole lovely, divine utterance; that such things are all and altogether the invention of men—honest invention, in part at least, I grant, but yet not true. Thank God, we are nowise bound to accept any man's explanation of God's ways and God's doings, however good the man may be, if it do not

commend itself to our conscience. The man's conscience may be a bet-
ter conscience than ours, and his judgment clearer; nothing the more
can we accept while we cannot see good: to do so would be to sin.

But it is by no means my object to set forth what I believe or do not
believe; a time may come for that; my design is now very different
indeed. I desire to address those who call themselves Christians, and
expostulate with them thus:—

Whatever be your *opinions* on the greatest of all subjects, is it well
that the impression with regard to Christianity made upon your genera-
tion, should be that of your opinions, and not of something beyond
opinion? Is Christianity capable of being represented by opinion, even
the best? If it were, how many of us are such as God would choose to
represent his thoughts and intents by our opinions concerning them?
Who is there of his friends whom any thoughtful man would depute to
represent his thoughts to his fellows? If you answer, 'The opinions I
hold and by which I represent Christianity, are those of the Bible,' I
reply, that none can understand, still less represent, the opinions of
another, but such as are of the same mind with him— certainly none
who mistake his whole scope and intent so far as in supposing *opinion*
to be the object of any writer in the Bible. Is Christianity a system of
articles of belief, let them be correct as language can give them? Nev-
er. So far am I from believing it, that I would rather have a man
holding, as numbers of you do, what seem to me the most obnoxious
untruths, opinions the most irreverent and gross, if at the same time he
lived in the faith of the Son of God, that is, trusted in God as the Son
of God trusted in him, than I would have a man with every one of
whose formulas of belief I utterly coincided, but who knew nothing of
a daily life and walk with God. The one, holding doctrines of devils, is
yet a child of God; the other, holding the doctrines of Christ and his
Apostles, is of the world, yea, of the devil.

'How! a man hold the doctrine of devils, and yet be of God?'

Yes; for to hold a thing with the intellect, is not to believe it. A
man's real belief is that which he lives by; and that which the man I
mean lives by, is the love of God, and obedience to his law, so far as
he has recognized it. Those hideous doctrines are outside of him; he
thinks they are inside, but no matter; they are not true, and they cannot
really be inside any good man. They are sadly against him; for he can-
not love to dwell upon any of those supposed characteristics of his
God; he acts and lives nevertheless in a measure like the true God.
What a man believes, is the thing he does. This man would shrink with
loathing from actions such as he thinks God justified in doing; like

God, he loves and helps and saves. Will the living God let such a man's opinions damn him? No more than he will let the correct opinions of another, who lives for himself, save him. The best salvation even the latter could give would be but damnation. What I come to and insist upon is, that, supposing your theories right, and containing all that is to be believed, yet those theories are not what makes you Christians, if Christians indeed you are. On the contrary, they are, with not a few of you, just what keeps you from being Christians. For when you say that, to be saved, a man must hold this or that, then are you leaving the living God and his will, and putting trust in some notion about him or his will. To make my meaning clearer,—some of you say we must trust in the finished work of Christ; or again, our faith must be in the merits of Christ—in the atonement he has made—in the blood he has shed: all these statements are a simple repudiation of the living Lord, *in whom* we are told to believe, who, by his presence with and in us, and our obedience to him, lifts us out of darkness into light, leads us from the kingdom of Satan into the glorious liberty of the sons of God. No manner or amount of belief *about him* is the faith of the New Testament. With such teaching I have had a lifelong acquaintance, and declare it most miserably false. But I do not now mean to dispute against it; except the light of the knowledge of the glory of God in the face of Christ Jesus make a man sick of his opinions, he may hold them to doomsday for me; for no opinion, I repeat, is Christianity, and no preaching of any plan of salvation is the preaching of the glorious gospel of the living God. Even if your plan, your theories, were absolutely true, the holding of them with sincerity, the trusting in this or that about Christ, or in anything he did or could do, the trusting in anything but himself, his own living self, is a delusion. Many will grant this heartily, and yet the moment you come to talk with them, you find they insist that to believe in Christ is to believe in the atonement, meaning by that only and altogether their special theory about the atonement; and when you say we must believe in the atoning Christ, and cannot possibly believe in any theory concerning the atonement, they go away and denounce you, saying, 'He does not believe in the atonement!' If I explain the atonement otherwise than they explain it, they assert that I deny the atonement; nor count it of any consequence that I say I believe in the atoner with my whole heart, and soul, and strength, and mind. This they call *contending for the truth*! Because I refuse an explanation which is not in the New Testament, though they believe it is, because they can think of no other, one which seems to me as false in logic as detestable in morals, not to say that there is no spirituality in it whatever, therefore I am not a Christian! What wonder men such as I have quoted refuse the Christianity they suppose such 'believers' to represent! I do not say that with this sad folly may not mingle a potent faith in the Lord himself; but I do say that the importance they place on theory is even more sadly obstructive to true faith than such theories themselves: while the mind is occupied in enquiring,

'Do I believe or feel this thing right?'—the true question is forgotten: 'Have I left all to follow him?' To the man who gives himself to the living Lord, every belief will necessarily come right; the Lord himself will see that his disciple believe aright concerning him. If a man cannot trust him for this, what claim can he make to faith in him? It is because he has little or no faith, that he is left clinging to preposterous and dishonouring ideas, the traditions of men concerning his Father, and neither his teaching nor that of his apostles. The living Christ is to them but a shadow; the all but obliterated Christ of their theories no soul can thoroughly believe in: the disciple of such a Christ rests on his work, or his merits, or his atonement!

What I insist upon is, that a man's faith shall be in the living, loving, ruling, helping Christ, devoted to us as much as ever he was, and with all the powers of the Godhead for the salvation of his brethren. It is not faith that he did this, that his work wrought that—it is faith in the man who did and is doing everything for us that will save him: without this he cannot work to heal spiritually, any more than he would heal physically, when he was present to the eyes of men. Do you ask, 'What is faith in him?' I answer, The leaving of your way, your objects, your self, and the taking of his and him; the leaving of your trust in men, in money, in opinion, in character, in atonement itself, *and doing as he tells you.* I can find no words strong enough to serve for the weight of this necessity—this obedience. It is the one terrible heresy of the church, that it has always been presenting something else than obedience as faith in Christ. The work of Christ is not the Working Christ, any more than the clothing of Christ is the body of Christ. If the woman who touched the hem of his garment had trusted in the garment and not in him who wore it, would she have been healed? And the reason that so many who believe *about* Christ rather than in him, get the comfort they do, is that, touching thus the mere hem of his garment, they cannot help believing a little in the live man inside the garment. It is not wonderful that such believers should so often be miserable; they lay themselves down to sleep with nothing but the skirt of his robe in their hand—a robe too, I say, that never was his, only by them is supposed his—when they might sleep in peace with the living Lord in their hearts. Instead of so knowing Christ that they have him in them saving them, they lie wasting themselves in soul-sickening self-examination as to whether they are believers, whether they are really trusting in the atonement, whether they are truly sorry for their sins—the way to madness of the brain, and despair of the heart. Some even ponder the imponderable— whether they are of the elect, whether they have an interest in the blood shed for sin, whether theirs is a saving faith—when all the time the man who died for them is waiting to begin to save them from every evil—and first from this self which is consuming them with trouble about its salvation; he will set them free, and take them home to the bosom of the Father—if only they will mind what he says to them—which is the beginning, middle, and end of faith. If, instead of searching into the mysteries of corruption in their own charnel-houses, they would but awake and arise from the dead, and come out into the light which Christ is waiting to give them, he would begin at once to fill them with the fulness of God.

'But I do not know how to awake and arise!'

I will tell you:—Get up, and do something the master tells you; so make yourself his disciple at once. Instead of asking yourself whether you believe or not, ask yourself whether you have this day done one thing because he said, Do it, or once abstained because he said, Do not do it. It is simply absurd to say you believe, or even want to believe in him, if you do not anything he tells you. If you can think of nothing he ever said as having had an atom of influence on your doing or not doing, you have too good ground to consider yourself no disciple of his. Do not, I pray you, worse than waste your time in trying to convince yourself that you are his disciple notwithstanding—that for this reason or that you still have cause to think you believe in him. What though you should succeed in persuading yourself to absolute certainty that you are his disciple, if, after all, he say to you, 'Why did you not do the things I told you? Depart from me; I do not know you!' Instead of trying to persuade yourself, if the thing be true you can make it truer; if it be not true, you can begin at once to make it true, to *be* a disciple of the Living One—by obeying him in the first thing you can think of in which you are not obeying him. We must learn to obey him in everything, and so must begin somewhere: let it be at once, and in the very next thing that lies at the door of our conscience! Oh fools and slow of heart, if you think of nothing but Christ, and do not set yourselves to do his words! you but build your houses on the sand. What have such teachers not to answer for who have turned your regard away from the direct words of the Lord himself, which are spirit and life, to contemplate plans of salvation tortured out of the words of his apostles, even were those plans as true as they are false! There is but one plan of salvation, and that is to believe in the Lord Jesus Christ; that is, to take him for what he is—our master, and his words as if he meant them, which assuredly he did. To do his words is to enter into vital relation with him, to obey him is the only way to be one with him. The relation between him and us is an absolute one; it can nohow begin to *live* but in obedience: it is obedience. There can be no truth, no reality, in any initiation of atonement with him, that is not obedience. What! have I the poorest notion of a God, and dare think of entering into relations with him, the very first of which is not that what he saith, I will do? The thing is eternally absurd, and comes of the father of lies. I know what he whispers to those to whom such teaching as this is distasteful: 'It is the doctrine of works!' But one word of the Lord humbly heard and received will suffice to send all the demons of false theology into the abyss. He says the man that does not do the things he tells him, builds his house to fall in utter ruin. He instructs his messengers to go and baptize all nations, 'teaching them to observe all things whatsoever I have commanded you.' Tell me it is faith he requires: do I not know it? and is not faith the highest act of which the human mind is capable? But faith in what? Faith in what he is, in what he says—a faith which can have no existence except in obedience—a faith which is obedience. To do what he wishes is to put forth faith in him. For this the teaching of men has substituted this or that belief *about* him, faith in this or that supposed design of his manifestation in the flesh. It was himself, and God in him that he manifested; but faith in him and his father thus manifested, they make altogether secondary to acceptance of the paltry contrivance of a juggling morality, which they attribute to God and his Christ, imagining it the atonement, and 'the plan of salvation.' 'Do you put faith in *him*,' I ask, 'or in the doctrines and commandments of men?' If you say 'In him,'—'Is it then possible,' I return, 'that you do not see that, above all things and all thoughts, you are bound to obey him?' Do you not mourn that you cannot trust in him as you would, that you find it too hard? Too hard it is for you, and too hard it will remain, while the things he tells you to do—the things you can do—even those you will not try! How should you be capable of trusting in the true one while you are nowise true to him? How are you to believe he will do his part by you, while you are not such as to do your part by him? How are you to believe while you are not faithful? How, I say, should you be capable of trusting in him? The very thing to make you able to trust in him, and so receive all things from him, you turn your back upon: obedience you decline, or at least neglect. You say you do not refuse to obey him? I care not whether you refuse or not, while you do not obey. Remember the parable: 'I go, sir, and went not.' What have you done this day because it was the will of Christ? Have you dismissed, once dismissed, an anxious thought for the morrow? Have you ministered to any needy soul or body, and kept your right hand from knowing what your left hand did? Have you begun to leave all and follow him? Did you set yourself to judge righteous judgment? Are you being ware of covetousness? Have you forgiven your enemy? Are you seeking the kingdom of God and his righteousness before all other things? Are you hungering and thirsting after righteousness? Have you given to some one that asked of you? Tell me something that you have done, are doing, or are trying to do because he told you. If you do nothing that he says, it is no wonder that you cannot trust in him, and are therefore driven to seek refuge in the atonement, as if something he had done, and not he himself in his doing were the atonement. *That is not as you understand it?* What does it matter how you understand, or what you understand, so long as you are not of one mind with the Truth, so long as you and God are not *at one*, do not atone together? How should you understand? Knowing that you do not heed his word, why should I heed your explanation of it? You do not his will, and so you cannot understand him; you do not know him, that is why you cannot trust in him. You think your common sense enough to let you know what he means? Your common sense ought to be enough to know itself unequal to the task. It is the heart of the child that alone can understand the Father. Would you have me think you guilty of the sin against the Holy Ghost—that you *understand* Jesus Christ and yet will not obey him? That were too dreadful. I believe you do not understand him. No man can do yet what he tells him aright—but are you trying? Obedience is not perfection, but trying. You count him a hard master, and will not stir. Do you suppose he ever gave a commandment knowing it was of no use for it could not be done? He tells us a thing knowing that we must do it, or be lost; that not his Father himself could save us but by getting us at length to do everything he commands, for not otherwise can we know life, can we learn the holy secret of divine being. He knows that you can try, and that in your trying and failing he will be able to help you, until at length you shall do the will of God even as he does it himself. He takes the will in the imperfect deed, and makes the deed at last perfect. Correctest notions without obedience are worthless. The doing of the will of God is the way to oneness with God, which alone is salvation. Sitting at the gate of heaven, sitting on the footstool of the throne itself, yea, clasping the knees of the Father, you could not be at peace, except in their every vital movement, in every their smallest point of consciousness, your heart, your soul, your mind, your brain, your body, were one with the living God. If you had one brooding thought that was not a joy in him, you would not be at peace; if you had one desire you could not leave absolutely to his will you would not be at peace; you would not be saved, therefore could not feel saved. God, all and in all, ours to the fulfilling of our very being, is the religion of the perfect, son- hearted Lord Christ.

Well do I know it is faith that saves us—but not faith in any work of God—it is faith in God himself. If I did not believe God as good as the tenderest human heart, the fairest, the purest, the most unselfish human heart could imagine him, yea, an infinitude better, higher than we as the heavens are higher than the earth—believe it, not as a proposition, or even as a thing I was convinced of, but with the responsive condition and being of my whole nature; if I did not feel every fibre of heart and brain and body safe with him because he is the Father who made me that I am—I would not be saved, for this faith is salvation; it is God and the man one. God and man together, the vital energy flowing unchecked from the creator into his creature—that is the salvation of the creature. But the poorest faith in the living God, the God revealed in Christ Jesus, if it be vital, true, that is obedient, is the beginning of the way to know him, and to know him is eternal life. If you mean by faith anything of a different kind, that faith will not save you. A faith, for instance, that God does not forgive me because he loves me, but because he loves Jesus Christ, cannot save me, because it is a falsehood against God: if the thing were true, such a gospel would be the preaching of a God that was not love, therefore in whom was no salvation, a God to know whom could not be eternal life. Such a faith would damn, not save a man; for it would bind him to a God who was anything but perfect. Such assertions going by the name of Christianity, are nothing but the poor remnants of paganism; and it is only with that part of our nature not yet Christian that we are able to believe them—so far indeed as it is possible a lie should be believed. We must forsake all our fears and distrusts for Christ. We must receive his teaching heartily, nor let the interpretation of it attributed to his apostles make us turn aside from it. I say interpretation attributed to them; for what they teach is never against what Christ taught, though very often the exposition of it is—and that from no fault in the apostles, but from the grievous fault of those who would understand, and even explain, rather than obey. We may be sure of this, that no man will be condemned for any sin that is past; that, if he be condemned, it will be because he would not come to the light when the light came to him; because he would not cease to do evil and learn to do well; because he hid his unbelief in the garment of a false faith, and would not obey; because he imputed to himself a righteousness that was not his; because he preferred imagining himself a worthy person, to confessing himself everywhere in the wrong, and repenting. We may be sure also of this, that, if a man becomes the disciple of Christ, he will not leave him in ignorance as to what he has to believe; he shall know the truth of everything it is needful for him to understand. If we do what he tells us, his light will go up in our hearts. Till then we could not understand even if he explained to us. If you cannot trust him to let you know what is right, but think you must hold this or that before you can come to him, then I justify your doubts in what you call your worst times, but which I suspect are your best times in which you come nearest to the truth—those, namely, in which you fear you have no faith.

So long as a man will not set himself to obey the word spoken, the word written, the word printed, the word read, of the Lord Christ, I would not take the trouble to convince him concerning the most obnoxious doctrines that they were false as hell. It is those who would fain believe, but who by such doctrines are hindered, whom I would help. Disputation about things but hides the living Christ who alone can teach the truth, who is the truth, and the knowledge of whom is life; I write for the sake of those whom the false teaching that claims before all to be true has driven away from God—as well it might, for the God so taught is not a God worthy to be believed in. A stick, or a stone, or a devil, is all that some of our brethren of mankind have to believe in: he who believes in a God not altogether unselfish and good, a God who does not do all he can for his creatures, belongs to the same class; his is not the God who made the heaven and the earth and the sea and the fountains of water—not the God revealed in Christ. If a man see in God any darkness at all, and especially if he defend that darkness, attempting to justify it as one who respects the person of God, I cannot but think his blindness must have followed his mockery of '*Lord! Lord!*' Surely, if he had been strenuously obeying Jesus, he would ere now have received the truth that God is light, and in him is no darkness—a truth which is not acknowledged by calling the darkness attributed to him light, and the candle of the Lord in the soul of man darkness. It is one thing to believe that God can do nothing wrong, quite another to call whatever presumption may attribute to him right.

The whole secret of progress is the doing of the thing we know. There is no other way of progress in the spiritual life; no other way of progress in the understanding of that life: only as we do, can we know.

Is there then anything you will not leave for Christ? You cannot know him—and yet he is the Truth, the one thing alone that can be known! Do you not care to be imperfect? would you rather keep this or that, with imperfection, than part with it to be perfect? You cannot know Christ, for the very principle of his life was the simple absolute relation of realities; his one idea was to be a perfect child to his Father. He who will not part with all for Christ, is not worthy of him, and cannot know him; and the Lord is true, and cannot acknowledge him: how could he receive to his house, as one of his kind, a man who prefers something to his Father; a man who is not for God; a man who will strike a bargain with God, and say, 'I will give up so much, if thou wilt spare me'! To yield all to him who has only made us and given us everything, yea his very self by life and by death, such a man counts too much. His conduct says, 'I never asked thee to do so much for me, and I cannot make the return thou demandest.' The man will have to be left to himself. He must find what it is to be without God! Those who know God, or have but begun to catch a far-off glimmer of his gloriousness, of what he is, regard life as insupportable save God be the All in all, the first and the last.

To let their light shine, not to force on them their interpretations of God's designs, is the duty of Christians towards their fellows. If you who set yourselves to explain the theory of Christianity, had set yourselves instead to do the will of the Master, the one object for which the Gospel was preached to you, how different would now be the condition of that portion of the world with which you come into contact! Had you given yourselves to the understanding of his word that you might do it, and not to the quarrying from it of material wherewith to buttress your systems, in many a heart by this time would the name of the Lord be loved where now it remains unknown. The word of life would then by you have been held out indeed. Men, undeterred by your explanations of Christianity, for you would not be forcing them on their acceptance, and attracted by your behaviour, would be saying to each other, as Moses said to himself when he saw the bush that burned with fire and was not consumed, 'I will now turn aside and see this great sight!' they would be drawing nigh to behold how these Christians loved one another, and how just and fair they were to every one that had to do with them! to note that their goods were the best, their weight surest, their prices most *reasonable*, their word most certain! that in their families was neither jealousy nor emulation! that mammon was not there worshipped! that in their homes selfishness was neither the hidden nor the openly ruling principle; that their children were as diligently taught to share, as some are to save, or to lay out only upon self—their mothers more anxious lest a child should hoard than lest he should squander; that in no house of theirs was religion one thing, and the daily life another; that the ecclesiastic did not think first of his church, nor the peer of his privileges.

What do I hear you say?—'*How then shall the world go on?*' The Lord's world will go on, and that without you; the devil's world will go on, and that with you. The objection is but another and overwhelming proof of your unbelief. Either you do not believe the word the Lord spake— that, if we seek first the kingdom of God and his righteousness, all things needful will be added to us; or what he undertakes does not satisfy you; it is not enough; you want more; you prefer the offers of Mammon. You are nowise anxious to be saved from the too-much that is a snare; you want what you call a fortune—the freedom of the world. You would not live under such restrictions as the Lord might choose to lay upon you if he saw that something might be made of you precious in his sight! You would inherit the earth, and not by meekness; you would have the life of this world sweet, come of the life eternal, the life that God shares with you, what may: so much as that comes to, you would gladly leave God to look after, if only you might be sure of not sharing with the rich man when you die. But you find that, unable to trust him for this world, neither can you trust him for the world to come. Refusing to obey him in your life, how can you trust him for your life? Hence the various substitutes you seek for faith in him: you would hold him to his word, bind him by his promises, appeal to the atonement, to the satisfaction made to his justice, as you call it—while you will take no trouble to fulfil the absolutely reasonable and necessary condition, yea, morally and spiritually imperative condition—condition and means in one—on which he offers, and through which alone he can offer you deliverance from the burden of life into the strength and glory of life—that you shall be true, and to him obedient children. You say 'Christ has satisfied the law,' but you will not satisfy him! He says, 'Come unto me,' and you will not rise and go to him. You say, 'Lord I believe; help mine unbelief,' but when he says, 'Leave everything behind you, and be as I am towards God, and you shall have peace and rest,' you turn away, muttering about *figurative language*. If you had been true, had been living *the* life, had been Christians indeed, you would, however little, have drawn the world after you. In your churches you would be receiving truest nourishment, yea strength to live—thinking far less of serving God on the Sunday, and far more of serving your neighbour in the week. The sociable vile, the masterful rich, the deceitful trader, the ambitious poor, whom you have attracted to your communities with the offer of a salvation other than deliverance from sin, would not be lording it over them and dragging them down; they would be the cleaner and the stronger for their absence; while the publicans and the sinners would have been drawn instead, and turned into true men and women; and the Israelite indeed, who is yet more repelled by your general worldliness than by your misrepresentations of God, showing him selfish like yourselves who is the purity of the creation— the Israelite in whom is no guile would have hastened to the company of the loving men and true, eager to learn what it was that made them so good, so happy, so unselfish, so free of care, so ready to die, so willing to live, so hopeful, so helpful, so careless to possess, so undeferential to possession. Finding you to hold, from the traditional force of false teaching, such things as you do, he would have said, 'No! such beliefs can never account for such mighty results!' You would have answered, 'Search the Scriptures and see.' He would have searched, and found—not indeed the things you imagine there, but things infinitely better and higher, things that indeed account for the result he wondered at; he would have found such truth as he who has found will hold for ever as the only gladness of his being. There you would have had your reward for being true Christians in spite of the evil doctrines you had been taught and teaching: you would have been taught in return the truth of the matter by him whom your true Christianity had enticed to itself, and sent to the fountainhead free of the prejudices that disabled your judgment. Thus delivered from the false notions which could not fail to have stunted your growth hitherto, how rapid would it not have become!

If any of you tell me my doctrine is presumptuous, that it is contrary to what is taught in the New Testament, and what the best of men have always believed, I will not therefore proceed to defend even my beliefs, the principles on which I try to live—how much less my opinions! I appeal to you instead, whether or not I have spoken the truth concerning our paramount obligation to do the word of Christ. If you answer that I have not, I have nothing more to say; there is no other ground on which we can meet. But if you allow that it is a prime, even if you do not allow it *the* prime duty, then what I insist upon is, that you should do it, so and not otherwise recommending the knowledge of him. I do not attempt to change your opinions; if they are wrong, the obedience alone on which I insist can enable you to set them right; I only pray you to obey, and assert that thus only can you fit your-selves for understanding the mind of Christ. I say none but he who does right, can think right; you cannot *know* Christ to be right until you do as he does, as he tells you to do; neither can you set him forth, until you know him as he means himself to be known, that is, as he is. If you are serving and trusting in Mammon, how can you know the living God who, the source of life, is alone to be trusted in! If you do not admit that it is the duty of a man to do the word of Christ, or if, admitting the duty, you yet do not care to perform it, why should I care to convince you that my doctrine is right? What is it to any true man what you think of his doctrine? What does it matter what you think of any doctrine? If I could convince your judgment, your hearts remain-ing as they are, I should but add to your condemnation. The true heart must see at once, that, however wrong I may or may not be in other things, at least I am right in this, that Jesus must be obeyed, and at once obeyed, in the things he did say: it will not long imagine to obey him in things he did not say. If a man do what is unpleasing to Christ, believing it his will, he shall yet gain thereby, for it gives the Lord a hold of him, which he will use; but before he can reach liberty, he must be delivered from that falsehood. For him who does not choose to see that Christ must be obeyed, he must be left to the teaching of the Father, who brings all that hear and learn of him to Christ, that they may learn what he is who has taught them and brought them. He will leave no man to his own way, however much he may prefer it. The Lord did not die to provide a man with the wretched heaven he may invent for himself, or accept invented for him by others; he died to give him life, and bring him to the heaven of the Father's peace; the children must share in the essential bliss of the Father and the Son. This is and has been the Father's work from the beginning—to bring us into the home of his heart, where he shares the glories of life with the Living One, in whom was born life to light men back to the original life. This is our destiny; and however a man may refuse, he will find it hard to fight with God—useless to kick against the goads of his love. For the Father is goading him, or will goad him, if needful, into life by unrest and trouble; hell-fire will have its turn if less will not do: can any need it more than such as will neither enter the kingdom of heaven themselves, nor suffer them to enter it that would? The old race of the

Pharisees is by no means extinct; they were St Paul's great trouble, and are yet to be found in every religious community under the sun.

The one only thing truly to reconcile all differences is, to walk in the light. So St Paul teaches us in his epistle to the Philippians, the third chapter and sixteenth verse. After setting forth the loftiest idea of human endeavour in declaring the summit of his own aspiration, he says—not, 'This must be your endeavour also, or you cannot be saved;' but, 'If in anything ye be otherwise minded, God shall reveal even this unto you. Nevertheless whereto we have already attained, let us walk by that same.' Observe what widest conceivable scope is given by the apostle to honest opinion, even in things of grandest import!—the one only essential point with him is, that whereto we have attained, what we have seen to be true, *we walk by that*. In such walking, and in such walking only, love will grow, truth will grow; the soul, then first in its genuine element and true relation towards God, will see into reality that was before but a blank to it; and he who has promised to teach, will teach abundantly. Faster and faster will the glory of the Lord dawn upon the hearts and minds of his people so walking—then his people indeed; fast and far will the knowledge of him spread, for truth of action, both preceding and following truth of word, will prepare the way before him. The man walking in that whereto he has attained, will be able to think aright; the man who does not think right, is unable because he has not been walking right; only when he begins to do the thing he knows, does he begin to be able to think aright; then God comes to him in a new and higher way, and works along with the spirit he has created. The soul, without its heaven above its head, without its life-breath around it, without its love-treasure in its heart, without its origin one with it and bound up in it, without its true self and originating life, cannot think to any real purpose— nor ever would to all eternity. When man joins with God, then is all impotence and discord cast out. Until then, there can be but jar; God is in contest with the gates of hell that open in the man, and can but hold his own; when the man joins him, then is Satan foiled. For then first nature receives her necessity: no such necessity has she as this law of all laws—that God and man are one. Until they begin to be one in the reality as in the divine idea, in the flower as in the root, in the finishing as in the issuing creation, nothing can go right with the man, and God can have no rest from his labour in him. As the greatest orbs in heaven are drawn by the least, God himself must be held in divine disquiet until every one of his family be brought home to his heart, to be one with him in a unity too absolute, profound, far- reaching, fine, and intense, to be understood by any but the God from whom it comes, yet to be guessed at by the soul from the unspeakableness of its delight when at length it is with the *only* that can be its own, the one that it can possess, the one that can possess it. For God is the heritage of the soul in the ownness of origin; man is the offspring of his making will, of his life; God himself is his birth-place; God is the self that makes the soul able to say *I too, I myself.* This absolute unspeakable bliss of the creature is that for which the Son died, for which the Father suffered with him. Then only is life itself; then only is it right, is it one; then only is it as designed and necessitated by the eternal life-outgiving Life.

Whereto then we have attained let us walk by that same!

END OF THE SECOND SERIES.

UNSPOKEN SERMONS SERIES THREE

TO MY WIFE

Sun and wind and rain, the Lord
Is to seed his Father buried
For he is the living Word,
And the quickening Spirit.
BORDIGHERA:
May 3, 1889.

THE CREATION IN CHRIST.

All things were made by him, and without him was not anything made that was made. In him was life, and the life was the light of men.—John i. 3-4.

It seems to me that any lover of the gospel given to thinking, and especially one accustomed to the effort of uttering thought, can hardly have failed to feel dissatisfaction, more or less definite, with the close of the third verse, as here presented to English readers. It seems to me in its feebleness, unlike, and rhetorically unworthy of the rest. That it is no worse than pleonastic, that is, redundant, therefore only unnecessary, can be no satisfaction to the man who would find perfection, if he may, in the words of him who was nearer the Lord than any other. The phrase 'that was made' seems, from its uselessness, weak even to foolishness after what precedes: 'All things were made by him, and without him was not anything made *that was made*.'

My hope was therefore great when I saw, in reading the Greek, that the shifting of a period would rid me of the pleonasm. If thereupon any precious result of meaning should follow, the change would not merely be justifiable—seeing that points are of no authority with anyone accustomed to the vagaries of scribes, editors, and printers—but one for which to give thanks to God. And I found the change did unfold such a truth as showed the rhetoric itself in accordance with the highest thought of the apostle. So glad was I, that it added little to my satisfaction to find the change supported by the best manuscripts and versions. It could add none to learn that the passage had been, in respect of the two readings, a cause of much disputation: the ground of argument on the side of the common reading, seemed to me worse than worthless.

Let us then look at the passage as I think it ought to be translated, and after that, seek the meaning for the sake of which it was written. It is a meaning indeed by no means dependent for its revelation on this passage, belonging as it does to the very truth as it is in Jesus; but it is therein magnificently expressed by the apostle, and differently from anywhere else—that is, if I am right in the interpretation which suggested itself the moment I saw the probable rhetorical relation of the words.

'All things were made through him, and without him was made not one thing. That which was made in him was life, and the life was the light of men.'

Note the antithesis of the *through* and the *in*.

In this grand assertion seems to me to lie, more than shadowed, the germ of creation and redemption—of all the divine in its relation to all the human.

In attempting to set forth what I find in it, I write with no desire to provoke controversy, which I loathe, but with some hope of presenting to the minds of such as have become capable of seeing it, the glory of the truth of the Father and the Son, as uttered by this first of seers, after the grandest fashion of his insight. I am as indifferent to a reputation for orthodoxy as I despise the championship of novelty. To the untrue, the truth itself must seem unsound, for the light that is in them is darkness.

I believe, then, that Jesus Christ is the eternal son of the eternal father; that from the first of firstness Jesus is the son, because God is the father—a statement imperfect and unfit because an attempt of human thought to represent that which it cannot grasp, yet which it so believes that it must try to utter it even in speech that cannot be right. I believe therefore that the Father is the greater, that if the Father had not been, the Son could not have been. I will not apply logic to the thesis, nor would I state it now but for the sake of what is to follow. The true heart will remember the inadequacy of our speech, and our thought also, to the things that lie near the unknown roots of our existence. In saying what I do, I only say what Paul implies when he speaks of the Lord giving up the kingdom to his father, that God may be all in all. I worship the Son as the human God, the divine, the only Man, deriving his being and power from the Father, equal with him as a son is the equal at once and the subject of his father—but *making himself the equal of his father in what is most precious in Godhead, namely, Love*—which is, indeed, the essence of that statement of the evangelist with which I have now to do—a higher thing than the making of the worlds and the things in them, which he did by the power of the Father, not by a self-existent power in himself, whence the apostle, to whom the Lord must have said things he did not say to the rest, or who was better able to receive what he said to all, says, 'All things were made' not *by*, but '*through* him.'

We must not wonder things away into nonentity, but try to present them to ourselves after what fashion we are able—our shadows of the heavenly. For our very beings and understandings and consciousnesses, though but shadows in regard to any perfection either of outline or operation, are yet shadows of his being, his understanding, his consciousness, and he has cast those shadows; they are no more causally our own than his power of creation is ours. In our shadow-speech then, and following with my shadow-understanding as best I can the words of the evangelist, I say, The Father, in bringing out of the unseen the things that are seen, made essential use of the Son, so that all that exists was created *through* him. What the difference between the part in creation of the Father and the part of the Son may be, who can understand?—but perhaps we may one day come to see into it a little; for I dare hope that, through our willed sonship, we shall come far nearer ourselves to creating. The word *creation* applied to the loftiest success of human genius, seems to me a mockery of humanity, itself in process of creation.

Let us read the text again: 'All things were made *through* him, and without him was made not one thing. That which was made *in* him was life.' You begin to see it? The power by which he created the worlds was given him by his father; he had in himself a greater power than that by which he made the worlds. There was something made, not *through* but *in* him; something brought into being by himself. Here he creates in his grand way, in himself, as did the Father. 'That which was made *in* him was *life*'

What does this mean? What is the *life* the apostle intends? Many forms of life have come to being through the Son, but those were results, not forms of the life that was brought to existence *in* him. He could not have been employed by the Father in creating, save in virtue of the life that was *in* him.

As to what the life of God is to himself, we can only know that we cannot know it—even that not being absolute ignorance, for no one can see that, from its very nature, he cannot understand a thing without therein approaching that thing in a most genuine manner. As to what the life of God is in relation to us, we know that it is the causing life of everything that we call life—of everything that is; and in knowing this, we know something of that life, by the very forms of its force. But the one interminable mystery, for I presume the two make but one mystery—a mystery that must be a mystery to us for ever, not because God will not explain it, but because God himself could not make us understand it—is first, how he can be self-existent, and next, how he can make other beings exist: self-existence and creation no man will ever understand. Again, regarding the matter from the side of the creature—the cause of his being is antecedent to that being; he can therefore have no knowledge of his own creation; neither could he understand that which he can do nothing like. If we could make ourselves, we should understand our creation, but to do that we must be God. And of all ideas this—that, with the self-dissatisfied, painfully circumscribed consciousness I possess, I could in any way have caused myself, is the most dismal and hopeless. Nevertheless, if I be a child of God, I must be *like* him, like him even in the matter of this creative energy. There must be something in me that corresponds in its childish way to the eternal might in him. But I am forestalling. The question now is: What was that life, the thing made *in* the Son—made by him inside himself, not outside him—made not *through* but *in him*—the life that was his own, as God's is his own?

It was, I answer, that act in him that corresponded in him, as the son, to the self-existence of his father. Now what is the deepest in God? His power? No, for power could not make him what we mean when we say *God*. Evil could, of course, never create one atom; but let us understand very plainly, that a being whose essence was only power would be such a negation of the divine that no righteous worship could be offered him: his service must be fear, and fear only. Such a being, even were he righteous in judgment, yet could not be God. The God himself whom we love could not be righteous were he not something deeper and better still than we generally mean by the word—but, alas, how little can language say without seeming to say something wrong! In one word, God is Love. Love is the deepest depth, the essence of his nature, at the root of all his being. It is not merely that he could not be God, if he had made no creatures to whom to be God; but love is the heart and hand of his creation; it is his right to create, and his power to create as well. The love that foresees creation is itself the power to create. Neither could he be righteous—that is, fair to his creatures—but that his love created them. His perfection is his love. All his divine rights rest upon his love. Ah, he is not the great monarch! The simplest peasant loving his cow, is more divine than any monarch whose monarchy is his glory. If God would not punish sin, or if he did it for

256

anything but love, he would not be the father of Jesus Christ, the God who works as Jesus wrought. What then, I say once more, is in Christ correspondent to the creative power of God? It must be something that comes also of love; and in the Son the love must be to the already existent. Because of that eternal love which has no beginning, the Father must have the Son. God could not love, could not be love, without making things to love: Jesus has God to love; the love of the Son is responsive to the love of the Father. The response to self-existent love is self-abnegating love. The refusal of himself is that in Jesus which corresponds to the creation of God. His love takes action, creates, in self-abjuration, in the death of self as motive; in the drowning of self in the life of God, where it lives only as love. What is life in a child? Is it not perfect response to his parents? thorough oneness with them? A child at strife with his parents, one in whom their will is not his, is no child; as a child he is dead, and his death is manifest in rigidity and contortion. His spiritual order is on the way to chaos. Disintegration has begun. Death is at work in him. See the same child yielding to the will that is righteously above his own; see the life begin to flow from the heart through the members; see the relaxing limbs; see the light rise like a fountain in his eyes, and flash from his face! Life has again its lordship!

The life of Christ is this—negatively, that he does nothing, cares for nothing for his own sake; positively, that he cares with his whole soul for the will, the pleasure of his father. Because his father is his father, therefore he will be his child. The truth in Jesus is his relation to his father; the righteousness of Jesus is his fulfilment of that relation. Meeting this relation, loving his father with his whole being, he is not merely alive as born of God; but, giving himself with perfect will to God, choosing to die to himself and live to God, he therein creates in himself a new and higher life; and, standing upon himself, has gained the power to awake life, the divine shadow of his own, in the hearts of us his brothers and sisters, who have come from the same birth-home as himself, namely, the heart of his God and our God, his father and our father, but who, without our elder brother to do it first, would never have chosen that self-abjuration which is life, never have become alive like him. To will, not from self, but with the Eternal, is to live.

This choice of his own being, in the full knowledge of what he did; this active willing to be the Son of the Father, perfect in obedience—is that in Jesus which responds and corresponds to the self-existence of God. Jesus rose at once to the height of his being, set himself down on the throne of his nature, in the act of subjecting himself to the will of the Father as his only good, the only *reason* of his existence. When he died on the cross, he did that, in the wild weather of his outlying provinces in the torture of the body of his revelation, which he had done at home in glory and gladness. From the infinite beginning—for here I can speak only by contradictions-he completed and held fast the eternal circle of his existence in saying, 'Thy will, not mine, be done!' He made himself what he is by *deathing* himself into the will of the eternal Father, through which will he was the eternal Son—thus plunging into the fountain of his own life, the everlasting Fatherhood, and taking the Godhead of the Son. This is the life that was made *in* Jesus: 'That which was made in him was life.' This life, self-willed in Jesus, is the one thing that makes such life—the eternal life, the true life, possible—nay, imperative, essential, to every man, woman, and child, whom the Father has sent into the outer, that he may go back into the inner world, his heart. As the self-existent life of the Father has given us being, so the willed devotion of Jesus is his power to give us eternal life like his own—to enable us to do the same. There is no life for any man, other than the same kind that Jesus has; his disciple must live by the same absolute devotion of his will to the Father's; then is his life one with the life of the Father.

Because we are come out of the divine nature, which chooses to be divine, we must *choose* to be divine, to be of God, to be one with God, loving and living as he loves and lives, and so be partakers of the divine nature, or we perish. Man cannot originate this life; it must be shown him, and he must choose it. God is the father of Jesus and of us—of every possibility of our being; but while God is the father of his children, Jesus is the father of their sonship; for in him is made the life which is sonship to the Father—the recognition, namely, in fact and life, that the Father has his claim upon his sons and daughters. We are not and cannot become true sons without our will willing his will, our doing following his making. It was the will of Jesus to be the thing God willed and meant him, that made him the true son of God. He was not the son of God because he could not help it, but because he willed to be in himself the son that he was in the divine idea. So with us: we must *be* the sons we are. We are not made to be what we cannot help being; sons and daughters are not after such fashion! We are sons and daughters in God's claim; we must be sons and daughters in our will. And we can be sons and daughters, saved into the original necessity and bliss of our being, only by choosing God for the father he is, and doing his will—yielding ourselves true sons to the absolute Father.

Therein lies human bliss—only and essential. The working out of this our salvation must be pain, and the handing of it down to them that are below must ever be in pain; but the eternal form of the will of God in and for us, is intensity of bliss.

'And the life was the light of men.'

The life of which I have now spoken became light to men in the appearing of him in whom it came into being. The life became light that men might see it, and themselves live by choosing that life also, by choosing so to live, such to be.

There is always something deeper than anything said—something of which all human, all divine words, figures, pictures, motion-forms, are but the outer laminar spheres through which the central reality shines more or less plainly. Light itself is but the poor outside form of a deeper, better thing, namely, life. The life is Christ. The light too is Christ, but only the body of Christ. The life is Christ himself. The light is what we *see* and shall see in him; the life is what we may *be* in him. The life 'is a light by abundant clarity invisible;' it is the unspeakable unknown; it must become light such as men can see before men can know it. Therefore the obedient human God appeared as the obedient divine man, doing the works of his father—the things, that is, which his father did—doing them humbly before unfriendly brethren. The Son of the Father must take his own form in the substance of flesh, that he may be seen of men, and so become the light of men—not that men may have light, but that men may have life;—that, seeing what they could not originate, they may, through the life that is in them, begin to hunger after the life of which they are capable, and which is essential to their being;—that the life in them may long for him who is their life, and thirst for its own perfection, even as root and stem may thirst for the flower for whose sake, and through whose presence in them, they exist. That the child of God may become the son of God by beholding *the* Son, the life revealed in light; that the radiant heart of the Son of God may be the sunlight to his fellows; that the idea may be drawn out by the presence and drawing of the Ideal—that Ideal, the perfect Son of the Father, was sent to his brethren.

Let us not forget that the devotion of the Son could never have been but for the devotion of the Father, who never seeks his own glory one atom more than does the Son; who is devoted to the Son, and to all his sons and daughters, with a devotion perfect and eternal, with fathomless unselfishness. The whole being and doing of Jesus on earth is the same as his being and doing from all eternity, that whereby he is the blessed son-God of the father-God; it is the shining out of that life that men might see it. It is a being like God, a doing of the will of God, a working of the works of God, therefore an unveiling of the Father in the Son, that men may know him. It is the prayer of the Son to the rest of the sons to come back to the Father, to be reconciled to the Father, to behave to the Father as he does. He seems to me to say: 'I know your father, for he is my father; I know him because I have been with him from eternity. You do not know him; I have come to you to tell you that as I am, such is he; that he is just like me, only greater and better. He only is the true, original good; I am true because I seek nothing but his will. He only is all in all; I am not all in all, but he is my father, and I am the son in whom his heart of love is satisfied. Come home with me, and sit with me on the throne of my obedience. Together we will do his will, and be glad with him, for his will is the only good. You may do with me as you please; I will not defend myself. Because I speak true, my witness is unswerving; I stand to it, come what may. If I held my face to my testimony only till danger came close, and then prayed the Father for twelve legions of angels to deliver me, that would be to say the Father would do anything for his children until it began to hurt him. I bear witness that my father is such as I. In the face of death I assert it, and dare death to disprove it. Kill me; do what you will and can against me; my father is true, and I am true in saying that he is true. Danger or hurt cannot turn me aside from this my witness. Death can only kill my body; he cannot make me his captive. Father, thy will be done! The pain will pass; it will be but for a time! Gladly will I suffer that men may know that I live, and that thou art my life. Be with me, father, that it may not be more than I can bear.'

Friends, if you think anything less than this could redeem the world, or make blessed any child that God has created, you know neither the Son nor the Father.

The bond of the universe, the chain that holds it together, the one active unity, the harmony of things, the negation of difference, the reconciliation of all forms, all shows, all wandering desires, all returning loves; the fact at the root of every vision, revealing that 'love is the only good in the world,' and selfishness the one thing hateful, in the city of the living God unutterable, is the devotion of the Son to the Father. It is the life of the universe. It is not the fact that God created all things, that makes the universe a whole; but that he through whom he created them loves him perfectly, is eternally content in his father, is satisfied to be because his father is with him. It is not the fact that God is all in all, that unites the universe; it is the love of the Son to the

Father. For of no onehood comes unity; there can be no oneness where there is only one. For the very beginnings of unity there must be two. Without Christ, therefore, there could be no universe. The reconciliation wrought by Jesus is not the primary source of unity, of safety to the world; that reconciliation was the necessary working out of the eternal antecedent fact, the fact making itself potent upon the rest of the family—that God and Christ are one, are father and son, the Father loving the Son as only the Father can love, the Son loving the Father as only the Son can love. The prayer of the Lord for unity between men and the Father and himself, springs from the eternal need of love. The more I regard it, the more I am lost in the wonder and glory of the thing. But for the Father and the Son, no two would care a jot the one for the other. It might be the right way for creatures to love because of mere existence, but what two creatures would ever have originated the loving? I cannot for a moment believe it would have been I. Even had I come into being as now with an inclination to love, selfishness would soon have overborne it. But if the Father loves the Son, if the very music that makes the harmony of life lies, not in the theory of love in the heart of the Father, but in the fact of it, in the burning love in the hearts of Father and Son, then glory be to the Father and to the Son, and to the spirit of both, the fatherhood of the Father meeting and blending with the sonhood of the Son, and drawing us up into the glory of their joy, to share in the thoughts of love that pass between them, in their thoughts of delight and rest in each other, in their thoughts of joy in all the little ones. The life of Jesus is the light of men, revealing to them the Father.

But light is not enough; light is for the sake of life. We too must have life in ourselves. We too must, like the Life himself, live. We can live in no way but that in which Jesus lived, in which life was made in him. That way is, to give up our life. This is the one supreme action of life possible to us for the making of life in ourselves. Christ did it of himself, and so became light to us, that we might be able to do it in ourselves, after him, and through his originating act. We must do it ourselves, I say. The help that he has given and gives, the light and the spirit-working of the Lord, the spirit, in our hearts, is all in order that we may, as we must, do it ourselves. Till then we are not alive; life is not made in us. The whole strife and labour and agony of the Son with every man, is to get him to die as he died. All preaching that aims not at this, is a building with wood and hay and stubble. If I say not with whole heart, 'My father, do with me as thou wilt, only help me against myself and for thee;' if I cannot say, 'I am thy child, the inheritor of thy spirit, thy being, a part of thyself, glorious in thee, but grown poor in me: let me be thy dog, thy horse, thy anything thou willest; let me be thine in any shape the love that is my Father may please to have me; let me be thine in any way, and my own or another's in no way but thine;'—if we cannot, fully as this, give ourselves to the Father, then we have not yet laid hold upon that for which Christ has laid hold upon us. The faith that a man may, nay, must put in God, reaches above earth and sky, stretches beyond the farthest outlying star of the creatable universe. The question is not at present, however, of removing mountains, a thing that will one day be simple to us, but of waking and rising from the dead now.

When a man truly and perfectly says with Jesus, and as Jesus said it, 'Thy will be done,' he closes the everlasting life-circle; the life of the Father and the Son flows through him; he is a part of the divine organism. Then is the prayer of the Lord in him fulfilled: 'I in them and thou in me, that they made be made perfect in one.' The Christ in us, is the spirit of the perfect child toward the perfect father. The Christ in us is our own true nature made blossom in us by the Lord, whose life is the light of men that it may become the life of men; for our true nature is childhood to the Father.

Friends, those of you who know, or suspect, that these things are true, let us arise and live—arise even in the darkest moments of spiritual stupidity, when hope itself sees nothing to hope for. Let us not trouble ourselves about the cause of our earthliness, except we know it to be some unrighteousness in us, but go at once to the Life. Never, never let us accept as consolation the poor suggestion, that the cause of our deadness is physical. Can it be comfort to know that this body of ours, because of the death in it, is too much for the spirit—which ought not merely to triumph over it, but to inspire it with subjection and obedience? Let us comfort ourselves in the thought of the Father and the Son. So long as there dwells harmony, so long as the Son loves the Father with all the love the Father can welcome, all is well with the little ones. God is all right—why should we mind standing in the dark for a minute outside his window? Of course we miss the *inness*, but there is a bliss of its own in waiting. What if the rain be falling, and the wind blowing; what if we stand alone, or, more painful still, have some dear one beside us, sharing our *outness*; what even if the window be not shining, because of the curtains of good inscrutable drawn across it; let us think to ourselves, or say to our friend, 'God is; Jesus is not dead; nothing can be going wrong, however it may look so to hearts unfinished in childness.' Let us say to the Lord, 'Jesus, art thou loving the Father in there? Then we out here will do his will, patiently waiting till he open the door. We shall not mind the wind or the rain much. Perhaps thou art saying to the Father, "Thy little ones need some wind and rain: their buds are hard; the flowers do not come out. I cannot get them made blessed without a little more winter-weather." Then perhaps the Father will say, "Comfort them, my son Jesus, with the memory of thy patience when thou wast missing me. Comfort them that thou wast sure of me when everything about thee seemed so unlike me, so unlike the place thou hadst left.'" In a word, let us be at peace, because peace is at the heart of things—peace and utter satisfaction between the Father and the Son—in which peace they call us to share; in which peace they promise that at length, when they have their good way with us, we shall share.

Before us, then, lies a bliss unspeakable, a bliss beyond the thought or invention of man, to every child who will fall in with the perfect imagination of the Father. His imagination is one with his creative will. The thing that God imagines, that thing exists. When the created falls in with the will of him who 'loved him into being,' then all is well; thenceforward the mighty creation goes on in him upon higher and yet higher levels, in more and yet more divine airs. Thy will, O God, be done! Nought else is other than loss, than decay, than corruption. There is no life but that born of the life that the Word made in himself by doing thy will, which life is the light of men. Through that light is born the life of men—the same life in them that came first into being in Jesus. As he laid down his life, so must men lay down their lives, that as he liveth they may live also. That which was made in him was life, and the life is the light of men; and yet his own, to whom he was sent, *did not believe him.*

THE KNOWING OF THE SON.

Ye have neither heard his voice at any time, nor seen his shape. And ye have not his word abiding in you; for whom he hath sent, him ye believe not.— John v. 37-38.

We shall know one day just how near we come in the New Testament to the very words of the Lord. That we have them with a difference, I cannot doubt. For one thing, I do not believe he spoke in Greek. He was sent to the lost sheep of the house of Israel, and would speak their natural language, not that which, at best, they knew in secondary fashion. That the thoughts of God would come out of the heart of Jesus in anything but the mother-tongue of the simple men to whom he spoke, I cannot think. He may perhaps have spoken to the Jews of Jerusalem in Greek, for they were less simple; but at present I do not see ground to believe he did.

Again, are we bound to believe that John Boanerges, who indeed best, and in some things alone, understood him, was able, after such a lapse of years, to give us in his gospel, supposing the Lord to have spoken to his disciples in Greek, the *very* words in which he uttered the simplest profundities ever heard in the human world? I do not say he was not able; I say—Are we bound to believe he was able? When the disciples became, by the divine presence in their hearts, capable of understanding the Lord, they remembered things he had said which they had forgotten; possibly the very words in which he said them returned to their memories; but must we believe the evangelists always precisely recorded his words? The little differences between their records is answer enough. The gospel of John is the outcome of years and years of remembering, recalling, and pondering the words of the Master, one thing understood recalling another. We cannot tell of how much the memory, in best condition—that is, with God in the man—may not be capable; but I do not believe that John would have always given us the very words of the Lord, even if, as I do not think he did, he had spoken them in Greek. God has not cared that we should anywhere have assurance of his very words; and that not merely, perhaps, because of the tendency in his children to word-worship, false logic, and corruption of the truth, but because he would not have them oppressed by words, seeing that words, being human, therefore but partially capable, could not absolutely contain or express what the Lord meant, and that even he must depend for being understood upon the spirit of his disciple. Seeing it could not give life, the letter should not be throned with power to kill; it should be but the handmaid to open the door of the truth to the mind that was *of* the truth.

'Then you believe in an individual inspiration to anyone who chooses to lay claim to it!'

Yes—to everyone who claims it from God; not to everyone who claims from men the recognition of his possessing it. He who has a thing, does not need to have it recognized. If I did not believe in a special inspiration to every man who asks for the holy spirit, the good thing of God, I should have to throw aside the whole tale as an imposture; for the Lord has, according to that tale, promised such inspiration to those who ask it. If an objector has not this spirit, is not inspired with the truth, he knows nothing of the words that are spirit and life; and his objection is less worth heeding than that of a savage to the assertion of a chemist. His assent equally is but the blowing of an idle horn.

'But how is one to tell whether it be in truth the spirit of God that is speaking in a man?'

You are not called upon to tell. The question for you is whether you have the spirit of Christ yourself. The question is for you to put to yourself, the question is for you to answer to yourself: Am I alive with the life of Christ? Is his spirit dwelling in me? Everyone who desires to follow the Master has the spirit of the Master, and will receive more, that he may follow closer, nearer, in his very footsteps. He is not called upon to prove to this or that or any man that he has the light of Jesus; he has to let his light shine. It does not follow that his work is to teach others, or that he is able to speak large truths in true forms. When the strength or the joy or the pity of the truth urges him, let him speak it out and not be afraid—content to be condemned for it; comforted that if he mistake, the Lord himself will condemn him, and save him 'as by fire.' The condemnation of his fellow men will not hurt him, nor a whit the more that it be spoken in the name of Christ. If he speak true, the Lord will say 'I sent him.' For all truth is of him; no man can see a true thing to be true but by the Lord, the spirit.

'How am I to know that a thing is true?'

By *doing* what you know to be true, and calling nothing true until you see it to be true; by shutting your mouth until the truth opens it. Are you meant to be silent? Then woe to you if you speak.

'But if I do not take the words attributed to him by the evangelists, for the certain, absolute, very words of the Master, how am I to know that they represent his truth?'

By seeing in them what corresponds to the plainest truth he speaks, and commends itself to the power that is working in you to make of you a true man; by their appeal to your power of judging what is true; by their rousing of your conscience. If they do not seem to you true, either they are not the words of the Master, or you are not true enough to understand them. Be certain of this, that, if any words that are his do not show their truth to you, you have not received his message in them; they are not yet to you the word of God, for they are not in you spirit and life. They may be the nearest to the truth that words can come; they may have served to bring many into contact with the heart of God; but for you they remain as yet sealed. If yours be a true heart, it will revere them because of the probability that they are words with the meaning of the Master behind them; to you they are the rock in the desert before Moses spoke to it. If you wait, your ignorance will not hurt you; if you presume to reason from them, you are a blind man disputing of that you never saw. To reason from a thing not understood, is to walk straight into the mire. To dare to reason of truth from words that do not show to us that they are true, is the presumption of Pharisaical *hypocrisy*. Only they who are not true, are capable of doing it. Humble mistake will not hurt us: the truth is there, and the Lord will see that we come to know it. We may think we know it when we have scarce a glimpse of it; but the error of a true heart will not be allowed to ruin it. Certainly that heart would not have mistaken the truth except for the untruth yet remaining in it; but he who casts out devils will cast out that devil.

In the saying before us, I see enough to enable me to believe that its words embody the mind of Christ. If I could not say this, I should say, 'The apostle has here put on record a saying of Christ's; I have not yet been able to recognise the mind of Christ in it; therefore I conclude that I cannot have understood it, for to understand what is true is to know it true.' I have yet seen no words credibly reported as the words of Jesus, concerning which I dared to say, 'His mind is not therein, therefore the words are not his.' The mind of man call receive any word only in proportion as it is the word of Christ, and in proportion as he is one with Christ. To him who does verily receive his word, it is a power, not of argument, but of life. The words of the Lord are not for the logic that deals with words as if they were things; but for the spiritual logic that reasons from divine thought to divine thought, dealing with spiritual facts.

No thought, human or divine, can be conveyed from man to man save through the symbolism of the creation. The heavens and the earth are around us that it may be possible for us to speak of the unseen by the seen; for the outermost husk of creation has correspondence with the deepest things of the Creator. He is not a God that hideth himself, but a God who made that he might reveal; he is consistent and one throughout. There are things with which an enemy hath meddled; but there are more things with which no enemy could meddle, and by which we may speak of God. They may not have revealed him to us, but at least when he is revealed, they show themselves so much of his nature, that we at once use them as spiritual tokens in the commerce of the spirit, to help convey to other minds what we may have seen of the unseen. Belonging to this sort of mediation are the words of the Lord I would now look into.

'And the Father himself which hath sent me, hath borne witness of me. Ye have neither heard his voice at any time, nor seen his shape. And ye have not his word abiding in you: for whom he hath sent, him ye believe not.'

If Jesus said these words, he meant more, not less, than lies on their surface. They cannot be mere assertion of what everybody knew; neither can their repetition of similar negations be tautological. They were not intended to inform the Jews of a fact they would not have dreamed of denying. Who among them would say he had ever heard God's voice, or seen his shape? John himself says 'No man hath seen God at any time.' What is the tone of the passage? It is reproach. Then he reproaches them that they had not seen God, when no man hath seen God at any time, and Paul says no man can see him! Is there here any paradox? There cannot be the sophism: 'No man hath seen God; ye are to blame that ye have not seen God; therefore all men are to blame that they have not seen God!' If we read, 'No man hath seen God, but some men ought to have seen him,' we do not reap such hope for the race as will give the aspect of a revelation to the assurance that not one of those capable of seeing him has ever seen him!

The one utterance is of John; the other of his master: if there is any contradiction between them, of course the words of John must be thrown away. But there can hardly be contradiction, since he who says the one thing, is recorder of the other as said by his master, him to whom he belonged, whose disciple he was, whom he loved as never man loved man before.

The word *see* is used in one sense in the one statement, and in another sense in the other. In the one it means *see with the eyes*; in the other, *with the soul*. The one statement is made of all men; the other is made to certain of the Jews of Jerusalem concerning themselves. It is true that no man hath seen God, and true that some men ought to have seen him. No man hath seen him with his bodily eyes; these Jews ought to have seen him with their spiritual eyes.

No man has ever seen God in any outward, visible, close-fitting form of his own: he is revealed in no shape save that of his son. But multitudes of men have with their mind's, or rather their heart's eye, seen more or less of God; and perhaps every man might have and ought to have seen something of him. We cannot follow God into his infinitesimal intensities of spiritual operation, any more than into the atomic life-potencies that lie deep beyond the eye of the microscope: God may be working in the heart of a savage, in a way that no wisdom of his wisest, humblest child can see, or imagine that it sees. Many who have never beheld the face of God, may yet have caught a glimpse of the hem of his garment; many who have never seen his shape, may yet have seen the vastness of his shadow; thousands who have never felt the warmth of its folds, have yet been startled by

No face: only the sight
Of a sweepy garment vast and white.

Some have dreamed his hand laid upon them, who never knew themselves gathered to his bosom. The reproach in the words of the Lord is the reproach of men who ought to have had an experience they had not had. Let us look a little nearer at his words.

'Ye have not heard his voice at any time,' might mean, '*Ye have never listened to his voice*,' or '*Ye have never obeyed his voice*' but the following phrase, 'nor seen his shape,' keeps us rather to the primary sense of the word *hear*: '*The sound of his voice is unknown to you;*' '*You have never heard his voice so as to know it for his.*' 'You have not seen his shape;'—'*You do not know what he is like.*' Plainly he implies, '*You ought to know his voice; you ought to know what he is like.*' 'You have not his word abiding in you;'—'*The word that is in you from the beginning, the word of God in your conscience, you have not kept with you, it is not dwelling in you; by yourselves accepted as the witness of Moses, the scripture in which you think you have eternal life does not abide with you, is not at home in you. It comes to you and goes from you. You hear, heed not, and forget. You do not dwell with it, and brood upon it, and obey it. It finds no acquaintance in you. You are not of its kind. You are not of those to whom the word of God comes. Their ears are ready to hear; they hunger after the word of the Father.*'

On what does the Lord found this his accusation of them? What is the sign in them of their ignorance of God?—For whom he hath sent, him ye believe not.'

'How so?' the Jews might answer. 'Have we not asked from thee a sign from heaven, and hast thou not pointblank refused it?'

The argument of the Lord was indeed of small weight with, and of little use to, those to whom it most applied, for the more it applied, the more incapable were they of seeing that it did apply; but it would be of great force upon some that stood listening, their minds more or less open to the truth, and their hearts drawn to the man before them. His argument was this: 'If ye had ever heard the Father's voice; if ye had ever known his call; if you had ever imagined him, or a God anything like him; if you had cared for his will so that his word was at home in your hearts, you would have known me when you saw me—known that I must come from him, that I must be his messenger, and would have listened to me. The least acquaintance with God, such as any true heart must have, would have made you recognize that I came from the God of whom you knew that something. You would have been capable of knowing me by the light of his word abiding in you; by the shape you had beheld however vaguely; by the likeness of my face and my voice to those of my father. You would have seen my father in me; you would have known me by the little you knew of him. The family-feeling would have been awake in you, the holy instinct of the same spirit, making you know your elder brother. That you do not know me now, as I stand here speaking to you, is that you do not know your own father, even my father; that throughout your lives you have re-fused to do his will, and so have not heard his voice; that you have shut your eyes from seeing him, and have thought of him only as a partisan of your ambitions. If you had loved my father, you would have known his son.' And I think he might have said, 'If even you had loved your neighbour, you would have known me, neighbour to the deepest and best in you.' If the Lord were to appear this day in Eng-

land as once in Palestine, he would not come in the halo of the paint-
ers, or with that wintry shine of effeminate beauty, of sweet weakness,
in which it is their helpless custom to represent him. Neither would he
probably come as carpenter, or mason, or gardener. He would come in
such form and condition as might bear to the present England, Scot-
land, and Ireland, a relation like that which the form and condition he
then came in, bore to the motley Judea, Samaria, and Galilee. If he
came thus, in form altogether unlooked for, who would they be that
recognized and received him? The idea involves no absurdity. He is
not far from us at any moment—if the old story be indeed more than
the best and strongest of the fables that possess the world. He might at
any moment appear: who, I ask, would be the first to receive him?
Now, as then, it would of course be the childlike in heart, the truest,
the least selfish. They would not be the highest in the estimation of
any church, for the childlike are not yet the many. It might not even be
those that knew most about the former visit of the Master, that had
pondered every word of the Greek Testament. The first to cry, 'It is the
Lord!' would be neither 'good churchman' nor 'good dissenter.' It
would be no one with so little of the mind of Christ as to imagine him
caring about stupid outside matters. It would not be the man that holds
by the mooring-ring of the letter, fast in the quay of what he calls the-
ology, and from his rotting deck abuses the presumption of those that
go down to the sea in ships—lets the wind of the spirit blow where it
listeth, but never blow him out among its wonders in the deep. It
would not be he who, obeying a command, does not care to see reason
in the command; not he who, from very barrenness of soul, cannot re-
ceive the meaning and will of the Master, and so fails to fulfil the letter
of his word, making it of none effect. It would certainly, if any, be
those who were likest the Master—those, namely, that did the will of
their father and his father, that built their house on the rock by hearing
and doing his sayings. But are there any enough like him to know him
at once by the sound of his voice, by the look of his face. There are
multitudes who would at once be taken by a false Christ fashioned af-
ter their fancy, and would at once reject the Lord as a poor impostor.
One thing is certain: they who first recognized him would be those that
most loved righteousness and hated iniquity.

But I would not forget that there are many in whom foolish forms
cover a live heart, warm toward everything human and divine; for the
worst-fitting and ugliest robe may hide the loveliest form. Every cov-
ering is not a clothing. The grass clothes the fields; the glory
surpassing Solomon's clothes the grass; but the traditions of the wor-

thiest elders will not clothe any soul—how much less the traditions of the unworthy! Its true clothing must grow out of the live soul itself. Some naked souls need but the sight of truth to rush to it, as Dante says, like a wild beast to his den; others, heavily clad in the garments the scribes have left behind them, and fearful of rending that which is fit only to be trodden underfoot, right cautiously approach the truth, go round and round it like a shy horse that fears a hidden enemy. But let each be true after the fashion possible to him, and he shall have the Master's praise.

If the Lord were to appear, the many who take the common presentation of thing or person for the thing or person, could never recognize the new vision as another form of the old: the Master has been so misrepresented by such as have claimed to present him, and especially in the one eternal fact of facts—the relation between him and his father—that it is impossible they should see any likeness. For my part, I would believe in no God rather than in such a God as is generally offered for believing in. How far those may be to blame who, righteously disgusted, cast the idea from them, nor make inquiry whether something in it may not be true, though most must be false, neither grant it any claim to investigation on the chance that some that call themselves his prophets may have taken spiritual bribes

To mingle beauty with infirmities,
And pure perfection with impure defeature—

how far those may be to blame, it is not my work to inquire. Some would grasp with gladness the hope that such chance might be proved a fact; others would not care to discern upon the palimpsest, covered but not obliterated, a credible tale of a perfect man revealing a perfect God: they are not true enough to desire that to be fact which would immediately demand the modelling of their lives upon a perfect idea, and the founding of their every hope upon the same.

But we all, beholding the glory of the Lord, are changed into the same image.

THE MIRRORS OF THE LORD.

But we all, with open face beholding as in a glass the glory of the Lord, are changed into the same image from glory to glory, even as by the spirit of the Lord.—II. Corinthians iii. 18.

We may see from this passage how the apostle Paul received the Lord, and how he understands his life to be the light of men, and so their life also.

Of all writers I know, Paul seems to me the most plainly, the most determinedly practical in his writing. What has been called his mysticism is at one time the exercise of a power of seeing, as by spiritual refraction, truths that had not, perhaps have not yet, risen above the human horizon; at another, the result of a wide-eyed habit of noting the analogies and correspondences between the concentric regions of creation; it is the working of a poetic imagination divinely alive, whose part is to foresee and welcome approaching truth; to discover the same principle in things that look unlike; to embody things discovered, in forms and symbols heretofore unused, and so present to other minds the deeper truths to which those forms and symbols owe their being.

I find in Paul's writing the same artistic fault, with the same resulting difficulty, that I find in Shakspere's—a fault that, in each case, springs from the admirable fact that the man is much more than the artist—the fault of trying to say too much at once, of pouring out stintless the plethora of a soul swelling with life and its thought, through the too narrow neck of human utterance. Thence it comes that we are at times bewildered between two or more meanings, equally good in themselves, but perplexing as to the right deduction, as to the line of the thinker's reasoning. The uncertainty, however, lies always in the intellectual region, never in the practical. What Paul cares about is plain enough to the true heart, however far from plain to the man whose desire to understand goes ahead of his obedience, who starts with the notion that Paul's design was to teach a system, to explain instead of help to see God, a God that can be revealed only to childlike insight, never to keenest intellect. The energy of the apostle, like that of his master, went forth to rouse men to seek the kingdom of God over them, his righteousness in them; to dismiss the lust of possession and passing pleasure; to look upon the glory of the God and Father, and turn to him from all that he hates; to recognize the brotherhood of men, and the hideousness of what is unfair, unloving, and self-exalting. His design was not to teach any plan of salvation other than obedience to the Lord of Life. He knew nothing of the so-called Christian systems that change the glory of the perfect God into the likeness of the low intellects and dull consciences of men—a worse corruption than the representing of him in human shape. What kind of soul is it that would not choose the Apollo of light, the high-walking Hyperion, to the notion of the dull, self-cherishing monarch, the law-dispensing magistrate, or the cruel martinet, generated in the pagan arrogance of Rome, and accepted by the world in the church as the portrait of its God! Jesus Christ is the *only* likeness of the living Father.

Let us see then what Paul teaches us in this passage about the life which is the light of men. It is his form of bringing to bear upon men the truth announced by John.

When Moses came out from speaking with God, his face was radiant; its shining was a wonder to the people, and a power upon them. But the radiance began at once to diminish and die away, as was natural, for it was not indigenous in Moses. Therefore Moses put a veil upon his face that they might not see it fade. As to whether this was right or wise, opinion may differ: it is not my business to discuss the question. When he went again into the tabernacle, he took off his veil, talked with God with open face, and again put on the veil when he came out. Paul says that the veil which obscured the face of Moses lies now upon the hearts of the Jews, so that they cannot understand him, but that when they turn to the Lord, go into the tabernacle with Moses, the veil shall be taken away, and they shall see God. Then will they understand that the glory is indeed faded upon the face of Moses, but by reason of the glory that excelleth, the glory of Jesus that overshines it. Here, after all, I can hardly help asking—Would not Moses have done better to let them see that the glory of their leader was altogether

273

dependent on the glory within the veil, whither they were not worthy to enter? Did that veil hide Moses's face only? Did he not, however unintentionally, lay it on their hearts? Did it not cling there, and help to hide God from them, so that they could not perceive that the greater than Moses was come, and stormed at the idea that the glory of their prophet must yield? Might not the absence of that veil from his face have left them a little more able to realize that his glory was a glory that must pass, a glory whose glory was that it prepared the way for a glory that must extinguish it? Moses had put the veil for ever from his face, but they clutched it to their hearts, and it blinded them—admirable symbol of the wilful blindness of old Mosaist or modern Wesleyan, admitting no light that his Moses or his Wesley did not see, and thus losing what of the light he saw and reflected.

Paul says that the sight of the Lord will take that veil from their hearts. His light will burn it away. His presence gives liberty. Where he is, there is no more heaviness, no more bondage, no more wilderness or Mount Sinai. The Son makes free with sonship.

And now comes the passage whose import I desire to make more clear:

'But we all,' having this presence and this liberty, 'with open face beholding as in a glass the glory of the Lord, are changed into the same image,' that of the Lord, 'from glory to glory, even as of the Lord, the spirit.'

'We need no Moses, no earthly mediator, to come between us and the light, and bring out for us a little of the glory. We go into the presence of the Son revealing the Father—into the presence of the Light of men. Our mediator is the Lord himself, the spirit of light, a mediator not sent by us to God to bring back his will, but come from God to bring us himself. We enter, like Moses, into the presence of the visible, radiant God—only how much more visible, more radiant! As Moses stood with uncovered face receiving the glory of God full upon it, so with open, with uncovered face, full in the light of the glory of God, in the place of his presence, stand we—you and I, Corinthians. It is no reflected light we see, but the glory of God shining *in*, shining out of, shining in and from the face of Christ, the glory of the Father, one with the Son. Israel saw but the fading reflection of the glory of God on the face of Moses; we see the glory itself in the face of Jesus.'

But in what follows, it seems to me that the revised version misses the meaning almost as much as the authorized, when, instead of 'beholding as in a glass,' it gives 'reflecting as a mirror.' The former is wrong; the latter is far from right. The idea, with the figure, is that of a poet, not a man of science. The poet deals with the outer show of things, which outer show is infinitely deeper in its relation to truth, as well as more practically useful, than the analysis of the man of science. Paul never thought of the mirror as reflecting, as throwing back the rays of light from its surface; he thought of it as receiving, taking into itself, the things presented to it—here, as filling its bosom with the glory it looks upon. When I see the face of my friend in a mirror, the mirror seems to hold it in itself, to surround the visage with its liquid embrace. The countenance is *there*—down there in the depth of the mirror. True, it shines radiant out of it, but it is not the shining out of it that Paul has in his thought; it is the fact—the *visual* fact, which, according to Wordsworth, the poet always seizes—of the mirror holding in it the face.

That this is the way poet or prophet—Paul was both—would think of the thing, especially in the age of the apostle, I shall be able to make appear even more probable by directing your notice to the following passage from Dante—whose time, though so much farther from that of the apostle than our time from Dante's, was in many respects much liker Paul's than ours.

The passage is this:—Dell' Inferno: Canto xxiii. 25-27:

E quei: 'S'io fossi d'impiombato vetro,
L'immagine di fuor tua non trarrei
Piu tosto a me, che quella dentro impetro.'

Here Virgil, with reference to the power he had of reading the thoughts of his companion, says to Dante:

'If I were of leaded glass,'—meaning, 'If I were glass covered at the back with lead, so that I was a mirror,'—'I should not draw thy outward image to me more readily than I gain thy inner one;'—meaning, 'than now I know your thoughts.'

It seems, then, to me, that the true simple word to represent the Greek, and the most literal as well by which to translate it, is the verb *mirror*—when the sentence, so far, would run thus: 'But we all, with unveiled face, mirroring the glory of the Lord,—.'

I must now go on to unfold the idea at work in the heart of the apostle. For the mere correctness of a translation is nothing, except it bring us something deeper, or at least some fresher insight: with him who cares for the words apart from what the writer meant them to convey, I have nothing to do: he must cease to 'pass for a man' and begin to be a man indeed, on the way to be a live soul, before I can desire his intercourse. The prophet-apostle seems to me, then, to say, 'We all, with clear vision of the Lord, mirroring in our hearts his glory, even as a mirror would take into itself his face, are thereby changed into his likeness, his glory working our glory, by the present power, in our inmost being, of the Lord, the spirit.' Our mirroring of Christ, then, is one with the presence of his spirit in us. The idea, you see, is not the reflection, the radiating of the light of Christ on others, though that were a figure lawful enough; but the taking into, and having in us, him working to the changing of us.

That the thing signified transcends the sign, outreaches the figure, is no discovery; the thing figured always belongs to a higher stratum, to which the simile serves but as a ladder; when the climber has reached it, 'he then unto the ladder turns his back.' It is but according to the law of symbol, that the thing symbolized by the mirror should have properties far beyond those of leaded glass or polished metal, seeing it is a live soul understanding that which it takes into its deeps—holding it, and conscious of what it holds. It mirrors by its will to hold in its mirror. Unlike its symbol, it can hold not merely the outward visual resemblance, but the inward likeness of the person revealed by it; it is open to the influences of that which it embraces, and is capable of active co-operation with them: the mirror and the thing mirrored are of one origin and nature, and in closest relation to each other. Paul's idea is, that when we take into our understanding, our heart, our conscience, our being, the glory of God, namely Jesus Christ as he shows himself to our eyes, our hearts, our consciences, he works upon us, and will keep working, till we are changed to the very likeness we have thus mirrored in us; for with his likeness he comes himself, and dwells in us. He will work until the same likeness is wrought out and perfected in us, the image, namely, of the humanity of God, in which image we were made at first, but which could never be developed in us except by the indwelling of the perfect likeness. By the power of Christ thus received and at home in us, we are changed—the glory in him becoming glory in us, his glory changing us to glory.

But we must beware of receiving this or any symbol *after the flesh*, beware of interpreting it in any fashion that partakes of the character of the mere physical, psychical, or spirituo-mechanical. The symbol deals with things far beyond the deepest region whence symbols can be drawn. The indwelling of Jesus in the soul of man, who shall declare! But let us note this, that the dwelling of Jesus in us is the power of the spirit of God upon us; for 'the Lord is that spirit,' and that Lord dwelling in us, we are changed 'even as from the Lord the spirit.' When we think Christ, Christ comes; when we receive his image into our spiritual mirror, he enters with it. Our thought is not cut off from his. Our open receiving thought is his door to come in. When our hearts turn to him, that is opening the door to him, that is holding up our mirror to him; then he comes in, not by our thought only, not in our idea only, but he comes himself, and of his own will—comes in as we could not take him, but as he can come and we receive him— enabled to receive by his very coming the one welcome guest of the whole universe. Thus the Lord, the spirit, becomes the soul of our souls, becomes spiritually what he always was creatively; and as our spirit informs, gives shape to our bodies, in like manner his soul informs, gives shape to our souls. In this there is nothing unnatural, nothing at conflict with our being. It is but that the deeper soul that willed and wills our souls, rises up, the infinite Life, into the Self we call *I* and *me*, but which lives immediately from him, and is his very own property and nature—unspeakably more his than ours: this deeper creative soul, working on and with his creation upon higher levels, makes the *I* and *me* more and more his, and himself more and more ours; until at length the glory of our existence flashes upon us, we face full to the sun that enlightens what it sent forth, and know ourselves alive with an infinite life, even the life of the Father; know that our existence is not the moonlight of a mere consciousness of being, but the sun-glory of a life justified by having become one with its origin, thinking and feeling with the primal Sun of life, from whom it was dropped away that it might know and bethink itself, and return to circle for ever in exultant harmony around him. Then indeed we *are*; then indeed we have life; the life of Jesus has, through light, become life in us; the glory of God in the face of Jesus, mirrored in our hearts, has made us alive; we are one with God for ever and ever.

What less than such a splendour of hope would he worthy the revelation of Jesus? Filled with the soul of their Father, men shall inherit the glory of their Father; filled with themselves, they cast him out, and rot. The company of the Lord, soul to soul, is that which saves with life, his life of God-devotion, the souls of his brethren. No other saving can save them. They must receive the Son, and through the Son the Father. What it cost the Son to get so near to us that we could say *Come in*, is the story of his life. He stands at the door and knocks, and when we open to him he comes in, and dwells with us, and we are transformed to the same image of truth and purity and heavenly childhood. Where power dwells, there is no force; where the spirit-Lord is, there is liberty. The Lord Jesus, by free, potent communion with their inmost being, will change his obedient brethren till in every thought and impulse they are good like him, unselfish, neighbourly, brotherly like him, loving the Father perfectly like him, ready to die for the truth like him, caring like him for nothing in the universe but the will of God, which is love, harmony, liberty, beauty, and joy.

I do not know if we may call this having life in ourselves; but it is the waking up, the perfecting in us of the divine life inherited from our Father in heaven, who made us in his own image, whose nature remains in us, and makes it the deepest reproach to a man that he has neither heard his voice at any time, nor seen his shape. He who would thus live must, as a mirror draws into its bosom an outward glory, receive into his 'heart of heart' the inward glory of Jesus Christ, *the Truth*.

THE TRUTH.

I am the truth.—John xiv. 6.

When the man of the five senses talks of *truth*, he regards it but as a predicate of something historical or scientific proved a fact; or, if he allows that, for aught he knows, there may be higher truth, yet, as he cannot obtain proof of it from without, he acts as if under no conceivable obligation to seek any other satisfaction concerning it. Whatever appeal be made to the highest region of his nature, such a one behaves as if it were the part of a wise man to pay it no heed, because it does not come within the scope of the lower powers of that nature. According to the word of *the* man, however, truth means more than fact, more than relation of facts or persons, more than loftiest abstraction of metaphysical entity—means being and life, will and action; for he says, '*I am the truth.*'

I desire to help those whom I may to understand more of what is meant by *the truth*, not for the sake of definition, or logical discrimination, but that, when they hear the word from the mouth of the Lord, the right idea may rise in their minds; that the word may neither be to them a void sound, nor call up either a vague or false notion of what he meant by it. If he says, 'I am the truth,' it must, to say the least, be well to know what he means by the word with whose idea he identifies himself. And at once we may premise that he can mean nothing merely intellectual, such as may be set forth and left there; he means something vital, so vital that the whole of its necessary relations are subject to it, so vital that it includes everything else which, in any lower plane, may go or have gone by the same name. Let us endeavour to arrive at his meaning by a gently ascending stair.

A thing being so, the word that says it is so, is the truth. But the fact may be of no value in itself, and our knowledge of it of no value either. Of most facts it may be said that the truth concerning them is of no consequence. For instance, it cannot be in itself important whether on a certain morning I took one side of the street or the other. It may be of importance to some one to know which I took, but in itself it is of none. It would therefore be felt unfit if I said, 'It is a *truth* that I walked on the sunny side.' The correct word would be a *fact*, not a truth. If the question arose whether a statement concerning the thing were correct, we should still be in the region of fact or no fact; but when we come to ask whether the statement was true or false, then we are concerned with the matter as the assertion of a human being, and ascend to another plane of things. It may be of no consequence which side I was upon, or it may be of consequence to some one to know which, but it is of vital importance to the witness and to any who love him, whether or not he believes the statement he makes—whether the man himself is true or false. Concerning the thing it can be but a question of *fact*; it remains a question of fact even whether the man has or has not spoken the truth; but concerning the man it is a question of truth: he is either a pure soul, so far as this thing witnesses, or a false soul, capable and guilty of a lie. In this relation it is of no consequence whether the man spoke the fact or not; if he meant to speak the fact, he remains a true man.

Here I would anticipate so far as to say that there are *truths* as well as *facts*, and lies against truths as well as against facts. When the Pharisees said *Corban*, they lied against the truth that a man must honour his father and mother.

Let us go up now from the region of facts that seem casual, to those facts that are invariable, by us unchangeable, which therefore involve what we call *law*. It will be seen at once that the *fact* here is of more dignity, and the truth or falsehood of a statement in this region of more consequence in itself. It is a small matter whether the water in my jug was frozen on such a morning; but it is a fact of great importance that at thirty-two degrees of Fahrenheit water always freezes. We rise a step here in the nature of the facts concerned: are we come therefore into the region of truths? Is it a truth that water freezes at thirty-two degrees? I think not. There is no principle, open to us, involved in the changeless fact. The principle that lies at the root of it in the mind of God must be a truth, but to the human mind the fact is as yet only a fact. The word truth ought to be kept for higher things. There are those that think such facts the highest that can be known; they put therefore the highest word they know to the highest thing they know, and call the facts of nature truths; but to me it seems that, however high you come in your generalization, however wide you make your law—-including, for instance, all solidity under the law of freezing—you have not risen higher than the statement that such and such is an invariable fact. Call it a law if you will—a law of nature if you choose—that it always is so, but not a truth. It cannot be to us a truth until we descry the reason of its existence, its relation to mind and intent, yea to self-existence. Tell us why it *must* be so, and you state a truth. When we come to see that a law is such, because it is the embodiment of a certain eternal thought, beheld by us in it, a fact of the being of God, the facts of which alone are truths, then indeed it will be to us, not a law merely, but an embodied truth. A law of God's nature is a way he would have us think of him; it is a necessary truth of all being. When a law of Nature makes us see this; when we say, I understand that law; I see why it ought to be; it is just like God; then it rises, not to the dignity of a truth in itself, but to the truth of its own nature—namely, a revelation of character, nature, and will in God. It is a picture of something in God, a word that tells a fact about God, and is therefore far nearer being called a truth than anything below it. As a simple illustration: What notion should we have of the unchanging and unchangeable, without the solidity of matter? If, such as we are, we had nothing solid about us, where would be our thinking about God and truth and law?

But there is a region perhaps not so high as this from the scientific point of view, where yet the word truth may begin to be rightly applied. I believe that every fact in nature is a revelation of God, is there such as it is because God is such as he is; and I suspect that all its facts impress us so that we learn God unconsciously. True, we cannot think of any one fact thus, except as we find the soul of it—its fact of God; but from the moment when first we come into contact with the world, it is to us a revelation of God, his things seen, by which we come to know the things unseen. How should we imagine what we may of God, without the firmament over our heads, a visible sphere, yet a formless infinitude! What idea could we have of God without the sky? The truth of the sky is what it makes us feel of the God that sent it out to our eyes. If you say the sky could not but be so and such, I grant it—with God at the root of it. There is nothing for us to conceive in its stead—therefore indeed it must be so. In its discovered laws, light seems to me to be such because God is such. Its so-called laws are the waving of his garments, waving so because he is thinking and loving and walking inside them.

We are here in a region far above that commonly claimed for science, open only to the heart of the child and the childlike man and woman—a region in which the poet is among his own things, and to which he has often to go to fetch them. For things as they are, not as science deals with them, are the revelation of God to his children. I would not be misunderstood: there is no fact of science not yet incorporated in a law, no law of science that has got beyond the hypothetic and tentative, that has not in it the will of God, and therefore may not reveal God; but neither fact nor law is there for the sake of fact or law; each is but a mean to an end; in the perfected end we find the intent, and there God—not in the laws themselves, save as his means. For that same reason, human science cannot discover God; for human science is but the backward undoing of the tapestry-web of God's science, works with its back to him, and is always leaving him—his intent, that is, his perfected work—behind it, always going farther and farther away from the point where his work culminates in revelation. Doubtless it thus makes some small intellectual approach to him, but at best it can come only to his back; science will never find the face of God; while those who would reach his heart, those who, like Dante, are returning thither where they are, will find also the spring-head of his science. Analysis is well, as death is well; analysis is death, not life. It discovers a little of the way God walks to his ends, but in so doing it forgets and leaves the end itself behind. I do not say the man of science does so, but the very process of his work is such a leaving of God's ends behind. It is a following back of his footsteps, too often without appreciation of the result for which the feet took those steps. To rise from the perfected work is the swifter and loftier ascent. If the man could find out why God worked so, then he would be discovering God; but even then he would not be discovering the best and the deepest of God; for his means cannot be so great as his ends. I must make myself clearer.

Ask a man of mere science, what is the truth of a flower: he will pull it to pieces, show you its parts, explain how they operate, how they minister each to the life of the flower; he will tell you what changes are wrought in it by scientific cultivation; where it lives originally, where it can live; the effects upon it of another climate; what part the insects bear in its varieties—and doubtless many more facts about it. Ask the poet what is the truth of the flower, and he will answer: 'Why, the flower itself, the perfect flower, and what it cannot help saying to him who has ears to hear it.' The truth of the flower is, not the facts about it, be they correct as ideal science itself, but the shining, glowing, gladdening, patient thing throned on its stalk—the compeller of smile and tear from child and prophet. The man of science laughs at this, because he is only a man of science, and does not know what it means; but the poet and the child care as little for his laughter as the birds of God, as Dante calls the angels, for his treatise on aerostation. The children of God must always be mocked by the children of the world, whether in the church or out of it—children with sharp ears and eyes, but dull hearts. Those that hold love the only good in the world, understand and smile at the world's children, and can do very well without anything they have got to tell them. In the higher state to which their love is leading them, they will speedily outstrip the men of science, for they have that which is at the root of science, that for the revealing of which God's science exists. What shall it profit a man to know all things, and lose the bliss, the consciousness of well-being, which alone can give value to his knowledge?

God's science in the flower exists for the existence of the flower in its relation to his children. If we understand, if we are at one with, if we love the flower, we have that for which the science is there, that which alone can equip us for true search into the means and ways by which the divine idea of the flower was wrought out to be presented to us. The idea of God *is* the flower; his idea is not the botany of the flower. Its botany is but a thing of ways and means—of canvas and colour and brush in relation to the picture in the painter's brain. The mere intellect can never find out that which owes its being to the heart supreme. The relation of the intellect to that which is born of the heart is an unreal except it be a humble one. The idea of God, I repeat, is the flower. He thought it; invented its means; sent it, a gift of himself, to the eyes and hearts of his children. When we see how they are loved by the ignorant and degraded, we may well believe the flowers have a place in the history of the world, as written for the archives of heaven, which we are yet a long way from understanding, and which science could not, to all eternity, understand, or enable to understand. Watch that child! He has found one of his silent and motionless brothers, with God's clothing upon it, God's thought in its face. In what a smile breaks out the divine understanding between them! Watch his mother when he takes it home to her—no nearer understanding it than he! It is no old association that brings those tears to her eyes, powerful in that way as are flowers, and things far inferior to flowers; it is God's thought, unrecognized as such, holding communion with her. She weeps with a delight inexplicable. It is only a daisy! only a primrose! only a pheasant-eye-narcissus! only a lily of the field! only a snowdrop! only a sweet-pea! only a brave yellow crocus! But here to her is no mere fact; here is no law of nature; here is a truth of nature, the truth of a flower—a perfect thought from the heart of God—a truth of God!—not an intellectual truth, but a divine fact, a dim revelation, a movement of the creative soul! Who but a father could think the flowers for his little ones? We are nigh the region now in which the Lord's word is at home—'I am the truth.'

I will take an illustrative instance altogether to my mind and special purpose. What, I ask, is the truth of water? Is it that it is formed of hydrogen and oxygen?—That the chemist has now another mode of stating the *fact* of water, will not affect my illustration. His new mode will probably be one day yet more antiquated than mine is now.—Is it for the sake of the fact that hydrogen and oxygen combined form water, that the precious thing exists? Is oxygen-and-hydrogen the divine idea of water? Or has God put the two together only that man might separate and find them out? He allows his child to pull his toys to pieces; but were they made that he might pull them to pieces? He were a child not to be envied for whom his inglorious father would make toys to such an end! A school-examiner might see therein the best use of a toy, but not a father! Find for us what in the constitution of the two gases makes them fit and capable to be thus honoured in forming the lovely thing, and you will give us a revelation about more than water, namely about the God who made oxygen and hydrogen. There is no water in oxygen, no water in hydrogen: it comes bubbling fresh from the imagination of the living God, rushing from under the great white throne of the glacier. The very thought of it makes one gasp with an elemental joy no metaphysician can analyse. The water itself, that dances, and sings, and slakes the wonderful thirst—symbol and picture of that draught for which the woman of Samaria made her prayer to Jesus—this lovely thing itself, whose very wetness is a delight to every inch of the human body in its embrace—this live thing which, if I might, I would have running through my room, yea, babbling along my table—this water is its own self its own truth, and is therein a truth of God. Let him who would know the love of the maker, become sorely athirst, and drink of the brook by the way—then lift up his heart—not at that moment to the maker of oxygen and hydrogen, but to the inventor and mediator of thirst and water, that man might foresee a little of what his soul may find in God. If he become not then as a hart panting for the water-brooks, let him go back to his science and its husks: they will at last make him thirsty as the victim in the dust-tower of the Persian. As well may a man think to describe the joy of drinking by giving thirst and water for its analysis, as imagine he has revealed anything about water by resolving it into its scientific elements. Let a man go to the hillside and let the brook sing to him till he loves it, and he will find himself far nearer the fountain of truth than the triumphal car of the chemist will ever lead the shouting crew of his half-comprehending followers. He will draw from the brook the water of joyous tears, 'and worship him that made heaven, and earth, and the sea, and the fountains of waters.'

The truth *of a thing*, then, is the blossom of it, the thing it is made for, the topmost stone set on with rejoicing; truth in a man's imagination is the power to recognize this truth of a thing; and wherever, in anything that God has made, in the glory of it, be it sky or flower or human face, we see the glory of God, there a true imagination is beholding a truth of God. And now we must advance to a yet higher plane.

We have seen that the moment whatever goes by the name of truth comes into connection with man; the moment that, instead of merely mirroring itself in his intellect as a thing outside of him, it comes into contact with him as a being of action; the moment the knowledge of it affects or ought to affect his sense of duty, it becomes a thing of far nobler import; the question of truth enters upon a higher phase, looks out of a loftier window. A fact which in itself is of no value, becomes at once a matter of life and death—moral life and death, when a man has the choice, the imperative choice of being true or false concerning it. When the truth, the heart, the summit, the crown of a thing, is perceived by a man, he approaches the fountain of truth whence the thing came, and perceiving God by understanding what is, becomes more of a man, more of the being he was meant to be. In virtue of this truth perceived, he has relations with the universe undeveloped in him till then. But far higher will the doing of the least, the most insignificant duty raise him. He begins thereby to be a true man. A man may delight in the vision and glory of a truth, and not himself be true. The man whose vision is weak, but who, as far as he sees, and desirous to see farther, does the thing he sees, is a true man. If a man knows what is, and says it is not, his knowing does not make him less than a liar. The man who recognizes the truth of any human relation, and neglects the duty involved, is not a true man. The man who knows the laws of nature, and does not heed them, the more he teaches them to others, the less is he a true man. But he may obey them all and be the falsest of men, because of far higher and closer duties which he neglects. The man who takes good care of himself and none of his brother and sister,

285

is false. A man may be a poet, aware of the highest truth of a thing, of that beauty which is the final cause of its existence; he may draw thence a notion of the creative loveliness that thought it out; he may be a man who would not tell a lie, or steal, or slander—and yet he may not be a true man, inasmuch as the essentials of manhood are not his aim: having nowise come to the flower of his own being, nowise, in his higher degree, attained the truth of *a thing*—namely, that for which he exists, the creational notion of him—neither is he striving after the same. There are relations closer than those of the facts around him, plainer than those that seem to bring the maker nigh to him, which he is failing to see, or seeing fails to acknowledge, or acknowledging fails to fulfil. Man is man only in the doing of the truth, perfect man only in the doing of the highest truth, which is the fulfilling of his relations to his origin. But he has relations with his fellow man, closer infinitely than with any of the things around him, and to many a man far plainer than his relations with God. Now the nearer is plainer that he may step on it, and rise to the higher, till then the less plain. These relations make a large part of his being, are essential to his very existence, and spring from the very facts of the origination of his being. They are the relation of thought to thought, of being to being, of duty to duty. The very nature of a man depends upon or is one with these relations. They are *truths*, and the man is a true man as he fulfils them. Fulfilling them perfectly, he is himself a *truth*, a living truth. As regarded merely by the intellect, these relations are facts of man's nature; but that they are of man's nature makes them truths, and the fulfilments of them are duties. He is so constituted as to understand them at first more than he can love them, with the resulting advantage of having thereby the opportunity of choosing them purely because they are true; so doing he chooses to love them, and is enabled to love them in the doing, which alone can truly reveal them to him, and make the loving of them possible. Then they cease to show themselves in the form of duties, and appear as they more truly are, absolute truths, essential realities, eternal delights. The man is a true man who chooses duty; he is a perfect man who at length never thinks of duty, who forgets the name of it. The duty of Jesus was the doing in lower forms than the perfect that which he loved perfectly, and did perfectly in the highest forms also. Thus he fulfilled all righteousness. One who went to the truth by mere impulse, would be a holy animal, not a true man. Relations, truths, duties, are shown to the man away beyond him, that he may choose them, and be a child of God, choosing righteousness like him. Hence the whole sad victorious human tale, and the glory to be revealed!

The moral philosopher who regards duties only as facts of his system; nay, even the man who rewards them as truths, essential realities of his humanity, but goes no farther, is essentially a liar, a man of untruth. He is a man indeed, but not a true man. He is a man in possibility, but not a real man yet. The recognition of these things is the imperative obligation to fulfil them. Not fulfilling these relations, the man is undoing the right of his own existence, destroying his *raison d'etre*, making of himself a monster, a live reason why he should not live, for nothing on those terms could ever have begun to be. His presence is a claim upon his creator for destruction.

The facts of human relation, then, are truths indeed, and of awfullest import. 'Whosoever hateth his brother is a murderer; and ye know that no murderer hath eternal life abiding in him!' The man who lives a hunter after pleasure, not a labourer in the fields of duty, who thinks of himself as if he were alone on the earth, is in himself a lie. Instead of being the man he looks, the man he was made to be, he lives as the beasts seem to live—with this difference, I trust, that they are rising, while he, so far as lies in himself, is sinking. But he cannot be allowed to sink beyond God's reach; hence all the holy—that is, healing—miseries that come upon him, of which he complains as so hard and unfair: they are for the compelling of the truth he will not yield—a painful suasion to be himself, to be a truth.

But suppose, for the sake of my progressive unfolding, that a man did everything required of him—fulfilled all the relations to his fellows of which I have been speaking, was toward them at least, a true man; he would yet feel, doubtless would feel it the more, that something was lacking to him—lacking to his necessary well-being. Like a live flower, he would feel that he had not yet blossomed, and could not tell what the blossom ought to be. In this direction the words of the Lord point, when he says to the youth, 'If thou wouldst be perfect.' The man whom I suppose, would feel that his existence was not yet justified to itself, that the truth of his being and nature was not yet revealed to his consciousness. He would remain unsatisfied; and the cause would be that there was in him a relation, and that the deepest, closest, and strongest, which had not yet come into live fact, which had not yet become a truth in him, toward which he was not true, whereby his being remained untrue, he was not himself, was not ripened into the divine idea, which alone can content itself. A child with a child's heart who does not even know that he has a father, yet misses him—with his whole nature, even if not with his consciousness. This relation has not yet so far begun to be fulfilled in him, as that the coming blossom should send before it patience and hope enough to enable him to live by faith without sight. When the flower begins to come, the human plant begins to rejoice in the glory of God not yet revealed, the inheritance of the saints in light; with uplifted stem and forward-leaning bud expects the hour when the lily of God's field shall know itself alive, with God himself for its heart and its atmosphere; the hour when God and the man shall be one, and all that God cares for shall be the man's. But again I forget my progression.

The highest truth to the intellect, the abstract truth, is the relation in which man stands to the source of his being—his will to the will whence it became a will, his love to the love that kindled his power to love, his intellect to the intellect that lighted his. If a man deal with these things only as things to be dealt with, as objects of thought, as ideas to be analysed and arranged in their due order and right relation, he treats them as facts and not as truths, and is no better, probably much the worse, for his converse with them, for he knows in a measure, and is false to all that is most worthy of his faithfulness.

But when the soul, or heart, or spirit, or what you please to call that which is the man himself and not his body, sooner or later becomes aware that he needs some one above him, whom to obey, in whom to rest, from whom to seek deliverance from what in himself is despicable, disappointing, unworthy even of his own interest; when he is aware of an opposition in him, which is not harmony; that, while he hates it, there is yet present with him, and seeming to be himself, what sometimes he calls *the old Adam*, sometimes *the flesh*, sometimes *his lower nature*, sometimes *his evil self*; and sometimes recognizes as simply that part of his being where God is not; then indeed is the man in the region of truth, and beginning to come true in himself. Nor will it be long ere he discover that there is no part in him with which he would be at strife, so God were there, so that it were true, what it ought to be—in right relation to the whole; for, by whatever name called, the old Adam, or antecedent horse, or dog, or tiger, it would then fulfil its part holily, intruding upon nothing, subject utterly to the rule of the higher; horse or dog or tiger, it would be good horse, good dog, good tiger.

When the man bows down before a power that can account for him, a power to whom he is no mystery as he is to himself; a power that knows whence he came and whither he is going; who knows why he loves this and hates that, why and where he began to go wrong; who can set him right, longs indeed to set him right, making of him a creature to look up to himself without shadow of doubt, anxiety or fear, confident as a child whom his father is leading by the hand to the heights of happy-making truth, knowing that where he is wrong, the father is right and will set him right; when the man feels his whole being in the embrace of self-responsible paternity—then the man is bursting into his flower; then the truth of his being, the eternal fact at the root of his new name, his real nature, his idea—born in God at first, and responsive to the truth, the being of God, his origin—begins to show itself; then his nature is almost in harmony with itself. For, obeying the will that is the cause of his being, the cause of that which demands of itself to be true, and that will being righteousness and love and truth, he begins to stand on the apex of his being, to know himself divine. He begins to feel himself free. The truth—not as known to his intellect, but as revealed in his own sense of being true, known by his essential consciousness of his divine condition, without which his nature is neither his own nor God's—trueness has made him free. Not any abstract truth, not all abstract truth, not truth its very metaphysical self, held by purest insight into entity, can make any man free; but the truth done, the truth loved, the truth lived by the man; the truth *of* and not merely *in* the man himself; the honesty that makes the man himself a child of the honest God.

When a man is, with his whole nature, loving and willing the truth, he is then a live truth. But this he has not originated in himself. He has seen it and striven for it, but not originated it. The one originating, living, visible truth, embracing all truths in all relations, is Jesus Christ. He is true; he is the live Truth. His truth, chosen and willed by him, the ripeness of his being, the flower of his sonship which is his nature, the crown of his one topmost perfect relation acknowledged and gloried in, is his absolute obedience to his father. The obedient Jesus is Jesus the Truth. He is true and the root of all truth and development of truth in men. Their very being, however far from the true human, is the undeveloped Christ in them, and his likeness to Christ is the truth of a man, even as the perfect meaning of a flower is the truth of a flower. Every man, according to the divine idea of him, must come to the truth of that idea; and under every form of Christ is the Christ. The truth of every man, I say, is the perfected Christ in him. As Christ is the blossom of humanity, so the blossom of every man is the Christ perfected in him. The vital force of humanity working in him is Christ; he is his root—the generator and perfecter of his individuality. The stronger the pure will of the man to be true; the freer and more active his choice; the more definite his individuality, ever the more is the man and all that is his, Christ's. Without him he could not have been; being, he could not have become capable of truth; capable of truth, he could never have loved it; loving and desiring it, he could not have attained to it. Nothing but the heart-presence, the humanest sympathy, and whatever deeper thing else may be betwixt the creating Truth and the responding soul, could make a man go on hoping, until at last he forget himself, and keep open house for God to come and go. He gives us the will wherewith to will, and the power to use it, and the help needed to supplement the power, whatever in any case the need may be; but we ourselves must will the truth, and for that the Lord is waiting, for the victory of God his father in the heart of his child. In this alone can he see of the travail of his soul, in this alone be satisfied. The work is his, but we must take our willing share. When the blossom breaks forth in us, the more it is ours the more it is his, for the highest creation of the Father, and that pre-eminently through the Son, is the being that can, like the Father and the Son, of his own self will what is right. The groaning and travailing, the blossom and the joy, are the Father's and the Son's and ours. The will, the power of willing, may be created, but the willing is begotten. Because God wills first, man wills also.

When my being is consciously and willedly in the hands of him who called it to live and think and suffer and be glad—given back to him by a perfect obedience—I thenceforward breathe the breath, share the life of God himself. Then I am free, in that I am true—which means one with the Father. And freedom knows itself to be freedom. When a man is true, if he were in hell he could not be miserable. He is right with himself because right with him whence he came. To be right with God is to be right with the universe; one with the power, the love, the will of the mighty Father, the cherisher of joy, the lord of laughter, whose are all glories, all hopes, who loves everything, and hates nothing but selfishness, which he will not have in his kingdom.

Christ then is the Lord of life; his life is the light of men; the light mirrored in them changes them into the image of him, the Truth; and thus *the truth, who is the Son, makes them free.*

FREEDOM.

The Truth shall make you free…. Whosoever committeth sin, is the servant of sin. And the servant abideth not in the house for ever: but the Son abideth ever. If the Son therefore shall make you free, ye shall be free indeed.—John viii. 32, 34-36.

As this passage stands, I have not been able to make sense of it. No man could be in the house of the Father in virtue of being the servant of sin; yet this man is in the house as a servant, and the house in which he serves is not the house of sin, but the house of the Father. The utterance is confused at best, and the reasoning faulty. He must be in the house of the Father on some other ground than sin. This, had no help come, would have been sufficient cause for leaving the passage alone, as one where, perhaps, the words of the Lord were misrepresented— where, at least, perceiving more than one fundamental truth involved in the passage, I failed to follow the argument. I do not see that I could ever have suggested where the corruption, if any, lay. Most difficulties of similar nature have originated, like this, I can hardly doubt, with some scribe who, desiring to explain what he did not understand, wrote his worthless gloss on the margin: the next copier took the words for an omission that ought to be replaced in the body of the text, and inserting them, falsified the utterance, and greatly obscured its intention. What do we not owe to the critics who have searched the scriptures, and found what really was written! In the present case, Dr. Westcott's notation gives us to understand that there is another with 'a reasonable probability of being the true reading.' The difference is indeed small to the eye, but is great enough to give us fine gold instead of questionable ore. In an alternative of the kind, I must hope in what seems logical against what seems illogical; in what seems radiant against what seems trite.

What I take for the true reading then, I English thus: 'Every one committing sin is a slave. But the slave does not remain in the house for ever; the son remaineth for ever. If then the son shall make you free, you shall in reality be free.' The authorized version gives, 'Whosoever committeth sin, is the servant of *sin*; 'the revised version gives, 'Every one that committeth sin is the bondservant of *sin*;' both accepting the reading that has the words, '*of sin*.' The statement is certainly in itself true, but appears to me useless for the argument that follows. And I think it may have been what I take to be the true reading, that suggested to the apostle Paul what he says in the beginning of the fourth chapter of his Epistle to the Galatians—words of spirit and life from which has been mistakenly drawn the doctrine of adoption, merest poison to the child-heart. The words of the Lord here are not that he who sins is the slave of sin, true utterly as that is; but that he is a slave, and the argument shows that he means a slave to God. The two are perfectly consistent. No amount of slavery to sin can keep a man from being as much the slave of God as God chooses in his mercy to make him. It is his sin makes him a slave instead of a child. His slavery to sin is his ruin; his slavery to God is his only hope. God indeed does not love slavery; he hates it; he will have children, not slaves; but he may keep a slave in his house a long time in the hope of waking up the poor slavish nature to aspire to the sonship which belongs to him, which is his birthright. But the slave is not to be in the house for ever. The father is not bound to keep his son a slave because the foolish child prefers it.

Whoever will not do what God desires of him, is a slave whom God can compel to do it, however he may bear with him. He who, knowing this, or fearing punishment, obeys God, is still a slave, but a slave who comes within hearing of the voice of his master. There are, however, far higher than he, who yet are but slaves. Those to whom God is not all in all, are slaves. They may not commit great sins; they may be trying to do right; but so long as they *serve* God, as they call it, from duty, and do not know him as their father, the joy of their being, they are slaves—good slaves, but slaves. If they did not try to do their duty, they would be bad slaves. They are by no means so slavish as those that serve from fear, but they are slaves; and because they are but slaves, they can fulfil no righteousness, can do no duty perfectly, but must ever be trying after it wearily and in pain, knowing well that if they stop trying, they are lost. They are slaves indeed, for they would be glad to be adopted by one who is their own father! Where then are the sons? I know none, I answer, who are yet utterly and entirely sons or daughters. There may be such—God knows; I have not known them; or, knowing them, have not been myself such as to be able to recognize them. But I do know some who are enough sons and daughters to be at war with the slave in them, who are not content to be slaves to their father. Nothing I have seen or known of sonship, comes near the glory of the thing; but there are thousands of sons and daughters, though their number be yet only a remnant, who are siding with the father of their spirits against themselves, against all that divides them from him from whom they have come, but out of whom they have never come, seeing that in him they live and move and have their being. Such are not slaves; they are true though not perfect children; they are fighting along with God against the evil separation; they are breaking at the middle wall of partition. Only the rings of their fetters are left, and they are struggling to take them off. They are children—with more or less of the dying slave in them; they know it is there, and what it is, and hate the slavery in them, and try to slay it. The real slave is he who does not seek to be a child; who does not desire to end his slavery; who looks upon the claim of the child as presumption; who cleaves to the traditional authorized service of forms and ceremonies, and does not know the will of him who made the seven stars and Orion, much less cares to obey it; who never lifts up his heart to cry 'Father, what wouldst thou have me to do?' Such are continually betraying their slavery by their complaints. 'Do we not well to be angry?' they cry with Jonah; and, truly, being slaves, I do not know how they are to help it. When they are sons and daughters, they will no longer complain of the hardships, and miseries, and troubles of life; no longer grumble at their aches and pains, at the pinching of their poverty, at the hunger that assails them; no longer be indignant at their rejection by what is called Society. Those who believe in their own perfect father, can ill blame him for anything they do not like. Ah, friend, it may be you and I are slaves, but there *are* such sons and daughters as I speak of.

The slaves of sin rarely grumble at that slavery; it is their slavery to God they grumble at; of that alone they complain—of the painful messengers he sends to deliver them from their slavery both to sin and to himself. They must be sons or slaves. They cannot rid themselves of their owner. Whether they deny God, or mock him by acknowledging and not heeding him, or treat him as an arbitrary, formal monarch; whether, taking no trouble to find out what pleases him, they do dull things for his service he cares nothing about, or try to propitiate him by assuming with strenuous effort some yoke the Son never wore, and never called on them to wear, they are slaves, and not the less slaves that they are slaves to God; they are so thoroughly slaves, that they do not care to get out of their slavery by becoming sons and daughters, by finding the good of life where alone it can or could lie. Could a creator make a creature whose well-being should not depend on himself? And if he could, would the creature be the greater for that? Which, the creature he made more, or the creature he made less dependent on himself, would be the greater? The slave in heart would immediately, with Milton's Satan, reply, that the farthest from him who made him must be the freest, thus acknowledging his very existence a slavery, and but two kinds in being—a creator, and as many slaves as he pleases to make, whose refusal to obey is their unknown protest against their own essence. *Being* itself must, for what they call liberty, be repudiated! Creation itself, to go by their lines of life, is an injustice! God had no right to create beings less than himself; and as he could not create equal, he ought not to have created! But they do not complain of having been created; they complain of being required to do justice. They will not obey, but, his own handiwork, ravish from his work every advantage they can! They desire to be free with another kind of freedom than that with which God is free; unknowing, they seek a more complete slavery. There is, in truth, no mid way between absolute harmony with the Father and the condition of slaves—submissive, or rebellious. If the latter, their very rebellion is by the strength of the Father in them. Of divine essence, they thrust their existence in the face of their essence, their own nature.

Yet is their very rebellion in some sense but the rising in them of his spirit against their false notion of him—against the lies they hold concerning him. They do not see that, if his work, namely, they themselves, are the chief joy to themselves, much more might the life that works them be a glory and joy to them the work—inasmuch as it is nearer to them than they to themselves, causing them to be, and extends, without breach of relation, so infinitely above and beyond them. For nothing can come so close as that which creates; the nearest, strongest, dearest relation possible is between creator and created. Where this is denied, the schism is the widest; where it is acknowledged and fulfilled, the closeness is unspeakable. But ever remains what cannot be said, and I sink defeated. The very protest of the rebel against slavery, comes at once of the truth of God in him, which he cannot all cast from him, and of a slavery too low to love truth—a meanness that will take all and acknowledge nothing, as if his very being was a disgrace to him. The liberty of the God that would have his creature free, is in contest with the slavery of the creature who would cut his own stem from his root that he might call it his own and love it; who rejoices in his own consciousness, instead of the life of that consciousness; who poises himself on the tottering wall of his own being, instead of the rock on which that being is built. Such a one regards his own dominion over himself—the rule of the greater by the less, inasmuch as the conscious self is less than the self—as a freedom infinitely greater than the range of the universe of God's being. If he says, 'At least I have it my own way!' I answer, You do not know what is your way and what is not. You know nothing of whence your impulses, your desires, your tendencies, your likings come. They may spring now from some chance, as of nerves diseased; now from some roar of a wandering bodiless devil; now from some infant hate in your heart; now from the greed or lawlessness of some ancestor you would be ashamed of if you knew him; or it may be now from some far-piercing chord of a heavenly orchestra: the moment it comes up into your consciousness, you call it your own way, and glory in it! Two devils amusing themselves with a duet of inspiration, one at each ear, might soon make that lordly *me* you are so in love with, rejoice in the freedom of willing the opposite each alternate moment; and at length drive you mad at finding that you could not, will as you would, make choice of a way and its opposite simultaneously. The whole question rests and turns on the relation of creative and created, of which relation few seem to have the consciousness yet developed. To live without the eternal creative life is an impossibility; freedom from God can only mean an incapacity for seeing the facts of existence, an incapability of understanding the glory of the creature who makes common cause with his creator in his creation of him, who wills that the lovely will calling him into life and giving him choice, should finish making him, should draw him into the circle of the creative heart, to joy that he lives by no poor power of his own will, but is one with the causing life of his life, in closest breathing and willing, vital and claimant oneness with the life of all life. Such a creature knows the life of the infinite Father as the very flame of his life, and joys that nothing is done or will be done in the universe in which the Father will not make him all of a sharer that it is possible for perfect generosity to make him. If you say this is irreverent, I doubt if you have seen the God manifest in Jesus. But all will be well, for the little god of your poor content will starve your soul to misery, and the terror of the eternal death creeping upon you, will compel you to seek a perfect father. Oh, ye hide-bound Christians, the Lord is not straitened, but ye are straitened in your narrow unwilling souls! Some of you need to be shamed before yourselves; some of you need the fire.

But one who reads may call out, in the agony and thirst of a child waking from a dream of endless seeking and no finding, 'I am bound like Lazarus in his grave-clothes! what am I to do?' Here is the answer, drawn from this parable of our Lord; for the saying is much like a parable, teaching more than it utters, appealing to the conscience and heart, not to the understanding: You are a slave; the slave has no hold on the house; only the sons and daughters have an abiding rest in the home of their father. God cannot have slaves about him always. You must give up your slavery, and be set free from it. That is what I am here for. If I make you free, you shall be free indeed; for I can make you free only by making you what you were meant to be, sons like myself. That is how alone the Son can work. But it is you who must become sons; you must will it, and I am here to help you.' It is as if he said, 'You shall have the freedom of my father's universe; for, free from yourselves, you will be free of his heart. Yourselves are your slavery. That is the darkness which you have loved rather than the light. You have given honour to yourselves, and not to the Father; you have sought honour from men, and not from the Father! Therefore, even in the house of your father, you have been but sojourning slaves. We in his family are all one; we have no party-spirit; we have no self-seeking: fall in with us, and you shall be free as we are free.'

If then the poor starved child cry—'How, Lord?' the answer will depend on what he means by that *how*. If he means, 'What plan wilt thou adopt? What is thy scheme for cutting my bonds and setting me free?' the answer may be a deepening of the darkness, a tightening of the bonds. But if he means, 'Lord, what wouldst thou have me to do?' the answer will not tarry. 'Give yourself to me to do what I tell you, to understand what I say, to be my good, obedient little brother, and I will wake in you the heart that my father put in you, the same kind of heart that I have, and it will grow to love the Father, altogether and absolutely, as mine does, till you are ready to be torn to pieces for him. Then you will know that you are at the heart of the universe, at the heart of every secret—at the heart of the Father. Not till then will you be free, then free indeed!'

Christ died to save us, not from suffering, but from ourselves; not from injustice, far less from justice, but from being unjust. He died that we might live—but live as he lives, by dying as he died who died to himself that he might live unto God. If we do not die to ourselves, we cannot live to God, and he that does not live to God, is dead. 'Ye shall know the truth,' the Lord says, 'and the truth shall make you free. I am the truth, and you shall be free as I am free. To be free, you must be sons like me. To be free you must *be* that which you have to be, that which you are created. To be free you must give the answer of sons to the Father who calls you. To be free you must fear nothing but evil, care for nothing but the will of the Father, hold to him in absolute confidence and infinite expectation. He alone is to be trusted.' He has shown us the Father not only by doing what the Father does, not only by loving his Father's children even as the Father loves them, but by his perfect satisfaction with him, his joy in him, his utter obedience to him. He has shown us the Father by the absolute devotion of a perfect son. He is the Son of God because the Father and he are one, have one thought, one mind, one heart. Upon this truth—I do not mean the dogma, but the truth itself of Jesus to his father—hangs the universe; and upon the recognition of this truth—that is, upon their becoming thus true—hangs the freedom of the children, the redemption of their whole world. 'I and the Father are one,' is the centre-truth of the Universe; and the circumfering truth is, 'that they also may be one in us.'

The only free man, then, is he who is a child of the Father. He is a servant of all, but can be made the slave of none: he is a son of the lord of the universe. He is in himself, in virtue of his truth, free. He is in himself a king. For the Son rests his claim to royalty on this, that *he was born and came into the world to bear witness to the truth.*

KINGSHIP.

Art thou a king then? Jesus answered, Thou sayest that I am a king! To this end was I born, and for this cause came I into the world, that I should bear witness unto the truth: every one that is of the truth heareth my voice.—John xviii. 37.

Pilate asks Jesus if he is a king. The question is called forth by what the Lord had just said concerning his kingdom, closing with the statement that it was not of this world. He now answers Pilate that he is a king indeed, but shows him that his kingdom is of a very different kind from what is called kingdom in this world. The rank and rule of this world are uninteresting to him. He might have had them. Calling his disciples to follow him, and his twelve legions of angels to help them, he might soon have driven the Romans into the abyss, piling them on the heap of nations they had tumbled there before. What easier for him than thus to have cleared the way, and over the tributary world reigned the just monarch that was the dream of the Jews, never seen in Israel or elsewhere, but haunting the hopes and longings of the poor and their helpers! He might from Jerusalem have ruled the world, not merely dispensing what men call justice, but compelling atonement. He did not care for government. No such kingdom would serve the ends of his father in heaven, or comfort his own soul. What was perfect empire to the Son of God, while he might teach one human being to love his neighbour, and be good like his father! To be love-helper to one heart, for its joy, and the glory of his father, was the beginning of true kingship! The Lord would rather wash the feet of his weary brothers, than be the one only perfect monarch that ever ruled in the world. It was empire he rejected when he ordered Satan behind him like a dog to his heel. Government, I repeat, was to him flat, stale, unprofitable.

What then is the kingdom over which the Lord cares to reign, for he says he came into the world to be a king? I answer, A kingdom of kings, and no other. Where every man is a king, there and there only does the Lord care to reign, in the name of his father. As no king in Europe would care to reign over a cannibal, a savage, or an animal race, so the Lord cares for no kingdom over anything this world calls a nation. A king must rule over his own kind. Jesus is a king in virtue of no conquest, inheritance, or election, but in right of essential being; and he cares for no subjects but such as are his subjects in the same right. His subjects must be of his own kind, in their very nature and essence kings. To understand his answer to Pilate, see wherein consists his kingship; what it is that makes him a king; what manifestation of his essential being gives him a claim to be king. The Lord's is a kingdom in which no man seeks to be above another: ambition is of the dirt of this world's kingdoms. He says, 'I am a king, for I was born for the purpose, I came into the world with the object of bearing witness to the truth. Everyone that is of my kind, that is of the truth, hears my voice. He is a king like me, and makes one of my subjects.' Pilate thereupon—as would most Christians nowadays, instead of setting about being true—requests a definition of truth, a presentation to his intellect in set terms of what the word 'truth' means; but instantly, whether confident of the uselessness of the inquiry, or intending to resume it when he has set the Lord at liberty, goes out to the people to tell them he finds no fault in him. Whatever interpretation we put on his action here, he must be far less worthy of blame than those 'Christians' who, instead of setting themselves to be pure 'even as he is pure,' to be their brother and sister's keeper, and to serve God by being honourable in shop and counting-house and labour-market, proceed to 'serve' him, some by going to church or chapel, some by condemning the opinions of their neighbours, some by teaching others what they do not themselves heed. Neither Pilate nor they ask the one true question, 'How am I to be a true man? How am I to become a man worth being a man?' The Lord is a king because his life, the life of his thoughts, of his imagination, of his will, of every smallest action, is true—true first to God in that he is altogether his, true to himself in that he forgets himself altogether, and true to his fellows in that he will endure anything they do to him, nor cease declaring himself the son and messenger and likeness of God. They will kill him, but it matters not: the truth is as he says!

Jesus is a king because his business is to bear witness to the truth. What truth? All truth; all verity of relation throughout the universe— first of all, that his father is good, perfectly good; and that the crown and joy of life is to desire and do the will of the eternal source of will, and of all life. He deals thus the death-blow to the power of hell. For the one principle of hell is—'I am my own. I am my own king and my own subject. *I* am the centre from which go out my thoughts; *I* am the object and end of my thoughts; back upon *me* as the alpha and omega of life, my thoughts return. My own glory is, and ought to be, my chief care; my ambition, to gather the regards of men to the one centre, my-self. My pleasure is *my* pleasure. My kingdom is—as many as I can bring to acknowledge my greatness over them. My judgment is the faultless rule of things. My right is—what I desire. The more I am all in all to myself, the greater I am. The less I acknowledge debt or obli-gation to another; the more I close my eyes to the fact that I did not make myself; the more self-sufficing I feel or imagine myself—the greater I am. I will be free with the freedom that consists in doing whatever I am inclined to do, from whatever quarter may come the inclination. To do my own will so long as I feel anything to be my will, is to be free, is to live. To all these principles of hell, or of this world—they are the same thing, and it matters nothing whether they are asserted or defended so long as they are acted upon—the Lord, the king, gives the direct lie. It is as if he said:—'I ought to know what I say, for I have been from all eternity the son of him from whom you issue, and whom you call your father, but whom you will not have your father: I know all he thinks and is; and I say this, that my perfect freedom, my pure individuality, rests on the fact that I have not anoth-er will than his. My will is all for his will, for his will is right. He is righteousness itself. His very being is love and equity and self-devotion, and he will have his children such as himself—creatures of love, of fairness, of self-devotion to him and their fellows. I was born to bear witness to the truth—in my own person to be the truth visi-ble—the very likeness and manifestation of the God who is true. My very being is his witness. Every fact of me witnesses him. He is the truth, and I am the truth. Kill me, but while I live I say, Such as I am he is. If I said I did not know him, I should be a liar. I fear nothing you can do to me. Shall the king who comes to say what is true, turn his back for fear of men? My Father is like me; I know it, and I say it. You do not like to hear it because you are not like him. I am low in your eyes which measure things by their show; therefore you say I blas-pheme. I should blaspheme if I said he was such as anything you are capable of imagining him, for you love show, and power, and the praise of men. I do not, and God is like me. I came into the world to show him. I am a king because he sent me to bear witness to his truth, and I bear it. Kill me, and I will rise again. You can kill me, but you cannot hold me dead. Death is my servant; you are the slaves of Death because you will not be true, and let the truth make you free. Bound, and in your hands, I am free as God, for God is my father. I know I shall suffer, suffer unto death, but if you knew my father, you would not wonder that I am ready; you would be ready too. He is my strength. My father is greater than I.'

Remember, friends, I said, 'It is as if he said.' I am daring to present a shadow of the Lord's witnessing, a shadow surely cast by his deeds and his very words! If I mistake, he will forgive me. I do not fear him; I fear only lest, able to see and write these things, I should fail of witnessing, and myself be, after all, a castaway—no king, but a talker; no disciple of Jesus, ready to go with him to the death, but an arguer about the truth; a hater of the lies men speak for God, and myself a truth-speaking liar, not a doer of the word.

We see, then, that the Lord bore his witness to the Truth, to the one God, by standing just what he was, before the eyes and the lies of men. The true king is the man who stands up a true man and speaks the truth, and will die but not lie. The robes of such a king may be rags or purple; it matters neither way. The rags are the more likely, but neither better nor worse than the robes. Then was the Lord dressed most royally when his robes were a jest, a mockery, a laughter. Of the men who before Christ bare witness to the truth, some were sawn asunder, some subdued kingdoms; it mattered nothing which: they witnessed.

The truth is God; the witness to the truth is Jesus. The kingdom of the truth is the hearts of men. The bliss of men is the true God. The thought of God is the truth of everything. All well-being lies in true relation to God. The man who responds to this with his whole being, is of the truth. The man who knows these things, and but knows them; the man who sees them to be true, and does not order life and action, judgment and love by them, is of the worst of lying; with hand, and foot, and face he casts scorn upon that which his tongue confesses.

Little thought the sons of Zebedee and their ambitious mother what the earthly throne of Christ's glory was which they and she begged they might share. For the king crowned by his witnessing, witnessed then to the height of his uttermost argument, when he hung upon the cross—like a sin, as Paul in his boldness expresses it. When his witness is treated as a lie, then most he witnesses, for he gives it still.

High and lifted up on the throne of his witness, on the cross of his torture, he holds to it: 'I and the Father are one.' Every mockery borne in witnessing, is a witnessing afresh. Infinitely more than had he sat on the throne of the whole earth, did Jesus witness to the truth when Pilate brought him out for the last time, and perhaps made him sit on the judgment-seat in his mockery of kingly garments and royal insignia, saying, 'Behold your king!' Just because of those robes and that crown, that sceptre and that throne of ridicule, he was the only real king that ever sat on any throne.

Is every Christian expected to bear witness? A man content to bear no witness to the truth is not in the kingdom of heaven. One who believes must bear witness. One who sees the truth, must live witnessing to it. Is our life, then, a witnessing to the truth? Do we carry ourselves in bank, on farm, in house or shop, in study or chamber or workshop, as the Lord would, or as the Lord would not? Are we careful to be true? Do we endeavour to live to the height of our ideas? Or are we mean, self-serving, world-flattering, fawning slaves? When contempt is cast on the truth, do we smile? Wronged in our presence, do we make no sign that we hold by it? I do not say we are called upon to dispute, and defend with logic and argument, but we are called upon to show that we are on the other side. But when I say *truth,* I do not mean *opinion*: to treat opinion as if that were truth, is grievously to wrong the truth. The soul that loves the truth and tries to be true, will know when to speak and when to be silent; but the true man will never look as if he did not care. We are not bound to say all we think, but we are bound not even to look what we do not think. The girl who said before a company of mocking companions, 'I believe in Jesus,' bore true witness to her Master, the Truth. David bore witness to God, the Truth, when he said, '*Unto thee, O Lord, belongeth mercy, for thou renderest to every man according to his work.*'

JUSTICE.

Also unto thee, O Lord, belongeth mercy; for thou renderest to every man according to his work.— Psalm lxii. 12.

Some of the translators make it *kindness* and *goodness*; but I presume there is no real difference among them as to the character of the word which here, in the English Bible, is translated mercy.

The religious mind, however, educated upon the theories yet prevailing in the so-called religious world, must here recognize a departure from the presentation to which they have been accustomed: to make the psalm speak according to prevalent theoretic modes, the verse would have to be changed thus:—'To thee, O Lord, belongeth justice, for thou renderest to every man according to his work.'

Let the reason of my choosing this passage, so remarkable in itself, for a motto to the sermon which follows, remain for the present doubtful. I need hardly say that I mean to found no logical argument upon it.

Let us endeavour to see plainly what we mean when we use the word *justice,* and whether we mean what we ought to mean when we use it—especially with reference to God. Let us come nearer to knowing what we ought to understand by justice, that is, the justice of God; for his justice is the live, active justice, giving existence to the idea of justice in our minds and hearts. Because he is just, we are capable of knowing justice; it is because he is just, that we have the idea of justice so deeply imbedded in us.

What do we oftenest mean by *justice*? Is it not the carrying out of the law, the infliction of penalty assigned to offence? By a just judge we mean a man who administers the law without prejudice, without favour or dislike; and where guilt is manifest, punishes as much as, and no more than, the law has in the case laid down. It may not be that justice has therefore been done. The law itself may be unjust, and the judge may mistake; or, which is more likely, the working of the law may be foiled by the parasites of law for their own gain. But even if the law be good, and thoroughly administered, it does not necessarily follow that justice is done.

Suppose my watch has been taken from my pocket; I lay hold of the thief; he is dragged before the magistrate, proved guilty, and sentenced to a just imprisonment: must I walk home satisfied with the result? Have I had justice done me? The thief may have had justice done him—but where is my watch? That is gone, and I remain a man wronged. Who has done me the wrong? The thief. Who can set right the wrong? The thief, and only the thief; nobody but the man that did the wrong. God may be able to move the man to right the wrong, but God himself cannot right it without the man. Suppose my watch found and restored, is the account settled between me and the thief? I may forgive him, but is the wrong removed? By no means. But suppose the thief to bethink himself, to repent. He has, we shall say, put it out of his power to return the watch, but he comes to me and says he is sorry he stole it and begs me to accept for the present what little he is able to bring, as a beginning of atonement: how should I then regard the matter? Should I not feel that he had gone far to make atonement—done more to make up for the injury he had inflicted upon me, than the mere restoration of the watch, even by himself, could reach to? Would there not lie, in the thief's confession and submission and initial restoration, an appeal to the divinest in me—to the eternal brotherhood? Would it not indeed amount to a sufficing atonement as between man and man? If he offered to bear what I chose to lay upon him, should I feel it necessary, for the sake of justice, to inflict some certain suffering as demanded by righteousness? I should still have a claim upon him for my watch, but should I not be apt to forget it? He who commits the offence can make up for it—and he alone.

One thing must surely be plain—that the punishment of the wrongdoer makes no atonement for the wrong done. How could it make up to me for the stealing of my watch that the man was punished? The wrong would be there all the same. I am not saying the man ought not to be punished—far from it; I am only saying that the punishment nowise makes up to the man wronged. Suppose the man, with the watch in his pocket, were to inflict the severest flagellation on himself: would that lessen my sense of injury? Would it set anything right? Would it anyway atone? Would it give him a right to the watch? Punishment may do good to the man who does the wrong, but that is a thing as different as important.

Another thing plain is, that, even without the material rectification of the wrong where that is impossible, repentance removes the offence which no suffering could. I at least should feel that I had no more quarrel with the man. I should even feel that the gift he had made me, giving into my heart a repentant brother, was infinitely beyond the restitution of what he had taken from me. True, he owed me both himself and the watch, but such a greater does more than include such a less. If it be objected, 'You may forgive, but the man has sinned against God!'—Then it is not a part of the divine to be merciful, I return, and a man may be more merciful than his maker! A man may do that which would be too merciful in God! Then mercy is not a divine attribute, for it may exceed and be too much; it must not be infinite, therefore cannot be God's own.

'Mercy may be against justice.' Never—if you mean by justice what I mean by justice. If anything be against justice, it cannot be called mercy, for it is cruelty. '*To thee, O Lord, belongeth mercy, for thou renderest to every man according to his work.*' There is *no* opposition, *no* strife whatever, between mercy and justice. Those who say justice means the punishing of sin, and mercy the not punishing of sin, and attribute both to God, would make a schism in the very idea of God. And this brings me to the question, What is meant by divine justice?

Human justice may be a poor distortion of justice, a mere shadow of it; but the justice of God must be perfect. We cannot frustrate it in its working; are we just to it in our idea of it? If you ask any ordinary Sunday congregation in England, what is meant by the justice of God, would not nineteen out of twenty answer, that it means his punishing of sin? Think for a moment what degree of justice it would indicate in a man—that he punished every wrong. A Roman emperor, a Turkish cadi, might do that, and be the most unjust both of men and judges. Ahab might be just on the throne of punishment, and in his garden the murderer of Naboth. In God shall we imagine a distinction of office and character? God is one; and the depth of foolishness is reached by that theology which talks of God as if he held different offices, and differed in each. It sets a contradiction in the very nature of God himself. It represents him, for instance, as having to do that as a magistrate which as a father he would not do! The love of the father makes him desire to be unjust as a magistrate! Oh the folly of any mind that would explain God before obeying him! that would map out the character of God, instead of crying, Lord, what wouldst thou have me to do? God is no magistrate; but, if he were, it would be a position to which his fatherhood alone gave him the right; his rights as a father cover every right he can be analytically supposed to possess. The justice of God is this, that—to use a boyish phrase, the best the language will now afford me because of misuse—he gives every man, woman, child, and beast, everything that has being, *fair play*; he renders to every man according to his work; and therein lies his perfect mercy; for nothing else could be merciful to the man, and nothing but mercy could be fair to him. God does nothing of which any just man, the thing set fairly and fully before him so that he understood, would not say, 'That is fair.' Who would, I repeat, say a man was a just man because he insisted on prosecuting every offender? A scoundrel might do that. Yet the justice of God, forsooth, is his punishment of sin! A just man is one who cares, and tries, and always tries, to give fair play to everyone in every thing. When we speak of the justice of God, let us see that we do mean justice! Punishment of the guilty may be involved in justice, but it does not constitute the justice of God one atom more than it would constitute the justice of a man.

'But no one ever doubts that God gives fair play!'

'That may be—but does not go for much, if you say that God does this or that which is not fair.'

'If he does it, you may be sure it is fair.'

'Doubtless, or he could not be God—except to devils. But you say he does so and so, and is just; I say, he does not do so and so, and is just. You say he does, for the Bible says so. I say, if the Bible said so, the Bible would lie; but the Bible does not say so. The lord of life complains of men for not judging right. To say on the authority of the Bible that God does a thing no honourable man would do, is to lie against God; to say that it is therefore right, is to lie against the very spirit of God. To uphold a lie for God's sake is to be against God, not for him. God cannot be lied for. He is the truth. The truth alone is on his side. While his child could not see the rectitude of a thing, he would infinitely rather, even if the thing were right, have him say, God could not do that thing, than have him believe that he did it. If the man were sure God did it, the thing he ought to say would be, 'Then there must be something about it I do not know, which if I did know, I should see the thing quite differently.' But where an evil thing is invented to explain and account for a good thing, and a lover of God is called upon to believe the invention or be cast out, he needs not mind being cast out, for it is into the company of Jesus. Where there is no ground to believe that God does a thing except that men who would

306

explain God have believed and taught it, he is not a true man who accepts men against his own conscience of God. I acknowledge no authority calling upon me to believe a thing of God, which I could not be a man and believe right in my fellow-man. I will accept no explanation of any way of God which explanation involves what I should scorn as false and unfair in a man. If you say, That may be right of God to do which it would not be right of man to do, I answer, Yes, because the relation of the maker to his creatures is very different from the relation of one of those creatures to another, and he has therefore duties toward his creatures requiring of him what no man would have the right to do to his fellow-man; but he can have no duty that is not both just and merciful. More is required of the maker, by his own act of creation, than can be required of men. More and higher justice and righteousness is required of him by himself, the Truth;—greater nobleness, more penetrating sympathy; and *nothing* but what, if an honest man understood it, he would say was right. If it be a thing man cannot understand, then man can say nothing as to whether it is right or wrong. He cannot even know that God does *it*, when the *it* is unintelligible to him. What he calls *it* may be but the smallest facet of a composite action. His part is silence. If it be said by any that God does a thing, and the thing seems to me unjust, then either I do not know what the thing is, or God does not do it. The saying cannot mean what it seems to mean, or the saying is not true. If, for instance, it be said that God visits the sins of the fathers on the children, a man who takes *visits upon* to mean *punishes,* and *the children* to mean *the innocent children,* ought to say, 'Either I do not understand the statement, or the thing is not true, whoever says it.' God *may* do what seems to a man not right, but it must so seem to him because God works on higher, on divine, on perfect principles, too right for a selfish, unfair, or unloving man to understand. But least of all must we accept some low notion of justice in a man, and argue that God is just in doing after that notion.

The common idea, then, is, that the justice of God consists in punishing sin: it is in the hope of giving a larger idea of the justice of God in punishing sin that I ask, '*Why is God bound to punish sin?*'

'How could he be a just God and not punish sin?'

'Mercy is a good and right thing,' I answer, 'and but for sin there could be no mercy. We are enjoined to forgive, to be merciful, to be as our father in heaven. Two rights cannot possibly be opposed to each other. If God punish sin, it must be merciful to punish sin; and if God forgive sin, it must be just to forgive sin. We are required to forgive, with the argument that our father forgives. It must, I say, be right to forgive. Every attribute of God must be infinite as himself. He cannot be sometimes merciful, and not always merciful. He cannot be just, and not always just. Mercy belongs to him, and needs no contrivance of theologic chicanery to justify it.'

'Then you mean that it is wrong to punish sin, therefore God does not punish sin?'

'By no means; God does punish sin, but there is no opposition between punishment and forgiveness. The one may be essential to the possibility of the other. Why, I repeat, does God punish sin? That is my point.'

'Because in itself sin deserves punishment.'

'Then how can he tell us to forgive it?'

'He punishes, and having punished he forgives?'

'That will hardly do. If sin demands punishment, and the righteous punishment is given, then the man is free. Why should he be forgiven?'

'He needs forgiveness because no amount of punishment will meet his deserts.'

I avoid for the present, as anyone may perceive, the probable expansion of this reply.

'Then why not forgive him at once if the punishment is not essential— if part can be pretermitted? And again, can that be required which, according to your showing, is not adequate? You will perhaps answer, 'God may please to take what little he can have;' and this brings me to the fault in the whole idea.

Punishment is *nowise* an *offset* to sin. Foolish people sometimes, in a tone of self-gratulatory pity, will say, 'If I have sinned I have suffered.' Yes, verily, but what of that? What merit is there in it? Even had you laid the suffering upon yourself, what did that do to make up for the wrong? That you may have bettered by your suffering is well for you, but what atonement is there in the suffering? The notion is a false one altogether. Punishment, deserved suffering, is no equipoise to sin. It is no use laying it in the other scale. It will not move it a hair's breadth. Suffering weighs nothing at all against sin. It is not of the same kind, not under the same laws, any more than mind and matter. We say a man deserves punishment; but when we forgive and do not punish him, we do not *always* feel that we have done wrong; neither when we do punish him do we feel that any amends has been made for his wrongdoing. If it were an offset to wrong, then God would be bound to punish for the sake of the punishment; but he cannot be, for he forgives. Then it is not for the sake of the punishment, as a thing that in itself ought to be done, but for the sake of something else, as a means to an end, that God punishes. It is not directly for justice, else how could he show mercy, for that would involve injustice?

Primarily, God is not bound to *punish* sin; he is bound to *destroy* sin. If he were not the Maker, he might not be bound to destroy sin—I do not know; but seeing he has created creatures who have sinned, and therefore sin has, by the creating act of God, come into the world, God is, in his own righteousness, bound to destroy sin.

'But that is to have no mercy.'

You mistake. God does destroy sin; he is always destroying sin. In him I trust that he is destroying sin in me. He is always saving the sinner from his sins, and that is destroying sin. But vengeance on the sinner, the law of a tooth for a tooth, is not in the heart of God, neither in his hand. If the sinner and the sin in him, are the concrete object of the divine wrath, then indeed there can be no mercy. Then indeed there will be an end put to sin by the destruction of the sin and the sinner together. But thus would no atonement be wrought—nothing be done to make up for the wrong God has allowed to come into being by creating man. There must be an atonement, a making-up, a bringing together—an atonement which, I say, cannot be made except by the man who has sinned.

Punishment, I repeat, is not the thing required of God, but the absolute destruction of sin. What better is the world, what better is the sinner, what better is God, what better is the truth, that the sinner should suffer—continue suffering to all eternity? Would there be less sin in the universe? Would there be any making-up for sin? Would it show God justified in doing what he knew would bring sin into the world, justified in making creatures who he knew would sin? What setting-right would come of the sinner's suffering? If justice demand it, if suffering be the equivalent for sin, then the sinner must suffer, then God is bound to exact his suffering, and not pardon; and so the making of man was a tyrannical deed, a creative cruelty. But grant that the sinner has deserved to suffer, no amount of suffering is any atonement for his sin. To suffer to all eternity could not make up for one unjust word. Does that mean, then, that for an unjust word I deserve to suffer to all eternity? The unjust word is an eternally evil thing; nothing but God in my heart can cleanse me from the evil that uttered it; but does it follow that I saw the evil of what I did so perfectly, that eternal punishment for it would be just? Sorrow and confession and self-abasing love will make up for the evil word; suffering will not. For evil in the abstract, nothing can be done. It is eternally evil. But I may be saved from it by learning to loathe it, to hate it, to shrink from it with an eternal avoidance. The only vengeance worth having on sin is to make the sinner himself its executioner. Sin and punishment are in no antagonism to each other in man, any more than pardon and punishment are in God; they can perfectly co-exist. The one naturally follows the other, punishment being born of sin, because evil exists only by the life of good, and has no life of its own, being in itself death. Sin and suffering are not natural opposites; the opposite of evil is good, not suffering; the opposite of sin is not suffering, but righteousness. The path across the gulf that divides right from wrong is not the fire, but repentance. If my friend has wronged me, will it console me to see him punished? Will that be a rendering to me of my due? Will his agony be a balm to my deep wound? Should I be fit for any friendship if that were possible even in regard to my enemy? But would not the shadow of repentant grief, the light of reviving love on his countenance, heal it at once however deep? Take any of those wicked people in Dante's hell, and ask wherein is justice served by their punishment. Mind, I am not saying it is not right to punish them; I am saying that justice is not, never can be, satisfied by suffering—nay, cannot have any satisfaction in or from suffering. Human resentment, human revenge, human hate may. Such justice as Dante's keeps wickedness alive in its most terrible forms. The life of God goes forth to inform, or at least give a home to victorious evil. Is he not defeated every time that one of those lost souls defies him? All hell cannot make Vanni Fucci say 'I was wrong.' God is triumphantly defeated, I say, throughout the hell of his vengeance. Although against evil, it is but the vain and wasted cruelty of a tyrant. There is no destruction of evil thereby, but an enhancing of its horrible power in the midst of the most agonizing and disgusting tortures a *divine* imagination can invent. If sin must be kept alive, then hell must be kept alive; but while I regard the smallest sin as infinitely loathsome, I do not believe that any being, never good enough to see the essential ugliness of sin, could sin so as to *deserve* such punishment. I am not now, however, dealing with the question of the duration of punishment, but with the idea of punishment itself; and would only say in passing, that the notion that a creature born imperfect, nay, born with impulses to evil not of his own generating, and which he could not help having, a creature to whom the true face of God was never presented, and by whom it never could have been seen, should be thus condemned, is as loathsome a lie against God as could find place in heart too undeveloped to understand what justice is, and too low to look up into the face of Jesus. It never in truth found place in any heart, though in many a pettifogging brain. There is but one thing lower than deliberately to believe such a lie, and that is to worship the God of whom it is believed. The one deepest, highest, truest, fittest, most wholesome suffering must be generated in the wicked by a vision, a true sight, more or less adequate, of the hideousness of their lives, of the horror of the wrongs they have done. Physical suffering may be a factor in rousing this mental pain; but 'I would I had never been born!' must be the cry of Judas, not because of the hell-fire around him, but because he loathes the man that betrayed his friend, the world's friend. When a man loathes himself, he has begun to be saved. Punishment tends to this result. Not for its own sake, not as a make-up for sin, not for divine revenge—horrible word, not for any satisfaction to justice, can punishment exist. Punishment is for the sake of amendment and atonement. God is bound by his love to punish sin in order to deliver his creature; he is bound by his justice to destroy sin in his creation. Love is justice—is the fulfilling of the law, for God as well as for his children. This is the reason of punishment; this is why justice requires that the wicked shall not go unpunished—that they, through the eye-opening power of pain, may come to see and do justice, may be brought to desire and make all possible amends, and so become just. Such punishment concerns justice in the deepest degree. For Justice, that is God, is bound in himself to see justice done by his children— not in the mere outward act, but in their very being. He is bound in himself to make up for wrong done by his children, and he can do nothing to make up for wrong done but by bringing about the repentance of the wrong-doer. When the man says, 'I did wrong; I hate myself and my deed; I cannot endure to think that I did it!' then, I say, is atonement begun. Without that, all that the Lord did would be lost. He would have made no atonement. Repentance, restitution, confession, prayer for forgiveness, righteous dealing thereafter, is the sole possible, the only true make-up for sin. For nothing less than this did Christ die. When a man acknowledges the right he denied before; when he says to the wrong, 'I abjure, I loathe you; I see now what you are; I could not see it before because I would not; God forgive me; make me clean, or let me die!' then justice, that is God, has conquered—and not till then.

'What atonement is there?'

Every atonement that God cares for; and the work of Jesus Christ on earth was the creative atonement, because it works atonement in every heart. He brings and is bringing God and man, and man and man, into perfect unity: 'I in them and thou in me, that they may be made perfect in one.'

'That is a dangerous doctrine!'

More dangerous than you think to many things—to every evil, to every lie, and among the rest to every false trust in what Christ did, instead of in Christ himself. Paul glories in the cross of Christ, but he does not trust in the cross: he trusts in the living Christ and his living father.

Justice then requires that sin should be put an end to; and not that only, but that it should be atoned for; and where punishment can do anything to this end, where it can help the sinner to know what he has been guilty of, where it can soften his heart to see his pride and wrong and cruelty, justice requires that punishment shall not be spared. And the more we believe in God, the surer we shall be that he will spare nothing that suffering can do to deliver his child from death. If suffering cannot serve this end, we need look for no more hell, but for the destruction of sin by the destruction of the sinner. That, however, would, it appears to me, be for God to suffer defeat, blameless indeed, but defeat.

If God be defeated, he must destroy—that is, he must withdraw life. How can he go on sending forth his life into irreclaimable souls, to keep sin alive in them throughout the ages of eternity? But then, I say, no atonement would be made for the wrongs they have done; God remains defeated, for he has created that which sinned, and which would not repent and make up for its sin. But those who believe that God will thus be defeated by many souls, must surely be of those who do not believe he cares enough to do his very best for them. He *is* their Father; he had power to make them out of himself, separate from himself, and capable of being one with him: surely he will somehow save and keep them! Not the power of sin itself can close *all* the channels between creating and created.

The notion of suffering as an offset for sin, the foolish idea that a man by suffering borne may get out from under the hostile claim to which his wrong-doing has subjected him, comes first of all, I think, from the satisfaction we feel when wrong comes to grief. Why do we feel this satisfaction? Because we hate wrong, but, not being righteous ourselves, more or less hate the wronger as well as his wrong, hence are not only righteously pleased to behold the law's disapproval proclaimed in his punishment, but unrighteously pleased with his suffering, because of the impact upon us of his wrong. In this way the inborn justice of our nature passes over to evil. It is no pleasure to God, as it so often is to us, to see the wicked suffer. To regard any suffering with satisfaction, save it be sympathetically with its curative quality, comes of evil, is inhuman because undivine, is a thing God is incapable of. His nature is always to forgive, and just because he forgives, he punishes. Because God is so altogether alien to wrong, because it is to him a heart-pain and trouble that one of his little ones should do the evil thing, there is, I believe, no extreme of suffering to which, for the sake of destroying the evil thing in them, he would not subject them. A man might flatter, or bribe, or coax a tyrant; but there is no refuge from the love of God; that love will, for very love, insist upon the uttermost farthing.

'That is not the sort of love I care about!'

No; how should you? I well believe it! You cannot care for it until you begin to know it. But the eternal love will not be moved to yield you to the selfishness that is killing you. What lover would yield his lady to her passion for morphia? You may sneer at such love, but the Son of God who took the weight of that love, and bore it through the world, is content with it, and so is everyone who knows it. The love of the Father is a radiant perfection. Love and not self-love is lord of the universe. Justice demands your punishment, because justice demands, and will have, the destruction of sin. Justice demands your punishment because it demands that your father should do his best for you. God, being the God of justice, that is of fair-play, and having made us what we are, apt to fall and capable of being raised again, is in himself bound to punish in order to deliver us—else is his relation to us poor beside that of an earthly father. 'To thee, O Lord, belongeth mercy, for thou renderest to every man according to his work.' A man's work is his character; and God in his mercy is not indifferent, but treats him according to his work.

The notion that the salvation of Jesus is a salvation from the consequences of our sins, is a false, mean, low notion. The salvation of Christ is salvation from the smallest tendency or leaning to sin. It is a deliverance into the pure air of God's ways of thinking and feeling. It is a salvation that makes the heart pure, with the will and choice of the heart to be pure. To such a heart, sin is disgusting. It sees a thing as it is,—that is, as God sees it, for God sees everything as it is. The soul thus saved would rather sink into the flames of hell than steal into heaven and skulk there under the shadow of an imputed righteousness. No soul is saved that would not prefer hell to sin. Jesus did not die to save us from punishment; he was called Jesus because he should save his people from their sins.

If punishment be no atonement, how does the fact bear on the popular theology accepted by every one of the opposers of what they call

Christianity, as representing its doctrines? Most of us have been more or less trained in it, and not a few of us have thereby, thank God, learned what it is—an evil thing, to be cast out of intellect and heart. Many imagine it dead and gone, but in reality it lies at the root (the intellectual root only, thank God) of much the greater part of the teaching of Christianity in the country; and is believed in—so far as the false *can* be believed in—by many who think they have left it behind, when they have merely omitted the truest, most offensive modes of expressing its doctrines. It is humiliating to find how many comparatively honest people think they get rid of a falsehood by softening the statement of it, by giving it the shape and placing it in the light in which it will least assert itself, and so have a good chance of passing both with such as hold it thoroughly, and such as might revolt against it more plainly uttered.

Once for all I will ease my soul regarding the horrid phantasm. I have passed through no change of opinion concerning it since first I began to write or speak; but I have written little and spoken less about it, because I would preach no mere negation. My work was not to destroy the false, except as it came in the way of building the true. Therefore I sought to speak but what I believed, saying little concerning what I did not believe; trusting, as now I trust, in the true to cast out the false, and shunning dispute. Neither will I now enter any theological lists to be the champion for or against mere doctrine. I have no desire to change the opinion of man or woman. Let everyone for me hold what he pleases. But I would do my utmost to disable such as think correct opinion essential to salvation from laying any other burden on the shoulders of true men and women than the yoke of their Master; and such burden, if already oppressing any, I would gladly lift. Let the Lord himself teach them, I say. A man who has not the mind of Christ—and no man has the mind of Christ except him who makes it his business to obey him—cannot have correct opinions concerning him; neither, if he could, would they be of any value to him: he would be nothing the better, he would be the worse for having them. Our business is not to think correctly, but to live truly; then first will there be a possibility of our thinking correctly. One chief cause of the amount of unbelief in the world is, that those who have seen something of the glory of Christ, set themselves to theorize concerning him rather than to obey him. In teaching men, they have not taught them Christ, but taught them about Christ. More eager after credible theory than after doing the truth, they have speculated in a condition of heart in which it was impossible they should understand; they have presumed to explain a Christ whom years and years of obedience could alone have made them able to comprehend. Their teaching of him, therefore, has been repugnant to the common sense of many who had not half their privileges, but in whom, as in Nathanael, there was no guile. Such, naturally, press their theories, in general derived from them of old time, upon others, insisting on their thinking about Christ as they think, instead of urging them to go to Christ to be taught by him whatever he chooses to teach them. They do their unintentional worst to stop all growth, all life. From such and their false teaching I would gladly help to deliver the true-hearted. Let the dead bury their dead, but I would do what I may to keep them from burying the living.

If there be no satisfaction to justice in the mere punishment of the wrong-doer, what shall we say of the notion of satisfying justice by causing one to suffer who is not the wrong-doer? And what, moreover, shall we say to the notion that, just because he is not the person who deserves to be punished, but is absolutely innocent, his suffering gives perfect satisfaction to the perfect justice? That the injustice be done with the consent of the person maltreated makes no difference: it makes it even worse, seeing, as they say, that justice requires the punishment of the *sinner*, and here is one far more than innocent. They have shifted their ground; it is no more punishment, but mere suffering the law requires! The thing gets worse and worse. I declare my utter and absolute repudiation of the idea in any form whatever. Rather than believe in a justice—that is, a God—to whose righteousness, abstract or concrete, it could be any satisfaction for the wrong-doing of a man that a man who did no wrong should suffer, I would be driven from among men, and dwell with the wild beasts that have not reason enough to be unreasonable. What! God, the father of Jesus Christ, like that! His justice contented with direst injustice! The anger of him who will nowise clear the guilty, appeased by the suffering of the innocent! Very God forbid! Observe: the evil fancy actually substitutes for punishment not mere suffering, but that suffering which is farthest from punishment; and this when, as I have shown, punishment, the severest, can be no satisfaction to justice! How did it come ever to be imagined? It sprang from the trustless dread that cannot believe in the forgiveness of the Father; cannot believe that even God will do anything for nothing; cannot trust him without a legal arrangement to bind him. How many, failing to trust God, fall back on a *text*, as they call it! It sprang from the pride that will understand what it cannot, before it will obey what it sees. He that will understand *first* will believe a lie—a lie from which obedience alone will at length deliver him. If anyone say, 'But I believe what you despise,' I answer, To believe it is your punishment for being able to believe it; you may call it your reward, if you will. You ought not to be able to believe it. It is the merest, poorest, most shameless fiction, invented without the perception that it was an invention—fit to satisfy the intellect, doubtless, of the inventor, else he could not have invented it. It has seemed to satisfy also many a humble soul, content to take what was given, and not think; content that another should think for him, and tell him what was the mind of his Father in heaven. Again I say, let the person who can be so satisfied be so satisfied; I have not to trouble myself with him. That he can be content with it, argues him unready to receive better. So long as he can believe false things concerning God, he is such as is capable of believing them—with how much or how little of blame, God knows. Opinion, right or wrong, will do nothing to save him. I would that he thought no more about this or any other opinion, but set himself to do the work of the Master. With his opinions, true or false, I have nothing to do. It is because such as he force evil things upon their fellows— utter or imply them from the seat of authority or influence—to their agony, their paralysation, their unbelief, their indignation, their stumbling, that I have any right to speak. I would save my fellows from having what notion of God is possible to them blotted out by a lie.

If it be asked how, if it be false, the doctrine of substitution can have been permitted to remain so long an article of faith to so many, I answer, On the same principle on which God took up and made use of the sacrifices men had, in their lack of faith, invented as a way of pleasing him. Some children will tell lies to please the parents that hate lying. They will even confess to having done a wrong they have not done, thinking their parents would like them to say they had done it, because they teach them to confess. God accepted men's sacrifices until he could get them to see—and with how many has he yet not succeeded, in the church and out of it!—that he does not care for such things.

'But,' again it may well be asked, 'whence then has sprung the undeniable potency of that teaching?'

I answer, From its having in it a notion of God and his Christ, poor indeed and faint, but, by the very poverty and untruth in its presentation, fitted to the weakness and unbelief of men, seeing it was by men invented to meet and ease the demand made upon their own weakness and unbelief. Thus the leaven spreads. The truth is there. It is Christ the glory of God. But the ideas that poor slavish souls breed concerning this glory the moment the darkness begins to disperse, is quite another thing. Truth is indeed too good for men to believe; they must dilute it before they can take it; they must dilute it before they dare give it. They must make it less true before they can believe it enough to get any good of it. Unable to believe in the love of the Lord Jesus Christ, they invented a mediator in his mother, and so were able to approach a little where else they had stood away; unable to believe in the forgivingness of their father in heaven, they invented a way to be forgiven that should not demand of him so much; which might make it right for him to forgive; which should save them from having to believe downright in the tenderness of his father-heart, for that they found impossible. They thought him bound to punish for the sake of punishing, as an offset to their sin; they could not believe in clear forgiveness; that did not seem divine; it needed itself to be justified; so they invented for its justification a horrible injustice, involving all that was bad in sacrifice, even human sacrifice. They invented a satisfaction for sin which was an insult to God. He sought no satisfaction, but an obedient return to the Father. What satisfaction was needed he made himself in what he did to cause them to turn from evil and go back to him. The thing was too simple for complicated unbelief and the arguing spirit. Gladly would I help their followers to loathe such thoughts of God; but for that, they themselves must grow better men and women. While they are capable of being satisfied with them, there would be no advantage in their becoming intellectually convinced that such thoughts were wrong. I would not speak a word to persuade them of it. Success would be worthless. They would but remain what they were—children capable of thinking meanly of their father. When the heart recoils, discovering how horrible it would be to have such an unreality for God, it will begin to search about and see whether it must indeed accept such statements concerning God; it will search after a real God by whom to hold fast, a real God to deliver them from the terrible idol. It is for those thus moved that I write, not at all for the sake of disputing with those who love the lie they may not be to blame for holding; who, like the Jews of old, would cast out of their synagogue the man who doubts the genuineness of their moral caricature of God, who doubts their travesty of the grandest truth in the universe, the atonement of Jesus Christ. Of such a man they will unhesitatingly report that he does not believe in the atonement. But a lie for God is against God, and carries the sentence of death in itself.

Instead of giving their energy to do the will of God, men of power have given it to the construction of a system by which to explain why Christ must die, what were the necessities and designs of God in permitting his death; and men of power of our own day, while casting from them not a little of the good in the teaching of the Roman Church, have clung to the morally and spiritually vulgar idea of justice and satisfaction held by pagan Rome, buttressed by the Jewish notion of sacrifice, and in its very home, alas, with the mother of all the western churches! Better the reformers had kept their belief in a purgatory, and parted with what is called vicarious sacrifice!

Their system is briefly this: God is bound to punish sin, and to punish it to the uttermost. His justice requires that sin be punished. But he loves man, and does not want to punish him if he can help it. Jesus Christ says, 'I will take his punishment upon me.' God accepts his offer, and lets man go unpunished—upon a condition. His justice is more than satisfied by the punishment of an infinite being instead of a world of worthless creatures. The suffering of Jesus is of greater value than that of all the generations, through endless ages, because he is infinite, pure, perfect in love and truth, being God's own everlasting son. God's condition with man is, that he believe in Christ's atonement thus explained. A man must say, 'I have sinned, and deserve to be tortured to all eternity. But Christ has paid my debts, by being punished instead of me. Therefore he is my Saviour. I am now bound by gratitude to him to turn away from evil.' Some would doubtless insist on his saying a good deal more, but this is enough for my purpose.

As to the justice of God requiring the punishment of the sinner, I have said enough. That the mere suffering of the sinner can be no satisfaction to justice, I have also tried to show. If the suffering of the sinner be indeed required by the justice of God, let it be administered. But what shall we say adequate to confront the base representation that it is not punishment, not the suffering of the sinner that is required, but suffering! nay, as if this were not depth enough of baseness to crown all heathenish representation of the ways of God, that the suffering of the innocent is unspeakably preferable in his eyes to that of the wicked, as a make-up for wrong done! nay, again, 'in the lowest deep a lower deep,' that the suffering of the holy, the suffering of the loving, the suffering of the eternally and perfectly good, is supremely satisfactory to the pure justice of the Father of spirits! Not all the suffering that could be heaped upon the wicked could buy them a moment's respite, so little is their suffering a counterpoise to their wrong; in the working of this law of equivalents, this *lex talionis*, the suffering of millions of years could not equal the sin of a moment, could not pay off one farthing of the deep debt. But so much more valuable, precious, and dear, is the suffering of the innocent, so much more of a satisfaction—observe—to the *justice* of God, that in return for that suffering another wrong is done: the sinners who deserve and ought to be punished are set free.

I know the root of all that can be said on the subject; the notion is imbedded in the gray matter of my Scotch brains; and if I reject it, I know what I reject. For the love of God my heart rose early against the low invention. Strange that in a Christian land it should need to be said, that to punish the innocent and let the guilty go free is unjust! It wrongs the innocent, the guilty, and God himself. It would be the worst of all wrongs to the guilty to treat them as innocent. The whole device is a piece of spiritual charlatanry—fit only for a fraudulent jail-delivery. If the wicked ought to be punished, it were the worst possible perversion of justice to take a righteous being however strong, and punish him instead of the sinner however weak. To the poorest idea of justice in punishment, it is essential that the sinner, and no other than the sinner, should receive the punishment. The strong being that was willing to bear such punishment might well be regarded as worshipful, but what of the God whose so-called justice he thus defeats? If you say it is justice, not God that demands the suffering, I say justice cannot demand that which is unjust, and the whole thing is unjust. God is absolutely just, and there is no deliverance from his justice, which is one with his mercy. The device is an absurdity—a grotesquely deformed absurdity. To represent the living God as a party to such a style of action, is to veil with a mask of cruelty and hypocrisy the face whose glory can be seen only in the face of Jesus; to put a tirade of vulgar Roman legality into the mouth of the Lord God merciful and gracious, who will by no means clear the guilty. Rather than believe such ugly folly of him whose very name is enough to make those that know him heave the breath of the hart panting for the waterbrooks; rather than think of him what in a man would make me avoid him at the risk of my life, I would say, 'There is no God; let us neither eat nor drink, that we may die! For lo, this is not our God! This is not he for whom we have waited!' But I have seen his face and heard his voice in the face and the voice of Jesus Christ; and I say this is our God, the very one whose being the Creator makes it an infinite gladness to be the created. I will not have the God of the scribes and the pharisees whether Jewish or Christian, protestant, Roman, or Greek, but thy father, O Christ! He is my God. If you say, 'That is our God, not yours!' I answer, 'Your portrait of your God is an evil caricature of the face of Christ.'

To believe in a vicarious sacrifice, is to think to take refuge with the Son from the righteousness of the Father; to take refuge with his work instead of with the Son himself; to take refuge with a theory of that work instead of the work itself; to shelter behind a false quirk of law instead of nestling in the eternal heart of the unchangeable and righteous Father, who is merciful in that he renders to every man according to his work, and compels their obedience, nor admits judicial quibble or subterfuge. God will never let a man off with any fault. He must have him clean. He will excuse him to the very uttermost of truth, but not a hair's-breadth beyond it; he is his true father, and will have his child true as his son Jesus Christ is true. He will impute to him nothing that he has not, will lose sight of no smallest good that he has; will quench no smoking flax, break no bruised reed, but send forth judgment unto victory. He is God beyond all that heart hungriest for love and righteousness could to eternity desire.

If you say the best of men have held the opinions I stigmatize, I answer, 'Some of the best of men have indeed held these theories, and of men who have held them I have loved and honoured some heartily and humbly—but because of what they *were*, not because of what they *thought*; and they were what they were in virtue of their obedient faith, not of their opinion. They were not better men because of holding these theories. In virtue of knowing God by obeying his son, they rose above the theories they had never looked in the face, and so had never recognized as evil. Many have arrived, in the natural progress of their sacred growth, at the point where they must abandon them. The man of whom I knew the most good gave them up gladly. Good to worshipfulness may be the man that holds them, and I hate them the more therefore; they are lies that, working under cover of the truth mingled with them, burrow as near the heart of the good man as they can go. Whoever, from whatever reason of blindness, may be the holder of a lie, the thing is a lie, and no falsehood must mingle with the justice we mete out to it. There is nothing for any lie but the pit of hell. Yet until the man sees the thing to be a lie, how shall he but hold it! Are there not mingled with it shadows of the best truth in the universe? So long as a man is able to love a lie, he is incapable of seeing it is a lie. He who is true, out and out, will know at once an untruth; and to that vision we must all come. I do not write for the sake of those who either make or heartily accept any lie. When they see the glory of God, they will see the eternal difference between the false and the true, and not till then. I write for those whom such teaching as theirs has folded in a cloud through which they cannot see the stars of heaven, so that some of them even doubt if there be any stars of heaven. For the holy ones who believed and taught these things in days gone by, all is well.

JUSTICE.

Many of the holiest of them cast the lies from them long ere the present teachers of them were born. Many who would never have invented them for themselves, yet receiving them with the seals affixed of so many good men, took them in their humility as recognized truths, instead of inventions of men; and, oppressed by authority, the authority of men far inferior to themselves, did not dare dispute them, but proceeded to order their lives by what truths they found in their company, and so had their reward, the reward of obedience, in being by that obedience brought to know God, which knowledge broke for them the net of a presumptuous self-styled orthodoxy. Every man who tries to obey the Master is my brother, whether he counts me such or not, and I revere him; but dare I give quarter to what I see to be a lie, because my brother believes it? The lie is not of God, whoever may hold it.

'Well, then,' will many say, 'if you thus unceremoniously cast to the winds the doctrine of vicarious sacrifice, what theory do you propose to substitute in its stead?'

'In the name of the truth,' I answer, *None*. I will send out no theory of mine to rouse afresh little whirlwinds of dialogistic dust mixed with dirt and straws and holy words, hiding the Master in talk about him. If I have any such, I will not cast it on the road as I walk, but present it on a fair patine to him to whom I may think it well to show it. Only eyes opened by the sun of righteousness, and made single by obedience, can judge even the poor moony pearl of formulated thought. Say if you will that I fear to show my opinion. Is the man a coward who will not fling his child to the wolves? What faith in this kind I have, I will have to myself before God, till I see better reason for uttering it than I do now.

'Will you then take from me my faith, and help me to no other?'

Your faith! God forbid. Your theory is not your faith, nor anything like it. Your faith is your obedience; your theory I know not what. Yes, I will gladly leave you without any of what you call faith. Trust in God. Obey the word—every word of the Master. That is faith; and so believing, your opinion will grow out of your true life, and be worthy of it. Peter says the Lord gives the spirit to them that obey him: the spirit of the Master, and that alone, can guide you to any theory that it will be of use to you to hold. A theory arrived at any other way is not worth the time spent on it. Jesus is the creating and saving lord of our intellects as well as of our more precious hearts; nothing that he does not think, is worth thinking; no man can think as he thinks, except he be pure like him; no man can be pure like him, except he go with him,

321

and learn from him. To put off obeying him till we find a credible theory concerning him, is to set aside the potion we know it our duty to drink, for the study of the various schools of therapy. You know what Christ requires of you is right—much of it at least you believe to be right, and your duty to do, whether he said it or not: *do it*. If you do not do what you know of the truth, I do not wonder that you seek it intellectually, for that kind of search may well be, as Milton represents it, a solace even to the fallen angels. But do not call anything that may be so gained, *The Truth*. How can you, not caring to *be* true, judge concerning him whose life was to do for very love the things you confess your duty, yet do them not? Obey the truth, I say, and let theory wait. Theory may spring from life, but never life from theory.

I will not then tell you what I think, but I will tell any man who cares to hear it what I believe. I will do it now. Of course what I say must partake thus much of the character of theory that I cannot prove it; I can only endeavour to order my life by it.

I believe in Jesus Christ, the eternal Son of God, my elder brother, my lord and master; I believe that he has a right to my absolute obedience whereinsoever I know or shall come to know his will; that to obey him is to ascend the pinnacle of my being; that not to obey him would be to deny him. I believe that he died that I might die like him—die to any ruling power in me but the will of God—live ready to be nailed to the cross as he was, if God will it. I believe that he is my Saviour from myself, and from all that has come of loving myself, from all that God does not love, and would not have me love—all that is not worth loving; that he died that the justice, the mercy of God, might have its way with me, making me just as God is just, merciful as he is merciful, perfect as my father in heaven is perfect. I believe and pray that he will give me what punishment I need to set me right, or keep me from going wrong. I believe that he died to deliver me from all meanness, all pretence, all falseness, all unfairness, all poverty of spirit, all cowardice, all fear, all anxiety, all forms of self-love, all trust or hope in possession; to make me merry as a child, the child of our father in heaven, loving nothing but what is lovely, desiring nothing I should be ashamed to let the universe of God see me desire. I believe that God is just like Jesus, only greater yet, for Jesus said so. I believe that God is absolutely, grandly beautiful, even as the highest soul of man counts beauty, but infinitely beyond that soul's highest idea—with the beauty that creates beauty, not merely shows it, or itself exists beautiful. I believe that God has always done, is always doing his best for every man; that no man is miserable because God is forgetting

322

him; that he is not a God to crouch before, but our father, to whom the child-heart cries exultant, 'Do with me as thou wilt.'

I believe that there is nothing good for me or for any man but God, and more and more of God, and that alone through knowing Christ can we come nigh to him.

I believe that no man is ever condemned for any sin except one—that he will not leave his sins and come out of them, and be the child of him who is his father.

I believe that justice and mercy are simply one and the same thing; without justice to the full there can be no mercy, and without mercy to the full there can be no justice; that such is the mercy of God that he will hold his children in the consuming fire of his distance until they pay the uttermost farthing, until they drop the purse of selfishness with all the dross that is in it, and rush home to the Father and the Son, and the many brethren—rush inside the centre of the life-giving fire whose outer circles burn. I believe that no hell will be lacking which would help the just mercy of God to redeem his children.

I believe that to him who obeys, and thus opens the doors of his heart to receive the eternal gift, God gives the spirit of his son, the spirit of himself, to be in him, and lead him to the understanding of all truth; that the true disciple shall thus always know what he ought to do, though not necessarily what another ought to do; that the spirit of the father and the son enlightens by teaching righteousness. I believe that no teacher should strive to make men think as he thinks, but to lead them to the living Truth, to the Master himself, of whom alone they can learn anything, who will make them in themselves know what is true by the very seeing of it. I believe that the inspiration of the Almighty alone gives understanding. I believe that to be the disciple of Christ is the end of being; that to persuade men to be his disciples is the end of teaching.

'The sum of all this is that you do not believe in the atonement?'

I believe in Jesus Christ. Nowhere am I requested to believe in any thing, or in any statement, but everywhere to believe in God and in Jesus Christ. In what you call the atonement, in what you mean by the word, what I have already written must make it plain enough I do not believe. God forbid I should, for it would be to believe a lie, and a lie which is to blame for much non-acceptance of the gospel in this and other lands. But, as the word was used by the best English writers at the time when the translation of the Bible was made—with all my heart, and soul, and strength, and mind, I believe in the atonement, call it the *a-tone-ment*, or the *at-one-ment*, as you please. I believe that Jesus Christ *is* our atonement; that through him we are reconciled to, made one with God. There is not one word in the New Testament about reconciling God to us; it is we that have to be reconciled to God. I am not writing, neither desire to write, a treatise on the atonement, my business being to persuade men to be atoned to God; but I will go so far to meet my questioner as to say—without the slightest expectation of satisfying him, or the least care whether I do so or not, for his *opinion* is of no value to me, though his truth is of endless value to me and to the universe—that, even in the sense of the atonement being a making-up for the evil done by men toward God, I believe in the atonement. Did not the Lord cast himself into the eternal gulf of evil yawning between the children and the Father? Did he not bring the Father to us, let us look on our eternal Sire in the face of his true son, that we might have that in our hearts which alone could make us love him—a true sight of him? Did he not insist on the one truth of the universe, the one saving truth, that God was just what he was? Did he not hold to that assertion to the last, in the face of contradiction and death? Did he not thus lay down his life persuading us to lay down ours at the feet of the Father? Has not his very life by which he died passed into those who have received him, and re-created theirs, so that now they live with the life which alone is life? Did he not foil and slay evil by letting all the waves and billows of its horrid sea break upon him, go over him, and die without rebound—spend their rage, fall defeated, and cease? Verily, he made atonement! *We* sacrifice to God!—it is God who has sacrificed his own son to us; there was no way else of getting the gift of himself into our hearts. Jesus sacrificed himself to his father and the children to bring them together—all the love on the side of the Father and the Son, all the selfishness on the side of the children. If the joy that alone makes life worth living, the joy that God is such as Christ, be a true thing in my heart, how can I but believe in the atonement of Jesus Christ? I believe it heartily, as God means it.

Then again, as the power that brings about a making-up for any wrong done by man to man, I believe in the atonement. Who that believes in Jesus does not long to atone to his brother for the injury he has done him? What repentant child, feeling he has wronged his father, does not desire to make atonement? Who is the mover, the causer, the persuader, the creator of the repentance, of the passion that restores fourfold?—Jesus, our propitiation, our atonement. He is the head and leader, the prince of the atonement. He could not do it without us, but he leads us up to the Father's knee: he makes us make atonement. Learning Christ, we are not only sorry for what we have done wrong,

324

we not only turn from it and hate it, but we become able to serve both God and man with an infinitely high and true service, a soul-service. We are able to offer our whole being to God to whom by deepest right it belongs. Have I injured anyone? With him to aid my justice, new risen with him from the dead, shall I not make good amends? Have I failed in love to my neighbour? Shall I not now love him with an infinitely better love than was possible to me before? That I will and can make atonement, thanks be to him who is my atonement, making me at one with God and my fellows! He is my life, my joy, my lord, my owner, the perfecter of my being by the perfection of his own. I dare not say with Paul that I am the slave of Christ; but my highest aspiration and desire is to be the slave of Christ.

'But you do not believe that the sufferings of Christ, as sufferings, justified the supreme ruler in doing anything which he would not have been at liberty to do but for those sufferings?'

I do not. I believe the notion as unworthy of man's belief, as it is dishonouring to God. It has its origin doubtless in a salutary sense of sin; but sense of sin is not inspiration, though it may lie not far from the temple-door. It is indeed an opener of the eyes, but upon home-defilement, not upon heavenly truth; it is not the revealer of secrets. Also there is another factor in the theory, and that is unbelief—incapacity to accept the freedom of God's forgiveness; incapacity to believe that it is God's chosen nature to forgive, that he is bound in his own divinely willed nature to forgive. No atonement is necessary to him but that men should leave their sins and come back to his heart. But men cannot believe in the forgiveness of God. Therefore they need, therefore he has given them a mediator. And yet they will not know him. They think of the father of souls as if he had abdicated his fatherhood for their sins, and assumed the judge. If he put off his fatherhood, which he cannot do, for it is an eternal fact, he puts off with it all relation to us. He cannot repudiate the essential and keep the resultant. Men cannot, or will not, or dare not see that nothing but his being our father gives him any right over us—that nothing but that could give him a perfect right. They regard the father of their spirits as their governor! They yield the idea of the Ancient of Days, 'the glad creator,' and put in its stead a miserable, puritanical martinet of a God, caring not for righteousness, but for his rights; not for the eternal purities, but the goody proprieties. The prophets of such a God take all the glow, all the hope, all the colour, all the worth, out of life on earth, and offer you instead what they call eternal bliss—a pale, tearless hell. Of all things, turn from a mean, poverty stricken faith. But, if you ate

straitened in your own mammon-worshipping soul, how shall you be-
lieve in a God any greater than can stand up in that prison-chamber?

I desire to wake no dispute, will myself dispute with no man, but
for the sake of those whom certain *believers* trouble, I have spoken my
mind. I love the one God seen in the face of Jesus Christ. From all
copies of Jonathan Edwards's portrait of God, however faded by time,
however softened by the use of less glaring pigments, I turn with
loathing. Not such a God is he concerning whom was the message
John heard from Jesus, *that he is light, and in him is no darkness at
all.*

LIGHT.

This then is the message which we have heard of him, and declare unto you, that God is light, and in him is no darkness at all.—1 John i. 5.

And this is the condemnation, that light is come into the world, and men loved darkness rather than light; because their deeds were evil.—John iii. 19.

We call the story of Jesus, told so differently, yet to my mind so consistently, by four narrators, *the gospel*. What makes this tale *the good news*? Is everything in the story of Christ's life on earth good news? Is it good news that the one only good man was served by his fellow-men as Jesus was served—cast out of the world in torture and shame? Is it good news that he came to his own, and his own received him not? What makes it fit, I repeat, to call the tale *good news*? If we asked this or that theologian, we should, in so far as he was a true man, and answered from his own heart and not from the tradition of the elders, understand what he saw in it that made it good news to him, though it might involve what would be anything but good news to some of us. The deliverance it might seem to this or that man to bring, might be founded on such notions of God as to not a few of us contain as little of good as of news. To share in the deliverance which some men find in what they call the gospel—for all do not apply the word to the tale itself, but to certain deductions made from the epistles and their own consciousness of evil—we should have to believe such things of God as would be the opposite of an evangel to us—yea, a message from hell itself; we should have to imagine that whose possibility would be worse than any ill from which their 'good news' might offer us deliverance: we must first believe in an unjust God, from whom we have to seek refuge. True, they call him just, but say he does that which seems to the best in me the essence of injustice. They will tell me I judge after the flesh: I answer, Is it then to the flesh the Lord appeals when he says, 'Yea, and why even of yourselves judge ye not what is right?' Is he not the light that lighteth every man that cometh into the world? They tell me I was born in sin, and I know it to be true; they tell me also that I am judged with the same severity as if I had been born in righteousness, and that I know to be false. They make it a consequence of the purity and justice of God that he will judge us, born in evil, for which birth we were not accountable, by our sinfulness, instead of by our guilt. They tell me, or at least give me to understand, that every wrong thing I have done makes me subject to be treated as if I had done that thing with the free will of one who had in him no taint of evil—when, perhaps, I did not at the time recognize the thing as evil, or recognized it only in the vaguest fashion. Is there any gospel in telling me that God is unjust, but that there is a way of deliverance from him? Show me my God unjust, and you wake in me a damnation from which no power can deliver me—least of all God himself. It may be good news to such as are content to have a God capable of unrighteousness, if only he be on their side!

Who would not rejoice to hear from Matthew, or Mark, or Luke, what, in a few words, he meant by the word *gospel*—or rather, what in the story of Jesus made him call it *good news*! Each would probably give a different answer to the question, all the answers consistent, and each a germ from which the others might be reasoned; but in the case of John, we have his answer to the question: he gives us in one sentence of two members, not indeed the gospel according to John, but the gospel according to Jesus Christ himself. He had often told the story of Jesus, the good news of what he was, and did, and said: what in it all did John look upon as the essence of the goodness of its news? In his gospel he gives us all *about* him, the message *concerning* him; now he tells us what in it makes it to himself and to us good news—tells us the very goodness of the good news. It is not now his own message about Jesus, but the soul of that message—that which makes it gospel—the news Jesus brought concerning the Father, and gave to the disciples as his message for them to deliver to men. Throughout the story, Jesus, in all he does, and is, and says, is telling the news concerning his father, which he was sent to give to John and his companions, that they might hand it on to their brothers; but here, in so many words, John tells us what he himself has heard from The Word—what in sum he has gathered from Jesus as the message he has to declare. He has received it in no systematic form; it is what a life, *the* life, what a man, *the* man, has taught him. The Word is the Lord; the Lord is the gospel. The good news is no fagot of sticks of a man's gathering on the Sabbath.

Every man must read the Word for himself. One may read it in one shape, another in another: all will be right if it be indeed the Word they read, and they read it by the lamp of obedience. He who is willing to do the will of the Father shall know the truth of the teaching of Jesus. The spirit is 'given to them that obey him.'

But let us hear how John reads the Word—near what is John's version of the gospel.

'This then is the message,' he says, 'which we have heard of him, and declare unto you, that God is light, and in him is no darkness at all.' Ah, my heart, this is indeed the good news for thee! This is a gospel! If God be light, what more, what else can I seek than God, than God himself! Away with your doctrines! Away with your salvation from the 'justice' of a God whom it is a horror to imagine! Away with your iron cages of false metaphysics! I am saved—for God is light! My God, I come to thee. That thou shouldst be thyself is enough for time and eternity, for my soul and all its endless need. Whatever seems to me darkness, that I will not believe of my God. If I should mistake, and call that darkness which is light, will he not reveal the matter to me, setting it in the light that lighteth every man, showing me that I saw but the husk of the thing, not the kernel? Will he not break open the shell for me, and let the truth of it, his thought, stream out upon me? He will not let it hurt me to mistake the light for darkness, while I take not the darkness for light. The one comes from blindness of the intellect, the other from blindness of heart and will. I love the light, and will not believe at the word of any man, or upon the conviction of any man, that that which seems to me darkness is in God. Where would the good news be if John said, 'God is light, but you cannot see his light; you cannot tell, you have no notion, what light is; what God means by light, is not what you mean by light; what God calls light may be horrible darkness to you, for you are of another nature from him!' Where, I say, would be the good news of that? It is true, the light of God may be so bright that we see nothing; but that is not darkness, it is infinite hope of light. It is true also that to the wicked 'the day of the Lord is darkness, and not light;' but is that because the conscience of the wicked man judges of good and evil oppositely to the conscience of the good man? When he says, 'Evil, be thou my good,' he means by *evil* what God means by evil, and by *good* he means *pleasure*. He cannot make the meanings change places. To say that what our deepest conscience calls darkness may be light to God, is blasphemy; to say light in God and light in man are of differing kinds, is to speak against the spirit of light. God is light far beyond what we can see, but what we mean by light, God means by light; and what is light to God is light to us, or would be light to us if we saw it, and will be light to us when we do see it. God means us to be jubilant in the fact that he is light—that he is what his children, made in his image, mean when they say *light*; that what in him is dark to them, is dark by excellent glory, by too much cause of jubilation; that, however dark it may be to their eyes, it is light even as they mean it, light for their eyes and souls and hearts to take in the moment they are enough of eyes, enough of souls, enough of hearts, to receive it in its very being. Living Light, thou wilt not have me believe anything dark of thee! thou wilt have me so sure of thee as to dare to say that is not of God which I see dark, see unlike the Master! If I am not honest enough, if the eye in me be not single enough to see thy light, thou wilt punish me, I thank thee, and purge my eyes from their darkness, that they may let the light in, and so I become an inheritor, with thy other children, of that light which is thy Godhead, and makes thy creatures need to worship thee. 'In thy light we shall see light.'

All man will not, in our present imperfection, see the same light; but light is light notwithstanding, and what each does see, is his safety if he obeys it. In proportion as we have the image of Christ mirrored in us, we shall know what is and is not light. But never will anything prove to be light that is not of the same kind with that which we mean by light, with that in a thing which makes us call it light. The darkness yet left in us makes us sometimes doubt of a thing whether it be light or darkness; but when the eye is single, the whole body will be full of light.

To fear the light is to be untrue, or at least it comes of untruth. No being, for himself or for another, needs fear the light of God. Nothing can be in light inimical to our nature, which is of God, or to anything in us that is worthy. All fear of the light, all dread lest there should be something dangerous in it, comes of the darkness still in those of us who do not love the truth with all our hearts; it will vanish as we are more and more interpenetrated with the light. In a word, there is no way of thought or action which we count admirable in man, in which God is not altogether adorable. There is no loveliness, nothing that makes man dear to his brother man, that is not in God, only it is infinitely better in God. He is God our saviour. Jesus is our saviour because God is our saviour. He is the God of comfort and consolation. He will soothe and satisfy his children better than any mother her infant. The only thing he will not give them is—leave to stay in the dark. If a child cry, 'I want the darkness,' and complain that he will not give it, yet he will not give it. He gives what his child needs—often by refusing what he asks. If his child say, 'I will not be good; I prefer to die; let me die!' his dealing with that child will be as if he said—'No; I have the right to content you, not giving you your own will but mine, which is your one good. You shall not die; you shall live to thank me that I would not hear your prayer. You know what you ask, but not what you refuse.' There are good things God must delay giving until his child has a pocket to hold them—till he gets his child to make that pocket. He must first make him fit to receive and to have. There is no part of our nature that shall not be satisfied—and that not by lessening it, but by enlarging it to embrace an ever-enlarging enough.

Come to God, then, my brother, my sister, with all thy desires and instincts, all thy lofty ideals, all thy longing for purity and unselfishness, all thy yearning to love and be true, all thy aspiration after self-forgetfulness and child-life in the breath of the Father; come to him with all thy weaknesses, all thy shames, all thy futilities; with all thy helplessness over thy own thoughts; with all thy failure, yea, with the sick sense of having missed the tide of true affairs; come to him with all thy doubts, fears, dishonesties, meannesses, paltrinesses, misjudgments, wearinesses, disappointments, and stalenesses: be sure he will take thee and all thy miserable brood, whether of draggle-winged angels, or covert-seeking snakes, into his care, the angels for life, the snakes for death, and thee for liberty in his limitless heart! For he is light, and in him is no darkness at all. If he were a king, a governor; if the name that described him were *The Almighty*, thou mightst well doubt whether there could be light enough in him for thee and thy darkness; but he is thy father, and more thy father than the word can mean in any lips but his who said, 'my father and your father, my God and your God;' and such a father is light, an infinite, perfect light. If he were any less or any other than he is, and thou couldst yet go on growing, thou must at length come to the point where thou wouldst be dissatisfied with him; but he is light, and in him is no darkness at all. If anything seem to be in him that you cannot be content with, be sure that the ripening of thy love to thy fellows and to him, the source of thy being, will make thee at length know that anything else than just what he is would have been to thee an endless loss. Be not afraid to build upon the rock Christ, as if thy holy imagination might build too high and heavy for that rock, and it must give way and crumble beneath the weight of thy divine idea. Let no one persuade thee that there is in him a little darkness, because of something he has said which his creature interprets into darkness. The interpretation is the work of the enemy—a handful of tares of darkness sown in the light. Neither let thy cowardly conscience receive any word as light because another calls it light, while it looks to thee dark. Say either the thing is not what it seems, or God never said or did it. But, of all evils, to misinterpret what God does, and then say the thing as interpreted must be right because God does it, is of the devil. Do not try to believe anything that affects thee as darkness. Even if thou mistake and refuse something true thereby, thou wilt do less wrong to Christ by such a refusal than thou wouldst by accepting as his what thou canst see only as darkness. It is impossible thou art seeing a true, a real thing—seeing it as it is, I mean—if it looks to thee darkness. But let thy words be few, lest thou say with thy tongue what thou wilt afterward repent with thy heart. Above all things believe in the light, that it is what thou callest light, though the darkness in thee may give thee cause at a time to doubt whether thou art verily seeing the light.

'But there is another side to the matter: God is light indeed, but there *is* darkness; darkness is death, and men are in it.'

Yes; darkness is death, but not death to him that comes out of it.

It may sound paradoxical, but no man is condemned for anything he has done; he is condemned for continuing to do wrong. He is condemned for not coming out of the darkness, for not coming to the light, the living God, who sent the light, his son, into the world to guide him home. Let us hear what John says about the darkness.

For here also we have, I think, the word of the apostle himself: at the 13th verse he begins, I think, to speak in his own person. In the 19th verse he says, 'And this is the condemnation,'—not that men are sinners—not that they have done that which, even at the moment, they were ashamed of—not that they have committed murder, not that they have betrayed man or woman, not that they have ground the faces of the poor, making money by the groans of their fellows—not for any hideous thing are they condemned, but that they will not leave such doings behind, and do them no more: 'This is the condemnation, that light is come into the world, and men' would not come out of the darkness to the light, but 'loved darkness rather than light, because their deeds were evil.' Choosing evil, clinging to evil, loving the darkness because it suits with their deeds, therefore turning their backs on the inbreaking light, how can they but be condemned—if God be true, if he be light, and darkness be alien to him! Whatever of honesty is in man, whatever of judgment is left in the world, must allow that their condemnation is in the very nature of things, that it must rest on them and abide.

But if one happens to utter some individual truth which another man has made into one of the cogs of his system, he is in danger of being supposed to accept all the toothed wheels and their relations in that system. I therefore go on to say that it does not follow, because light has come into the world, that it has fallen upon this or that man. He has his portion of the light that lighteth every man, but the revelation of God in Christ may not yet have reached him. A man might see and pass the Lord in a crowd, nor be to blame like the Jews of Jerusalem for not knowing him. A man like Nathanael might have started and stopped at the merest glimpse of him, but all growing men are not yet like him without guile. Everyone who has not yet come to the light is not necessarily keeping his face turned away from it. We dare not say that this or that man would not have come to the light had he seen it; we do not know that he will not come to the light the moment he does see it. God gives every man time. There is a light that lightens sage and savage, but the glory of God in the face of Jesus may not have shined on this sage or that savage. The condemnation is of those who, having seen Jesus, refuse to come to him, or pretend to come to him but do not the things he says. They have all sorts of excuses at hand; but as soon as a man begins to make excuse, the time has come when he might be doing that from which he excuses himself. How many are there not who, believing there is something somewhere with the claim of light upon them, go on and on to get more out of the darkness! This consciousness, all neglected by them, gives broad ground for the expostulation of the Lord—'Ye will not come unto me that ye might have life!'

'All manner of sin and blasphemy,' the Lord said, 'shall be forgiven unto men; but the blasphemy against the spirit shall not be forgiven.' God speaks, as it were, in this manner: 'I forgive you everything. Not a word more shall be said about your sins—only come out of them; come out of the darkness of your exile; come into the light of your home, of your birthright, and do evil no more. Lie no more; cheat no more; oppress no more; slander no more; envy no more; be neither greedy nor vain; love your neighbour as I love you; be my good child; trust in your father. I am light; come to me, and you shall see things as

I see them, and hate the evil thing. I will make you love the thing which now you call good and love not. I forgive all the past.'

'I thank thee, Lord, for forgiving me, but I prefer staying in the darkness: forgive me that too.'

'No; that cannot be. The one thing that cannot be forgiven is the sin of choosing to be evil, of refusing deliverance. It is impossible to forgive that sin. It would be to take part in it. To side with wrong against right, with murder against life, cannot be forgiven. The thing that is past I pass, but he who goes on doing the same, annihilates this my forgiveness, makes it of no effect. Let a man have committed any sin whatever, I forgive him; but to choose to go on sinning—how can I forgive that? It would be to nourish and cherish evil! It would be to let my creation go to ruin. Shall I keep you alive to do things hateful in the sight of all true men? If a man refuse to come out of his sin, he must suffer the vengeance of a love that would be no love if it left him there. Shall I allow my creature to be the thing my soul hates?'

There is no excuse for this refusal. If we were punished for every fault, there would be no end, no respite; we should have no quiet wherein to repent; but God passes by all he can. He passes by and forgets a thousand sins, yea, tens of thousands, forgiving them all—only we must begin to be good, begin to do evil no more. He who refuses must be punished and punished—punished through all the ages— punished until he gives way, yields, and comes to the light, that his deeds may be seen by himself to be what they are, and be by himself reproved, and the Father at last have his child again. For the man who in this world resists to the full, there may be, perhaps, a whole age or era in the history of the universe during which his sin shall not be forgiven; but *never* can it be forgiven until he repents. How can they who will not repent be forgiven, save in the sense that God does and will do all he can to make them repent? Who knows but such sin may need for its cure the continuous punishment of an aeon?

There are three conceivable kinds of punishment—first, that of mere retribution, which I take to be entirely and only human— therefore, indeed, more properly inhuman, for that which is not divine is not essential to humanity, and is of evil, and an intrusion upon the human; second, that which works repentance; and third, that which refines and purifies, working for holiness. But the punishment that falls on whom the Lord loveth because they have repented, is a very different thing from the punishment that falls on those whom he loveth in deed but cannot forgive because they hold fast by their sins.

There are also various ways in which the word *forgive* can be used. A man might say to his son—'My boy, I forgive you. You did not know what you were doing. I will say no more about it.' Or he might say—'My boy, I forgive you; but I must punish you, for you have done the same thing several times, and I must make you remember.' Or, again, he might say—'I am seriously angry with you. I cannot forgive you. I must punish you severely. The thing was too shameful! I cannot pass it by.' Or, once more, he might say—'Except you alter your ways entirely, I shall have nothing more to do with you. You need not come to me. I will not take the responsibility of anything you do. So far from answering for you, I shall feel bound in honesty to warn my friends not to put confidence in you. Never, never, till I see a greater difference in you than I dare hope to see in this world, will I forgive you. I can no more regard you as one of the family. I would die to save you, but I cannot forgive you. There is nothing in you now on which to rest forgiveness. To say, I forgive you, would be to say, Do anything you like; I do not care what you do.' So God may forgive and punish; and he may punish and not forgive, that he may rescue. To forgive the sin against the holy spirit would be to damn the universe to the pit of lies, to render it impossible for the man so forgiven ever to be saved. He cannot forgive the man who will not come to the light because his deeds are evil. Against that man his fatherly heart is *moved with indignation.*

THE DISPLEASURE OF JESUS.

When Jesus therefore saw her weeping, and the Jews also weeping which came with her, he groaned in the spirit, and was troubled.—John xi. 33.

Grimm, in his lexicon to the New Testament, after giving as the equivalent of the word [Greek: embrimaomai] in pagan use, 'I am moved with anger,' 'I roar or growl,' 'I snort at,' 'I am vehemently angry or indignant with some one,' tells us that in Mark i. 43, and Matthew ix. 30, it has a meaning different from that of the pagans, namely, 'I command with severe admonishment.' That he has any authority for saying so, I do not imagine, and believe the statement a blunder. The Translators and Revisers, however, have in those passages used the word similarly, and in one place, the passage before us, where a true version is of yet more consequence, have taken another liberty and rendered the word 'groaned.' The Revisers, at the same time, place in the margin what I cannot but believe its true meaning—'was moved with indignation.'

Let us look at all the passages in which the word is used of the Lord, and so, if we may, learn something concerning him. The only place in the gospel where it is used of any but the Lord is Mark xiv. 5. Here both versions say of the disciples that they 'murmured at' the waste of the ointment by one of the women who anointed the Lord. With regard to this rendering I need only remark that surely 'murmured at' can hardly be strong enough, especially seeing 'they had indignation among themselves' at the action.

It is indeed right and necessary to insist that many a word must differ in moral weight and colour as used of or by persons of different character. The anger of a good man is a very different thing from the anger of a bad man; the displeasure of Jesus must be a very different thing from the displeasure of a tyrant. But they are both anger, both displeasure, nevertheless. We have no right to change a root-meaning, and say in one case that a word means *he was indignant*, in another that it means *he straitly or strictly charged*, and in a third that it means *he groaned*. Surely not thus shall we arrive at the truth! If any statement is made, any word employed, that we feel unworthy of the Lord, let us refuse it; let us say, 'I do not believe that;' or, 'There must be something there that I cannot see into: I must wait; it cannot be what it looks to me, and be true of the Lord!' But to accept the word as used of the Lord, and say it means something quite different from what it means when used by the same writer of some one else, appears to me untruthful.

We shall take first the passage, Mark i. 43—in the authorized version, 'And he straitly charged him;' in the revised, 'And he strictly charged him,' with '*sternly*' in the margin. Literally, as it seems to me, it reads, and ought to be read, 'And being angry' or 'displeased' or 'vexed' 'with him, he immediately dismissed him.' There is even some dissatisfaction implied, I think, in the word I have translated 'dismissed.' The word in John ix. 34, 'they cast him out,' is the same, only a little intensified.

This adds something to the story, and raises the question, Why should Jesus have been angry? If we can find no reason for his anger, we must leave the thing as altogether obscure; for I do not know where to find another meaning for the word, except in the despair of a would-be interpreter.

Jesus had cured the leper—not with his word only, which would have been enough for the mere cure, but was not enough without the touch of his hand—the Sinaitic version says '*his hands*'—to satisfy the heart of Jesus—a touch defiling him, in the notion of the Jews, but how cleansing to the sense of the leper! The man, however, seems to have been unworthy of this delicacy of divine tenderness. The Lord, who could read his heart, saw that he made him no true response—that there was not awaked in him the faith he desired to rouse: he had not drawn the soul of the man to his. The leper was jubilant in the removal of his pain and isolating uncleanness, in his deliverance from suffering and scorn; he was probably elated with the pride of having had a miracle wrought for *him*. In a word, he was so full of himself that he did not think truly of his deliverer.

The Lord, I say, saw this, or something of this kind, and was not satisfied. He had wanted to give the man something so much better than a pure skin, and had only roused in him an unseemly delight in his own cleanness—*unseemly*, for it was such that he paid no heed to the Lord, but immediately disobeyed his positive command. The moral position the man took was that which displeased the Lord, made him angry. He saw in him positive and rampant self-will and disobedience, an impertinent assurance and self-satisfaction. Filled, not with pure delight, or the child-like merriment that might well burst forth, min-gled with tears, at such deliverance; filled, not with gratitude, but gratification, the keener that he had been so long an object of loathing to his people; filled with arrogance because of the favour shown to him, of all men, by the great prophet, and swelling with boast of the same, he left the presence of the healer to thwart his will, and, com-manded to tell no man, at once 'began'—the frothy, volatile, talking soul—'to publish it much, and to blaze abroad the matter, insomuch that Jesus could no more openly enter into a city, but was without in desert places.'

Let us next look at the account of the healing of the two blind men, given in the ninth chapter of Matthew's gospel. In both the versions the same phrases are used in translation of the word in question, as in the story of the leper in Mark's gospel—'straitly,' 'strictly,' 'sternly charged them.' I read the passage thus: 'And Jesus was displeased'—or, per-haps, 'much displeased'—'with them, saying, See that no man know it.'

'But they went forth, and spread abroad his fame in all that land.' Surely here we have light on the cause of Jesus' displeasure with the blind men! it was the same with them as with the leper: they showed themselves bent on their own way, and did not care for his. Doubtless they were, in part, all of them moved by the desire to spread abroad his fame; that may even have seemed to them the best acknowledgment they could render their deliverer. They never suspected that a great man might desire to avoid fame, laying no value upon it, knowing it for a foolish thing. They did not understand that a man desirous of helping his fellows might yet avoid a crowd as obstructive to his ob-ject. 'What is a prophet without honour?' such virtually ask, nor understand the answer, 'A man the more likely to prove a prophet.' These men would repay their healer with trumpeting, not obedience. By them he should have his right—but as they not he judged fit! In his modesty he objected, but they would take care he should not go with-out his reward! Through them he should reap the praises of men! 'Not tell!' they exclaim. 'Indeed, we will tell!' They were too grateful not to rumour him, not grateful enough to obey him.

THE DISPLEASURE OF JESUS.

We cannot surely be amazed at their self-sufficiency. How many are there not who seem capable of anything for the sake of the church or Christianity, except the one thing its Lord cares about—that they should do what he tells them! He would deliver them from themselves into the liberty of the sons of God, make them his brothers; they leave him to vaunt their church. His commandments are not grievous; they invent commandments for him, and lay them, burdens grievous to be borne, upon the necks of their brethren. God would have us sharers in his bliss—in the very truth of existence; they worship from afar, and will not draw nigh. It was not, I think, the obstruction to his work, not the personal inconvenience it would cause him, that made the Lord angry, but that they would not be his friends, would not do what he told them, would not be the children of his father, and help him to save their brethren. When Peter in his way next—much the same way as theirs—opposed the will of the Father, saying, 'That be far from thee, Lord!' he called him Satan, and ordered him behind him.

Does it affect anyone to the lowering of his idea of the Master that he should ever be angry? If so, I would ask him whether his whole conscious experience of anger be such, that he knows but one kind of anger. There is a good anger and a bad anger. There is a wrath of God, and there is a wrath of man that worketh not the righteousness of God. Anger may be as varied as the colour of the rainbow. God's anger can be nothing but Godlike, therefore divinely beautiful, at one with his love, helpful, healing, restoring; yet is it verily and truly what we call anger. How different is the anger of one who loves, from that of one who hates! yet is anger anger. There is the degraded human anger, and the grand, noble, eternal anger. Our anger is in general degrading, because it is in general impure.

It is to me an especially glad thought that the Lord came so near us as to be angry with us. The more we think of Jesus being angry with us, the more we feel that we must get nearer and nearer to him—get within the circle of his wrath, out of the sin that makes him angry, and near to him where sin cannot come. There is no quenching of his love in the anger of Jesus. The anger of Jesus is his recognition that we are to blame; if we were not to blame, Jesus could never be angry with us; we should not be of his kind, therefore not subject to his blame. To recognize that we are to blame, is to say that we ought to be better, that we are able to do right if we will. We are able to turn our faces to the light, and come out of the darkness; the Lord will see to our growth.

It is a serious thought that the disobedience of the men he had set free from blindness and leprosy should be able to hamper him in his

339

work for his father. But his best friends, his lovers did the same. That he should be crucified was a horror to them; they would have made him a king, and ruined his father's work. He preferred the cruelty of his enemies to the kindness of his friends. The former with evil intent wrought his father's will; the latter with good intent would have frustrated it. His disciples troubled him with their unbelieving expostulations. Let us know that the poverty of our idea of Jesus—how much more our disobedience to him!—thwarts his progress to victory, delays the coming of the kingdom of heaven. Many a man valiant for Christ, but not understanding him, and laying on himself and his fellows burdens against nature, has therein done will-worship and would-be service for which Christ will give him little thanks, which indeed may now be moving his holy anger. Where we do that we ought not, and could have helped it, be moved to anger against us, O Christ! do not treat us as if we were not worth being displeased with; let not our faults pass as if they were of no weight. Be angry with us, holy brother, wherein we are to blame; where we do not understand, have patience with us, and open our eyes, and give us strength to obey, until at length we are the children of the Father even as thou. For though thou art lord and master and saviour of them that are growing, thou art perfect lord only of the true and the safe and the free, who live in thy light and are divinely glad: we keep thee back from thy perfect lordship. Make us able to be angry and not sin; to be angry nor seek revenge the smallest; to be angry and full of forgiveness. We will not be content till our very anger is love.

The Lord did not call the leprosy to return and seize again upon the man who disobeyed him. He may have deserved it, but the Lord did not do it. He did not wrap the self-confident seeing men in the cloud of their old darkness because they wrapped themselves in the cloud of disobedience. He let them go. Of course they failed of their well-being by it; for to say a man might disobey and be none the worse, would be to say that *no* may be *yes*, and light sometimes darkness; it would be to say that the will of God is not man's bliss. But the Lord did not directly punish them, any more than he does tens of thousands of wrongs in the world. Many wrongs punish themselves against the bosses of armed law; many wrong-doers cut themselves, like the priests of Baal, with the knives of their own injustice; and it is his will it should be so; but, whether he punish directly or indirectly, he is always working to deliver. I think sometimes his anger is followed, yea, accompanied by an astounding gift, fresh from his heart of grace. He knows what to do, for he is love. He is love when he gives, and love when he withholds;

love when he heals, and love when he slays. Lord, if thus thou lookest upon men in thine anger, what must a full gaze be from thine eyes of love!

Let us now look at the last case in which this word [Greek: embrimaomai] is used in the story of our Lord—that form of it, at least, which we have down here, for sure they have a fuller gospel in the Father's house, and without spot of blunder in it: let us so use that we have that we be allowed at length to look within the leaves of the other!

In the authorized version of the gospel of John, the eleventh chapter, the thirty-third verse, we have the words: 'When Jesus therefore saw her weeping, and the Jews also weeping which came with her, he groaned in the spirit and was troubled;'—according to the margin of the revised version, 'he was moved with indignation in the spirit, and troubled himself.' Also in the thirty-eighth verse we read, according to the margin of the revised version, 'Jesus therefore again being moved with indignation in himself cometh to the tomb.'

Indignation—anger at the very tomb! in the presence of hearts torn by the loss of a brother four days dead, whom also he loved! Yes, verily, friends! such indignation, such anger as, at such a time, in such a place, it was eternally right the heart of Jesus should be moved withal. I can hardly doubt that he is in like manner moved by what he sees now at the death-beds and graves of not a few who are not his enemies, and yet in the presence of death seem no better than pagans. What have such gained by being the Christians they say they are? They fix their eyes on a grisly phantasm they call Death, and never lift them to the radiant Christ standing by bed or grave! For them Christ has not conquered Death:

Thou art our king, O Death! to thee we groan!

They would shudder at the thought of saying so in words; they say it in the bitterness of their tears, in their eyes of despair, in their black garments, in their instant retreat from the light of day to burrow in the bosom of darkness? 'What, would you have us not weep?' Weep freely, friends; but let your tears be those of expectant Christians, not hopeless pagans. Let us look at the story.

The Lord had all this time been trying to teach his friends about his father—what a blessed and perfect father he was, who had sent him that men might look on his very likeness, and know him greater than any likeness could show him; and all they had gained by it seemed not to amount to an atom of consolation when the touch of death came. He had said hundreds of things to Martha and Mary that are not down in the few pages of our earthly gospel; but the fact that God loves them, and that God has Lazarus, seems nothing to them because they have not Lazarus! The Lord himself, for all he has been to them, cannot console them, even with his bodily presence, for the bodily absence of their brother. I do not mean that God would have even his closest presence make us forget or cease to desire that of our friend. God forbid! The love of God is the perfecting of every love. He is not the God of oblivion, but of eternal remembrance. There is no past with him. So far is he from such jealousy as we have all heard imputed to him, his determination is that his sons and daughters shall love each other perfectly. He gave us to each other to belong to each other for ever. He does not give to take away; with him is no variableness or shadow of turning. But if my son or daughter be gone from me for a season, should not the coming of their mother comfort me? Is it nothing that he who is the life should be present, assuring the well-being of the life that has vanished, and the well-being of the love that misses it? Why should the Lord have come to the world at all, if these his friends were to take no more good of him than this? Having the elder brother, could they not do for a little while without the younger? Must they be absolutely miserable without him? All their cry was, 'Lord, if thou hadst been here, my brother had not died!' You may say they did not know Christ well enough yet. That is plain—but Christ had expected more of them, and was disappointed. You may say, 'How could that be, seeing he knew what was in man?' I doubt if you think rightly how much the Lord gave up in coming to us. Perhaps you have a poor idea of how much the Son was able to part with, or rather could let the Father take from him, without his sonship, the eternal to the eternal, being touched by it, save to show it deeper and deeper, closer and closer. That he did not in this world know everything, is plain from his own words, and from signs as well: I should scorn to imagine that ignorance touching his Godhead, that his Godhead could be hurt by what enhances his devotion. It enhances in my eyes the idea of his Godhead. Here, I repeat, I cannot but think that he was disappointed with his friends Martha and Mary. Had he done no more for them than this? Was his father and their father no comfort to them? Was this the way his best friends treated his father, who was doing everything for them possible for a father to do for his children! He cared so dearly for their hearts that he could not endure to see them weeping so that they shut out his father. His love was vexed with them that they would sit in ashes when they ought to be out in his father's sun and wind. And all for a lie!— since the feeling in their hearts that made them so weep, was a false one. Remember, it was not their love, but a false notion of loss. Were they no nearer the light of life than that? To think they should believe in death and the grave, not in him, the Life! Why should death trouble them? Why grudge the friendly elements their grasp on the body, restoring it whence it came, because Lazarus was gone home to God, and needed it no more? I suspect that, looking into their hearts, he saw them feeling and acting just as if Lazarus had ceased to exist.

'Lord, if thou hadst been here, my brother had not died. But I know, that even now, whatsoever thou wilt ask of God, God will give it thee.'

'Thy brother shall rise again.'

'I know that he shall rise again in the resurrection at the last day.'

'I am the resurrection, and the life: he that believeth in me, though he were dead, yet shall he live. And whosoever liveth, and believeth in me, shall never die.'

I will not now endeavour to disclose anything of the depth of this word of the Lord. It will suffice for my present object to say that the sisters must surely have known that he raised up the daughter of Jairus and the son of the widow of Nain; and if the words he had just spoken, 'Thy brother shall rise again,' seemed to Martha too good to be true in the sense that he was going to raise him now, both she and Mary believing he could raise him if he would, might at least have known that if he did not, it must be for reasons as lovely as any for which he might have done it. If he could, and did not, must it not be as well as, yes, better than if he did?

Martha had gone away, for the moment at least, a little comforted; and now came Mary, who knew the Lord better than her sister—alas, with the same bitter tears flowing from her eyes, and the same hopeless words, almost of reproach, falling from her lips! Then it was—at the sight of her and the Jews with her weeping, that the spirit of the Lord was moved with indignation. They wept as those who believe in death, not in life. Mary wept as if she had never seen with her eyes, never handled with her hands the Word of life! He was troubled with their unbelief, and troubled with their trouble. What was to be done with his brothers and sisters who *would* be miserable, who would not believe in his father! What a life of pain was theirs! How was he to comfort them? They would not be comforted! What a world was it that would go on thus—that would not free itself from the clutch of death, even after death was dead, but would weep and weep for thousands of years to come, clasped to the bosom of dead Death! Was existence, the glorious out-gift of his father, to be the most terrible of miseries, because some must go home before others? It was all so sad!—and all because they would not know his father! Then came the reaction from his indignation, and the labouring heart of the Lord found relief in tears.

The Lord was standing, as it were, on the watershed of life. On one side of him lay what Martha and Mary called the world of life, on the other what he and his father and Lazarus called more abundant life. The Lord saw into both worlds—saw Martha and Mary on the one side weeping, on the other Lazarus waiting for them in peace. He would do his best for them—for the sisters—not for Lazarus! It was hard on Lazarus to be called back into the winding-sheet of the body, a sacrifice to their faithlessness, but it should be done! Lazarus should suffer for his sisters! Through him they should be compelled to believe in the Father, and so be delivered from bondage! Death should have no more dominion over them!

He was vexed with them, I have said, for not believing in God, his and their father; and at the same time was troubled with their trouble. The cloud of his loving anger and disappointed sympathy broke in tears; and the tears eased his heart of the weight of its divine grief. He turned, not to them, not to punish them for their unbelief, not even to chide them for their sorrow; he turned to his father to thank him.

He thanks him for hearing a prayer he had made—whether a moment before, or ere he left the other side of the Jordan, I cannot tell. What was the prayer for having heard which he now thanks his father? Surely he had spoken about bringing Lazarus back, and his father had shown himself of one mind with him. 'And I knew that thou hearest me always, but because of the multitude which standeth around I said it, that they may believe that thou didst send me.' 'I said it:' said what? He had said something for the sake of the multitude; what was it? The thanksgiving he had just uttered. He was not in the way of thanking his father in formal words; and now would not naturally have spoken his thanks aloud; for he was always speaking to the Father, and the Father was always hearing him; but he had a reason for doing so, and was now going to give his reason. He had done the unusual thing for the sake of being heard do it, and for holy honesty-sake he tells the fact, speaking to his father so as the people about him may hear, and there be no shadow of undisclosed doubleness in the action—nothing covert, however perfect in honesty. His design in thus thanking aloud must be made patent! 'I thank thee, father, for hearing me; and I say it, not as if I had had any doubt of thy hearing me, but that the people may understand that I am not doing this thing of myself, but as thy messenger. It is thou, father, art going to do it; I am doing it as thy right hand.—Lazarus, come forth.'

I have said the trouble of the Lord was that his friends would not trust his father. He did not want any reception of himself that was not a reception of his father. It was his father, not he, that did the works! From this disappointment came, it seems to me, that sorrowful sigh, 'Nevertheless, when the son of man cometh, shall he find faith on the earth?'

The thought of the Lord in uttering this prayer is not his own justification, but his father's reception by his children. If ever the Lord claims to be received as a true man, it is for the sake of his father and his brethren, that in the receiving of him, he may be received who sent him. Had he now desired the justification of his own claim, the thing he was about to do would have been powerful to that end; but he must have them understand clearly that the Father was one with him in it— that they were doing it together—that it was the will of the Father— that he had sent him.

Lazarus must come and help him with these sisters whom he could not get to believe! Lazarus had tasted of death, and knew what it was: he must come and give his testimony! 'They have lost sight of you, Lazarus, and fancy you gone to the nowhere of their unbelief. Come forth; come out of the unseen. We will set them at rest.' It was hard, I repeat, upon Lazarus; he was better where he was; but he must come and bear the Lord company a little longer, and then be left behind with his sisters, that they and millions more like them might know that God is the God of the living, and not of the dead.

The Jews said, 'Behold how he loved him!' but can any Christian believe it was from love to Lazarus that Jesus wept? It was from love to God, and to Martha and Mary. He had not lost Lazarus; but Martha and Mary were astray from their father in heaven. 'Come, my brother; witness!' he cried; and Lazarus came forth, bound hand and foot. 'Loose him and let him go,' he said—a live truth walking about the world: he had never been dead, and was come forth; he had not been lost, and was restored! It was a strange door he came through, back to his own—a door seldom used, known only to one—but there he was! Oh, the hearts of Martha and Mary! Surely the Lord had some recompense for his trouble, beholding their joy!

Any Christian woman who has read thus far, I now beg to reflect on what

I am going to put before her.

345

Lazarus had to die again, and thanked God, we may be sure, for the glad fact. Did his sisters, supposing them again left behind him in the world, make the same lamentations over him as the former time he went? If they did, if they fell again into that passion of grief, lamenting and moaning and refusing to be comforted, what would you say of them? I imagine something to this effect: 'It was most unworthy of them to be no better for such a favour shown them. It was to behave like the naughtiest of faithless children. Did they not know that he was not lost?—that he was with the Master, who had himself seemed lost for a few days, but came again? He was no more lost now than the time he went before! Could they not trust that he who brought him back once would take care they should have him for ever at last!' Would you not speak after some such fashion? Would you not remember that he who is the shepherd of the sheep will see that the sheep that love one another shall have their own again, in whatever different pastures they may feed for a time? Would it not be hard to persuade you that they ever did so behave? They must have felt that he was but 'gone for a minute … from this room into the next;' and that, however they might miss him, it would be a shame not to be patient when they knew there was nothing to fear. It was all right with him, and would soon be all right with them also!

'Yes,' I imagine you saying, 'that is just how they would feel!'

'Then,' I return, 'why are *you* so miserable? Or why is it but the cold frost of use and forgetting that makes you less miserable than you were a year ago?'

'Ah,' you answer, 'but I had no such miracle wrought for me! Ah, if I had such a miracle wrought for me, you should see then!'

'You mean that if your husband, your son, your father, your brother, your lover, had been taken from you once and given to you again, you would not, when the time came that he must go once more, dream of calling him a second time from the good heaven? You would not be cruel enough for that! You would not bemoan or lament! You would not make the heart of the Lord sad with your hopeless tears! Ah, how little you know yourself! Do you not see that, so far as truth and reason are concerned, you are now in precisely the position supposed—the position of those sisters after Lazarus was taken from them the second time? You know now all they knew then. They had no more of a revelation by the recall of Lazarus than you have. For you profess to believe the story, though you make that doubtful enough by your disregard of the very soul of it. Is it possible that, so far as you are concerned, Lazarus might as well not have risen? What difference is

346

there between your position now and theirs? Lazarus was with God, and they knew he had gone, come back, and gone again. You know that he went, came, and went again. Your friend is gone as Lazarus went twice, and you behave as if you knew nothing of Lazarus. You make a lamentable ado, vexing Jesus that you will not be reasonable and trust his father! When Martha and Mary behaved as you are doing, they had not had Lazarus raised; you have had Lazarus raised, yet you go on as they did then!

'You give too good reason to think that, if the same thing were done for you, you would say he was only in a cataleptic fit, and in truth was never raised from the dead. Or is there another way of understanding your behaviour: you do not believe that God is unchangeable, but think he acts one way one time and another way another time just from caprice? He might give back a brother to sisters who were favourites with him, but no such gift is to be counted upon? Why then, I ask, do you worship such a God?'

'But you know he does *not* do it! That was a mere exceptional case.'

'If it was, it is worthless indeed—as worthless as your behaviour would make it. But you are dull of heart, as were Martha and Mary. Do you not see that he is as continually restoring as taking away—that every bereavement is a restoration—that when you are weeping with void arms, others, who love as well as you, are clasping in ecstasy of reunion?'

'Alas, we know nothing about that!'

'If you have learned no more I must leave you, having no ground in you upon which my words may fall. You deceived me; you called yourself a Christian. You cannot have been doing the will of the Father, or you would not be as you are.'

'Ah, you little know my loss!'

'Indeed it is great! it seems to include God! If you knew what he knows about death you would clap your listless hands. But why should I seek in vain to comfort you? You must be made miserable, that you may wake from your sleep to know that you need God. If you do not find him, endless life with the living whom you bemoan would become and remain to you unendurable. The knowledge of your own heart will teach you this— not the knowledge you have, but the knowledge that is on its way to you through suffering. Then you will feel that existence itself is the prime of evils, without *the righteousness which is of God by faith.*'

RIGHTEOUSNESS.

—that I may win Christ, and be found in him, not having mine own righteousness, which is of the law, but that which is through the faith of Christ, the righteousness which is of God by faith.—Ep. to the Philippians iii. 8-9.

What does the apostle mean by the righteousness that is of God by faith? He means the same righteousness Christ had by his faith in God, the same righteousness God himself has.

In his second epistle to the Corinthians he says, 'He hath made him to be sin for us who knew no sin, that we might be made the righteousness of God in him;'—'He gave him to be treated like a sinner, killed and cast out of his own vineyard by his husbandmen, that we might in him be made righteous like God.' As the antithesis stands it is rhetorically correct. But if the former half means, 'he made him to be treated as if he were a sinner,' then the latter half should, in logical precision, mean, 'that we might be treated as if we were righteous.'

'That is just what Paul does mean,' insist not a few. 'He means that Jesus was treated by God as if he were a sinner, our sins being imputed to him, in order that we might be treated as if we were righteous, his righteousness being imputed to us.'

That is, that, by a sort of legal fiction, Jesus was treated as what he was not, in order that we might be treated as what we are not. This is the best device, according to the prevailing theology, that the God of truth, the God of mercy, whose glory is that he is just to men by forgiving their sins, could fall upon for saving his creatures!

I had thought that this most contemptible of false doctrines had nigh ceased to be presented, though I knew it must be long before it ceased to exercise baneful influence; but, to my astonishment, I came upon it lately in quite a modern commentary which I happened to look into in a friend's house. I say, to my astonishment, for the commentary was the work of one of the most liberal and lovely of Christians, a dignitary high in the church of England, a man whom I knew and love, and hope ere long to meet where there are no churches. In the comment that came under my eye, he refers to the doctrine of imputed righteousness as the possible explanation of a certain passage—refers to it as to a doctrine concerning whose truth was no question.

It seems to me that, seeing much duplicity exists in the body of Christ, every honest member of it should protest against any word tending to imply the existence of falsehood in the indwelling spirit of that body. I now protest against this so-called *doctrine*, counting it the rightful prey of the foolishest wind in the limbo of vanities, whither I would gladly do my best to send it. It is a mean, nauseous invention, false, and productive of falsehood. Say it is a figure, I answer it is not only a false figure but an embodiment of untruth; say it expresses a reality, and I say it teaches the worst of lies; say there is a shadow of truth in it, and I answer it may be so, but there is no truth touched in it that could not be taught infinitely better without it. It is the meagre misshapen offspring of the legalism of a poverty-stricken mechanical fancy, unlighted by a gleam of divine imagination. No one who knows his New Testament will dare to say that the figure is once used in it.

I have dealt already with the source of it. They say first, God must punish the sinner, for justice requires it; then they say he does not punish the sinner, but punishes a perfectly righteous man instead, attributes his righteousness to the sinner, and so continues just. Was there ever such a confusion, such an inversion of right and wrong! Justice *could not* treat a righteous man as an unrighteous; neither, if justice required the punishment of sin, *could* justice let the sinner go unpunished. To lay the pain upon the righteous in the name of justice is simply monstrous. No wonder unbelief is rampant. Believe in Moloch if you will, but call him Moloch, not Justice. Be sure that the thing that God gives, the righteousness that is of God, is a real thing, and not a contemptible legalism. Pray God I have no righteousness imputed to me. Let me be regarded as the sinner I am; for nothing will serve my need but to be made a righteous man, one that will no more sin.

We have the word *imputed* just once in the New Testament. Whether the evil doctrine may have sprung from any possible misunderstanding of the passage where it occurs, I hardly care to inquire.

The word as Paul uses it, and the whole of the thought whence his use of it springs, appeals to my sense of right and justice as much as the common use of it arouses my abhorrence. The apostle says that a certain thing was imputed to Abraham for righteousness; or, as the revised version has it, 'reckoned unto him:' what was it that was thus imputed to Abraham? The righteousness of another? God forbid! It was his own faith. The faith of Abraham is reckoned to him for righteousness. To impute the righteousness of one to another, is simply to act a falsehood; to call the faith of a man his righteousness is simply to speak the truth. Was it not righteous in Abraham to obey God? The Jews placed righteousness in keeping all the particulars of the law of Moses: Paul says faith in God was counted righteousness before Moses was born. You may answer, Abraham was unjust in many things, and by no means a righteous man. True; he was not a righteous man in any complete sense; his righteousness would never have satisfied Paul; neither, you may be sure, did it satisfy Abraham; but his faith was nevertheless righteousness, and if it had not been counted to him for righteousness, there would have been falsehood somewhere, for such faith as Abraham's *is righteousness*. It was no mere intellectual recognition of the existence of a God, which is consistent with the deepest atheism; it was that faith which is one with action: 'He went out, not knowing whither he went.' The very act of believing in God after such fashion that, when the time of action comes, the man will obey God, is the highest act, the deepest, loftiest righteousness of which man is capable, is at the root of all other righteousness, and the spirit of it will work till the man is perfect. If you define righteousness in the common-sense, that is, in the divine fashion—for religion is nothing if it be not the deepest common-sense—as a giving to everyone his due, then certainly the first due is to him who makes us capable of owing, that is, makes us responsible creatures. You may say this is not one's first feeling of duty. True; but the first in reality is seldom the first perceived. The first duty is too high and too deep to come first into consciousness. If any one were born perfect, which I count an eternal impossibility, then the highest duty would come first into the consciousness. As we are born, it is the doing of, or at least the honest trying to do many another duty, that will at length lead a man to see that his duty to God is the first and deepest and highest of all, including and requiring the performance of all other duties whatever. A man might live a thousand years in neglect of duty, and never come to see that any obligation was upon him to put faith in God and do what he told him—never have a glimpse of the fact that he owed him something. I will allow that if God were what he thinks him he would indeed owe him little; but he thinks him such in consequence of not doing what he knows he ought to do. He has not come to the light. He has deadened, dulled, hardened his nature. He has not been a man without guile, has not been true and fair.

But while faith in God is the first duty, and may therefore well be called righteousness in the man in whom it is operative, even though it be imperfect, there is more reason than this why it should be counted to a man for righteousness. It is the one spiritual act which brings the man into contact with the original creative power, able to help him in every endeavour after righteousness, and ensure his progress to perfection. The man who exercises it may therefore also well be called a righteous man, however far from complete in righteousness. We may call a woman beautiful who is not perfect in beauty; in the Bible men are constantly recognized as righteous men who are far from perfectly righteous. The Bible never deals with impossibilities, never demands of any man at any given moment a righteousness of which at that moment he is incapable; neither does it lay upon any man any other law than that of perfect righteousness. It demands of him righteousness; when he yields that righteousness of which he is capable, content for the moment, it goes on to demand more: the common-sense of the Bible is lovely.

To the man who has no faith in God, faith in God cannot look like righteousness; neither can he know that it is creative of all other righteousness toward equal and inferior lives: he cannot know that it is not merely the beginning of righteousness, but the germ of life, the active potency whence life-righteousness grows. It is not like some single separate act of righteousness; it is the action of the whole man, turning to good from evil—turning his back on all that is opposed to righteousness, and starting on a road on which he cannot stop, in which he must go on growing more and more righteous, discovering more and more what righteousness is, and more and more what is unrighteous in himself. In the one act of believing in God—that is, of giving himself to do what he tells him—he abjures evil, both what he knows and what he does not yet know in himself. A man may indeed have turned to obey God, and yet be capable of many an injustice to his neighbour which he has not yet discovered to be an injustice; but as he goes on obeying, he will go on discovering. Not only will he grow more and more determined to be just, but he will grow more and more sensitive to the idea of injustice—I do not mean in others, but in himself. A man who continues capable of a known injustice to his neighbour, cannot be believed to have turned to God. At all events, a man cannot be near God, so as to be learning what is just toward God, and not be near his neighbour, so as to be learning what is unfair to him; for his will, which is the man, lays hold of righteousness, chooses to be righteous. If a man is to be blamed for not choosing righteousness, for not turning to the light, for not coming out of the darkness, then the man who does choose and turn and come out, is to be justified in his deed, and declared to be righteous. He is not yet thoroughly righteous, but is growing in and toward righteousness. He needs creative God, and time for will and effort. Not yet quite righteous, he cannot yet act quite righteously, for only the man in whom the image of God is perfected can live perfectly. Born into the world without righteousness, he cannot see, he cannot know, he is not in touch with perfect righteousness, and it would be the deepest injustice to demand of him, with a penalty, at any given moment, more than he knows how to yield; but it is the highest lore constantly to demand of him perfect righteousness as what he must attain to. With what life and possibility is in him, he must keep turning to righteousness and abjuring iniquity, ever aiming at the perfection of God. Such an obedient faith is most justly and fairly, being all that God himself can require of the man, called by God righteousness in the man. It would not be enough for the righteousness of God, or Jesus, or any perfected saint, because they are capable of perfect righteousness, and, knowing what is perfect righteousness, choose to be perfectly righteous; but, in virtue of the life and growth in it, it is enough at a given moment for the disciple of the Perfect. The righteousness of Abraham was not to compare with the righteousness of Paul. He did not fight with himself for righteousness, as did Paul— not because he was better than Paul and therefore did not need to fight, but because his idea of what was required of him was not within sight of that of Paul; yet was he righteous in the same way as Paul was righteous: he had begun to be righteous, and God called his righteousness righteousness, for faith is righteousness. His faith was an act recognizing God as his law, and that is not a partial act, but an all-embracing and all-determining action. A single righteous deed toward one's fellow could hardly be imputed to a man as righteousness. A man who is not trying after righteousness may yet do many a righteous act: they will not be forgotten to him, neither will they be imputed to him as righteousness. Abraham's action of obedient faith was righteousness none the less that his righteousness was far behind Paul's. Abraham started at the beginning of the long, slow, disappointing preparation of the Jewish people; Paul started at its close, with the story of Jesus behind him. Both believed, obeying God, and therefore both were righteous. They were righteous because they gave themselves up to God to make them righteous; and not to call such men righteous, not to impute their faith to them for righteousness, would be unjust. But God is utterly just, and nowise resembles a legal-minded Roman emperor, or a bad pope formulating the doctrine of vicarious sacrifice.

What, then, is the righteousness which is of God by faith? It is simply the thing that God wants every man to be, wrought out in him by constant obedient contact with God himself. It is not an attribute either of God or man, but a fact of character in God and in man. It is God's righteousness wrought out in us, so that as he is righteous we too are righteous. It does not consist in obeying this or that law; not even the keeping of every law, so that no hair's-breadth did we run counter to one of them, would be righteousness. To be righteous is to be such a heart, soul, mind, and will, as, without regard to law, would recoil with horror from the lightest possible breach of any law. It is to be so in love with what is fair and right as to make it impossible for a man to do anything that is less than absolutely righteous. It is not the love of righteousness in the abstract that makes anyone righteous, but such a love of fairplay toward everyone with whom we come into contact, that anything less than the fulfilling, with a clear joy, of our divine relation to him or her, is impossible. For the righteousness of God goes far beyond mere deeds, and requires of us love and helping mercy as our highest obligation and justice to our fellow men—those of them too who have done nothing for us, those even who have done us wrong. Our relations with others, God first and then our neighbour in order and degree, must one day become, as in true nature they are, the gladness of our being; and nothing then will ever appear good for us, that is not in harmony with those blessed relations. Every thought will not merely be just, but will be just because it is something more, because it is live and true. What heart in the kingdom of heaven would ever dream of constructing a metaphysical system of what we owed to God and why we owed it? The light of our life, our sole, eternal, and infinite joy, is simply God—God—God—nothing but God, and all his creatures in him. He is all and in all, and the children of the kingdom know it. He includes all things; not to be true to anything he has made is to be untrue to him. God is truth, is life; to be in God is to know him and need no law. Existence will be eternal Godness.

You would not like that way of it? There is, there can be, no other; but before you can judge of it, you must know at least a little of God as he is, not as you imagine him. I say *as you imagine him*, because it cannot be that any creature should know him as he is and not desire him. In proportion as we know him we must desire him, until at length we live in and for him with all our conscious heart. That is why the Jews did not like the Lord: he cared so simply for his father's will, and not for anything they called his will.

The righteousness which is of God by faith in the source, the prime of that righteousness, is then just the same kind of thing as God's righteousness, differing only as the created differs from the creating. The righteousness of him who does the will of his father in heaven, is the righteousness of Jesus Christ, is God's own righteousness. The righteousness which is of God by faith in God, is God's righteousness. The man who has this righteousness, thinks about things as God thinks about them, loves the things that God loves, cares for nothing that God does not care about. Even while this righteousness is being born in him, the man will say to himself, 'Why should I be troubled about this thing or that? Does God care about it? No. Then why should I care? I must not care. I will not care! 'If he does not know whether God cares about it or not, he will say, 'If God cares I should have my desire, he will give it me; if he does not care I should have it, neither will I care. In the meantime I will do my work.' The man with God's righteousness does not love a thing merely because it is right, but loves the very rightness in it. He not only loves a thought, but he loves the man in his thinking that thought; he loves the thought alive in the man. He does not take his joy from himself. He feels joy in himself, but it comes to him from others, not from himself—from God first, and from some-body, anybody, everybody next. He would rather, in the fulness of his content, pass out of being, rather himself cease to exist, than that an-other should. He could do without knowing himself, but he could not know himself and spare one of the brothers or sisters God had given him. The man who really knows God, is, and always will be, content with what God, who is the very self of his self, shall choose for him; he is entirely God's, and not at all his own. His consciousness of him-self is the reflex from those about him, not the result of his own turning in of his regard upon himself. It is not the contemplation of what God has made him, it is the being what God has made him, and the contemplation of what God himself is, and what he has made his fellows, that gives him his joy. He wants nothing, and feels that he has all things, for he is in the bosom of his father, and the thoughts of his father come to him. He knows that if he needs anything, it is his before he asks it; for his father has willed him, in the might and truth of his fatherhood, to be one with himself.

This then, or something like this, for words are poor to tell the best things, is the righteousness which is of God by faith—so far from being a thing built on the rubbish heap of legal fiction called vicarious sacrifice, or its shadow called imputed righteousness, that only the child with the child-heart, so far ahead of and so different from the wise and prudent, can understand it. The wise and prudent interprets God by himself, and does not understand him; the child interprets God by himself, and does understand him. The wise and prudent must make a system and arrange things to his mind before he can say, *I believe*. The child sees, believes, obeys—and knows he must be perfect as his father in heaven is perfect. If an angel, seeming to come from heaven, told him that God had let him off, that he did not require so much of him as that, but would be content with less; that he could not indeed allow him to be wicked, but would pass by a great deal, modifying his demands because it was so hard for him to be quite good, and he loved him so dearly, the child of God would at once recognize, woven with the angel's starry brilliancy, the flicker of the flames of hell, and would say to the shining one, 'Get thee behind me, Satan.' Nor would there be the slightest wonder or merit in his doing so, for at the words of the deceiver, if but for briefest moment imagined true, the shadow of a rising hell would gloom over the face of creation; hope would vanish; the eternal would be as the carcase of a dead man; the glory would die out of the face of God—until the groan of a thunderous *no* burst from the caverns of the universe, and the truth, flashing on his child's soul from the heart of the Eternal, Immortal, Invisible, withered up the lie of the messenger of darkness.

'But how can God bring this about in me?'

Let him do it, and perhaps you will know; if you never know, yet there it will be. Help him to do it, or he cannot do it. He originates the possibility of your being his son, his daughter; he makes you able to will it, but you must will it. If he is not doing it in you—that is, if you have as yet prevented him from beginning, why should I tell you, even if I knew the process, how he would do what you will not let him do? Why should you know? What claim have you to know? But indeed how should you be able to know? For it must deal with deeper and higher things than you *can* know anything of till the work is at least begun. Perhaps if you approved of the plans of the glad creator, you would allow him to make of you something divine! To teach your intellect what has to be learned by your whole being, what cannot be understood without the whole being, what it would do you no good to understand save you understood it in your whole being—if this be the province of any man, it is not mine. Let the dead bury their dead, and the dead teach their dead; for me, I will try to wake them. To those who are awake, I cry, 'For the sake of your father and the first-born among many brethren to whom we belong, for the sake of those he has given us to love the most dearly, let patience have her perfect work. Statue under the chisel of the sculptor, stand steady to the blows of his mallet. Clay on the wheel, let the fingers of the divine potter model you at their will. Obey the Father's lightest word; hear the Brother who knows you, and died for you; beat down your sin, and trample it to death.

Brother, when thou sittest at home in thy house, which is the temple of the Lord, open all thy windows to breathe the air of his approach; set the watcher on thy turret, that he may listen out into the dark for the sound of his coming, and thy hand be on the latch to open the door at his first knock. Shouldst thou open the door and not see him, do not say he did not knock, but understand that he is there, and wants thee to go out to him. It may be he has something for thee to do for him. Go and do it, and perhaps thou wilt return with a new prayer, to find a new window in thy soul.

Never wait for fitter time or place to talk to him. To wait till thou go to church, or to thy closet, is to make *him* wait. He will listen as thou walkest in the lane or the crowded street, on the common or in the place of shining concourse.

Remember, if indeed thou art able to know it, that not in any church is the service done that he requires. He will say to no man, 'You never went to church: depart from me; I do not know you;' but, 'Inasmuch as you never helped one of my father's children, you have done nothing for me.' Church or chapel is *not* the place for divine service. It is a place of prayer, a place of praise, a place to feed upon good things, a place to learn of God, as what place is not? It is a place to look in the eyes of your neighbour, and love God along with him. But the world in which you move, the place of your living and loving and labour, not the church you go to on your holiday, is the place of divine service. Serve your neighbour, and you serve him.

Do not heed much if men mock you and speak lies of you, or in goodwill defend you unworthily. Heed not much if even the righteous turn their backs upon you. Only take heed that you turn not from them. Take courage in the fact that *there is nothing covered, that shall not be revealed; and hid, that shall not be known.*

THE FINAL UNMASKING.

***For there is nothing covered, that shall not be re-
vealed; and hid, that shall not be known.*— Matthew
x. 26; Luke xii. 2.**

God is not a God that hides, but a God that reveals. His whole work
in relation to the creatures he has made—and where else can lie his
work?—is revelation—the giving them truth, the showing of himself
to them, that they may know him, and come nearer and nearer to him,
and so he have his children more and more of companions to him.
That we are in the dark about anything is never because he hides it, but
because we are not yet such that he is able to reveal that thing to us.

That God could not do the thing at once which he takes time to do,
we may surely say without irreverence. His will cannot finally be
thwarted; where it is thwarted for a time, the very thwarting subserves
the working out of a higher part of his will. He gave man the power to
thwart his will, that, by means of that same power, he might come at
last to do his will in a higher kind and way than would otherwise have
been possible to him. God sacrifices his will to man that man may be-
come such as himself, and give all to the truth; he makes man able to
do wrong, that he may choose and love righteousness.

The fact that all things are slowly coming into the light of the
knowledge of men—so far as this may be possible to the created—is
used in three different ways by the Lord, as reported by his evangelist.
In one case, with which we will not now occupy ourselves—*Mark* iv.
22; *Luke* viii. 16—he uses it to enforce the duty of those who have
received light to let it shine: they must do their part to bring all things
out. In *Luke* xii. 2, is recorded how he brought it to bear on hypocrisy,
showing its uselessness; and, in the case recorded in *Matthew* x. 25, he

uses the fact to enforce fearlessness as to the misinterpretation of our words and actions.

In whatever mode the Lord may intend that it shall be wrought out, he gives us to understand, as an unalterable principle in the government of the universe, that all such things as the unrighteous desire to conceal, and such things as it is a pain to the righteous to have concealed, shall come out into the light.

'Beware of hypocrisy,' the Lord says, 'for there is nothing covered, that shall not be revealed, neither hid, that shall not be known,' What is hypocrisy? The desire to look better than you are; the hiding of things you do, because you would not be supposed to do them, because you would be ashamed to have them known where you are known. The doing of them is foul; the hiding of them, in order to appear better than you are, is fouler still. The man who does not live in his own consciousness as in the open heavens, is a hypocrite—and for most of us the question is, are we growing less or more of such hypocrites? Are we ashamed of not having been open and clear? Are we fighting the evil thing which is our temptation to hypocrisy? The Lord has not a thought in him to be ashamed of before God and his universe, and he will not be content until he has us in the same liberty. For our encouragement to fight on, he tells us that those that hunger and thirst after righteousness shall be filled, that they shall become as righteous as the spirit of the Father and the Son in them can make them desire.

The Lord says also, 'If they have called the master of the house Beelzebub, how much more shall they call them of his household! Fear them not therefore: for there is nothing covered, that shall not be revealed; and hid, that shall not be known.' To a man who loves righteousness and his fellow men, it must always be painful to be misunderstood; and misunderstanding is specially inevitable where he acts upon principles beyond the recognition of those around him, who, being but half-hearted Christians, count themselves the law-givers of righteousness, and charge him with the very things it is the aim of his life to destroy. The Lord himself was accused of being a drunkard and a keeper of bad company—and perhaps would in the present day be so regarded by not a few calling themselves by his name, and teaching temperance and virtue. He lived upon a higher spiritual platform than they understand, acted from a height of the virtues they would inculcate, loftier than their eyes can scale. His Himalays are not visible from their sand-heaps. The Lord bore with their evil tongues, and was neither dismayed nor troubled; but from this experience of his own, comforts those who, being his messengers, must fare as he. 'If they have called the master of the house Beelzebub, how much more shall they call them of his household!'—'If they insult a man, how much more will they not insult his servants!' While men count themselves Christians on any other ground than that they are slaves of Jesus Christ, the children of God, and free from themselves, so long will they use the servants of the Master despitefully. 'Do not hesitate,' says the Lord, 'to speak the truth that is in you; never mind what they call you; proclaim from the housetop; fear nobody.'

He spoke the words to the men to whom he looked first to spread the news of the kingdom of heaven; but they apply to all who obey him. Few who have endeavoured to do their duty, have not been annoyed, disappointed, enraged perhaps, by the antagonism, misunderstanding, and false representation to which they have been subjected therein—issuing mainly from those and the friends of those who have benefited by their efforts to be neighbours to all. The tales of heartlessness and ingratitude one must come across, compel one to see more and more clearly that humanity, without willed effort after righteousness, is mean enough to sink to any depth of disgrace. The judgments also of imagined superiority are hard to bear. The rich man who will screw his workmen to the lowest penny, will read his poor relation a solemn lecture on extravagance, because of some humblest little act of generosity! He takes the end of the beam sticking out of his eye to pick the mote from the eye of his brother withal! If, in the endeavour to lead a truer life, a man merely lives otherwise than his neighbours, strange motives will be invented to account for it. To the honest soul it is a comfort to believe that the truth will one day be known, that it will cease to be supposed that he was and did as dull heads and hearts reported of him. Still more satisfactory will be the unveiling where a man is misunderstood by those who ought to know him better—who, not even understanding the point at issue, take it for granted he is about to do the wrong thing, while he is crying for courage to heed neither himself nor his friends, but only the Lord. How many hear and accept the words, 'Be not conformed to this world,' without once perceiving that what they call Society and bow to as supreme, is the World and nothing else, or that those who mind what people think, and what people will say, are conformed to—that is, take the shape of—the world. The true man feels he has nothing to do with Society as judge or lawgiver: he is under the law of Jesus Christ, and it sets him free from the law of the World. Let a man do right, nor trouble himself about worthless opinion; the less he heeds tongues, the less difficult will he find it to love men. Let him comfort himself with the thought that the truth must out. He will not have to pass through eternity with the brand of ignorant or malicious judgment upon him. He shall find his peers and be judged of them.

But, thou who lookest for the justification of the light, art thou verily prepared for thyself to encounter such exposure as the general unveiling of things must bring? Art thou willing for the truth whatever it be? I nowise mean to ask, Have you a conscience so void of offence, have you a heart so pure and clean, that you fear no fullest exposure of what is in you to the gaze of men and angels?—as to God, he knows it all now! What I mean to ask is, Do you so love the truth and the right, that you welcome, or at least submit willingly to the idea of an exposure of what in you is yet unknown to yourself—an exposure that may redound to the glory of the truth by making you ashamed and humble? It may be, for instance, that you were wrong in regard to those, for the righting of whose wrongs to you, the great judgment of God is now by you waited for with desire: will you welcome any discovery, even if it work for the excuse of others, that will make you more true, by revealing what in you was false? Are you willing to be made glad that you were wrong when you thought others were wrong? If you can with such submission face the revelation of things hid, then you are of the truth, and need not be afraid; for, whatever comes, it will and can only make you more true and humble and pure.

Does the Lord mean that everything a man has ever done or thought must be laid bare to the universe?

So far, I think, as is necessary to the understanding of the man by those who have known, or are concerned to know him. For the time to come, and for those who are yet to know him, the man will henceforth, if he is a true man, be transparent to all that are capable of reading him. A man may not then, any more than now, be intelligible to those beneath him, but all things will be working toward revelation, nothing toward concealment or misunderstanding. Who in the kingdom will desire concealment, or be willing to misunderstand? Concealment is darkness; misunderstanding is a fog. A man will hold the door open for anyone to walk into his house, for it is a temple of the living God—with some things worth looking at, and nothing to hide. The glory of the true world is, that there is nothing in it that needs to be covered, while ever and ever there will be things uncovered. Every man's light will shine for the good and glory of his neighbour.

'Will all my weaknesses, all my evil habits, all my pettinesses, all the wrong thoughts which I cannot help—will all be set out before the universe?'

Yes, if they so prevail as to constitute your character—that is, if they are you. But if you have come out of the darkness, if you are fighting it, if you are honestly trying to walk in the light, you may hope in God your father that what he has cured, what he is curing, what he has forgiven, will be heard of no more, not now being a constituent part of you. Or if indeed some of your evil things must yet be seen, the truth of them will be seen—that they are things you are at strife with, not things you are cherishing and brooding over. God will be fair to you—so fair!—fair with the fairness of a father loving his own—who will have you clean, who will neither spare you any needful shame, nor leave you exposed to any that is not needful. The thing we have risen above, is dead and forgotten, or if remembered, there is God to comfort us. 'If any man sin, we have a comforter with the Father.' We may trust God with our past as heartily as with our future. It will not hurt us so long as we do not try to hide things, so long as we are ready to bow our heads in hearty shame where it is fit we should be ashamed. For to be ashamed is a holy and blessed thing. Shame is a thing to shame only those who want to appear, not those who want to be. Shame is to shame those who want to pass their examination, not those who would get into the heart of things. In the name of God let us henceforth have nothing to be ashamed of, and be ready to meet any shame on its way to meet us. For to be humbly ashamed is to be plunged in the cleansing bath of the truth.

As to the revelation of the ways of God, I need not speak; he has been always, from the first, revealing them to his prophet, to his child, and will go on doing so for ever. But let me say a word about another kind of revelation—that of their own evil to the evil.

The only terrible, or at least the supremely terrible revelation is that of a man to himself. What a horror will it not be to a vile man—more than all to a man whose pleasure has been enhanced by the suffering of others—a man that knew himself such as men of ordinary morals would turn from with disgust, but who has hitherto had no insight into what he is—what a horror will it not be to him when his eyes are opened to see himself as the pure see him, as God sees him! Imagine such a man waking all at once, not only to see the eyes of the universe fixed upon him with loathing astonishment, but to see himself at the same moment as those eyes see him! What a waking!—into the full blaze of fact and consciousness, of truth and violation!

To know my deed, 'twere best not know myself!

Or think what it must be for a man counting himself religious, orthodox, exemplary, to perceive suddenly that there was no religion in him, only love of self; no love of the right, only a great love of being in the right! What a discovery—that he was simply a hypocrite—one who loved to *appear*, and *was* not! The rich seem to be those among whom will occur hereafter the sharpest reverses, if I understand aright the parable of the rich man and Lazarus. Who has not known the insolence of their meanness toward the poor, all the time counting themselves of the very elect! What riches and fancied religion, with the self-sufficiency they generate between them, can make man or woman capable of, is appalling. Mammon, the most contemptible of deities, is the most worshipped, both outside and in the house of God: to many of the religious rich in that day, the great damning revelation will be their behaviour to the poor to whom they thought themselves very kind. 'He flattereth himself in his own eyes until his iniquity is found to be hateful.' A man may loathe a thing in the abstract for years, and find at last that all the time he has been, in his own person, guilty of it. To carry a thing under our cloak caressingly, hides from us its identity with something that stands before us on the public pillory. Many a man might read this and assent to it, who cages in his own bosom a carrion-bird that he never knows for what it is, because there are points of difference in its plumage from that of the bird he calls by an ugly name.

Of all who will one day stand in dismay and sickness of heart, with the consciousness that their very existence is a shame, those will fare the worst who have been consciously false to their fellows; who, pretending friendship, have used their neighbour to their own ends; and especially those who, pretending friendship, have divided friends. To such Dante has given the lowest hell. If there be one thing God hates, it must be treachery. Do not imagine Judas the only man of whom the Lord would say, 'Better were it for that man if he had never been born!' Did the Lord speak out of personal indignation, or did he utter a spiritual fact, a live principle? Did he speak in anger at the treachery of his apostle to himself, or in pity for the man that had better not have been born? Did the word spring from his knowledge of some fearful punishment awaiting Judas, or from his sense of the horror it was to be such a man? Beyond all things pitiful is it that a man should carry about with him the consciousness of being such a person—should know himself and not another that false one! 'O God,' we think, 'how terrible if it were I!' Just so terrible is it that it should be Judas! And have I not done things with the same germ in them, a germ which, brought to its evil perfection, would have shown itself the cankerworm, treachery? Except I love my neighbour as myself, I may one day betray him! Let us therefore be compassionate and humble, and hope for every man.

A man may sink by such slow degrees that, long after he is a devil, he may go on being a good churchman or a good dissenter, and thinking himself a good Christian. Continuously repeated sin against the poorest consciousness of evil must have a dread rousing. There are men who never wake to know how wicked they are, till, lo, the gaze of the multitude is upon them!—the multitude staring with self-righteous eyes, doing like things themselves, but not yet found out; sinning after another pattern, therefore the hardest judges, thinking by condemnation to escape judgment. But there is nothing covered that shall not be revealed. What if the only thing to wake the treacherous, money-loving thief, Judas, to a knowledge of himself, was to let the thing go on to the end, and his kiss betray the Master? Judas did not hate the Master when he kissed him, but not being a true man, his very love betrayed him.

The good man, conscious of his own evil, and desiring no refuge but the purifying light, will chiefly rejoice that the exposure of evil makes for the victory of the truth, the kingdom of God and his Christ. He sees in the unmasking of the hypocrite, in the unveiling of the covered, in the exposure of the hidden, God's interference, for him and all the race, between them and the lie.

The only triumph the truth can ever have is its recognition by the heart of the liar. Its victory is in the man who, not content with saying, 'I was blind and now I see,' cries out, 'Lord God, just and true, let me perish, but endure thou! Let me live because thou livest, because thou savest me from the death in myself, the untruth I have nourished in me, and even called righteousness! Hallowed be thy name, for thou only art true; thou only lovest; thou only art holy, for thou only art humble! Thou only art unselfish; thou only hast never sought thine own, but the things of thy children! Yea, O father, be thou true, and every man a liar!'

There is no satisfaction of revenge possible to the injured. The severest punishment that can be inflicted upon the wrong-doer is simply to let him know what he is; for his nature is of God, and the deepest in him is the divine. Neither can any other punishment than the sinner's being made to see the enormity of his injury, give satisfaction to the injured. While the wronger will admit no wrong, while he mocks at the idea of amends, or while, admitting the wrong, he rejoices in having done it, no suffering could satisfy revenge, far less justice. Both would continually know themselves foiled. Therefore, while a satisfied justice is an unavoidable eternal event, a satisfied revenge is an eternal impossibility. For the moment that the sole adequate punishment, a vision of himself, begins to take true effect upon the sinner, that moment the sinner has begun to grow a righteous man, and the brother human whom he has offended has no choice, has nothing left him but to take the offender to his bosom—the more tenderly that his brother is a repentant brother, that he was dead and is alive again, that he was lost and is found. Behold the meeting of the divine extremes—the extreme of punishment, the embrace of heaven! They run together; 'the wheel is come full circle.' For, I venture to think, there can be no such agony for created soul, as to see itself vile—vile by its own action and choice. Also I venture to think there can be no delight for created soul—short, that is, of being one with the Father—so deep as that of seeing the heaven of forgiveness open, and disclose the shining stair that leads to its own natural home, where the eternal father has been all the time awaiting this return of his child.

So, friends, how ever indignant we may be, however intensely and however justly we may feel our wrongs, there is no revenge possible for us in the universe of the Father. I may say to myself with heartiest vengeance, 'I should just like to let that man see what a wretch he is— what all honest men at this moment think of him!' but, the moment come, the man will loathe himself tenfold more than any other man could, and that moment my heart will bury his sin. Its own ocean of pity will rush from the divine depths of its God-origin to overwhelm it. Let us try to forethink, to antedate our forgiveness. Dares any man suppose that Jesus would have him hate the traitor through whom he came to the cross? Has he been pleased through all these ages with the manner in which those calling themselves by his name have treated, and are still treating his nation? We have not yet sounded the depths of forgiveness that are and will be required of such as would be his disciples!

Our friends will know us then: for their joy, will it be, or their sorrow? Will their hearts sink within them when they look on the real likeness of us? Or will they rejoice to find that we were not so much to be blamed as they thought, in this thing or that which gave them trouble?

Let us remember, however, that not evil only will be unveiled; that many a masking misconception will uncover a face radiant with the loveliness of the truth. And whatever disappointments may fall, there is consolation for every true heart in the one sufficing joy—that it

364

stands on the border of the kingdom, about to enter into ever fuller, ever-growing possession *of the inheritance of the saints in light.*

THE INHERITANCE.

Giving thanks unto the Father, which hath made us meet to be partakers of the inheritance of the saints in light.— Ep. to the Colossians i. 12.

To have a share in any earthly inheritance, is to diminish the share of the other inheritors. In the inheritance of the saints, that which each has, goes to increase the possession of the rest. Hear what Dante puts in the mouth of his guide, as they pass through Purgatory:—

> Perche s'appuntano i vostri desiri
>   Dove per compagnia parte si scema,
>   Invidia muove il mantaco a' sospiri.
> Ma se l'amor della spera suprema
>   Torcesse 'n suso 'l desiderio vostro,
>   Non vi sarebbe al petto quella tema;
> Che per quanto si dice piu li nostro,
>   Tanto possiede piu di ben ciascuno,
>   E piu di caritade arde in quel chiostro.
> Because you point and fix your longing eyes
>   On things where sharing lessens every share,
>   The human bellows heave with envious sighs.
> But if the loftiest love that dwelleth there
>   Up to the heaven of heavens your longing turn,
>   Then from your heart will pass this fearing care:
> The oftener there the word *our* they discern,
>   The more of good doth everyone possess,
>   The more of love doth in that cloister burn.

THE INHERITANCE.

Dante desires to know how it can be that a distributed good should make the receivers the richer the more of them there are; and Virgil answers—

> Perocche tu rificchi
> La mente pure alle cose terrene,
> Di vera luce tenebre dispicchi.
> Quello 'nfinito ed ineffabil bene,
> Che lassu e, cosi corre ad amore,
> Com' a lucido corpo raggio viene.
> Tanto si da, quanto trova d' ardore:
> Si che quantunque carita si stende,
> Cresce sovr' essa l' eterno valore.
> E quanta gente pin lassu s' intende,
> Piu v' e da bene amare, e pin vi s' ama,
> E come specchio, l' uno all' altro rende.
> Because thy mind doth stick
> To earthly things, and on them only brood,
> From the true light thou dost but darkness pick.
> That same ineffable and infinite Good,
> Which dwells up there, to Love doth run as fleet
> As sunrays to bright things, for sisterhood.
> It gives itself proportionate to the heat:
> So that, wherever Love doth spread its reign,
> The growing wealth of God makes that its seat.
> And the more people that up thither strain,
> The more there are to love, the more they love,
> And like a mirror each doth give and gain.

In this inheritance then a man may desire and endeavour to obtain his share without selfish prejudice to others; nay, to fail of our share in it, would be to deprive others of a portion of theirs. Let us look a little nearer, and see in what the inheritance of the saints consists.

It might perhaps be to commit some small logical violence on the terms of the passage to say that 'the inheritance of the saints in light' *must* mean purely and only 'the possession of light which is the inheritance of the saints.' At the same time the phrase is literally 'the inheritance of the saints *in the light*;' and this perhaps makes it the more likely that, as I take it, Paul had in his mind the light as itself the inheritance of the saints—that he held the very substance of the inheritance to be the light. And if we remember that God is light; also that the highest prayer of the Lord for his friends was that they might be one in him and his father; and recall what the apostle said to the Ephesians, that 'in him we live and move and have our being,' we may be prepared to agree that, although he may not mean to include all possible phases of the inheritance of the saints in the one word *light*, as I think he does, yet the idea is perfectly consistent with his teaching. For the one only thing to make existence a good, the one thing to make it worth having, is just that there should be no film of separation between our life and the life of which ours is an outcome; that we should not only *know* that God is our life, but be aware, in some grand consciousness beyond anything imagination can present to us, of the presence of the making God, in the very process of continuing us the live things he has made us. This is only another way of saying that the very inheritance upon which, as the twice-born sons of our father, we have a claim—which claim his sole desire for us is that we should, so to say, enforce—that this inheritance is simply the light, God himself, the Light. If you think of ten thousand things that are good and worth having, what is it that makes them good or worth having but the God in them? That the loveliness of the world has its origin in the making will of God, would not content me; I say, the very loveliness of it is the loveliness of God, for its loveliness is his own lovely thought, and must be a revelation of that which dwells and moves in himself. Nor is this all: my interest in its loveliness would vanish, I should feel that the soul was out of it, if you could persuade me that God had ceased to care for the daisy, and now cared for something else instead. The faces of some flowers lead me back to the heart of God; and, as his child, I hope I feel, in my lowly degree, what he felt when, brooding over them, he said, 'They are good;' that is, 'They are what I mean.'

The thing I am reasoning toward is this: that, if everything were thus seen in its derivation from God, then the inheritance of the saints, whatever the form of their possession, would be seen to be light. All things are God's, not as being in his power—that of course—but as coming from him. The darkness itself becomes light around him when we think that verily he hath created the darkness, for there could have been no darkness but for the light Without God there would not even have been nothing; there would not have existed the idea of nothing, any more than any reality of nothing, but that he exists and called *something* into being.

Nothingness owes its very name and nature to the being and reality of God. There is no word to represent that which is not God, no word for the *where* without God in it; for it is not, could not be. So I think we may say that the inheritance of the saints is the share each has in the Light.

But how can any share exist where all is open?

The true share, in the heavenly kingdom throughout, is not what you have to keep, but what you have to give away. The thing that is mine is the thing I have with the power to give it. The thing I have *no* power to give a share in, is nowise mine; the thing I cannot share with everyone, cannot be essentially my own. The cry of the thousand splendours which Dante, in the fifth canto of the 'Paradiso,' tells us he saw gliding toward them in the planet Mercury, was—

Ecco chi crescera li nostri amori!

Lo, here comes one who will increase our loves!

All the light is ours. God is all ours. Even that in God which we cannot understand is ours. If there were anything in God that was not ours, then God would not be one God. I do not say we must, or can ever know all in God; not throughout eternity shall we ever comprehend God, but he is our father, and must think of us with every part of him—so to speak in our poor speech; he must know us, and that in himself which we cannot know, with the same thought, for he is one. We and that which we do not or cannot know, come together in his thought. And this helps us to see how, claiming all things, we have yet shares. For the infinitude of God can only begin and only go on to be revealed, through his infinitely differing creatures—all capable of wondering at, admiring, and loving each other, and so bound all in one in him, each to the others revealing him. For every human being is like a facet cut in the great diamond to which I may dare liken the father of him who likens his kingdom to a pearl. Every man, woman, child—for the incomplete also is his, and in its very incompleteness reveals him as a progressive worker in his creation—is a revealer of God. I have my message of my great Lord, you have yours. Your dog, your horse tells you about him who cares for all his creatures. None of them came from his *hands*. Perhaps the precious things of the earth, the coal and the diamonds, the iron and clay and gold, may be said to have come from his hands; but the live things come from his heart—from near the same region whence ourselves we came. How much my horse may, in his own fashion—that is, God's equine way—know of him, I cannot tell, because he cannot tell. Also, we do not know what the horses know, because they are horses, and we are at best, in relation to them, only horsemen. The ways of God go down into microscopic depths, as well as up into telescopic heights—and with more marvel, for there lie the beginnings of life: the immensities of stars and worlds all exist for the sake of less things than they. So with mind; the ways of God go into the depths yet unrevealed to us; he knows his horses and dogs as we cannot know them, because we are not yet pure sons of God. When through our sonship, as Paul teaches, the redemption of these lower brothers and sisters shall have come, then we shall understand each other better. But now the lord of life has to look on at the wilful torture of multitudes of his creatures. It must be that offences come, but woe unto that man by whom they come! The Lord may seem not to heed, but he sees and knows.

I say, then, that every one of us is something that the other is not, and therefore knows some thing—it may be without knowing that he knows it—which no one else knows; and that it is every one's business, as one of the kingdom of light, and inheritor in it all, to give his portion to the rest; for we are one family, with God at the head and the heart of it, and Jesus Christ, our elder brother, teaching us of the Father, whom he only knows.

We may say, then, that whatever is the source of joy or love, whatever is pure and strong, whatever wakes aspiration, whatever lifts us out of selfishness, whatever is beautiful or admirable—in a word, whatever is of the light—-must make a part, however small it may then prove to be in its proportion, of the inheritance of the saints in the light; for, as in the epistle of James, 'Every good gift, and every perfect gift is from above, and cometh down from the Father of lights, with whom is no variableness, neither shadow of turning.'

Children fear heaven, because of the dismal notions the unchildlike give them of it, who, without imagination, receive unquestioning what others, as void of imagination as themselves, represent concerning it. I do not see that one should care to present an agreeable picture of it; for, suppose I could persuade a man that heaven was the perfection of all he could desire around him, what would the man or the truth gain by it? If he knows the Lord, he will not trouble himself about heaven; if he does not know him, he will not be drawn to *him* by it. I would not care to persuade the feeble Christian that heaven was a place worth going to; I would rather persuade him that no spot in space, no hour in eternity is worth anything to one who remains such as he is. But would that none presumed to teach the little ones what they know nothing of themselves! What have not children suffered from strong endeavour to desire the things they could not love! Well do I remember the pain of the prospect—no, the trouble at not being pleased with the prospect— of being made a pillar in the house of God, and going no more out! Those words were not spoken to the little ones. Yet are they, literally taken, a blessed promise compared with the notion of a continuous church-going! Perhaps no one teaches such a thing; but somehow the children get the dreary fancy: there are ways of involuntary teaching more potent than words. What boy, however fain to be a disciple of Christ and a child of God, would prefer a sermon to his glorious kite, that divinest of toys, with God himself for his playmate, in the blue wind that tossed it hither and thither in the golden void! He might be ready to part with kite and wind and sun, and go down to the grave for his brothers—but surely not that they might be admitted to an everlasting prayer-meeting! For my own part, I *rejoice* to think that there will be neither church nor chapel in the high countries; yea, that there will be nothing there called religion, and no law but the perfect law of liberty. For how should there be law or religion where every throb of the heart says *God*! where every song-throat is eager with thanksgiving! where such a tumult of glad waters is for ever bursting from beneath the throne of God, the tears of the gladness of the universe! Religion? Where will be the room for it, when the essence of every thought must be God? Law? What room will there be for law, when everything upon which law could lay a *shalt not* will be too loathsome to think of? What room for honesty, where love fills full the law to overflowing—where a man would rather drop sheer into the abyss, than wrong his neighbour one hair's-breadth?

Heaven will be continuous touch with God. The very sense of being will in itself be bliss. For the sense of true life, there must be actual, conscious contact with the source of the life; therefore mere life—in itself, in its very essence good—good as the life of God which is our life—must be such bliss as, I think, will need the mitigation of the loftiest joys of communion with our blessed fellows; the mitigation of art in every shape, and of all combinations of arts; the mitigation of countless services to the incomplete, and hard toil for those who do not yet know their neighbour or their Father. The bliss of pure being will, I say, need these mitigations to render the intensity of it endurable by heart and brain.

To those who care only for things, and not for the souls of them, for the truth, the reality of them, the prospect of inheriting light can have nothing attractive, and for their comfort—how false a comfort!—they may rest assured there is no danger of their being required to take up their inheritance at present. Perhaps they will be left to go on sucking *things* dry, constantly missing the loveliness of them, until they come at last to loathe the lovely husks, turned to ugliness in their false imaginations. Loving but the body of Truth, even here they come to call it a lie, and break out in maudlin moaning over the illusions of life. The soul of Truth they have lost, because they never loved her. What may

371

they not have to pass through, what purifying fires, before they can even behold her!

The notions of Christians, so called, concerning the state into which they suppose their friends to have entered, and which they speak of as a place of blessedness, are yet such as to justify the bitterness of their lamentation over them, and the heathenish doubt whether they shall know them again. Verily it were a wonder if they did! After a year or two of such a fate, they might well be unrecognizable! One is almost ashamed of writing about such follies. The nirvana is grandeur contrasted with their heaven. The early Christians might now and then plague Paul with a foolish question, the answer to which plagues us to this day; but was there ever one of them doubted he was going to find his friends again? It is a mere form of Protean unbelief. They believe, they say, that God is love; but they cannot quite believe that he does not make the love in which we are most like him, either a mockery or a torture. Little would any promise of heaven be to me if I might not hope to say, 'I am sorry; forgive me; let what I did in anger or in coldness be nothing, in the name of God and Jesus!' Many such words will pass, many a self-humiliation have place. The man or woman who is not ready to confess, who is not ready to pour out a heartful of regrets—can such a one be an inheritor of the light? It is the joy of a true heart of an heir of light, of a child of that God who loves an open soul—the joy of any man who hates the wrong the more because he has done it, to say, 'I was wrong; I am sorry.' Oh, the sweet winds of repentance and reconciliation and atonement, that will blow from garden to garden of God, in the tender twilights of his kingdom! Whatever the place be like, one thing is certain, that there will be endless, infinite atonement, ever-growing love. Certain too it is that whatever the divinely human heart desires, it shall not desire in vain. The light which is God, and which is our inheritance because we are the children of God, insures these things. For the heart which desires is made thus to desire. God is; let the earth be glad, and the heaven, and the heaven of heavens! Whatever a father can do to make his children blessed, that will God do for his children. Let us, then, live in continual expectation, looking for the good things that God will give to men, being their father and their everlasting saviour. If the things I have here come from him, and are so plainly but a beginning, shall I not take them as an earnest of the better to follow? How else can I regard them? For never, in the midst of the good things of this lovely world, have I felt quite at home in it. Never has it shown me things lovely or grand enough to satisfy me. It is not all I should like for a place to live in. It may be that my unsatisfaction comes from not having eyes open enough, or keen enough, to see and understand what he has given; but it matters little whether the cause lie in the world or in myself, both being incomplete: God is, and all is well. All that is needed to set the world right enough for me—and no empyrean heaven could be right for me without it—is, that I care for God as he cares for me; that my will and desires keep time and harmony with his music; that I have no thought that springs from myself apart from him; that my individuality have the freedom that belongs to it as born of his individuality, and be in no slavery to my body, or my ancestry, or my prejudices, or any impulse whatever from region unknown; that I be free by obedience to the law of my being, the live and live-making will by which life is life, and my life is myself. What springs from myself and not from God, is evil; it is a perversion of something of God's. Whatever is not of faith is sin; it is a stream cut off—a stream that cuts itself off from its source, and thinks to run on without it. But light is my inheritance through him whose life is the light of men, to wake in them the life of their father in heaven. Loved be the Lord who in himself generated that life which is the light of men!

END OF THE THIRD SERIES.

A BOOK OF STRIFE IN THE FORM OF

THE DIARY OF AN OLD SOUL

DEDICATION

Sweet friends, receive my offering. You will find

Against each worded page a white page set:—
This is the mirror of each friendly mind
Reflecting that. In this book we are met.
Make it, dear hearts, of worth to you indeed:—
Let your white page be ground, my print be seed,
Growing to golden ears, that faith and hope shall feed.

YOUR OLD SOUL

(This edition does not have alternate blank pages, but there is plenty of space around the poetry),

JANUARY.

1.

LORD, what I once had done with youthful might,
Had I been from the first true to the truth,
Grant me, now old, to do—with better sight,
And humbler heart, if not the brain of youth;
So wilt thou, in thy gentleness and ruth,
Lead back thy old soul, by the path of pain,
Round to his best—young eyes and heart and brain.

2.

A dim aurora rises in my east,
Beyond the line of jagged questions hoar,
As if the head of our intombed High Priest
Began to glow behind the unopened door:
Sure the gold wings will soon rise from the gray!—
They rise not. Up I rise, press on the more,
To meet the slow coming of the Master's day.

3.

Sometimes I wake, and, lo! I have forgot,
And drifted out upon an ebbing sea!
My soul that was at rest now resteth not,
For I am with myself and not with thee;
Truth seems a blind moon in a glaring morn,
Where nothing is but sick-heart vanity:
Oh, thou who knowest! save thy child forlorn.

4.

Death, like high faith, levelling, lifteth all.
When I awake, my daughter and my son,
Grown sister and brother, in my arms shall fall,
Tenfold my girl and boy. Sure every one
Of all the brood to the old wings will run.
Whole-hearted is my worship of the man
From whom my earthly history began.

5.

Thy fishes breathe but where thy waters roll;
Thy birds fly but within thy airy sea;
My soul breathes only in thy infinite soul;
I breathe, I think, I love, I live but thee.
Oh breathe, oh think,—O Love, live into me;
Unworthy is my life till all divine,
Till thou see in me only what is thine.

6.

Then shall I breathe in sweetest sharing, then
Think in harmonious consort with my kin;
Then shall I love well all my father's men,
Feel one with theirs the life my heart within.
Oh brothers! sisters holy! hearts divine!
Then I shall be all yours, and nothing mine—
To every human heart a mother-twin.

7.

I see a child before an empty house,
Knocking and knocking at the closed door;
He wakes dull echoes—but nor man nor mouse,
If he stood knocking there for evermore.—
A mother angel, see! folding each wing,
Soft-walking, crosses straight the empty floor,
And opens to the obstinate praying thing.

8.

Were there but some deep, holy spell, whereby
Always I should remember thee—some mode
Of feeling the pure heat-throb momently
Of the spirit-fire still uttering this I!—
Lord, see thou to it, take thou remembrance' load:
Only when I bethink me can I cry;
Remember thou, and prick me with love's goad.

9.

If to myself—"God sometimes interferes"—
I said, my faith at once would be struck blind.
I see him all in all, the lifing mind,
Or nowhere in the vacant miles and years.
A love he is that watches and that hears,
Or but a mist fumed up from minds of men,
Whose fear and hope reach out beyond their ken.

10.

When I no more can stir my soul to move,
And life is but the ashes of a fire;
When I can but remember that my heart
Once used to live and love, long and aspire,—
Oh, be thou then the first, the one thou art;
Be thou the calling, before all answering love,
And in me wake hope, fear, boundless desire.

11.

I thought that I had lost thee; but, behold!
Thou comest to me from the horizon low,
Across the fields outspread of green and gold—
Fair carpet for thy feet to come and go.
Whence I know not, or how to me thou art come!—
Not less my spirit with calm bliss doth glow,
Meeting thee only thus, in nature vague and dumb.

12.

Doubt swells and surges, with swelling doubt behind!
My soul in storm is but a tattered sail,
Streaming its ribbons on the torrent gale;
In calm, 'tis but a limp and flapping thing:
Oh! swell it with thy breath; make it a wing,—
To sweep through thee the ocean, with thee the wind
Nor rest until in thee its haven it shall find.

13.

The idle flapping of the sail is doubt;
Faith swells it full to breast the breasting seas.
Bold, conscience, fast, and rule the ruling helm;
Hell's freezing north no tempest can send out,
But it shall toss thee homeward to thy leas;
Boisterous wave-crest never shall o'erwhelm
Thy sea-float bark as safe as field-borne rooted elm.

14.

Sometimes, hard-trying, it seems I cannot pray—
For doubt, and pain, and anger, and all strife.
Yet some poor half-fledged prayer-bird from the nest
May fall, flit, fly, perch—crouch in the bowery breast
Of the large, nation-healing tree of life;—
Moveless there sit through all the burning day,
And on my heart at night a fresh leaf cooling lay.

15.

My harvest withers. Health, my means to live—
All things seem rushing straight into the dark.
But the dark still is God. I would not give
The smallest silver-piece to turn the rush
Backward or sideways. Am I not a spark
Of him who is the light?—Fair hope doth flush
My east.—Divine success—Oh, hush and hark!

16.

Thy will be done. I yield up everything.
"The life is more than meat"—then more than health;
"The body more than raiment"—then than wealth;
The hairs I made not, thou art numbering.
Thou art my life—I the brook, thou the spring.
Because thine eyes are open, I can see;
Because thou art thyself, 'tis therefore I am me.

17.

No sickness can come near to blast my health;
My life depends not upon any meat;
My bread comes not from any human tilth;
No wings will grow upon my changeless wealth;
Wrong cannot touch it, violence or deceit;
Thou art my life, my health, my bank, my barn—
And from all other gods thou plain dost warn.

18.

Care thou for mine whom I must leave behind;
Care that they know who 'tis for them takes care;
Thy present patience help them still to bear;
Lord, keep them clearing, growing, heart and mind;
In one thy oneness us together bind;
Last earthly prayer with which to thee I cling—
Grant that, save love, we owe not anything.

19.

'Tis well, for unembodied thought a live,
True house to build—of stubble, wood, nor hay;
So, like bees round the flower by which they thrive,
My thoughts are busy with the informing truth,
And as I build, I feed, and grow in youth—
Hoping to stand fresh, clean, and strong, and gay,
When up the east comes dawning His great day.

20.

Thy will is truth—'tis therefore fate, the strong.
Would that my will did sweep full swing with thine!
Then harmony with every spheric song,
And conscious power, would give sureness divine.
Who thinks to thread thy great laws' onward throng,
Is as a fly that creeps his foolish way
Athwart an engine's wheels in smooth resistless play.

21.

Thou in my heart hast planted, gardener divine,
A scion of the tree of life: it grows;
But not in every wind or weather it blows;
The leaves fall sometimes from the baby tree,
And the life-power seems melting into pine;
Yet still the sap keeps struggling to the shine,
And the unseen root clings cramplike unto thee.

22.

Do thou, my God, my spirit's weather control;
And as I do not gloom though the day be dun,
Let me not gloom when earth-born vapours roll
Across the infinite zenith of my soul.
Should sudden brain-frost through the heart's summer run,
Cold, weary, joyless, waste of air and sun,
Thou art my south, my summer-wind, my all, my one.

23.

O Life, why dost thou close me up in death?
O Health, why make me inhabit heaviness?—
I ask, yet know: the sum of this distress,
Pang-haunted body, sore-dismayed mind,
Is but the egg that rounds the winged faith;
When that its path into the air shall find,
My heart will follow, high above cold, rain, and wind.

24.

I can no more than lift my weary eyes;
Therefore I lift my weary eyes—no more.
But my eyes pull my heart, and that, before
'Tis well awake, knocks where the conscience lies;
Conscience runs quick to the spirit's hidden door:
Straightway, from every sky-ward window, cries
Up to the Father's listening ears arise.

25.

Not in my fancy now I search to find thee;
Not in its loftiest forms would shape or bind thee;
I cry to one whom I can never know,
Filling me with an infinite overflow;
Not to a shape that dwells within my heart,
Clothed in perfections love and truth assigned thee,
But to the God thou knowest that thou art.

26.

Not, Lord, because I have done well or ill;
Not that my mind looks up to thee clear-eyed;
Not that it struggles in fast cerements tied;
Not that I need thee daily sorer still;
Not that I wretched, wander from thy will;
Not now for any cause to thee I cry,
But this, that thou art thou, and here am I.

27.

Yestereve, Death came, and knocked at my thin door.
I from my window looked: the thing I saw,
The shape uncouth, I had not seen before.
I was disturbed—with fear, in sooth, not awe;
Whereof ashamed, I instantly did rouse
My will to seek thee—only to fear the more:
Alas! I could not find thee in the house.

28.

I was like Peter when he began to sink.
To thee a new prayer therefore I have got—
That, when Death comes in earnest to my door,
Thou wouldst thyself go, when the latch doth clink,
And lead him to my room, up to my cot;
Then hold thy child's hand, hold and leave him not,
Till Death has done with him for evermore.

29.

Till Death has done with him?—Ah, leave me then!
And Death has done with me, oh, nevermore!
He comes—and goes—to leave me in thy arms,
Nearer thy heart, oh, nearer than before!
To lay thy child, naked, new-born again
Of mother earth, crept free through many harms,
Upon thy bosom—still to the very core.

30.

Come to me, Lord: I will not speculate how,
Nor think at which door I would have thee appear,
Nor put off calling till my floors be swept,
But cry, "Come, Lord, come any way, come now."
Doors, windows, I throw wide; my head I bow,
And sit like some one who so long has slept
That he knows nothing till his life draw near.

31.

O Lord, I have been talking to the people;
Thought's wheels have round me whirled a fiery zone,
And the recoil of my words' airy ripple
My heart unheedful has puffed up and blown.
Therefore I cast myself before thee prone:
Lay cool hands on my burning brain, and press
From my weak heart the swelling emptiness.

FEBRUARY.

1.

I TO myself have neither power nor worth,
Patience nor love, nor anything right good;
My soul is a poor land, plenteous in dearth—
Here blades of grass, there a small herb for food—
A nothing that would be something if it could;
But if obedience, Lord, in me do grow,
I shall one day be better than I know.

2.

The worst power of an evil mood is this—
It makes the bastard self seem in the right,
Self, self the end, the goal of human bliss.
But if the Christ-self in us be the might
Of saving God, why should I spend my force
With a dark thing to reason of the light—
Not push it rough aside, and hold obedient course?

3.

Back still it comes to this: there was a man
Who said, "I am the truth, the life, the way:"—
Shall I pass on, or shall I stop and hear?—
"Come to the Father but by me none can:"
What then is this?—am I not also one
Of those who live in fatherless dismay?
I stand, I look, I listen, I draw near.

4.

My Lord, I find that nothing else will do,
But follow where thou goest, sit at thy feet,
And where I have thee not, still run to meet.
Roses are scentless, hopeless are the morns,
Rest is but weakness, laughter crackling thorns,
If thou, the Truth, do not make them the true:
Thou art my life, O Christ, and nothing else will do.

5.

Thou art here—in heaven, I know, but not from here—
Although thy separate self do not appear;
If I could part the light from out the day,
There I should have thee! But thou art too near:
How find thee walking, when thou art the way?
Oh, present Christ! make my eyes keen as stings,
To see thee at their heart, the glory even of things.

6.

That thou art nowhere to be found, agree
Wise men, whose eyes are but for surfaces;
Men with eyes opened by the second birth,
To whom the seen, husk of the unseen is,
Descry thee soul of everything on earth.
Who know thy ends, thy means and motions see:
Eyes made for glory soon discover thee.

7.

Thou near then, I draw nearer—to thy feet,
And sitting in thy shadow, look out on the shine;
Ready at thy first word to leave my seat—
Not thee: thou goest too. From every clod
Into thy footprint flows the indwelling wine;
And in my daily bread, keen-eyed I greet
Its being's heart, the very body of God.

8.

Thou wilt interpret life to me, and men,
Art, nature, yea, my own soul's mysteries—
Bringing, truth out, clear-joyous, to my ken,
Fair as the morn trampling the dull night. Then
The lone hill-side shall hear exultant cries;
The joyous see me joy, the weeping weep;
The watching smile, as Death breathes on me his cold sleep.

9.

I search my heart—I search, and find no faith.
Hidden He may be in its many folds—
I see him not revealed in all the world
Duty's firm shape thins to a misty wraith.
No good seems likely. To and fro I am hurled.
I have no stay. Only obedience holds:—
I haste, I rise, I do the thing he saith.

10.

Thou wouldst not have thy man crushed back to clay;
It must be, God, thou hast a strength to give
To him that fain would do what thou dost say;
Else how shall any soul repentant live,
Old griefs and new fears hurrying on dismay?
Let pain be what thou wilt, kind and degree,
Only in pain calm thou my heart with thee.

11.

I will not shift my ground like Moab's king,
But from this spot whereon I stand, I pray—
From this same barren rock to thee I say,
"Lord, in my commonness, in this very thing
That haunts my soul with folly—through the clay
Of this my pitcher, see the lamp's dim flake;
And hear the blow that would the pitcher break."

12.

Be thou the well by which I lie and rest;
Be thou my tree of life, my garden ground;
Be thou my home, my fire, my chamber blest,
My book of wisdom, loved of all the best;
Oh, be my friend, each day still newer found,
As the eternal days and nights go round!
Nay, nay—thou art my God, in whom all loves are bound!

13.

Two things at once, thou know'st I cannot think.
When busy with the work thou givest me,
I cannot consciously think then of thee.
Then why, when next thou lookest o'er the brink
Of my horizon, should my spirit shrink,
Reproached and fearful, nor to greet thee run?
Can I be two when I am only one.

14.

My soul must unawares have sunk awry.
Some care, poor eagerness, ambition of work,
Some old offence that unforgiving did lurk,
Or some self-gratulation, soft and sly—
Something not thy sweet will, not the good part,
While the home-guard looked out, stirred up the old murk,
And so I gloomed away from thee, my Heart.

15.

Therefore I make provision, ere I begin
To do the thing thou givest me to do,
Praying,—Lord, wake me oftener, lest I sin.
Amidst my work, open thine eyes on me,
That I may wake and laugh, and know and see
Then with healed heart afresh catch up the clue,
And singing drop into my work anew.

16.

If I should slow diverge, and listless stray
Into some thought, feeling, or dream unright,
O Watcher, my backsliding soul affray;
Let me not perish of the ghastly blight.
Be thou, O Life eternal, in me light;
Then merest approach of selfish or impure
Shall start me up alive, awake, secure.

17.

Lord, I have fallen again—a human clod!
Selfish I was, and heedless to offend;
Stood on my rights. Thy own child would not send
Away his shreds of nothing for the whole God!
Wretched, to thee who savest, low I bend:
Give me the power to let my rag-rights go
In the great wind that from thy gulf doth blow.

18.

Keep me from wrath, let it seem ever so right:
My wrath will never work thy righteousness.
Up, up the hill, to the whiter than snow-shine,
Help me to climb, and dwell in pardon's light.
I must be pure as thou, or ever less
Than thy design of me—therefore incline
My heart to take men's wrongs as thou tak'st mine.

19.

Lord, in thy spirit's hurricane, I pray,
Strip my soul naked—dress it then thy way.
Change for me all my rags to cloth of gold.
Who would not poverty for riches yield?
A hovel sell to buy a treasure-field?
Who would a mess of porridge careful hold
Against the universe's birthright old?

20.

Help me to yield my will, in labour even,
Nor toil on toil, greedy of doing, heap—
Fretting I cannot more than me is given;
That with the finest clay my wheel runs slow,
Nor lets the lovely thing the shapely grow;
That memory what thought gives it cannot keep,
And nightly rimes ere morn like cistus-petals go.

21.

'Tis—shall thy will be done for me?—or mine,
And I be made a thing not after thine—
My own, and dear in paltriest details?
Shall I be born of God, or of mere man?
Be made like Christ, or on some other plan?—
I let all run:—set thou and trim my sails;
Home then my course, let blow whatever gales.

22.

With thee on board, each sailor is a king
Nor I mere captain of my vessel then,
But heir of earth and heaven, eternal child;
Daring all truth, nor fearing anything;
Mighty in love, the servant of all men;
Resenting nothing, taking rage and blare
Into the Godlike silence of a loving care.

23.

I cannot see, my God, a reason why
From morn to night I go not gladsome free;
For, if thou art what my soul thinketh thee,
There is no burden but should lightly lie,
No duty but a joy at heart must be:
Love's perfect will can be nor sore nor small,
For God is light—in him no darkness is at all.

24.

'Tis something thus to think, and half to trust—
But, ah! my very heart, God-born, should lie
Spread to the light, clean, clear of mire and rust,
And like a sponge drink the divine sunbeams.
What resolution then, strong, swift, and high!
What pure devotion, or to live or die!
And in my sleep, what true, what perfect dreams!

25.

There is a misty twilight of the soul,
A sickly eclipse, low brooding o'er a man,
When the poor brain is as an empty bowl,
And the thought-spirit, weariful and wan,
Turning from that which yet it loves the best,
Sinks moveless, with life-poverty opprest:—
Watch then, O Lord, thy feebly glimmering coal.

26.

I cannot think; in me is but a void;
I have felt much, and want to feel no more;
My soul is hungry for some poorer fare—
Some earthly nectar, gold not unalloyed:—
The little child that's happy to the core,
Will leave his mother's lap, run down the stair,
Play with the servants—is his mother annoyed?

27.

I would not have it so. Weary and worn,
Why not to thee run straight, and be at rest?
Motherward, with toy new, or garment torn,
The child that late forsook her changeless breast,
Runs to home's heart, the heaven that's heavenliest:
In joy or sorrow, feebleness or might,
Peace or commotion, be thou, Father, my delight.

28.

The thing I would say, still comes forth with doubt
And difference:—is it that thou shap'st my ends?
Or is it only the necessity
Of stubborn words, that shift sluggish about,
Warping my thought as it the sentence bends?—
Have thou a part in it, O Lord, and I
Shall say a truth, if not the thing I try.

29.

Gather my broken fragments to a whole,
As these four quarters make a shining day.
Into thy basket, for my golden bowl,
Take up the things that I have cast away
In vice or indolence or unwise play.
Let mine be a merry, all-receiving heart,
But make it a whole, with light in every part.

MARCH.

1.

THE song birds that come to me night and morn,
Fly oft away and vanish if I sleep,
Nor to my fowling-net will one return:
Is the thing ever ours we cannot keep?—
But their souls go not out into the deep.
What matter if with changed song they come back?
Old strength nor yet fresh beauty shall they lack.

2.

Gloriously wasteful, O my Lord, art thou!
Sunset faints after sunset into the night,
Splendorously dying from thy window-sill—
For ever. Sad our poverty doth bow
Before the riches of thy making might:
Sweep from thy space thy systems at thy will—
In thee the sun sets every sunset still.

3.

And in the perfect time, O perfect God,
When we are in our home, our natal home,
When joy shall carry every sacred load,
And from its life and peace no heart shall roam,
What if thou make us able to make like thee—
To light with moons, to clothe with greenery,
To hang gold sunsets o'er a rose and purple sea!

4.

Then to his neighbour one may call out, "Come!
Brother, come hither—I would show you a thing;"
And lo, a vision of his imagining,
Informed of thought which else had rested dumb,
Before the neighbour's truth-delighted eyes,
In the great æther of existence rise,
And two hearts each to each the closer cling!

5.

We make, but thou art the creating core.
Whatever thing I dream, invent, or feel,
Thou art the heart of it, the atmosphere.
Thou art inside all love man ever bore;
Yea, the love itself, whatever thing be dear.
Man calls his dog, he follows at his heel,
Because thou first art love, self-caused, essential, mere.

6.

This day be with me, Lord, when I go forth,
Be nearer to me than I am able to ask.
In merriment, in converse, or in task,
Walking the street, listening to men of worth,
Or greeting such as only talk and bask,
Be thy thought still my waiting soul around,
And if He come, I shall be watching found.

7.

What if, writing, I always seem to leave
Some better thing, or better way, behind,
Why should I therefore fret at all, or grieve!
The worse I drop, that I the better find;
The best is only in thy perfect mind.
Fallen threads I will not search for—I will weave.
Who makes the mill-wheel backward strike to grind!

8.

Be with me, Lord. Keep me beyond all prayers:
For more than all my prayers my need of thee,
And thou beyond all need, all unknown cares;
What the heart's dear imagination dares,
Thou dost transcend in measureless majesty
All prayers in one—my God, be unto me
Thy own eternal self, absolutely.

9.

Where should the unknown treasures of the truth
Lie, but there whence the truth comes out the most—
In the Son of man, folded in love and ruth?
Fair shore we see, fair ocean; but behind
Lie infinite reaches bathing many a coast—
The human thought of the eternal mind,
Pulsed by a living tide, blown by a living wind.

10.

Thou, healthful Father, art the Ancient of Days,
And Jesus is the eternal youth of thee.
Our old age is the scorching of the bush
By life's indwelling, incorruptible blaze.
O Life, burn at this feeble shell of me,
Till I the sore singed garment off shall push,
Flap out my Psyche wings, and to thee rush.

11.

But shall I then rush to thee like a dart?
Or lie long hours æonian yet betwixt
This hunger in me, and the Father's heart?—
It shall be good, how ever, and not ill;
Of things and thoughts even now thou art my next;
Sole neighbour, and no space between, thou art—
And yet art drawing nearer, nearer still.

12.

Therefore, my brothers, therefore, sisters dear,
However I, troubled or selfish, fail
In tenderness, or grace, or service clear,
I every moment draw to you more near;
God in us from our hearts veil after veil
Keeps lifting, till we see with his own sight,
And all together run in unity's delight.

13.

I love thee, Lord, for very greed of love—
Not of the precious streams that towards me move,
But of the indwelling, outgoing, fountain store.
Than mine, oh, many an ignorant heart loves more!
Therefore the more, with Mary at thy feet,
I must sit worshipping—that, in my core,
Thy words may fan to a flame the low primeval heat.

14.

Oh my beloved, gone to heaven from me!
I would be rich in love to heap you with love;
I long to love you, sweet ones, perfectly—
Like God, who sees no spanning vault above,
No earth below, and feels no circling air—
Infinitely, no boundary anywhere.
I am a beast until I love as God doth love.

15.

Ah, say not, 'tis but perfect self I want
But if it were, that self is fit to live
Whose perfectness is still itself to scant,
Which never longs to have, but still to give.
A self I must have, or not be at all:
Love, give me a self self-giving—or let me fall
To endless darkness back, and free me from life's thrall.

16.

"Back," said I! Whither back? How to the dark?
From no dark came I, but the depths of light;
From the sun-heart I came, of love a spark:
What should I do but love with all my might?
To die of love severe and pure and stark,
Were scarcely loss; to lord a loveless height—
That were a living death, damnation's positive night.

17.

But love is life. To die of love is then
The only pass to higher life than this.
All love is death to loving, living men;
All deaths are leaps across clefts to the abyss.
Our life is the broken current, Lord, of thine,
Flashing from morn to morn with conscious shine—
Then first by willing death self-made, then life divine.

18.

I love you, my sweet children, who are gone
Into another mansion; but I know
I love you not as I shall love you yet.
I love you, sweet dead children; there are none
In the land to which ye vanished to go,
Whose hearts more truly on your hearts are set—
Yet should I die of grief to love you only so.

19.

"I am but as a beast before thee, Lord."—
Great poet-king, I thank thee for the word.—
Leave not thy son half-made in beastly guise—
Less than a man, with more than human cries—
An unshaped thing in which thyself cries out!
Finish me, Father; now I am but a doubt;
Oh! make thy moaning thing for joy to leap and shout.

20.

Let my soul talk to thee in ordered words,
O king of kings, O lord of only lords!—
When I am thinking thee within my heart,
From the broken reflex be not far apart.
The troubled water, dim with upstirred soil,
Makes not the image which it yet can spoil:—
Come nearer, Lord, and smooth the wrinkled coil.

21.

O Lord, when I do think of my departed,
I think of thee who art the death of parting;
Of him who crying Father breathed his last,
Then radiant from the sepulchre upstarted.—
Even then, I think, thy hands and feet kept smarting:
With us the bitterness of death is past,
But by the feet he still doth hold us fast.

22.

Therefore our hands thy feet do hold as fast.
We pray not to be spared the sorest pang,
But only—be thou with us to the last.
Let not our heart be troubled at the clang
Of hammer and nails, nor dread the spear's keen fang,
Nor the ghast sickening that comes of pain,
Nor yet the last clutch of the banished brain.

23.

Lord, pity us: we have no making power;
Then give us making will, adopting thine.
Make, make, and make us; temper, and refine.
Be in us patience—neither to start nor cower.
Christ, if thou be not with us—not by sign,
But presence, actual as the wounds that bleed—
We shall not bear it, but shall die indeed.

24.

O Christ, have pity on all men when they come
Unto the border haunted of dismay;
When that they know not draweth very near—
The other thing, the opposite of day,
Formless and ghastly, sick, and gaping-dumb,
Before which even love doth lose his cheer:
O radiant Christ, remember then thy fear.

25.

Be by me, Lord, this day. Thou know'st I mean—
Lord, make me mind thee. I herewith forestall
My own forgetfulness, when I stoop to glean
The corn of earth—which yet thy hand lets fall.
Be for me then against myself. Oh lean
Over me then when I invert my cup;
Take me, if by the hair, and lift me up.

26.

Lord of essential life, help me to die.
To will to die is one with highest life,
The mightiest act that to Will's hand doth lie—
Born of God's essence, and of man's hard strife:
God, give me strength my evil self to kill,
And die into the heaven of thy pure will.—
Then shall this body's death be very tolerable.

27.

As to our mothers came help in our birth—
Not lost in lifing us, but saved and blest—
Self bearing self, although right sorely prest,
Shall nothing lose, but die and be at rest
In life eternal, beyond all care and dearth.
God-born then truly, a man does no more ill,
Perfectly loves, and has whate'er he will.

28.

As our dear animals do suffer less
Because their pain spreads neither right nor left,
Lost in oblivion and foresightlessness—
Our suffering sore by faith shall be bereft
Of all dismay, and every weak excess.
His presence shall be better in our pain,
Than even self-absence to the weaker brain.

29.

"Father, let this cup pass." He prayed—was heard.
What cup was it that passed away from him?
Sure not the death-cup, now filled to the brim!
There was no quailing in the awful word;
He still was king of kings, of lords the lord:—
He feared lest, in the suffering waste and grim,
His faith might grow too faint and sickly dim.

30.

Thy mind, my master, I will dare explore;
What we are told, that we are meant to know.
Into thy soul I search yet more and more,
Led by the lamp of my desire and woe.
If thee, my Lord, I may not understand,
I am a wanderer in a houseless land,
A weeping thirst by hot winds ever fanned.

31.

Therefore I look again—and think I see
That, when at last he did cry out, "My God,
Why hast thou me forsaken?" straight man's rod
Was turned aside; for, that same moment, he
Cried "Father!" and gave up will and breath and spirit
Into his hands whose all he did inherit—
Delivered, glorified eternally.

APRIL.

1.

LORD, I do choose the higher than my will.
I would be handled by thy nursing arms
After thy will, not my infant alarms.
Hurt me thou wilt—but then more loving still,
If more can be and less, in love's perfect zone!
My fancy shrinks from least of all thy harms,
But do thy will with me—I am thine own.

2.

Some things wilt thou not one day turn to dreams?
Some dreams wilt thou not one day turn to fact?
The thing that painful, more than should be, seems,
Shall not thy sliding years with them retract—
Shall fair realities not counteract?
The thing that was well dreamed of bliss and joy—
Wilt thou not breathe thy life into the toy?

3.

I have had dreams of absolute delight,
Beyond all waking bliss—only of grass,
Flowers, wind, a peak, a limb of marble white;
They dwell with me like things half come to pass,
True prophecies:—when I with thee am right,
If I pray, waking, for such a joy of sight,
Thou with the gold, wilt not refuse the brass.

4.

I think I shall not ever pray for such;
Thy bliss will overflood my heart and brain,
And I want no unripe things back again.
Love ever fresher, lovelier than of old—
How should it want its more exchanged for much?
Love will not backward sigh, but forward strain,
On in the tale still telling, never told.

5.

What has been, shall not only be, but is.
The hues of dreamland, strange and sweet and tender
Are but hint-shadows of full many a splendour
Which the high Parent-love will yet unroll
Before his child's obedient, humble soul.
Ah, me, my God! in thee lies every bliss
Whose shadow men go hunting wearily amiss.

6.

Now, ere I sleep, I wonder what I shall dream.
Some sense of being, utter new, may come
Into my soul while I am blind and dumb—
With shapes and airs and scents which dark hours teem,
Of other sort than those that haunt the day,
Hinting at precious things, ages away
In the long tale of us God to himself doth say.

7.

Late, in a dream, an unknown lady I saw
Stand on a tomb; down she to me stepped thence.
"They tell me," quoth I, "thou art one of the dead!"
And scarce believed for gladness the yea she said;
A strange auroral bliss, an arctic awe,
A new, outworldish joy awoke intense,
To think I talked with one that verily was dead.

8.

Thou dost demand our love, holy Lord Christ,
And batest nothing of thy modesty;—
Thou know'st no other way to bliss the highest
Than loving thee, the loving, perfectly.
Thou lovest perfectly—that is thy bliss:
We must love like thee, or our being miss—
So, to love perfectly, love perfect Love, love thee.

9.

Here is my heart, O Christ; thou know'st I love thee.
But wretched is the thing I call my love.
O Love divine, rise up in me and move me—
I follow surely when thou first dost move.
To love the perfect love, is primal, mere
Necessity; and he who holds life dear,
Must love thee every hope and heart above.

10.

Might I but scatter interfering things—
Questions and doubts, distrusts and anxious pride,
And in thy garment, as under gathering wings,
Nestle obedient to thy loving side,
Easy it were to love thee. But when thou
Send'st me to think and labour from thee wide,
Love falls to asking many a why and how.

11.

Easier it were, but poorer were the love.
Lord, I would have me love thee from the deeps—
Of troubled thought, of pain, of weariness.
Through seething wastes below, billows above,
My soul should rise in eager, hungering leaps;
Through thorny thicks, through sands unstable press—
Out of my dream to him who slumbers not nor sleeps.

12.

I do not fear the greatness of thy command—
To keep heart-open-house to brother men;
But till in thy God's love perfect I stand,
My door not wide enough will open. Then
Each man will be love-awful in my sight;
And, open to the eternal morning's might,
Each human face will shine my window for thy light.

13.

Make me all patience and all diligence;
Patience, that thou mayst have thy time with me;
Diligence, that I waste not thy expense
In sending out to bring me home to thee.
What though thy work in me transcends my sense—
Too fine, too high, for me to understand—
I hope entirely. On, Lord, with thy labour grand.

14.

Lest I be humbled at the last, and told
That my great labour was but for my peace
That not for love or truth had I been bold,
But merely for a prisoned heart's release;
Careful, I humble me now before thy feet:
Whate'er I be, I cry, and will not cease—
Let me not perish, though favour be not meet.

15.

For, what I seek thou knowest I must find,
Or miserably die for lack of love.
I justify thee: what is in thy mind,
If it be shame to me, all shame above.
Thou know'st I choose it—know'st I would not shove
The hand away that stripped me for the rod—
If so it pleased my Life, my love-made-angry God.

16.

I see a door, a multitude near by,
In creed and quarrel, sure disciples all!
Gladly they would, they say, enter the hall,
But cannot, the stone threshold is so high.
From unseen hand, full many a feeding crumb,
Slow dropping o'er the threshold high doth come:
They gather and eat, with much disputing hum.

17.

Still and anon, a loud clear voice doth call—
"Make your feet clean, and enter so the hall."
They hear, they stoop, they gather each a crumb.
Oh the deaf people! would they were also dumb!
Hear how they talk, and lack of Christ deplore,
Stamping with muddy feet about the door,
And will not wipe them clean to walk upon his floor!

18.

But see, one comes; he listens to the voice;
Careful he wipes his weary dusty feet!
The voice hath spoken—to him is left no choice;
He hurries to obey—that only is meet.
Low sinks the threshold, levelled with the ground;
The man leaps in—to liberty he's bound.
The rest go talking, walking, picking round.

19.

If I, thus writing, rebuke my neighbour dull,
And talk, and write, and enter not the door,
Than all the rest I wrong Christ tenfold more,
Making his gift of vision void and null.
Help me this day to be thy humble sheep,
Eating thy grass, and following, thou before;
From wolfish lies my life, O Shepherd, keep.

20.

God, help me, dull of heart, to trust in thee.
Thou art the father of me—not any mood
Can part me from the One, the verily Good.
When fog and failure o'er my being brood.
When life looks but a glimmering marshy clod,
No fire out flashing from the living God—
Then, then, to rest in faith were worthy victory!

21.

To trust is gain and growth, not mere sown seed!
Faith heaves the world round to the heavenly dawn,
In whose great light the soul doth spell and read
Itself high-born, its being derived and drawn
From the eternal self-existent fire;
Then, mazed with joy of its own heavenly breed,
Exultant-humble falls before its awful sire.

22.

Art thou not, Jesus, busy like to us?
Thee shall I image as one sitting still,
Ordering all things in thy potent will,
Silent, and thinking ever to thy father,
Whose thought through thee flows multitudinous?
Or shall I think of thee as journeying, rather,
Ceaseless through space, because thou everything dost fill?

23.

That all things thou dost fill, I well may think—
Thy power doth reach me in so many ways.
Thou who in one the universe dost bind,
Passest through all the channels of my mind;
The sun of thought, across the farthest brink
Of consciousness thou sendest me thy rays;
Nor drawest them in when lost in sleep I sink.

24.

So common are thy paths, thy coming seems
Only another phase oft of my me;
But nearer is my I, O Lord, to thee,
Than is my I to what itself it deems;
How better then couldst thou, O master, come,
Than from thy home across into my home,
Straight o'er the marches that I cannot see!

25.

Marches?—'Twixt thee and me there's no division,
Except the meeting of thy will and mine,
The loves that love, the wills that will the same.
Where thine meets mine is my life's true condition;
Yea, only there it burns with any flame.
Thy will but holds me to my life's fruition.
O God, I would—I have no mine that is not thine.

26.

I look for thee, and do not see thee come.—
If I could see thee, 'twere a commoner thing,
And shallower comfort would thy coming bring.
Earth, sea, and air lie round me moveless dumb,
Never a tremble, an expectant hum,
To tell the Lord of Hearts is drawing near:
Lo! in the looking eyes, the looked for Lord is here.

27.

I take a comfort from my very badness:
It is for lack of thee that I am bad.
How close, how infinitely closer yet
Must I come to thee, ere I can pay one debt
Which mere humanity has on me set!
"How close to thee!"—no wonder, soul, thou art glad!
Oneness with him is the eternal gladness.

28.

What can there be so close as making and made?
Nought twinned can be so near; thou art more nigh
To me, my God, than is this thinking I
To that I mean when I by me is said;
Thou art more near me, than is my ready will
Near to my love, though both one place do fill;—
Yet, till we are one,—Ah me! the long until!

29.

Then shall my heart behold thee everywhere.
The vision rises of a speechless thing,
A perfectness of bliss beyond compare!
A time when I nor breathe nor think nor move,
But I do breathe and think and feel thy love,
The soul of all the songs the saints do sing!—
And life dies out in bliss, to come again in prayer.

30.

In the great glow of that great love, this death
Would melt away like a fantastic cloud;
I should no more shrink from it than from the breath
That makes in the frosty air a nimbus-shroud;
Thou, Love, hast conquered death, and I aloud
Should triumph over him, with thy saintly crowd,
That where the Lamb goes ever followeth.

MAY.

1.

WHAT though my words glance sideways from the thing
Which I would utter in thine ear, my sire!
Truth in the inward parts thou dost desire—
Wise hunger, not a fitness fine of speech:
The little child that clamouring fails to reach
With upstretched hand the fringe of her attire,
Yet meets the mother's hand down hurrying.

2.

Even when their foolish words they turned on him,
He did not his disciples send away;
He knew their hearts were foolish, eyes were dim,
And therefore by his side needs must they stay.
Thou will not, Lord, send me away from thee.
When I am foolish, make thy cock crow grim;
If that is not enough, turn, Lord, and look on me.

3.

Another day of gloom and slanting rain!
Of closed skies, cold winds, and blight and bane!
Such not the weather, Lord, which thou art fain
To give thy chosen, sweet to heart and brain!—
Until we mourn, thou keep'st the merry tune;
Thy hand unloved its pleasure must restrain,
Nor spoil both gift and child by lavishing too soon.

4.

But all things shall be ours! Up, heart, and sing.
All things were made for us—we are God's heirs—
Moon, sun, and wildest comets that do trail
A crowd of small worlds for a swiftness-tail!
Up from Thy depths in me, my child-heart bring—
The child alone inherits anything:
God's little children-gods—all things are theirs!

5.

Thy great deliverance is a greater thing
Than purest imagination can foregrasp;
A thing beyond all conscious hungering,
Beyond all hope that makes the poet sing.
It takes the clinging world, undoes its clasp,
Floats it afar upon a mighty sea,
And leaves us quiet with love and liberty and thee.

6.

Through all the fog, through all earth's wintery sighs,
I scent Thy spring, I feel the eternal air,
Warm, soft, and dewy, filled with flowery eyes,
And gentle, murmuring motions everywhere—
Of life in heart, and tree, and brook, and moss;
Thy breath wakes beauty, love, and bliss, and prayer,
And strength to hang with nails upon thy cross.

7.

If thou hadst closed my life in seed and husk,
And cast me into soft, warm, damp, dark mould,
All unaware of light come through the dusk,
I yet should feel the split of each shelly fold,
Should feel the growing of my prisoned heart,
And dully dream of being slow unrolled,
And in some other vagueness taking part.

8.

And little as the world I should foreknow
Up into which I was about to rise—
Its rains, its radiance, airs, and warmth, and skies,
How it would greet me, how its wind would blow—
As little, it may be, I do know the good
Which I for years half darkling have pursued—
The second birth for which my nature cries.

9.

The life that knows not, patient waits, nor longs:—
I know, and would be patient, yet would long.
I can be patient for all coming songs,
But let me sing my one monotonous song.
To me the time is slow my mould among;
To quicker life I fain would spur and start
The aching growth at my dull-swelling heart.

10.

Christ is the pledge that I shall one day see;
That one day, still with him, I shall awake,
And know my God, at one with him and free.
O lordly essence, come to life in me;
The will-throb let me feel that doth me make;
Now have I many a mighty hope in thee,
Then shall I rest although the universe should quake.

11.

Haste to me, Lord, when this fool-heart of mine
Begins to gnaw itself with selfish craving;
Or, like a foul thing scarcely worth the saving,
Swoln up with wrath, desireth vengeance fine.
Haste, Lord, to help, when reason favours wrong;
Haste when thy soul, the high-born thing divine,
Is torn by passion's raving, maniac throng.

12.

Fair freshness of the God-breathed spirit air,
Pass through my soul, and make it strong to love;
Wither with gracious cold what demons dare
Shoot from my hell into my world above;
Let them drop down, like leaves the sun doth sear,
And flutter far into the inane and bare,
Leaving my middle-earth calm, wise, and clear.

13.

Even thou canst give me neither thought nor thing,
Were it the priceless pearl hid in the land,
Which, if I fix thereon a greedy gaze,
Becomes not poison that doth burn and cling;
Their own bad look my foolish eyes doth daze,
They see the gift, see not the giving hand—
From the living root the apple dead I wring.

14.

This versing, even the reading of the tale
That brings my heart its joy unspeakable,
Sometimes will softly, unsuspectedly hale
That heart from thee, and all its pulses quell.
Discovery's pride, joy's bliss, take aback my sail,
And sweep me from thy presence and my grace,
Because my eyes dropped from the master's face.

15.

Afresh I seek thee. Lead me—once more I pray—
Even should it be against my will, thy way.
Let me not feel thee foreign any hour,
Or shrink from thee as an estranged power.
Through doubt, through faith, through bliss, through stark dismay,
Through sunshine, wind, or snow, or fog, or shower,
Draw me to thee who art my only day.

16.

I would go near thee—but I cannot press
Into thy presence—it helps not to presume.
Thy doors are deeds; the handles are their doing.
He whose day-life is obedient righteousness,
Who, after failure, or a poor success,
Rises up, stronger effort yet renewing—
He finds thee, Lord, at length, in his own common room.

17.

Lord, thou hast carried me through this evening's duty;
I am released, weary, and well content.
O soul, put on the evening dress of beauty,
Thy sunset-flush, of gold and purple blent!—
Alas, the moment I turn to my heart,
Feeling runs out of doors, or stands apart!
But such as I am, Lord, take me as thou art.

18.

The word he then did speak, fits now as then,
For the same kind of men doth mock at it.
God-fools, God-drunkards these do call the men
Who think the poverty of their all not fit,
Borne humbly by their art, their voice, their pen,
Save for its allness, at thy feet to fling,
For whom all is unfit that is not everything.

19.

O Christ, my life, possess me utterly.
Take me and make a little Christ of me.
If I am anything but thy father's son,
'Tis something not yet from the darkness won.
Oh, give me light to live with open eyes.
Oh, give me life to hope above all skies.
Give me thy spirit to haunt the Father with my cries.

20.

'Tis hard for man to rouse his spirit up—
It is the human creative agony,
Though but to hold the heart an empty cup,
Or tighten on the team the rigid rein.
Many will rather lie among the slain
Than creep through narrow ways the light to gain—
Than wake the will, and be born bitterly.

21.

But he who would be born again indeed,
Must wake his soul unnumbered times a day,
And urge himself to life with holy greed;
Now ope his bosom to the Wind's free play;
And now, with patience forceful, hard, lie still,
Submiss and ready to the making will,
Athirst and empty, for God's breath to fill.

22.

All times are thine whose will is our remede.
Man turns to thee, thou hast not turned away;
The look he casts, thy labour that did breed—
It is thy work, thy business all the day:
That look, not foregone fitness, thou dost heed.
For duty absolute how be fitter than now?
Or learn by shunning?—Lord, I come; help thou.

23.

Ever above my coldness and my doubt
Rises up something, reaching forth a hand:
This thing I know, but cannot understand.
Is it the God in me that rises out
Beyond my self, trailing it up with him,
Towards the spirit-home, the freedom-land,
Beyond my conscious ken, my near horizon's brim?

416

24.

O God of man, my heart would worship all
My fellow men, the flashes from thy fire;
Them in good sooth my lofty kindred call,
Born of the same one heart, the perfect sire;
Love of my kind alone can set me free;
Help me to welcome all that come to me,
Not close my doors and dream solitude liberty!

25.

A loving word may set some door ajar
Where seemed no door, and that may enter in
Which lay at the heart of that same loving word.
In my still chamber dwell thou always, Lord;
Thy presence there will carriage true afford;
True words will flow, pure of design to win;
And to my men my door shall have no bar.

26.

My prayers, my God, flow from what I am not;
I think thy answers make me what I am.
Like weary waves thought follows upon thought,
But the still depth beneath is all thine own,
And there thou mov'st in paths to us unknown.
Out of strange strife thy peace is strangely wrought;
If the lion in us pray—thou answerest the lamb.

27.

So bound in selfishness am I, so chained,
I know it must be glorious to be free
But know not what, full-fraught, the word doth mean.
By loss on loss I have severely gained
Wisdom enough my slavery to see;
But liberty, pure, absolute, serene,
No freëst-visioned slave has ever seen.

28.

For, that great freedom how should such as I
Be able to imagine in such a self?
Less hopeless far the miser man might try
To image the delight of friend-shared pelf.
Freedom is to be like thee, face and heart;
To know it, Lord, I must be as thou art,
I cannot breed the imagination high.

29.

Yet hints come to me from the realm unknown;
Airs drift across the twilight border land,
Odoured with life; and as from some far strand
Sea-murmured, whispers to my heart are blown
That fill me with a joy I cannot speak,
Yea, from whose shadow words drop faint and weak:
Thee, God, I shadow in that region grand.

30.

O Christ, who didst appear in Judah land,
Thence by the cross go back to God's right hand,
Plain history, and things our sense beyond,
In thee together come and correspond:
How rulest thou from the undiscovered bourne
The world-wise world that laughs thee still to scorn?
Please, Lord, let thy disciple understand.

31.

'Tis heart on heart thou rulest. Thou art the same
At God's right hand as here exposed to shame,
And therefore workest now as thou didst then—
Feeding the faint divine in humble men.
Through all thy realms from thee goes out heart-power,
Working the holy, satisfying hour,
When all shall love, and all be loved again.

JUNE.

1.

FROM thine, as then, the healing virtue goes
Into our hearts—that is the Father's plan.
From heart to heart it sinks, it steals, it flows,
From these that know thee still infecting those.
Here is my heart—from thine, Lord, fill it up,
That I may offer it as the holy cup
Of thy communion to my every man.

2.

When thou dost send out whirlwinds on thy seas,
Alternatest thy lightning with its roar,
Thy night with morning, and thy clouds with stars
Or, mightier force unseen in midst of these,
Orderest the life in every airy pore;
Guidest men's efforts, rul'st mishaps and jars,—
'Tis only for their hearts, and nothing more.

3.

This, this alone thy father careth for—
That men should live hearted throughout with thee—
Because the simple, only life thou art,
Of the very truth of living, the pure heart.
For this, deep waters whelm the fruitful lea,
Wars ravage, famine wastes, plague withers, nor
Shall cease till men have chosen the better part.

4.

But, like a virtuous medicine, self-diffused
Through all men's hearts thy love shall sink and float;
Till every feeling false, and thought unwise,
Selfish, and seeking, shall, sternly disused,
Wither, and die, and shrivel up to nought;
And Christ, whom they did hang 'twixt earth and skies,
Up in the inner world of men arise.

5.

Make me a fellow worker with thee, Christ;
Nought else befits a God-born energy;
Of all that's lovely, only lives the highest,
Lifing the rest that it shall never die.
Up I would be to help thee—for thou liest
Not, linen-swathed in Joseph's garden-tomb,
But walkest crowned, creation's heart and bloom.

6.

My God, when I would lift my heart to thee,
Imagination instantly doth set
A cloudy something, thin, and vast, and vague,
To stand for him who is the fact of me;
Then up the Will, and doth her weakness plague
To pay the heart her duty and her debt,
Showing the face that hearkeneth to the plea.

7.

And hence it comes that thou at times dost seem
To fade into an image of my mind;
I, dreamer, cover, hide thee up with dream,—
Thee, primal, individual entity!—
No likeness will I seek to frame or find,
But cry to that which thou dost choose to be,
To that which is my sight, therefore I cannot see.

8.

No likeness? Lo, the Christ! Oh, large Enough!
I see, yet fathom not the face he wore.
He is—and out of him there is no stuff
To make a man. Let fail me every spark
Of blissful vision on my pathway rough,
I have seen much, and trust the perfect more,
While to his feet my faith crosses the wayless dark.

9.

Faith is the human shadow of thy might.
Thou art the one self-perfect life, and we
Who trust thy life, therein join on to thee,
Taking our part in self-creating light.
To trust is to step forward out of the night—
To be—to share in the outgoing Will
That lives and is, because outgoing still.

10.

I am lost before thee, Father! yet I will
Claim of thee my birthright ineffable.
Thou lay'st it on me, son, to claim thee, sire;
To that which thou hast made me, I aspire;
To thee, the sun, upflames thy kindled fire.
No man presumes in that to which he was born;
Less than the gift to claim, would be the giver to scorn.

11.

Henceforth all things thy dealings are with me
For out of thee is nothing, or can be,
And all things are to draw us home to thee.
What matter that the knowers scoffing say,
"This is old folly, plain to the new day"?—
If thou be such as thou, and they as they,
Unto thy Let there be, they still must answer Nay.

12.

They will not, therefore cannot, do not know him.
Nothing they could know, could be God. In sooth,
Unto the true alone exists the truth.
They say well, saying Nature doth not show him:
Truly she shows not what she cannot show;
And they deny the thing they cannot know.
Who sees a glory, towards it will go.

13.

Faster no step moves God because the fool
Shouts to the universe God there is none;
The blindest man will not preach out the sun,
Though on his darkness he should found a school.
It may be, when he finds he is not dead,
Though world and body, sight and sound are fled,
Some eyes may open in his foolish head.

14.

When I am very weary with hard thought,
And yet the question burns and is not quenched,
My heart grows cool when to remembrance wrought
That thou who know'st the light-born answer sought
Know'st too the dark where the doubt lies entrenched—
Know'st with what seemings I am sore perplexed,
And that with thee I wait, nor needs my soul be vexed.

15.

Who sets himself not sternly to be good,
Is but a fool, who judgment of true things
Has none, however oft the claim renewed.
And he who thinks, in his great plenitude,
To right himself, and set his spirit free,
Without the might of higher communings,
Is foolish also—save he willed himself to be.

16.

How many helps thou giv'st to those would learn!
To some sore pain, to others a sinking heart;
To some a weariness worse than any smart;
To some a haunting, fearing, blind concern;
Madness to some; to some the shaking dart
Of hideous death still following as they turn;
To some a hunger that will not depart.

17.

To some thou giv'st a deep unrest—a scorn
Of all they are or see upon the earth;
A gaze, at dusky night and clearing morn,
As on a land of emptiness and dearth;
To some a bitter sorrow; to some the sting
Of love misprized—of sick abandoning;
To some a frozen heart, oh, worse than anything!

18.

To some a mocking demon, that doth set
The poor foiled will to scoff at the ideal,
But loathsome makes to them their life of jar.
The messengers of Satan think to mar,
But make—driving the soul from false to feal—
To thee, the reconciler, the one real,
In whom alone the would be and the is are met.

19.

Me thou hast given an infinite unrest,
A hunger—not at first after known good,
But something vague I knew not, and yet would—
The veiled Isis, thy will not understood;
A conscience tossing ever in my breast;
And something deeper, that will not be expressed,
Save as the Spirit thinking in the Spirit's brood.

20.

But now the Spirit and I are one in this—
My hunger now is after righteousness;
My spirit hopes in God to set me free
From the low self loathed of the higher me.
Great elder brother of my second birth,
Dear o'er all names but one, in heaven or earth,
Teach me all day to love eternally.

21.

Lo, Lord, thou know'st, I would not anything
That in the heart of God holds not its root;
Nor falsely deem there is any life at all
That doth in him nor sleep nor shine nor sing;
I know the plants that bear the noisome fruit
Of burning and of ashes and of gall—
From God's heart torn, rootless to man's they cling.

22.

Life-giving love rots to devouring fire;
Justice corrupts to despicable revenge;
Motherhood chokes in the dam's jealous mire;
Hunger for growth turns fluctuating change;
Love's anger grand grows spiteful human wrath,
Hunting men out of conscience' holy path;
And human kindness takes the tattler's range.

23.

Nothing can draw the heart of man but good;
Low good it is that draws him from the higher—
So evil—poison uncreate from food.
Never a foul thing, with temptation dire,
Tempts hellward force created to aspire,
But walks in wronged strength of imprisoned Truth,
Whose mantle also oft the Shame indu'th.

24.

Love in the prime not yet I understand—
Scarce know the love that loveth at first hand:
Help me my selfishness to scatter and scout;
Blow on me till my love loves burningly;
Then the great love will burn the mean self out,
And I, in glorious simplicity,
Living by love, shall love unspeakably.

25.

Oh, make my anger pure—let no worst wrong
Rouse in me the old niggard selfishness.
Give me thine indignation—which is love
Turned on the evil that would part love's throng;
Thy anger scathes because it needs must bless,
Gathering into union calm and strong
All things on earth, and under, and above.

26.

Make my forgiveness downright—such as I
Should perish if I did not have from thee;
I let the wrong go, withered up and dry,
Cursed with divine forgetfulness in me.
'Tis but self-pity, pleasant, mean, and sly,
Low whispering bids the paltry memory live:—
What am I brother for, but to forgive!

27.

"Thou art my father's child—come to my heart:"
Thus must I say, or Thou must say, "Depart;"
Thus I would say—I would be as thou art;
Thus I must say, or still I work athwart
The absolute necessity and law
That dwells in me, and will me asunder draw,
If in obedience I leave any flaw.

28.

Lord, I forgive—and step in unto thee.
If I have enemies, Christ deal with them:
He hath forgiven me and Jerusalem.
Lord, set me from self-inspiration free,
And let me live and think from thee, not me—
Rather, from deepest me then think and feel,
At centre of thought's swift-revolving wheel.

29.

I sit o'ercanopied with Beauty's tent,
Through which flies many a golden-winged dove,
Well watched of Fancy's tender eyes up bent;
A hundred Powers wait on me, ministering;
A thousand treasures Art and Knowledge bring;
Will, Conscience, Reason tower the rest above;
But in the midst, alone, I gladness am and love.

30.

'Tis but a vision, Lord; I do not mean
That thus I am, or have one moment been—
'Tis but a picture hung upon my wall,
To measure dull contentment therewithal,
And know behind the human how I fall;—
A vision true, of what one day shall be,
When thou hast had thy very will with me.

JULY.

1.

ALAS, my tent! see through it a whirlwind sweep!
Moaning, poor Fancy's doves are swept away.
I sit alone, a sorrow half asleep,
My consciousness the blackness all astir.
No pilgrim I, a homeless wanderer—
For how canst Thou be in the darkness deep,
Who dwellest only in the living day?

2.

It must be, somewhere in my fluttering tent,
Strange creatures, half tamed only yet, are pent—
Dragons, lop-winged birds, and large-eyed snakes!
Hark! through the storm the saddest howling breaks!
Or are they loose, roaming about the bent,
The darkness dire deepening with moan and scream?—
My Morning, rise, and all shall be a dream.

3.

Not thine, my Lord, the darkness all is mine—
Save that, as mine, my darkness too is thine:
All things are thine to save or to destroy—
Destroy my darkness, rise my perfect joy;
Love primal, the live coal of every night,
Flame out, scare the ill things with radiant fright,
And fill my tent with laughing morn's delight.

4.

Master, thou workest with such common things—
Low souls, weak hearts, I mean—and hast to use,
Therefore, such common means and rescuings,
That hard we find it, as we sit and muse,
To think thou workest in us verily:
Bad sea-boats we, and manned with wretched crews—
That doubt the captain, watch the storm-spray flee.

5.

Thou art hampered in thy natural working then
When beings designed on freedom's holy plan
Will not be free: with thy poor, foolish men,
Thou therefore hast to work just like a man.
But when, tangling thyself in their sore need,
Thou hast to freedom fashioned them indeed,
Then wilt thou grandly move, and Godlike speed.

6.

Will this not then show grandest fact of all—
In thy creation victory most renowned—
That thou hast wrought thy will by slow and small,
And made men like thee, though thy making bound
By that which they were not, and could not be
Until thou mad'st them make along with thee?—
Master, the tardiness is but in me.

7.

Hence come thy checks—because I still would run
My head into the sand, nor flutter aloft
Towards thy home, with thy wind under me.
'Tis because I am mean, thy ways so oft
Look mean to me; my rise is low begun;
But scarce thy will doth grasp me, ere I see,
For my arrest and rise, its stern necessity.

8.

Like clogs upon the pinions of thy plan
We hang—like captives on thy chariot-wheels,
Who should climb up and ride with Death's conqueror;
Therefore thy train along the world's highway steals
So slow to the peace of heart-reluctant man.
What shall we do to spread the wing and soar,
Nor straiten thy deliverance any more?

9.

The sole way to put flight into the wing,
To preen its feathers, and to make them grow,
Is to heed humbly every smallest thing
With which the Christ in us has aught to do.
So will the Christ from child to manhood go,
Obedient to the father Christ, and so
Sweet holy change will turn all our old things to new.

10.

Creation thou dost work by faint degrees,
By shade and shadow from unseen beginning;
Far, far apart, in unthought mysteries
Of thy own dark, unfathomable seas,
Thou will'st thy will; and thence, upon the earth—
Slow travelling, his way through centuries winning—
A child at length arrives at never ending birth.

11.

Well mayst thou then work on indocile hearts
By small successes, disappointments small;
By nature, weather, failure, or sore fall;
By shame, anxiety, bitterness, and smarts;
By loneliness, by weary loss of zest:—
The rags, the husks, the swine, the hunger-quest,
Drive home the wanderer to the father's breast.

12.

How suddenly some rapid turn of thought
May throw the life-machine all out of gear,
Clouding the windows with the steam of doubt,
Filling the eyes with dust, with noise the ear!
Who knows not then where dwells the engineer,
Rushes aghast into the pathless night,
And wanders in a land of dreary fright.

13.

Amazed at sightless whirring of their wheels,
Confounded with the recklessness and strife,
Distract with fears of what may next ensue,
Some break rude exit from the house of life,
And plunge into a silence out of view—
Whence not a cry, no wafture once reveals
What door they have broke open with the knife.

14.

Help me, my Father, in whatever dismay,
Whatever terror in whatever shape,
To hold the faster by thy garment's hem;
When my heart sinks, oh, lift it up, I pray;
Thy child should never fear though hell should gape,
Not blench though all the ills that men affray
Stood round him like the Roman round Jerusalem.

15.

Too eager I must not be to understand.
How should the work the master goes about
Fit the vague sketch my compasses have planned?
I am his house—for him to go in and out.
He builds me now—and if I cannot see
At any time what he is doing with me,
'Tis that he makes the house for me too grand.

16.

The house is not for me—it is for him.
His royal thoughts require many a stair,
Many a tower, many an outlook fair,
Of which I have no thought, and need no care.
Where I am most perplexed, it may be there
Thou mak'st a secret chamber, holy-dim,
Where thou wilt come to help my deepest prayer.

17.

I cannot tell why this day I am ill;
But I am well because it is thy will—
Which is to make me pure and right like thee.
Not yet I need escape—'tis bearable
Because thou knowest. And when harder things
Shall rise and gather, and overshadow me,
I shall have comfort in thy strengthenings.

18.

How do I live when thou art far away?—
When I am sunk, and lost, and dead in sleep,
Or in some dream with no sense in its play?
When weary-dull, or drowned in study deep?—
O Lord, I live so utterly on thee,
I live when I forget thee utterly—
Not that thou thinkest of, but thinkest me.

19.

Thou far!—that word the holy truth doth blur.
Doth the great ocean from the small fish run
When it sleeps fast in its low weedy bower?
Is the sun far from any smallest flower,
That lives by his dear presence every hour?
Are they not one in oneness without stir—
The flower the flower because the sun the sun?

20.

"Dear presence every hour"!—what of the night,
When crumpled daisies shut gold sadness in;
And some do hang the head for lack of light,
Sick almost unto death with absence-blight?—
Thy memory then, warm-lingering in the ground,
Mourned dewy in the air, keeps their hearts sound,
Till fresh with day their lapsed life begin.

21.

All things are shadows of the shining true:
Sun, sea, and air—close, potent, hurtless fire—
Flowers from their mother's prison—dove, and dew—
Every thing holds a slender guiding clue
Back to the mighty oneness:—hearts of faith
Know thee than light, than heat, endlessly nigher,
Our life's life, carpenter of Nazareth.

22.

Sometimes, perhaps, the spiritual blood runs slow,
And soft along the veins of will doth flow,
Seeking God's arteries from which it came.
Or does the etherial, creative flame
Turn back upon itself, and latent grow?—
It matters not what figure or what name,
If thou art in me, and I am not to blame.

23.

In such God-silence, the soul's nest, so long
As all is still, no flutter and no song,
Is safe. But if my soul begin to act
Without some waking to the eternal fact
That my dear life is hid with Christ in God—
I think and move a creature of earth's clod,
Stand on the finite, act upon the wrong.

24.

My soul this sermon hence for itself prepares:—
"Then is there nothing vile thou mayst not do,
Buffeted in a tumult of low cares,
And treacheries of the old man 'gainst the new."—
Lord, in my spirit let thy spirit move,
Warning, that it may not have to reprove:—
In my dead moments, master, stir the prayers.

25.

Lord, let my soul o'erburdened then feel thee
Thrilling through all its brain's stupidity.
If I must slumber, heedless of ill harms,
Let it not be but in my Father's arms;
Outside the shelter of his garment's fold,
All is a waste, a terror-haunted wold.—
Lord, keep me. 'Tis thy child that cries. Behold.

26.

Some say that thou their endless love host won
By deeds for them which I may not believe
Thou ever didst, or ever willedst done:
What matter, so they love thee? They receive
Eternal more than the poor loom and wheel
Of their invention ever wove and spun.—
I love thee for I must, thine all from head to heel.

27.

The love of thee will set all notions right.
Right save by love no thought can be or may;
Only love's knowledge is the primal light.
Questions keep camp along love's shining coast—
Challenge my love and would my entrance stay:
Across the buzzing, doubting, challenging host,
I rush to thee, and cling, and cry—Thou know'st.

28.

Oh, let me live in thy realities,
Nor substitute my notions for thy facts,
Notion with notion making leagues and pacts;
They are to truth but as dream-deeds to acts,
And questioned, make me doubt of everything.—
"O Lord, my God," my heart gets up and cries,
"Come thy own self, and with thee my faith bring."

29.

O master, my desires to work, to know,
To be aware that I do live and grow—
All restless wish for anything not thee,
I yield, and on thy altar offer me.
Let me no more from out thy presence go,
But keep me waiting watchful for thy will—
Even while I do it, waiting watchful still.

30.

Thou art the Lord of life, the secret thing.
Thou wilt give endless more than I could find,
Even if without thee I could go and seek;
For thou art one, Christ, with my deepest mind,
Duty alive, self-willed, in me dost speak,
And to a deeper purer being sting:
I come to thee, my life, my causing kind.

31.

Nothing is alien in thy world immense—
No look of sky or earth or man or beast;
"In the great hand of God I stand, and thence"
Look out on life, his endless, holy feast.
To try to feel is but to court despair,
To dig for a sun within a garden-fence:
Who does thy will, O God, he lives upon thy air.

AUGUST.

1.

SO shall abundant entrance me be given
Into the truth, my life's inheritance.
Lo! as the sun shoots straight from out his tomb,
God-floated, casting round a lordly glance
Into the corners of his endless room,
So, through the rent which thou, O Christ, hast riven,
I enter liberty's divine expanse.

2.

It will be so—ah, so it is not now!
Who seeks thee for a little lazy peace,
Then, like a man all weary of the plough,
That leaves it standing in the furrow's crease,
Turns from thy presence for a foolish while,
Till comes again the rasp of unrest's file,
From liberty is distant many a mile.

3.

Like one that stops, and drinks, and turns, and goes
Into a land where never water flows,
There travels on, the dry and thirsty day,
Until the hot night veils the farther way,
Then turns and finds again the bubbling pool—
Here would I build my house, take up my stay,
Nor ever leave my Sychar's margin cool.

4.

Keep me, Lord, with thee. I call from out the dark—
Hear in thy light, of which I am a spark.
I know not what is mine and what is thine—
Of branch and stem I miss the differing mark—
But if a mere hair's-breadth me separateth,
That hair's-breadth is eternal, infinite death.
For sap thy dead branch calls, O living vine!

5.

I have no choice, I must do what I can;
But thou dost me, and all things else as well;
Thou wilt take care thy child shall grow a man.
Rouse thee, my faith; be king; with life be one;
To trust in God is action's highest kind;
Who trusts in God, his heart with life doth swell;
Faith opens all the windows to God's wind.

6.

O Father, thou art my eternity.
Not on the clasp Of consciousness—on thee
My life depends; and I can well afford
All to forget, so thou remember, Lord.
In thee I rest; in sleep thou dost me fold;
In thee I labour; still in thee, grow old;
And dying, shall I not in thee, my Life, be bold?

7.

In holy things may be unholy greed.
Thou giv'st a glimpse of many a lovely thing,
Not to be stored for use in any mind,
But only for the present spiritual need.
The holiest bread, if hoarded, soon will breed
The mammon-moth, the having-pride, I find.
'Tis momently thy heart gives out heart-quickening.

8.

It is thyself, and neither this nor that,
Nor anything, told, taught, or dreamed of thee,
That keeps us live. The holy maid who sat
Low at thy feet, choosing the better part,
Rising, bore with her—what a memory!
Yet, brooding only on that treasure, she
Had soon been roused by conscious loss of heart.

9.

I am a fool when I would stop and think,
And lest I lose my thoughts, from duty shrink.
It is but avarice in another shape.
'Tis as the vine-branch were to hoard the grape,
Nor trust the living root beneath the sod.
What trouble is that child to thee, my God,
Who sips thy gracious cup, and will not drink!

10.

True, faithful action only is the life,
The grapes for which we feel the pruning knife.
Thoughts are but leaves; they fall and feed the ground.
The holy seasons, swift and slow, go round;
The ministering leaves return, fresh, large, and rife—
But fresher, larger, more thoughts to the brain:—
Farewell, my dove!—come back, hope-laden, through the rain.

11.

Well may this body poorer, feebler grow!
It is undressing for its last sweet bed;
But why should the soul, which death shall never know,
Authority, and power, and memory shed?
It is that love with absolute faith would wed;
God takes the inmost garments off his child,
To have him in his arms, naked and undefiled.

12.

Thou art my knowledge and my memory,
No less than my real, deeper life, my love.
I will not fool, degrade myself to trust
In less than that which maketh me say Me,
In less than that causing itself to be.
Then art within me, behind, beneath, above—
I will be thine because I may and must.

13.

Thou art the truth, the life. Thou, Lord, wilt see
To every question that perplexes me.
I am thy being; and my dignity
Is written with my name down in thy book;
Thou wilt care for it. Never shall I think
Of anything that thou mightst overlook:—
In faith-born triumph at thy feet I sink.

14.

Thou carest more for that which I call mine,
In same sort—better manner than I could,
Even if I knew creation's ends divine,
Rousing in me this vague desire of good.
Thou art more to me than my desires' whole brood;
Thou art the only person, and I cry
Unto the father I of this my I.

15.

Thou who inspirest prayer, then bend'st thine ear;
It, crying with love's grand respect to hear!
I cannot give myself to thee aright—
With the triumphant uttermost of gift;
That cannot be till I am full of light—
To perfect deed a perfect will must lift:—
Inspire, possess, compel me, first of every might.

16.

I do not wonder men can ill believe
Who make poor claims upon thee, perfect Lord;
Then most I trust when most I would receive.
I wonder not that such do pray and grieve—
The God they think, to be God is not fit.
Then only in thy glory I seem to sit,
When my heart claims from thine an infinite accord.

17.

More life I need ere I myself can be.
Sometimes, when the eternal tide ebbs low,
A moment weary of my life I grow—
Weary of my existence' self, I mean,
Not of its plodding, not its wind and snow
Then to thy knee trusting I turn, and lean:
Thou will'st I live, and I do will with thee.

18.

Dost thou mean sometimes that we should forget thee,
Dropping the veil of things 'twixt thee and us?—
Ah, not that we should lose thee and regret thee!
But that, we turning from our windows thus,
The frost-fixed God should vanish from the pane,
Sun-melted, and a moment, Father, let thee
Look like thyself straight into heart and brain.

19.

For sometimes when I am busy among men,
With heart and brain an open thoroughfare
For faces, words, and thoughts other than mine,
And a pause comes at length—oh, sudden then,
Back throbs the tide with rush exultant rare;
And for a gentle moment I divine
Thy dawning presence flush my tremulous air.

20.

If I have to forget thee, do thou see
It be a good, not bad forgetfulness;
That all its mellow, truthful air be free
From dusty noes, and soft with many a yes;
That as thy breath my life, my life may be
Man's breath. So when thou com'st at hour unknown,
Thou shalt find nothing in me but thine own.

21.

Thou being in me, in my deepest me,
Through all the time I do not think of thee,
Shall I not grow at last so true within
As to forget thee and yet never sin?
Shall I not walk the loud world's busy way,
Yet in thy palace-porch sit all the day?
Not conscious think of thee, yet never from thee stray?

22.

Forget!—Oh, must it be?—Would it were rather
That every sense was so filled with my father
That not in anything could I forget him,
But deepest, highest must in all things set him!—
Yet if thou think in me, God, what great matter
Though my poor thought to former break and latter—
As now my best thoughts; break, before thee foiled, and scatter!

23.

Some way there must be of my not forgetting,
And thither thou art leading me, my God.
The child that, weary of his mother's petting,
Runs out the moment that his feet are shod,
May see her face in every flower he sees,
And she, although beyond the window sitting,
Be nearer him than when he sat upon her knees.

24.

What if, when I at last, at the long last,
Shall see thy face, my Lord, my life's delight,
It should not be the face that hath been glassed
In poor imagination's mirror slight!
Will my soul sink, and shall I stand aghast,
Beggared of hope, my heart a conscious blight,
Amazed and lost—death's bitterness come and not passed?

25.

Ah, no! for from thy heart the love will press,
And shining from thy perfect human face,
Will sink into me like the father's kiss;
And deepening wide the gulf of consciousness
Beyond imagination's lowest abyss,
Will, with the potency of creative grace,
Lord it throughout the larger thinking place.

26.

Thus God-possessed, new born, ah, not for long
Should I the sight behold, beatified,
Know it creating in me, feel the throng
Of speechless hopes out-throbbing like a tide,
And my heart rushing, borne aloft the flood,
To offer at his feet its living blood—
Ere, glory-hid, the other face I spied.

27.

For out imagination is, in small,
And with the making-difference that must be,
Mirror of God's creating mirror; all
That shows itself therein, that formeth he,
And there is Christ, no bodiless vanity,
Though, face to face, the mighty perfectness
With glory blurs the dim-reflected less.

28.

I clasp thy feet, O father of the living!
Thou wilt not let my fluttering hopes be more,
Or lovelier, or greater, than thy giving!
Surely thy ships will bring to my poor shore,
Of gold and peacocks such a shining store
As will laugh all the dreams to holy scorn,
Of love and sorrow that were ever born.

29.

Sometimes it seems pure natural to trust,
And trust right largely, grandly, infinitely,
Daring the splendour of the giver's part;
At other times, the whole earth is but dust,
The sky is dust, yea, dust the human heart;
Then art thou nowhere, there is no room for thee
In the great dust-heap of eternity.

30.

But why should it be possible to mistrust—
Nor possible only, but its opposite hard?
Why should not man believe because he must—
By sight's compulsion? Why should he be scarred
With conflict? worn with doubting fine and long?—
No man is fit for heaven's musician throng
Who has not tuned an instrument all shook and jarred.

31.

Therefore, O Lord, when all things common seem,
When all is dust, and self the centre clod,
When grandeur is a hopeless, foolish dream,
And anxious care more reasonable than God,—
Out of the ashes I will call to thee—
In spite of dead distrust call earnestly:—
Oh thou who livest, call, then answer dying me.

SEPTEMBER.

1.

WE are a shadow and a shining, we!
One moment nothing seems but what we see,
Nor aught to rule but common circumstance—
Nought is to seek but praise, to shun but chance;
A moment more, and God is all in all,
And not a sparrow from its nest can fall
But from the ground its chirp goes up into his hall.

2.

I know at least which is the better mood.
When on a heap of cares I sit and brood,
Like Job upon his ashes, sorely vext,
I feel a lower thing than when I stood
The world's true heir, fearless as, on its stalk,
A lily meeting Jesus in his walk:
I am not all mood—I can judge betwixt.

3.

Such differing moods can scarce to one belong;
Shall the same fountain sweet and bitter yield?
Shall what bore late the dust-mood, think and brood
Till it bring forth the great believing mood?
Or that which bore the grand mood, bald and peeled,
Sit down to croon the shabby sensual song,
To hug itself, and sink from wrong to meaner wrong?

4.

In the low mood, the mere man acts alone,
Moved by impulses which, if from within,
Yet far outside the centre man begin;
But in the grand mood, every softest tone
Comes from the living God at very heart—
From thee who infinite core of being art,
Thee who didst call our names ere ever we could sin.

5.

There is a coward sparing in the heart,
Offspring of penury and low-born fear:—
Prayer must take heed nor overdo its part,
Asking too much of him with open ear!
Sinners must wait, not seek the very best,
Cry out for peace, and be of middling cheer:—
False heart! thou cheatest God, and dost thy life molest.

6.

Thou hungerest not, thou thirstest not enough.
Thou art a temporizing thing, mean heart.
Down-drawn, thou pick'st up straws and wretched stuff,
Stooping as if the world's floor were the chart
Of the long way thy lazy feet must tread.
Thou dreamest of the crown hung o'er thy head—
But that is safe—thou gatherest hairs and fluff!

7.

Man's highest action is to reach up higher,
Stir up himself to take hold of his sire.
Then best I love you, dearest, when I go
And cry to love's life I may love you so
As to content the yearning, making love,
That perfects strength divine in weakness' fire,
And from the broken pots calls out the silver dove.

8.

Poor am I, God knows, poor as withered leaf;
Poorer or richer than, I dare not ask.
To love aright, for me were hopeless task,
Eternities too high to comprehend.
But shall I tear my heart in hopeless grief,
Or rise and climb, and run and kneel, and bend,
And drink the primal love—so love in chief?

9.

Then love shall wake and be its own high life.
Then shall I know 'tis I that love indeed—
Ready, without a moment's questioning strife,
To be forgot, like bursting water-bead,
For the high good of the eternal dear;
All hope, all claim, resting, with spirit clear,
Upon the living love that every love doth breed.

10.

Ever seem to fail in utterance.
Sometimes amid the swift melodious dance
Of fluttering words—as if it had not been,
The thought has melted, vanished into night;
Sometimes I say a thing I did not mean,
And lo! 'tis better, by thy ordered chance,
Than what eluded me, floating too feathery light.

11.

If thou wouldst have me speak, Lord, give me speech.
So many cries are uttered now-a-days,
That scarce a song, however clear and true,
Will thread the jostling tumult safe, and reach
The ears of men buz-filled with poor denays:
Barb thou my words with light, make my song new,
And men will hear, or when I sing or preach.

12.

Can anything go wrong with me? I ask—
And the same moment, at a sudden pain,
Stand trembling. Up from the great river's brim
Comes a cold breath; the farther bank is dim;
The heaven is black with clouds and coming rain;
High soaring faith is grown a heavy task,
And all is wrong with weary heart and brain.

13.

"Things do go wrong. I know grief, pain, and fear.
I see them lord it sore and wide around."
From her fair twilight answers Truth, star-crowned,
"Things wrong are needful where wrong things abound.
Things go not wrong; but Pain, with dog and spear,
False faith from human hearts will hunt and hound.
The earth shall quake 'neath them that trust the solid ground."

14.

Things go not wrong when sudden I fall prone,
But when I snatch my upheld hand from thine,
And, proud or careless, think to walk alone.
Then things go wrong, when I, poor, silly sheep,
To shelves and pits from the good pasture creep;
Not when the shepherd leaves the ninety and nine,
And to the mountains goes, after the foolish one.

15.

Lo! now thy swift dogs, over stone and bush,
After me, straying sheep, loud barking, rush.
There's Fear, and Shame, and Empty-heart, and Lack,
And Lost-love, and a thousand at their back!
I see thee not, but know thou hound'st them on,
And I am lost indeed—escape is none.
See! there they come, down streaming on my track!

16.

I rise and run, staggering—double and run.—
But whither?—whither?—whither for escape?
The sea lies all about this long-necked cape—
There come the dogs, straight for me every one—
Me, live despair, live centre of alarms!—
Ah! lo! 'twixt me and all his barking harms,
The shepherd, lo!—I run—fall folded in his arms.

17.

There let the dogs yelp, let them growl and leap;
It is no matter—I will go to sleep.
Like a spent cloud pass pain and grief and fear,
Out from behind it unchanged love shines clear.—
Oh, save me, Christ!—I know not what I am,
I was thy stupid, self-willed, greedy lamb,
Would be thy honest and obedient sheep.

18.

Why is it that so often I return
From social converse with a spirit worn,
A lack, a disappointment—even a sting
Of shame, as for some low, unworthy thing?—
Because I have not, careful, first of all,
Set my door open wide, back to the wall,
Ere I at others' doors did knock and call.

19.

Yet more and more of me thou dost demand;
My faith and hope in God alone shall stand,
The life of law—not trust the rain and sun
To draw the golden harvest o'er the land.
I must not say—"This too will pass and die,"
"The wind will change," "Round will the seasons run."
Law is the body of will, of conscious harmony.

20.

Who trusts a law, might worship a god of wood;
Half his soul slumbers, if it be not dead.
He is a live thing shut in chaos crude,
Hemmed in with dragons—a remorseless head
Still hanging over its uplifted eyes.
No; God is all in all, and nowhere dies—
The present heart and thinking will of good.

21.

Law is our schoolmaster. Our master, Christ,
Lived under all our laws, yet always prayed—
So walked the water when the storm was highest.—
Law is Thy father's; thou hast it obeyed,
And it thereby subject to thee hast made—
To rule it, master, for thy brethren's sakes:—
Well may he guide the law by whom law's maker makes.

22.

Death haunts our souls with dissolution's strife;
Soaks them with unrest; makes our every breath
A throe, not action; from God's purest gift
Wipes off the bloom; and on the harp of faith
Its fretted strings doth slacken still and shift:
Life everywhere, perfect, and always life,
Is sole redemption from this haunting death.

23.

God, thou from death dost lift me. As I rise,
Its Lethe from my garment drips and flows.
Ere long I shall be safe in upper air,
With thee, my life—with thee, my answered prayer
Where thou art God in every wind that blows,
And self alone, and ever, softly dies,
There shall my being blossom, and I know it fair.

24.

I would dig, Master, in no field but thine,
Would build my house only upon thy rock,
Yet am but a dull day, with a sea-sheen!
Why should I wonder then that they should mock,
Who, in the limbo of things heard and seen,
Hither and thither blowing, lose the shine
Of every light that hangs in the firmament divine.

25.

Lord, loosen in me the hold of visible things;
Help me to walk by faith and not by sight;
I would, through thickest veils and coverings,
See into the chambers of the living light.
Lord, in the land of things that swell and seem,
Help me to walk by the other light supreme,
Which shows thy facts behind man's vaguely hinting dream.

26.

I see a little child whose eager hands
Search the thick stream that drains the crowded street
For possible things hid in its current slow.
Near by, behind him, a great palace stands,
Where kings might welcome nobles to their feet.
Soft sounds, sweet scents, fair sights there only go—
There the child's father lives, but the child does not know.

27.

On, eager, hungry, busy-seeking child,
Rise up, turn round, run in, run up the stair.
Far in a chamber from rude noise exiled,
Thy father sits, pondering how thou dost fare.
The mighty man will clasp thee to his breast:
Will kiss thee, stroke the tangles of thy hair,
And lap thee warm in fold on fold of lovely rest.

28.

The prince of this world came, and nothing found
In thee, O master; but, ah, woe is me!
He cannot pass me, on other business bound,
But, spying in me things familiar, he
Casts over me the shadow of his flight,
And straight I moan in darkness—and the fight
Begins afresh betwixt the world and thee.

29.

In my own heart, O master, in my thought,
Betwixt the woolly sheep and hairy goat
Not clearly I distinguish; but I think
Thou knowest that I fight upon thy side.
The how I am ashamed of; for I shrink
From many a blow—am borne on the battle-tide,
When I should rush to the front, and take thy foe by the throat.

30.

The enemy still hath many things in me;
Yea, many an evil nest with open hole
Gapes out to him, at which he enters free.
But, like the impact of a burning coal,
His presence mere straight rouses the garrison,
And all are up in arms, and down on knee,
Fighting and praying till the foe is gone.

OCTOBER.

1.

REMEMBER, Lord, thou hast not made me good.
Or if thou didst, it was so long ago
I have forgotten—and never understood,
I humbly think. At best it was a crude,
A rough-hewn goodness, that did need this woe,
This sin, these harms of all kinds fierce and rude,
To shape it out, making it live and grow.

2.

But thou art making me, I thank thee, sire.
What thou hast done and doest thou know'st well,
And I will help thee:—gently in thy fire
I will lie burning; on thy potter's-wheel
I will whirl patient, though my brain should reel;
Thy grace shall be enough the grief to quell,
And growing strength perfect through weakness dire.

3.

I have not knowledge, wisdom, insight, thought,
Nor understanding, fit to justify
Thee in thy work, O Perfect. Thou hast brought
Me up to this—and, lo! what thou hast wrought,
I cannot call it good. But I can cry—
"O enemy, the maker hath not done;
One day thou shalt behold, and from the sight wilt run."

4.

The faith I will, aside is easily bent;
But of thy love, my God, one glimpse alone
Can make me absolutely confident—
With faith, hope, joy, in love responsive blent.
My soul then, in the vision mighty grown,
Its father and its fate securely known,
Falls on thy bosom with exultant moan.

5.

Thou workest perfectly. And if it seem
Some things are not so well, 'tis but because
They are too loving-deep, too lofty-wise,
For me, poor child, to understand their laws:
My highest wisdom half is but a dream;
My love runs helpless like a falling stream:
Thy good embraces ill, and lo! its illness dies!

6.

From sleep I wake, and wake to think of thee.
But wherefore not with sudden glorious glee?
Why burst not gracious on me heaven and earth
In all the splendour of a new-day-birth?
Why hangs a cloud betwixt my lord and me?
The moment that my eyes the morning greet,
My soul should panting rush to clasp thy father-feet.

7.

Is it because it is not thou I see,
But only my poor, blotted fancy of thee?
Oh! never till thyself reveal thy face,
Shall I be flooded with life's vital grace.
Oh make my mirror-heart thy shining-place,
And then my soul, awaking with the morn,
Shall be a waking joy, eternally new-born.

OCTOBER.

8.

Lord, in my silver is much metal base,
Else should my being by this time have shown
Thee thy own self therein. Therefore do I
Wake in the furnace. I know thou sittest by,
Refining—look, keep looking in to try
Thy silver; master, look and see thy face,
Else here I lie for ever, blank as any stone.

9.

But when in the dim silver thou dost look,
I do behold thy face, though blurred and faint.
Oh joy! no flaw in me thy grace will brook,
But still refine: slow shall the silver pass
From bright to brighter, till, sans spot or taint,
Love, well content, shall see no speck of brass,
And I his perfect face shall hold as in a glass.

10.

With every morn my life afresh must break
The crust of self, gathered about me fresh;
That thy wind-spirit may rush in and shake
The darkness out of me, and rend the mesh
The spider-devils spin out of the flesh—
Eager to net the soul before it wake,
That it may slumberous lie, and listen to the snake.

11.

'Tis that I am not good—that is enough;
I pry no farther—that is not the way.
Here, O my potter, is thy making stuff!
Set thy wheel going; let it whir and play.
The chips in me, the stones, the straws, the sand,
Cast them out with fine separating hand,
And make a vessel of thy yielding clay.

12.

What if it take a thousand years to make me,
So me he leave not, angry, on the floor!—
Nay, thou art never angry!—that would break me!
Would I tried never thy dear patience sore,
But were as good as thou couldst well expect me,
Whilst thou dost make, I mar, and thou correct me!
Then were I now content, waiting for something more.

13.

Only, my God, see thou that I content thee—
Oh, take thy own content upon me, God!
Ah, never, never, sure, wilt thou repent thee,
That thou hast called thy Adam from the clod!
Yet must I mourn that thou shouldst ever find me
One moment sluggish, needing more of the rod
Than thou didst think when thy desire designed me.

14.

My God, it troubles me I am not better.
More help, I pray, still more. Thy perfect debtor
I shall be when thy perfect child I am grown.
My Father, help me—am I not thine own?
Lo, other lords have had dominion o'er me,
But now thy will alone I set before me:
Thy own heart's life—Lord, thou wilt not abhor me!

15.

In youth, when once again I had set out
To find thee, Lord, my life, my liberty,
A window now and then, clouds all about,
Would open into heaven: my heart forlorn
First all would tremble with a solemn glee,
Then, whelmed in peace, rest like a man outworn,
That sees the dawn slow part the closed lids of the morn.

16.

Now I grow old, and the soft-gathered years
Have calmed, yea dulled the heart's swift fluttering beat;
But a quiet hope that keeps its household seat
Is better than recurrent glories fleet.
To know thee, Lord, is worth a many tears;
And when this mildew, age, has dried away,
My heart will beat again as young and strong and gay.

17.

Stronger and gayer tenfold!—but, O friends,
Not for itself, nor any hoarded bliss.
I see but vaguely whither my being tends,
All vaguely spy a glory shadow-blent,
Vaguely desire the "individual kiss;"
But when I think of God, a large content
Fills the dull air of my gray cloudy tent.

18.

Father of me, thou art my bliss secure.
Make of me, maker, whatsoe'er thou wilt.
Let fancy's wings hang moulting, hope grow poor,
And doubt steam up from where a joy was spilt—
I lose no time to reason it plain and clear,
But fly to thee, my life's perfection dear:—
Not what I think, but what thou art, makes sure.

19.

This utterance of spirit through still thought,
This forming of heart-stuff in moulds of brain,
Is helpful to the soul by which 'tis wrought,
The shape reacting on the heart again;
But when I am quite old, and words are slow,
Like dying things that keep their holes for woe,
And memory's withering tendrils clasp with effort vain?

20.

Thou, then as now, no less wilt be my life,
And I shall know it better than before,
Praying and trusting, hoping, claiming more.
From effort vain, sick foil, and bootless strife,
I shall, with childness fresh, look up to thee;
Thou, seeing thy child with age encumbered sore,
Wilt round him bend thine arm more carefully.

21.

And when grim Death doth take me by the throat,
Thou wilt have pity on thy handiwork;
Thou wilt not let him on my suffering gloat,
But draw my soul out—gladder than man or boy,
When thy saved creatures from the narrow ark
Rushed out, and leaped and laughed and cried for joy,
And the great rainbow strode across the dark.

22.

Against my fears, my doubts, my ignorance,
I trust in thee, O father of my Lord!
The world went on in this same broken dance,
When, worn and mocked, he trusted and adored:
I too will trust, and gather my poor best
To face the truth-faced false. So in his nest
I shall awake at length, a little scarred and scored.

23.

Things cannot look all right so long as I
Am not all right who see—therefore not right
Can see. The lamp within sends out the light
Which shows the things; and if its rays go wry,
Or are not white, they must part show a lie.
The man, half-cured, did men not trees conclude,
Because he moving saw what else had seemed a wood.

24.

Give me, take from me, as thou wilt. I learn—
Slowly and stubbornly I learn to yield
With a strange hopefulness. As from the field
Of hard-fought battle won, the victor chief
Turns thankfully, although his heart do yearn,
So from my old things to thy new I turn,
With sad, thee-trusting heart, and not in grief.

25.

If with my father I did wander free,
Floating o'er hill and field where'er we would,
And, lighting on the sward before the door,
Strange faces through the window-panes should see,
And strange feet standing where the loved had stood,
The dear old place theirs all, as ours before—
Should I be sorrowful, father, having thee?

26.

So, Lord, if thou tak'st from me all the rest,
Thyself with each resumption drawing nigher,
It shall but hurt me as the thorn of the briar,
When I reach to the pale flower in its breast.
To have thee, Lord, is to have all thy best,
Holding it by its very life divine—
To let my friend's hand go, and take his heart in mine.

27.

Take from me leisure, all familiar places;
Take all the lovely things of earth and air
Take from me books; take all my precious faces;
Take words melodious, and their songful linking;
Take scents, and sounds, and all thy outsides fair;
Draw nearer, taking, and, to my sober thinking,
Thou bring'st them nearer all, and ready to my prayer.

28.

No place on earth henceforth I shall count strange,
For every place belongeth to my Christ.
I will go calm where'er thou bid'st me range;
Whoe'er my neighbour, thou art still my nighest.
Oh my heart's life, my owner, will of my being!
Into my soul thou every moment diest,
In thee my life thus evermore decreeing.

29.

What though things change and pass, nor come again!
Thou, the life-heart of all things, changest never.
The sun shines on; the fair clouds turn to rain,
And glad the earth with many a spring and river.
The hearts that answer change with chill and shiver,
That mourn the past, sad-sick, with hopeless pain,
They know not thee, our changeless heart and brain.

30.

My halting words will some day turn to song—
Some far-off day, in holy other times!
The melody now prisoned in my rimes
Will one day break aloft, and from the throng
Of wrestling thoughts and words spring up the air;
As from the flower its colour's sweet despair
Issues in odour, and the sky's low levels climbs.

31.

My surgent thought shoots lark-like up to thee.
Thou like the heaven art all about the lark.
Whatever I surmise or know in me,
Idea, or but symbol on the dark,
Is living, working, thought-creating power
In thee, the timeless father of the hour.
I am thy book, thy song—thy child would be.

NOVEMBER

1.

THOU art of this world, Christ. Thou know'st it all;
Thou know'st our evens, our morns, our red and gray;
How moons, and hearts, and seasons rise and fall;
How we grow weary plodding on the way;
Of future joy how present pain bereaves,
Rounding us with a dark of mere decay,
Tossed with a drift Of summer-fallen leaves.

2.

Thou knowest all our weeping, fainting, striving;
Thou know'st how very hard it is to be;
How hard to rouse faint will not yet reviving;
To do the pure thing, trusting all to thee;
To hold thou art there, for all no face we see;
How hard to think, through cold and dark and dearth,
That thou art nearer now than when eye-seen on earth.

3.

Have pity on us for the look of things,
When blank denial stares us in the face.
Although the serpent mask have lied before,
It fascinates the bird that darkling sings,
And numbs the little prayer-bird's beating wings.
For how believe thee somewhere in blank space,
If through the darkness come no knocking to our door?

4.

If we might sit until the darkness go,
Possess our souls in patience perhaps we might;
But there is always something to be done,
And no heart left to do it. To and fro
The dull thought surges, as the driven waves fight
In gulfy channels. Oh! victorious one,
Give strength to rise, go out, and meet thee in the night.

5.

"Wake, thou that sleepest; rise up from the dead,
And Christ will give thee light." I do not know
What sleep is, what is death, or what is light;
But I am waked enough to feel a woe,
To rise and leave death. Stumbling through the night,
To my dim lattice, O calling Christ! I go,
And out into the dark look for thy star-crowned head.

6.

There are who come to me, and write, and send,
Whom I would love, giving good things to all,
But friend—that name I cannot on them spend;
'Tis from the centre of self-love they call
For cherishing—for which they first must know
How to be still, and take the seat that's low:
When, Lord, shall I be fit—when wilt thou call me friend?

7.

Wilt thou not one day, Lord? In all my wrong,
Self-love and weakness, laziness and fear,
This one thing I can say: I am content
To be and have what in thy heart I am meant
To be and have. In my best times I long
After thy will, and think it glorious-dear;
Even in my worst, perforce my will to thine is bent.

8.

My God, I look to thee for tenderness
Such as I could not seek from any man,
Or in a human heart fancy or plan—
A something deepest prayer will not express:
Lord, with thy breath blow on my being's fires,
Until, even to the soul with self-love wan,
I yield the primal love, that no return desires.

9.

Only no word of mine must ever foster
The self that in a brother's bosom gnaws;
I may not fondle failing, nor the boaster
Encourage with the breath of my applause.
Weakness needs pity, sometimes love's rebuke;
Strength only sympathy deserves and draws—
And grows by every faithful loving look.

10.

'Tis but as men draw nigh to thee, my Lórd,
They can draw nigh each other and not hurt.
Who with the gospel of thy peace are girt,
The belt from which doth hang the Spirit's sword,
Shall breathe on dead bones, and the bones shall live,
Sweet poison to the evil self shall give,
And, clean themselves, lift men clean from the mire abhorred.

11.

My Lord, I have no clothes to come to thee;
My shoes are pierced and broken with the road;
I am torn and weathered, wounded with the goad,
And soiled with tugging at my weary load:
The more I need thee! A very prodigal
I stagger into thy presence, Lord of me:
One look, my Christ, and at thy feet I fall!

12.

Why should I still hang back, like one in a dream,
Who vainly strives to clothe himself aright,
That in great presence he may seemly seem?
Why call up feeling?—dress me in the faint,
Worn, faded, cast-off nimbus of some saint?
Why of old mood bring back a ghostly gleam—
While there He waits, love's heart and loss's blight!

13.

Son of the Father, elder brother mine,
See thy poor brother's plight; See how he stands
Defiled and feeble, hanging down his hands!
Make me clean, brother, with thy burning shine;
From thy rich treasures, householder divine,
Bring forth fair garments, old and new, I pray,
And like thy brother dress me, in the old home-bred way.

14.

My prayer-bird was cold—would not away,
Although I set it on the edge of the nest.
Then I bethought me of the story old—
Love-fact or loving fable, thou know'st best—
How, when the children had made sparrows of clay,
Thou mad'st them birds, with wings to flutter and fold:
Take, Lord, my prayer in thy hand, and make it pray.

15.

My poor clay-sparrow seems turned to a stone,
And from my heart will neither fly nor run.
I cannot feel as thou and I both would,
But, Father, I am willing—make me good.
What art thou father for, but to help thy son?
Look deep, yet deeper, in my heart, and there,
Beyond where I can feel, read thou the prayer.

16.

Oh what it were to be right sure of thee!
Sure that thou art, and the same as thy son, Jesus!
Oh, faith is deeper, wider than the sea,
Yea, than the blue of heaven that ever flees us!
Yet simple as the cry of sore-hurt child,
Or as his shout, with sudden gladness wild,
When home from school he runs, till morn set free.

17.

If I were sure thou, Father, verily art,
True father of the Nazarene as true,
Sure as I am of my wife's shielding heart,
Sure as of sunrise in the watching blue,
Sure as I am that I do eat and drink,
And have a heart to love and laugh and think,
Meseems in flame the joy might from my body start.

18.

But I must know thee in a deeper way
Than any of these ways, or know thee not;
My heart at peace far loftier proof must lay
Than if the wind thou me the wave didst roll,
Than if I lay before thee a sunny spot,
Or knew thee as the body knows its soul,
Or even as the part doth know its perfect whole.

19.

There is no word to tell how I must know thee;
No wind clasped ever a low meadow-flower
So close that as to nearness it could show thee;
No rainbow so makes one the sun and shower.
A something with thee, I am a nothing fro' thee.
Because I am not save as I am in thee,
My soul is ever setting out to win thee.

20.

I know not how—for that I first must know thee.
I know I know thee not as I would know thee,
For my heart burns like theirs that did not know him,
Till he broke bread, and therein they must know him.
I know thee, knowing that I do not know thee,
Nor ever shall till one with me I know thee—
Even as thy son, the eternal man, doth know thee.

21.

Creation under me, in, and above,
Slopes upward from the base, a pyramid,
On whose point I shall stand at last, and love.
From the first rush of vapour at thy will,
To the last poet-word that darkness chid,
Thou hast been sending up creation's hill,
To lift thy souls aloft in faithful Godhead free.

22.

I think my thought, and fancy I think thee.—
Lord, wake me up; rend swift my coffin-planks;
I pray thee, let me live—alive and free.
My soul will break forth in melodious thanks,
Aware at last what thou wouldst have it be,
When thy life shall be light in me, and when
My life to thine is answer and amen.

23.

How oft I say the same things in these lines!
Even as a man, buried in during dark,
Turns ever where the edge of twilight shines,
Prays ever towards the vague eternal mark;
Or as the sleeper, having dreamed he drinks,
Back straightway into thirstful dreaming sinks,
So turns my will to thee, for thee still longs, still pines.

24.

The mortal man, all careful, wise, and troubled,
The eternal child in the nursery doth keep.
To-morrow on to-day the man heaps doubled;
The child laughs, hopeful, even in his sleep.
The man rebukes the child for foolish trust;
The child replies, "Thy care is for poor dust;
Be still, and let me wake that thou mayst sleep."

25.

Till I am one, with oneness manifold,
I must breed contradiction, strife, and doubt;
Things tread Thy court—look real—take proving hold—
My Christ is not yet grown to cast them out;
Alas! to me, false-judging 'twixt the twain,
The Unseen oft fancy seems, while, all about,
The Seen doth lord it with a mighty train.

26.

But when the Will hath learned obedience royal,
He straight will set the child upon the throne;
To whom the seen things all, grown instant loyal,
Will gather to his feet, in homage prone—
The child their master they have ever known;
Then shall the visible fabric plainly lean
On a Reality that never can be seen.

27.

Thy ways are wonderful, maker of men!
Thou gavest me a child, and I have fed
And clothed and loved her, many a growing year;
Lo! now a friend of months draws gently near,
And claims her future—all beyond his ken—
There he hath never loved her nor hath led:
She weeps and moans, but turns, and leaves her home so dear.

28.

She leaves, but not forsakes. Oft in the night,
Oft at mid-day when all is still around,
Sudden will rise, in dim pathetic light,
Some childish memory of household bliss,
Or sorrow by love's service robed and crowned;
Rich in his love, she yet will sometimes miss
The mother's folding arms, the mother's sealing kiss.

29.

Then first, I think, our eldest-born, although
Loving, devoted, tender, watchful, dear,
The innermost of home-bred love shall know!
Yea, when at last the janitor draws near,
A still, pale joy will through the darkness go,
At thought of lying in those arms again,
Which once were heaven enough for any pain.

30.

By love doth love grow mighty in its love:
Once thou shalt love us, child, as we love thee.
Father of loves, is it not thy decree
That, by our long, far-wandering remove
From thee, our life, our home, our being blest,
We learn at last to love thee true and best,
And rush with all our loves back to thy infinite rest?

DECEMBER.

1.

I AM a little weary of my life—
Not thy life, blessed Father! Or the blood
Too slowly laves the coral shores of thought,
Or I am weary of weariness and strife.
Open my soul-gates to thy living flood;
I ask not larger heart-throbs, vigour-fraught,
I pray thy presence, with strong patience rife.

2.

I will what thou will'st—only keep me sure
That thou art willing; call to me now and then.
So, ceasing to enjoy, I shall endure
With perfect patience—willing beyond my ken
Beyond my love, beyond my thinking scope;
Willing to be because thy will is pure;
Willing thy will beyond all bounds of hope.

3.

This weariness of mine, may it not come
From something that doth need no setting right?
Shall fruit be blamed if it hang wearily
A day before it perfected drop plumb
To the sad earth from off its nursing tree?
Ripeness must always come with loss of might.
The weary evening fall before the resting night.

4.

Hither if I have come through earth and air,
Through fire and water—I am not of them;
Born in the darkness, what fair-flashing gem
Would to the earth go back and nestle there?
Not of this world, this world my life doth hem;
What if I weary, then, and look to the door,
Because my unknown life is swelling at the core?

5.

All winged things came from the waters first;
Airward still many a one from the water springs
In dens and caves wind-loving things are nursed:—
I lie like unhatched bird, upfolded, dumb,
While all the air is trembling with the hum
Of songs and beating hearts and whirring wings,
That call my slumbering life to wake to happy things.

6.

I lay last night and knew not why I was sad.
"'Tis well with God," I said, "and he is the truth;
Let that content me."—'Tis not strength, nor youth,
Nor buoyant health, nor a heart merry-mad,
That makes the fact of things wherein men live:
He is the life, and doth my life outgive;
In him there is no gloom, but all is solemn-glad,

7.

I said to myself, "Lo, I lie in a dream
Of separation, where there comes no sign;
My waking life is hid with Christ in God,
Where all is true and potent—fact divine."
I will not heed the thing that doth but seem;
I will be quiet as lark upon the sod;
God's will, the seed, shall rest in me the pod.

8.

And when that will shall blossom—then, my God,
There will be jubilation in a world!
The glad lark, soaring heavenward from the sod,
Up the swift spiral of its own song whirled,
Never such jubilation wild out-poured
As from my soul will break at thy feet, Lord,
Like a great tide from sea-heart shoreward hurled.

9.

For then thou wilt be able, then at last,
To glad me as thou hungerest to do;
Then shall thy life my heart all open find,
A thoroughfare to thy great spirit-wind;
Then shall I rest within thy holy vast,
One with the bliss of the eternal mind;
And all creation rise in me created new.

10.

What makes thy being a bliss shall then make mind
For I shall love as thou, and love in thee;
Then shall I have whatever I desire,
My every faintest wish being all divine;
Power thou wilt give me to work mightily,
Even as my Lord, leading thy low men nigher,
With dance and song to cast their best upon thy fire.

11.

Then shall I live such an essential life
That a mere flower will then to me unfold
More bliss than now grandest orchestral strife—
By love made and obedience humble-bold,
I shall straight through its window God behold.
God, I shall feed on thee, thy creature blest
With very being—work at one with sweetest rest.

12.

Give me a world, to part for praise and sunder.
The brooks be bells; the winds, in caverns dumb,
Wake fife and flute and flageolet and voice;
The fire-shook earth itself be the great drum;
And let the air the region's bass out thunder;
The firs be violins; the reeds hautboys;
Rivers, seas, icebergs fill the great score up and under!

13.

But rather dost thou hear the blundered words
Of breathing creatures; the music-lowing herds
Of thy great cattle; thy soft-bleating sheep;
O'erhovered by the trebles of thy birds,
Whose Christ-praised carelessness song-fills the deep;
Still rather a child's talk who apart doth hide him,
And make a tent for God to come and sit beside him.

14.

This is not life; this being is not enough.
But thou art life, and thou hast life for me.
Thou mad'st the worm—to cast the wormy slough,
And fly abroad—a glory flit and flee.
Thou hast me, statue-like, hewn in the rough,
Meaning at last to shape me perfectly.
Lord, thou hast called me fourth, I turn and call on thee.

15.

'Tis thine to make, mine to rejoice in thine.
As, hungering for his mother's face and eyes,
The child throws wide the door, back to the wall,
I run to thee, the refuge from poor lies:
Lean dogs behind me whimper, yelp, and whine;
Life lieth ever sick, Death's writhing thrall,
In slavery endless, hopeless, and supine.

16.

The life that hath not willed itself to be,
Must clasp the life that willed, and be at peace;
Or, like a leaf wind-blown, through chaos flee;
A life-husk into which the demons go,
And work their will, and drive it to and fro;
A thing that neither is, nor yet can cease,
Which uncreation can alone release.

17.

But when I turn and grasp the making hand,
And will the making will, with confidence
I ride the crest of the creation-wave,
Helpless no more, no more existence' slave;
In the heart of love's creating fire I stand,
And, love-possessed in heart and soul and sense,
Take up the making share the making Master gave.

18.

That man alone who does the Father's works
Can be the Father's son; yea, only he
Who sonlike can create, can ever be;
Who with God wills not, is no son, not free.
O Father, send the demon-doubt that lurks
Behind the hope, out into the abyss;
Who trusts in knowledge all its good shall miss.

19.

Thy beasts are sinless, and do live before thee;
Thy child is sinful, and must run to thee.
Thy angels sin not and in peace adore thee;
But I must will, or never more be free.
I from thy heart came, how can I ignore thee?—
Back to my home I hurry, haste, and flee;
There I shall dwell, love-praising evermore thee.

20.

My holy self, thy pure ideal, lies
Calm in thy bosom, which it cannot leave;
My self unholy, no ideal, hies
Hither and thither, gathering store to grieve—
Not now, O Father! now it mounts, it flies,
To join the true self in thy heart that waits,
And, one with it, be one with all the heavenly mates.

21.

Trusting thee, Christ, I kneel, and clasp thy knee;
Cast myself down, and kiss thy brother-feet—
One self thou and the Father's thought of thee!
Ideal son, thou hast left the perfect home,
Ideal brother, to seek thy brothers come!
Thou know'st our angels all, God's children sweet,
And of each two wilt make one holy child complete.

22.

To a slow end I draw these daily words,
Nor think such words often to write again—
Rather, as light the power to me affords,
Christ's new and old would to my friends unbind;
Through words he spoke help to his thought behind;
Unveil the heart with which he drew his men;
Set forth his rule o'er devils, animals, corn, and wind.

23.

I do remember how one time I thought,
"God must be lonely—oh, so lonely lone!
I will be very good to him—ah, nought
Can reach the heart of his great loneliness!
My whole heart I will bring him, with a moan
That I may not come nearer; I will lie prone
Before the awful loveliness in loneliness' excess."

24.

A God must have a God for company.
And lo! thou hast the Son-God to thy friend.
Thou honour'st his obedience, he thy law.
Into thy secret life-will he doth see;
Thou fold'st him round in live love perfectly—
One two, without beginning, without end;
In love, life, strength, and truth, perfect without a flaw.

25.

Thou hast not made, or taught me, Lord, to care
For times and seasons—but this one glad day
Is the blue sapphire clasping all the lights
That flash in the girdle of the year so fair—
When thou wast born a man, because alway
Thou wast and art a man, through all the flights
Of thought, and time, and thousandfold creation's play.

26.

We all are lonely, Maker—each a soul
Shut in by itself, a sundered atom of thee.
No two yet loved themselves into a whole;
Even when we weep together we are two.
Of two to make one, which yet two shall be,
Is thy creation's problem, deep, and true,
To which thou only hold'st the happy, hurting clue.

27.

No less than thou, O Father, do we need
A God to friend each lonely one of us.
As touch not in the sack two grains of seed,
Touch no two hearts in great worlds populous.
Outside the making God we cannot meet
Him he has made our brother: homeward, thus,
To find our kin we first must turn our wandering feet.

28.

It must be possible that the soul made
Should absolutely meet the soul that makes;
Then, in that bearing soul, meet every other
There also born, each sister and each brother.
Lord, till I meet thee thus, life is delayed;
I am not I until that morning breaks,
Not I until my consciousness eternal wakes.

29.

Again I shall behold thee, daughter true;
The hour will come when I shall hold thee fast
In God's name, loving thee all through and through.
Somewhere in his grand thought this waits for us.
Then shall I see a smile not like thy last—
For that great thing which came when all was past,
Was not a smile, but God's peace glorious.

30.

Twilight of the transfiguration-joy,
Gleam-faced, pure-eyed, strong-willed, high-hearted boy!
Hardly thy life clear forth of heaven was sent,
Ere it broke out into a smile, and went.
So swift thy growth, so true thy goalward bent,
Thou, child and sage inextricably blent,
Wilt one day teach thy father in some heavenly tent

31.

Go, my beloved children, live your life.
Wounded, faint, bleeding, never yield the strife.
Stunned, fallen-awake, arise, and fight again.
Before you victory stands, with shining train
Of hopes not credible until they are.
Beyond morass and mountain swells the star
Of perfect love—the home of longing heart and brain

THE HOPE OF
THE GOSPEL

SALVATION FROM SIN.

—and thou shalt call his name Jesus; for he shall save his people from their sins.—*Matthew* i. 21.

I would help some to understand what Jesus came from the home of our Father to be to us and do for us. Everything in the world is more or less misunderstood at first: we have to learn what it is, and come at length to see that it must be so, that it could not be otherwise. Then we know it; and we never know a thing *really* until we know it thus.

I presume there is scarce a human being who, resolved to speak openly, would not confess to having something that plagued him, something from which he would gladly be free, something rendering it impossible for him, at the moment, to regard life as an altogether good thing. Most men, I presume, imagine that, free of such and such things antagonistic, life would be an unmingled satisfaction, worthy of being prolonged indefinitely. The causes of their discomfort are of all kinds, and the degrees of it reach from simple uneasiness to a misery such as makes annihilation the highest hope of the sufferer who can persuade himself of its possibility. Perhaps the greater part of the energy of this world's life goes forth in the endeavour to rid itself of discomfort. Some, to escape it, leave their natural surroundings behind them, and with strong and continuous effort keep rising in the social scale, to discover at every new ascent fresh trouble, as they think, awaiting them, whereas in truth they have brought the trouble with them. Others, making haste to be rich, are slow to find out that the poverty of their souls, none the less that their purses are filling, will yet keep them unhappy. Some court endless change, nor know that on themselves the change must pass that will set them free. Others expand their souls with knowledge, only to find that content will not dwell in the great house they have built. To number the varieties of human endeavour to escape discomfort would be to enumerate all the modes of such life as does not know how to live. All seek the thing whose defect appears the *cause* of their misery, and is but the variable *occasion* of it, the cause of the shape it takes, not of the misery itself; for, when one apparent cause is removed, another at once succeeds. The real cause of his trouble is a something the man has not perhaps recognized as even existent; in any case he is not yet acquainted with its true nature.

However absurd the statement may appear to one who has not yet discovered the fact for himself, the cause of every man's discomfort is evil, moral evil—first of all, evil in himself, his own sin, his own wrongness, his own unrightness; and then, evil in those he loves: with this latter I have not now to deal; the only way to get rid of it, is for the man to get rid of his own sin. No special sin may be recognizable as having caused this or that special physical discomfort—which may indeed have originated with some ancestor; but evil in ourselves is the cause of its continuance, the source of its necessity, and the preventive of that patience which would soon take from it, or at least blunt its sting. The evil is *essentially* unnecessary, and passes with the attainment of the object for which it is permitted—namely, the development of pure will in man; the suffering also is essentially unnecessary, but while the evil lasts, the suffering, whether consequent or merely concomitant, is absolutely necessary. Foolish is the man, and there are many such men, who would rid himself or his fellows of discomfort by setting the world right, by waging war on the evils around him, while he neglects that integral part of the world where lies his business, his first business—namely, his own character and conduct. Were it possible—an absurd supposition—that the world should thus be righted from the outside, it would yet be impossible for the man who had contributed to the work, remaining what he was, ever to enjoy the perfection of the result; himself not in tune with the organ he had tuned, he must imagine it still a distracted, jarring instrument. The philanthropist who regards the wrong as in the race, forgetting that the race is made up of conscious and wrong individuals, forgets also that wrong is always generated in and done by an individual; that the wrongness exists in the individual, and by him is passed over, as tendency, to the race; and that no evil can be cured in the race, except by its being cured in its individuals: tendency is not absolute evil; it is there that it may be resisted, not yielded to. There is no way of making three men right but by making right each one of the three; but a cure in one man who repents and turns, is a beginning of the cure of the whole human race.

SALVATION FROM SIN.

Even if a man's suffering be a far inheritance, for the curing of which by faith and obedience this life would not be sufficiently long, faith and obedience will yet render it endurable to the man, and overflow in help to his fellow-sufferers. The groaning body, wrapt in the garment of hope, will, with outstretched neck, look for its redemption, and endure.

The one cure for any organism, is to be set right—to have all its parts brought into harmony with each other; the one comfort is to know this cure in process. Rightness alone is cure. The return of the organism to its true self, is its only possible ease. To free a man from suffering, he must be set right, put in health; and the health at the root of man's being, his rightness, is to be free from wrongness, that is, from sin. A man is right when there is no wrong in him. The wrong, the evil is in him; he must be set free from it. I do not mean set free from the sins he has done: that will follow; I mean the sins he is doing, or is capable of doing; the sins in his being which spoil his nature—the wrongness in him—the evil he consents to; the sin he is, which makes him do the sin he does.

To save a man from his sins, is to say to him, in sense perfect and eternal, 'Rise up and walk. Be at liberty in thy essential being. Be free as the son of God is free.' To do this for us, Jesus was born, and remains born to all the ages. When misery drives a man to call out to the source of his life,—and I take the increasing outcry against existence as a sign of the growth of the race toward a sense of the need of regeneration—the answer, I think, will come in a quickening of his conscience. This earnest of the promised deliverance may not, in all probability will not be what the man desires; he will want only to be rid of his suffering; but that he cannot have, save in being delivered from its essential root, a thing infinitely worse than any suffering it can produce. If he will not have that deliverance, he must keep his suffering. Through chastisement he will take at last the only way that leads into the liberty of that which is and must be. There can be no deliverance but to come out of his evil dream into the glory of God.

It is true that Jesus came, in delivering us from our sins, to deliver us also from the painful consequences of our sins. But these consequences exist by the one law of the universe, the true will of the Perfect. That broken, that disobeyed by the creature, disorganization renders suffering inevitable; it is the natural consequence of the unnatural—and, in the perfection of God's creation, the result is curative of the cause; the pain at least tends to the healing of the breach. The Lord never came to deliver men from the consequences of their sins while yet those sins remained: that would be to cast out of window the medicine of cure while yet the man lay sick; to go dead against the very laws of being. Yet men, loving their sins, and feeling nothing of their dread hatefulness, have, consistently with their low condition, constantly taken this word concerning the Lord to mean that he came to save them from the punishment of their sins. The idea—the miserable fancy rather—has terribly corrupted the preaching of the gospel. The message of the good news has not been truly delivered. Unable to believe in the forgiveness of their Father in heaven, imagining him not at liberty to forgive, or incapable of forgiving forthright; not really believing him God our Saviour, but a God bound, either in his own nature or by a law above him and compulsory upon him, to exact some recompense or satisfaction for sin, a multitude of teaching men have taught their fellows that Jesus came to bear our punishment and save us from hell. They have represented a result as the object of his mission—the said result nowise to be desired by true man save as consequent on the gain of his object. The mission of Jesus was from the same source and with the same object as the punishment of our sins. He came to work along with our punishment. He came to side with it, and set us free from our sins. No man is safe from hell until he is free from his sins; but a man to whom his sins, that is the evil things in him, are a burden, while he may indeed sometimes feel as if he were in hell, will soon have forgotten that ever he had any other hell to think of than that of his sinful condition. For to him his sins are hell; he would go to the other hell to be free of them; free of them, hell itself would be endurable to him. For hell is God's and not the devil's. Hell is on the side of God and man, to free the child of God from the corruption of death. Not one soul will ever be redeemed from hell but by being saved from his sins, from the evil in him. If hell be needful to save him, hell will blaze, and the worm will writhe and bite, until he takes refuge in the will of the Father. 'Salvation from hell, is salvation as conceived by such to whom hell and not evil is the terror.' But if even for dread of hell a poor soul seek the Father, he will be heard of him in his terror, and, taught of him to seek the immeasurably greater gift, will in the greater receive the less.

There is another important misapprehension of the words of the messengers of the good tidings—that they threaten us with punishment because of the sins we have committed, whereas their message is of forgiveness, not of vengeance; of deliverance, not of evil to come. Not for anything he has committed do they threaten a man with the outer darkness. Not for any or all of his sins that are past shall a man be condemned; not for the worst of them needs he dread remaining un-forgiven. The sin he dwells in, the sin he will not come out of, is the sole ruin of a man. His present, his live sins—those pervading his thoughts and ruling his conduct; the sins he keeps doing, and will not give up; the sins he is called to abandon, and clings to; the same sins which are the cause of his misery, though he may not know it—these are they for which he is even now condemned. It is true the memory of the wrongs we have done is, or will become very bitter; but not for those is condemnation; and if that in our character which made them possible were abolished, remorse would lose its worst bitterness in the hope of future amends. 'This is the condemnation, that light is come into the world, and men loved darkness rather than light, because their deeds were evil.'

It is the indwelling badness, ready to produce bad actions, that we need to be delivered from. Against this badness if a man will not strive, he is left to commit evil and reap the consequences. To be saved from these consequences, would be no deliverance; it would be an immediate, ever deepening damnation. It is the evil in our being—no essential part of it, thank God!—the miserable fact that the very child of God does not care for his father and will not obey him, causing us to desire wrongly, act wrongly, or, where we try not to act wrongly, yet making it impossible for us not to feel wrongly—this is what he came to deliver us from;—not the things we have done, but the possi-bility of doing such things any more. With the departure of this possibility, and with the hope of confession hereafter to those we have wronged, will depart also the power over us of the evil things we have done, and so we shall be saved from them also. The bad that lives in us, our evil judgments, our unjust desires, our hate and pride and envy and greed and self-satisfaction—these are the souls of our sins, our live sins, more terrible than the bodies of our sins, namely the deeds we do, inasmuch as they not only produce these loathsome things, but make us loathsome as they. Our wrong deeds are our dead works; our evil thoughts are our live sins. These, the essential opposites of faith and love, the sins that dwell and work in us, are the sins from which Jesus came to deliver us. When we turn against them and refuse to obey them, they rise in fierce insistence, but the same moment begin to die. We are then on the Lord's side, as he has always been on ours, and he begins to deliver us from them.

Anything in you, which, in your own child, would make you feel him not so pleasant as you would have him, is something wrong. This may mean much to one, little or nothing to another. Things in a child which to one parent would not seem worth minding, would fill another with horror. After his moral development, where the one parent would smile, the other would look aghast, perceiving both the present evil, and the serpent-brood to follow. But as the love of him who is love, transcends ours as the heavens are higher than the earth, so must he desire in his child infinitely more than the most jealous love of the best mother can desire in hers. He would have him rid of all discontent, all fear, all grudging, all bitterness in word or thought, all gauging and measuring of his own with a different rod from that he would apply to another's. He will have no curling of the lip; no indifference in him to the man whose service in any form he uses; no desire to excel another, no contentment at gaining by his loss. He will not have him receive the smallest service without gratitude; would not hear from him a tone to jar the heart of another, a word to make it ache, be the ache ever so transient. From such, as from all other sins, Jesus was born to deliver us; not, primarily, or by itself, from the punishment of any of them. When all are gone, the holy punishment will have departed also. He came to make us good, and therein blessed children.

One master-sin is at the root of all the rest. It is no individual action, or anything that comes of mood, or passion; it is the non-recognition by the man, and consequent inactivity in him, of the highest of all relations, that relation which is the root and first essential condition of every other true relation of or in the human soul. It is the absence in the man of harmony with the being whose thought is the man's existence, whose word is the man's power of thought. It is true that, being thus his offspring, God, as St Paul affirms, cannot be far from any one of us: were we not in closest contact of creating and created, we could not exist; as we have in us no power to be, so have we none to continue being; but there is a closer contact still, as absolutely necessary to our well-being and highest existence, as the other to our being at all, to the mere capacity of faring well or ill. For the highest creation of God in man is his will, and until the highest in man meets the highest in God, their true relation is not yet a spiritual fact. The flower lies in the root, but the root is not the flower. The relation exists, but while one of the parties neither knows, loves, nor acts upon it, the relation is, as it were, yet unborn. The highest in man is neither his intellect nor his imagination nor his reason; all are inferior to his will, and indeed, in a grand way, dependent upon it: his will must meet God's—a will *distinct* from God's, else were no *harmony* possible between them. Not the less, therefore, but the more, is all God's. For God creates in the man the power to will His will. It may cost God a suffering man can never know, to bring the man to the point at which he will will His will; but when he is brought to that point, and declares for the truth, that is, for the will of God, he becomes one with God, and the end of God in the man's creation, the end for which Jesus was born and died, is gained. The man is saved from his sins, and the universe flowers yet again in his redemption. But I would not be supposed, from what I have said, to imagine the Lord without sympathy for the sorrows and pains which reveal what sin is, and by means of which he would make men sick of sin. With everything human he sympathizes. Evil is not human; it is the defect and opposite of the human; but the suffering that follows it is human, belonging of necessity to the human that has sinned: while it is by cause of sin, suffering is *for* the sinner, that he may be delivered from his sin. Jesus is in himself aware of every human pain. He feels it also. In him too it is pain. With the energy of tenderest love he wills his brothers and sisters free, that he may fill them to overflowing with that essential thing, joy. For that they were indeed created. But the moment they exist, truth becomes the first thing, not happiness; and he must make them true. Were it possible, however, for pain to continue after evil was gone, he would never rest while one ache was yet in the world. Perfect in sympathy, he feels in himself, I say, the tortured presence of every nerve that lacks its repose. The man may recognize the evil in him only as pain; he may know little and care nothing about his sins; yet is the Lord sorry for his pain. He cries aloud, 'Come unto me, all ye that labour and are heavy laden, and I will give you rest.' He does not say, 'Come unto me, all ye that feel the burden of your sins;' he opens his arms to all weary enough to come to him in the poorest hope of rest. Right gladly would he free them from their misery—but he knows only one way: he will teach them to be like himself, meek and lowly, bearing with gladness the yoke of his father's will. This is the one, the only right, the only possible way of freeing them from their sins, the cause of their unrest. With them the weariness comes first; with him the sins: there is but one cure for both—the will of the Father. That which is his joy will be their deliverance! He might indeed, it may be, take from them the human, send them down to some lower stage of being, and so free them from suffering—but that must be either a descent toward annihilation, or a fresh beginning to grow up again toward the region of suffering they have left; for that which is not growing must at length die out of creation. The disobedient and selfish would fain in the hell of their hearts possess the liberty and gladness that belong to purity and love, but they cannot have them; they are weary and heavy-laden, both with what they are, and because of what they were made for but are not. The Lord knows what they need; they know only what they want. They want ease; he knows they need purity. Their very existence is an evil, of which, but for his resolve to purify them, their maker must rid his universe. How can he keep in his sight a foul presence? Must the creator send forth his virtue to hold alive a thing that will be evil—a thing that ought not to be, that has no claim but to cease? The Lord himself would not live save with an existence absolutely good.

It may be my reader will desire me to say *how* the Lord will deliver him from his sins. That is like the lawyer's 'Who is my neighbour?' The spirit of such a mode of receiving the offer of the Lord's deliverance, is the root of all the horrors of a corrupt theology, so acceptable to those who love weak and beggarly hornbooks of religion. Such questions spring from the passion for the fruit of the tree of knowledge, not the fruit of the tree of life. Men would understand: they do not care to *obey*,—understand where it is impossible they should understand save by obeying. They would search into the work of the Lord instead of doing their part in it—thus making it impossible both for the Lord to go on with his work, and for themselves to become capable of seeing and understanding what he does. Instead of immediately obeying the Lord of life, the one condition upon which he can help them, and in itself the beginning of their deliverance, they set themselves to question their unenlightened intellects as to his plans for their deliverance—and not merely how he means to effect it, but how he can be able to effect it. They would bind their Samson until they have scanned his limbs and thews. Incapable of understanding the first motions of freedom in themselves, they proceed to interpret the riches of his divine soul in terms of their own beggarly notions, to paraphrase his glorious verse into their own paltry commercial prose; and then, in the growing presumption of imagined success, to insist upon their neighbours' acceptance of their distorted shadows of 'the plan of salvation' as the truth of him in whom is no darkness, and the one condition of their acceptance with him. They delay setting their foot on the stair which alone can lead them to the house of wisdom, until they shall have determined the material and mode of its construction. For the sake of knowing, they postpone that which alone can enable them to know, and substitute for the true understanding which lies beyond, a false persuasion that they already understand. They will not accept, that is, act upon, their highest privilege, that of obeying the Son of God. It is on them that do his will, that the day dawns; to them the day-star arises in their hearts. Obedience is the soul of knowledge.

SALVATION FROM SIN.

By obedience, I intend no kind of obedience to man, or submission to authority claimed by man or community of men. I mean obedience to the will of the Father, however revealed in our conscience.

God forbid I should seem to despise understanding. The New Testament is full of urgings to understand. Our whole life, to be life at all, must be a growth in understanding. What I cry out upon is the misunderstanding that comes of man's endeavour to understand while not obeying. Upon obedience our energy must be spent; understanding will follow. Not anxious to know our duty, or knowing it and not doing it, how shall we understand that which only a true heart and a clean soul can ever understand? The power in us that would understand were it free, lies in the bonds of imperfection and impurity, and is therefore incapable of judging the divine. It cannot see the truth. If it could see it, it would not know it, and would not have it. Until a man begins to obey, the light that is in him is darkness.

Any honest soul may understand this much, however—for it is a thing we may of ourselves judge to be right—that the Lord cannot save a man from his sins while he holds to his sins. An omnipotence that could do and not do the same thing at the same moment, were an idea too absurd for mockery; an omnipotence that could at once make a man a free man, and leave him a self-degraded slave—make him the very likeness of God, and good only because he could not help being good, would be an idea of the same character—equally absurd, equally self-contradictory.

But the Lord is not unreasonable; he requires no high motives where such could not yet exist. He does not say, 'You must be sorry for your sins, or you need not come to me:' to be sorry for his sins a man must love God and man, and love is the very thing that has to be developed in him. It is but common sense that a man, longing to be freed from suffering, or made able to bear it, should betake himself to the Power by whom he is. Equally is it common sense that, if a man would be delivered from the evil in him, he must himself begin to cast it out, himself begin to disobey it, and work righteousness. As much as either is it common sense that a man should look for and expect the help of his Father in the endeavour. Alone, he might labour to all eternity and not succeed. He who has not made himself, cannot set himself right without him who made him. But his maker is in him, and is his strength. The man, however, who, instead of doing what he is told, broods speculating on the metaphysics of him who calls him to his work, stands leaning his back against the door by which the Lord would enter to help him. The moment he sets about putting straight the thing that is crooked—I mean doing right where he has been doing wrong, he withdraws from the entrance, gives way for the Master to come in. He cannot make himself pure, but he can leave that which is impure; he can spread out the 'defiled, discoloured web' of his life before the bleaching sun of righteousness; he cannot save himself, but he can let the Lord save him. The struggle of his weakness is as essential to the coming victory as the strength of Him who resisted unto death, striving against sin.

The sum of the whole matter is this:—The Son has come from the Father to set the children free from their sins; the children must hear and obey him, that he may send forth judgment unto victory.

Son of our Father, help us to do what thou sayest, and so with thee die unto sin, that we may rise to the sonship for which we were created. Help us to repent even to the sending away of our sins.

THE REMISSION OF SINS.

John did baptize in the wilderness, and preach the baptism of repentance for the remission of sins.— *Mark* **i. 4.**

God and man must combine for salvation from sin, and the same word, here and elsewhere translated *remission*, seems to be employed in the New Testament for the share of either in the great deliverance.

But first let me say something concerning the word here and everywhere translated *repentance*. I would not even suggest a mistranslation; but the idea intended by the word has been so misunderstood and therefore mistaught, that it requires some consideration of the word itself to get at a right recognition of the moral fact it represents.

The Greek word then, of which the word *repentance* is the accepted synonym and fundamentally the accurate rendering, is made up of two words, the conjoint meaning of which is, *a change of mind* or *thought*. There is in it no intent of, or hint at *sorrow* or *shame*, or any other of the mental conditions that, not unfrequently accompanying repentance, have been taken for essential parts of it, sometimes for its very essence. Here, the last of the prophets, or the evangelist who records his doings, qualifies the word, as if he held it insufficient in itself to convey the Baptist's meaning, with the three words that follow it— *[Greek: eis aPhesin amartiôn:—kaerussôn Baptisma metauoias eis aphesin amartiôn]*—'preaching a baptism of repentance—*unto a sending away of sins'*. I do not say the phrase *[Greek: aphesis amartiôn]* never means *forgiveness,* one form at least of *God's* sending away of sins; neither do I say that the taking of the phrase to mean *repentance for the remission of sins*, namely, repentance in order to obtain the pardon of God, involves any inconsistency; but I say that the word *[Greek: eis]* rather *unto* than *for;* that the word *[Greek: aphesis],* translated *remission*, means, fundamentally, a *sending away,* a *dismissal;* and that the writer seems to use the added phrase to make certain what he means by *repentance;* a repentance, namely, that reaches to the sending away, or abjurement of sins. I do not think *a change of mind unto the remission or pardon of sin* would be nearly so logical a phrase as *a change of mind unto the dismission of sinning.* The revised version refuses the word *for* and chooses *unto,* though it retains *remission,* which word, now, conveys no meaning except the forgiveness of God. I think that here the same word is used for man's dismission of his sins, as is elsewhere used for God's dismission or remission of them. In both uses, it is a sending away of sins, with the difference of meaning that comes from the differing sources of the action. Both God and man send away sins, but in the one case God sends away the sins of the man, and in the other the man sends away his own sins. I do not enter into the question whether God's aphesis may or may not mean as well the sending of his sins out of a man, as the pardon of them; whether it may not sometimes mean *dismission,* and sometimes *remission*: I am sure the one deed cannot be separated from the other.

That the phrase here intends repentance unto the ceasing from sin, the giving up of what is wrong, I will try to show at least probable.

In the first place, the user of the phrase either defines the change of mind he means as one that has for its object the pardon of God, or as one that reaches to a new life: the latter seems to me the more natural interpretation by far. The kind and scope of the repentance or change, and not any end to be gained by it, appears intended. The change must be one of will and conduct—a radical change of life on the part of the man: he must repent—that is, change his mind—not to a different opinion, not even to a mere betterment of his conduct—not to anything less than a sending away of his sins. This interpretation of the preaching of the Baptist seems to me, I repeat, the more direct, the fuller of meaning, the more logical.

Next, in St Matthew's gospel, the Baptist's buttressing argument, or imminent motive for the change he is pressing upon the people is, that the kingdom of heaven is at hand: 'Because the king of heaven is coming, you must give up your sinning.' The same argument for immediate action lies in his quotation from Isaiah,—'Prepare ye the way of the Lord; make straight in the desert a highway for our God.' The only true, the only possible preparation for the coming Lord, is to cease from doing evil, and begin to do well—to send away sin. They must cleanse, not the streets of their cities, not their houses or their garments or even their persons, but their hearts and their doings. It is true the Baptist did not see that the kingdom coming was not of this world, but of the higher world in the hearts of men; it is true that his faith failed him in his imprisonment, because he heard of no martial movement on the part of the Lord, no assertion of his sovereignty, no convincing show of his power; but he did see plainly that righteousness was essential to the kingdom of heaven. That he did not yet perceive that righteousness *is* the kingdom of heaven; that he did not see that the Lord was already initiating his kingdom by sending away sin out of the hearts of his people, is not wonderful. The Lord's answer to his fore-runner's message of doubt, was to send his messenger back an eye-witness of what he was doing, so to wake or clarify in him the perception that his kingdom was not of this world—that he dealt with other means to another end than John had yet recognized as his mission or object; for obedient love in the heart of the poorest he healed or persuaded, was his kingdom come.

Again, observe that, when the Pharisees came to John, he said to them, 'Bring forth therefore fruits meet for repentance:' is not this the same as, 'Repent unto the sending away of your sins'?

Note also, that, when the multitudes came to the prophet, and all, with the classes most obnoxious to the rest, the publicans and the soldiers, asked what he would have them do—thus plainly recognizing that something was required of them—his instruction was throughout in the same direction: they must send away their sins; and each must begin with the fault that lay next him. The kingdom of heaven was at hand: they must prepare the way of the Lord by beginning to do as must be done in his kingdom.

They could not rid themselves of their sins, but they could set about sending them away; they could quarrel with them, and proceed to turn them out of the house: the Lord was on his way to do his part in their final banishment. Those who had repented to the sending away of their sins, he would baptize with a holy power to send them away indeed. The operant will to get rid of them would be baptized with a fire that should burn them up. When a man breaks with his sins, then the wind of the Lord's fan will blow them away, the fire of the Lord's heart will consume them.

I think, then, that the part of the repentant man, and not the part of God, in the sending away of sins, is intended here. It is the man's one preparation for receiving the power to overcome them, the baptism of fire.

Not seldom, what comes in the name of the gospel of Jesus Christ, must seem, even to one not far from the kingdom of heaven, no good news at all. It does not draw him; it wakes in him not a single hope. He has no desire after what it offers him as redemption. The God it gives him news of, is not one to whom he would draw nearer. But when such a man comes to see that the very God must be his Life, the heart of his consciousness; when he perceives that, rousing himself to put from him what is evil, and do the duty that lies at his door, he may fearlessly claim the help of him who 'loved him into being,' then his will immediately sides with his conscience; he begins to try to *be*; and—first thing toward being—to rid himself of what is antagonistic to all being, namely *wrong*. Multitudes will not even approach the appalling task, the labour and pain of *being*. God is doing his part, is undergoing the mighty toil of an age-long creation, endowing men with power to be; but few as yet are those who take up their part, who respond to the call of God, who will to be, who put forth a divine effort after real existence. To the many, the spirit of the prophet cries, 'Turn ye, and change your way! The kingdom of heaven is near you. Let your king possess his own. Let God throne himself in you, that his liberty be your life, and you free men. That he may enter, clear the house for him. Send away the bad things out of it. Depart from evil, and do good. The duty that lieth at thy door, do it, be it great or small.'

For indeed in this region there is no great or small. 'Be content with your wages,' said the Baptist to the soldiers. To many people now, the word would be, 'Rule your temper;' or, 'Be courteous to all;' or, 'Let each hold the other better than himself;' or, 'Be just to your neighbour that you may love him.' To make straight in the desert a highway for our God, we must bestir ourselves in the very spot of the desert on which we stand; we must cast far from us our evil thing that blocks the way of his chariot-wheels. If we do not, never will those wheels roll through our streets; never will our desert blossom with his roses.

The message of John to his countrymen, was then, and is yet, the one message to the world:—'Send away your sins, for the kingdom of heaven is near.' Some of us—I cannot say *all*, for I do not know—who have already repented, who have long ago begun to send away our sins, need fresh repentance every day—how many times a day, God only knows. We are so ready to get upon some path that seems to run parallel with the narrow way, and then take no note of its divergence! What is there for us when we discover that we are out of the way, but to bethink ourselves and turn? By those 'who need no repentance,' the Lord may have meant such as had repented perfectly, had sent away

490

all their sins, and were now with him in his Father's house; also such as have never sinned, and such as no longer turn aside for any temptation.

We shall now, perhaps, be able to understand the relation of the Lord himself to the baptism of John.

He came to John to be baptized; and most would say John's baptism was of repentance for the remission or pardon of sins. But the Lord could not be baptized for the remission of sins, for he had never done a selfish, an untrue, or an unfair thing. He had never wronged his Father, any more than ever his Father had wronged him. Happy, happy Son and Father, who had never either done the other wrong, in thought, word, or deed! As little had he wronged brother or sister. He needed no forgiveness; there was nothing to forgive. No more could he be baptized for repentance: in him repentance would have been to turn to evil! Where then was the propriety of his coming to be baptized by John, and insisting on being by him baptized? It must lie elsewhere.

If we take the words of John to mean 'the baptism of repentance unto the sending away of sins;' and if we bear in mind that in his case repentance could not be, inasmuch as what repentance is necessary to bring about in man, was already existent in Jesus; then, altering the words to fit the case, and saying, 'the baptism of willed devotion to the sending away of sin,' we shall see at once how the baptism of Jesus was a thing right and fit.

That he had no sin to repent of, was not because he was so constituted that he could not sin if he would; it was because, of his own will and judgment, he sent sin away from him—sent it from him with the full choice and energy of his nature. God knows good and evil, and, blessed be his name, chooses good. Never will his righteous anger make him unfair to us, make him forget that we are dust. Like him, his son also chose good, and in that choice resisted all temptation to help his fellows otherwise than as their and his father would. Instead of crushing the power of evil by divine force; instead of compelling justice and destroying the wicked; instead of making peace on the earth by the rule of a perfect prince; instead of gathering the children of Jerusalem under his wings whether they would or not, and saving them from the horrors that anguished his prophetic soul—he let evil work its will while it lived; he contented himself with the slow unencouraging ways of help essential; making men good; casting out, not merely controlling Satan; carrying to their perfect issue on earth the old primeval principles because of which the Father honoured him: 'Thou hast loved righteousness and hated iniquity; therefore God, even thy God, hath anointed thee with the oil of gladness above thy fellows.' To love righteousness is to make it grow, not to avenge it; and to win for righteousness the true victory, he, as well as his brethren, had to send away evil. Throughout his life on earth, he resisted every impulse to work more rapidly for a lower good,—strong perhaps when he saw old age and innocence and righteousness trodden under foot. What but this gives any worth of reality to the temptation in the wilderness, to the devil's departing from him for a season, to his coming again to experience a like failure? Ever and ever, in the whole attitude of his being, in his heart always lifted up, in his unfailing readiness to pull with the Father's yoke, he was repelling, driving away sin—away from himself, and, as Lord of men, and their saviour, away from others also, bringing them to abjure it like himself. No man, least of all any lord of men, can be good without willing to be good, without setting himself against evil, without sending away sin. Other men have to send it away out of them; the Lord had to send it away from before him, that it should not enter into him. Therefore is the stand against sin common to the captain of salvation and the soldiers under him.

What did Jesus come into the world to do? The will of God in saving his people from their sins—not from the punishment of their sins, that blessed aid to repentance, but from their sins themselves, the paltry as well as the heinous, the venial as well as the loathsome. His whole work was and is to send away sin—to banish it from the earth, yea, to cast it into the abyss of non-existence behind the back of God. His was the holy war; he came carrying it into our world; he resisted unto blood; the soldiers that followed him he taught and trained to resist also unto blood, striving against sin; so he became the captain of their salvation, and they, freed themselves, fought and suffered for others. This was the task to which he was baptized; this is yet his enduring labour. 'This is my blood of the new covenant which is shed for many unto the sending away of sins.' What was the new covenant? 'I will make a new covenant with the house of Israel and with the house of Judah; not according to the covenant which they brake, but this: I will put my law in their inward parts, and write it in their hearts, and will be their God, and they shall be my people.'

John baptized unto repentance because those to whom he was sent had to repent. They must bethink themselves, and send away the sin that was in them. But had there been a man, aware of no sin in him, but aware that life would be no life were not sin kept out of him, that man would have been right in receiving the baptism of John unto the continuous dismission of the sin ever wanting to enter in at his door.

The object of the baptism was the sending away of sin; its object was repentance only where necessary to, only as introducing, as resulting in that. He to whom John was not sent, He whom he did not call, He who needed no repentance, was baptized for the same object, to the same conflict for the same end—the banishment of sin from the dominions of his father—and that first by his own sternest repudiation of it in himself. Thence came his victory in the wilderness: he would have his fathers way, not his own. Could he be less fitted to receive the baptism of John, that the object of it was no new thing with him, who had been about it from the beginning, yea, from all eternity? We shall be about it, I presume, to all eternity.

Such, then, as were baptized by John, were initiated into the company of those whose work was to send sin out of the world, and first, by sending it out of themselves, by having done with it. Their earliest endeavour in this direction would, as I have said, open the door for that help to enter without which a man could never succeed in the divinely arduous task—could not, because the region in which the work has to be wrought lies in the very roots of his own being, where, knowing nothing of the secrets of his essential existence, he can immediately do nothing, where the maker of him alone is potent, alone is consciously present. The change that must pass in him more than equals a new creation, inasmuch as it is a higher creation. But its necessity is involved in the former creation; and thence we have a right to ask help of our creator, for he requires of us what he has created us unable to effect without him. Nay, nay!—could we do anything without him, it were a thing to leave undone. Blessed fact that he hath made us so near him! that the scale of our being is so large, that we are completed only by his presence in it! that we are not men without him! that we can be one with our self-existent creator! that we are not cut off from the original Infinite! that in him we must share infinitude, or be enslaved by the finite! The very patent of our royalty is, that not for a moment can we live our true life without the eternal life present in and with our spirits. Without him at our unknown root, we cease to be. True, a dog cannot live without the presence of God; but I presume a dog may live a good dog-life without knowing the presence of his origin: man is dead if he know not the Power which is his cause, his deepest selfing self; the Presence which is not himself, and is nearer to him than himself; which is infinitely more himself, more his very being, than he is himself. The being of which we are conscious, is not our full self; the extent of our consciousness of our self is no measure of our self; our consciousness is infinitely less than we; while God is more necessary even to that poor consciousness of self than our self-consciousness is necessary to our humanity. Until a man become the power of his own existence, become his own God, the sole thing necessary to his existing is the will of God; for the well-being and perfecting of that existence, the sole thing necessary is, that the man should know his maker present in him. All that the children want is their Father.

The one true end of all speech concerning holy things is—the persuading of the individual man to cease to do evil, to set himself to do well, to look to the lord of his life to be on his side in the new struggle. Supposing the suggestions I have made correct, I do not care that my reader should understand them, except it be to turn against the evil in him, and begin to cast it out. If this be not the result, it is of no smallest consequence whether he agree with my interpretation or not. If he do thus repent, it is of equally little consequence; for, setting himself to do the truth, he is on the way to know all things. Real knowledge has begun to grow possible for him.

I am not sure what the Lord means in the words, 'Thus it becometh us to fulfil all righteousness.' Baptism could not be the fulfilling of all righteousness! Perhaps he means, 'We must, by a full act of the will, give ourselves altogether to righteousness. We must make it the business of our lives to send away sin, and do the will of the Father. That is my work as much as the work of any man who must repent ere he can begin. I will not be left out when you call men to be pure as our father is pure.'

To be certain whom he intends by *us* might perhaps help us to see his meaning. Does he intend *all of us men*? Does he intend 'my father and me'? Or does he intend 'you and me, John'? If the saying mean what I have suggested, then the *us* would apply to all that have the knowledge of good and evil. 'Every being that can, must devote himself to righteousness. To be right is no adjunct of completeness; it is the ground and foundation of existence.' But perhaps it was a lesson for John himself, who, mighty preacher of righteousness as he was, did not yet count it the all of life. I cannot tell.

Note that when the Lord began his teaching, he employed, neither using nor inculcating any rite, the same words as John,—'Repent, for the kingdom of heaven is at hand.'

That kingdom had been at hand all his infancy, boyhood, and young manhood: he was in the world with his father in his heart: that was the kingdom of heaven. Lonely man on the hillside, or boy the cynosure of doctor-eyes, his father was everything to him:—'Wist ye not that I must be in my father's things?'

JESUS IN THE WORLD.

'Son, why hast thou thus dealt with us? behold, thy father and I have sought thee sorrowing.' And he said unto them, 'How is it that ye sought me? wist ye not that I must be about my father's business?' And they understood not the saying which he spake unto them.—*Luke* ii. 48-50.

Was that his saying? Why did they not understand it? Do we understand it? What did his saying mean? The Greek is not absolutely clear. Whether the Syriac words he used were more precise, who in this world can tell? But had we heard his very words, we too, with his father and mother, would have failed to understand them. Must we fail still?

It will show at once where our initial difficulty lies, if I give the latter half of the saying as presented in the revised English version: its departure from the authorized reveals the point of obscurity:—'Wist ye not that I must be in my father's house?' His parents had his exact words, yet did not understand. We have not his exact words, and are in doubt as to what the Greek translation of them means.

If the authorized translation be true to the intent of the Greek, and therefore to that of the Syriac, how could his parents, knowing him as they did from all that had been spoken before concerning him, from all they had seen in him, from the ponderings in Mary's own heart, and from the precious thoughts she and Joseph cherished concerning him, have failed to understand him when he said that wherever he was, he must be about his father's business? On the other hand, supposing them to know and feel that he must be about his father's business, would that have been reason sufficient, in view of the degree of spiritual development to which they had attained, for the Lord's expecting them not to be anxious about him when they had lost him? Thousands on thousands who trust God for their friends in things spiritual, do not trust him for them in regard of their mere health or material well-being. His parents knew how prophets had always been treated in the land; or if they did not think in that direction, there were many dangers to which a boy like him would seem exposed, to rouse an anxiety that could be met only by a faith equal to saying, 'Whatever has happened to him, death itself, it can be no evil to one who is about his father's business;' and such a faith I think the Lord could not yet have expected of them. That what the world counts misfortune might befall him on his father's business, would have been recognized by him, I think, as reason for their parental anxiety—so long as they had not learned God—that he is what he is—the thing the Lord had come to teach his father's men and women. His words seem rather to imply that there was no need to be anxious about his personal safety. Fear of some accident to him seems to have been the cause of their trouble; and he did not mean, I think, that they ought not to mind if he died doing his father's will, but that he was in no danger as regarded accident or misfortune. This will appear more plainly as we proceed. So much for the authorized version.

Let us now take the translation given us by the Revisers:—'Wist ye not that I must be in my father's house?'

Are they authorized in translating the Greek thus? I know no justification for it, but am not learned enough to say they have none. That the Syriac has it so, is of little weight; seeing it is no original Syriac, but retranslation. If he did say '*my father's house*', could he have meant the temple and his parents not have known what he meant? And why should he have taken it for granted they would know, or judge that they ought to have known, that he was there? So little did the temple suggest itself to them, that either it was the last place in which they sought him, or they had been there before, and had *not* found him. If he meant that they might have known this without being told, why was it that, even when he set the thing before them, they did not understand him? I do not believe he meant the temple; I do not think he said or meant '*in my fathers house*'.

What then makes those who give us this translation, prefer it to the phrase in the authorized version, '*about my Father's business*'?

One or other of two causes—most likely both together: an ecclesiastical fancy, and the mere fact that he was found in the temple. A mind ecclesiastical will presume the temple the fittest, therefore most likely place, for the Son of God to betake himself to, but such a mind would not be the first to reflect that the temple was a place where the Father was worshipped neither in spirit nor in truth—a place built by one of the vilest rulers of this world, less fit than many another spot for the special presence of him of whom the prophet bears witness: 'Thus saith the high and lofty One that inhabiteth eternity, whose name is Holy; I dwell in the high and holy place, with him also that is of a contrite and humble spirit, to revive the spirit of the humble, and to revive the heart of the contrite ones.' Jesus himself, with the same breath in which once he called it his father's house, called it a den of thieves. His expulsion from it of the buyers and sellers, was the first waft of the fan with which he was come to purge his father's dominions. Nothing could ever cleanse that house; his fanning rose to a tempest, and swept it out of his father's world.

For the second possible cause of the change from *business* to *temple*—the mere fact that he was found in the temple, can hardly be a reason for his expecting his parents to know that he was there; and if it witnessed to some way of thought or habit of his with which they were acquainted, it is, I repeat, difficult to see why the parents should fail to perceive what the interpreters have found so easily. But the parents looked for a larger meaning in the words of such a son—whose meaning at the same time was too large for them to find.

When, according to the Greek, the Lord, on the occasion already alluded to, says 'my father's house,' he says it plainly; he uses the word *house*: here he does not.

Let us see what lies in the Greek to guide us to the thought in the mind of the Lord when he thus reasoned with the apprehensions of his father and mother. The Greek, taken literally, says, 'Wist ye not that I must be in the——of my father?' The authorized version supplies *business*; the revised, *house*. There is no noun in the Greek, and the article 'the' is in the plural. To translate it as literally as it can be translated, making of it an English sentence, the saying stands, 'Wist ye not that I must be in the things of my father?' The plural article implies the English *things*; and the question is then, What *things* does he mean? The word might mean *affairs* or *business*; but why the plural article should be contracted to mean *house*, *I* do not know. In a great wide sense, no doubt, the word *house* might be used, as I am about to show, but surely not as meaning the temple.

He was arguing for confidence in God on the part of his parents, not for a knowledge of his whereabout. The same thing that made them anxious concerning him, prevented them from understanding his words—lack, namely, of faith in the Father. This, the one thing he came into the world to teach men, those words were meant to teach his parents. They are spirit and life, involving the one principle by which men shall live. They hold the same core as his words to his disciples in the storm, 'Oh ye of little faith!' Let us look more closely at them.

'Why did you look for me? Did you not know that I must be among my father's things?' What are we to understand by 'my father's things'? The translation given in the authorized version is, I think, as to the words themselves, a thoroughly justifiable one: 'I must be about my father's business,' or 'my father's affairs'; I refuse it for no other reason than that it does not fit the logic of the narrative, as does the word *things*, which besides opens to us a door of large and joyous prospect. Of course he was about his father's business, and they might know it and yet be anxious about him, not having a perfect faith in that father. But, as I have said already, it was not anxiety as to what might befall him because of doing the will of the Father; he might well seem to them as yet too young for danger from that source; it was but the vague perils of life beyond their sight that appalled them; theirs was just the uneasiness that possesses every parent whose child is missing; and if they, like him, had trusted in their father, they would have known what their son now meant when he said that he was in the midst of his father's things—namely, that the very things from which they dreaded evil accident, were his own home-surroundings; that he was not doing the Father's business in a foreign country, but in the Father's own house. Understood as meaning the world, or the universe, the phrase, 'my father's house,' would be a better translation than the authorized; understood as meaning the poor, miserable, God-forsaken temple—no more the house of God than a dead body is the house of a man—it is immeasurably inferior.

It seems to me, I say, that the Lord meant to remind them, or rather to make them feel, for they had not yet learned the fact, that he was never away from home, could not be lost, as they had thought him; that he was in his father's house all the time, where no hurt could come to him. 'The things' about him were the furniture and utensils of his home; he knew them all and how to use them. 'I must be among my father's belongings.' The world was his home because his father's house. He was not a stranger who did not know his way about in it. He was no lost child, but with his father all the time.

Here we find one main thing wherein the Lord differs from us: we are not at home in this great universe, our father's house. We ought to be, and one day we shall be, but we are not yet. This reveals Jesus more than man, by revealing him more man than we. We are not complete men, we are not anything near it, and are therefore out of harmony, more or less, with everything in the house of our birth and habitation. Always struggling to make our home in the world, we have not yet succeeded. We are not at home in it, because we are not at home with the lord of the house, the father of the family, not one with our elder brother who is his right hand. It is only the son, the daughter, that abideth ever in the house. When we are true children, if not the world, then the universe will be our home, felt and known as such, the house we are satisfied with, and would not change. Hence, until then, the hard struggle, the constant strife we hold with *Nature*—as we call the things of our father; a strife invaluable for our development, at the same time manifesting us not yet men enough to be lords of the house built for us to live in. We cannot govern or command in it as did the Lord, because we are not at one with his father, therefore neither in harmony with his things, nor rulers over them. Our best power in regard to them is but to find out wonderful facts concerning them and their relations, and turn these facts to our uses on systems of our own. For we discover what we seem to discover, by working inward from without, while he works outward from within; and we shall never understand the world, until we see it in the direction in which he works making it—namely from within outward. This of course we cannot do until we are one with him. In the meantime, so much are both we and his things his, that we can err concerning them only as he has made it possible for us to err; we can wander only in the direction of the truth—if but to find that we can find nothing.

Think for a moment how Jesus was at home among the things of his father. It seems to me, I repeat, a spiritless explanation of his words—that the temple was the place where naturally he was at home. Does he make the least lamentation over the temple? It is Jerusalem he weeps over—the men of Jerusalem, the killers, the stoners. What was his place of prayer? Not the temple, but the mountain-top. Where does he find symbols whereby to speak of what goes on in the mind and before the face of his father in heaven? Not in the temple; not in its rites; not on its altars; not in its holy of holies; he finds them in the world and its lovely-lowly facts; on the roadside, in the field, in the vineyard, in the garden, in the house; in the family, and the commonest of its affairs—the lighting of the lamp, the leavening of the meal, the neighbour's borrowing, the losing of the coin, the straying of the sheep. Even in the unlovely facts also of the world which he turns to holy use, such as the unjust judge, the false steward, the faithless labourers, he ignores the temple. See how he drives the devils from the souls and bodies of men, as we the wolves from our sheepfolds! how before him the diseases, scaly and spotted, hurry and flee! The world has for him no chamber of terror. He walks to the door of the sepulchre, the sealed cellar of his father's house, and calls forth its four days dead. He rebukes the mourners, he stays the funeral, and gives back the departed children to their parents' arms. The roughest of its servants do not make him wince; none of them are so arrogant as to disobey his word; he falls asleep in the midst of the storm that threatens to swallow his boat. Hear how, on that same occasion, he rebukes his disciples! The children to tremble at a gust of wind in the house! God's little ones afraid of a storm! Hear him tell the watery floor to be still, and no longer toss his brothers! see the watery floor obey him and grow still! See how the wandering creatures under it come at his call! See him leave his mountain-closet, and go walking over its heaving surface to the help of his men of little faith! See how the world's water turns to wine! how its bread grows more bread at his word! See how he goes from the house for a while, and returning with fresh power, takes what shape he pleases, walks through its closed doors, and goes up and down its invisible stairs!

All his life he was among his father's things, either in heaven or in the world—not then only when they found him in the temple at Jerusalem. He is still among his father's things, everywhere about in the world, everywhere throughout the wide universe. Whatever he laid aside to come to us, to whatever limitations, for our sake, he stooped his regal head, he dealt with the things about him in such lordly, child-like manner as made it clear they were not strange to him, but the things of his father. He claimed none of them as his own, would not have had one of them his except through his father. Only as his father's could he enjoy them;—only as coming forth from the Father, and full of the Father's thought and nature, had they to him any existence. That the things were his fathers, made them precious things to him. He had no care for having, as men count having. All his having was in the Father. I wonder if he ever put anything in his pocket: I doubt if he had one. Did he ever say, 'This is mine, not yours'? Did he not say, 'All things are mine, therefore they are yours'? Oh for his liberty among the things of the Father! Only by knowing them the things of our Father, can we escape enslaving ourselves to them. Through the false, the infernal idea of *having*, of *possessing* them, we make them our tyrants, make the relation between them and us an evil thing. The world was a blessed place to Jesus, because everything in it was his father's. What pain must it not have been to him, to see his brothers so vilely misuse the Father's house by grasping, each for himself, at the family things! If the knowledge that a spot in the landscape retains in it some pollution, suffices to disturb our pleasure in the whole, how must it not have been with him, how must it not be with him now, in regard to the disfigurements and defilements caused by the greed of men, by their haste to be rich, in his father's lovely house!

Whoever is able to understand Wordsworth, or Henry Vaughan, when either speaks of the glorious insights of his childhood, will be able to imagine a little how Jesus must, in his eternal childhood, regard the world.

Hear what Wordsworth says:—

2

Hear what Henry Vaughan says:—

2

Whoever has thus gazed on flower or cloud; whoever can recall poorest memory of the trail of glory that hung about his childhood, must have some faint idea how his father's house and the things in it always looked, and must still look to the Lord. With him there is no fading into the light of common day. He has never lost his childhood, the very essence of childhood being nearness to the Father and the outgoing of his creative love; whence, with that insight of his eternal childhood of which the insight of the little ones here is a fainter repetition, he must see everything as the Father means it. The child sees things as the Father means him to see them, as he thought of them when he uttered them. For God is not only the father of the child, but of the childhood that constitutes him a child, therefore the childness is of the divine nature. The child may not indeed be capable of looking into the father's method, but he can in a measure understand his work, has therefore free entrance to his study and workshop both, and is welcome to find out what he can, with fullest liberty to ask him questions. There are men too, who, at their best, see, in their lower measure, things as they are—as God sees them always. Jesus saw things just as his father saw them in his creative imagination, when willing them out to the eyes of his children. But if he could always see the things of his father even as some men and more children see them at times, he might well feel *almost* at home among them. He could not cease to admire, cease to love them. I say *love,* because the life in them, the presence of the creative one, would ever be plain to him. In the Perfect, would familiarity ever destroy wonder at things essentially wonderful because essentially divine? To cease to wonder is to fall plumbdown from the childlike to the commonplace—the most undivine of all moods intellectual. Our nature can never be at home among things that are not wonderful to us.

Could we see things always as we have sometimes seen them—and as one day we must always see them, only far better—should we ever know dullness? Greatly as we might enjoy all forms of art, much as we might learn through the eyes and thoughts of other men, should we fly to these for deliverance from *ennui*, from any haunting discomfort? Should we not just open our own child-eyes, look upon the things themselves, and be consoled?

Jesus, then, would have his parents understand that he was in his father's world among his father's things, where was nothing to hurt him; he knew them all, was in the secret of them all, could use and order them as did his father. To this same I think all we humans are destined to rise. Though so many of us now are ignorant what kind of home we need, what a home we are capable of having, we too shall inherit the earth with the Son eternal, doing with it as we would—willing with the will of the Father. To such a home as we now inhabit, only perfected, and perfectly beheld, we are travelling—never to reach it save by the obedience that makes us the children, therefore the heirs of God. And, thank God! there the father does not die that the children may inherit; for, bliss of heaven! we inherit with the Father.

All the dangers of Jesus came from the priests, and the learned in the traditional law, whom his parents had not yet begun to fear on his behalf. They feared the dangers of the rugged way, the thieves and robbers of the hill-road. For the scribes and the pharisees, the priests and the rulers—they would be the first to acknowledge their Messiah, their king! Little they imagined, when they found him where he ought to have been safest had it been indeed his father's house, that there he sat amid lions—the great doctors of the temple! He could rule all the *things* in his father's house, but not the men of religion, the men of the temple, who called his father their Father. True, he might have compelled them with a word, withered them by a glance, with a finger-touch made them grovel at his feet; but such supremacy over his brothers the Lord of life despised. He must rule them as his father ruled himself; he would have them know themselves of the same family with himself; have them at home among the things of God, caring for the things he cared for, loving and hating as he and his father loved and hated, ruling themselves by the essential laws of being. Because they would not be such, he let them do to him as they would, that he might get at their hearts by some unknown unguarded door in their diviner part. 'I will be God among you; I will be myself to you.—You will not have me? Then do to me as you will. The created shall have power over him through whom they were created, that they may be compelled to know him and his father. They shall look on him whom they have pierced.'

His parents found him in the temple; they never really found him until he entered the true temple—their own adoring hearts. The temple that knows not its builder, is no temple; in it dwells no divinity. But at length he comes to his own, and his own receive him;—comes to them in the might of his mission to preach good tidings to the poor, to heal the broken-hearted, to preach deliverance, and sight, and liberty, and the Lord's own good time.

JESUS AND HIS FELLOW TOWNSMEN.

And he came to Nazareth, where he had been brought up: and, as his custom was, he went into the synagogue on the sabbath day, and stood up for to read. And there was delivered unto him the book of the prophet Esaias. And when he had opened the book, he found the place where it was written, 'The spirit of the Lord is upon me, because he hath anointed me to preach the gospel to the poor; he hath sent me to heal the brokenhearted, to preach deliverance to the captives, and recovering of sight to the blind, to set at liberty them that are bruised, to preach the acceptable year of the Lord.' And he closed the book, and he gave it again to the minister, and sat down. And the eyes of all them that were in the synagogue were fastened on him. And he began to say unto them, 'This day is this scripture fulfilled in your ears.'—*Luke* iv. 14-21.

The Lord's sermon upon the mount seems such an enlargement of these words of the prophet as might, but for the refusal of the men of Nazareth to listen to him, have followed his reading of them here recorded. That, as given by the evangelist, they correspond to neither of the differing originals of the English and Greek versions, ought to be enough in itself to do away with the spiritually vulgar notion of the verbal inspiration of the Scriptures.

The point at which the Lord stops in his reading, is suggestive: he closes the book, leaving the words 'and the day of vengeance of our God,' or, as in the Septuagint, 'the day of recompense,' unread: God's vengeance is as holy a thing as his love, yea, is love, for God is love and God is not vengeance; but, apparently, the Lord would not give the word a place in his announcement of his mission: his hearers would not recognize it as a form of the Father's love, but as vengeance on their enemies, not vengeance on the selfishness of those who would not be their brother's keeper.

He had not begun with Nazareth, neither with Galilee. 'A prophet has no honour in his own country,' he said, and began to teach where it was more likely he would be heard. It is true that he wrought his first miracle in Cana, but that was at his mother's request, not of his own intent, and he did not begin his teaching there. He went first to Jerusalem, there cast out the buyers and sellers from the temple, and did other notable things alluded to by St John; then went back to Galilee, where, having seen the things he did in Jerusalem, his former neighbours were now prepared to listen to him. Of these the Nazarenes, to whom the sight of him was more familiar, retained the most prejudice against him: he belonged to their very city! they had known him from a child!—and low indeed are they in whom familiarity with the high and true breeds contempt! they are judged already. Yet such was the fame of the new prophet, that even they were willing to hear in the synagogue what he had to say to them—thence to determine for themselves what claim he had to an honourable reception. But the eye of their judgment was not single, therefore was their body full of darkness. Should Nazareth indeed prove, to their self-glorifying satisfaction, the city of the great Prophet, they were more than ready to grasp at the renown of having produced him: he was indeed the great Prophet, and within a few minutes they would have slain him for the honour of Israel. In the ignoble even the love of their country partakes largely of the ignoble.

There was a shadow of the hateless vengeance of God in the expulsion of the dishonest dealers from the temple with which the Lord initiated his mission: that was his first parable to Jerusalem; to Nazareth he comes with the sweetest words of the prophet of hope in his mouth—good tidings of great joy—of healing and sight and liberty; followed by the godlike announcement, that what the prophet had promised he was come to fulfil. His heart, his eyes, his lips, his hands—his whole body is full of gifts for men, and that day was that scripture fulfilled in their ears. The prophecy had gone before that he should save his people from their sins; he brings an announcement they will better understand: he is come, he says, to deliver men from sorrow and pain, ignorance and oppression, everything that makes life hard and unfriendly. What a gracious speech, what a daring pledge to a world whelmed in tyranny and wrong! To the women of it, I imagine, it sounded the sweetest, in them woke the highest hopes. They had scarce had a hearing when the Lord came; and thereupon things began to mend with them, and are mending still, for the Lord is at work, and will be. He is the refuge of the oppressed. By its very woes, as by bitterest medicine, he is setting the world free from sin and woe. This very hour he is curing its disease, the symptoms of which are so varied and so painful; working none the less faithfully that the sick, taking the symptoms for the disease, cry out against the incompetence of their physician. 'What power can heal the broken-hearted?' they cry. And indeed it takes a God to do it, but the God is here! In yet better words than those of the prophet, spoken straight from his own heart, he cries: 'Come unto me, all ye that labour and are heavy laden, and I will give you rest.' He calls to him every heart knowing its own bitterness, speaks to the troubled consciousness of every child of the Father. He is come to free us from everything that makes life less than bliss essential. No other could be a gospel worthy of the God of men.

Every one will, I presume, confess to more or less misery. Its apparent source may be this or that; its real source is, to use a poor figure, a dislocation of the juncture between the created and the creating life. This primal evil is the parent of evils unnumbered, hence of miseries multitudinous, under the weight of which the arrogant man cries out against life, and goes on to misuse it, while the child looks around for help—and who shall help him but his father! The Father is with him all the time, but it may be long ere the child knows himself in his arms. His heart may be long troubled as well as his outer life. The dank mists of doubtful thought may close around his way, and hide from him the Light of the world! cold winds from the desert of foiled endeavour may sorely buffet and for a time baffle his hope; but every now and then the blue pledge of a great sky will break through the clouds over his head; and a faint aurora will walk his darkest East. Gradually he grows more capable of imagining a world in which every good thing thinkable may be a fact. Best of all, the story of him who is himself the good news, the gospel of God, becomes not only more and more believable to his heart, but more and more ministrant to his life of conflict, and his assurance of a living father who hears when his children cry. The gospel according to this or that expounder of it, may repel him unspeakably; the gospel according to Jesus Christ, attracts him supremely, and ever holds where it has drawn him. To the priest, the scribe, the elder, exclaiming against his self-sufficiency in refusing what they teach, he answers, 'It is life or death to me. Your gospel I cannot take. To believe as you would have me believe, would be to lose my God. Your God is no God to me. I do not desire him. I would rather die the death than believe in such a God. In the name of the true God, I cast your gospel from me; it is no gospel, and to believe it would be to wrong him in whom alone lies my hope.'

'But to believe in such a man,' he might go on to say, 'with such a message, as I read of in the New Testament, is life from the dead. I have yielded myself, to live no more in the idea of self, but with the life of God. To him I commit the creature he has made, that he may live in it, and work out its life—develop it according to the idea of it in his own creating mind. I fall in with his ways for me. I believe in him. I trust him. I try to obey him. I look to be rendered capable of and receive a pure vision of his will, freedom from the prison-house of my limitation, from the bondage of a finite existence. For the finite that dwells in the infinite and in which the infinite dwells, is finite no longer. Those who are thus children indeed, are little Gods, the divine brood of the infinite Father. No mere promise of deliverance from the consequences of sin, would be any gospel to me. Less than the liberty of a holy heart, less than the freedom of the Lord himself, will never satisfy one human soul. Father, set me free in the glory of thy will, so that I will only as thou willest. Thy will be at once thy perfection and mine. Thou alone art deliverance—absolute safety from every cause and kind of trouble that ever existed, anywhere now exists, or ever can exist in thy universe.'

But the people of the Lord's town, to whom he read, appropriating them, the gracious words of the prophet, were of the wise and prudent of their day. With one and the same breath, they seem to cry, 'These things are good, it is true, but they must come after our way. We must have the promise to our fathers fulfilled—that we shall rule the world, the chosen of God, the children of Abraham and Israel. We want to be a free people, manage our own affairs, live in plenty, and do as we please. Liberty alone can ever cure the woes of which you speak. We do not need to be better; we are well enough. Give us riches and honour, and keep us content with ourselves, that we may be satisfied with our own likeness, and thou shalt be the Messiah.' Never, perhaps, would such be men's spoken words, but the prevailing condition of their minds might often well take form in such speech. Whereon will they ground their complaint should God give them their hearts' desire? When that desire given closes in upon them with a torturing sense of slavery; when they find that what they have imagined their own will, was but a suggestion they knew not whence; when they discover that life is not good, yet they cannot die; will they not then turn and entreat their maker to save them after his own fashion?

Let us try to understand the brief, elliptical narrative of what took place in the synagogue of Nazareth on the occasion of our Lord's announcement of his mission.

'This day,' said Jesus, 'is this scripture fulfilled in your ears;' and went on with his divine talk. We shall yet know, I trust, what 'the gracious words' were 'which proceeded out of his mouth': surely some who heard them, still remember them, for 'all bare him witness, and wondered at' them! How did they bear him witness? Surely not alone by the intensity of their wondering gaze! Must not the narrator mean that their hearts bore witness to the power of his presence, that they felt the appeal of his soul to theirs, that they said in themselves, 'Never man spake like this man'? Must not the light of truth in his face, beheld of such even as knew not the truth, have lifted their souls up truthward? Was it not the something true, common to all hearts, that bore the wondering witness to the graciousness of his words? Had not those words found a way to the pure human, that is, the divine in the men? Was it not therefore that they were drawn to him—all but ready to accept him?—on their own terms, alas, not his! For a moment he seemed to them a true messenger, but truth in him was not truth to them: had he been what they took him for, he would have been no saviour. They were, however, though partly by mistake, well disposed toward him, and it was with a growing sense of being honoured by his relation to them, and the property they had in him, that they said, 'Is not this Joseph's son?'

But the Lord knew what was in their hearts; he knew the false notion with which they were almost ready to declare for him; he knew also the final proof to which they were in their wisdom and prudence about to subject him. He did not look likely to be a prophet, seeing he had grown up among them, and had never shown any credentials: they had a right to proof positive! They had heard of wonderful things he had done in other places: why had they not first of all been done in *their* sight? Who had a claim equal to theirs? who so capable as they to pronounce judgment on his mission whether false or true: had they not known him from childhood? His words were gracious, but words were nothing: he must *do* something—something wonderful! Without such conclusive, satisfying proof, Nazareth at least would never acknowledge him!

They were quite ready for the honour of having any true prophet, such as it seemed not impossible the son of Joseph might turn out to be, recognized as their towns-man, one of their own people: if he were such, theirs was the credit of having produced him! Then indeed they were ready to bear witness to him, take his part, adopt his cause, and before the world stand up for him! As to his being the Messiah, that was merest absurdity: did they not all know his father, the carpenter? He might, however, be the prophet whom so many of the best in the nation were at the moment expecting! Let him do something wonderful!

They were not a gracious people, or a good. The Lord saw their thought, and it was far from being to his mind. He desired no such reception as they were at present equal to giving a prophet. His mighty works were not meant for such as they—to convince them of what they were incapable of understanding or welcoming! Those who would not believe without signs and wonders, could never believe worthily with any number of them, and none should be given them! His mighty works were to rouse the love, and strengthen the faith of the meek and lowly in heart, of such as were ready to come to the light, and show that they were of the light. He knew how poor the meaning the Nazarenes put on the words he had read; what low expectations they had of the Messiah when most they longed for his coming. They did not hear the prophet while he read the prophet! At sight of a few poor little wonders, nothing to him, to them sufficient to prove him such a Messiah as *they* looked for, they would burst into loud acclaim, and rush to their arms, eager, his officers and soldiers, to open the one triumphant campaign against the accursed Romans, and sweep them beyond the borders of their sacred country. Their Messiah would make of their nation the redeemed of the Lord, themselves the favourites of his court, and the tyrants of the world! Salvation from their sins was not in their hearts, not in their imaginations, not at all in their thoughts. They had heard him read his commission to heal the brokenhearted; they would rush to break hearts in his name. The Lord knew them, and their vain expectations. He would have no such followers— no followers on false conceptions—no followers whom wonders would delight but nowise better! The Nazarenes were not yet of the sort that needed but one change to be his people. He had come to give them help; until they accepted his, they could have none to give him.

The Lord never did mighty work in proof of his mission; to help a growing faith in himself and his father, he would do anything! He healed those whom healing would deeper heal—those in whom suffering had so far done its work, that its removal also would carry it on. To the Nazarenes he would not manifest his power; they were not in a condition to get good from such manifestation: it would but confirm their present arrogance and ambition. Wonderful works can only nourish a faith already existent; to him who believes without it, a miracle *may* be granted. It was the Israelite indeed, whom the Lord met with miracle: 'Because I said unto thee, I saw thee under the fig-tree, believest thou? Thou shalt see the angels of God ascending and descending on the Son of Man.' Those who laughed him to scorn were not allowed to look on the resurrection of the daughter of Jairus. Peter, when he would walk on the water, had both permission and power given him to do so. The widow received the prophet, and was fed; the Syrian went to the prophet, and was cured. In Nazareth, because of unbelief, the Lord could only lay his hands on a few sick folk; in the rest was none of that leaning toward the truth, which alone can make room for the help of a miracle. This they soon made manifest.

The Lord saw them on the point of challenging a display of his power, and anticipated the challenge with a refusal.

For the better understanding of his words, let me presume to paraphrase them: 'I know you will apply to me the proverb, Physician, heal thyself, requiring me to prove what is said of me in Capernaum, by doing the same here; but there is another proverb, No prophet is accepted in his own country. Unaccepted I do nothing wonderful. In the great famine, Elijah was sent to no widow of the many in Israel, but to a Sidonian; and Elisha cured no leper of the many in Israel, but Naaman the Syrian. There are those fit to see signs and wonders; they are not always the kin of the prophet.'

The Nazarenes heard with indignation. Their wonder at his gracious words was changed to bitterest wrath. The very beams of their ugly religion were party-spirit, exclusiveness, and pride in the fancied favour of God for them only of all the nations: to hint at the possibility of a revelation of the glory of God to a stranger; far more, to hint that a stranger might be fitter to receive such a revelation than a Jew, was an offence reaching to the worst insult; and it was cast in their teeth by a common man of their own city! 'Thou art but a well-known carpenter's son, and dost thou teach *us*! Darest thou imply a divine preference for Capernaum over Nazareth?' In bad odour with the rest of their countrymen, they were the prouder of themselves.

The *whole* synagogue, observe, rose in a fury. Such a fellow a prophet! He was worse than the worst of Gentiles! he was a false Jew! a traitor to his God! a friend of the idol-worshipping Romans! Away with him! His townsmen led the van in his rejection by his own. The men of Nazareth would have forestalled his crucifixion by them of Jerusalem. What! a Sidonian woman fitter to receive the prophet than any Jewess! a heathen worthier to be kept alive by miracle in time of famine, than a worshipper of the true God! a leper of Damascus less displeasing to God than the lepers of his chosen race! It was no longer condescending approval that shone in their eyes. He a prophet! They had seen through him! Soon had they found him out! The moment he perceived it useless to pose for a prophet with them, who had all along known the breed of him, he had turned to insult them! He dared not attempt in his own city the deceptions with which, by the help of Satan, he had made such a grand show, and fooled the idiots of Capernaum! He saw they knew him too well, were too wide-awake to be cozened by him, and to avoid their expected challenge, fell to reviling the holy nation. Let him take the consequences! To the brow of the hill with him!

How could there be any miracle for such! They were well satisfied with themselves, and

2

Need and the upward look, the mood ready to believe when and where it can, the embryonic faith, is dear to Him whose love would have us trust him. Let any man seek him—not in curious inquiry whether the story of him may be true or cannot be true—in humble readiness to accept him altogether if only he can, and he shall find him; we shall not fail of help to believe because we doubt. But if the questioner be such that the dispersion of his doubt would but leave him in disobedience, the Power of truth has no care to effect his conviction. Why cast out a devil that the man may the better do the work of the devil? The childlike doubt will, as it softens and yields, minister nourishment with all that was good in it to the faith-germ at its heart; the wise and prudent unbelief will be left to develop its own misery. The Lord could easily have satisfied the Nazarenes that he was the Messiah: they would but have hardened into the nucleus of an army for the subjugation of the world. To a warfare with their own sins, to the subjugation of their doing and desiring to the will of the great Father, all the miracles in his power would never have persuaded them. A true convincement is not possible to hearts and minds like theirs.

Not only is it impossible for a low man to believe a thousandth part of what a noble man can, but a low man cannot believe anything as a noble man believes it. The men of Nazareth could have believed in Jesus as their saviour from the Romans; as their saviour from their sins they could not believe in him, for they loved their sins. The king of heaven came to offer them a share in his kingdom; but they were not poor in spirit, and the kingdom of heaven was not for them. Gladly would they have inherited the earth; but they were not meek, and the earth was for the lowly children of the perfect Father.

THE HEIRS OF HEAVEN AND EARTH.

And he opened his mouth and taught them, saying, 'Blessed are the poor in spirit; for theirs is the kingdom of heaven.' ...'Blessed are the meek; for they shall inherit the earth.'—*Matthew* v. 2-3, 5.

The words of the Lord are the seed sown by the sower. Into our hearts they must fall that they may grow. Meditation and prayer must water them, and obedience keep them in the sunlight. Thus will they bear fruit for the Lord's gathering.

Those of his disciples, that is, obedient hearers, who had any experience in trying to live, would, in part, at once understand them; but as they obeyed and pondered, the meaning of them would keep growing. This we see in the writings of the apostles. It will be so with us also, who need to understand everything he said neither more nor less than they to whom first he spoke; while our obligation to understand is far greater than theirs at the time, inasmuch as we have had nearly two thousand years' experience of the continued coming of the kingdom he then preached: it is not yet come; it has been all the time, and is now, drawing slowly nearer.

The sermon on the mount, as it is commonly called, seems the Lord's first free utterance, in the presence of any large assembly, of the good news of the kingdom. He had been teaching his disciples and messengers; and had already brought the glad tidings that his father was their father, to many besides—to Nathanael for one, to Nicodemus, to the woman of Samaria, to every one he had cured, every one whose cry for help he had heard: his epiphany was a gradual thing, beginning, where it continues, with the individual. It is impossible even to guess at what number may have heard him on this occasion: he seems to have gone up the mount because of the crowd—to secure a somewhat opener position whence he could better speak; and thither followed him those who desired to be taught of him, accompanied doubtless by not a few in whom curiosity was the chief motive. Disciple or gazer, he addressed the individuality of every one that had ears to hear. Peter and Andrew, James and John, are all we know as his recognized disciples, followers, and companions, at the time; but, while his words were addressed to such as had come to him desiring to learn of him, the things he uttered were eternal truths, life in which was essential for every one of his father's children, therefore they were for all: he who heard to obey, was his disciple.

How different, at the first sound of it, must the good news have been from the news anxiously expected by those who waited for the Messiah! Even the Baptist in prison lay listening after something of quite another sort. The Lord had to send him a message, by eye-witnesses of his doings, to remind him that God's thoughts are not as our thoughts, or his ways as our ways—that the design of God is other and better than the expectation of men. His summary of the gifts he was giving to men, culminated with the preaching of the good news to the poor. If John had known these his doings before, he had not recognized them as belonging to the Lord's special mission: the Lord tells him it is not enough to have accepted him as the Messiah; he must recognize his doings as the work he had come into the world to do, and as in their nature so divine as to be the very business of the Son of God in whom the Father was well pleased.

Wherein then consisted the goodness of the news which he opened his mouth to give them? What was in the news to make the poor glad? Why was his arrival with such words in his heart and mouth, the coming of the kingdom?

All good news from heaven, is of *truth*—essential truth, involving duty, and giving and promising help to the performance of it. There can be no good news for us men, except of uplifting love, and no one can be lifted up who will not rise. If God himself sought to raise his little ones without their consenting effort, they would drop from his foiled endeavour. He will carry us in his arms till we are able to walk; he will carry us in his arms when we are weary with walking; he will not carry us if we will not walk.

Very different are the good news Jesus brings us from certain prevalent representations of the gospel, founded on the pagan notion that suffering is an offset for sin, and culminating in the vile assertion that the suffering of an innocent man, just because he is innocent, yea per-

515

fect, is a satisfaction to the holy Father for the evil deeds of his children. As a theory concerning the atonement nothing could be worse, either intellectually, morally, or spiritually; announced as the gospel itself, as the good news of the kingdom of heaven, the idea is monstrous as any Chinese dragon. Such a so-called gospel is no gospel, however accepted as God sent by good men of a certain development. It is evil news, dwarfing, enslaving, maddening—news to the child-heart of the dreariest damnation. Doubtless some elements of the gospel are mixed up with it on most occasions of its announcement; none the more is it the message received from him. It can be good news only to such as are prudently willing to be delivered from a God they fear, but unable to accept the gospel of a perfect God, in whom to trust perfectly.

The good news of Jesus was just the news of the thoughts and ways of the Father in the midst of his family. He told them that the way men thought for themselves and their children was not the way God thought for himself and his children; that the kingdom of heaven was founded, and must at length show itself founded on very different principles from those of the kingdoms and families of the world, meaning by the world that part of the Father's family which will not be ordered by him, will not even try to obey him. The world's man, its great, its successful, its honorable man, is he who may have and do what he pleases, whose strength lies in money and the praise of men; the greatest in the kingdom of heaven is the man who is humblest and serves his fellows the most. Multitudes of men, in no degree notable as ambitious or proud, hold the ambitious, the proud man in honour, and, for all deliverance, hope after some shadow of his prosperity. How many even of those who look for the world to come, seek to the powers of this world for deliverance from its evils, as if God were the God of the world to come only! The oppressed of the Lord's time looked for a Messiah to set their nation free, and make it rich and strong; the oppressed of our time believe in money, knowledge, and the will of a people which needs but power to be in its turn the oppressor. The first words of the Lord on this occasion were:—'Blessed are the poor in spirit, for theirs is the kingdom of heaven,'

It is not the proud, it is not the greedy of distinction, it is not those who gather and hoard, not those who lay down the law to their neighbours, not those that condescend, any more than those that shrug the shoulder and shoot out the lip, that have any share in the kingdom of the Father. That kingdom has no relation with or resemblance to the kingdoms of this world, deals with no one thing that distinguishes their rulers, except to repudiate it. The Son of God will favour no smallest ambition, be it in the heart of him who leans on his bosom. The kingdom of God, the refuge of the oppressed, the golden age of the new world, the real Utopia, the newest yet oldest Atlantis, the home of the children, will not open its gates to the most miserable who would rise above his equal in misery, who looks down on any one more miserable than himself. It is the home of perfect brotherhood. The poor, the beggars in spirit, the humble men of heart, the unambitious, the unselfish; those who never despise men, and never seek their praises; the lowly, who see nothing to admire in themselves, therefore cannot seek to be admired of others; the men who give themselves away—these are the freemen of the kingdom, these are the citizens of the new Jerusalem. The men who are aware of their own essential poverty; not the men who are poor in friends, poor in influence, poor in acquirements, poor in money, but those who are poor in spirit, who *feel themselves poor creatures*; who know nothing to be pleased with themselves for, and desire nothing to make them think well of themselves; who know that they need much to make their life worth living, to make their existence a good thing, to make them fit to live; these humble ones are the poor whom the Lord calls blessed. When a man says, I am low and worthless, then the gate of the kingdom begins to open to him, for there enter the true, and this man has begun to know the truth concerning himself. Whatever such a man has attained to, he straightway forgets; it is part of him and behind him; his business is with what he has not, with the things that lie above and before him. The man who is proud of anything he thinks he has reached, has not reached it. He is but proud of himself, and imagining a cause for his pride. If he had reached, he would already have begun to forget. He who delights in contemplating whereto he has attained, is not merely sliding back; he is already in the dirt of self-satisfaction. The gate of the kingdom is closed, and he outside. The child who, clinging to his Father, dares not think he has in any sense attained while as yet he is not as his Father—his Father's heart, his Father's heaven is his natural home. To find himself thinking of himself as above his fellows, would be to that child a shuddering terror; his universe would contract around him, his ideal wither on its throne. The least motion of self-satisfaction, the first thought of placing himself in the forefront of estimation, would be to him a flash from the nether abyss. God is his life and his lord. That his father should be content with him must be all his care. Among his relations with his neighbour, infinitely precious, comparison with his neighbour has no place. Which is the greater is of no account. He would not choose to be less than his neighbour; he would choose his neighbour to be greater than he. He looks up to every man. Otherwise gifted than he, his neighbour is more than he. All come from the one mighty father: shall he judge the live thoughts of God, which is greater and which is less? In thus denying, thus turning his back on himself, he has no thought of saintliness, no thought but of his father and his brethren. To such a child heaven's best secrets are open. He clambers about the throne of the Father unrebuked; his back is ready for the smallest heavenly playmate; his arms are an open refuge for any blackest little lost kid of the Father's flock; he will toil with it up the heavenly stair, up the very steps of the great white throne, to lay it on the Father's knees. For the glory of that Father is not in knowing himself God, but in giving himself away—in creating and redeeming and glorifying his children.

The man who does not house self, has room to be his real self— God's eternal idea of him. He lives eternally; in virtue of the creative power present in him with momently, unimpeded creation, he *is*. How should there be in him one thought of ruling or commanding or surpassing! He can imagine no bliss, no good in being greater than some one else. He is unable to wish himself other than he is, except more what God made him for, which is indeed the highest willing of the will of God. His brother's wellbeing is essential to his bliss. The thought of standing higher in the favour of God than his brother, would make him miserable. He would lift every brother to the embrace of the Father. Blessed are the poor in spirit, for they are of the same spirit as God, and of nature the kingdom of heaven is theirs.

'Blessed are the meek, for they shall inherit the earth,' expresses the same principle: the same law holds in the earth as in the kingdom of heaven. How should it be otherwise? Has the creator of the ends of the earth ceased to rule it after his fashion, because his rebellious children have so long, to their own hurt, vainly endeavoured to rule it after theirs? The kingdom of heaven belongs to the poor; the meek shall inherit the earth. The earth as God sees it, as those to whom the kingdom of heaven belongs also see it, is good, all good, very good, fit for the meek to inherit; and one day they shall inherit it—not indeed as men of the world count inheritance, but as the maker and owner of the world has from the first counted it. So different are the two ways of inheriting, that one of the meek may be heartily enjoying his possession, while one of the proud is selfishly walling him out from the spot in it he loves best.

The meek are those that do not assert themselves, do not defend themselves, never dream of avenging themselves, or of returning aught but good for evil. They do not imagine it their business to take care of themselves. The meek man may indeed take much thought, but it will not be for himself. He never builds an exclusive wall, shuts any honest neighbour out. He will not always serve the wish, but always the good of his neighbour. His service must be true service. Self shall be no umpire in affair of his. Man's consciousness of himself is but a shadow: the meek man's self always vanishes in the light of a real presence. His nature lies open to the Father of men, and to every good impulse is as it were empty. No bristling importance, no vain attendance of fancied rights and wrongs, guards his door, or crowds the passages of his house; they are for the angels to come and go. Abandoned thus to the truth, as the sparks from the gleaming river dip into the flowers of Dante's unperfected vision, so the many souls of the visible world, lights from the father of lights, enter his heart freely; and by them he inherits the earth he was created to inherit—possesses it as his father made him capable of possessing, and the earth of being possessed. Because the man is meek, his eye is single; he sees things as God sees them, as he would have his child see them: to confront creation with pure eyes is to possess it.

How little is the man able to make his own, who would ravish all! The man who, by the exclusion of others from the space he calls his, would grasp any portion of the earth as his own, befools himself in the attempt. The very bread he has swallowed cannot so in any real sense be his. There does not exist such a power of possessing as he would arrogate. There is not such a sense of having as that of which he has conceived the shadow in his degenerate and lapsing imagination. The real owner of his demesne is that pedlar passing his gate, into a divine soul receiving the sweetnesses which not all the greed of the so-counted possessor can keep within his walls: they overflow the cup-lip of the coping, to give themselves to the footfarer. The motions aerial, the sounds, the odours of those imprisoned spaces, are the earnest of a possession for which is ever growing his power of possessing. In no wise will such inheritance interfere with the claim of the man who calls them his. Each possessor has them his, as much as each in his own way is capable of possessing them. For possession is determined by the kind and the scope of the power of possessing; and the earth has a fourth dimension of which the mere owner of its soil knows nothing.

The child of the maker is naturally the inheritor. But if the child try to possess as a house the thing his father made an organ, will he succeed in so possessing it? Or if he do nestle in a corner of its case, will he oust thereby the Lord of its multiplex harmony, sitting regnant on the seat of sway, and drawing with 'volant touch' from the house of the child the liege homage of its rendered wealth? To the poverty of such a child are all those left, who think to have and to hold after the corrupt fancies of a greedy self.

We cannot see the world as God means it, save in proportion as our souls are meek. In meekness only are we its inheritors. Meekness alone makes the spiritual retina pure to receive God's things as they are, mingling with them neither imperfection nor impurity of its own. A thing so beheld that it conveys to me the divine thought issuing in its form, is mine; by nothing but its mediation between God and my life, can anything be mine. The man so dull as to insist that a thing is his because he has bought it and paid for it, had better bethink himself that not all the combined forces of law, justice, and goodwill, can keep it his; while even death cannot take the world from the man who possesses it as alone the maker of him and it cares that he should possess it. This man leaves it, but carries it with him; that man carries with him only its loss. He passes, unable to close hand or mouth upon any portion of it. Its *ownness* to him was but the changes he could make in it, and the nearness into which he could bring it to the body he lived in. That body the earth in its turn possesses now, and it lies very still, changing nothing, but being changed. Is this the fine of the great buyer of land, to have his fine pate full of fine dirt? In the soul of the meek, the earth remains an endless possession—his because he who made it is his—his as nothing but his maker could ever be the creature's. He has the earth by his divine relation to him who sent it forth from him as a tree sends out its leaves. To inherit the earth is to grow ever more alive to the presence, in it and in all its parts, of him who is the life of men. How far one may advance in such inheritance while yet in the body, will simply depend on the meekness he attains while yet in the body; but it may be, as Frederick Denison Maurice, the servant of God, thought while yet he was with us, that the new heavens and the new earth are the same in which we now live, righteously inhabited by the meek, with their deeper-opened eyes. What if the meek of the dead be thus possessing it even now! But I do not care to speculate. It is enough that the man who refuses to assert himself, seeking no recognition by men, leaving the care of his life to the Father, and occupying himself with the will of the Father, shall find himself, by and by, at home in the Father's house, with all the Father's property his.

Which is more the possessor of the world—he who has a thousand houses, or he who, without one house to call his own, has ten in which his knock at the door would rouse instant jubilation? Which is the richer—the man who, his large money spent, would have no refuge; or he for whose necessity a hundred would sacrifice comfort? Which of the two possessed the earth—king Agrippa or tent-maker Paul?

Which is the real possessor of a book—the man who has its original and every following edition, and shows, to many an admiring and envying visitor, now this, now that, in binding characteristic, with possessor-pride; yea, from secret shrine is able to draw forth and display the author's manuscript, with the very shapes in which his thoughts came forth to the light of day,—or the man who cherishes one little, hollow-backed, coverless, untitled, bethumbed copy, which he takes with him in his solitary walks and broods over in his silent chamber, always finding in it some beauty or excellence or aid he had not found before—which is to him in truth as a live companion?

For what makes the thing a book? Is it not that it has a soul—the mind in it of him who wrote the book? Therefore only can the book be possessed, for life alone can be the possession of life. The dead possess their dead only to bury them.

Does not he then, who loves and understands his book, possess it with such possession as is impossible to the other? Just so may the world itself be possessed—either as a volume unread, or as the wine of a soul, 'the precious life-blood of a master-spirit, embalmed and treasured up on purpose to a life beyond life.' It may be possessed as a book filled with words from the mouth of God, or but as the golden-clasped covers of that book; as an embodiment or incarnation of God himself; or but as a house built to sell. The Lord loved the world and the things of the world, not as the men of the world love them, but finding his father in everything that came from his father's heart.

The same spirit, then, is required for possessing the kingdom of heaven, and for inheriting the earth. How should it not be so, when the one Power is the informing life of both? If we are the Lord's, we possess the kingdom of heaven, and so inherit the earth. How many who call themselves by his name, would have it otherwise: they would possess the earth and inherit the kingdom! Such fill churches and chapels on Sundays: anywhere suits for the worship of Mammon.

Yet verily, earth as well as heaven may be largely possessed even now.

Two men are walking abroad together; to the one, the world yields thought after thought of delight; he sees heaven and earth embrace one another; he feels an indescribable presence over and in them; his joy will afterward, in the solitude of his chamber, break forth in song;—to the other, oppressed with the thought of his poverty, or ruminating how to make much into more, the glory of the Lord is but a warm summer day; it enters in at no window of his soul; it offers him no gift; for, in the very temple of God, he looks for no God in it. Nor must there needs be two men to think and feel thus differently. In what diverse fashion will any one *subject* to ever-changing mood see the same world of the same glad creator! Alas for men, if it changed as we change, if it grew meaningless when we grow faithless! Thought for a morrow that may never come, dread of the dividing death which works for endless companionship, anger with one we love, will cloud the radiant morning, and make the day dark with night. At evening, having bethought ourselves, and returned to him that feeds the ravens, and watches the dying sparrow, and says to his children 'Love one another,' the sunset splendour is glad over us, the western sky is refulgent as the court of the Father when the glad news is spread abroad that a sinner has repented. We have mourned in the twilight of our little faith, but, having sent away our sin, the glory of God's heaven over his darkening earth has comforted us.

SORROW THE PLEDGE OF JOY.

'Blessed are they that mourn, for they shall be comforted.'—*Matthew* v. 4.

Grief, then, sorrow, pain of heart, mourning, is no partition-wall between man and God. So far is it from opposing any obstacle to the passage of God's light into man's soul, that the Lord congratulates them that mourn. There is no evil in sorrow. True, it is not an essential good, a good in itself, like love; but it will mingle with any good thing, and is even so allied to good that it will open the door of the heart for any good. More of sorrowful than of joyful men are always standing about the everlasting doors that open into the presence of the Most High. It is true also that joy is in its nature more divine than sorrow; for, although man must sorrow, and God share in his sorrow, yet in himself God is not sorrowful, and the 'glad creator' never made man for sorrow: it is but a stormy strait through which he must pass to his ocean of peace. He 'makes the joy the last in every song.' Still, I repeat, a man in sorrow is in general far nearer God than a man in joy. Gladness may make a man forget his thanksgiving; misery drives him to his prayers. For we *are* not yet, we are only *becoming*. The endless day will at length dawn whose every throbbing moment will heave our hearts Godward; we shall scarce need to lift them up: now, there are two door-keepers to the house of prayer, and Sorrow is more on the alert to open than her grandson Joy.

The gladsome child runs farther afield; the wounded child turns to go home. The weeper sits down close to the gate; the lord of life draws nigh to him from within. God loves not sorrow, yet rejoices to see a man sorrowful, for in his sorrow man leaves his heavenward door on the latch, and God can enter to help him. He loves, I say, to see him sorrowful, for then he can come near to part him from that which makes his sorrow a welcome sight. When Ephraim bemoans himself, he is a pleasant child. So good a medicine is sorrow, so powerful to slay the moths that infest and devour the human heart, that the Lord is glad to see a man weep. He congratulates him on his sadness. Grief is an ill-favoured thing, but she is Love's own child, and her mother loves her.

The promise to them that mourn, is not *the kingdom of heaven*, but that their mourning shall be ended, that they shall be comforted. To mourn is not to fight with evil; it is only to miss that which is good. It is not an essential heavenly condition, like poorness of spirit or meekness. No man will carry his mourning with him into heaven—or, if he does, it will speedily be turned either into joy, or into what will result in joy, namely, redemptive action.

Mourning is a canker-bitten blossom on the rose-tree of love. Is there any mourning worthy the name that has not love for its root? Men mourn because they love. Love is the life out of which are fashioned all the natural feelings, every emotion of man. Love modelled by faith, is hope; love shaped by wrong, is anger—verily anger, though pure of sin; love invaded by loss, is grief.

The garment of mourning is oftenest a winding-sheet; the loss of the loved by death is the main cause of the mourning of the world. The Greek word here used to describe the blessed of the Lord, generally means *those that mourn for the dead*. It is not in the New Testament employed exclusively in this sense, neither do I imagine it stands here for such only: there are griefs than death sorer far, and harder far to comfort—harder even for God himself, with whom all things are possible; but it may give pleasure to know that the promise of comfort to those that mourn, may specially apply to those that mourn because their loved have gone out of their sight, and beyond the reach of their cry. Their sorrow, indeed, to the love divine, involves no difficulty; it is a small matter, easily met. The father, whose elder son is ever with him, but whose younger is in a far country, wasting his substance with riotous living, is unspeakably more to be pitied, and is harder to help, than that father both of whose sons lie in the sleep of death.

Much of what goes by the name of comfort, is merely worthless; and such as could be comforted by it, I should not care to comfort. Let time do what it may to bring the ease of oblivion; let change of scene do what in it lies to lead thought away from the vanished; let new loves bury grief in the grave of the old love: consolation of such sort could never have crossed the mind of Jesus. Would The Truth call a man blessed because his pain would sooner or later depart, leaving him at best no better than before, and certainly poorer—not only the beloved gone, but the sorrow for him too, and with the sorrow the love that had caused the sorrow? Blessed of God because restored to an absence of sorrow? Such a God were fitly adored only where not one heart worshipped in spirit and in truth.

'The Lord means of course,' some one may say, 'that the comfort of the mourners will be the restoration of that which they have lost. He means, "Blessed are ye although ye mourn, for your sorrow will be turned into joy."'

Happy are they whom nothing less than such restoration will comfort! But would such restoration be comfort enough for the heart of Jesus to give? Was ever love so deep, so pure, so perfect, as to be good enough for him? And suppose the love between the parted two had been such, would the mere restoration in the future of that which once he had, be ground enough for so emphatically proclaiming the man blessed now, blessed while yet in the midnight of his loss, and knowing nothing of the hour of his deliverance? To call a man *blessed* in his sorrow because of something to be given him, surely implies a something better than what he had before! True, the joy that is past may have been so great that the man might well feel blessed in the merest hope of its restoration; but would that be meaning enough for the word in the mouth of the Lord? That the interruption of his blessedness was but temporary, would hardly be fit ground for calling the man *blessed* in that interruption. *Blessed* is a strong word, and in the mouth of Jesus means all it can mean. Can his saying here mean less than—'Blessed are they that mourn, for they shall be comforted with a bliss well worth all the pain of the medicinal sorrow'? Besides, the benediction surely means that the man is blessed *because* of his condition of mourning, not in spite of it. His mourning is surely a part at least of the Lord's ground for congratulating him: is it not the present operative means whereby the consolation is growing possible? In a word, I do not think the Lord would be content to call a man blessed on the mere ground of his going to be restored to a former bliss by no means perfect; I think he congratulated the mourners upon the grief they were enduring, because he saw the excellent glory of the comfort that was drawing nigh; because he knew the immeasurably greater joy to which the sorrow was at once clearing the way and conducting the mourner. When I say *greater*, God forbid I should mean *other!* I mean the same bliss, divinely enlarged and divinely purified—passed again through the hands of the creative Perfection. The Lord knew all the history of love and loss; beheld throughout the universe the winged Love discrowning the skeleton Fear. God's comfort must ever be larger than man's grief, else were there gaps in his Godhood. Mere restoration would leave a hiatus, barren and growthless, in the development of his children.

But, alas, what a pinched hope, what miserable expectations, most who call themselves the Lord's disciples derive from their notions of his teaching! Well may they think of death as the one thing to be right zealously avoided, and for ever lamented! Who would forsake even the window-less hut of his sorrow for the poor mean place they imagine the Father's house! Why, many of them do not even expect to know their friends there! do not expect to distinguish one from another of all the holy assembly! They will look in many faces, but never to recognize old friends and lovers! A fine saviour of men is their Jesus! Glorious lights they shine in the world of our sorrow, holding forth a word of darkness, of dismallest death! Is the Lord such as they believe him? 'Good-bye, then, good Master!' cries the human heart. 'I thought thou couldst save me, but, alas, thou canst not. If thou savest the part of our being which can sin, thou lettest the part that can love sink into hopeless perdition: thou art not he that should come; I look for another! Thou wouldst destroy and not save me! Thy father is not my father; thy God is not my God! Ah, to whom shall we go? He has not the words of eternal life, this Jesus, and the universe is dark as chaos! O father, this thy son is good, but we need a greater son than he. Never will thy children love thee under the shadow of this new law, that they are not to love one another as thou lovest them!' How does that man love God—of what kind is the love he bears him—who is unable to believe that God loves every throb of every human heart toward another? Did not the Lord die that we should love one another, and be one with him and the Father, and is not the knowledge of difference essential to the deepest love? Can there be oneness without difference? harmony without distinction? Are all to have the same face? then why faces at all? If the plains of heaven are to be crowded with the same one face over and over for ever, but one moment will pass ere by monotony bliss shall have grown ghastly. Why not perfect spheres of featureless ivory rather than those multitudinous heads with one face! Or are we to start afresh with countenances all new, each beautiful, each lovable, each a revelation of the infinite father, each distinct from every other, and therefore all blending toward a full revealing—but never more the dear old precious faces, with its whole story in each, which seem, at the very thought of them, to draw our hearts out of our bosoms? Were they created only to become dear, and be destroyed? Is it in wine only that the old is better? Would such a new heaven be a thing to thank God for? Would this be a prospect on which the Son of Man would congratulate the mourner, or at which the mourner for the dead would count himself blessed? It is a shame that such a preposterous, monstrous unbelief should call for argument.

A heaven without human love it were inhuman, and yet more undivine to desire; it ought not to be desired by any being made in the image of God. The lord of life died that his father's children might grow perfect in love—might love their brothers and sisters as he loved them: is it to this end that they must cease to know one another? To annihilate the past of our earthly embodiment, would be to crush under the heel of an iron fate the very idea of tenderness, human or divine.

We shall all doubtless be changed, but in what direction?—to something less, or to something greater?—to something that is less we, which means degradation? to something that is not we, which means annihilation? or to something that is more we, which means a farther development of the original idea of us, the divine germ of us, holding in it all we ever were, all we ever can and must become? What is it constitutes this or that man? Is it what he himself thinks he is? Assuredly not. Is it what his friends at any given moment think him? Far from it. In which of his changing moods is he more himself? Loves any lover so little as to desire *no* change in the person loved—no something different to bring him or her closer to the indwelling ideal? In the loveliest is there not something not like her—something less lovely than she—some little thing in which a change would make her, not less, but more herself? Is it not of the very essence of the Christian hope, that we shall be changed from much bad to all good? If a wife so love that she would keep every opposition, every inconsistency in her husband's as yet but partially harmonious character, she does not love well enough for the kingdom of heaven. If its imperfections be essential to the individuality she loves, and to the repossession of her joy in it, she may be sure that, if he were restored to her as she would have him, she would soon come to love him less—perhaps to love him not at all; for no one who does not love perfection, will ever keep constant in loving. Fault is not lovable; it is only the good in which the alien fault dwells that causes it to seem capable of being loved. Neither is it any man's peculiarities that make him beloved; it is the essential humanity underlying those peculiarities. They may make him interesting, and, where not offensive, they may come to be loved for the sake of the man; but in themselves they are of smallest account.

We must not however confound peculiarity with diversity. Diversity is in and from God; peculiarity in and from man. The real man is the divine idea of him; the man God had in view when he began to send him forth out of thought into thinking; the man he is now working to perfect by casting out what is not he, and developing what is he. But in God's real men, that is, his ideal men, the diversity is infinite; he does not repeat his creations; every one of his children differs from every other, and in every one the diversity is lovable. God gives in his children an analysis of himself, an analysis that will never be exhausted. It is the original God-idea of the individual man that will at length be given, without spot or blemish, into the arms of love.

Such, surely, is the heart of the comfort the Lord will give those whose love is now making them mourn; and their present blessedness must be the expectation of the time when the true lover shall find the restored the same as the lost—with precious differences: the things that were not like the true self, gone or going; the things that were loveliest, lovelier still; the restored not merely more than the lost, but more the person lost than he or she that was lost. For the things which made him or her what he or she was, the things that rendered lovable, the things essential to the person, will be more present, because more developed.

Whether or not the Lord was here thinking specially of the mourners for the dead, as I think he was, he surely does not limit the word of comfort to them, or wish us to believe less than that his father has perfect comfort for every human grief. Out upon such miserable theologians as, instead of receiving them into the good soil of a generous heart, to bring forth truth an hundred fold, so cut and pare the words of the Lord as to take the very life from them, quenching all their glory and colour in their own inability to believe, and still would have the dead letter of them accepted as the comfort of a creator to the sore hearts he made in his own image! Here, 'as if they were God's spies,' some such would tell us that the Lord proclaims the blessedness of those that mourn for their sins, and of them only. What mere honest man would make a promise which was all a reservation, except in one unmentioned point! Assuredly they who mourn for their sins will be gloriously comforted, but certainly such also as are bowed down with any grief. The Lord would have us know that sorrow is not a part of life; that it is but a wind blowing throughout it, to winnow and cleanse. Where shall the woman go whose child is at the point of death, or whom the husband of her youth has forsaken, but to her Father in heaven? Must she keep away until she knows herself sorry for her sins? How should that woman care to be delivered from her sins, how could she accept any comfort, who believed the child of her bosom lost to her for ever? Would the Lord have such a one be of good cheer, of merry heart, because her sins were forgiven her? Would such a mother be a woman of whom the saviour of men might have been born? If a woman forget the child she has borne and nourished, how shall she remember the father from whom she has herself come? The Lord came to heal the broken-hearted; therefore he said, 'Blessed are the mourners.' Hope in God, mother, for the deadest of thy children, even for him who died in his sins. Thou mayest have long to wait for him—but he will be found. It may be, thou thyself wilt one day be sent to seek him and find him. Rest thy hope on no excuse thy love would make for him, neither upon any quibble theological or sacerdotal; hope on in him who created him, and who loves him more than thou. God will excuse him better than thou, and his uncovenanted mercy is larger than that of his ministers. Shall not *the* Father do *his* best to find his prodigal? the good shepherd to find his lost sheep? The angels in his presence know the Father, and watch for the prodigal. Thou shalt be comforted.

There is one phase of our mourning for the dead which I must not leave unconsidered, seeing it is the pain within pain of all our mourning—the sorrow, namely, with its keen recurrent pangs because of things we have said or done, or omitted to say or do, while we companied with the departed. The very life that would give itself to the other, aches with the sense of having, this time and that, not given what it might. We cast ourselves at their feet, crying, Forgive me, my heart's own! but they are pale with distance, and do not seem to hear. It may be that they are longing in like agony of love after us, but know better, or perhaps only are more assured than we, that we shall be comforted together by and by.

Bethink thee, brother, sister, I say; bethink thee of the splendour of God, and answer—Would he be perfect if in his restitution of all things there were no opportunity for declaring our bitter grief and shame for the past? no moment in which to sob—Sister, brother, I am thy slave? no room for making amends? At the same time, when the desired moment comes, one look in the eyes may be enough, and we shall know one another even as God knows us. Like the purposed words of the prodigal in the parable, it may be that the words of our confession will hardly find place. Heart may so speak to heart as to forget there were such things. Mourner, hope in God, and comfort where thou canst, and the lord of mourners will be able to comfort thee the sooner. It may be thy very severity with thyself, has already moved the Lord to take thy part.

Such as mourn the loss of love, such from whom the friend, the brother, the lover, has turned away—what shall I cry to them?—You too shall be comforted—only hearken: Whatever selfishness clouds the love that mourns the loss of love, that selfishness must be taken out of it—burned out of it even by pain extreme, if such be needful. By cause of that in thy love which was not love, it may be thy loss has come; anyhow, because of thy love's defect, thou must suffer that it may be supplied. God will not, like the unjust judge, avenge thee to escape the cry that troubles him. No crying will make him comfort thy selfishness. He will not render thee incapable of loving truly. He despises neither thy love though mingled with selfishness, nor thy suffering that springs from both; he will disentangle thy selfishness from thy love, and cast it into the fire. His cure for thy selfishness at once and thy suffering, is to make thee love more—and more truly; not with the love of love, but with the love of the person whose lost love thou bemoanest. For the love of love is the love of thyself. Begin to love as God loves, and thy grief will assuage; but for comfort wait his time. What he will do for thee, he only knows. It may be thou wilt never know what he will do, but only what he has done: it was too good for thee to know save by receiving it. The moment thou art capable of it, thine it will be.

One thing is clear in regard to every trouble—that the natural way with it is straight to the Father's knee. The Father is father *for* his children, else why did he make himself their father? Wouldst thou not, mourner, be comforted rather after the one eternal fashion—the child by the father—than in such poor temporary way as would but leave thee the more exposed to thy worst enemy, thine own unreclaimed self?—an enemy who has but this one good thing in him—that he will always bring thee to sorrow!

The Lord has come to wipe away our tears. He is doing it; he will have it done as soon as he can; and until he can, he would have them flow without bitterness; to which end he tells us it is a blessed thing to mourn, because of the comfort on its way. Accept his comfort now, and so prepare for the comfort at hand. He is getting you ready for it, but you must be a fellow worker with him, or he will never have done. He *must* have you pure in heart, eager after righteousness, a very child of his father in heaven.

GOD'S FAMILY.

'Blessed are the pure in heart, for they shall see God.' 'Blessed are they which do hunger and thirst after righteousness, for they shall be filled.' 'Blessed are the peace-makers, for they shall be called the children of God.'—*Matthew* v. 8, 6, 9.

The cry of the deepest in man has always been, to see God. It was the cry of Moses and the cry of Job, the cry of psalmist and of prophet; and to the cry, there has ever been faintly heard a far approach of coming answer. In the fullness of time the Son appears with the proclamation that a certain class of men shall behold the Father: 'Blessed are the pure in heart,' he cries, 'for they shall see God.' He who saw God, who sees him now, who always did and always will see him, says, 'Be pure, and you also shall see him.' To see God was the Lord's own, eternal, one happiness; therefore he knew that the essential bliss of the creature is to behold the face of the creator. In that face lies the mystery of a man's own nature, the history of a man's own being. He who can read no line of it, can know neither himself nor his fellow; he only who knows God a little, can at all understand man. The blessed in Dante's Paradise ever and always read each other's thoughts in God. Looking to him, they find their neighbour. All that the creature needs to see or know, all that the creature can see or know, is the face of him from whom he came. Not seeing and knowing it, he will never be at rest; seeing and knowing it, his existence will yet indeed be a mystery to him and an awe, but no more a dismay. To know that it is, and that it has power neither to continue nor to cease, must to any soul alive enough to appreciate the fact, be merest terror, save also it knows one with it the Power by which it exists. From the man who comes to know and feel that Power in him and one with him, loneliness, anxiety, and fear vanish; he is no more an orphan without a home, a little one astray on the cold waste of a helpless consciousness. 'Father,' he cries, 'hold me fast to thy creating will, that I may know myself one with it, know myself its outcome, its willed embodiment, and rejoice without trembling. Be this the delight of my being, that thou hast willed, hast loved me forth; let me know that I am thy child, born to obey thee. Dost thou not justify thy deed to thyself by thy tenderness toward me? dost thou not justify it to thy child by revealing to him his claim on thee because of thy disparture of him from thyself, because of his utter dependence on thee? Father, thou art in me, else I could not be in thee, could have no house for my soul to dwell in, or any world in which to walk abroad,'

These truths are, I believe, the very necessities of fact, but a man does not therefore, at a given moment, necessarily know them. It is absolutely necessary, none the less, to his real being, that he should know these spiritual relations in which he stands to his Origin; yea, that they should be always present and potent with him, and become the heart and sphere and all-pervading substance of his consciousness, of which they are the ground and foundation. Once to have seen them, is not always to see them. There are times, and those times many, when the cares of this world—with no right to any part in our thought, seeing either they are unreasonable or God imperfect—so blind the eyes of the soul to the radiance of the eternally true, that they see it only as if it ought to be true, not as if it must be true; as if it might be true in the region of thought, but could not be true in the region of fact. Our very senses, filled with the things of our passing sojourn, combine to cast discredit upon the existence of any world for the sake of which we are furnished with an inner eye, an eternal ear. But had we once seen God face to face, should we not be always and for ever sure of him? we have had but glimpses of the Father. Yet, if we had seen God face to face, but had again become impure of heart—if such a fearful thought be a possible idea—we should then no more believe that we had ever beheld him. A sin-beclouded soul could never recall the vision whose essential verity was its only possible proof. None but the pure in heart see God; only the growing-pure hope to see him. Even those who saw the Lord, the express image of his person, did not see God. They only saw Jesus—and then but the outside Jesus, or a little more. They were not pure in heart; they saw him and did not see him. They saw him with their eyes, but not with those eyes which alone can see God. Those were not born in them yet. Neither the eyes of the resurrection-body, nor the eyes of unembodied spirits can see God; only the eyes of that eternal something that is of the very essence of God, the thought-eyes, the truth-eyes, the love-eyes, can see him. It is not because we are created and he uncreated, it is not because of any difference involved in that difference of all differences, that we cannot see him. If he pleased to take a shape, and that shape were presented to us, and we saw that shape, we should not therefore be seeing God. Even if we knew it was a shape of God—call it even God himself our eyes rested upon; if we had been told the fact and believed the report; yet, if we did not see the *Godness*, were not capable of recognizing him, so as without the report to know the vision him, we should not be seeing God, we should only be seeing the tabernacle in which for the moment he dwelt. In other words, not seeing what in the form made it a form fit for him to take, we should not be seeing a presence which could only be God.

To see God is to stand on the highest point of created being. Not until we see God—no partial and passing embodiment of him, but the abiding presence—do we stand upon our own mountain-top, the height of the existence God has given us, and up to which he is leading us. That there we should stand, is the end of our creation. This truth is at the heart of everything, means all kinds of completions, may be uttered in many ways; but language will never compass it, for form will never contain it. Nor shall we ever see, that is know God perfectly. We shall indeed never absolutely know man or woman or child; but we may know God as we never can know human being—as we never can know ourselves. We not only may, but we must so know him, and it can never be until we are pure in heart. Then shall we know him with the infinitude of an ever-growing knowledge.

'What is it, then, to be pure in heart?'

I answer, It is not necessary to define this purity, or to have in the mind any clear form of it. For even to know perfectly, were that possible, what purity of heart is, would not be to be pure in heart.

'How then am I to try after it? can I do so without knowing what it is?'

Though you do not know any definition of purity, you know enough to begin to be pure. You do not know what a man is, but you know how to make his acquaintance—perhaps even how to gain his friendship. Your brain does not know what purity is; your heart has some acquaintance with purity itself. Your brain in seeking to know what it is, may even obstruct your heart in bettering its friendship with it. To know what purity is, a man must already be pure; but he who can put the question, already knows enough of purity, I repeat, to begin to become pure. If this moment you determine to start for purity, your conscience will at once tell you where to begin. If you reply, 'My conscience says nothing definite'; I answer, 'You are but playing with your conscience. Determine, and it will speak.'

If you care to see God, be pure. If you will not be pure, you will grow more and more impure; and instead of seeing God, will at length find yourself face to face with a vast inane—a vast inane, yet filled full of one inhabitant, that devouring monster, your own false self. If for this neither do you care, I tell you there is a Power that will not have it so; a Love that will make you care by the consequences of not caring.

You who seek purity, and would have your fellow-men also seek it, spend not your labour on the stony ground of their intellect, endeavouring to explain what purity is; give their imagination the one pure man; call up their conscience to witness against their own deeds; urge upon them the grand resolve to be pure. With the first endeavour of a soul toward her, Purity will begin to draw nigh, calling for admittance; and never will a man have to pause in the divine toil, asking what next is required of him; the demands of the indwelling Purity will ever be in front of his slow-labouring obedience.

If one should say, 'Alas, I am shut out from this blessing! I am not pure in heart: never shall I see God!' here is another word from the same eternal heart to comfort him, making his grief its own consolation. For this man also there is blessing with the messenger of the Father. Unhappy men were we, if God were the God of the perfected only, and not of the growing, the becoming! 'Blessed are they,' says the Lord, concerning the not yet pure, 'which do hunger and thirst after righteousness, for they shall be filled.' Filled with righteousness, they are pure; pure, they shall see God.

Long ere the Lord appeared, ever since man was on the earth, nay, surely, from the very beginning, was his spirit at work in it for righteousness; in the fullness of time he came in his own human person, to fulfil all righteousness. He came to his own of the same mind with himself, who hungered and thirsted after righteousness. They should be fulfilled of righteousness!

To hunger and thirst after anything, implies a sore personal need, a strong desire, a passion for that thing. Those that hunger and thirst after righteousness, seek with their whole nature the design of that nature. Nothing less will give them satisfaction; that alone will set them at ease. They long to be delivered from their sins, to send them away, to be clean and blessed by their absence—in a word to become men, God's men; for, sin gone, all the rest is good. It was not in such hearts, it was not in any heart that the revolting legal fiction of imputed righteousness arose. Righteousness itself, God's righteousness, rightness in their own being, in heart and brain and hands, is what they desire. Of such men was Nathanael, in whom was no guile; such, perhaps, was Nicodemus too, although he did come to Jesus by night; such was Zacchaeus. The temple could do nothing to deliver them; but, by their very futility, its observances had done their work, developing the desires they could not meet, making the men hunger and thirst the more after genuine righteousness: the Lord must bring them this bread from heaven. With him, the live, original rightness, in their hearts, they must speedily become righteous. With that Love their friend, who is at once both the root and the flower of things, they would strive vigorously as well as hunger eagerly after righteousness. Love is the father of righteousness. It could not be, and could not be hungered after, but for love. The lord of righteousness himself could not live without Love, without the Father in him. Every heart was created for, and can live no otherwise than in and upon love eternal, perfect, pure, unchanging; and love necessitates righteousness. In how many souls has not the very thought of a real God waked a longing to be different, to be pure, to be right! The fact that this feeling is possible, that a soul can become dissatisfied with itself, and desire a change in itself, reveals God as an essential part of its being; for in itself the soul is aware that it cannot be what it would, what it ought—that it cannot set itself right: a need has been generated in the soul for which the soul can generate no supply; a presence higher than itself must have caused that need; a power greater than itself must supply it, for the soul knows its very need, its very lack, is of something greater than itself.

But the primal need of the human soul is yet greater than this; the longing after righteousness is only one of the manifestations of it; the need itself is that of *existence not self-existent* for the consciousness of the presence of the causing Self-existent. It is the man's need of God. A moral, that is, a human, a spiritual being, must either be God, or one with God. This truth begins to reveal itself when the man begins to feel that he cannot cast out the thing he hates, cannot be the thing he loves. That he hates thus, that he loves thus, is because God is in him, but he finds he has not enough of God. His awaking strength manifests itself in his sense of weakness, for only strength can know itself weak. The negative cannot know itself at all. Weakness cannot know itself weak. It is a little strength that longs for more; it is infant righteousness that hungers after righteousness.

To every soul dissatisfied with itself, comes this word, at once rousing and consoling, from the Power that lives and makes him live—that in his hungering and thirsting he is blessed, for he shall be filled. His hungering and thirsting is the divine pledge of the divine meal. The more he hungers and thirsts the more blessed is he; the more room is there in him to receive that which God is yet more eager to give than he to have. It is the miserable emptiness that makes a man hunger and thirst; and, as the body, so the soul hungers after what belongs to its nature. A man hungers and thirsts after righteousness because his nature needs it—needs it because it was made for it; his soul desires its own. His nature is good, and desires more good. Therefore, that he is empty of good, needs discourage no one; for what is emptiness but room to be filled? Emptiness is need of good; the emptiness that desires good, is itself good. Even if the hunger after righteousness should in part spring from a desire after self-respect, it is not therefore *all* false. A man could not even be ashamed of himself, without some 'feeling sense' of the beauty of rightness. By divine degrees the man will at length grow sick of himself, and desire righteousness with a pure hunger—just as a man longs to eat that which is good, nor thinks of the strength it will restore.

To be filled with righteousness, will be to forget even righteousness itself in the bliss of being righteous, that is, a child of God. The thought of righteousness will vanish in the fact of righteousness. When a creature is just what he is meant to be, what only he is fit to be; when, therefore, he is truly himself, he never thinks what he is. He *is* that thing; why think about it? It is no longer outside of him that he should contemplate or desire it.

God made man, and woke in him the hunger for righteousness; the Lord came to enlarge and rouse this hunger. The first and lasting effect of his words must be to make the hungering and thirsting long yet more. If their passion grow to a despairing sense of the unattainable, a hopelessness of ever gaining that without which life were worthless, let them remember that the Lord congratulates the hungry and thirsty, so sure does he know them of being one day satisfied. Their hunger is a precious thing to have, none the less that it were a bad thing to retain unappeased. It springs from the lack but also from the love of good, and its presence makes it possible to supply the lack. Happy, then, ye pining souls! The food you would have, is the one thing the Lord would have you have, the very thing he came to bring you! Fear not, ye hungering and thirsting; you shall have righteousness enough, though none to spare—none to spare, yet enough to overflow upon every man. See how the Lord goes on filling his disciples, John and Peter and James and Paul, with righteousness from within! What honest soul, interpreting the servant by the master, and unbiassed by the tradition of them that would shut the kingdom of heaven against men, can doubt what Paul means by 'the righteousness which is of God by faith'? He was taught of Jesus Christ through the words he had spoken; and the man who does not understand Jesus Christ, will never understand his apostles. What righteousness could St Paul have meant but the same the Lord would have men hunger and thirst after—the very righteousness wherewith God is righteous! They that hunger and thirst after such only righteousness, shall become pure in heart, and shall see God.

If your hunger seems long in being filled, it is well it should seem long. But what if your righteousness tarry, because your hunger after it is not eager? There are who sit long at the table because their desire is slow; they eat as who should say, We need no food. In things spiritual, increasing desire is the sign that satisfaction is drawing nearer. But it were better to hunger after righteousness for ever than to dull the sense of lack with the husks of the Christian scribes and lawyers: he who trusts in the atonement instead of in the father of Jesus Christ, fills his fancy with the chimeras of a vulgar legalism, not his heart with the righteousness of God.

Hear another like word of the Lord. He assures us that the Father hears the cries of his elect—of those whom he seeks to worship him because they worship in spirit and in truth. 'Shall not God avenge his own elect,' he says, 'which cry day and night unto him?' Now what can God's elect have to keep on crying for, night and day, but righteousness? He allows that God seems to put off answering them, but assures us he will answer them speedily. Even now he must be busy answering their prayers; increasing hunger is the best possible indication that he is doing so. For some divine reason it is well they should not yet know in themselves that he is answering their prayers; but the day must come when we shall be righteous even as he is righteous; when no word of his will miss being understood because of our lack of righteousness; when no unrighteousness shall hide from our eyes the face of the Father.

These two promises, of seeing God, and being filled with righteousness, have place between the individual man and his father in heaven directly; the promise I now come to, has place between a man and his God as the God of other men also, as the father of the whole family in heaven and earth: 'Blessed are the peace-makers, for they shall be called the children of God.'

Those that are on their way to see God, those who are growing pure in heart through hunger and thirst after righteousness, are indeed the children of God; but specially the Lord calls those his children who, on their way home, are peace-makers in the travelling company; for, surely, those in any family are specially the children, who make peace with and among the rest. The true idea of the universe is the whole family in heaven and earth. All the children in this part of it, the earth, at least, are not good children; but however far, therefore, the earth is from being a true portion of a real family, the life-germ at the root of the world, that by and for which it exists, is its relation to God the father of men. For the development of this germ in the consciousness of the children, the church—whose idea is the purer family within the more mixed, ever growing as leaven within the meal by absorption, but which itself is, alas! not easily distinguishable from the world it would change—is one of the passing means. For the same purpose, the whole divine family is made up of numberless human families, that in these, men may learn and begin to love one another. God, then, would make of the world a true, divine family. Now the primary necessity to the very existence of a family is peace. Many a human family is no family, and the world is no family yet, for the lack of peace. Wherever peace is growing, there of course is the live peace, counteracting disruption and disintegration, and helping the development of the true essential family. The one question, therefore, as to any family is, whether peace or strife be on the increase in it; for peace alone makes it possible for the binding grass-roots of life—love, namely, and justice—to spread throughout what were else but a wind-blown heap of still drifting sand. The peace-makers quiet the winds of the world ever ready to be up and blowing; they tend and cherish the interlacing roots of the ministering grass; they spin and twist many uniting cords, and they weave many supporting bands; they are the servants, for the truth's sake, of the individual, of the family, of the world, of the great universal family of heaven and earth. They are the true children of that family, the allies and ministers of every clasping and consolidating force in it; fellow-workers they are with God in the creation of the family; they help him to get it to his mind, to perfect his father-idea. Ever radiating peace, they welcome love, but do not seek it; they provoke no jealousy. They are the children of God, for like him they would be one with his creatures. His eldest son, his very likeness, was the first of the family-peace-makers. Preaching peace to them that were afar off and them that were nigh, he stood undefended in the turbulent crowd of his fellows, and it was only over his dead body that his brothers began to come together in the peace that will not be broken. He rose again from the dead; his peace-making brothers, like himself, are dying unto sin; and not yet have the evil children made their father hate, or their elder brother flinch.

On the other hand, those whose influence is to divide and separate, causing the hearts of men to lean away from each other, make themselves the children of the evil one: born of God and not of the devil, they turn from God, and adopt the devil their father. They set their God-born life against God, against the whole creative, redemptive purpose of his unifying will, ever obstructing the one prayer of the first-born—that the children may be one with him in the Father. Against the heart-end of creation, against that for which the Son yielded himself utterly, the sowers of strife, the fomenters of discord, contend ceaseless. They do their part with all the other powers of evil to make the world which the love of God holds together—a world at least, though not yet a family—one heaving mass of dissolution. But they labour in vain. Through the mass and through it, that it may cohere, this way and that, guided in dance inexplicable of prophetic harmony, move the children of God, the lights of the world, the lovers of men, the fellow-workers with God, the peace-makers—ever weaving, after a pattern devised by, and known only to him who orders their ways, the web of the world's history. But for them the world would have no history; it would vanish, a cloud of windborne dust. As in his labour, so shall these share in the joy of God, in the divine fruition of victorious endeavour. Blessed are the peace-makers, for they shall be called the children of God—*the* children because they set the Father on the throne of the Family.

The main practical difficulty, with some at least of the peace-makers, is, how to carry themselves toward the undoers of peace, the disuniters of souls. Perhaps the most potent of these are not those powers of the church visible who care for canon and dogma more than for truth, and for the church more than for Christ; who take uniformity for unity; who strain at a gnat and swallow a camel, nor knowing what spirit they are of; such men, I say, are perhaps neither the most active nor the most potent force working for the disintegration of the body of Christ. I imagine also that neither are the party-liars of politics the worst foes to divine unity, ungenerous, and often knowingly false as they are to their opponents, to whom they seem to have no desire to be honest and fair. I think, rather, they must be the babbling liars of the social circle, and the faithless brothers and unloving sisters of disunited human families. But why inquire? Every self-assertion, every form of self-seeking however small or poor, world-noble or grotesque, is a separating and scattering force. And these forces are multitudinous, these points of radial repulsion are innumerable, because of the prevailing passion of mean souls to seem great, and feel important. If such cannot hope to attract the attention of the great-little world, if they cannot even become 'the cynosure of neighbouring eyes,' they will, in what sphere they may call their own, however small it be, try to make a party for themselves; each, revolving on his or her own axis, will attempt to self-centre a private whirlpool of human monads. To draw such a surrounding, the partisan of self will sometimes gnaw asunder the most precious of bonds, poison whole broods of infant loves. Such real schismatics go about, where not inventing evil, yet rejoicing in iniquity; mishearing; misrepresenting; paralyzing affection; separating hearts. Their chosen calling is that of the strife-maker, the child of the dividing devil. They belong to the class of *the perfidious*, whom Dante places in the lowest infernal gulf as their proper home. Many a woman who now imagines herself standing well in morals and religion, will find herself at last just such a child of the devil; and her misery will be the hope of her redemption.

But it is not for her sake that I write these things: would such a woman recognize her own likeness, were I to set it down as close as words could draw it? I am rather as one groping after some light on the true behaviour toward her kind. Are we to treat persons known for liars and strife-makers as the children of the devil or not? Are we to turn away from them, and refuse to acknowledge them, rousing an ignorant strife of tongues concerning our conduct? Are we guilty of connivance, when silent as to the ambush whence we know the wicked arrow privily shot? Are we to call the traitor to account? or are we to give warning of any sort? I have no answer. Each must carry the question that perplexes to the Light of the World. To what purpose is the spirit of God promised to them that ask it, if not to help them order their way aright?

One thing is plain—that we must love the strife-maker; another is nearly as plain—that, if we do not love him, we must leave him alone; for without love there can be no peace-making, and words will but occasion more strife. To be kind neither hurts nor compromises. Kindness has many phases, and the fitting form of it may avoid offence, and must avoid untruth.

GOD'S FAMILY.

We must not fear what man can do to us, but commit our way to the Father of the Family. We must be nowise anxious to defend ourselves; and if not ourselves because God is our defence, then why our friends? is he not their defence as much as ours? Commit thy friend's cause also to him who judgeth righteously. Be ready to bear testimony for thy friend, as thou wouldst to receive the blow struck at him; but do not plunge into a nest of scorpions to rescue his handkerchief. Be true to him thyself, nor spare to show thou lovest and honourest him; but defence may dishonour: men may say, What! is thy friend's esteem then so small? He is unwise who drags a rich veil from a cactus-bush.

Whatever our relation, then, with any peace-breaker, our mercy must ever be within call; and it may help us against an indignation too strong to be pure, to remember that when any man is reviled for righteousness-sake, then is he blessed.

THE REWARD OF OBEDIENCE.

'Blessed are the merciful, for they shall obtain mercy.' 'Blessed are they which are persecuted for righteousness' sake, for theirs is the kingdom of heaven. Blessed are ye when men shall revile you and persecute you, and shall say all manner of evil against you falsely, for my sake. Rejoice and be exceeding glad, for great is your reward in heaven; for so persecuted they the prophets which were before you.'—*Matthew* v. 7, 10 11, 12.

Mercy cannot get in where mercy goes not out. The outgoing makes way for the incoming. God takes the part of humanity against the man. The man must treat men as he would have God treat him. 'If ye forgive men their trespasses,' the Lord says, 'your heavenly father will also forgive you; but if ye forgive not men their trespasses, neither will your father forgive your trespasses. And in the prophecy of the judgment of the Son of man, he represents himself as saying, 'Inasmuch as ye have done it unto one of the least of these my brethren, ye have done it unto me.'

But the demand for mercy is far from being for the sake only of the man who needs his neighbour's mercy; it is greatly more for the sake of the man who must show the mercy. It is a small thing to a man whether or not his neighbour be merciful to him; it is life or death to him whether or not he be merciful to his neighbour. The greatest mercy that can be shown to man, is to make him merciful; therefore, if he will not be merciful, the mercy of God must compel him thereto. In the parable of the king taking account of his servants, he delivers the unmerciful debtor to the tormentors, 'till he should pay all that was due unto him.' The king had forgiven his debtor, but as the debtor refuses to pass on the forgiveness to his neighbour—the only way to make a return in kind—the king withdraws his forgiveness. If we forgive not men their trespasses, our trespasses remain. For how can God in any sense forgive, remit, or send away the sin which a man insists on retaining? Unmerciful, we must be given up to the tormentors until we learn to be merciful. God is merciful: we must be merciful. There is no blessedness except in being such as God; it would be altogether unmerciful to leave us unmerciful. The reward of the merciful is, that by their mercy they are rendered capable of receiving the mercy of God— yea, God himself, who is Mercy.

That men may be drawn to taste and see and understand, the Lord associates reward with righteousness. The Lord would have men love righteousness, but how are they to love it without being acquainted with it? How are they to go on loving it without a growing knowledge of it? To draw them toward it that they may begin to know it, and to encourage them when assailed by the disappointments that accompany endeavour, he tells them simply a truth concerning it—that in the doing of it, there is great reward. Let no one start with dismay at the idea of a reward of righteousness, saying virtue is its own reward. Is not virtue then a reward? Is any other imaginable reward worth mentioning beside it? True, the man may, after this mode or that, mistake the reward promised; not the less must he have it, or perish. Who will count himself deceived by overfulfilment? Would a parent be deceiving his child in saying, 'My boy, you will have a great reward if you learn Greek,' foreseeing his son's delight in Homer and Plato—now but a valueless waste in his eyes? When his reward comes, will the youth feel aggrieved that it is Greek, and not bank-notes?

The nature indeed of the Lord's promised rewards is hardly to be mistaken; yet the foolish remarks one sometimes hears, make me wish to point out that neither is the Lord proclaiming an ethical system, nor does he make the blunder of representing as righteousness the doing of a good thing because of some advantage to be thereby gained. When he promises, he only states some fact that will encourage his disciples—that is, all who learn of him—to meet the difficulties in the way of doing right and so learning righteousness, his object being to make men righteous, not to teach them philosophy. I doubt if those who would, on the ground of mentioned reward, set aside the teaching of the Lord, are as anxious to be righteous as they are to prove him unrighteous. If they were, they would, I think, take more care to represent him truly; they would make farther search into the thing, nor be willing that he whom the world confesses its best man, and whom they themselves, perhaps, confess their superior in conduct, should be found less pure in theory than they. Must the Lord hide from his friends that they will have cause to rejoice that they have been obedient? Must he give them no help to counterbalance the load with which they start on their race? Is he to tell them the horrors of the persecutions that await them, and not the sweet sympathies that will help them through? Was it wrong to assure them that where he was going they should go also? The Lord could not demand of them more righteousness than he does: 'Be ye therefore perfect as your father in heaven is perfect;' but not to help them by word of love, deed of power, and promise of good, would have shown him far less of a brother and a saviour. It is the part of the enemy of righteousness to increase the difficulties in the way of becoming righteous, and to diminish those in the way of seeming righteous. Jesus desires no righteousness for the pride of being righteous, any more than for advantage to be gained by it; therefore, while requiring such purity as the man, beforehand, is unable to imagine, he gives him all the encouragement he can. He will not enhance his victory by difficulties—of them there are enough—but by completeness. He will not demand the loftiest motives in the yet far from loftiest soul: to those the soul must grow. He will hearten the child with promises, and fulfil them to the contentment of the man.

Men cannot be righteous without love; to love a righteous man is the best, the only way to learn righteousness: the Lord gives us himself to love, and promises his closest friendship to them that overcome.

God's rewards are always in kind. 'I am your father; be my children, and I will be your father.' Every obedience is the opening of another door into the boundless universe of life. So long as the constitution of that universe remains, so long as the world continues to be made by God, righteousness can never fail of perfect reward. Before it could be otherwise, the government must have passed into other hands.

The idea of merit is nowise essential to that of reward. Jesus tells us that the lord who finds his servant faithful, will make him sit down to meat, and come forth and serve him; he says likewise, 'When ye have done all, say we are unprofitable servants; we have done only that which it was our duty to do.' Reward is the rebound of Virtue's well-served ball from the hand of Love; a sense of merit is the most sneaking shape that self-satisfaction can assume. God's reward lies closed in all well-doing: the doer of right grows better and humbler, and comes

544

nearer to God's heart as nearer to his likeness; grows more capable of God's own blessedness, and of inheriting the kingdoms of heaven and earth. To be made greater than one's fellows is the offered reward of hell, and involves no greatness; to be made greater than one's self, is the divine reward, and involves a real greatness. A man might be set above all his fellows, to be but so much less than he was before; a man cannot be raised a hair's-breadth above himself, without rising nearer to God. The reward itself, then, is righteousness; and the man who was righteous for the sake of such reward, knowing what it was, would be righteous for the sake of righteousness,—which yet, however, would not be perfection. But I must distinguish and divide no farther now.

The reward of mercy is not often of this world; the merciful do not often receive mercy in return from their fellows; perhaps they do not often receive much gratitude. None the less, being the children of their father in heaven, will they go on to show mercy, even to their enemies. They must give like God, and like God be blessed in giving.

There is a mercy that lies in the endeavour to share with others the best things God has given: they who do so will be persecuted, and reviled, and slandered, as well as thanked and loved and befriended. The Lord not only promises the greatest possible reward; he tells his disciples the worst they have to expect. He not only shows them the fair countries to which they are bound; he tells them the truth of the rough weather and the hardships of the way. He will not have them choose in ignorance. At the same time he strengthens them to meet coming difficulty, by instructing them in its real nature. All this is part of his preparation of them for his work, for taking his yoke upon them, and becoming fellow-labourers with him in his father's vineyard. They must not imagine, because they are the servants of his father, that therefore they shall find their work easy; they shall only find the reward great. Neither will he have them fancy, when evil comes upon them, that something unforeseen, unprovided for, has befallen them. It is just then, on the contrary, that their reward comes nigh: when men revile them and persecute them, then they may know that they are blessed. Their suffering is ground for rejoicing, for exceeding gladness. The ignominy cast upon them leaves the name of the Lord's Father written upon their foreheads, the mark of the true among the false, of the children among the slaves. With all who suffer for the world, persecution is the seal of their patent, a sign that they were sent: they fill up that which is behind of the afflictions of Christ for his body's sake.

Let us look at the similar words the Lord spoke in a later address to his disciples, in the presence of thousands, on the plain,— supplemented with lamentation over such as have what they desire: St Luke vi. 20-26.

'Blessed be ye poor, for yours is the kingdom of God. Blessed are ye that hunger now, for ye shall be filled. Blessed are ye that weep now, for ye shall laugh. Blessed are ye when men shall hate you, and when they shall separate you from their company, and shall reproach you, and cast out your name as evil, for the Son of Man's sake. Rejoice ye in that day, and leap for joy, for behold your reward is great in heaven; for in the like manner did their fathers unto the prophets.

'But woe unto you that are rich! for ye have received your consolation. Woe unto you that are full, for ye shall hunger. Woe unto you that laugh now, for ye shall mourn and weep. Woe unto you when all men shall speak well of you; for so did their fathers to the false prophets.'

On this occasion he uses the word *hunger* without limitation. Every true want, every genuine need, every God-created hunger, is a thing provided for in the idea of the universe; but no attempt to fill a void otherwise than the Heart of the Universe intended and intends, is or can be anything but a woe. God forgets none of his children—the naughty ones any more than the good. Love and reward is for the good: love and correction for the bad. The bad ones will trouble the good, but shall do them no hurt. The evil a man does to his neighbour, shall do his neighbour no harm, shall work indeed for his good; but he himself will have to mourn for his doing. A sore injury to himself, it is to his neighbour a cause of jubilation—not for the evil the man does to himself—over that there is sorrow in heaven—but for the good it occasions his neighbour. The poor, the hungry, the weeping, the hated, may lament their lot as if God had forgotten them; but God is all the time caring for them. Blessed in his sight now, they shall soon know themselves blessed. 'Blessed are ye that weep now, for ye shall laugh.'—Welcome words from the glad heart of the Saviour! Do they not make our hearts burn within us?—They shall be comforted even to laughter! The poor, the hungry, the weeping, the hated, the persecuted, are the powerful, the opulent, the merry, the loved, the victorious of God's kingdom,—to be filled with good things, to laugh for very delight, to be honoured and sought and cherished!

But such as have their poor consolation in this life—alas for them!—for those who have yet to learn what hunger is! for those whose laughter is as the crackling of thorns! for those who have loved and gathered the praises of men! for the rich, the jocund, the full-fed!

Silent-footed evil is on its way to seize them. Dives must go without; Lazarus must have. God's education makes use of terrible extremes. There are last that shall be first, and first that shall be last.

The Lord knew what trials, what tortures even awaited his disciples after his death; he knew they would need every encouragement he could give them to keep their hearts strong, lest in some moment of dismay they should deny him. If they had denied him, where would our gospel be? If there are none able and ready to be crucified for him now, alas for the age to come! What a poor travesty of the good news of God will arrive at their doors!

Those whom our Lord felicitates are all the children of one family; and everything that can be called blessed or blessing comes of the same righteousness. If a disciple be blessed because of any one thing, every other blessing is either his, or on the way to become his; for he is on the way to receive the very righteousness of God. Each good thing opens the door to the one next it, so to all the rest. But as if these his assurances and promises and comfortings were not large enough; as if the mention of any condition whatever might discourage some humble man of heart with a sense of unfitness, with the fear, perhaps conviction that the promise was not for him; as if some one might say, 'Alas, I am proud, and neither poor in spirit nor meek; I am at times not at all hungry after righteousness; I am not half merciful, and am very ready to feel hurt and indignant: I am shut out from every blessing!' the Lord, knowing the multitudes that can urge nothing in their own favour, and sorely feel they are not blessed, looks abroad over the wide world of his brothers and sisters, and calls aloud, including in the boundless invitation every living soul with but the one qualification of unrest or discomfort, 'Come unto me all ye that labour and are heavy laden, and I will give you rest.'

THE YOKE OF JESUS.

At that time Jesus answered and said,—according to Luke, In that hour Jesus rejoiced in spirit, and said,—'I thank thee, O Father, Lord of heaven and earth, because thou hast hid these things from the wise and prudent, and hast revealed them unto babes. Even so, Father, for so it seemed good in thy sight.
'All things are delivered unto me of my father; and no man knoweth the son,'—according to Luke, 'who the son is,'—'but the father; neither knoweth any man the father,'—according to Luke, 'who the father is,'—'save the son, and he to whomsoever the son will reveal him.'—*Matthew* xi. 25-27; *Luke* x. 21-22.
'Come unto me, all ye that labour, and are heavy laden, and I will give you rest. Take my yoke upon you, and learn of me, for I am meek and lowly in heart; and ye shall find rest unto your souls. For my yoke is easy, and my burden is light.' *Matthew* xi. 28-30.

The words of the Lord in the former two of these paragraphs, are represented, both by Matthew and by Luke, as spoken after the denunciation of the cities of Chorazin, Bethsaida, and Capernaum; only in

Luke's narrative, the return of the seventy is mentioned between; and there the rejoicing of the Lord over the Father's revelation of himself to babes, appears to have reference to the seventy. The fact that the return of the seventy is not mentioned elsewhere, leaves us free to suppose that the words were indeed spoken on that occasion. The circumstances, however, as circumstances, are to us of little importance, not being necessary to the understanding of the words.

The Lord makes no complaint against the wise and prudent; he but recognizes that they are not those to whom his father reveals his best things; for which fact and the reasons of it, he thanks, or praises his father. 'I bless thy will: I see that thou art right: I am of one mind with thee:' something of each of these phases of meaning seems to belong to the Greek word.

'But why not reveal true things first to the wise? Are they not the fittest to receive them?' Yes, if these things and their wisdom lie in the same region—not otherwise. No amount of knowledge or skill in physical science, will make a man the fitter to argue a metaphysical question; and the wisdom of this world, meaning by the term, the philosophy of prudence, self-protection, precaution, specially unfits a man for receiving what the Father has to reveal: in proportion to our care about our own well being, is our incapability of understanding and welcoming the care of the Father. The wise and the prudent, with all their energy of thought, could never see the things of the Father sufficiently to recognize them as true. Their sagacity labours in earthly things, and so fills their minds with their own questions and conclusions, that they cannot see the eternal foundations God has laid in man, or the consequent necessities of their own nature. They are proud of finding out things, but the things they find out are all less than themselves. Because, however, they have discovered them, they imagine such things the goal of the human intellect. If they grant there may be things beyond those, they either count them beyond their reach, or declare themselves uninterested in them: for the wise and prudent, they do not exist. They work only to gather by the senses, and deduce from what they have so gathered, the prudential, the probable, the expedient, the protective. They never think of the essential, of what in itself must be. They are cautious, wary, discreet, judicious, circumspect, provident, temporizing. They have no enthusiasm, and are shy of all forms of it—a clever, hard, thin people, who take *things* for the universe, and love of facts for love of truth. They know nothing deeper in man than mere surface mental facts and their relations. They do not perceive, or they turn away from any truth which the intellect cannot formulate. Zeal for God will never eat them up: why should it? he is not interesting to them: theology may be; to such men religion means theology. How should the treasure of the Father be open to such? In their hands his rubies would draw in their fire, and cease to glow. The roses of paradise in their gardens would blow withered. They never go beyond the porch of the temple; they are not sure whether there be any *adytum*, and they do not care to go in and see: why indeed should they? it would but be to turn and come out again. Even when they know their duty, they must take it to pieces, and consider the grounds of its claim before they will render it obedience. All those evil doctrines about God that work misery and madness, have their origin in the brains of the wise and prudent, not in the hearts of the children. These wise and prudent, careful to make the words of his messengers rime with their conclusions, interpret the great heart of God, not by their own hearts, but by their miserable intellects; and, postponing the obedience which alone can give power to the understanding, press upon men's minds their wretched interpretations of the will of the Father, instead of the doing of that will upon their hearts. They call their philosophy the truth of God, and say men must hold it, or stand outside. They are the slaves of the letter in all its weakness and imperfection,— and will be until the spirit of the Word, the spirit of obedience shall set them free.

The babes must beware lest the wise and prudent come between them and the Father. They must yield no claim to authority over their belief, made by man or community, by church any more than by synagogue. That alone is for them to believe which the Lord reveals to their souls as true; that alone is it possible for them to believe with what he counts belief. The divine object for which teacher or church exists, is the persuasion of the individual heart to come to Jesus, the spirit, to be taught what he alone can teach.

Terribly has his gospel suffered in the mouths of the wise and prudent: how would it be faring now, had its first messages been committed to persons of repute, instead of those simple fishermen? It would be nowhere, or, if anywhere, unrecognizable. From the first we should have had a system founded on a human interpretation of the divine gospel, instead of the gospel itself, which would have disappeared. As it is, we have had one dull miserable human system after another usurping its place; but, thank God, the gospel remains! The little child, heedless of his trailing cloud of glory, and looking about him aghast in an unknown world, may yet see and run to the arms open to the children. How often has not some symbol employed in the

New Testament been forced into the service of argument for one or another contemptible scheme of redemption, which were no redemption; while the truth for the sake of which the symbol was used, the thing meant to be conveyed by it, has lain unregarded beside the heap of rubbish! Had the wise and prudent been the confidants of God, I repeat, the letter would at once have usurped the place of the spirit; the ministering slave would have been set over the household; a system of religion, with its rickety, malodorous plan of salvation, would not only have at once been put in the place of a living Christ, but would yet have held that place. The great brother, the human God, the eternal Son, the living one, would have been as utterly hidden from the tearful eyes and aching hearts of the weary and heavy-laden, as if he had never come from the deeps of love to call the children home out of the shadows of a self-haunted universe. But the Father revealed the Father's things to his babes; the babes loved, and began to do them, therewith began to understand them, and went on growing in the knowledge of them and in the power of communicating them; while to the wise and prudent, the deepest words of the most babe-like of them all, John Boanerges, even now appear but a finger-worn rosary of platitudes. The babe understands the wise and prudent, but is understood only by the babe.

The Father, then, revealed his things to babes, because the babes were his own little ones, uncorrupted by the wisdom or the care of this world, and therefore able to receive them. The others, though his children, had not begun to be like him, therefore could not receive them. The Father's things could not have got anyhow into their minds without leaving all their value, all their spirit, outside the unchildlike place. The babes are near enough whence they come, to understand a little how things go in the presence of their father in heaven, and thereby to interpret the words of the Son. The child who has not yet 'walked above a mile or two from' his 'first love,' is not out of touch with the mind of his Father. Quickly will he seal the old bond when the Son himself, the first of the babes, the one perfect babe of God, comes to lead the children out of the lovely 'shadows of eternity' into the land of the 'white celestial thought.' As God is the one only real father, so is it only to God that any one can be a perfect child. In his garden only can childhood blossom.

The leader of the great array of little ones, himself, in virtue of his firstborn childhood, the first recipient of the revelations of his father, having thus given thanks, and said why he gave thanks, breaks out afresh, renewing expression of delight that God had willed it thus:

'Even so, father, for so it seemed good in thy sight!' I venture to trans-late, 'Yea, O Father, for thus came forth satisfaction before thee!' and think he meant, 'Yea, Father, for thereat were all thy angels filled with satisfaction,' The babes were the prophets in heaven, and the angels were glad to find it was to be so upon the earth also; they rejoiced to see that what was bound in heaven, was bound on earth; that the same principle held in each. Compare Matt. xviii. 10 and 14; also Luke xv. 10. 'See that ye despise not one of these little ones; for I say unto you that their angels in heaven do always behold the face of my father which is in heaven.... Thus it is not the will before your father which is in heaven,'—*among the angels who stand before him*, I think he means,—'that one of these little ones should perish.' 'Even so, I say unto you, there is joy in the presence of the angels of God over one sinner that repenteth.'

Having thus thanked his father that he has done after his own 'good and acceptable and perfect will', he turns to his disciples, and tells them that he knows the Father, being his Son, and that he only can re-veal the Father to the rest of his children: 'All things are delivered unto me of my father; and no one knoweth the son but the father; neither knoweth any one the father save the son, and he to whomsoever the son willeth to reveal him.' It is almost as if his mention of the babes brought his thoughts back to himself and his father, between whom lay the secret of all life and all sending—yea, all loving. The relation of the Father and the Son contains the idea of the universe. Jesus tells his disciples that his father had no secrets from him; that he knew the Fa-ther as the Father knew him. The Son must know the Father; he only could know him—and knowing, he could reveal him; the Son could make the other, the imperfect children, know the Father, and so be-come such as he. All things were given unto him by the Father, because he was the Son of the Father: for the same reason he could reveal the things of the Father to the child of the Father. The child-relation is the one eternal, ever enduring, never changing relation.

Note that, while the Lord here represents the knowledge his father and he have each of the other as limited to themselves, the statement is one of fact only, not of design or intention: his presence in the world is for the removal of that limitation. The Father knows the Son and sends him to us that we may know him; the Son knows the Father, and dies to reveal him. The glory of God's mysteries is—that they are for his children to look into.

When the Lord took the little child in the presence of his disciples, and declared him his representative, he made him the representative of his father also; but the eternal child alone can reveal him. To reveal is immeasurably more than to represent; it is to present to the eyes that know the true when they see it. Jesus represented God; the spirit of Jesus reveals God. The represented God a man may refuse; many refused the Lord; the revealed God no one can refuse; to see God and to love him are one. He can be revealed only to the child; perfectly, to the pure child only. All the discipline of the world is to make men children, that God may be revealed to them.

No man, when first he comes to himself, can have any true knowledge of God; he can only have a desire after such knowledge. But while he does not know him at all, he cannot become in his heart God's child; so the Father must draw nearer to him. He sends therefore his first born, who does know him, is exactly like him, and can represent him perfectly. Drawn to him, the children receive him, and then he is able to reveal the Father to them. No wisdom of the wise can find out God; no words of the God-loving can reveal him. The simplicity of the whole natural relation is too deep for the philosopher. The Son alone can reveal God; the child alone understand him. The elder brother companies with the younger, and makes him yet more a child like himself. He interpenetrates his willing companion with his obedient glory. He lets him see how he delights in his father, and lets him know that God is his father too. He rouses in his little brother the sense of their father's will; and the younger, as he hears and obeys, begins to see that his elder brother must be the very image of their father. He becomes more and more of a child, and more and more the Son reveals to him the Father. For he knows that to know the Father is the one thing needful to every child of the Father, the one thing to fill the divine gulf of his necessity. To see the Father is the cry of every child-heart in the universe of the Father—is the need, where not the cry, of every living soul. Comfort yourselves then, brothers and sisters; he to whom the Son will reveal him shall know the Father; and the Son came to us that he might reveal him. 'Eternal Brother,' we cry, 'show us the Father. Be thyself to us, that in thee we may know him. We too are his children: let the other children share with thee in the things of the Father.'

Having spoken to his father first, and now to his disciples, the Lord turns to the whole world, and lets his heart overflow:—St Matthew alone has saved for us the eternal cry:—'Come unto me all ye that labour and are heavy laden, and I will give you rest.'—'I know the Father; come then to me, all ye that labour and are heavy laden.' He does not here call those who want to know the Father; his cry goes far beyond them; it reaches to the ends of the earth. He calls those who are weary; those who do not know that ignorance of the Father is the cause of all their labour and the heaviness of their burden. 'Come unto me,' he says, 'and I will give you rest.'

This is the Lord's own form of his gospel, more intensely personal and direct, at the same time of yet wider inclusion, than that which, at Nazareth, he appropriated from Isaiah; differing from it also in this, that it is interfused with strongest persuasion to the troubled to enter into and share his own eternal rest. I will turn his argument a little. 'I have rest because I know the Father. Be meek and lowly of heart toward him as I am; let him lay his yoke upon you as he lays it on me. I do his will, not my own. Take on you the yoke that I wear; be his child like me; become a babe to whom he can reveal his wonders. Then shall you too find rest to your souls; you shall have the same peace I have; you will be weary and heavy laden no more. I find my yoke easy, my burden light.'

We must not imagine that, when the Lord says, 'Take my yoke upon you,' he means a yoke which he lays on those that come to him; 'my yoke' is the yoke he wears himself, the yoke his father lays upon him, the yoke out of which, that same moment, he speaks, bearing it with glad patience. 'You must take on you the yoke I have taken: the Father lays it upon us.'

The best of the good wine remains; I have kept it to the last. A friend pointed out to me that the Master does not mean we must take on us a yoke like his; we must take on us the very yoke he is carrying.

Dante, describing how, on the first terrace of Purgatory, he walked stooping, to be on a level with Oderisi, who went bowed to the ground by the ponderous burden of the pride he had cherished on earth, says— 'I went walking with this heavy-laden soul, just as oxen walk in the yoke': this picture almost always comes to me with the words of the Lord, 'Take my yoke upon you, and learn of me.' Their intent is, 'Take the other end of my yoke, doing as I do, being as I am.' Think of it a moment:—to walk in the same yoke with the Son of Man, doing the same labour with him, and having the same feeling common to him and us! This, and nothing else, is offered the man who would have rest to his soul; is required of the man who would know the Father; is by the Lord pressed upon him to whom he would give the same peace which pervades and sustains his own eternal heart.

But a yoke is for drawing withal: what load is it the Lord is drawing? Wherewith is the cart laden which he would have us help him draw? With what but the will of the eternal, the perfect Father? How should the Father honour the Son, but by giving him his will to embody in deed, by making him hand to his father's heart!—and hardest of all, in bringing home his children! Specially in drawing this load must his yoke-fellow share. How to draw it, he must learn of him who draws by his side.

Whoever, in the commonest duties that fall to him, does as the Father would have him do, bears His yoke along with Jesus; and the Father takes his help for the redemption of the world—for the deliverance of men from the slavery of their own rubbish-laden waggons, into the liberty of God's husbandmen. Bearing the same yoke with Jesus, the man learns to walk step for step with him, drawing, drawing the cart laden with the will of the father of both, and rejoicing with the joy of Jesus. The glory of existence is to take up its burden, and exist for Existence eternal and supreme—for the Father who does his divine and perfect best to impart his glad life to us, making us sharers of that nature which is bliss, and that labour which is peace. He lives for us; we must live for him. The little ones must take their full share in the great Father's work: his work is the business of the family.

Starts thy soul, trembles thy brain at the thought of such a burden as the will of the eternally creating, eternally saving God? 'How shall mortal man walk in such a yoke,' sayest thou, 'even with the Son of God bearing it also?'

Why, brother, sister, it is the only burden bearable—the only burden that can be borne of mortal! Under any other, the lightest, he must at last sink outworn, his very soul gray with sickness!

He on whom lay the other half of the burden of God, the weight of his creation to redeem, says, 'The yoke I bear is easy; the burden I draw is light'; and this he said, knowing the death he was to die. The yoke did not gall his neck, the burden did not overstrain his sinews, neither did the goal on Calvary fright him from the straight way thither. He had the will of the Father to work out, and that will was his strength as well as his joy. He had the same will as his father. To him the one thing worth living for, was the share the love of his father gave him in his work. He loved his father even to the death of the cross, and eternally beyond it.

When we give ourselves up to the Father as the Son gave himself, we shall not only find our yoke easy and our burden light, but that they communicate ease and lightness; not only will they not make us weary, but they will give us rest from all other weariness. Let us not waste a moment in asking how this can be; the only way to know that, is to take the yoke on us. That rest is a secret for every heart to know, for never a tongue to tell. Only by having it can we know it. If it seem impossible to take the yoke on us, let us attempt the impossible; let us lay hold of the yoke, and bow our heads, and try to get our necks under it. Giving our Father the opportunity, he will help and not fail us. He is helping us every moment, when least we think we need his help; when most we think we do, then may we most boldly, as most earnestly we must, cry for it. What or how much his creatures can do or bear, God only understands; but when most it seems impossible to do or bear, we must be most confident that he will neither demand too much, nor fail with the vital creator-help. That help will be there when wanted—that is, the moment it can be help. To be able beforehand to imagine ourselves doing or bearing, we have neither claim nor need.

It is vain to think that any weariness, however caused, any burden, however slight, may be got rid of otherwise than by bowing the neck to the yoke of the Father's will. There can be no other rest for heart and soul that he has created. From every burden, from every anxiety, from all dread of shame or loss, even loss of love itself, that yoke will set us free.

These words of the Lord—so many as are reported in common by St Matthew and St Luke, namely his thanksgiving, and his statement concerning the mutual knowledge of his father and himself, meet me like a well known face unexpectedly encountered: they come to me like a piece of heavenly bread cut from the gospel of St John. The words are not in that gospel, and in St Matthew's and St Luke's there is nothing more of the kind—in St Mark's nothing like them. The passage seems to me just one solitary flower testifying to the presence in the gospels of Matthew and Luke of the same root of thought and feeling which everywhere blossoms in that of John. It looks as if it had crept out of the fourth gospel into the first and third, and seems a true sign, though no proof, that, however much the fourth be unlike the other gospels, they have all the same origin. Some disciple was able to remember one such word of which the promised comforter brought many to the remembrance of John. I do not see how the more phenomenal gospels are ever to be understood, save through a right perception of the relation in which the Lord stands to his father, which relation is the main subject of the gospel according to St John.

As to the loving cry of the great brother to the whole weary world which Matthew alone has set down, I seem aware of a certain indescribable individuality in its tone, distinguishing it from all his other sayings on record.

THE YOKE OF JESUS.

Those who come at the call of the Lord, and take the rest he offers them, learning of him, and bearing the yoke of the Father, are the salt of the earth, the light of the world.

THE SALT AND THE LIGHT OF THE WORLD.

'Ye are the salt of the earth; but if the salt have lost his savour, wherewith shall it be salted? It is thenceforth good for nothing, but to be cast out, and to be trodden under foot of men. Ye are the light of the world. A city that is set on an hill, cannot be hid. Neither do men light a candle, and put it under a bushel, but on a candlestick, and it giveth light unto all that are in the house. Let your light so shine before men, that they may see your good works, and glorify your father which is in heaven.'—*Matthew* v. 3-16.

The Lord knew these men, and had their hearts in his hand; else would he have told them they were the salt of the earth and the light of the world? They were in danger, it is true, of pluming themselves on what he had said of them, of taking their importance to their own credit, and seeing themselves other than God saw them. Yet the Lord does not hesitate to call his few humble disciples the salt of the earth; and every century since has borne witness that such indeed they were—that he spoke of them but the simple fact. Where would the world be now but for their salt and their light! The world that knows neither their salt nor their light may imagine itself now at least greatly retarded by the long-drawn survival of their influences; but such as have chosen aspiration and not ambition, will cry, But for those men, whither should we at this moment be bound! Their Master set them to be salt against corruption, and light against darkness; and our souls answer and say, Lord, they have been the salt, they have been the light of the world!

No sooner has he used the symbol of the salt, than the Lord proceeds to supplement its incompleteness. They were salt which must remember that it is salt; which must live salt, and choose salt, and be salt. For the whole worth of salt lies in its being salt; and all the saltness of the moral salt lies in the will to be salt. To lose its saltness, then, is to cease to exist, save as a vile thing whose very being is unjustifiable. What is to be done with saltless salt!—with such as would teach religion, and know not God!

Having thus carried the figure as far as it will serve him, the Master changes it for another, which he can carry farther. For salt only preserves from growing bad; it does not cause anything to grow better. His disciples are the salt of the world, but they are more. Therefore, having warned the human salt to look to itself that it be indeed salt, he proceeds: 'Ye are the light of the world, a city, a candle,' and so resumes his former path of persuasion and enforcement: 'It is so, therefore make it so.'—'Ye are the salt of the earth; therefore be salt.'—'Ye are the light of the world; therefore shine.'—'Ye are a city; be seen upon your hill.'—'Ye are the Lord's candles; let no bushels cover you. Let your light shine.' Every disciple of the Lord must be a preacher of righteousness.

Cities are the best lighted portions of the world; and perhaps the Lord meant, 'You are a live city, therefore light up your city.' Some connection of the city with light seems probably in his thought, seeing the allusion to the city on the hill comes in the midst of what he says about light in relation to his disciples as the light of the world. Anyhow the city is the best circle in which, and the best centre from which to diffuse moral light. A man brooding in the desert may find the very light of light, but he must go to the city to let it shine.

From the general idea of light, however, associated with the city as visible to all the country around, the Lord turns at once, in this probably fragmentary representation of his words, to the homelier, the more individual and personally applicable figure of the lamp: 'Neither do men light a lamp, and put it under a bushel, but on a lampstand, and it giveth light to all that are in the house,'

Here let us meditate a moment. For what is a lamp or a man lighted? For them that need light, therefore for all. A candle is not lighted for itself; neither is a man. The light that serves self only, is no true light; its one virtue is that it will soon go out. The bushel needs to be

559

lighted, but not by being put over the lamp. The man's own soul needs to be lighted, but light for itself only, light covered by the bushel, is darkness whether to soul or bushel. Light unshared is darkness. To be light indeed, it must shine out. It is of the very essence of light, that it is for others. The thing is true of the spiritual as of the physical light—of the truth as of its type.

The lights of the world are live lights. The lamp that the Lord kindles is a lamp that can will to shine, a soul that must shine. Its true relation to the spirits around it—to God and its fellows, is its light. Then only does it fully shine, when its love, which is its light, shows it to all the souls within its scope, and all those souls to each other, and so does its part to bring all together toward one. In the darkness each soul is alone; in the light the souls are a family. Men do not light a lamp to kill it with a bushel, but to set it on a stand, that it may give light to all that are in the house. The Lord seems to say, 'So have I lighted you, not that you may shine for yourselves, but that you may give light unto all. I have set you like a city on a hill, that the whole earth may see and share in your light. Shine therefore; so shine before men, that they may see your good things and glorify your father for the light with which he has lighted you. Take heed to your light that it be such, that it so shine, that in you men may see the Father—may see your works so good, so plainly his, that they recognize his presence in you, and thank him for you.' There was the danger always of the shadow of the self-bushel clouding the lamp the Father had lighted; and the moment they ceased to show the Father, the light that was in them was darkness. God alone is the light, and our light is the shining of his will in our lives. If our light shine at all, it must be, it can be only in showing the Father; nothing is light that does not bear him witness. The man that sees the glory of God, would turn sick at the thought of glorifying his own self, whose one only possible glory is to shine with the glory of God. When a man tries to shine from the self that is not one with God and filled with his light, he is but making ready for his own gathering contempt. The man who, like his Lord, seeks not his own, but the will of him who sent him, he alone shines. He who would shine in the praises of men, will, sooner or later, find himself but a Gideon's-pitcher left broken on the field.

Let us bestir ourselves then to keep this word of the Lord; and to this end inquire how we are to let our light shine.

To the man who does not try to order his thoughts and feelings and judgments after the will of the Father, I have nothing to say; he can have no light to let shine. For to let our light shine is to see that in every, even the smallest thing, our lives and actions correspond to what we know of God; that, as the true children of our father in heaven, we do everything as he would have us do it. Need I say that to let our light shine is to be just, honourable, true, courteous, more careful over the claim of our neighbour than our own, as knowing ourselves in danger of overlooking it, and not bound to insist on every claim of our own! The man who takes no count of what is fair, friendly, pure, unselfish, lovely, gracious,—where is his claim to call Jesus his master? where his claim to Christianity? What saves his claim from being merest mockery?

The outshining of any human light must be obedience to truth recognized as such; our first show of light as the Lord's disciples must be in doing the things he tells us. Naturally thus we declare him our master, the ruler of our conduct, the enlightener of our souls; and while in the doing of his will a man is learning the loveliness of righteousness, he can hardly fail to let some light shine across the dust of his failures, the exhalations from his faults. Thus will his disciples shine as lights in the world, holding forth the Word of life.

To shine, we must keep in his light, sunning our souls in it by thinking of what he said and did, and would have us think and do. So shall we drink the light like some diamonds, keep it, and shine in the dark. Doing his will, men will see in us that we count the world his, hold that his will and not ours must be done in it. Our very faces will then shine with the hope of seeing him, and being taken home where he is. Only let us remember that trying to look what we ought to be, is the beginning of hypocrisy.

If we do indeed expect better things to come, we must let our hope appear. A Christian who looks gloomy at the mention of death, still more, one who talks of his friends as if he had lost them, turns the bushel of his little-faith over the lamp of the Lord's light. Death is but our visible horizon, and our look ought always to be focussed beyond it. We should never talk as if death were the end of anything.

To let our light shine, we must take care that we have no respect for riches: if we have none, there is no fear of our showing any. To treat the poor man with less attention or cordiality than the rich, is to show ourselves the servants of Mammon. In like manner we must lay no value on the praise of men, or in any way seek it. We must honour no man because of intellect, fame, or success. We must not shrink, in fear of the judgment of men, from doing openly what we hold right; or at all acknowledge as a law-giver what calls itself Society, or harbour the least anxiety for its approval.

In business, the custom of the trade must be understood by both contracting parties, else it can have no place, either as law or excuse, with the disciple of Jesus. The man to whom business is one thing and religion another, is not a disciple. If he refuses to harmonize them by making his business religion, he has already chosen Mammon; if he thinks not to settle the question, it is settled. The most futile of all human endeavours is, to serve God and Mammon. The man who makes the endeavour, betrays his Master in the temple and kisses him in the garden; takes advantage of him in the shop, and offers him 'divine service!' on Sunday. His very church-going is but a further service of Mammon! But let us waste no strength in despising such men; let us rather turn the light upon ourselves: are we not in some way denying him? Is our light bearing witness? Is it shining before men so that they glorify God for it? If it does not shine, it is darkness. In the darkness which a man takes for light, he will thrust at the heart of the Lord himself.

He who goes about his everyday duty as the work the Father has given him to do, is he who lets his light shine. But such a man will not be content with this: he must yet let his light shine. Whatever makes his heart glad, he will have his neighbour share. The body is a lantern; it must not be a dark lantern; the glowing heart must show in the shining face. His glad thought may not be one to impart to his neighbour, but he must not quench the vibration of its gladness ere it reach him. What shall we say of him who comes from his closet, his mountain-top, with such a veil over his face as masks his very humanity? Is it with the Father that man has had communion, whose every movement is self-hampered, and in whose eyes dwell no smiles for the people of his house? The man who receives the quiet attentions, the divine ministrations, of wife or son or daughter, without token of pleasure, without sign of gratitude, can hardly have been with Jesus. Or can he have been with him, and have left him behind in his closet? If his faith in God take from a man his cheerfulness, how shall the face of a man ever shine? And why are they always glad before the face of the Father in heaven? It is true that pain or inward grief may blameless banish all smiling, but even heaviness of heart has no right so to tumble the bushel over the lamp that no ray can get out to tell that love is yet burning within. The man must at least let his dear ones know that something else than displeasure with them is the cause of his clouded countenance.

What a sweet colour the divine light takes to itself in courtesy, whose perfection is the recognition of every man as a temple of the

562

THE SALT AND THE LIGHT OF THE WORLD.

living God. Sorely ruined, sadly defiled the temple may be, but if God had left it, it would be a heap and not a house.

Next to love, specially will the light shine out in fairness. What light can he have in him who is always on his own side, and will never descry reason or right on that of his adversary? And certainly, if he that showeth mercy, as well he that showeth justice, ought to do it with cheerfulness.

But if all our light shine out, and none of our darkness, shall we not be in utmost danger of hypocrisy? Yes, if we but hide our darkness, and do not strive to slay it with our light: what way have we to show it, while struggling to destroy it? Only when we cherish evil, is there hypocrisy in hiding it. A man who is honestly fighting it and showing it no quarter, is already conqueror in Christ, or will soon be—and more than innocent. But our good feelings, those that make for righteousness and unity, we ought to let shine; they claim to commune with the light in others. Many parents hold words unsaid which would lift hundred-weights from the hearts of their children, yea, make them leap for joy. A stern father and a silent mother make mournful, or, which is far worse, hard children. Need I add that, if any one, hearing the injunction to let his light shine, makes himself shine instead, it is because the light is not in him!

But what shall I say of such as, in the name of religion, let only their darkness out—the darkness of worshipped opinion, the darkness of lip-honour and disobedience! Such are those who tear asunder the body of Christ with the explosives of dispute, on the plea of such a unity as alone they can understand, namely a paltry uniformity. What have not the 'good church-man' and the 'strong dissenter' to answer for, who, hiding what true light they have, if indeed they have any, each under the bushel of his party-spirit, radiate only repulsion! There is no schism, none whatever, in using diverse forms of thought or worship: true honesty is never schismatic. The real schismatic is the man who turns away love and justice from the neighbour who holds theories in religious philosophy, or as to church-constitution, different from his own; who denies or avoids his brother because he follows not with him; who calls him a schismatic because he prefers this or that mode of public worship not his. The other *may* be schismatic; he himself certainly *is*. He walks in the darkness of opinion, not in the light of life, not in the faith which worketh by love. Worst of all is division in the name of Christ who came to make one. Neither Paul nor Apollos nor Cephas would—least of all will Christ be the leader of any party save that of his own elect, the party of love—of love which suffereth long and is kind; which envieth not, is not puffed up, doth not behave itself unseemly, seeketh not its own, is not easily provoked, thinketh no evil, rejoiceth not in iniquity, but rejoiceth in the truth, beareth all things, believeth all things, hopeth all things, endureth all things.

'Let your light shine,' says the Lord:—if I have none, the call cannot apply to me; but I must bethink me, lest, in the night I am cherishing about me, the Lord come upon me like a thief. There may be those, however, and I think they are numerous, who, having some, or imagining they have much light, yet have not enough to know the duty of letting it shine on their neighbours. The Lord would have his men so alive with his light, that it should for ever go flashing from each to all, and all, with eternal response, keep glorifying the Father. Dost thou look for a good time coming, friend, when thou shalt know as thou art known? Let the joy of thy hope stream forth upon thy neighbours. Fold them round in that which maketh thyself glad. Let thy nature grow more expansive and communicative. Look like the man thou art—a man who knows something very good. Thou believest thyself on the way to the heart of things: walk so, shine so, that all that see thee shall want to go with thee.

What light issues from such as make their faces long at the very name of death, and look and speak as if it were the end of all things and the worst of evils? Jesus told his men not to fear death; told them his friends should go to be with him; told them they should live in the house of his father and their father; and since then he has risen himself from the tomb, and gone to prepare a place for them: who, what are these miserable refusers of comfort? Not Christians, surely! Oh, yes, they are Christians! 'They are gone,' they say, 'to be for ever with the Lord;' and then they weep and lament, and seem more afraid of starting to join them than of aught else under the sun! To the last attainable moment they cling to what they call life. They are children—were there ever any other such children?—who hang crying to the skirts of their mother, and will not be lifted to her bosom. They are not of Paul's mind: to be with Him is not better! They worship their physician; and their prayer to the God of their life is to spare them from more life. What sort of Christians are they? Where shines their light? Alas for thee, poor world, hadst thou no better lights than these!

You who have light, show yourselves the sons and daughters of Light, of God, of Hope—the heirs of a great completeness. Freely let your light shine.

Only take heed that ye do not your righteousness before men, to be seen of them.

THE RIGHT HAND AND THE LEFT.

Take heed that ye do not your righteousness before men to be seen of them; otherwise ye have no reward of your father which is in heaven.... But when thou doest alms, let not thy left hand know what thy right hand doeth; that thine alms may be in secret; and thy father which seeth in secret, himself shall reward thee.— *Matthew* vi. 1,3.

Let your light out freely, that men may see it, but not that men may see you. If I do anything, not because it has to be done, not because God would have it so, not that I may do right, not because it is honest, not that I love the thing, not that I may be true to my Lord, not that the truth may be recognized as truth and as his, but that I may be seen as the doer, that I may be praised of men, that I may gain repute or fame; be the thing itself ever so good, I may look to men for my reward, for there is none for me with the Father. If, that light being my pleasure, I do it that the light may shine, and that men may know *the* Light, the father of lights, I do well; but if I do it that I may be seen shining, that the light may be noted as emanating from me and not from another, then am I of those that seek glory of men, and worship Satan; the light that through me may possibly illuminate others, will, in me and for me, be darkness.

But when thou doest alms, let not thy left hand know what thy right hand doeth.

How, then, am I to let my light shine, if I take pains to hide what I do?

The injunction is not to hide what you do from others, but to hide it from yourself. The Master would have you not plume yourself upon it, not cherish the thought that you have done it, or confer with yourself in satisfaction over it. You must not count it to your praise. A man must not desire to be satisfied with himself. His right hand must not seek the praise of his left hand. His doing must not invite his after-thinking. The right hand must let the thing done go, as a thing done-with. We must meditate nothing either as a fine thing for us to do, or a fine thing for us to have done. We must not imagine any merit in us: it would be to love a lie, for we can have none; there is no such thing possible. Is there anything to be proud of in refusing to worship the devil? Is it a grand thing, is it a meritorious thing, not to be vile? When we have done all, we are unprofitable servants. Our very best is but decent. What more could it be? Why then think of it as anything more? What things could we or any one do, worthy of being brooded over as possessions. Good to do, they were; bad to pride ourselves upon, they are. Why should a man meditate with satisfaction on having denied himself some selfish indulgence, any more than on having washed his hands? May we roll the rejection of a villainy as a sweet morsel under our tongues? They were the worst villains of all who could be proud of not having committed a villainy; and their pride would but render them the more capable of the villainy, when next the temptation to it came. Even if our supposed merit were of the positive order, and we did every duty perfectly, the moment we began to pride ourselves upon the fact, we should drop into a hell of worthlessness. What are we for but to do our duty? We must do it, and think nothing of ourselves for that, neither care what men think of us for anything. With the praise or blame of men we have nought to do. Their blame may be a good thing, their praise cannot be. But the worst sort of the praise of men is the praise we give ourselves. We must do nothing to be seen of ourselves. We must seek no approbation even, but that of God, else we shut the door of the kingdom from the outside. His approbation will but quicken our sense of unworthiness. What! seek the praise of men for being fair to our own brothers and sisters? What! seek the praise of God for laying our hearts at the feet of him to whom we utterly belong? There is no pride so mean—and all pride is absolutely, essentially mean—as the pride of being holier than our fellow, except the pride of being holy. Such imagined holiness is foulness. Religion itself in the hearts of the unreal, is a dead thing; what seems life in it, is the vermiculate life of a corpse.

THE RIGHT HAND AND THE LEFT.

There is one word in the context, as we have it in the authorized version, that used to trouble me, seeming to make its publicity a portion of the reward for doing certain right things in secret: I mean the word *openly*, at the ends of the fourth, the sixth, and the eighteenth verses, making the Lord seem to say, 'Avoid the praise of men, and thou shalt at length have the praise of men.'—'Thy father, which seeth in secret, shall reward thee openly.' *Thy reward shall be seen of men! and thou seen as the receiver of the reward!* In what other way could the word, then or now, be fairly understood? It must be the interpolation of some Jew scribe, who, even after learning a little of the Christ, continued unable to conceive as reward anything that did not draw part at least of its sweetness from the gazing eyes of the multitude. Glad was I to find that the word is not in the best manuscripts; and God be thanked that it is left out in the revised version. What shall we think of the daring that could interpolate it! But of like sort is the daring of much exposition of the Master's words. What men have not faith enough to receive, they will still dilute to the standard of their own faculty of reception. If any one say, 'Why did the Lord let the word remain there so long, if he never said it?' I answer: Perhaps that the minds of his disciples might be troubled at its presence, arise against it, and do him right by casting it out—and so Wisdom be justified of her children.

But there are some who, if the notion of reward is not naturally a trouble to them, yet have come to feel it such, because of the words of certain objectors who think to take a higher stand than the Christian, saying the idea of reward for doing right is a low, an unworthy idea. Now, verily, it would be a low thing for any child to do his father's will in the hope that his father would reward him for it; but it is quite another thing for a father whose child endeavours to please him, to let him know that he recognizes his childness toward him, and will be fatherly good to him. What kind of a father were the man who, because there could be no merit or desert in doing well, would not give his child a smile or a pleased word when he saw him trying his best? Would not such acknowledgment from the father be the natural correlate of the child's behaviour? and what would the father's smile be but the perfect reward of the child? Suppose the father to love the child so that he wants to give him everything, but dares not until his character is developed: must he not be glad, and show his gladness, at every shade of a progress that will at length set him free to throne his son over all that he has? 'I am an unprofitable servant,' says the man who has done his duty; but his lord, coming unexpectedly, and finding him at his post, girds himself, and makes him sit down to meat, and comes forth and serves him. How could the divine order of things, founded for growth and gradual betterment, hold and proceed without the notion of return for a thing done? Must there be only current and no tide? How can we be workers with God at his work, and he never say 'Thank you, my child'? Will he take joy in his success and give none? Is he the husbandman to take all the profit, and muzzle the mouth of his ox? When a man does work for another, he has his wages for it, and society exists by the dependence of man upon man through work and wages. The devil is not the inventor of this society; he has invented the notion of a certain degradation in work, a still greater in wages; and following this up, has constituted a Society after his own likeness, which despises work, leaves it undone, and so can claim its wages without disgrace.

If you say, 'No one ought to do right for the sake of reward,' I go farther and say, 'No man *can* do right for the sake of reward. A man may do a thing indifferent, he may do a thing wrong, for the sake of reward; but a thing in itself right, done for reward, would, in the very doing, cease to be right.' At the same time, if a man does right, he cannot escape being rewarded for it; and to refuse the reward, would be to refuse life, and foil the creative love. The whole question is of the kind of reward expected. What first reward for doing well, may I look for? To grow purer in heart, and stronger in the hope of at length seeing God. If a man be not after this fashion rewarded, he must perish. As to happiness or any lower rewards that naturally follow the first—is God to destroy the law of his universe, the divine sequence of cause and effect in order to say: 'You must do well, but you shall gain no good by it; you must lead a dull joyless existence to all eternity, that lack of delight may show you pure'? Could Love create with such end in view? Righteousness does not demand creation; it is Love, not Righteousness, that cannot live alone. The creature must already be, ere Righteousness can put in a claim. But, hearts and souls there, Love itself, which created for love and joy, presses the demand of Righteousness first.

A righteousness that created misery in order to up-hold itself, would be a righteousness that was unrighteous. God will die for righteousness, but never create for a joyless righteousness. To call into being the necessarily and hopelessly incomplete, would be to wrong creation in its very essence. To create for the knowledge of himself, and then not give himself, would be injustice even to cruelty; and if God give himself, what other reward—there can be no *further*—is not included, seeing he is Life and all her children—the All in all? It will take the utmost joy God can give, to let men know him; and what man, knowing him, would mind losing every other joy? Only what other joy could keep from entering, where the God of joy already dwelt? The law of the universe holds, and will hold, the name of the Father be praised:—'Whatsoever a man soweth, that shall he also reap.' 'They have sown the wind, and they shall reap the whirlwind.' 'He that soweth to his flesh, shall of the flesh reap corruption; but he that soweth to the spirit, shall of the spirit reap life everlasting.' 'Whosoever hath, to him shall be given, and he shall have more abundance; but whosoever hath not, from him shall be taken away even that he hath.'

To object to Christianity as selfish, is utter foolishness; Christianity alone gives any hope of deliverance from selfishness. Is it selfish to desire to love? Is it selfish to hope for purity and the sight of God? What better can we do for our neighbour than to become altogether righteous toward him? Will he not be the nearer sharing in the exceeding great reward of a return to the divine idea?

Where is the evil toward God, where the wrong to my neighbour, if I think sometimes of the joys to follow in the train of perfect loving? Is not the atmosphere of God, love itself, the very breath of the Father, wherein can float no thinnest pollution of selfishness, the only material wherewithal to build the airy castles of heaven? 'Creator,' the childlike heart might cry, 'give me all the wages, all the reward thy perfect father-heart can give thy unmeriting child. My fit wages may be pain, sorrow, humiliation of soul: I stretch out my hands to receive them. Thy reward will be to lift me out of the mire of self-love, and bring me nearer to thyself and thy children: welcome, divinest of good things! Thy highest reward is thy purest gift; thou didst make me for it from the first; thou, the eternal life, hast been labouring still to fit me for receiving it—the vision, the knowledge, the possession of thyself. I can seek but what thou waitest and watchest to give: I would be such into whom thy love can flow.'

It seems to me that the only merit that could live before God, is the merit of Jesus—who of himself, at once, untaught, unimplored, laid himself aside, and turned to the Father, refusing his life save in the Father. Like God, of himself he chose righteousness, and so merited to sit on the throne of God. In the same spirit he gave himself afterward to his father's children, and merited the power to transfuse the life-redeeming energy of his spirit into theirs: made perfect, he became the author of eternal salvation unto all them that obey him. But it is a word of little daring, that Jesus had no thought of merit in what he did—that he saw only what he had to be, what he must do.—I speak after the poor fashion of a man lost in what is too great for him, yet is his very life.—Where can be a man's merit in refusing to go down to an abyss of loss—loss of the right to be, loss of his father, loss of himself? Would Satan, with all the instincts and impulses of his origin in him, have *merited* eternal life by refusing to be a devil? Not the less would he have had eternal life; not the less would he have been wrapt in the love and confidence of the Father. He would have had his reward. I cannot imagine thing created meriting aught save by divine courtesy.

I suspect the notion of merit belongs to a low development, and the higher a man rises, the less will he find it worth a thought. Perhaps we shall come to see that it owes what being it has, to man, that it is a thing thinkable only by man. I suspect it is not a thought of the eternal mind, and has in itself no existence, being to God merely a thing thought by man.

2

The man, then, who does right, and seeks no praise from men, while he merits nothing, shall be rewarded by his Father, and his reward will be right precious to him.

We must let our light shine, make our faith, our hope, our love, manifest—that men may praise, not us for shining, but the Father for creating the light. No man with faith, hope, love, alive in his soul, could make the divine possessions a show to gain for himself the admiration of men: not the less must they appear in our words, in our looks, in our carriage—above all, in honourable, unselfish, hospitable, helpful deeds. Our light must shine in cheerfulness, in joy, yea, where a man has the gift, in merriment; in freedom from care save for one another, in interest in the things of others, in fearlessness and tenderness, in courtesy and graciousness. In our anger and indignation, specially, must our light shine. But we must give no quarter to the most shadowy thought of how this or that will look. From the faintest thought of the praise of men, we must turn away. No man can be the disciple of Christ and desire fame. To desire fame is ignoble; it is a beggarly greed. In the noble mind, it is the more of an infirmity. There is no aspiration in it—nothing but ambition. It is simply selfishness that would be proud if it could. Fame is the applause of the many, and the judgment of the many is foolish; therefore the greater the fame, the more is the foolishness that swells it, and the worse is the foolishness that longs after it. Aspiration is the sole escape from ambition. He who aspires—that is, does his endeavour to rise above himself—neither lusts to be higher than his neighbour, nor seeks to mount in his opinion. What light there is in him shines the more that he does nothing to be seen of men. He stands in the mist between the gulf and the glory, and looks upward. He loves not his own soul, but longs to be clean.

2

O Lord, the earnest expectation of thy creature waiteth for the manifestation of the sons of God.

THE HOPE OF THE UNIVERSE.

For the earnest expectation of the creature waiteth for the manifestation of the sons of God.—*Romans* viii. 19.

Let us try, through these words, to get at the idea in St Paul's mind for which they stand, and have so long stood. It can be no worthless idea they represent—no mere platitude, which a man, failing to understand it at once, may without loss leave behind him. The words mean something which Paul believes vitally associated with the life and death of his Master. He had seen Jesus with his bodily eyes, I think, but he had not seen him with those alone; he had seen and saw him with the real eyes, the eyes that do not see except they understand; and the sight of him had uplifted his whole nature—first his pure will for righteousness, and then his hoping imagination; and out of these, in the knowledge of Jesus, he spoke.

The letters he has left behind him, written in the power of this uplifting, have waked but poor ideas in poor minds; for words, if they seem to mean anything, must always seem to mean something within the scope of the mind hearing them. Words cannot convey the thought of a thinker to a no-thinker; of a largely aspiring and self-discontented soul, to a creature satisfied with his poverty, and counting his meagre faculty the human standard. Neither will they readily reveal the mind of one old in thought, to one who has but lately begun to think. The higher the reader's notion of what St Paul intends—the higher the idea, that is, which his words wake in him, the more likely is it to be the same which moved the man who had seen Jesus, and was his own no more. If a man err in his interpretation, it will hardly be by attributing to his words an intent too high.

First then, what does Paul, the slave of Christ, intend by 'the creature' or 'the creation'? If he means the *visible world*, he did not surely, and without saying so, mean to exclude the noblest part of it—the sentient! If he did, it is doubly strange that he should immediately attribute not merely sense, but conscious sense, to that part, the insentient, namely, which remained. If you say he does so but by a figure of speech, I answer that a figure that meant less than it said—and how much less would not this?—would be one altogether unworthy of the Lord's messenger.

First, I repeat, to exclude the sentient from the term common to both in the word *creation* or *creature*—and then to attribute the capabilities of the sentient to the insentient, as a mere figure to express the hopes of men with regard to the perfecting of the insentient for the comfort of men, were a violence as unfit in rhetoric as in its own nature. Take another part of the same utterance: 'For we know that the whole creation groaneth and travaileth in pain together until now:' is it not manifest that to interpret such words as referring to the mere imperfections of the insensate material world, would be to make of the phrase a worthless hyperbole? I am inclined to believe the apostle regarded the whole visible creation as, in far differing degrees of consciousness, a live outcome from the heart of the living one, who is all and in all: such view, at the same time, I do not care to insist upon; I only care to argue that the word *creature* or *creation* must include everything in creation that has sentient life. That I should in the class include a greater number of phenomena than a reader may be prepared to admit, will nowise affect the force of what I have to say, seeing my point is simply this: that in the term *creation*, Paul comprises all creatures capable of suffering; the condition of which sentient, therefore superior portion, gives him occasion to speak of the whole creation as suffering in the process of its divine evolution or development, groaning and travailing as in the pangs of giving birth to a better self, a nobler world. It is not necessary to the idea that the creation should know what it is groaning after, or wherein the higher condition constituting its deliverance must consist. The human race groans for deliverance: how much does the race know that its redemption lies in becoming one with the Father, and partaking of his glory? Here and there one of the race knows it—which is indeed a pledge for the race—but the race cannot be said to know its own lack, or to have even a far-off notion of what alone can stay its groaning. In like manner the whole creation is groaning after an unforeseen yet essential birth—groans with the necessity of being freed from a state that is but a transitional and not a true one, from a condition that nowise answers to the intent in which existence began. In both the lower creation and the higher, this same groaning of the fettered idea after a freer life, seems the first enforced decree of a holy fate, and itself the first movement of the hampered thing toward the liberty of another birth.

To believe that God made many of the lower creatures merely for prey, or to be the slaves of a slave, and writhe under the tyrannies of a cruel master who will not serve his own master; that he created and is creating an endless succession of them to reap little or no good of life but its cessation—a doctrine held by some, and practically accepted by multitudes—is to believe in a God who, so far as one portion at least of his creation is concerned, is a demon. But a creative demon is an absurdity; and were such a creator possible, he would not be God, but must one day be found and destroyed by the real God. Not the less the fact remains, that miserable suffering abounds among them, and that, even supposing God did not foresee how creation would turn out for them, the thing lies at his door. He has besides made them so far dumb that they cannot move the hearts of the oppressors into whose hands he has given them, telling how hard they find the world, how sore their life in it. The apostle takes up their case, and gives us material for an answer to such as blame God for their sad condition.

There are many, I suspect, who from the eighth chapter of St Paul's epistle to the Romans, gather this much and no more:—that the lower animals alive at the coming of the Lord, whensoever that may be, will thenceforward, with such as thereafter may come into existence, lead a happy life for the time allotted them! Strong champions of God, these profound believers! What lovers of life, what disciples of St Paul, nay, what disciples of Jesus, to whom such a gloss is consolation for the moans of a universe! Truly, the furnace of affliction they would extinguish thus, casts out the more an evil odour! For all the creatures who through ages of misery have groaned and travailed and died, to these mild Christians it is enough that they are dead, therefore, as they would argue, out of it now! 'It is well with them,' I seem to hear such say; 'they are mercifully dealt with; their sufferings are over; they had not to live on for ever in oppression. The God of their life has taken from them their past, and troubles them with no future!' It is true this were no small consolation concerning such as are gone away! Surely rest is better than ceaseless toil and pain! But what shall we say of such a heedless God as those Christians are content to worship! Is he a merciful God? Is he a loving God? How shall he die to escape the remorse of the authorship of so much misery? Our pity turns from the dead creature to the live creator who could live and know himself the maker of so many extinguished hearts, whose friend was—not he, but Death. Blessed be the name of the Father of Jesus, there is no such creator!

Be we have not to do with the dead only; there are those which live and suffer: is there no comfort concerning them, but that they too shall at length die and leave their misery? And what shall we say of those coming, and yet to come and pass—evermore issuing from the fountain of life, daily born into evil things? Will the consolation that they will soon die, suffice for the heart of the child who laments over his dead bird or rabbit, and would fain love that father in heaven who keeps on making the creatures? Alas, they are crowding in; they cannot help themselves; their misery is awaiting them! Would those Christians have me believe in a God who differentiates creatures from himself, only that they may be the prey of other creatures, or spend a few hours or years, helpless and lonely, speechless and without appeal, in merciless hands, then pass away into nothingness? I will not; in the name of Jesus, I will not. Had he not known something better, would he have said what he did about the father of men and the sparrows?

What many men call their beliefs, are but the prejudices they happen to have picked up: why should such believers waste a thought as to how their paltry fellow-inhabitants of the planet fare? Many indeed have all their lives been too busy making their human fellows groan and sweat for their own fancied well-being, to spare a thought for the fate of the yet more helpless. But there are not a few, who would be indignant at having their belief in God questioned, who yet seem greatly to fear imagining him better than he is: whether is it he or themselves they dread injuring by expecting too much of him? 'You see the plain facts of the case!' they say. 'There is no questioning them! What can be done for the poor things—except indeed you take the absurd notion into your head, that they too have a life beyond the grave?'

Why should such a notion seem to you absurd? I answer. The teachers of the nation have unwittingly, it seems to me through unbelief, wronged the animals deeply by their silence anent the thoughtless popular presumption that they have no hereafter; thus leaving them deprived of a great advantage to their position among men. But I suppose they too have taken it for granted that the Preserver of man and beast never had a thought of keeping one beast alive beyond a certain time; in which case heartless men might well argue he did not care how they wronged them, for he meant them no redress. Their immortality is no new faith with me, but as old as my childhood.

Do you believe in immortality for yourself? I would ask any reader who is not in sympathy with my hope for the animals. If not, I have no argument with you. But if you do, why not believe in it for them? Verily, were immortality no greater a thing for the animals than it seems for men to some who yet profess to expect it, I should scarce care to insist upon their share in it. But if the thought be anywise precious to you, is it essential to your enjoyment in it, that nothing less than yourself should share its realization? Are you the lowest kind of creature that *could* be permitted to live? Had God been of like heart with you, would he have given life and immortality to creatures so much less than himself as we? Are these not worth making immortal? How, then, were they worth calling out of the depth of no-being? It is a greater deed, to make be that which was not, than to seal it with an infinite immortality: did God do that which was not worth doing? What he thought worth making, you think not worth continuing made! You would have him go on for ever creating new things with one hand, and annihilating those he had made with the other—for I presume you would not prefer the earth to be without animals! If it were harder for God to make the former go on living, than to send forth new, then his creatures were no better than the toys which a child makes, and destroys as he makes them. For what good, for what divine purpose is the maker of the sparrow present at its death, if he does not care what becomes of it? What is he there for, I repeat, if he have no care that it go well with his bird in its dying, that it be neither comfortless nor lost in the abyss? If his presence be no good to the sparrow, are you very sure what good it will be to you when your hour comes? Believe it is not by a little only that the heart of the universe is tenderer, more loving, more just and fair, than yours or mine.

If you did not believe you were yourself to out-live death, I could not blame you for thinking all was over with the sparrow; but to believe in immortality for yourself, and not care to believe in it for the sparrow, would be simply hard-hearted and selfish. If it would make you happy to think there was life beyond death for the sparrow as well as for yourself, I would gladly help you at least to hope that there may be.

I know of no reason why I should not look for the animals to rise again, in the same sense in which I hope myself to rise again—which is, to reappear, clothed with another and better form of life than before. If the Father will raise his children, why should he not also raise those whom he has taught his little ones to love? Love is the one bond of the universe, the heart of God, the life of his children: if animals can be loved, they are loveable; if they can love, they are yet more plainly loveable: love is eternal; how then should its object perish? Must the very immortality of love divide the bond of love? Must the love live on for ever without its object? or worse still, must the love die with its object, and be eternal no more than it? What a mis-invented correlation in which the one side was eternal, the other, where not yet annihilated, constantly perishing! Is not our love to the animals a precious variety of love? And if God gave the creatures to us, that a new phase of love might be born in us toward another kind of life from the same fountain, why should the new life be more perishing than the new love? Can you imagine that, if, here-after, one of God's little ones were to ask him to give again one of the earth's old loves—kitten, or pony, or squirrel, or dog, which he had taken from him, the Father would say no? If the thing was so good that God made it for and gave it to the child at first who never asked for it, why should he not give it again to the child who prays for it because the Father had made him love it? What a child may ask for, the Father will keep ready.

That there are difficulties in the way of believing thus, I grant; that there are impossibilities, I deny. Perhaps the first difficulty that occurs is, the many forms of life which we cannot desire again to see. But while we would gladly keep the perfected forms of the higher animals, we may hope that those of many other kinds are as transitory as their bodies, belonging but to a stage of development. All animal forms tend to higher: why should not the individual, as well as the race, pass through stages of ascent. If I have myself gone through each of the typical forms of lower life on my way to the human—a supposition by antenatal history rendered probable—and therefore may have passed through any number of individual forms of life, I do not see why each of the lower animals should not as well pass upward through a succession of bettering embodiments. I grant that the theory requires another to complement it; namely, that those men and women, who do not even approximately fulfil the conditions of their elevated rank, who will not endeavour after the great human-divine idea, striving to ascend, are sent away back down to that stage of development, say of fish or insect or reptile, beyond which their moral nature has refused to advance. Who has not seen or known men who *appeared* not to have passed, or indeed in some things to have approached the development of the more human of the lower animals! Let those take care who look contemptuously upon the animals, lest, in misusing one of them, they misuse some ancestor of their own, sent back, as the one mercy for him, to reassume far past forms and conditions—far past in physical, that is, but not in moral development—and so have another opportunity of passing the self-constituted barrier. The suggestion may appear very ridiculous, and no doubt lends itself to humorous comment; but what if it should be true! what if the amused reader should himself be getting ready to follow the remanded ancestor! Upon it, however, I do not care to spend thought or time, least of all argument; what I care to press is the question—If we believe in the progress of creation as hitherto manifested, also in the marvellous changes of form that take place in every individual of certain classes, why should there be any difficulty in hoping that old lives may reappear in new forms? The typical soul reappears in higher formal type; why may not also the individual soul reappear in higher form?

Multitudes evidently count it safest to hold by a dull scheme of things: can it be because, like David in Browning's poem *Saul*, they dread lest they should worst the Giver by inventing better gifts than his? That we do not know, is the best reason for hoping to the full extent God has made possible to us. If then we go wrong, it will be in the direction of the right, and with such aberration as will be easier to correct than what must come of refusing to imagine, and leaving the dullest traditional prepossessions to rule our hearts and minds, with no claim but the poverty of their expectation from the paternal riches. Those that hope little cannot grow much. To them the very glory of God must be a small thing, for their hope of it is so small as not to be worth rejoicing in. That he is a faithful creator means nothing to them for far the larger portion of the creatures he has made! Truly their notion of faithfulness is poor enough; how then can their faith be strong! In the very nature of divine things, the common-place must be false. The stupid, self-satisfied soul, which cannot know its own stupidity, and will not trouble itself either to understand or to imagine, is the farthest behind of all the backward children in God's nursery.

As I say, then, I know no cause of reasonable difficulty in regard to the continued existence of the lower animals, except the present nature of some of them. But what Christian will dare to say that God does not care about them?—and he knows them as we cannot know them. Great or small, they are his. Great are all his results; small are all his beginnings. That we have to send many of his creatures out of this phase of their life because of their hurtfulness in this phase of ours, is to me no stumbling-block. The very fact that this has always had to be done, the long protracted combat of the race with such, and the constantly repeated though not invariable victory of the man, has had an essential and incalculable share in the development of humanity, which is the rendering of man capable of knowing God; and when their part to that end is no longer necessary, changed conditions may speedily so operate that the wolf shall dwell with the lamb, and the leopard lie down with the kid. The difficulty may go for nothing in view of the forces of that future with which this loving speculation concerns itself.

I would now lead my companion a little closer to what the apostle says in the nineteenth verse; to come closer, if we may, to the idea that burned in his heart when he wrote what we call the eighth chapter of his epistle to the Romans. Oh, how far ahead he seems, in his hope for the creation, of the footsore and halting brigade of Christians at present crossing the world! He knew Christ, and could therefore look into the will of the Father.

For the earnest expectation of the creature waiteth for the manifestation of the sons of God!

At the head of one of his poems, Henry Vaughan has this Latin translation of the verse: I do not know whether he found or made it, but it is closer to its sense than ours:—

'Etenim res creatae exerto capite observantes expectant revelationem filiorum Dei.'—'For the things created, watching with head thrust out, await the revelation of the sons of God.'

Why?

Because God has subjected the creation to vanity, in the hope that the creation itself shall be delivered from the bondage of corruption into the glorious liberty of the children of God. For this double deliverance—from corruption and the consequent subjection to vanity, the creation is eagerly watching.

The bondage of corruption God encounters and counteracts by subjection to vanity. Corruption is the breaking up of the essential idea; the falling away from the original indwelling and life-causing thought. It is met by the suffering which itself causes. That suffering is for redemption, for deliverance. It is the life in the corrupting thing that makes the suffering possible; it is the live part, not the corrupted part that suffers; it is the redeemable, not the doomed thing, that is subjected to vanity. The race in which evil—that is, corruption, is at work, needs, as the one means for its rescue, subjection to vanity; it is the one hope against the supremacy of corruption; and the whole encircling, harboring, and helping creation must, for the sake of man, its head, and for its own further sake too, share in this subjection to vanity with its hope of deliverance.

Corruption brings in vanity, causes empty aching gaps in vitality. This aching is what most people regard as evil: it is the unpleasant cure of evil. It takes all shapes of suffering—of the body, of the mind, of the heart, of the spirit. It is altogether beneficent: without this ever invading vanity, what hope would there be for the rich and powerful, accustomed to, and set upon their own way? what hope for the self-indulgent, the conceited, the greedy, the miserly? The more things men seek, the more varied the things they imagine they need, the more are they subject to vanity—all the forms of which may be summed in the word disappointment. He who would not house with disappointment, must seek the incorruptible, the true. He must break the bondage of havings and shows; of rumours, and praises, and pretences, and selfish pleasures. He must come out of the false into the real; out of the darkness into the light; out of the bondage of corruption into the glorious liberty of the children of God. To bring men to break with corruption, the gulf of the inane yawns before them. Aghast in soul, they cry, 'Vanity of vanities! all is vanity!' and beyond the abyss begin to espy the eternal world of truth.

Note now 'the hope that the creation itself also,' as something besides and other than God's men and women, 'shall be delivered from the bondage of corruption, into the liberty of the glory of the children of God.' The creation then is to share in the deliverance and liberty and glory of the children of God. Deliverance from corruption, liberty from bondage, must include escape from the very home and goal of corruption, namely death,—and that in all its kinds and degrees. When you say then that for the children of God there is no more death, remember that the deliverance of the creature is from the bondage of corruption into the glorious liberty of the children of God. Dead, in bondage to corruption, how can they share in the liberty of the children of Life? Where is their deliverance?

If such then be the words of the apostle, does he, or does he not, I ask, hold the idea of the immortality of the animals? If you say all he means is, that the creatures alive at the coming of the Lord will be set free from the tyranny of corrupt man, I refer you to what I have already said of the poverty of such an interpretation, accepting the failure of justice and love toward those that have passed away, are passing, and must yet, ere that coming, be born to pass away for ever. For the man whose heart aches to adore a faithful creator, what comfort lies in such good news! He must perish for lack of a true God! Oh lame conclusion to the grand prophecy! Is God a mocker, who will not be mocked? Is there a past to God with which he has done? Is Time too much for him? Is he God enough to care for those that happen to live at one present time, but not God enough to care for those that happened to live at another present time? Or did he care for them, but could not help them? Shall we not rather believe that the vessels of less honour, the misused, the maltreated, shall be filled full with creative wine at last? Shall not the children have little dogs under the Father's table, to which to let fall plenty of crumbs? If there was such provision for the sparrows of our Lord's time of sojourn, and he will bring yet better with him when he comes again, how should the dead sparrows and their sorrows be passed over of him with whom is no variableness, neither shadow of turning? Or would the deliverance of the creatures into the groaned-for liberty have been much worth mentioning, if within a few years their share in the glory of the sons of God was to die away in death? But the gifts of God are without repentance.

How St Paul longs for and loves liberty! Only true lover of liberty is he, who will die to give it to his neighbour! St Paul loved liberty more than his own liberty. But then see how different his notion of the liberty on its way to the children of God, from the dull modern fancies of heaven still set forth in the popular hymn-books! The new heaven and the new earth will at least be a heaven and an earth! What would the newest earth be to the old children without its animals? Barer than the heavens emptied of the constellations that are called by their names. Then, if the earth must have its animals, why not the old ones, already dear? The sons of God are not a new race of sons of God, but the old race glorified:—why a new race of animals, and not the old ones glorified?

The apostle says they are to share in the liberty of the sons of God: will it not then be a liberty like ours, a liberty always ready to be offered on the altar of love? What sweet service will not that of the animals be, thus offered! How sweet also to minister to them in their turns of need! For to us doubtless will they then flee for help in any difficulty, as now they flee from us in dread of our tyranny. What lovelier feature in the newness of the new earth, than the old animals glorified with us, in their home with us—our common home, the house of our father—each kind an unfailing pleasure to the other! Ah, what horses! Ah, what dogs! Ah, what wild beasts, and what birds in the air! The whole redeemed creation goes to make up St Paul's heaven. He had learned of him who would leave no one out; who made the excuse for his murderers that they did not know what they were doing.

Is not the prophecy on the groaning creation to have its fulfilment in the new heavens and the new earth, wherein dwelleth righteousness? Does not this involve its existence beyond what we call this world? Why should it not then involve immortality? Would it not be more like the king eternal, immortal, invisible, to know no life but the immortal? to create nothing that could die; to slay nothing but evil? 'For he is not a God of the dead, but of the living; for all live unto him.'

But what is this liberty of the children of God, for which the whole creation is waiting? The children themselves are waiting for it: when they have it, then will their house and retinue, the creation, whose fate hangs on that of the children, share it with them: what is this liberty?

All liberty must of course consist in the realization of the ideal harmony between the creative will and the created life; in the correspondence of the creature's active being to the creator's idea, which is his substantial soul. In other words the creature's liberty is what his obedience to the law of his existence, the will of his maker, effects for him. The instant a soul moves counter to the will of its prime cause, the universe is its prison; it dashes against the walls of it, and the sweetest of its uplifting and sustaining forces at once become its manacles and fetters. But St Paul is not at the moment thinking either of the metaphysical notion of liberty, or of its religious realization; he has in his thought the birth of the soul's consciousness of freedom.

'And not only so'—that the creation groaneth and travaileth—'but ourselves also, which have the first fruits of the spirit, even we ourselves groan within ourselves, waiting for.... the redemption of our body.'—We are not free, he implies, until our body is redeemed; then all the creation will be free with us. He regards the creation as part of our embodiment. The whole creation is waiting for the manifestation of the sons of God—that is, the redemption of their body, the idea of which extends to their whole material envelopment, with all the life that belongs to it. For this as for them, the bonds of corruption must fall away; it must enter into the same liberty with them, and be that for which it was created—a vital temple, perfected by the unbroken indwelling of its divinity.

The liberty here intended, it may be unnecessary to say, is not that essential liberty—freedom from sin, but the completing of the redemption of the spirit by the redemption of the body, the perfecting of the greater by its necessary complement of the less. Evil has been constantly at work, turning our house of the body into a prison; rendering it more opaque and heavy and insensible; casting about it bands and cerements, and filling it with aches and pains. The freest soul, the purest of lovers, the man most incapable of anything mean, would not, for all his mighty liberty, yet feel absolutely at large while chained to a dying body—nor the less hampered, but the more, that that dying body was his own. The redemption of the body, therefore, the making of it for the man a genuine, perfected, responsive house-alive, is essential to the apostle's notion of a man's deliverance. The new man must have a new body with a new heaven and earth. St Paul never thinks of himself as released from body; he desires a perfect one, and of a nobler sort; he would inhabit a heaven-made house, and give up the earth-made one, suitable only to this lower stage of life, infected and unsafe from the first, and now much dilapidated in the service of the Master who could so easily give him a better. He wants a spiritual body—a body that will not thwart but second the needs and aspirations of the spirit. He had in his mind, I presume, such a body as the Lord died with, changed by the interpenetrating of the creative indwelling will, to a heavenly body, the body with which he rose. A body like the Lord's is, I imagine, necessary to bring us into true and perfect contact with the creation, of which there must be multitudinous phases whereof we cannot now be even aware.

The way in which both good and indifferent people alike lay the blame on their bodies, and look to death rather than God-aided struggle to set them at liberty, appears to me low and cowardly: it is the master fleeing from the slave, despising at once and fearing him. We must hold the supremacy over our bodies, but we must not despise body; it is a divine thing. Body and soul are in the image of God; and the lord of life was last seen in the glorified body of his death. I believe that he still wears that body. But we shall do better without these bodies that suffer and grow old—which may indeed, as some think, be but the outer cases, the husks of our real bodies. Endlessly helpful as they have been to us, and that, in a measure incalculable, through their very subjection to vanity, we are yet surely not in altogether and only helpful company, so long as the houses wherein we live have so many spots and stains in them which friendly death, it may be, can alone wash out—so many weather-eaten and self-engendered sores which the builder's hand, pulling down and rebuilding of fresh and nobler material, alone can banish.

When the sons, then, are free, when their bodies are redeemed, they will lift up with them the lower creation into their liberty. St Paul seems to believe that perfection in their kind awaits also the humbler inhabitants of our world, its advent to follow immediately on the manifestation of the sons of God: for our sakes and their own they have been made subject to vanity; for our sakes and their own they shall be restored and glorified, that is, raised higher with us.

Has the question no interest for you? It would have much, had you now what you must one day have—a heart big enough to love any life God has thought fit to create. Had the Lord cared no more for what of his father's was lower than himself, than you do for what of your father's is lower than you, you would not now be looking for any sort of redemption.

I have omitted in my quotations the word *adoption* used in both English versions: it is no translation of the Greek word for which it stands. It is used by St Paul as meaning the same thing with the phrase, 'the redemption of the body'—a fact to bring the interpretation given it at once into question. Falser translation, if we look at the importance of the thing signified, and its utter loss in the word used to represent it, not to mention the substitution for that of the apostle, of an idea not only untrue but actively mischievous, was never made. The thing St Paul means in the word he uses, has simply nothing to do with adoption—nothing whatever. In the beginning of the fourth chapter of his epistle to the Galatians, he makes perfectly clear what he intends by it. His unusual word means the father's recognition, when he comes of age, of the child's relation to him, by giving him his fitting place of dignity in the house; and here the deliverance of the body is the act of this recognition by the great Father, completing and crowning and declaring the freedom of the man, the perfecting of the last lingering remnant of his deliverance. St Paul's word, I repeat, has nothing to do with *adoption*; it means the manifestation of the grown-up sons of God; the showing of those as sons, who have always been his children; the bringing of them out before the universe in such suitable attire and with such fit attendance, that to look at them is to see what they are, the sons of the house—such to whom their elder brother applied the words: 'I said ye are Gods.'

If then the sons groan within themselves, looking to be lifted up, and the other inhabitants of the same world groan with them and cry, shall they not also be lifted up? Have they not also a faithful creator? He must be a selfish man indeed who does not desire that it should be so.

It appears then, that, in the expectation of the apostle, the new heavens and the new earth in which dwell the sons of God, are to be inhabited by blessed animals also—inferior, but risen—and I think, yet to rise in continuous development.

Here let me revert a moment, and say a little more clearly and strongly a thing I have already said:—

584

When the apostle speaks of the whole creation, is it possible he should have dismissed the animals from his thoughts, to regard the trees and flowers bearing their part in the groaning and travailing of the sore burdened world? Or could he, animals and trees and flowers forgotten, have intended by the creation that groaned and travailed, only the bulk of the earth, its mountains and valleys, plains and seas and rivers, its agglomeration of hard and soft, of hot and cold, of moist and dry? If he could, then the portion that least can be supposed to feel or know, is regarded by the apostle of love as immeasurably more important than the portion that loves and moans and cries. Nor is this all; for thereupon he attributes the suffering-faculty of the excluded, far more sentient portion at least, to the altogether inferior and less sentient, and upon the ground of that faculty builds the vision of its redemption! If it could be so, then how should the seeming apostle's affected rhapsody of hope be to us other than a mere puff-ball of falsest rhetoric, a special-pleading for nothing, as degrading to art as objectless in nature?

Much would I like to know clearly what animals the apostle saw on his travels, or around his home when he had one—their conditions, and their relations to their superiors. Anyhow they were often suffering creatures; and Paul was a man growing hourly in likeness to his maker and theirs, therefore overflowing with sympathy. Perhaps as he wrote, there passed through his mind a throb of pity for the beasts he had to kill at Ephesus.

If the Lord said very little about animals, could he have done more for them than tell men that his father cared for them? He has thereby wakened and is wakening in the hearts of men a seed his father planted. It grows but slowly, yet has already borne a little precious fruit. His loving friend St Francis has helped him, and many others have tried, and are now trying to help him: whoever sows the seed of that seed the Father planted is helping the Son. Our behaviour to the animals, our words concerning them, are seed, either good or bad, in the hearts of our children. No one can tell to what the animals might not grow, even here on the old earth under the old heaven, if they were but dealt with according to their true position in regard to us. They are, in sense very real and divine, our kindred. If I call them our poor relations, it is to suggest that poor relations are often ill used. Relatives, poor or rich, may be such ill behaved, self-assertive, disagreeable persons, that we cannot treat them as we gladly would; but our endeavour should be to develop every true relation. He who is prejudiced against a relative because he is poor, is himself an ill-bred relative, and to be ill-bred is an excluding fault with the court of the high countries. There, poverty is welcome, vulgarity inadmissible.

Those who love certain animals selfishly, pampering them, as so many mothers do their children with worse results, that they may be loved of them in return, betray them to their enemies. They are not lovers of animals, but only of favourites, and do their part to make the rest of the world dislike animals. Theirs are the dogs that inhospitably growl and bark and snap, moving the indifferent to dislike, and confirming the unfriendly in their antagonism. Any dog-parliament, met in the interests of their kind, would condemn such dogs to be discreetly bitten, and their mistresses to be avoided. And certainly, if animals are intended to live and grow, she is the enemy of any individual animal, who stunts his moral and intellectual development by unwise indulgence. Of whatever nature be the heaven of the animals, that animal is not in the fair way to enter it. The education of the lower lies at the door of the higher, and in true education is truest kindness.

But what shall I say of such as for any kind of end subject animals to torture? I dare hardly trust myself to the expression of my judgment of their conduct in this regard.

'We are investigators; we are not doing it for our own sakes, but for the sake of others, our fellow-men.'

The higher your motive for it, the greater is the blame of your unrighteousness. Must we congratulate you on such a love for your fellows as inspires you to wrong the weaker than they, those that are without helper against you? Shall we count the man worthy who, for the sake of his friend, robbed another man too feeble to protect himself, and too poor to punish his assailant? For the sake of your children, would you waylay a beggar? No real good can grow in the soil of injustice.

I cannot help suspecting, however, that the desire to know has a greater share in the enormity than the desire to help. Alas for the science that will sacrifice the law of righteousness but to behold a law of sequence! The tree of knowledge will never prove to man the tree of life. There is no law says, Thou shalt know; a thousand laws cry out, Thou shalt do right. These men are a law unto themselves—and what a law! It is the old story: the greed of knowing casts out righteousness, and mercy, and faith. Whatever believed a benefit may or may not thus be wrought for higher creatures, the injustice to the lower is nowise affected. Justice has no respect of persons, but they are surely the weaker that stand more in need of justice!

Labour is a law of the universe, and is not an evil. Death is a law of this world at least, and is not an evil. Torture is the law of no world but the hell of human invention. Labour and death are for the best good of those that labour and die; they are laws of life. Torture is doubtless over-ruled for the good of the tortured, but it will one day burn a very hell in the hearts of the torturers.

Torture can be inflicted only by the superior. The divine idea of a superior, is one who requires duty, and protects, helps, delivers: our relation to the animals is that of their superiors in the family, who require labour, it may be, but are just, helpful, protective. Can they know anything of the Father who neither love nor rule their inferiors, but use them as a child his insensate toys, pulling them to pieces to know what is inside them? Such men, so-called of science—let them have the dignity to the fullness of its worth—lust to know as if a man's life lay in knowing, as if it were a vile thing to be ignorant—so vile that, for the sake of his secret hoard of facts, they do right in breaking with torture into the house of the innocent! Surely they shall not thus find the way of understanding! Surely there is a maniac thirst for knowledge, as a maniac thirst for wine or for blood! He who loves knowledge the most genuinely, will with the most patience wait for it until it can be had righteously.

Need I argue the injustice? Can a sentient creature come forth without rights, without claim to well-being, or to consideration from the other creatures whom they find, equally without action of their own, present in space? If one answer, 'For aught I know, it may be so,'—Where then are thy own rights? I ask. If another have none, thine must lie in thy superior power; and will there not one day come a stronger than thou? Mayst thou not one day be in Naboth's place, with an Ahab getting up to go into thy vineyard to possess it? The rich man may come prowling after thy little ewe lamb, and what wilt thou have to say? He may be the stronger, and thou the weaker! That the rights of the animals are so much less than ours, does not surely argue them the less rights! They have little, and we have much; ought they therefore to have less and we more? Must we not rather be the more honourably anxious that they have their little to the full. Every gain of injustice is a loss to the world; for life consists neither in length of days nor in ease of body. Greed of life and wrong done to secure it, will never work anything but direst loss. As to knowledge, let justice guide thy search and thou wilt know the sooner. Do the will of God, and thou shalt know God, and he will open thine eyes to look into the very heart of knowledge. Force thy violent way, and gain knowledge, to miss truth.

Thou mayest wound the heart of God, but thou canst not rend it asunder to find the Truth that sits there enthroned.

What man would he be who accepted the offer to be healed and kept alive by means which necessitated the torture of certain animals? Would he feel himself a gentleman—walking the earth with the sense that his life and conscious well-being were informed and upheld by the agonies of other lives?

'I hope, sir, your health is better than it has been?'

'Thank you, I am wonderfully restored—have entered in truth upon a fresh lease of life. My organism has been nourished with the agonies of several dogs, and the pangs of a multitude of rabbits and guinea-pigs, and I am aware of a marvellous change for the better. They gave me their lives, and I gave them in return worse pains than mine. The bargain has proved a quite satisfactory one! True, their lives were theirs, not mine; but then their sufferings were theirs, not mine! They could not defend themselves; they had not a word to say, so reasonable was the exchange. Poor fools! they were neither so wise, nor so strong, nor such lovers of comfort as I! If they could not take care of themselves, that was their look-out, not mine! Every animal for himself!'

There was a certain patriotic priest who thought it better to put a just man to death than that a whole nation should perish. Precious salvation that might be wrought by injustice! But then the just man taught that the rich man and the beggar must one day change places.

'To set the life of a dog against the life of a human being!'

No, but the torture of a dog against the prolonged life of a being capable of torturing him. Priceless gain, the lengthening of such a life, to the man and his friends and his country!

That the animals do not suffer so much as we should under like inflictions, I hope true, and think true. But is toothache nothing, because there are yet worse pains for head and face?

Not a few who now regard themselves as benefactors of mankind, will one day be looked upon with a disapprobation which no argument will now convince them they deserve. But yet another day is coming, when they will themselves right sorrowfully pour out disapprobation upon their own deeds; for they are not stones but men, and must repent. Let them, in the interests of humanity, give their own entrails to the knife, their own silver cord to be laid bare, their own golden bowl to be watched throbbing, and I will worship at their feet. But shall I admire their discoveries at the expense of the stranger—nay, no stranger—the poor brother within their gates?

Your conscience does not trouble you? Take heed that the light that is in you be not darkness. Whatever judgment mean, will it suffice you in that hour to say, 'My burning desire to know how life wrought in him, drove me through the gates and bars of his living house'? I doubt if you will add, in your heart any more than with your tongue, 'and I did well.'

To those who expect a world to come, I say then, Let us take heed how we carry ourselves to the creation which is to occupy with us the world to come.

To those whose hearts are sore for that creation, I say, The Lord is mindful of his own, and will save both man and beast.

THE END.

Spurgeon's Sermons – Collected in 62 Volumes
Benediction Classics, 2011
c 700 pages each
Vol 1 – ISBN: 978-1849024457
Vol 2 – ISBN: 978-1849024426

Available from www.amazon.com, www.amazon.co.uk

Charles H. Spurgeon was known as the Prince of Preachers and aged 22 he was preaching to audiences of over 10,000 people. His sermons emphasised the demands of Christ upon believers' lives. They are easy to read and understand, with practical examples and witty comments. They contain a scriptural index, for easy reference.

G K Chesterton's Christian Writings (unabridged): Everlasting Man, Orthodoxy, Heretics, St Francis of Assisi, St. Thomas Aquinas and The Man who was Thursday
G K Chesterton
Benediction Classics, 2012
724 pages
ISBN: 978-1-78139-320-8

Available from www.amazon.com, www.amazon.co.uk

This Omnibus edition contains six of G K Chesterton's most famous writings

The Forbidden Texts - Gospels and Epistles that were banned from the Bible - Including: The Gospel of Peter; The Didache; The Gospel Of The Birth Of Mary; The Gospel Called The Protevangelion; St. Thomas's Gospel Of The Infancy Of Jesus Christ; The Gospel Of Nicodemus
Walter R. Cassels
Benediction Classics, 2012
514 pages
ISBN: 978-1-78139-216-4

Available from www.amazon.com, www.amazon.co.uk

Several Gospels and Epistles were considered not suitable to be included in the Canon of Scripture. These texts are fascinating writings, offering theological and social insights.

The Andrew Murray Collection, including the books Holy in Christ, Jesus Himself, Lord, Teach Us to Pray, The Master's Indwelling, The Ministry of Intercession
Andrew Murray
Benediction Classics, 2012
424 pages
ISBN: 978-1-78139-309-3

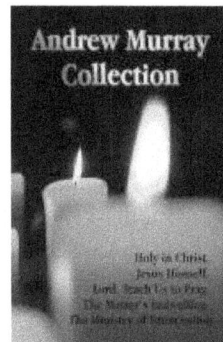

Available from www.amazon.com, www.amazon.co.uk

Andrew Murray is the master of devotional literature. His books are short, easy to read and profoundly challenging. These five books would be a great addition to any bookcase, providing a great source of Christian insight. With added Biblical Index.

Also from Benediction Books …
Wandering Between Two Worlds: Essays on Faith and Art
Anita Mathias
Benediction Books, 2007
152 pages
ISBN: 0955373700

Available from www.amazon.com, www.amazon.co.uk

In these wide-ranging lyrical essays, Anita Mathias writes, in lush, lovely prose, of her naughty Catholic childhood in Jamshedpur, India; her large, eccentric family in Mangalore, a sea-coast town converted by the Portuguese in the sixteenth century; her rebellion and atheism as a teenager in her Himalayan boarding school, run by German missionary nuns, St. Mary's Convent, Nainital; and her abrupt religious conversion after which she entered Mother Teresa's convent in Calcutta as a novice. Later rich, elegant essays explore the dualities of her life as a writer, mother, and Christian in the United States-- Domesticity and Art, Writing and Prayer, and the experience of being "an alien and stranger" as an immigrant in America, sensing the need for roots.

About the Author

Anita Mathias is the author of *Wandering Between Two Worlds: Essays on Faith and Art*. She has a B.A. and M.A. in English from Somerville College, Oxford University, and an M.A. in Creative Writing from the Ohio State University, USA. Anita won a National Endowment of the Arts fellowship in Creative Nonfiction in 1997. She lives in Oxford, England with her husband, Roy, and her daughters, Zoe and Irene.

Anita's website:
    http://www.anitamathias.com, and
Anita's blog Dreaming Beneath the Spires:
    http://dreamingbeneaththespires.blogspot.com

The Church That Had Too Much
Anita Mathias
Benediction Books, 2010
52 pages
ISBN: 9781849026567

Available from www.amazon.com, www.amazon.co.uk

The Church That Had Too Much was very well-intentioned. She wanted to love God, she wanted to love people, but she was both hampered by her muchness and the abundance of her possessions, and beset by ambition, power struggles and snobbery. Read about the surprising way The Church That Had Too Much began to resolve her problems in this deceptively simple and enchanting fable.

About the Author

Anita Mathias is the author of *Wandering Between Two Worlds: Essays on Faith and Art*. She has a B.A. and M.A. in English from Somerville College, Oxford University, and an M.A. in Creative Writing from the Ohio State University, USA. Anita won a National Endowment of the Arts fellowship in Creative Nonfiction in 1997. She lives in Oxford, England with her husband, Roy, and her daughters, Zoe and Irene.

Anita's website:
    http://www.anitamathias.com, and
Anita's blog Dreaming Beneath the Spires:
    http://dreamingbeneaththespires.blogspot.com

www.ingramcontent.com/pod-product-compliance
Lightning Source LLC
Chambersburg PA
CBHW020358100426
42812CB00001B/114